HEROD

*King of the Jews and
Friend of the Romans*

0   1   2cm

Top: Obverse and reverse, bronze coin of King Herod, undated. From the Armenian Gardens excavations, Old City, Jerusalem, site of Herod's large palace. Obverse, anchor; around, inscription ΗΡΩΔΟΥ ΒΑΣΙΛΕΩΣ ("Herod the King"). Reverse, double cornucopia with caduceus (?) between.

Bottom: Obverse and reverse, bronze coin of King Herod, dated year three (37 BCE). Provenance unknown (museum collections). Obverse, tripod with basin; in field to left, "year three"; to right, monogram ("TR." perhaps a reference to Tyre's mint); around, inscription ΗΡΩΔΟΥ ΒΑΣΙΛΕΩΣ ("Herod the King"). Reverse, Dioscuri helmet (?), on either side, palm branch.

Both coins reproduced to same scale. Courtesy of the Royal Ontario Museum, Toronto.

HEROD

King of the Jews and Friend of the Romans

Peter Richardson

UNIVERSITY OF SOUTH CAROLINA PRESS

Studies on Personalities of the New Testament
D. Moody Smith, General Editor

Copyright © 1996 University of South Carolina

Published in Columbia, South Carolina, by the
University of South Carolina Press

Manufactured in the United States of America

00 99 98 97 96   5 4 3 2 1

Library of Congress Cataloging-in-Publication Data

Richardson, Peter, 1935–
    Herod : king of the Jews and friend of the Romans / Peter
Richardson.
        p.   cm. – (Studies on personalities of the New Testament)
    Includes bibliographical references and index.
    ISBN 1–57003–136–3
    1. Herod I, King of Judea, 73–4 B.C.   2. Jews—History 168
B.C.–135 A.D.   3. Jews—Kings and rulers—Biography.   4. Bible.
N.T.   I. Title.   II. Series.
DS122.3.R53   1996
933′.05′092—dc20
    [B]   96–25248

To Nancy

who has basked in the sun
throughout Herod's domain
eaten sparse lunches
in some of his buildings
slept soundly
in a few of his palaces
and shared fully
in the excitement of the chase.

CONTENTS

List of Maps   xi

Preface and Acknowledgments   xii

Chronology of Herod's Life   xv

List of Abbreviations   xxi

Introduction

Rome: Extract from the *Acta Diurna*   1

Petra: Transcript of Herald's Report   4

Letter from Manaean of Damascus to Ephraim in Palmyra   5

Jerusalem: *Journal*, Obituary Notice   6

Yodefat: Report of Police Agent on a Speech by Judas   10

Competing Views of Herod   11

The "Great"?   12

1. In the End Is the Beginning (4 BCE)

The Eagle, or Eclipse of a King   15

Death of a King   18

Family Squabbles in Rome   20

Augustus's Indecision   25

The Delegations' Evaluations   30

2. Family Matters

Herod's Wills   33

Family Financial Provisions   38

Genealogy and Descent   40

Marriage and Divorce   43

Conclusion   45

Appendix: Herod's Family Tree   46

3. From Idumaea to Petra (to 64 BCE)

Introduction   52

Idumaeans   54

Nabateans   62

Ituraeans   68

Hasmoneans   73

Hyrcanus II and Aristobulus II   76

Antipater   78

4. Late Hellenism in the Near East

Syria   81

Dependent Kingdoms   83

The Decapolis   88

The Coastal Cities   91

5. From Petra to Rome (64–40 BCE)

Pompey, Gabinius, and Antipater's Rise to Power   95

Caesar, Cassius, Antipater, and Roman Troubles   103

Herod and His Trial   108

Civil War   113

Parthia   119

Herod and Antigonus   121

King of Judea   129

6. The Kingdom

Galilee   131

Judea   134

Samaritis   137

Gaulanitis, Batanea, Auranitis, and Trachonitis   139

Peraea   142

Conclusion   144

7. From Rome to Rhodes (40–30 BCE)

Up to Jerusalem: The First Season's Campaign   153

Up to Jerusalem: The Second Season's Campaign   156

The Battle for Jerusalem   158

Alexandra, Cleopatra, and the Death of Aristobulus III   162

The Nabatean War   165

The End of Hyrcanus II   169

Herod and Octavian at Rhodes   171

8. Herod's Buildings

Introduction   174

Geographic Location   174

Major Projects   177

Fortresses and Palaces   179

Religious Buildings   183

Cultural Buildings   186

Commercial Construction and Infrastructure   188

Strategy and Rationale   191

Concluding Comments   195

Appendix A: List of Herod's Buildings   197

Appendix B: Inscriptions and Coins   203

9. From Rhodes to Rome (30–17 BCE)

The Death of Mariamme   216

Appended Note   218

The Deaths of Alexandra and Costobar   220

Judean Society   222

Herod and Augustus   226

Internal Matters   234

To Rome   239

10. **Herod and Religion**

Introduction   240

Herod and the Temple   241

Josephus's Account of Herod and the Temple   247

Herod and Groups or Parties   249

Conclusion   260

11. **From Rome to Jericho (17–4 BCE)**

Augustus, Marcus Agrippa, and Herod   262

The Diaspora   264

A Synagogue in Rome?   266

The Decrees   269

Suit of the Ionian Jews   270

Benefactions   272

The Household   273

To Rome Again   278

The Nabatean War (12–9 BCE)   279

In Jerusalem   281

Archelaus, Eurycles, and Eunuchs   284

The Execution of Alexander and Aristobulus   286

Antipater   288

12. **The Herods and Christianity**

Herod: The Birth of Jesus and the Massacre of the Children   295

Archelaus of Judea, the Throne Claimant, and Quirinius's Census   298

Philip of Batanea, Auranitis, Gaulanitis, Trachonitis, and Ituraea   301

Antipas: The Deaths of John and Jesus   305

The Herodian Family   313

13. **"The Achievements of King Herod" (4 BCE)**   315

Select Bibliography   319

Index of References to Ancient Texts   331

Index of Modern Authors   345

Index of Places   349

Index of Subjects   355

MAPS

Pages 146–152

1. Late Hellenistic and Pre-Hasmonean Palestine
2. Hasmonean conquests
3. The Near East
4. Herod's kingdom
5. Herod's building activity in his own regions
6. Herod's building activity outside Judea
7. Post-Herodian divisions

PREFACE AND ACKNOWLEDGMENTS

Herod the Great, as he is usually called, was much like Henry VIII, Catherine the Great, or Peter the Great: talented, vigorous, lusty, skillful, charismatic, attractive, decisive, influential—but a disaster in his personal life. Like them, Herod changed his nation's history.

In a biographical study an author need not like the subject, but it helps if there is something to admire. Herod's personality is not attractive; had I been a contemporary I should not have wanted to spend much time with him. But I find much to admire in Herod, and it will show, I expect, in this study. My admiration derives from the finesse and grandeur in his architectural projects; when I first saw the archaeological evidence I was struck with curiosity about how to imagine reconstructions of his buildings and urban projects. I had spent many years thinking about texts and how texts permit scholars to reconstruct groups and tensions and problems. I realized that my training in architecture allowed another vantage point on a similar set of interests: the reconstruction of society and its concerns, the sense of cultural and religious conflict on a larger scale. No one in Herod's period built so extensively with projects that shed such a bright light on that world. I have tried, however, not to let my architectural interest intrude too much, not because architecture is not important but because this is a biographical study.

A study of Herod can investigate his life in a traditional biographical fashion with some hope of precision. The sources are better than those available for studies of Paul or Jesus or Seneca. In addition to archaeological remains, there are inscriptions and coins, second- and thirdhand appreciations, and a connected narrative of which he is the center. Nevertheless, though he is said to have written his own memoirs, nothing he wrote survived.

Every study of Herod is necessarily a study in Josephus, the main source of information for Herod's life, so assumptions are required about how to use Josephus, what to think of his sources, how to deal with the perplexing differences between *History of the Jewish War* and *Antiquities of the Jews*. At numerous points I have tried to show how I made my choices, but I have aimed to avoid this becoming too obtrusive.

The first centuries BCE and CE constitute one of the most enduringly fascinating periods in human history, not least in the religious events at the center of early Christianity. Herod was a marginal figure in that history, yet he was important for several reasons: (1) he shaped the world in which early Christianity began, adopting a political and religious and cultural program that departed from the stated—though not always the actual—program of his predecessors; (2) he was king when Jesus was born, responsible (according to legend) for a bloody massacre of other children; (3) his descendants, who occupied positions of power into the second century CE, continued to influence Christian history; (4) later, Christians regarded him as an archetypal villain, opposed to everything Christian.

Herod's fascination is also linked with political history. The rise of new Imperial forms of governance changed the Mediterranean world. Virtually all the influential characters—great, mean, weak, ill-starred—crossed Herod's path during the unsettled period of the civil wars and the rise of the principate, and their support was a significant feature in his rise to power; indeed, the whole Herodian family seemed to know how to turn at decisive moments, balancing Roman demands with Judean needs.

This was a period of transforming societal change. Class boundaries were altered during the transition from Republic to Empire. Important developments took place in literature and poetry, painting and sculpture, architecture and engineering; in some cases Herod was on the "cutting edge." Maps showed the extension of the bounds of the Empire to include diverse peoples at the edges of the known world, with profound cultural and social change altering forever conditions wherever the Romans touched, even while they fostered a notion of peace, the *pax romana*.

Herod should not be viewed as a "half-Jew" but as a third-generation Jew who was attentive to his religion—a Jew, however, who was a Roman citizen and a Hellenist, who shared the religious outlook of most Roman citizens. He had little hesitation in acknowledging the new status of Octavian in the cult of Roma and Augustus, and he supported other temple cults such as Pythian Apollo on Rhodes or Ba'al Shamim at Si'a. A one-sided view will not do. Much of the time his priorities lay more in accommodation to Augustus than in obedience to Torah. In some respects he was Torah-observant, but not consistently and not, I suspect, outside Judea. He was a Jew who was convinced about Judaism but far from scrupulous. Augustus's often-quoted comment about Herod, "I would rather be Herod's pig than his son," implies that Herod had a reputation for not eating pork. But scrupulous about not eating it? I doubt it. That remark criticized Herod's treatment of his children, and his inability to deal with the tensions and conflicts of his own household. His fear, mistrust, suspicion, jealousy, resentment, and the like allow unlimited amateur psychologizing, a temptation I have tried to avoid.

Herod's story is told in chapters 1, 3, 5, 7, 9, 11, and 13; his context and cultural accommodations are described in chapters 2, 4, 6, 8, and 10; and chapter 12 brings the story into the early Christian period.

Thanks to the University of Toronto for a full year's research leave in 1989–90 and a half-year's leave in the winter of 1994, and to its Office of Research Administration for various small grants for research and travel; to the Centre and the Department for the Study of Religion for travel and other assistance; to the Faculty of Architecture for office space during a leave; to the École Biblique (and especially to Jerome Murphy-O'Connor) and to Tantur (and especially to William Klassen and Dona Harvey), both in Jerusalem; to the American Center for Oriental Research in Amman (and especially to Bert de Vries); and to the American School of Classical Studies in Athens for kindnesses while I was pursuing the research. I have profited from opportunities to try out my views on a variety of academic audiences in North America, Europe, and the Middle East, and on nonacademic groups in Temple Emmanuel and Yorkminster Park Baptist Church in Toronto. I am especially indebted to graduate students at the University of Toronto who have tracked down some of the arcane pieces of information I needed to know: Michael Barnes, Alicia Batten, Ed Broeder, Nicola Denzey, Meerabelle Dey, Andrew Duffy, Leigh Gibson, Peter Gooch, Philip Harland, Paul Heger, Derrick Heuchan, Valerie Heuchan, Jackie Isaacs, Ernest Janzen, Michele Murray, Elaine Myers, Mike Nittoly, Martin B. Shukster, Kelly Spoerl, Rachel Urowitz (who prepared the indexes), Linda Wheatley-Irving, and Reena Zeidman, in particular.

I am grateful to the *Biblical Theology Bulletin*, Seton Hall University, South Orange, New Jersey, for permission to use and adapt the table by K. C. Hanson in the appendix following chapter 2; to Doubleday, a division of Bantam Doubleday Dell Publishing Group, Inc., for permission to quote in chapter 5 from R. B. Wright, "The Psalms of Solomon," in James H. Charlesworth, ed., *The Old Testament Pseudepigrapha* (Garden City, NY: Doubleday, 1983), 2: 651–52, 658–59.

Nancy, to whom the book is dedicated, must feel a little like Herod's eleventh wife, though she has not had any of the fringe benefits that living with him would have brought; but then, she has not had to face his wrath either, only my relentlessness.

CHRONOLOGY OF HEROD'S LIFE

73 BCE	BIRTH OF HEROD THE GREAT
73–71	Slave revolt in Italy (Spartacus)
69	Birth of Cleopatra VII
67	Pompey's campaign against the pirates
	Death of Queen Alexandra (76–67)
	Herod taken to Petra
	Hyrcanus II high priest (76–66?) with royal power (69–66?)
	Hyrcanus cedes lands to Aretas, King of Nabatea (85–62)
66	Hyrcanus deposed by Aristobulus II, king and high priest (66–63)
	First Catiline conspiracy; final defeat of Mithridates
65	Pompey in Syria; end of Seleucid monarchy
64	End of Roman war against Pontus
	Annexation of Seleucid kingdom and creation of Province of Syria
	Hurricane destroys crop in Judea; food shortage
63	Second Catiline conspiracy
	Birth of Octavian (Augustus)
	Aristobulus II defeats Hyrcanus II and Aretas of Nabatea at Papyron
	Pompey sides with Hyrcanus II; capture of Jerusalem
	Pharisees encourage Pompey to suppress monarchy
	Hyrcanus II re-appointed high priest and ethnarch (63–40)
	Antipater sides with Pompey, gains administrative responsibility
	Aristobulus II retires to Alexandreion; surrenders to Pompey
	Aristobulus II exiled
63/62	Pompey organizes new provinces of the East
	Aretas of Nabatea left independent; succeeded by Obodas II (62–57)
	Pompey establishes autonomous cities; Samaritans independent
61	Pompey's triumph in Rome
60	First Roman triumvirate (Caesar, Pompey, Crassus)
57	Hyrcanus loses power (57–55); Gabinius sets up five *synedria*

	Malichus I king of Nabatea (57–28) Herod meets Mark Antony (83–30)
57–55	Aristobulus II and sons revolt against Rome; put down by Gabinius
56	Birth of Nicolas of Damascus
55	Antipater helps Gabinius in Egypt; made procurator (55–43)
54	Crassus governor of Syria (55–53); pillages Temple Defeat of Crassus by Parthians at Carrhae Cassius governor of Syria (53–51)
51	Cleopatra VII rules Egypt
49	Caesar crosses the Rubicon Civil War between Pompey and Julius Caesar; Caesar declared dictator
48	Pompey assassinated Antipater rebuilds the walls of Jerusalem
47	Sextus Caesar governor of Syria (47–46) Julius Caesar in Egypt, Syria and Asia Caesar reinstates Cleopatra as queen of Egypt (47–30) Antipater made Roman citizen Antipater appointed procurator, Hyrcanus named ethnarch Caesar gives Joppa and Esdraelon to Judea; returns to Italy in July Phasael appointed governor of Jerusalem Herod appointed governor of Galilee, puts down revolt of Hezekiah Proceedings in Jerusalem against Herod Herod marries Doris
46	Herod appointed governor of Coele-Syria by Sextus Caesar Caecilius Bassus governor of Syria (46–44)
45	Herod assists Caesar's troops at Apamea Jewish embassy to Caesar results in new concessions Caesar adopts Octavian Birth of Antipater to Herod and Doris
44	Assassination of Julius Caesar (15 March) Cassius proconsul of Syria (44–42); terrorizes Judea; razes several towns; sells inhabitants into slavery
43	Second triumvirate (Antony, Octavian, Lepidus) Antipater poisoned by Malichus
42	Herod appointed governor of Coele-Syria (second time) by Cassius Herod settles affairs in Samaria; goes to Damascus Troubles with Marion of Tyre Octavian and Antony defeat Brutus and Cassius at Philippi Julius Caesar deified; birth of Tiberius Herod betrothed to Mariamme I; banishes Doris
41	Herod meets Antony in Bithynia

Antony rejects demands for Herod's ouster, at Daphne and Tyre
Herod and Phasael appointed joint tetrarchs

40 Parthians (Pacorus and Barzapharnes) invade Palestine with
    Antigonus
Antigonus named king by Parthians
Jerusalem revolts against Herod and Phasael
Phasael and Hyrcanus II submit to Barzapharnes
Phasael commits suicide, Hyrcanus is disfigured and taken to Parthia
Herod escapes via Masada to Alexandria, Rhodes and Rome (first
    trip)
Antigonus Mattathias (son of Aristobulus II) gains power (40–37)
Antigonus appointed high priest
Herod named king of Judea, Galilee, and Peraea by Senate of Rome

39 Ventidius Bassus governor of Syria (39–38)
Mark Antony in east
Western Idumaea and Samaritis added to Herod's territory
Herod lands at Ptolemais; takes Joppa, Masada, Orhesa;
    attacks Jerusalem but breaks off and returns to Galilee

38 Sossius governor of Syria (38–37)
Herod takes Sepphoris, Arbela caves; assists Mark Antony at Samosata
Pheroras rebuilds Alexandreion
Joseph killed at Jericho; Herod routs Pappus at Isana

37 Herod besieges Jerusalem
Marries Mariamme I in Samaria
Takes control in Jerusalem (July)
Purges Sanhedrin
Costobar (Herod's brother-in-law) named governor of Idumaea and
    Gaza
Antigonus executed by Antony at Antioch

37/36 Sabbatical year with famine

36 Birth of Alexander to Herod and Mariamme
Ananel (from Babylonia) appointed high priest (36–35)
Cleopatra VII gains Ituraea, Samaritis, coastland, parts of Nabatea
Hyrcanus II returns from Parthian imprisonment

35 Birth of Aristobulus to Herod and Mariamme I
Ananel deposed; Aristobulus III appointed high priest
Death of Aristobulus III by drowning at Jericho
Ananel re-appointed high priest (35–30)
Joseph (Salome's husband) executed by Herod

34 Herod questioned by Antony at Laodicea on death of Aristobulus
Cleopatra visits Jerusalem; gains Jericho and parts of coastal plain

32–31 War with Nabateans (Dium, Canatha)

32   Breach between Octavian and Mark Antony; Herod supports Antony
31   Herod takes Heshbon from Nabateans
      Earthquake in Palestine (spring)
      Octavian defeats Antony and Cleopatra at Actium (2 September)
      Hyrcanus II executed
30   Octavian confirms Herod king of Judea in meeting at Rhodes
          (spring)
      Jesus son of Phiabi appointed high priest (30–24)
      Herod entertains Octavian in Ptolemais
      Herod helps to supply Egyptian campaign; visits Octavian in Egypt
      Suicides of Antony and Cleopatra (August)
      Various cities added to Herod's territory
      Herod accompanies Octavian from Egypt to Antioch
29   Marcus Tullius Cicero governor of Syria (29–27)
      Execution of Mariamme
      Herod ill in Samaria; epidemic in Judea
28   Obodas III king of Nabatea (28–9)
      Alexandra intrigues for power; executed
      Salome divorces Costobar; Costobar executed
28/27 Sons of Baba executed by Herod
      Famine and plague
      Games in Jerusalem
27   Senate passes Acts of Settlement
      Senate proclaims Octavian Imperator Caesar Augustus (16 January)
      Herod marries Malthace
25   Herod marries Cleopatra of Jerusalem
25/24 Herod and Obodas assist Aelius Gallus on expedition to Arabia
24   Herod marries Mariamme II (daughter of Simon, son of Boethos)
24/23 "Zenodorus affair"
      Herod pacifies and gains Batanea, Trachonitis and Auranitis
23   M. Agrippa vice-gerent in the East (23–13)
      Alexander and Aristobulus (sons of Mariamme I) to Rome for
          education
      Birth of Archelaus to Herod and Malthace
23/22 Herod visits M. Agrippa in Lesbos
22   Gadara sends delegation to Agrippa in Lesbos
      Boethos appointed high priest (22–5)
      Augustus in Greece and Asia (22–19)
      Herod marries Pallas
22/21 Rebellion of Gadara against Herod
      Remission of one-third of taxes following sabbatical year (33/32)

21   Birth of Antipas to Herod and Malthace
      Marriage of M. Agrippa and Julia
20   Augustus visits Herod in Galilee and Samaritis (and Judea?)
      Augustus adds Gaulanitis, Hulata and Panias to Herod's territory
      Augustus appoints Herod *epitropos* of Coele-Syria (third time)
      Pheroras appointed tetrarch of Peraea
      Birth of Philip to Herod and Cleopatra of Jerusalem
18   M. Agrippa co-regent of Augustus
      Herod *socius et amicus populi Romani*
      Herod marries Elpis
17   Herod goes to Rome to fetch sons (second trip to Rome)
      Herod's first will names Alexander and Aristobulus
      M. Agrippa again sent out to the East (17–13)
      Augustus adopts Gaius and Lucius (Agrippa's children)
16   Alexander married to Glaphyra, daughter of the king of Cappadocia
      Aristobulus married to Berenice, daughter of Salome
      Herod visits M. Agrippa in Lesbos
15   M. Agrippa makes state visit to Judea
      Salome and Syllaeus fall in love in Jerusalem
15/14 Household problems
14   Herod joins M. Agrippa's expedition to Black Sea and Pontus
      Herod intercedes on behalf of Ilium with M. Agrippa
      Herod quarrels with Alexander and Aristobulus
      Antipater restored to favor
      Remits taxes on return, after sabbatical year of 16/15
13   M. Titius governor of Syria (13–10)
      Herod sails to Ionia to see M. Agrippa off
      Antipater sent to Rome with M. Agrippa (13–12)
      Doris restored to favor
      Herod's second will names Antipater heir
12   Herod accuses Alexander and Aristobulus before Augustus (third trip)
      Reunited; Herod, Antipater, Alexander, Aristobulus return together
      Third will favors Antipater; Alexander and Aristobulus subordinate
      Augustus gives Herod half of income of Cyprus copper mines
      Opening of Caesarea Maritima
      Herod breaks open Tomb of David
      Augustus becomes *pontifex maximus;* death of M. Agrippa
      Herod becomes President of Olympic Games (or 8?)
11   Revolt in Trachonitis
10   Imprisons Alexander and Aristobulus
      Accuses Syllaeus before Saturninus

9   Aretas IV king of Nabatea (9 BCE–40 CE)
     Invades Nabatea, captures Raepta: Augustus disciplines Herod
     Loses right to name successor; loses Augustus's favor
8   Herod visits Rome (? fourth trip); Antipas in Rome for his education
     Nicolas of Damascus reconciles Herod and Augustus
     Augustus wishes to cede Herod Nabatea
     Archelaus of Cappadocia reconciles Herod and Alexander
7   Birth of Jesus (probable date)
     Alexander and Aristobulus condemned at Berytus, strangled at
         Sebaste
     Herod's fourth will names Antipater heir with Philip succeeding him
     Antipater intrigues against his half-brother and his father
6   Varus governor of Syria (6–4)
     Herod breaks with the Pharisees; executions
     Syllaeus affair finally concluded in Rome
     Archelaus and Antipas return to Jerusalem
     Antipater goes to Rome with fifth will
     Antipater heir, Herod (son of Mariamme II) heir presumptive
     Breach with Pheroras
5   Pheroras dies; Antipater returns to Judea; trial; imprisonment
     Herod divorces Mariamme II
     Herod's sixth will names Antipas sole heir
     Mattathiah son of Theophilus appointed high priest (5–4)
4   Joseph son of Elam appointed high priest (one day)
     Revolt of Judas and Matthias; "Eagle affair"
     Joezar son of Boethos appointed high priest
     Eleazar son of Boethos appointed high priest
     Antipater executed
     Herod's seventh will names Archelaus, Antipas and Philip heirs
     DEATH OF HEROD THE GREAT in Jericho, late March
     Archelaus ethnarch: Judea, Samaritis, Idumaea, Caesarea and Sebaste
     Philip tetrarch: Trachonitis, Batanea, Gaulanitis, Auranitis, Panias
     Herod Antipas tetrarch: Galilee and Peraea
     Salome (Herod's sister): Jamnia, Azotus, Phasaelis
     Syria is given Gaza, Gadara, Hippos
2   Augustus named *pater patriae*
1   Gaius visits Judea; refrains from visiting Temple
     Joshua son of See appointed high priest (1 BCE–6 CE)
6 CE Archelaus deposed; replaced by prefects/procurators
     Census of Judea by Quirinius
     Annas appointed high priest (6–15)

ABBREVIATIONS

ABD Freedman, D. N., gen. ed., *The Anchor Bible Dictionary*. New York: Doubleday, 1992.

Abel, *Géographie* Abel, F.-M., *Géographie de Palestine*. Paris: Lecoffre, 1967 [1933].

Aharoni and Avi-Yonah, *Atlas* Aharoni, Y., M. Avi-Yonah, et al., *The Macmillan Bible Atlas,* 3rd ed. New York: Macmillan/Jerusalem: Carta, 1993.

AJA *American Journal of Archaeology* (1885–).

ANRW Temporini, Hilda, et al., eds., *Aufstieg und Niedergang der römischen Welt*. Berlin: de Gruyter, 1972– .

Ant. Josephus, *Jewish Antiquities*. In *Josephus*. Loeb Classical Library. Cambridge, MA: Harvard University Press, 1930.

Appian Appian, *Roman History*. Loeb Classical Library. Cambridge, MA: Harvard University Press, 1912–13.

Apion Josephus, *Against Apion*. In *Josephus*. Loeb Classical Library. Cambridge, MA: Harvard University Press, 1926.

BA *Biblical Archaeologist* (1938–).

Baly and Tushingham, *Atlas* Baly, Denis, and A. D. Tushingham, *Atlas of the Biblical World*. New York: World, 1971.

BAR *Biblical Archaeology Review* (1974–).

BAR/IS *Biblical Archaeology Reports/ International Series*.

BibZeit *Biblische Zeitschrift* (1903–).

BIES *Bulletin of the Israel Exploration Society* (1951–).

Bowersock, *Roman Arabia* Bowersock, G. W., *Roman Arabia*. Cambridge, MA: Harvard University Press, 1983.

Brown, John   Brown, R. E., *The Gospel According to John*. Garden City, NY: Doubleday, 1978 [1966].

CAH   Bury, J. B., S. A. Cook, and F. E. Adcock, eds., *The Cambridge Ancient History*. 1st and 2nd eds. Cambridge: Cambridge University Press.

Cassius Dio   Cassius Dio, *Roman History*. Harmondsworth: Penguin, 1987.

CBQ   *Catholic Biblical Quarterly* (1939–).

Charlesworth, Pseudepigrapha   Charlesworth, J., ed. *The Old Testament Pseudepigrapha*. Garden City, NY: Doubleday, 1983.

CIJ   Frey, J. B., *Corpus Inscriptionum Iudaicarum* (1936–).

CIL   *Corpus Inscriptionum Latinarum* (Berlin, 1962–).

CRINT   See Stern.

DBSupl   Picot, L., ed., *Dictionnaire de la Bible Supplément*. Paris: Letouzey, 1928ff.

DSS   Dead Sea Scrolls, cited after G. Vermes, *The Dead Sea Scrolls in English*. London: Penguin, 1990.

EJ   *Encyclopedia Judaica*. Jerusalem: Encyclopedia Judaica, 1972.

ER   Eliade, M., ed., *Encyclopedia of Religion*. New York: Macmillan, 1986.

ExT   *Expository Times* (1889–).

FGrH   Jacoby, F., *Die Fragmente der griechischen Historiker*. Leiden: Brill, 1954 [1876].

FHG   Nicolas of Damascus. *Fragmenta historicorum graecorum,* ed. C. Müller, T. Müller, et al. Paris: Didot, 1853–70.

Fiensy, Social History   Fiensy, D. A., *The Social History of Palestine in the Herodian Period*. Lewiston, NY: Mellen, 1991.

Grant   Grant, M., *Herod the Great*. New York: American Heritage, 1971.

Hoehner, Herod Antipas   Hoehner, H., *Herod Antipas: A Contemporary of Jesus Christ*. Grand Rapids: Zondervan, 1980 [1972].

HTR   *Harvard Theological Review* (1908–).

IDB   Buttrick, G. A., ed., *Interpreter's Dictionary of the Bible*. New York: Abingdon, 1962.

IEJ *Israel Exploration Journal* (1949/50–).

IGR Cagnat, R., ed., *Inscriptiones Graecae ad Res Romanas Pertinentes.* Rome: L'Erma 1964 [1911].

ILS Dessau, H., *Inscriptiones Latinae Selectae.* Dublin: Apud Weidmannos, 1974 [1892].

JAOS *Journal of the American Oriental Society* (1843–).

JBL *Journal of Biblical Literature* (1881–).

Jones Jones, A. H. M., *The Herods of Judea.* Oxford: Clarendon, 1967 [1938].

Josephus See *Ant.; Apion; Life; War*

JQR *Jewish Quarterly Review* (1888–).

JRS *Journal of Roman Studies* (1911–).

JTS *Journal of Theological Studies* (1899–).

Life Josephus, *Life of Josephus.* In *Josephus.* Loeb Classical Library. Cambridge, MA: Harvard University Press, 1926.

Louw and Nida Louw, J. P., and E. A. Nida, *Greek-English Lexicon on the New Testament Based on Semantic Domains,* 2d ed. New York: United Bible Societies, 1989.

LSJ Liddell, H. G., R. Scott, and H. S. Jones, *A Greek-English Lexicon: A New Edition.* Oxford: Clarendon, 1940.

Meshorer, *Ancient Jewish Coinage* Meshorer, Y., *Ancient Jewish Coinage: Herod the Great through Bar Cochba,* vol. 2. New York: Amphora, 1982.

Meshorer, *Jewish Coins* Meshorer, Y., *Jewish Coins of the Second Temple Period.* Tel Aviv: Am Hassefer, 1967.

Millar, *Roman Near East* Millar, F., *The Roman Near East, 31 BC–AD 337.* Cambridge, MA: Harvard University Press, 1993.

NEAEHL Stern, E., ed., *New Encyclopedia of Archaeological Excavations of the Holy Land.* Jerusalem: Israel Exploration Society, 1994.

OGIS Dittenberger, W., *Orientis Graeci Inscriptiones Selectae.* Leipzig: Hirzel, 1903–5.

PEFQS *Palestine Exploration Fund Quarterly Statement* (1869–1936).

PEQ *Palestine Exploration Quarterly* (1937–).

Perowne Perowne, S. G., *The Life and Times of Herod the Great.* London: Hodder and Stoughton, 1956.

Philo, *De vita* *De vita contemplativa* ("On the Contemplative Life"). In Philo, *Complete Works*. Loeb Classical Library. Cambridge, MA: Harvard University Press, 1941.

Philo, *De virtutibus* *De virtutibus* ("On Virtues"). In Philo, *Complete Works*. Loeb Classical Library. Cambridge, MA: Harvard University Press, 1929.

Philo, *In Flacc.* *In Flaccum* ("Against Flaccus"). In Philo, *Complete Works*. Loeb Classical Library. Cambridge, MA: Harvard University Press, 1941.

Philo, *Legatio* *Legatio ad Gaium* ("On the Embassy to Gaius"). In Philo, *Complete Works*. Loeb Classical Library. Cambridge, MA: Harvard University Press, 1962.

Philo, *Quod Omnis* *Quod omnis probus liber sit* ("Every Good Man"). In Philo, *Complete Works*. Loeb Classical Library. Cambridge, MA: Harvard University Press, 1929.

Philo, *Spec. leg.* *De specialibus legibus* ("On the Special Laws"). In Philo, *Complete Works*. Loeb Classical Library. Cambridge, MA: Harvard University Press, 1937–39.

PIR *Prosopographia Imperii Romani*. Berlin: de Gruyter, 1933–1987.

Pliny, *NH* Pliny the Elder, *Natural History*. Loeb Classical Library; Cambridge, MA: Harvard University Press, 1938–63.

Plutarch, *Antony* Plutarch, *Makers of Rome: Mark Antony*. London: Penguin, 1965.

RB *Revue Biblique* (1892–).

Sanders, *Jewish Law* Sanders, E. P., *Jewish Law from Jesus to the Mishnah*. London: SCM, 1990.

Sanders, *Judaism* Sanders, E. P., *Judaism: Practice and Belief 63 BCE–66 CE*. London: SCM, 1992.

Schalit Schalit, A., *König Herodes. Der Mann und sein Werk*. Berlin: de Gruyter, 1969.

Schürer Schürer, E., rev. and ed. G. Vermes and F. Millar, *The History of the Jewish People in the Age of Jesus Christ (175 BC–AD 135)*. Edinburgh: T. & T. Clark, 1973–87.

SCI *Scripta Classica Israelica* (1974–).

SEG *Supplementum Epigraphicum Graecum* (1923–).

Shatzman, *Armies* Shatzman, I., *The Armies of the Hasmoneans and Herod*. Tübingen: J. C. B. Mohr, 1991.

Smallwood, *Jews* Smallwood, E. M., *The Jews under Roman Rule*. Leiden: Brill, 1976.

Stern, *CRINT* Safrai, S., and M. Stern, eds., *Compendia Rerum Iudaicarum ad Novum Testamentum*. Assen: van Gorcum/Philadelphia: Fortress, 1974– .

Stern, *Greek and Latin Authors* Stern, M., *Greek and Latin Authors on Jews and Judaism*. Jerusalem: Israel Academy of Sciences and Humanities, 1974–84.

Strabo, *Geog.* Strabo, *Geography*. Loeb Classical Library. Cambridge, MA: Harvard University Press, 1917–32.

Sullivan, *Near Eastern Royalty* Sullivan, R. D., *Near Eastern Royalty 100–30 BC*. Toronto: University of Toronto Press, 1990.

War Josephus, *The Jewish War*. In *Josephus*. Loeb Classical Library. Cambridge, MA: Harvard University Press, 1927–28.

ZPE *Zeitschrift für Papyrologie und Epigraphik* (1967–).

HEROD

King of the Jews and
Friend of the Romans

INTRODUCTION

ROME: EXTRACT FROM THE *ACTA DIURNA*

Herod, Friend of Romans, Dead at Seventy

ROME—Herod, son of Antipater, dependent king of Judea, whose death in Jericho has just been announced, was one of the most striking and vigorous personalities of our time. As an Idumaean Jew by birth he suffered from the prejudice attaching to that origin and had little prospect of reaching the place that under the princeps he actually achieved.[1]

His indomitable energy and his keen political sense kept him in the forefront of the affairs of the Eastern Mediterranean for over forty years. He was an intimate of our beloved Augustus and his much lamented son-in-law Marcus Agrippa; his children were educated in Rome in close touch with the Imperial family; he was the linchpin of the Senate's eastern policy.

It is rumored that the kingdom may be split between three of his surviving sons—Antipas, Philip, and Archelaus—all of whom have many friends here in the capital. Augustus will soon consider Herod's final will.

During the last few years, Herod was troubled by family intrigues, making the succession a matter of constant concern. Just last week his oldest son, Antipater, was executed in Jericho for plotting Herod's death, thus removing the strongest and most obvious successor. Three years ago two promising but disappointing sons, Alexander and Aristobulus, were tried and executed for plotting a coup and suborning the military. The great Augustus, a keen judge of character and sympathetic to Herod's troubles, was heard to say one evening at that

---

1. The *Acta Diurna* were handwritten newsheets posted daily in Rome and distributed to the provinces (see Tacitus, *Annals* 16.22, re 66 CE). This daily "gazette" included crimes, divorces, gladiatorial events, and horoscopes. None has survived.

1

time: "Gentlemen, it is better to be Herod's pig [Ed: a reference to a Jewish custom of avoiding pork] than to be his son."

Herod was married ten times; Romans have said openly that his family troubles were caused by this eastern practice of multiple marriages. One of his wives, Mariamme I, of royal Jewish blood, was executed on his orders many years ago. Many believe that Herod regretted her death. Of his surviving wives, Doris, Malthace, Cleopatra, and a second Mariamme are poised to influence the succession. His sister Salome is also reckoned to be a factor.

Citizens know Herod's reputation as a patron of the arts; the *Acta Diurna* has noted many of his buildings over the years. Vitruvius has reviewed several projects, most recently the substantial completion of the new temple in Jerusalem for the Jewish god. He reported on several novel features of the project: its size in a constrained urban site, the creation of pedestrian overpasses to relieve the pressure of too many visitors during major pilgrimages, the plating of much of the holy building with gold, the immense size of the stones. The *temenos* is among the largest religious precincts in Roman territory.

It is a striking testimony to the king's devotion to Augustus and his family that several of his major projects carry familiar names; Caesarea-by-the-Sea with its extremely large harbor and the city called Sebaste both make unmistakable reference to the emperor. Herod built magnificent buildings for the goddess Roma and the Imperial cult in both these large cities, and another in the provincial city of Panias. The king dedicated two towns to our great mother Livia and another to Marcus Agrippa.

Herod first came to public attention as a result of his father Antipater's appointment as procurator of Judea by the divine Julius Caesar, three years before Caesar's assassination. Antipater deputized Herod to govern Galilee, a troublesome northern region of Judea whose borders were infested by brigands, like other regions of the Empire in those difficult days before the princeps brought peace and security. The young Herod, only 25 at the time, eradicated the brigands in the region, allowing trade to flourish freely.

When Caesar's assassin, Cassius, seized control briefly of the Province of Syria he too recognized Herod's ability by giving him responsibilities in Coele-Syria. And when the Great Triumvirate revenged the murder of Caesar, the princeps and Antony jointly requested the Senate to appoint Herod king of Judea, so impressed were they with his vigorous leadership. Because of Parthian mobilization against Rome the Senate wished a king who had proven military genius. Herod was their man, and the gods of Rome smiled on this choice. In the obscure politics of Judea into which he was thrust, Herod was opposed by some Judeans who defied Rome's wisdom. They were assisted by a Parthian raiding party. Three years later, with the assistance of victorious Roman troops, Herod occupied his capital city, Jerusalem.

The Senate's confidence in Herod's wise political sense, advanced economic views, and sensitive religious policies was fully justified. During his long reign of 37 years—from two years after Augustus's defeat of Cassius and Brutus at Philippi to the present, the twenty-eighth year since Augustus's defeat of Antony and Cleopatra at Actium—Herod has been Rome's strongest supporter in the region.

Herod and Augustus's friendship began in Rhodes, following Actium, when Herod was confirmed as king of Judea. Herod admitted openly that he had faithfully served Antony; Augustus was won over by Herod's candor and his promise to serve Augustus as loyally as he had Antony. Since the region was volatile, the finances of the east were in a shambles, and Herod was a tried administrator, Augustus concluded that here was a Jew who could keep the region quiet and serve Rome's interests.

With only rare lapses Herod administered this border region well. He enthusiastically embraced the great *pax romana,* for which our generation shall be remembered until the fish disappear from the Middle Sea. He rebuilt roads, opened trade routes, created new harbors, collected taxes faithfully, lived peacefully with his Arab and Egyptian neighbors, and steered a middle course between the competing religious claims of rising sectarian groups in Judea.

Judean matters did not hold Herod's attention full time; he took a lively interest in Roman affairs, faithfully supporting the policies of the Senate, most actively when he led his new navy to join M. Agrippa in the Black Sea. On their overland route back they encouraged tolerant policies toward Jews.

Though Herod lacked the advantages of the Roman education that he was to give his sons, he was as cultivated as others of his rank. In his earlier years he was a prominent athlete. He was a patron of games and drama, and gave theaters, stadia, and amphitheaters to cities. The Trustees of the Olympic Games appointed him president for life; the Boule of Athens erected statues on the Acropolis and in the Forum. He devoted large sums of money to other projects in Syrian Antioch, Rhodes, Chios, Cos, and Lesbos.

He lived life exuberantly, though he could also be reclusive, suffering from a depressive disorder that Rome's best doctors could not treat successfully. His final illness was brought about by acute symptoms stemming, it is rumored, from a common social disease complicated by depression over his son's recent execution.

Herod will be interred in his favorite villa, Herodium, a wilderness retreat while he lived and now an imaginative mausoleum, in form like Augustus's on the banks of the Tiber.

Romans will mourn the loss of this friend, though the grief will be mixed with gratitude to Fortuna for a long and stable reign. The Senate has expressed its condolences to his large family and to the members of the Synagogue of the Herodians here in the capital.

CAESAREA MARITIMA—Nicolas of Damascus has just sent this report: "There was shock in Caesarea and Jerusalem, and as far away as Damascus and Ashkelon, at news of the death of King Herod, a wise administrator, able politician, and brilliant military commander. He worked hard to become a writer, and his memoirs will be consulted for years to come for their insights into the often turbulent political relationships of this region. Under the patronage of Augustus, the East has been unusually quiet; indeed it has flourished as never before. Right-thinking Jews applauded King Herod's efforts to end Judea's isolation and bring it and its dependent areas into the modern world. Like his friend Pompey, Herod may well be known as 'the Great.' He will be missed."

PETRA: TRANSCRIPT OF HERALD'S REPORT

King Herod Dies

PETRA—By Special Dispatch: The family of Herod announced in Jericho that the king of Judea, Idumaea, Samaritis, and Galilee is dead. Almost an adopted son, Herod spent many of his formative years in Petra. In Judea the news has received a mixed reception. His surviving children are testing the waters with a view to succeeding him.

Herod's father, Antipater, was an Idumaean notable who served Hyrcanus II of Judea, the Jewish pretender, and then later the Romans. Herod was proud of his descent from Cypros (whom he honored with a fortress near Jericho), the illustrious kinswoman of King Aretas. His relationships with Nabatea were often strained. His aggressive efforts to increase his territory brought him into conflict with Nabatea in Peraea, Auranitis, Trachonitis, and Batanea. With Herod's death, it is expected that territories still in dispute will be returned to Nabatea.

Herod had a lively interest both in Nabatea and Idumaea because of his royal estates, his dependence on commercial duties, his sense of the importance of Nabatean trade routes, and the fact that parts of his own wealth came from the region, especially from the lush fig and date groves at Jericho. His border post at Machaerus and the hot spring at Calirrhoe, both of which are in Nabatean territory, were two of his favorite places. He contributed generously to the three-temple holy city of Si'a, near Canatha in Auranitis. He dedicated a remarkable structure to the patriarchs Abraham, Isaac and Jacob, together with their wives, at Hebron in Idumaea—a memorial that was a model for his temple to the Jewish god in Jerusalem.

The late traitor Syllaeus created difficulties between Judea and Nabatea; now that Augustus has removed him from the scene it is hoped that relations between the two countries, so closely tied together in the person of Herod, will become more stable. The succession is still undecided.

LETTER FROM MANAEAN IN DAMASCUS TO EPHRAIM IN PALMYRA

From Manaean, member of the tribe of Naphtali living in Damascus, to Ephraim in Palmyra, peace to you in the name of the Lord. I thank the God of Israel, blessed be he, on every remembrance of you.

Word has just arrived by Imperial Post of King Herod's death. His passing will change the political balances in the region; some have already said they hope the government of Judea and its border regions will be handed over to Syria or be created a Senatorial Province on its own. It is rumored that Governor Varus welcomes an addition to his mandate. Some Jews have wondered if they should make plans to return to Judea now that the king is dead.

You probably recall that at various times Herod held important posts in Coele-Syria. As a young man he put an end to the brigands, and Damscene merchants still recall with gratitude the ease with which their goods now move south without risk. Herod adopted a large view of the region's good; he put himself at the disposal of the Roman authorities of Syria, assisting in making Syria's borders secure and assisting in internal affairs.

Herod had a close relationship with Jews in Damascus. Our good friends Nicolas and Ptolemy, native sons of this city, have been at the royal court and key advisers in Herod's government over the years. Nicolas has been court historian, scholar, confidant, and apologist, following his successful but ill-advised role in Egypt as tutor to Queen Cleopatra's children. Ptolemy has been a key economic adviser to Herod, shaping the policies that have reinvigorated the economy of Judea, shattered by the Hasmonean dynastic struggles.

Herod was generous to Damascus; did I mention when we attended the theater on your last visit that the building had been donated by the king? Not only did it make it possible for touring companies from distant Rome or Athens to put Damascus on their itinerary, it was a crucial step in the restoration of that quarter of the city near the Temple of Jupiter. I don't know whether Herod's largess extended to include Palmyra, but he made gifts to Tyre, Sidon, Beirut, and Laodicea. Perhaps you have seen his innovative project in Antioch-on-the-Orontes, repaving the main street and building colonnades along the whole street, making it possible for everyone to shop in the rain without getting wet.

Long ago, when the Parthians overran you and threatened Syria, Herod helped to oppose them. His loyalty to Augustus was legendary; there were rumors that Augustus wanted to reward Herod with a further grant of lands, including even Syria.

His passing will leave a vacuum, so that Augustus must act decisively to forestall dynastic struggles or—worse still—revolts. While I did not like Herod very much—I met him socially a few times—I understand what Cassius, Mark Antony, and Augustus saw in him. Herod became a major player on the world's stage, and he did it as a Jew! Few of our countrymen have done that.

Be of good cheer. Work hard. Keep Torah. I hope to visit you soon, but it will not be until the succession has been arranged to Augustus's satisfaction. I hear that several delegations are making their way to Rome to press their cases on the princeps. When it is settled I will find some business to do in Palmyra, and we can talk over these matters face to face.

Peace be upon you and upon all Israel.

P.S. Attached is a copy of the Praetorian announcement from Antioch. "Governor Varus has offered the province's sympathies to the family and people of Herod, King of Judea. Varus has emphasized that King Herod was a good friend of Rome and a close personal colleague. He said it was sad that in his final years King Herod had to face so many domestic tragedies. Over the many years of his rule, the King's policies transformed a petty territory into one of the robust economies of the East, a success story of large proportions."

JERUSALEM: JOURNAL, OBITUARY NOTICE

Herod, King of Judea, Joins His Fathers

JERUSALEM—The king is dead! King Herod's heart stopped beating late yesterday, in the thirty-seventh year of his reign, after a long and painful illness. For some years he had been in failing health. The end came quietly in the royal palace in Jericho, following Herod's last visit to the hot spring at Calirrhoe in Peraea. In last week's issue may be found the details of the execution of Prince Antipater, King Herod's eldest son and the odds-on favorite to succeed him. No details are known as we go to press of how other sons, in the wake of Antipater's execution, are poised to succeed Herod.

A state funeral for the king will be staged, with a military parade proceeding from Jericho past the intimidating Hyrcania fortress to the wilderness retreat of Herodium near Bethlehem. In an exclusive interview Nicolas of Damascus noted that this fortified palace was designed as a mausoleum. The king will be interred in a secret part of the palace complex tomorrow. The public is not invited. It is not known whether Temple representatives will attend.

The late king's reign was marked by the expansion of the country's borders, integration within the economy of Rome, extensive rebuilding projects including whole new cities, and close supervision of the daily life of the citizens. A religious observer who wished to remain anonymous said that Herod's reign was characterized by laxity toward Torah, disregard of the requirements for the high priesthood, and tensions among the various groups within Judea. Our religion reporter expects unrest in coming months.

King Herod was a third-generation proselyte. His father was a leading Idumaean noble when King Alexander Jannaeus, may he rest in peace, incorporated Idumaea into Judea. Herod's mother, Cypros, was a Nabatean noble of the house of Aretas. Of Herod's siblings only Salome is still alive; his older brother Phasael committed suicide under Parthian arrest at the time of the Hasmonean civil war, his brother Joseph was killed in a military action at about the same time, and his brother Pheroras died recently in disgrace. Though there was widespread religious concern when Herod took the throne, he was proud of his family's Jewish religious ties and upheld many of the requirements of Torah, though some observers thought him superficial.

At the time of his birth, in the fourth year of the pious Queen Alexandra, Herod was a commoner and an unlikely successor to her throne. Chutzpah, innate ability, hard work, ruthlessness, and clever alliances took him from obscurity—some of his youth was spent in Petra with his mother's family—to notoriety during the reign of the ethnarch Hyrcanus II. When his father Antipater was appointed procurator, first by the notorious Gabinius and later by Julius Caesar (may the Lord honor his efforts for the Diaspora), he appointed the twenty-five-year-old Herod governor of Galilee.

Herod waged a merciless campaign against peasants who had been dispossessed of houses and lands and had to live in caves. In wiping out the "brigands," as he liked to call them, Herod found a ready-made opportunity for his organizational and military abilities. Rome was impressed with the young man; his vigor and ruthlessness suited the Roman needs. The authorities in Jerusalem were less impressed. Young Herod was brought before the Court and charged with illegal executions of Jewish citizens, particularly the respected Hezekiah. There was no verdict; it was commonly said at the time that Sextus Caesar, Governor of Syria, had interfered in the case.

Herod was appointed Governor of Coele-Syria under three different provincial administrations. His ability to win everyone's confidence was one of the hallmarks of his career: in succession he sided with Caesar, Caesar's assassins Cassius and Brutus, their revengers Antony and Octavian, then with Antony and Cleopatra, and then with Octavian. Herod's ability to land on his feet served him well.

During the fratricidal war that brought the Hasmonean house to its end, Herod and his brother Phasael positioned themselves to assume power with Roman help. Herod's decisive moment came when Antigonus chased him from Jerusalem and almost wiped him out. Herod turned disaster to opportunity by going to Rome, where he was surprised to find it suited Rome's purposes to make him king of Judea. Three years later he entered Jerusalem to a mixed reception.

Herod extended the kingdom almost to the borders of the great King David, may his kingdom be soon restored! To the initial grant of Judea, Galilee, and Peraea the Roman Senate soon added Western Idumaea and Samaritis. He temporarily lost control of some territories that Antony gave to Cleopatra, but Herod soon gained these back peacefully. The expansion was a mixed blessing, for it brought into the kingdom Hellenistic cities both on the coast and inland. Later Augustus added another mixed blessing, the northeastern territories of Gaulanitis, Auranitis, Batanea, Trachonitis, Hulata, and Panias. Reports circulated that Augustus considered even larger extensions to the kingdom, perhaps incorporating Syria or Arabia; these reports were premature.

Herod had ten wives, nine of whom are still alive. According to palace gossip, he was obsessively attached to Mariamme, the daughter of Alexander and granddaughter of Hyrcanus II, through whom Herod was connected to Hasmonean royalty, though this marriage failed to mold popular opinion in his favor as he had hoped. The marriage was stormy, with accusations of infidelity and intended regicide. After her execution, Mariamme was interred in his family tomb outside the Damascus Gate.

In an interview with Nicolas of Damascus our reporter inquired about Herod's economic policies. Nicolas said Herod had pursued a consistent policy to stimulate the economy of Judea, using even his own private resources, through public works projects that would put cash into people's pockets, allowing them to feed their families and pay their taxes. Though he remitted taxes occasionally, fiscal matters caused him difficulties. Critics, who wish to remain anonymous, claim that small landholders lost their houses and farms to wealthy absentee landlords. In next week's issue our business reporter will have a fuller evaluation of the state of the economy.

Herod's economic policies depended on his building projects. He spent more, it is said, than Augustus or Marcus Agrippa, with whom he competed to be the world's greatest patron. It is said of Augustus that, having inherited Rome as a city of stone, he intends to leave it a city of marble. But it is also said that he who has not seen Herod's Temple in Jerusalem has not seen a beautiful building.

Several of Herod's projects have been reviewed in journals in Athens and Rome, where there is an interest in architectural innovation. Local religious leaders and nationalist groups have been concerned by his expenditures in foreign cities and for non-Jewish purposes, with large sums going to hippodromes, theaters, amphitheaters, and Gentile temples. It is said that he never assisted in the construction of a synagogue.

Public reaction is muted while the people await some indication of what will follow after this long reign of almost thirty-seven years. A team of reporters sought reactions on Jerusalem's streets.

Devorah, Housewife: My poor Yehudah was always grateful for the work he got on the Temple colonnades, but no Jew could like all of those wives falling over each other in the palace. And the way he treated his kids and they him—oy vay.

Yehoshua, Torah Student: I can never forgive the execution of my friends last month for their noble effort to rid the Temple of the hated eagle sculpture. May Herod rot in Hell!

Miriam, Resident of Bethlehem: I got work occasionally at Herodium making beds, though I never liked the long walk. It always surprised me that even his bedrooms did not have any Gentile decorations; I thought he was supposed to be almost a Gentile himself.

Joseph, Pilgrim from Galilee: My neighbors don't much like the way Sepphoris dominates the Galilee and alters its traditions, but I say if it helps put bread and occasionally meat on our tables, good for him.

Gamaliel, Scholar: His building activities may be remarkable, and even the Temple is unusual in its own way, but we shall have to wait for a careful assessment of the total impact of his reign. We all hope that the Emperor, may he rule in peace, will make a wise decision when he considers the will.

Theodoros, Pilgrim from Ephesus: Here in Jerusalem you've probably never heard how your king helped us get our rights in Ephesus about ten years ago. I'll tell you, he did more for Jews in the Diaspora than anyone else ever did. It sure helped that he was such good friends with Augustus and old Marcus Agrippa. Now all our half-shekel taxes get to Jerusalem, and it's easier to make the long trip ourselves. He may have been a dirty old man, but he made a difference.

Rachel, Widow of an Agricultural Worker: My David died in misery and hopelessness just three years after we lost our small farm to one of those rich cronies of the king's. I'm happy to see the back of Herod. Maybe now all those high and mighty mucky-mucks will get what's coming to 'em.

Jose, Pilgrim from Babylon: Some of my friends from home resettled in King Herod's new colony in Batanea recently, because he gave them a deal on land and taxes—the whole package was grand. I'm visiting them next week on the way home to decide if I'll move too. Besides, he appointed a high priest from Babylon. No one else ever did that.

Amir, Arab Slave: Who cares?

Joel, Ship Captain, on a Recruiting Drive: The late king was the first person in almost a millennium to restore Judea's international dignity. He built a navy and made us a force to be reckoned with internationally. Now when I sail the Inland Sea, I can keep my head high. I'll miss him, but I'll think of him every time I see one of those coins he minted with the ship on it.

Shlomo and Ruth, Merchants: Well, it's hard to say. He kept the trade routes open so we never had any troubles with brigands for the last twenty-five years. But you know, he was too diligent collecting his duties and shipping fees. Like, how much of it went into his own pockets?

Hananiah, Levite: As a singer in the Temple services, I am satisfied with the attention he gave to music in the worship of G—d. Some Levites approve of the increased water supply, the easy cleaning of the precincts and the smooth crowd control. So he may have had a good side to him—but he was still a scoundrel.

Daniel, Recluse from the Dead Sea Area: God's just retribution has overtaken him at last! May his name be blotted from the book of life! He was in league with the sons of darkness! His rebuilding of the Holy Place was an act of impiety unequalled in our days! May it soon be destroyed and replaced by a copy of the heavenly Jerusalem! Woe on the renegade! Woe!

Rivka, Visiting from Alexandria: My last trip to Jerusalem was more than twenty years ago, with my husband Jason, may his soul rest in peace. The thing I notice most is the rebuilt Temple; now women can take their rightful place in worship right in the Temple courtyards.

Alexander, Entrepreneur: The king involved Judea in the great Roman free-trade zone. It was a move that had to come, and it opened up new opportunities for foreign trade, at the same time lowering the price of goods here in Jerusalem. Without him how could we enjoy fine Nabatean dinnerware on our tables, French and Italian wines, spices from the East, or the best Egyptian wheat? I owe much to Herod.

Phineas, Street Person: Herod was no king. The day is coming soon when all who are in Rome's pocket will meet their just end, the poor and hungry will be filled and freedom will reign. Death to despots!

YODEFAT: REPORT OF POLICE AGENT ON A SPEECH BY JUDAS

YODEFAT—Pretending I was a visitor from Magdala, I mingled in a crowd that gathered as a messenger delivered the news that the king had died. Even before the herald had finished, a noisy demonstration erupted on the streets of the city. The king's death was greeted with cheers and the singing of the Hallel. Nationalists seize every opportunity to promote so-called political independence and religious reform.

Also in town at the same time was Judas, son of Hezekiah the brigand-chief from Gush Halav whom the king executed years ago. He urged the crowd to damn the late king's memory. His message was simple, much like the messages of other revolutionaries noted in earlier reports, on file. A brief summary:

—not legitimate because not from David's family, nor Hasmonean;

—appointed by a godless Senate of Rome;

—not a proper Jew—just a half-Jew, no Jew;

—suppressed people, turned Israel into police state;

—eroded customs and traditions of Jewish life;

—army too powerful;

—traditional peasant landholdings, esp. of olive and wheat farmers, handed over to wealthy Jerusalemites;

—values and attachment to Torah weakened;

—tensions because of settlements in area (esp. military settlements);

—when Herod was tried years ago he should have been executed for murder of Judas's father, but they lost their nerve.

You get the idea and I need say no more. The most important feature of the mob scene was what followed. First, some hot-heads in the crowd asked what they could do. This whipped up the crowd; almost everyone wanted to do something. There were lots of crazy suggestions, not many of them serious. Judas let it go on for a while until the mob was explosive. Then he took control again. He's a dangerous man with a crowd—he seems to know when to let them get on with it and when to inflame them with his own noisy rhetoric. He said that with Herod dead now is the time for popular action. There is no obvious successor now that Antipater, Alexander, and Aristobulus have been executed. The rest are struggling for a little piece of the action. The Romans are far away in Antioch and their troops are scattered. Judas said that all that lies between Jews and a successful revolt are Herod's soldiers—and many of them are sympathetic. Judas told the crowd that if they could run Galilee effectively, the Romans would quietly acquiesce. Apparently similar proposals are being made elsewhere in Judea, Samaritis, Peraea, and Idumaea.

Assessment: Judas is a dangerous charismatic with clear goals. He may start a guerrilla-style action, like his father's years ago. If so, he will need weapons. (The nearest supply is in the armories at Sepphoris.)

Recommendations: Inform the commander at Sepphoris that trouble is brewing. Strengthen the detachment there. Keep the weapons under lock and key. Keep Judas under surveillance. Keep a lookout in other known trouble-spots throughout the realm.

Future Plans: Now that I have completed my tour of duty in the hills of Galilee I go on leave to visit my family at Bethsaida. Send further instructions there. The king is dead; long live the king!

COMPETING VIEWS OF HEROD

The evidence for Herod's life is ample: "There is no figure in all antiquity about whom we have more detailed information than Herod."[2] Most of the information comes to us from Josephus (*War* and *Antiquities*), but his purposes vary in the two rather different accounts, and he provides different evaluations of Herod less than 20 years apart. One way to begin this account of Herod

---

2. L. H. Feldman, "Josephus," *ABD* 3.989.

would be to comment on Josephus's different assessments of the "personality" of Herod. A comparison would offer insight into both Herod and Josephus, underscoring that no account of Herod, not even Jospehus's, gives the "truth." All accounts are more or less fictional.

I have taken a more deliberately fictional approach to introducing Herod in this set of "obituaries" of Herod, with different fictional settings in cities where Herod was known: Rome, Petra, Damascus, Jerusalem, Yodefat.[3] Together they provide assessments of Herod as contemporaries might have thought of him. In the quotes attached to the Jerusalem obituary notice I have hinted at more variety. My point is to emphasize at the outset how strikingly difficult is a coherent assessment of Herod. He was as complex as Peter the Great, Alexander the Great, Catherine the Great, or, my favorite historical figure for comparison, Henry VIII. In attempting to get at the "truth" of Herod, one inevitably puts on a set of spectacles, providing a frame through which to look at him. Any biographical study into his character or personality is inevitably relative.

THE "GREAT"?

In this book, the title "Herod the Great" is not used, though at one point (above) it was hinted at by Nicolas of Damascus. The reason is simple: there is no historical evidence that our Herod was ever referred to, or that he wished anyone to refer to him, by that title. It is one of the curious ironies that Agrippa I, Herod's grandson, styled himself "the great king" on some of his coins,[4] though he has not come down in history as Agrippa the Great, while Herod, who did not seek this title, has come to be called Herod the Great. Pompey, by comparison, deliberately wished to be known as Pompey the Great, imitating Alexander the Great, whom he may have resembled.[5] The adjective *great* is used once in Josephus (*Ant.* 17.28) with reference to Agrippa I, where it may mean "the elder" as compared with Agrippa II. That Josephus can refer to Agrippa I in this way, whatever he may mean by it, argues strongly against first-century use of the title "Herod the Great" of our Herod. It probably crept into usage first as a reference to Agrippa and only later was transferred to his more important grandfather.

---

3. I owe this idea to Hilaire Belloc, who wrote a fine obituary of Agrippa I. H. Belloc, *This and That and The Other* (London: Methuen, 1912), pp. 260–65. Some of the language and the style of the first "obituary" are borrowed from him.

4. E. W. Klimowsky, "Agrippa I as BASILEUS MEGAS," in *Recent Studies and Discoveries on Ancient Jewish and Syrian Coins,* vol. 1 (Jerusalem: Israel Numismatic Society, 1954), pp. 91–95.

5. Pompey was called *magnus* from 81 BCE, when he was saluted this way by his army. He extracted agreement to a triumph from Sulla, which he celebrated on 12 March 81 BCE. J. Leach, *Pompey the Great* (London: Croom Helm, 1978), pp. 30–33.

To demonstrate the contrasting views of Herod, I will note three nearly contemporaneous pieces of evidence. First, Nicolas of Damascus, whose work was available to Josephus and certainly influenced his treatment both in broad strokes and in fine detail, wrote extensively about Herod in his *Universal History of the World.*[6] Nicolas's testimony, which exists only in snippets, is slanted; he was after all Herod's court historian and apologist. But it is worth underscoring that Nicolas thought Herod a significant enough personality that about a third of his history treated Herod's life and times—and this from someone who had been Cleopatra's children's tutor! Sycophancy did not demand such a posthumous glorification of his patron.

Second, just a few years later, when Augustus summarized the signal events of his career in the *Res gestae,* he included not a line about Herod, despite the inclusion of other somewhat similar characters.[7] This can be read two ways. It may indicate that one can exaggerate the role of Herod in Roman politics, an exaggeration I may be guilty of from time to time. It is also evidence that Herod never caused Augustus any concern. He did not have to intervene in the affairs of Judea once the appointment of Herod was made, so that aspect of his own career did not need any elaboration.

Third, Strabo, another slightly younger contemporary of Herod's (64/63 BCE–21 CE), was in Rome at least twice when Herod visited there and may himself have traveled through Judea. He summarized Herod in this way: he was "so superior to his predecessors, particularly in intercourse with Romans and in his administration of affairs of state, that he received the title of king" (*Geog.* 16.2.46).

Obviously the primary sources tolerate different evaluations of the man. And while mine is not the only possible one, the somewhat more generous assessment of him which follows may be closer to the "truth" than the harsher evaluations of previous generations. It extends somewhat the much fuller treatment of Schalit and attempts to be consistent with recent ways of reading the evidence with a social-historical slant.

---

6. See Schürer 1.30–31. Perhaps as much as 48 of the 144 books of his history dealt with Herod and his period. He also wrote a *Biography of Augustus* and an *Autobiography,* only fragments of which remain.

7. P. A. Brunt and J. M. Monroe, *Res gestae divi Augusti: The Achievements of the Divine Augustus. Introduction and Commentary* (Oxford: Oxford University Press, 1967). Augustus referred to Gaul, Spain, Africa, Sicily, Sardinia (25), to the Cimbri, Charydis, Semnones, and also to Ethiopia and Arabia Felix (26), to Egypt, Greater Armenia, Cyrene (27), Dalmatia and Parthia (29), Pannonia, Illyrica, Dacia (30), even to India (31). He details difficulties with various kings of Armenia (27), and lists ten other kings who came as suppliants (32). Perhaps Judea is included in the "very many other peoples [who] have experienced the good faith of the Roman people which had never previously exchanged embassies or had friendly relations with the Roman people" (32), but it is likelier that Augustus assumed that previous embassies had created "friendly relations" and that Pompey's actions had brought Judea into direct contact with Rome. Syria, not coincidentally, is also not mentioned, nor is Galatia or Cappadocia.

CHAPTER 1

In the End Is the Beginning

THE EAGLE, OR ECLIPSE OF A KING

On the night of March 13, 4 BCE, there was an eclipse of the moon. On the previous day, in the denouement of the famous "eagle affair," the Rabbi and instigator, Matthias, and some students were executed.

A few days earlier, as it became widely known that Herod was facing death, Matthias the son of Margalus, and Judas the son of Sepphoraeus, teachers with a large following of students and much popular support, urged that the time was ripe to rid the Temple of the one object that defaced it—a great golden eagle. The law of Israel, they said, forbade images and likenesses of living things; and even if death should follow from their actions, the students would gain fame and honor by pulling it down (*War* 1.648–55; *Ant.* 17.149–67).

The students acted with bravado as great numbers of people strolled in the Temple precincts at midday. The eagle had been placed by Herod above the "great Gate," according to Josephus, so they were in clear view of both the people and the guards. The students got up on a roof, let themselves down with ropes, hacked off the golden eagle (probably a low relief stone sculpture covered with gold leaf), and were promptly arrested by the Temple captain with a band of Temple guards. The people fled, but forty students were seized along with Judas and Matthias and taken before Herod. They defended their actions on the basis of Torah, "the laws that Moses wrote as God prompted and taught him," and happily accepted punishment, even death, for their "piety."

Herod sent them to Jericho where Jewish officials were being gathered (*Ant.* 17.160). Sick almost to death, Herod accused them and raged against the ingratitude he had faced, then praised his own reconstruction of the Temple. The result was not in doubt; Matthias and the main perpetrators were burned alive while the others were simply executed. The date of the executions can be ascertained from Josephus's reference to an eclipse of the moon.[1] The eclipse might also serve to symbolize the eclipse of Herod himself; Herod's illness was nearing its climax. He had only days to live, and this fact began to release the tensions buried just beneath the surface of a calm kingdom, tensions motivated to a large extent by religious devotion, attachment to Torah, and hope for a state governed by obedience to God. The courage of those opposed to Herod and his rule increased as Herod's health deteriorated.

But how offensive was the golden eagle over the great gate? Had Herod deliberately flaunted a symbol of Roman control before his resistant subjects? Had Jews quietly accepted for some time the presence of the image of a living creature without protest? The answer to the last question is probably yes, and they had accepted it for years, not days or months, since the major portion of the work on the Temple was completed in 15 BCE. If, as some claim, the eagle was on the Holy Place, it might have been there since the late 20s.[2] In any case, until this particular incident there seems to have been no strong objection to the eagle's presence and no disability to sacrifice was created by it.[3]

Whether the offense was deliberate and great depends on the location of the eagle. It is not clear which gate the eagle was over. It may have been the same gate as the one referred to by Josephus elsewhere as "Agrippa's Gate" (*War* 1.416), for the symbolism of the eagle, perhaps representing Rome,[4] above a gate named after Augustus's chief lieutenant would have been doubly power-ful. But even so, we do not know which gate was Agrippa's. Wilkinson suggests that the eagle was positioned over the doors of the Temple proper (in a fre-quently reproduced reconstruction[5] that many scholars writing on the incident simply assume), but this seems unlikely for several reasons. (1) Herod avoided needless offense and would hardly have spent the huge sums he did on the Temple to curry Jewish favor only to lose it by putting an eagle right on the Holy Place. (2) The students would have profaned the Holy Place while letting themselves down by ropes from a roof above, since they were not priests—at least there is no evidence that they were. (3) It is likelier that the roof in ques-tion was the roof of one the stoas surrounding the Temple, to which access was publicly available. (4) If the gate was the Agrippa Gate it would have been in a

---

1. The debate on the year is discusssed in Schürer 1.326–29.

2. The usual view is 20/19 BCE (based on *Ant.* 15.380–425); I am more inclined to 23 BCE (based on *War* 1.401).

3. On the eagle's significance, Schalit, Anh. XLIV, p. 734. See Grant, pp. 206–10, who also inclines to the view it had been there for some time.

4. This is not certain, and is not said or implied by Josephus. It is equally likely—perhaps even likelier—that the eagle was a "Nabatean" eagle, with wings pulled back and sitting erect on a corner or in some other decorative position. The Roman eagle usually had wings spread in a more hostile mode.

5. J. Wilkinson, *Jerusalem As Jesus Knew It* (London: Thames and Hudson, 1978), p. 87.

ceremonial location, possibly at the bridge to the upper city or near the Antonia fortress.[6]

The evidence suggests that the eagle was not placed over the main door to the Holy Place, an offense almost too great to contemplate for most pious Jews. It was also not likely to have been placed over any one of the several gates to the Court of Women, though from an architectural point of view one of these would have been possible, and one, Nicanor's Gate, might be considered a *great* gate. It also seems unlikely that the eagle was over a gate that had symbolic significance for Jews such as the Huldah Gates, which led up from the City of David, or the Golden Gate in the East Wall of the platform, which led in from the Mount of Olives.

This inferential process leads to the supposition that the eagle was over the gate above what is now called Wilson's arch, the bridge leading to the Temple from the upper city. The plausibility of this view rests on several factors. (1) This was the route taken to the Temple by the upper classes living on the western hill, among whom were persons more tolerant of Hellenism and compliance with the Romans. (2) This was also the route from Herod's Palace, on the site of what is now the Citadel near the Jaffa Gate. (3) This was then the natural ceremonial route for distinguished visitors, such as Augustus or Agrippa, to visit the Temple precincts. (4) Such a location would allow that the eagle be placed either on the inside or outside face of the gate itself, though it seems likeliest that it was placed on the outside, not only because this was the normal position for symbolic architectural decoration[7] but also because an external location had the greatest impact on a first-time visitor. (5) In either location the students would have had access to the sculpture from the roof[8] and would have been able to be seen. (6) The uniqueness of this approach by bridge might well justify the term *great* being applied to the gate at the end of this imposing vista, rare—perhaps unique—in late Hellenistic and early Imperial cities.[9]

---

6. Further, see P. Richardson, "Why Turn the Tables? Jesus' Protest in the Temple Precincts," *SBL Seminar Papers 1992* (Atlanta: Scholars Press, 1992), pp. 507–23.

7. See the gates of the *theatron* at Siʿa (near Canatha) surrounding the Temple of Baʿal Shamim, especially relevant because of its use of the same eagle motif. The temple complex at Siʿa included both a Temple to Baʿal Shamim, which is to be connected with Herod himself (chaps. 3, 8) and a Temple of Dushara. For reconstruction drawings, see H. C. Butler, *Architecture, Southern Syria,* Division II A, Publications of the Princeton University Archaeological Expeditions to Syria, 1904–5 (Leiden: Brill, 1907), pp. 369–85, esp. 382.

8. Other descriptions in Josephus, some in the context of revolts, show how easy access to the roof of the stoas (or porticoes) was; e.g., *War* 2.48; *Ant.* 17.259.

9. Very frequently in other cities the main sanctuary is located on an *akropolis,* challenging the architect in a very different way to lead the worshipper to the place of worship. In Jerusalem the holy site is lower than the Western hill, the Mount of Olives, and suburbs to the north, but it is flanked by deep valleys. The architectural problem is thus quite different, except from the south. In the case of the Temple in Jerusalem, the Western approaches are dramtically designed.

We can now answer the question of whether Herod gave deliberate offense to Jews by the eagle. Yes and no. Offense there certainly was—but offense muted by the fact that Jews could not see the eagle from inside the Temple and could easily avoid it from the outside by using another gate. In any case, this decorative motif had ancient precedent in the Temple of Solomon, which was decorated extensively with "cherubim" (1 Kings 6:23–29) or, as Josephus says, "eagles" (*Ant.* 8.74, 81–83).

To sum up: (1) far from confirming a high degree of hellenization in Herod's buildings, the eagle and its offense were a variation from Herod's normal aniconic practice, which the religious authorities and the populace tolerated because it was so minor. (2) There was dissent, for Herod must have had a policy of "suppression." Some dissent was religiously motivated, possibly founded on scriptural study, and it was present both in Jerusalem and in more remote parts of the kingdom. (3) Herod balanced two competing needs: his commitment to Judaism caused him to give little offense in his buildings, especially the Temple in Jerusalem; but his attachment to Rome caused him to include, in as politically astute a way as possible, a symbol of Roman authority. The "eagle affair" was important in the eyes of both Herod and his critics. Herod was affronted by it; his critics saw it as a sign of how near the end was for a ruler who now had a fragile hold on power.

DEATH OF A KING

Later the same March (4 BCE) Herod died at his winter palace in Jericho of a painful disease, probably syphilis. His symptoms included fever, itching, pains in the colon, swollen feet, inflammation of the abdomen, gangrene of the penis, lung disease, convulsions, and eye problems.[10] He had gone to Jericho to try those accused in the "eagle affair," and then to the hot-springs on the east shore of the Dead Sea at Callirrhoe (where a splendid hotel now offers the same opportunity). All to no avail. The end was near.

Josephus's account is very dramatic.[11] When Herod saw no improvement from the hot-spring he despaired of recovery. His first reaction was to distribute fifty drachmas to each soldier, with more going to commanders and friends. Then, when he returned to Jericho, he determined that there would be an outpouring of grief at his death. To this end he gathered the elite of Jewish society together in the hippodrome at Jericho (presumably Josephus means

---

10. Dr. T. J. Murray (Dean of Medicine at Dalhousie University in Halifax, NS) offers four possible causes: tertiary syphilis, sarcoidosis, collagen vascular disease, and pemphigus (private communication).

11. I follow *War* 1.656–73; 2.1–100. The account in *Ant.* 17.168–323 is fuller; some of the differences will be alluded to in what follows. There is skepticism over Josephus's account, especially whether all the events can be fitted into the time available. It is a tight fit, but possible.

those gathered at the time of the "eagle affair"), closed the gates and instructed his sister Salome—who, with more dedication than insight, had stuck by him through thick and thin—and her husband Alexas to order the execution of these Jews at his death.

First a sub-plot had to be played out. Herod's relations with his oldest son, Antipater (named after his grandfather), had been very volatile. Antipater was now under sentence of death, a judicial decision that had been confirmed by Augustus in Rome.[12] But with Herod near death, a letter arrived stating that if Herod were inclined merely to banish Antipater the Emperor was agreeable. Josephus does not say whether Herod was so inclined.

Herod's despair was so great over his health problems—he was in his seventieth year and acutely ill—that he tried to kill himself with a paring knife. His cousin Achiab, who was attending him at the time, prevented him from carrying out this desperate act. The incident brought such a cry from those present that others in the palace, especially Antipater in his detention room, thought that Herod had died. Antipater was filled with hope, thinking that he had outlasted his father, and tried to bribe his jailer to let him go. But the jailer went straight to Herod's bedside and told him of Antipater's bribery attempt. Herod then ordered Antipater's immediate execution and burial at Hyrcanium, the nearest and most notorious of his wilderness fortified palaces. Herod immediately rewrote his will.[13]

He survived Antipater by only five days. Before it was known that he had expired, Salome dismissed the soldiers guarding the Jericho hippodrome and sent home the notables being held hostage. She later gathered the soldiers and whatever crowds she could into the hippodrome, where Ptolemy, Herod's chief financial minister, read a letter to the soldiers, asking them to be faithful to his successor. Ptolemy also read Herod's new will, which trifurcated his kingdom with Archelaus as king of Judea, Antipas as tetrarch of Galilee, and Philip as tetrarch of Trachonitis and the adjacent regions. Since the Emperor had to confirm these dispositions, Ptolemy was to take Herod's signet ring and his will to Rome for official action.[14]

Archelaus was congratulated by all; he set about making his father's funeral arrangements, having just looked after the funeral of his half-brother Antipater. We may suspect that in both cases he did so with relief or even pleasure. The royal jewels were displayed; Herod was laid out in purple grave clothes on a bier of gold decorated with precious gems, wearing a diadem of gold on his

---

12. Josephus usually refers to Augustus as Caesar; to avoid confusion with Julius Caesar I shall refer to him either as Augustus or, before the year 27 BCE, as Octavian.

13. On Herod's plans for the succession and his seven wills, see chap. 2.

14. In about 12 BCE Herod had been given the unusual privilege of naming his own successor. This arrangement was withdrawn in about 9 BCE, during the period when the relationship between Herod and Augustus was extremely strained (see chap. 11).

head, with a gold crown above that and holding a scepter in his hand. These accoutrements underlined that Herod was king of Judea and had been for over thirty-five years. The funeral procession included Herod's surviving children, first; then his other relatives; then his personal bodyguard, the Thracian regiment, the German regiment, and the Galatian regiment, all in battle dress, and then the rest of the army. Five hundred personal servants and freedmen followed carrying funeral spices. This impressive procession carried the funeral bier twenty-five miles to Herod's fortified palace on the edge of the Judean wilderness at Herodium, which had been specially designed to do double duty as a royal residence and a mausoleum (see chap. 8).

There Herod was buried. A mystery clouds his end, for no trace of his burial has been found despite the very extensive excavations at Herodium: no body, no artifacts, no evidence of grave robbery, no tomb. Indeed there is no place that seems both suitable and feasible for a burial chamber. It seems that in the end, Herod outwitted everyone.[15]

FAMILY SQUABBLES IN ROME

So ended Rome's most successful attempt to impose order on Judea. From that point on Rome's arrangements for keeping Judea pacified were, from both points of view, less satisfactory. The problems that led up to the revolt of 66 CE, and even later to the revolt of 132 CE, were in part the result of the longings for self-determination spawned under Herod among those who resisted the Idumaean "usurper," and in part the result of Rome's inability to understand Jewish convictions and aspirations.[16]

When Augustus divided the kingdom he did so under exceedingly awkward circumstances.[17] The chief members of Herod's court had traveled to Rome to argue their various cases before Augustus. There was no agreement

---

15. Ehud Netzer has made Herod's burial place a special concern. He has concluded that the most logical place, at the foot of the main circular tower in Herodium's upper palace, is impossible because it is solid masonry. He has investigated carefully the next likeliest place, the so-called Monumental Building on the lower level of Herodium, and can find no evidence for any burial there. The mystery remains.

16. The issues are of course complex: the Hasmonean revolt and the subsequent course of events, including the gradual hellenizing of an originally anti-Hellenistic revolt, account for many of the groups that developed during the second century BCE. Relatively few discrete shades of opinion were generated during the Herodian period itself; most seem to come from either before (Pharisees, Sadducees, Qumran) or after (Zealots, Sicarii, Baptists). See esp. chap. 10; M. Goodman, *The Ruling Class of Judea. The Origins of the Jewish Revolt against Rome A.D. 66–70* (Cambridge: Cambridge University Press, 1987); and R. Fenn, *The Death of Herod: An Essay in the Sociology of Religion* (Cambridge: Cambridge University Press, 1992).

17. For conditions generally, see Millar, *Roman Near East,* pp. 27–79 and 337–66, though he does not address these specific questions in detail.

among them as to what to recommend to him; indeed, many of the key persons changed their views along the way. Two of the three main beneficiaries were vying for sole rule or at least for the largest piece of the pie; a third was playing a waiting game. The decision was almost a *fait accompli,* since Herod's will had been read out at Jericho, and Archelaus had begun to act as if he were king. To complicate matters, there were earlier and quite different wills.[18]

Archelaus botched things in the first few days of his reign. After the requisite mourning period and a large funeral feast for the multitudes, several requests were made of him: lighten personal taxes; remove some of the duties on manufactured goods; release the prisoners. He acceded to these suggestions, with the expected result: a stepped-up set of new requests. These included punishment for those who had recently been honored by Herod, including those responsible for the executions of the students involved in the recent "eagle affair." Along with this came a demand that the high priest be removed from office and replaced by one not tarred with Herod's brush—one of greater piety and purity. These demands were too much. Archelaus, trapped by his earlier too-ready acquiescence, became upset when he realized that what he had agreed to was not enough. When he sent his general to tell those pressuring him to ease up, matters escalated, just as the Passover feast with its huge crowds was upon them. As the crowds noisily mourned the loss of Judas and Matthias, Archelaus instructed soldiers to keep the crowds quiet. The confrontation got out of hand, unintentionally it would seem, and many Passover pilgrims (three thousand, according to Josephus) were killed.

This incident poisoned the atmosphere as members of the court left for Rome; Josephus says some people changed their minds over the succession as a result of this confrontation since it was perceived as an indication of Archelaus's unsuitability to rule.

The scene in Rome when all the participants arrived was tense. The Senate assembled with Augustus present, along with his own heir, Gaius (his adopted son who was actually his grandson, the child of his daughter Julia and her husband Marcus Vipsanius Agrippa). Augustus had received written depositions by major actors in the drama: by Sabinus, procurator of Syria, accusing Archelaus and lauding Antipas; by Salome and her family, also accusing Archelaus; by Archelaus himself, providing confirmation of his claim; by Ptolemy, reckoning up Herod's accounts and handing over Herod's signet ring; and by Varus, governor (*legatus*) of Syria.

Present at the hearing were Archelaus and Antipas (full brothers), with their aunt, Salome. Philip (a half brother), who had been left at home to tend matters in Archelaus's place, arrived late.[19] Also present were Nicolas of Damas-

---

18. See chap. 2 for the wills.

19. According to Josephus, *War* 2.82–83 and *Ant.* 17.303, he headed for Rome at Varus's suggestion.

cus, Herod's chief adviser; Ptolemy of Damascus, Nicolas's brother and Herod's chief economic minister; Irenaeus, an orator retained to speak for Antipas; Antipater, Salome's son, speaking mainly against Archelaus. Though Salome and others had promised to support Archelaus, in fact they disliked him and transferred their support to Antipas; still, their first preference, according to Josephus in a surprising aside, was for autonomy under the protection of a Roman official.

The forces were neatly balanced. Archelaus, named king in his father's last will, was supported by Nicolas and Ptolemy and by his own half-brother Philip; this support was offset by the strong opposition of Sabinus and of most of the family. Antipas, placed second in his father's will, had been named sole heir in an earlier will; he was supported by most of the family members, even if lukewarmly, and by Sabinus (*War* 2.20–22). Archelaus and Antipas were the main combatants. But some suggested local autonomy under the Syrian governor. This must have been a viable possibility; dependent kingdoms, like Judea under Herod, usually lasted for relatively short times until they had been brought more fully into Roman culture and practices, at which point it would be natural to integrate them into the provincial system.

Having considered the depositions, Augustus convened the hearing. First on his feet was Antipater, Salome's son, first cousin of the main claimants.[20] Antipater made four points attempting to undercut Archelaus's claims: (1) Archelaus had preempted Augustus's decision by acting as if he were king, and this *lèse-majesté* disqualified him;[21] (2) he had encouraged unrest by appearing to mourn his father but secretly carousing at night; (3) as his grotesque butchery of a large number of pilgrims in the Temple showed, he was cruel, a character flaw that Herod had recognized by not giving him much hope of succession; (4) Herod's last will had been written when he was not of sound mind. Other relatives testified to the truth of these claims.

Nicolas, Herod's adviser and historian, defended Archelaus. Archelaus's actions were a sign of his loyalty, he said, for those killed in the Temple had been enemies of Augustus as much as of Archelaus. In fact, his actions had been advised by his accusers. Further, the last will was actually a very sensible document, for the naming of Archelaus as successor was just as sensible as the naming of Augustus as executor of the will (though this was the usual role of the Emperor in such matters). Then Archelaus fell on his knees before Augustus, who raised him up and said that he deserved to succeed his father. But Augustus

---

20. Antipater was married to his first cousin, Cypros, daughter of Herod and Mariamme I, the Ḥaṣmonean princess. He was thus doubly interested in the succession; curiously, he figures in the story only at this point.

21. Augustus insisted that client kings could not appoint their own successors but required the decision of the Emperor, Jones, pp. 66–67.

made no decision, and, according to Josephus, was of two minds: should he appoint one person only or divide the power so that the combatants would each have some support?

Events intervened. Varus, the Syrian governor, reported a major revolt ("Varus's War," as the *Talmud* calls it) at the feast of Pentecost, when large crowds were again up in Jerusalem. Pilgrims from Galilee and Idumaea had camped north of the Temple, those from Jericho and Peraea had camped to the south, and others from Judea had camped to the west. Whether by accident or design the Jews had Sabinus's troops surrounded. After an initial clash in the Temple, during which some of the colonnades were burned and much of the Temple treasure was looted by the Romans, the Jews surrounded Herod's palace, joined by deserters from the royal troops. There were also uprisings in the countryside: in Idumaea with Herodian veterans as the main corps; at Sepphoris led by Judas, son of the brigand chief Hezekiah (whose defeat by Herod had helped to make his early reputation); in Peraea where one mob, led by the royal slave Simon, burned the Winter Palace at Jericho, and another burned the royal palace at Betharamphtha; and in Judea, a mob led by Athronges and his four brothers. The spread of these uprisings—Jerusalem, Judea, Galilee, Peraea and Idumaea—must have been very threatening.[22]

Varus marched from Antioch to Ptolemais (Acco), on to Sepphoris (which he burned), then to Sebaste (which he saved, because it had not risen in revolt), and then up to Jerusalem (after plundering Arus, Sappho, and Emmaus). The pilgrims in Jerusalem now melted away to their distant homes at this display of Roman might, if they had not already done so. The inhabitants of Jerusalem disclaimed all responsibility. Varus rounded up the ringleaders throughout the country and brought them to Jerusalem, crucifying two thousand.

A particularly troublesome Idumaean rebel force decided—on the advice of Achiab, the cousin who had been with Herod at the time of his death—to surrender, and most were pardoned. Some Idumaean relatives of Herod's were sent to Rome in chains and executed by Augustus for fighting against a king of their own family. Their identity is not known.

In Rome, Archelaus—joined by Philip, who had become more independent and was vying for a share of the pie—was confronted by a delegation of fifty Judean ambassadors, supported by the Jewish community of Rome. As some of Herod's family had done earlier, these Judean ambassadors petitioned Augustus to unite Judea with Syria as long as there was a degree of separate administration. This compromise solution showed their loyalty to Rome, they claimed, and their willingness to submit to Roman authority and it would give them a safeguard against tyranny. The petition required them to make serious allegations about the late king's conduct, though Nicolas loyally refuted the

---

22. Goodman, *Ruling Class,* chap. 4; Fenn, *Death of Herod,* chap. 6.

charges and accused the Judeans of anarchism and persistent disloyalty. He linked this with a denunciation of Archelaus's relatives, who had swung over to the other side.

A second delegation must have appeared, though it is not mentioned by Josephus. Some cities of the Decapolis asked to be released from Jewish domination and attached to Syria (see chap. 4), successfully it seems, for Gadara, Hippos, and Gaza were detached from Judea, reshaping the settlement and adding to its complexity.[23]

Augustus had supported Herod from the spring of 30 BCE when Herod offered his allegiance, after Augustus, then known as Octavian, had defeated Mark Antony at the battle of Actium (31 BCE). Now, in 4 BCE, Augustus confirmed Herod's will, with several minor changes. Archelaus was named ethnarch, not king, of Judea, Samaritis, and Idumaea, including the important cities of Sebaste and Caesarea Maritima, both lavishly built by Herod. The title "ethnarch" implied that Archelaus ruled a "people," even though the "peoples" under his control were very disparate. Augustus held back from giving Archelaus the status, dignity, and role that went with the title "king." Antipas, who figures prominently in the gospels, became tetrarch of Galilee and Peraea, fertile areas with mixed but largely Jewish populations, separated by the Jordan River and by two cities of the Decapolis. Philip was allotted the northeast section of the kingdom: Trachonitis, Batanea, Gaulanitis, Auranitis, and the parts of Ituraea around Panias (soon to be re-christened Caesarea Philippi).[24]

Two other cities of the Decapolis that had been granted to Herod much earlier, Hippos (Susita) to the east and Gadara (Umm Qeis) to the southeast of the Sea of Galilee, were transferred to the province of Syria, as was Gaza, far to the southwest. Herod's sister Salome was rewarded with control of Phasaelis (named after her oldest brother), a new city in the Jordan valley, and two important cities near the coast, Jamnia (or Yavneh, where scribal learning later flourished) and Azotus (Ashdod).

Josephus subtly underscores, as he had earlier, the importance of the financial element and the potentially destabilizing effect of any decision that left principal players without adequate resources. Each of the heirs received an income sufficient to keep them in the style to which they had become accustomed: Archelaus four hundred talents, Antipas two hundred, Philip one hundred, Salome sixty. The sum of these figures approximated Herod's tax base and the relative wealth of each area. Augustus also confirmed dowries for two other daughters and arranged marriages for them. In a surprising act of generos-

---

23. Nicolas of Damascus, fragment 5 (*FHG* III, p. 354) = fragment 136,9 (*FGrH* IIA, no 90, p. 424). The contents of the negotiations are summarized in paragraphs 8–11 of the fragment; Josephus did not use this information, which he probably knew.

24. On these and other successors, see chap. 12.

ity and a mark of fondness for Herod, Augustus redistributed among Herod's family the one thousand talents that Herod willed him, keeping only a few sentimental items for himself. Whether Livia kept her five-hundred-talent bequest we are not told.

This division, predicated on an inability to select one trustworthy person, intensified the problems of the next century-and-a-half. Augustus unwisely acceded to Herod's last minute wishes and then complicated matters by subdividing the area still more.

AUGUSTUS'S INDECISION

This short period mirrored the turbulence of Herod's reign. Social unrest, high taxation, foreign use of funds, religion as a rallying point, unbridled ambition, distrust within the family, Roman failure to understand Judea, opportunism of the surrounding peoples—all are important themes in Herod's life and career, themes that reappear again and again.

The preference for the "Syrian option" expressed by three groups of Jews (family members around Salome, the Judean delegation,[25] and Rome's Jewish community) and, less surprisingly, by the independent delegation from the Decapolis, expressed judgment on Herod's strong centralist policy and confidence in Rome's policies. Herod's policies had not generated a desire for political independence.

Judea had achieved a place of influence in world affairs, buttressing one end of the Roman Empire; it should have troubled Augustus that disparate groups preferred direct Roman rule, with some local autonomy, to a dependent kingdom. Herod's long, prosperous, and relatively peaceful reign had not persuaded the population that this form of governance was preferable. When the Judean delegation argued vigorously for inclusion in Syria, they must have been motivated partly by dislike of Herod and partly by preference for religious self-determination over home-rule—an issue not stated in the texts but lurking below the surface. The preference for inclusion in Syria made sense to the delegation, though it made less sense to the family members. It seems the delegation was less concerned for "autonomy of the people" (as Josephus reports)[26] than for a course of action that would increase the degree of religious self-determination and assist in a return to a more theocratic state, even if theocratic principles were limited to a narrower sphere focused on cult and law.

Ironically, the argument to include Judea in Syria played straight into Au-

---

25. This delegation was instructed by Varus and sent with his concurrence; Varus had more than one iron in the fire. *War* 2.80; *Ant.* 17.300.

26. *War* 2.80; *peri tes tou ethnous autonomias,* which does not mean exactly "racial" (so Williamson) but rather "national autonomy," the same idea that stands behind the title "ethnarch."

gustus's hand; his own principles might have led him to think the time was ripe to convert Judea into a Roman province or to include it in Syria—in either case to have more direct Roman rule.[27] But he did not play the card offered to him. He may have deemed Judea still too troubled to be incorporated peacefully into Syria; he may have felt the area would benefit from more time under a strong dependent king before complete absorption took place. But if so, he faltered at the crucial moment, for he did not fashion a settlement calculated to continue Herod's strong rule.

Augustus took instead a weak course of action; he divided the kingdom as Herod had suggested. Augustus, the master of *Realpolitik,* failed to take a decisive course when faced with familial bitterness. The relations between Antipas and Archelaus must have been close to impossible, and Salome's change of heart to support Antipas against Archelaus was overlooked in the final settlement, for the cities she inherited were nominally in Archelaus's area. Only Philip emerged unscathed from the infighting. Augustus's decision to confirm the basic outlines of Herod's last will is surprising,[28] especially if that will was an act of desperation.

The role of Augustus's representatives in Syria is obscure. Is it significant that Sabinus, the procurator responsible for financial matters, supported Antipas, while Varus, the governor responsible for political and military affairs, supported Archelaus and then Philip? Romans on the scene did not echo family support for Antipas, who turned out to be rather able. Herod's earlier judgment in naming Antipas his sole heir may have been correct, as was the decision of Salome and others who shifted their support to Antipas, for Augustus had to depose Archelaus less than ten years later (in 6 CE) while Antipas survived as tetrarch of Galilee and Peraea until 39 CE when he too was deposed. Philip continued to rule Gaulanitis, Auranitis, and Trachonitis until he died in 34 CE.

The problems of the next generation were exacerbated partly by the family squabbles and partly by a divided kingdom but mostly by the inherent uncertainties of a weak solution. None of the brothers had a strong enough political and military base to impose order on the whole area, should that become necessary, as their father had done. When Archelaus was deposed as the result of the combined complaints of Judeans and Samaritans, Augustus allocated Judea neither to Antipas nor to Philip, though both were ruling moderately well. Instead he chose another confusing course of action—to annex Judea and govern it from Rome via Syria as a second-class province.

---

27. Galatia, on the death of Amyntas in 25 BCE, ceased to be a dependent kingdom and was created a new province. On the death of Deiotarus Philadelphus of Paphlagonia that kingdom was added to Galatia. When Archelaus failed to govern Judea adequately, Augustus made it a procuratorial province in 6 CE.

28. Perhaps Augustus believed the Syrian option would work only if there were some degree of religious self-determination, and that this disadvantage outweighed its potential advantages.

This settlement throws light on the evaluation of Herod in Rome. August-us's decision to divide the kingdom was political, though the factors that tipped the balance are unclear. Augustus was trying to fashion his own dynasty—his young grandson Gaius had just been introduced to public life and his other grandson Lucius was soon to be. But such familial concerns can hardly have influenced Augustus when it came to the turbulent eastern border, with its especially volatile Jewish peoples.[29] The settlement was unwise, even wrong. The popular revolts that followed Herod's death while the rival claimants were still in Rome cannot, of course, be attributed to Augustus's decision; at the time they broke out Augustus had not yet made up his mind. But they were a sign of deep political and social unrest, encouraged if not created by the stupidity and weakness of Archelaus in those first few days of his *de facto* rule. Once started, the revolts developed a life of their own, with leaders searching for a petty principality or instant aggrandizement. These revolts prefigure the later revolts of 6 CE under Judas and Zadok (see Acts 5:37; *War* 2.56) and the more destructive revolts of 66–74 CE and 132–35 CE.[30] A wise and strong successor to Herod might, with a different style from Herod's, have settled the issues in such a way that these later revolts would never have begun. It is even arguable that the Diaspora, calm and well-treated during Herod's reign, would have had no occasion to rise up in 115–17 CE had the decision in 4 BCE been different.

Augustus's decision must have had to do with conditions in Syria and Judea. Varus as governor and Sabinus as procurator differed in opinion; since Sabinus was the weaker of the two, little credence needed to be given to his support for Antipas, but Varus's support for Archelaus and Philip may have been a factor. Neither Varus nor Sabinus, however, was on the scene in Rome to offer advice directly to Augustus. Varus's encouragement of the delegation to plead their case for "ethnic autonomy" seems strange, but it underlines the ambivalence of informed Romans toward Judea's future. Was Varus hedging his bets? Was he playing one side against the other? Was he trying to enhance the province of Syria? Or was Varus genuinely more optimistic about Philip, the less deeply involved and perhaps less ambitious of the brothers?

Financial considerations probably played a part in Augustus's decision to accept a divided kingdom. (1) Josephus implies the need of support for Herod's many children as well as his sister Salome. An assured income for the children would contribute to political stability, because the aggrieved claimants to power

29. See Bowersock, *Roman Arabia*, pp. 45, 54, and all chap. 4.
30. See M. Hengel, *The Zealots* (Edinburgh: T. & T. Clark, 1989); an earlier study by W. Farmer, *Maccabees, Zealots and Jospehus* (New York: Columbia University Press, 1957) is still valuable; the studies by R. Horsley, *Jesus and the Spiral of Violence* (San Francisco: Harper & Row, 1987) and, with J. Hanson, *Bandits, Prophets, and Messiahs* (Minneapolis: Winston, 1985), take a social-historical approach and shed fresh light on the conditions. See also Fenn, *Death of Herod*, and Goodman, *Ruling Class*.

would be less likely to make trouble if they were comfortably well-off. The settlement was in this respect a success. (2) Most Jews voluntarily accepted their religious obligations to support the Temple and the priests through both the general Temple tax and the tithe and first-fruit offerings.[31] Since there was no offsetting tax credit for religious taxes paid, they had to pay the state-imposed head and property taxes as well as local manufacturing taxes and border-crossing duties. It is impossible to assess accurately the net effect of these stacked taxes, but it is likely that the peasants remained in a state of not-so-genteel poverty and that the urban proletariat scrambled to keep ahead of the tax collectors. There is not much direct evidence—some, but not much—that poverty was endemic, or that Jews were so badly off that revolt was the only recourse. (The gospels' concern with wealth and poverty is among the best kinds of evidence.[32]) (3) Herod's Keynesian economic policies had offset these relatively high taxes; he pumped large amounts of money, often his own money, into the economy to keep the country at work. His building projects scattered throughout the kingdom helped to create a measure of prosperity in all parts of the country. When things were particularly bad as a result of natural disaster he remitted taxes to keep money flowing. In general, though the taxes were heavy, the economy was healthy at his death.

Religion may also have played some part in Augustus's decision, though its role is more likely to have been negative than positive. None of the claimants was fired by the flames of religion, to judge from their later careers. All of them were like their father in that they did not see Judaism in exclusive terms. Augustus probably would have eliminated from contention anyone who showed too much enthusiasm for Judaism, for while he was willing to tolerate it, he was not inclined to increase its sense of importance or its degree of autonomy. This probably was exactly how he read the Jewish delegation's proposal: as they argued for inclusion in Syria they also argued for limited self-rule by which Judea would be administered through their own Jewish officials (*hêgemôn*). A system including the Temple hierarchy and a series of courts was already in place, though it had been overlooked or even abused during Herod's reign. That system could administer the laws of the country and exercise an appropriate range of penalties and judgments in accord with Torah. By enhancing that system religion would be reasserted; Torah would be back in its central place.[33] The delegation was religiously motivated, looking for a solution that

---

31. Sanders, *Judaism,* esp. chap. 9.

32. On the economic questions, I am indebted to Philip Harland's unpublished paper "The economy of Palestine: A survey of the secondary literature," which shows how variable are the taxation calculations and how dependent many of the studies are upon each other.

33. For a general assessment of Torah in the period, see P. Richardson et al., *Law in Religious Communities in the Roman Period: The Debate over Torah and Nomos in Post-Biblical Judaism and Early Christianity* (Waterloo, ON: Wilfrid Laurier University Press, 1991).

would break the stranglehold Herod had held on the religious life of the people through his appointment of high priests and his sidestepping of the religious courts of the land.[34] It was precisely this religious implication—not openly expressed but obvious to Augustus—that he was unwilling to accept, for he rejected any solution that encouraged an increasingly strong religious party. Ironically, the decision he made encouraged stronger and more extreme religious parties. Not by accident, Josephus records the rise of the Zealots as occurring in 6 CE when attempts at a settlement based mostly on religious grounds had been twice frustrated.[35]

The two heirs who might have combined a strong political solution and a sensitive religious outlook, Alexander and Aristobulus, had been executed three years earlier. They had in their favor their Hasmonean descent through their mother Mariamme I as well as personal popularity.[36] But these were flaws that proved to be fatal in Herod's view. Their maternity gave them the royal blood that Herod lacked and the claim of being descendants of an accepted high priest. By contrast, the mother of Archelaus and Antipas was Malthace, a Samaritan woman, and this fact must have cast a deep shadow on their suitability for office in the eyes of devout Jews. Philip's mother was Cleopatra of Jerusalem, of whom nothing is known.[37]

Augustus may have been influenced by his high personal regard for Herod, though at this stage it was seriously eroded due to Herod's bad judgment and vindictiveness, not to mention his paranoia and delusions. Augustus had been dependent on Herod to maintain his south-eastern flank. It is indicative of Augustus's continued regard for Herod that he went to such trouble to hear out the various parties as he made up his mind on Herod's will, and that he selected some mementos of Herod's for his own personal use. It seems likely that a factor in his decision was a preference to accept Herod's own wishes in the matter, no matter how desperate they were.

There is one other factor. The surviving children were young to be given full control; Archelaus was 19, Antipas 17, and Philip probably only 16.[38] Augustus probably felt unable to make a definitive decision before these young rulers had faced substantial challenges; by appointing all three he was biding his time until he could see how they behaved under pressure, possibly intending later to appoint one of them to kingship.

---

34. Both Fenn and Goodman undervalue the evidence of the delegation.

35. This connection has been contested from two sides: those who see the zealot ideals arising in the Maccabean period and those who believe that a zealot party only arose in the pre-revolt period. See below, chap. 10.

36. See Josephus's evaluation: *Ant.* 16.395–404.

37. On Herod's ten wives, see chap. 2.

38. In 44 CE, when Agrippa II was about sixteen, Claudius refused to appoint him king on Agrippa I's death.

THE DELEGATIONS' EVALUATIONS

The view of the Decapolis delegation has not been preserved. One can imagine the main lines of argument. First, the cities were created free. Second, they belong to the Hellenistic-Roman world, not the world of Judaism and the middle East. Third, Herod had exploited them. The result was loss of stature and of direct connection with Rome. Rome served itself best by restoring them to the status of free cities as outposts of Roman civilization and a bulwark against Arab influence.

The Judean delegation's (and also the Roman Jewish delegation's)[39] attitude toward Herod can be inferred from Josephus's description. The Judean delegation focused on Archelaus, because he was king-designate in his father's will and it was his soldiers who had killed the pilgrims in the Temple. Philip's role in the confrontation is unclear. Josephus singles him out for special comment but fails to give him a part other than that suggested by Varus—to cooperate with Archelaus (whom Varus was also supporting) if the decision seemed to be heading toward the selection of one successor, and to snatch a share of the prize if it was a split decision.

The Judean delegation's presentation fell into three parts: a diatribe against Herod, a diatribe against Archelaus, and a plea to be united with Syria. This last point was probably prompted by Varus and calculated to appeal to Augustus. To these were added protestations of loyalty: the Judeans were not seditious when well governed and were perfectly willing to recognize that Rome now exercised *de facto* authority in the East, as long as that exercise of authority was just, humane, and tolerant of Judea's distinctions. About Archelaus they needed only to say that they had readily received him as king (a sly reference to his presumptuousness?) and had prayed for a successful reign as they mourned Herod (a disingenuous claim belied by their earlier denunciation of him); but Archelaus's brutal slaughter of devout Jews in the Temple had shown that he was a true son of his father and unfit to rule.

Of most interest in Josephus's account are the three main accusations against Herod. (1) Herod was the most savage tyrant that had ever lived; they claimed he had executed many and tortured more—including whole cities. His reign of terror forced them to fall into passive subservience, almost slavery. They seemed to be hinting that they should have risen in revolt against Herod. (2) Herod had pillaged his own cities to adorn foreign cities, reducing their earlier prosperity to poverty. (3) Herod had deprived Jews of their ancestral laws so that now the Jewish people were "lawless." In other words, he had pre-

---

39. For more on the Jewish community in Rome, see chap. 5, where I argue for a strong debt of gratitude to Herod on the part of the community. That sense of debt need not extend to his children, several of whom were familiar because of their education at the Imperial court.

vented Torah from being applied to the political, religious, and cultural life of Judea as it should have been, thus eroding the place of the law of Moses.

These accusations seem a fair summary of what a delegation might have said to Augustus. That Josephus allowed these criticisms to occupy such a dramatic place in his narrative, with only the skimpiest of indications of Nicolas's rejoinder, is striking.[40] They can be used as a basis of a preliminary evaluation of Herod.

Their first accusation of tyranny and extreme cruelty is undoubtedly correct. Instances abound of solitary and arbitrary rule, of whimsical decisions that suited him and his needs and with little thought of others. Two qualifications of this popular judgment, however, need to be made. It was endemic in virtually all rulers of the period to engage in cruel and tyrannical acts—even Augustus could be faced with similar charges. In addition, Herod was faced with his subjects' "anarchic tendencies and habitual disloyalty to their kings" (to use Nicolas's words), so that, to be worthy of Augustus's confidence, Herod had to be decisive and often harsh in removing troublemakers.

The second accusation also contains an important element of truth. Herod beautified many foreign cities, including cities within his own realm which observant Jews would treat as if they were foreign cities. There is more than sufficient evidence of the accuracy of this basic observation.[41] But the linkage between Herod's beautification of cities and Judean poverty was almost certainly false. Herod spent far more money in his own lands than he did in any foreign ventures; the list of projects is tipped heavily in favor of Judea and the adjacent areas that formed part of his own domain. He was generous to other parts, often in areas in the Diaspora where there were sizable Jewish communities, but this generosity did not impoverish Judea. Employment was high, international trade was strong, and tariffs and duties brought in substantial amounts, even if much of the money went into Herod's or others' pockets.[42] Of course,

---

40. Josephus must be drawing on Nicolas, who will have had a full account of his rejoinders; Josephus simply chose to let the accusations stand in more or less the form they reached him.

41. In discussing Agrippa I Josephus drives a wedge between the character of Herod and his grandson Agrippa, saying that Herod "had an evil nature, relentless in punishment and unsparing in action against the objects of his hatred. It was generally admitted that he was on more friendly terms with Greeks than with Jews." Josephus goes on to contrast Herod's building activities at home and abroad: "he adorned the cities of foreigners by giving them money, building baths and theatres, erecting temples in some and porticoes in others, whereas there was not a single city of the Jews on which he deigned to bestow even a minor restoration or any gift worth mentioning" (*Ant.* 19.329). This seems a bizarre accusation when Josephus himself provides so much evidence to refute it and when he also shows a few paragraphs later that Agrippa I also built in foreign cities, in this case Berytus; see *Ant.* 19.335 and list of buildings in Appendix A, chap. 8.

42. A revealing parable of Jesus in Luke 19:11–27 (different in Matt. 25:14–30) may reflect Archelaus's journey to Rome to receive a kingdom. Its social realism says something about the sources of income of the wealthy in the period, the great wealth that flowed from high-risk, high-yield, carefully supervised investments.

there were huge imbalances between the rich and the poor, and there was much social unrest—much of it an expression of the poverty of the underprivileged. In short, Judea was much like other parts of the Empire.

The delegation's third accusation charged Herod with promoting "lawlessness," probably Torah disobedience. Again the accusation is essentially true. Herod undercut the authority of the high priest; much of the time he ignored the courts; he built cultural and athletic buildings in the land—even in Jerusalem—that symbolized a broader entente with Hellenism; he even built Temples to Roma and Augustus, and perhaps also to other deities (see chap. 8). These actions were offensive to Jews dedicated to a Judea governed according to Torah. In fact, however, the accusation implicitly acknowledges that many persons in Judea enjoyed this "lawless" state of affairs. For generations there had been a "Hellenist" sentiment in Judea. The Hasmonean family had soon followed this path and even high priestly families were tainted by certain kinds of "lawlessness." Archaeological evidence shows, for example, that at least the priestly family of Kathros, like other upper-class families, had figurative representations in the decorative plaster work of their mansions. By contrast, the excavations of Herod's own various palaces on Judean soil have provided no evidence of this kind of "lawlessness." So the delegation's charge is true but misleading.

Herod's people, by their revolutionary actions in several parts of the kingdom and by the Judean delegation's speech before Augustus, had indicated their contempt for Herod at the time of his death. His children were greedy to get what they could from his death—to seize the chance and look to their own advantage. Augustus and his deputies were not sure how to administer Judea. They groped for an adequate solution that would safeguard Rome's interests without giving much thought to the uniqueness of Israel's religion and the challenges it posed.

CHAPTER 2

Family Matters

HEROD'S WILLS

When Augustus dealt with Herod's seventh and last will, he had problems similar to Herod's in determining the succession. As events within the Seleucid, Armenian, Parthian, and Judean kingdoms—to name a few in the region—had shown, nothing fractured a state so easily as dynastic quarrels.[1] Augustus himself had tried to settle the marriages of his grandchildren to draw his family together. And just as Herod had included Alexander and Aristobulus in his first will, at precisely the same moment in 17 BCE, Augustus had made Gaius and Lucius his heirs by adopting these two children of M. Agrippa and Julia as his sons.[2]

Herod's problems with the succession, however, were substantially different from Augustus's; ultimately the Judean issues, though smaller than the Roman concerns, had been made more complex and intractable by his own actions. These difficulties of Herod's own making had to do in part with the complexity of dealing with his multiple wives[3] (in comparison, Augustus had to deal only with Livia); in part with which potential heir had the fewest disabilities; in part with the varied lineages of his children—ranging from children with Hasmonean blood to others with no "Jewish" blood at all; and in part with his many wills.[4]

---

1. Sullivan, *Near Eastern Royalty,* passim.

2. H. S. Jones, "The Princeps," *CAH* 10, chap. 5, esp. p. 151.

3. Josephus argues that Herod's wives were chosen for their beauty not their family; he also points out that polygamy was permitted and that the king gladly took advantage of this possibility. *War* 1.477.

4. See H. Hoehner, *Herod Antipas: A Contemporary of Jesus Christ* (Cambridge: Cambridge University Press, 1972), Appendix 1, pp. 269–76. My conclusions agree with his with the exception of my Will Five. Other commentators do not identify all the wills.

Will One

Although there is no certain documentary evidence of this first will, in 23/22 BCE,[5] when Herod was given the right to name his successor, it seems likely that he made a will immediately.[6] If so, the first will must have named Alexander heir;[7] it is possible that Aristobulus was also named in this will in some provisional way. The will gave effect to what was likely a condition of his marriage to Mariamme I: the putting away from the royal court of Doris and her son Antipater. Though it may seem surprising that seven years after Mariamme's execution and with other marriages intervening, Herod still honored the undertaking with Mariamme, it is not inexplicable. There are three reasons Herod's will may have honored Mariamme's wishes: (1) with the exception of Antipater, Alexander and Aristobulus were Herod's two oldest sons; (2) these sons were partially Hasmonean, so they offered Herod the advantages that caused him to be attracted to Mariamme in the first place: legitimacy and some hope of popular support; (3) Herod may well have still retained his old affection for Mariamme. The children were about nineteen and eighteen years of age, able to succeed should the need arise, and no doubt it was this more than anything else that triggered the discussions with Augustus over his right to name a successor. With other claimants on the scene (especially Antipater who was about 26) it was important to settle the succession.

Will Two

Because Alexander and Aristobulus had made themselves so unpopular, in 14/13 BCE Herod restored Doris to favor and brought her back to court (*War* 1.449–51; *Ant.* 16.81–86), along with her son Antipater. Antipater's restoration signified Herod's decision that Antipater should succeed Herod, thus excluding the other two brothers (*War* 1.151; *Ant.* 16.86). Consistent with Herod's decision there was a marital reconciliation between himself and Doris; *War* and *Antiquities* agree that Doris's return to Herod was engineered by Antipater, and if so he must have felt that reestablishing Doris's position would secure his position as successor. When Antipater traveled to Rome— presumably to take Herod's will to Augustus—his new position was immensely strengthened by his appearance, in full regalia, as a "friend of Caesar" (*Ant.* 16.86).

---

5. Hoehner dates the first will to 22 BCE.

6. Ibid., p. 269.

7. Ibid., pp. 269–71; in this first will only Alexander was named heir, referring to *War* 1.454, 456, 458; *Ant.* 15.343; 16.92, 95, 129, 133. Though the case is not certain, the focus of the narrative upon Alexander confirms the likelihood of this reconstruction.

Will Three

Herod's third will (12 BCE) followed the reconciliation—almost insisted upon by Augustus—of Herod with Mariamme's two sons.[8] It also followed Augustus's confirmation of Herod's right to name his own successor (or successors)—an indication of the unusual confidence Augustus had in Herod (*Ant.* 16.127–29; *War* 1.454). Herod named Antipater king, with Alexander and Aristobulus as "subordinate kings," according to Josephus. Herod publicly announced in Jerusalem the arrangements for sharing of royal power and warned against turning the royal successors against their father in his few remaining years (*War* 1.457–66; *Ant.* 16.132–35).

This will is interesting because: (1) it would have been unworkable, perhaps disastrous, given the relations among the three sons; (2) it was the first attempt to balance the claims of rival family branches; (3) it indicated that even at this period Herod thought it best to trifurcate the kingdom in some fashion, because each should have a share of the "honor" (*Ant.* 16.129); and (4) it suggested that Herod was declining in vigor and wished to give up rule altogether.

Will Four

By 7 BCE the behavior of Alexander and Aristobulus had again become intolerable or else the Machiavellian schemes of Antipater had become successful and the two brothers were tried and executed. Herod's new will still named Antipater his heir, but with a new twist; Herod Philip I (son of Mariamme II) was named Antipater's successor (*Ant.* 17.53; *War* 1.573).[9] Herod Philip I was about fifteen, hardly old enough to assume rule. And with this provision Herod passed over at least one older son, Archelaus who would have been about sixteen (Antipas was about fourteen; both were children of Malthace). The reason was probably that the children of Malthace would have been viewed as Samaritans, while Herod Philip I was a grandson of the ruling high priest, Simon the son of Boethos, and was more likely to be acceptable to the population at large.

Will Five

In 6 BCE Antipater was still named Herod's heir, but Herod Philip I (son of Mariamme II) was no longer Antipater's successor (*War* 1.599–600; *Ant.* 17.78). The change reflected who was in favor and who was not. This will, which I consider separate from Will Four (though Hoehner does not), was

---

8. Ibid., p. 271 n.4; Augustus preferred Alexander and Aristobulus, perhaps because of the intervention of Archelaus of Cappadocia. Hoehner also argues that it was only at this time that Augustus gave Herod the right to name more than one successor. See *Ant.* 15.342; 16.129, 133, where Josephus says "whichever of the sons, or even to apportion it."

9. Ibid., pp. 272–74.

necessitated by Herod's decision that Mariamme II was complicit in the "plot" against him. The repercussions fell on her (he divorced her), on her son (he was removed from the will), and on her father (he was removed from his position as high priest).[10]

Will Six

In the most interesting will of all, Herod returned to his original practice (and Augustus's preferred model) of naming one person his successor (5/4 BCE).[11] Antipater had been discredited, tried, and found guilty, and Herod had divorced Mariamme II. This required him—almost by necessity, given the shame that attaches to divorces—to dispossess the younger Herod and to fall back on the children of Malthace (*War* 1.646; *Ant.* 17.146–47). His attitude to Archelaus and Philip II, according to Josephus, was "hatred," because Antipater had poisoned his view of them, for they were obvious rivals in his desire to succeed alone. The sole remaining possibility for a successor was Antipas, at this time sixteen or seventeen years of age and just possible as a successor at this late point in Herod's life. Herod made a number of new provisions in the will, including bequests to his patrons Augustus and Livia, their children and friends and freedmen, to his own sons, and to Salome. Though similar provisions may have been included in previous wills, both *War* and *Antiquities* record them for the first time in Will Six.

Will Seven

Within a few months (4 BCE) the effects of Antipater's campaign against Archelaus and Philip had worn off, Antipater himself had been executed, and Herod had returned to his earlier practice of balancing rival claimants by naming Archelaus king (now nineteen years old), his full brother Antipas (about seventeen) and his half-brother Philip II (about sixteen) as tetrarchs (*War* 1.664; *Ant.* 17.188–90). Three cities were bequeathed to Salome and Herod's generous bequests to the Emperor and Livia and the others were continued.[12] Antipas was the clear loser in this final will, yet the sources report no indication of resentment over his demotion until much later when, according to Josephus, Antipas's wife pressured him to ask for the title of king.

---

10. Ibid., p. 273, nn.1, 2.

11. Hoehner errs in claiming that this is the first time that he has named as successor a child with no Hasmonean connection. He correctly points out that Antipater's wife was a Hasmonean (the daughter of Antigonus), but Herod had earlier named Herod Philip I, son of Mariamme II, as a successor.

12. Ibid., p. 275, n.2: Will Seven (in Hoehner's terms Will Six) was a codicil to Will Five (on his showing what I call Will Five is a codicil to Will Four). I have presented each will-drafting occasion as a new will, regardless of the degree of overlap with the previous one.

Herod's Intentions

After Herod's death Augustus accepted a slightly modified version of Will Seven (see chap. 1).[13] He was presented with three possible solutions: (1) incorporate Judea into the Roman provincial system by attaching it to Syria; (2) give the whole of Herod's kingdom to one strong king; (3) compromise and split the kingdom. The first of these was never considered by Herod, the second was occasionally tried, and the third was Herod's typical approach. Several additional observations are necessary.

First, in general Herod's various attempts to secure a stable succession had less to do with who was best suited to succeed than with which wife and sons, especially the older sons, were in or out of favor. Although the details Josephus provides are not as full as we might wish, with ten wives and an embarrassment of male children as potential successors, the rivalry within the palace walls for precedence was intense. Herod played his wives' and children's game.[14]

Second, along with the poisoned palace atmosphere that afflicted immediate family relationships, there were strong pressures to form alliances beyond the palace walls that would create a firm base for succession. Josephus provides some evidence, especially in the cases of Alexander and Aristobulus on the one hand and of Antipater on the other, that this was so. Claimants actively courted external support within the family's kinship connections and among the broader patronage connections outside the family, specifically the army.

Third, Herod's search for a successor became increasingly frantic as he aged and as his illness worsened. With the exceptions of his first, second, and sixth wills, he chose a combination of people to succeed him; even in the first will he may have referred to both brothers, with Alexander in the primary place. His practice of balancing potential successors might have been a sign of indecision on Herod's part or *Realpolitik*. Whichever was the case, such solutions were inherently unstable; Herod's inability to see this weakness and his unwillingness to trust fully any of his children were endemic aspects of the wavering efforts to find an adequate solution.[15]

Fourth, Herod preferred Hasmonean blood or connections initially. Except at the end, when he had no other choices, he leaned away from Malthace's children because of their Samaritan blood, though there is no evidence of this as a real or potential problem. (Josephus is silent on the politics of the Samaritan marriage.)

---

13. He also accepted, according to *Ant.* 17.189 (but not *War*), the allocation to Salome, Herod's sister, making her a fourth main inheritor.

14. On succession in Judaism, see Z. W. Falk, "Jewish Private Law," *CRINT* 1.504–34, esp. pp. 518–21.

15. Even given the Jewish custom that all male children inherit, there was no need for a king to split his kingdom to give all or several a share of the territory. Herod may have been influenced by this custom in the later days of his reign.

Fifth, when he divorced or banished a wife, the children of the marriage automatically fell out of favor because of the shame that accrued to the children of the divorced or banished wife.[16]

Sixth, the choice tended to fall on Antipater as the eldest (and probably also strongest and most ruthless), despite the unremarkable status of his wife and her family.[17] For much of the time—for longer than any of the other children—Antipater shared rule with Herod (*War* 1.458–65). The choice tended also to fall on children of sixteen or older, who might reasonably have been able to assume power whenever needed.

In sum, the family structure—Byzantine and unstable as a result of the many marriages, numerous children, internecine warfare, executions, accusations, charges and countercharges—interfered with Herod's finding a satisfactory solution to his need for a successor. His efforts were doomed, partly by his own failure to deal adequately with family members, partly by their unwillingness to accept one another, and partly by others' interference both inside (especially by mothers-in-law) and outside the family.

FAMILY FINANCIAL PROVISIONS

These seven successive wills were the visible aspects of a broader set of kinship questions, which have been studied in detail by K.C. Hanson.[18] Anthropologists and sociologists have shown us how to find information in the primary sources that lend fresh insights into the period. Nowhere is this more possible than in matters of kinship,[19] which are deeply embedded in politics, religion, and economics. Kinship questions bear mainly upon, but are not restricted to, matters of marriage; I here summarize and comment on a few issues as they bear on Herod himself.

Dowry

Among the economic aspects of kinship the questions of dowry, indirect dowry, bridewealth, and inheritance transactions are relevant. Dowry is "a pre-

---

16. This can be seen in the case of Doris's banishment, her subseequent reinstatement (see Will Two) and then later divorce (see Wills Six and Seven), and in the case of the divorce of Mariamme II (see Will Five). Curiously, it did not affect the children of the executed Mariamme I, presumably for the reasons noted above (see Wills One and Three).

17. Given the role that Doris occasionally played and Antipater's enormous importance, Josephus's silence has to be explained as a combination of ignorance of any details and the low status of her family.

18. K. C. Hanson, "The Herodians and Mediterranean Kinship," published as three articles in *Biblical Theology Bulletin,* "Part I: Genealogy and Descent" (19 [1989]: 75–84); "Part II: Marriage and Divorce" (19: 142–51); "Part III: Economics" (20 [1990]: 10–21). I am indebted to him for making them available.

19. B. J. Malina, *The New Testament World: Insights from Cultural Anthropology* (Louisville: John Knox, 1981), chap. 5.

mortem inheritance (full or partial) given to the daughter at the time of marriage"[20] and is a direct expression of a family's honor—its size being a public display of that honor, and its transmission assisting in the acquiring of more honor or perhaps a new client. Within Judaism these customs can be confirmed from the Hebrew Bible, the *Mishnah* and Tobit. Herodian dowries, in comparison to other known dowries, were at the upper end of the range on monetary transfers; for example, when Herod betrothed his daughter Salampsio to his brother Pheroras ("who shared with Herod all the honors of royalty except the diadem," *War* 1.483), the dowry was the enormous sum of 300 talents. When Pheroras reneged and Herod then betrothed her to Pheroras's son Phasael III, he added a further 100 talents (*Ant.* 16.228). Following Herod's death, Augustus betrothed Roxana and Salome, two other daughters of Herod, to members of the family and gave them each 25 talents for their dowries, still a significant sum (*Ant.* 17.322). Since all three betrothals were within the kinship system (endogamous), they show that wealth was being distributed within the family and to the next generation. In a corollary fashion, when Alexander was executed in 7 BCE, Glaphyra his wife returned with her dowry to her father in Cappadocia. The honor gained in the giving of the dowry required reciprocally that the dowry be returned in order to keep the honor intact and not incur shame.

Indirect Dowry and Bridewealth

" 'Indirect dowry' is property and/or cash given by the groom's kin either directly to the bride or indirectly through her kin."[21] Bridewealth covers a wider range of goods and services transferred from the groom's kin to the bride's kin. Together with dowry they were mechanisms for both families to bestow property on the new couple, thus balancing honor concerns between the two kin-groups and avoiding either one becoming the client of the other. These transfers protected the woman in the eventuality of widowhood or divorce and provided some redress in the case of unjust or dishonorable treatment. There are no unmistakably clear cases of indirect dowry in the Herodian kin-group, but Hanson plausibly suggests that Doris's expensive wardrobe retained by Herod upon their second divorce was a part of an indirect dowry.[22]

Inheritance

In the Roman world an important element in inheritance was the reciprocity of a client with his patron.[23] It is striking that Augustus and Livia were major

---

20. Hanson, "Kinship," 20: 11.

21. Ibid.

22. Ibid., 20: 15, citing *War* 1.590; *Ant.* 17.68.

23. There were important differences between Israelite, Attic, Hellenistic, Roman, and Mishnaic laws of inheritance; ibid., 20: 16–18.

heirs in Herod's final will, together to the sum of 1,500 talents plus gold and silver vessels and expensive clothes. The reciprocity of this relationship was enhanced by Augustus's decision to give Herod's legacies back to the family, thereby strengthening the bonds between the Imperial family and the Herodian family, a relationship that persisted for 160 years.

Herod's final will gave Archelaus, Antipas, and Philip a share of territory together with a substantial but proportional annual income. The eldest son, Archelaus, received the largest share as was customary in Jewish tradition; Antipas and Philip were unsuccessful in reversing this situation. Salome also inherited; she was made ruler (*despotês*) of three important cities (Jamnia/Yavneh, Azotus, Phasaelis), was given a one-time gift and an annual revenue, and inherited the royal palace in Ashkelon. (Salome later willed these possessions to the Empress Livia, her long-time friend.) These unusual arrangements for Salome, encouraged because the kingdom was divided, might be explained either as a result of Roman and Hellenistic practices or as an exception to the Jewish practices, predicated on Herod's closeness to Salome and her closeness to the Emperor's family.[24]

Almost all Herod's known children benefited from the will in some way. This fact speaks strongly against Smallwood's contention that Malthace, Cleopatra, Elpis, Phaedra, and Pallas were merely concubines. The status the children of these relationships obtained under the final will required that they were all full wives and that the children were all legitimate offspring.[25] For the most part, then, with the exception of his very generous treatment of Salome, "Herod followed the Jewish tradition of inheritance distribution."[26] These practices operated for daughters primarily at the time of betrothal and for sons primarily at the time of the death of the *pater familias,* though in unusual circumstances, as in the case of Salome, the will could be extended to include female kin. In short, rules of inheritance were not wooden or restricted.

GENEALOGY AND DESCENT

The first-century Roman family was an exogamous community family (based on equality of brothers, cohabitation of married sons with parents, no marriage between children of brothers, and monogamy); the Greek family was an egalitarian nuclear family (supposing equality of brothers, no cohabitation of married sons with parents, no marriage between children of brothers, and monogamy); the Jewish family was an endogamous community family (characterized by equality of brothers, cohabitation of married sons with parents, fre-

---

24. Ibid., 20: 19.
25. Ibid.
26. Ibid., 20: 20.

quent marriage between children of brothers, and polygamy [e.g., for kings up to 18 wives]).[27]

Family Tree

Hanson lays out in a columnar table arranged by generations all the kinship data of the Herodian family from the first generation (Antipater father of Herod) to the eighth generation. Hanson's table provides the most complete display yet of the whole family and corrects errors in previous family trees. Though difficult to use because it lacks the visual advantages of the more usual diagrammatic form, Hanson's table has the great advantage of completeness.[28] (A modified version of Hanson's table can be found in the appendix at the end of this chapter along with approximate dates for birth, death, marriage, and divorce where they can reasonably be deduced.) Josephus's information allows the conclusion that the Herodian family was not bound completely by traditional notions of patrilineal descent. Apparently the family also used cognatic descent (i.e., links based on female relationships, often in combination with male relationships). Josephus shows that descent from female members of the family, especially from Mariamme I, was important: "Aristobulus and Alexander would have no more ascribed honor than Antipater due to their mother's family's lineage, since the father of all three was Herod. But Mariamme's sons, though younger than Antipater, claimed greater honor on account of their Hasmonean descent, and ridiculed Antipater as being born of a non-royal mother, Doris."[29] There were substantial differences of opinion within the Herodian family on the matter of cognate descent, but those whose status depended on it, such as Alexander and Aristobulus, presupposed its legitimacy. It is not altogether clear whether or not Jewish society at large agreed.

Herod himself had only two endogamous marriages—one with a niece and another with a cousin—and they are listed last in Josephus's accounts. He lists no further information other than their childlessness (a mark of shame)—not even their names are given.[30] They were probably listed in last place because of their lack of honor, not for chronological reasons.[31] It is plausible that these marriages preceded Herod's marriage to Doris (which took place when he was about twenty-six, leaving ample room for earlier marriages). If so, he divorced the niece and the cousin when he divorced Doris and married Mariamme I.

---

27. Ibid., 19: 77, reviewing the work of Emmanuel Todd.
28. Ibid., 19: 78–81.
29. Ibid., 19: 82, referring to *War* 1.449.
30. Ibid., 19:83, citing *War* 1.563; *Ant.* 17.19.
31. Hanson notes that in *War* 1.562–63 Mariamme I is dropped to the end of the list after the shame of her execution.

A family tree that identifies all family members has the important advantage, in an endogamous strategy, of identifying all the potential marriage partners, and marriageable women were important assets. Such a tree also shows the exogamous strategy that has actually been followed in the family. Herod's strategy included his marriages into the Hasmonean royal family and into a priestly Jewish family, as well as marriages of six other exogamous partners: Salome's marriages to Joseph (a close friend) and to Costobar (a governor of Idumaea), and betrothal to Syllaeus (a Nabatean noble); the marriage of Antipater III to the daughter of Antigonus (Jewish royalty); the marriage of Alexander—and later also of Archelaus—to Glaphyra (daughter of the important dependent king of Cappadocia); the marriage of Antipas to the daughter of Aretas IV of Nabatea (another royal connection), Herod's nearest and most dangerous neighbor. It is apparent that Herod was more successful in arranging for elite, frequently royal, exogamous marriages for family and friends than he was in arranging marriages for himself. Of his own eight exogamous marriages, six were non-noble or non-royal.

This raises the important question: when did the standard view develop in Judaism that legitimacy was determined by the mother? Rituals of conversion to Judaism appeared for the first time in Rabbinic texts of the second and third centuries CE. Prior to that period—certainly in the Second Temple period—a woman was deemed a convert upon marriage to a Jew. If either Herod or his father Antipater II was considered a Jew, their wives were too. But were they *deemed* to be Jews? On this matter there were undoubtedly differences of opinion, not only among groups (11QT, for example, describes a specific and new court in the Temple to accommodate proselytes to Judaism) but also among later rabbinic authorities. The majority view, however, appears to have been that converts faced no disabilities—or only minor ones—and thus, for example, Cypros and Malthace (one a Nabatean and one a Samaritan) were Jews once they were married to Jews.[32]

Nevertheless, Herod's own descent was a matter of controversy in antiquity, but these disagreements confirm that "one's genealogy and descent are critical in determining one's honor, and are thus points of attack, as well as exaggeration."[33] The fuller a family tree is, the more it allows analysis of family honor, a crucial ingredient in evaluating status, "since honor and status are pivotal Mediterranean values."[34] It is not just the important political figures who shape these matters; a map of Herodian relationships and the ascribed honor

32. For several of these points, see S. J. D. Cohen, *From the Maccabees to the Mishnah* (Philadelphia: Westminster, 1987), pp. 46–59, esp. 52–54; see also B. J. Bamberger, *Proselytism in the Talmudic Period* (New York: KTAV, 1939).

33. Hanson, "Kinship," 19: 82, referring to Malina's study noted above.

34. Ibid., 19: 83.

that accrues within those relationships will thus include potential and actual endogamous marriage partners, actual exogamous marriage partners, birth-order, marriage-order, status, and rank.[35]

MARRIAGE AND DIVORCE

Endogamy

Biblical and post-Biblical evidence establishes that "endogamy was the Jewish ideal by the time of the Herodians," yet "the Herodians practiced a mixture of endogamy and exogamy."[36] Exogamy, however, should not be seen as a deviation; both strategies were used and brought advantages. Endogamous marriages can be analyzed according to whether they were consanguinal marriages (parallel-cousins, cross-cousins, cross-generational) or affinal marriages. Herod had no preference for one type of endogamy, though parallel cousins and uncle-niece marriages were the two most common. In the case of his brother Pheroras,[37] Herod first arranged for him to marry Mariamme I's sister; when she died he betrothed Pheroras to his oldest daughter by Mariamme, Salampsio, but Pheroras reneged. Later Herod betrothed Pheroras to Cypros, Salampsio's sister; Pheroras reneged again, affronting Herod's honor as head of the household and Jewish custom.

Exogamy

The family enhanced its "honor and power by establishing links with political and religious leaders throughout the Levant" by means of a substantial number of exogamous marriages.[38] Some marriages were to elite families, both royal and priestly, and some were to non-elite families or to those of unknown status. Herod himself accounts for five of the six instances of the last named strategy (Malthace, Cleopatra of Jerusalem, Elpis, Phaedra, Pallas). Despite the eight instances of marriage of males to daughters of royal families (fifteen, including females marrying rulers or sons of rulers), Herod himself only once married into a royal family (Mariamme I).[39] Herod's Hasmonean marriage was especially important to him; he married Pheroras to Mariamme's sister and his son Antipater to Antigonus's daughter. This three-pronged strategy was aimed at improving his popularity, enhancing his legitimacy, and tying together the two

---

35. Ibid., 19: 84.

36. Ibid., 19: 143.

37. Ibid., 19: 144.

38. Ibid., 19: 145.

39. Though this fact is to be accounted for by Herod's own commoner status, it still seems strange given his elevation to royal status in 40 BCE.

competing wings of the Hasmonean family under his own watchful eye, thereby neutralizing the threat of a Hasmonean revolt.

Liberty

As head of the kin-group, Herod played a crucial role arranging marriages for his own children, his siblings, and their children.[40] He negotiated at least ten marriages.[41] In some cases Herod's success was contingent on his own honor and status; in other cases Herod prevented a marriage taking place, as when he prevented Salome from marrying Syllaeus when Syllaeus refused to be circumcised (*War* 1.487; *Ant.* 16.220–25).

The restrictions on the liberty of family members in marital matters included their place of residence. Jewish families were patrilocal: married sons lived with their parents. The direct evidence for this custom in the case of the Herodian family is weak, but Josephus's narrative strongly implies that male children continued to live in the palace. Family members were on the same "gossip-reputation circuit" and the plots that were a part of the intra-generational rivalry suggest their living in close proximity.[42]

Divorce

Of the nine divorces among Herodians that Josephus mentions, four involve the husband divorcing his wife and five describe the wife divorcing her husband. This pattern holds true even in Herod's own generation: Herod divorced Doris (as well as his cousin and his niece if these were in fact earlier marriages) to marry Mariamme I; Doris was subsequently reinstated and divorced again; Herod divorced Mariamme II; Salome divorced Costobar; and Archelaus divorced his wife to marry Glaphyra, who had earlier been married to—and borne children with—Alexander. In four of the divorces, then, Herod was involved directly, or, if Salome's divorce is included, indirectly. These divorces presuppose family solidarity and loyalty; they show that competition for and maintenance of honor arose even between husband and wife, not just (contrary to what Malina says) outside the family. Though Josephus criticizes women for divorcing their husbands, the evidence for a fully Jewish family system suggests that "their status as non-priestly, urban elites gave them the

---

40. Hanson, "Kinship," 19: 147.

41. Ibid., 19: 147: Salome and Costobar (*Ant.* 15.254); Antipater III and Mariamme III, Antipater III's son and Pheroras's daughter (*War* 1.565); Cypros II and Antipater IV, Salampsio and Phaselus III (*Ant.* 17.22); Aristobulus I and Berenice I, Alexander II and Glaphyra (*Ant.* 16.11); Pheroras and Alexander I's daughter (*War* 1.483); Salome I and Alexas, and Salome I's daughter and Alexas's son (*War* 1.566).

42. Ibid., 19:148.

social flexibility to act in their own (and their family's) interests in terms of honor."[43]

CONCLUSION

This evidence is coherent and contradicts the standard scholarly views of random, capricious, and individually determined actions. Hanson states, "[The Herodians] were thoroughly Jewish in the structure of their kinship . . . [though] they employed some variations on what could be expected from urban and rural non-elites. Their family group exemplified the typical patriarchal family system of the eastern Mediterranean. They were patrilineal, patrilocal, and endogamous; they employed dowry, (probably) indirect dowry, and bridewealth, with the eldest son provided a larger share of the father's inheritance. They were also accountable to their Roman patrons when it came to inheritance. *Far from random or individually determined, the Herodians conformed to a family system both predictable and patterned.*"[44]

Hanson's analysis is extremely important and correct. Even if one or two niggling points were to fall (for instance, was Herod adopting in his final will the Jewish custom of a larger share of the estate for the eldest son?), his main case continues to be sound, especially the italicized conclusion. There was no essential difference between Herod's actions and those of other family members; they acted consistently. Herod's familial actions as king were not whimsical, they were not the result of passion, greed, anger, or resentment (though these may have been factors), they were part of a kinship system in which honor and shame were of deep concern.

Missing from Hanson's analysis is a consideration of the executions of family members. Though we will consider these executions further, here I suggest merely that they were extreme examples of that same kinship system in which the king's honor was at stake. Similar though less extreme actions were not unknown in Augustus's household, the most obvious case being that of his daughter Julia's banishment, which brought painful public shame upon him.

---

43. Ibid., 19:150.
44. Ibid., 20: 20; my italics.

Appendix
HEROD'S FAMILY TREE

In constructing this family tree I am indebted to Hanson's table "Kinship," 19: 79–81. I have simplified it somewhat, made a few minor corrections, added a few items he overlooked and modified it to agree with my independent decisions. The main difference between Hanson's table and my own is my attempt to supply dates; inevitably these are approximations only, but in some cases there is sufficient confirming evidence to suggest that the dates are close. When the evidence is still more tenuous I have supplied a question mark. Capital letters indicate an individual who held a governing position of some sort; [00] refers to a union that was childless. In a few cases a date in [ ] indicates a betrothal that was not consummated.

Name	Birth/ Death	Father Mother	Spouse	Birth/ Marriage/ Death	Spouse's Status
First Generation					
ANTIPATER I					
Second Generation					
ANTIPATER II	100?/43	ANTIPATER I	Cypros I		exogamous
Phallion	95?/40	ANTIPATER I	?		
Third Generation					
PHASAEL I	75?/40	ANTIPATER II Cypros I	?		
HEROD I	73/4	ANTIPATER II	Doris	/47/	exogamous; divorced
		Cypros I	Mariamme I	54?/37/29	royal; executed by Herod
			niece [00]	/30?/	brother's daughter
			cousin [00]	/29?/	father's brother's daughter
			Malthace	/27/4	exogamous
			Cleopatra	/25/	exogamous
			Mariamme II	/23/	priestly; divorced
			Pallas	/21/	exogamous
			Phaedra	/19/	exogamous
			Elpis	/17/	exogamous
			[Doris	/14/]	brought back to court
Joseph I	70?/38	ANTIPATER II Cypros I	?		
PHERORAS	68?/5	ANTIPATER II	daughter of Alexander I	50?/	brother's wife's sister
		Cypros I	a servant	/16/	exogamous

Name	Birth/ Death	Father Mother	Spouse	Birth/ Marriage/ Death	Spouse's Status
SALOME I	65?/10 CE	ANTIPATER II Cypros I	JOSEPH II COSTOBAR	/34 /28	ruler; executed royal; divorced; executed
			[SYLLAEUS]	/[16]/6	ruler; executed by Augustus
			Alexas	/9?/	exogamous
Achiab		Phallion?	?		
daughter		Phallion?	HEROD I	73/29/4	father's brother's son
Antiochus (buried at Scythopolis)		Phallion			

Fourth Generation

Name	Birth/ Death	Father Mother	Spouse	Birth/ Marriage/ Death	Spouse's Status
son? (*War* 1.275)	47?/	PHASAEL I			
Phasael III	44?/	PHASAEL I	Salampsio	33?/	father's brother's daughter
daughter	41?/	PHASAEL I	Herod I	73/30?/4	father's brother
Antipater III executed by Herod	45?/4	HEROD I Doris	daughter of ANTIGONUS	/14?/	royal
			Mariamme III	5?/	brother's daughter
Alexander II executed by Herod	36?/7	HEROD I Mariamme I	Glaphyra	/17/	royal
Aristobulus I executed by Herod	35?/7	HEROD I Mariamme I	Berenice I	36/17/	father's sister's daughter
son died in Rome	33?/	HEROD I Mariamme I			
Salampsio	33?/	HEROD I Mariamme I	Phasael III	44/7/	father's brother's son
Cypros II	32?/	HEROD I Mariamme I	Antipater IV	34?/7/	father's sister's son
Herod Philip I	22?/	HEROD I Mariamme II	Herodias		brother's daughter; divorced
ARCHELAUS I	23?/	HEROD I Malthace	Mariamme IV Glaphyra		exogamous; divorced brother's wife; royal
HEROD ANTIPAS	21?/	HEROD I Malthace	daughter ARETAS IV Herodias		royal; divorced brother's daughter

Continued on next page

Herod's Family Tree–*Continued*

Name	Birth/ Death	Father Mother	Spouse	Birth/ Marriage/ Death	Spouse's Status
Olympias	19?/	HEROD I Malthace	Joseph III	45?/	father's brother's son
HEROD PHILIP II	20?/34 CE	HEROD I Cleopatra	Salome III [00]		brother's daughter
Herod II	18?/ca.4	HEROD I Cleopatra	?		
Phasael II	19?/ca.4	HEROD I Pallas	?		
Roxana	18?/	HEROD I Phaedra	son of PHERORAS	30?/4/	father's brother's son; betrothed by Augustus
Salome II	17?/	HEROD I Elpis	son of PHERORAS	18?/4/	father's brother's son; betrothed by Augustus
Alexander III	42/	COSTOBAR SALOME I			
Herod III	39/	COSTOBAR SALOME I			
Berenice I	36/	COSTOBAR SALOME I	Aristobulus I	35?/17/7	mother's brother's son
			Theudion	/7/	mother's brother's wife's brother
Antipater IV	34/	COSTOBAR SALOME I	Cypros II	32?/	
daughter	31?/	COSTOBAR SALOME I	son of Alexas	/7/	mother's husband's son
Joseph III	45?/	Joseph I	Olympias	19?/	father's brother's daughter
son	20/	PHERORAS	Salome II	17?/4/	father's brother's daughter
son	18/	PHERORAS	Roxana	18?/4/	father's brother's daughter
daughter	13?/	PHERORAS	son Antipater III	13?/	father's brother's son's son
child	8?/	PHERORAS slave	?		

Name	Birth/Death	Father Mother	Spouse	Birth/Marriage/Death	Spouse's Status

Fifth Generation

Name	Birth/Death	Father Mother	Spouse	Birth/Marriage/Death	Spouse's Status
HEROD IV, CHALCIS	15/48 CE	Aristobulus I Berenice I	Mariamme V	1?/	father's brother's daughter
			Berenice III daughter of Antipater III	12?/	brother's daughter brother's daughter
MARCUS JULIUS HEROD AGRIPPA I	13?/44 CE	Aristobulus I Berenice I	Cypros III		father's sister's daughter
Aristobulus II	10?/	Aristobulus I Berenice I	Jotape I		royal
Herodias	8?/	Aristobulus I Berenice I	Herod Philip I	22?/	father's brother; divorced
			HEROD ANTIPAS	21?/	
Mariamme III	16?/	Aristobulus I Berenice I	Antipater III		father's brother
Antipater V	15?/	Phasael III Salampsio	?		
Herod V	13?/	Phasael III Salampsio	?		
Alexander IV	11?/	Phasael III Salampsio	?		
Alexandra II	9?/	Phasael III Salampsio	Timius of Cyprus [00]		
Cypros III	7?/	Phasael III Salampsio	AGRIPPA I	13?/ /44 CE	mother's brother's son
Cypros IV	12?/	Antipater IV Cypros II	Alexas Selcias		father's mother's husband's son
Mariamme V	1?/	Joseph III Olympias	HEROD IV		mother's father's son's son
Alexander V	14?/	Alexander II Glaphyra	?		
TIGRANES IV DHIKRAN	11?/36 CE	Alexander II Glaphyra	[00]		

Continued on next page

Herod's Family Tree—*Continued*

Name	Birth/ Death	Father Mother	Spouse	Birth/ Marriage/ Death	Spouse's Status
son	13?/	Antipater III daughter of ANTIGONUS	daughter of Pheroras	13?/	father's father's brother's daughter
daughter	12?/	Antipater III	HEROD IV	15?/ /48 CE	father's brother's son
Sixth Generation					
MARCUS JULIUS AGRIPPA II	27 CE/93 CE	AGRIPPA I Cypros III	[00]		
Drusus	23 CE	AGRIPPA I Cypros III	[00]		
Berenice III	30 CE	AGRIPPA I Cypros III	Marcus [00] HEROD IV POLEMO [00] [TITUS]	15?/ /48 CE 39 CE/ /81 CE	ruling family father's brother royal; divorced royal; [mistress]
Mariamme VI	32 CE?	AGRIPPA I Cypros III	Archelaus III DEMETRIUS		exogamous; divorced ruler
Drusilla		AGRIPPA I Cypros III	AZIZUS M. A. FELIX		royal; father's brother's wife's brother; divorced ruler
ARISTOBULUS IV		HEROD IV Mariamme V	Salome III		father's sister's daughter
Bernicianus		HEROD IV Berenice	?		
Hyrcanus		HEROD IV Berenice	?		
Salome III	14?/	Herod Philip I Herodias	HEROD PHILIP II ARISTOBULUS IV	20/30 CE/ 34 CE	father's brother father's brother's son's son
Jotape II		Aristobulus II [00] Jotape I			
TIGRANES V (DHIKRAN)		Alexander V	?		
Cypros V		Alexis Helcias Cypros IV	?		

Name	Birth/ Death	Father Mother	Spouse	Birth/ Marriage/ Death	Spouse's Status
Seventh Generation					
Herod VI		ARISTOBULUS IV Salome III	?		
Agrippa III		ARISTOBULUS IV Salome III	?		
Aristobulus V		ARISTOBULUS IV Salome III	?		
Berenice IV		Archelaus III Mariamme V	?		
Agrippinus		DEMETRIUS Mariamme V	?		
(Antonius)		M. A. FELIX	?		
Agrippa IV	/79 CE	Drusilla			
GAIUS JULIUS ALEXANDER VI		TIGRANES V	Iotape III		royal
Eighth Generation					
GAIUS JULIUS AGRIPPA		ALEXANDER VI Iotape III	?		
GAIUS JULIUS ALEXANDER BERENICIANUS		ALEXANDER VI Iotape III	?		

CHAPTER 3

From Idumaea to Petra (to 64 BCE)

INTRODUCTION

Conflicting origins for Herod were designed by the Roman, Christian, and Jewish communities to meet their different needs. On the Roman side, Strabo (late first century BCE to early first century CE) describes Herod as a "native of the country" who "slinked into the priesthood."[1] Eusebius preserves a Christian calumny (citing Julius Africanus[2]) that Herod's grandfather Antipas was a Gentile slave who had served in the Temple of Apollo in Ashkelon. This Christian apologetic aimed to diminish further the reputation of the "killer of the innocents" at Bethlehem. But there is no apparent source for the story;[3] it was made up of whole cloth in the early third century.

One Jewish tradition concerning Herod's origins (*Ant.* 14.403–4) refers to him as a "half-Jew." There are three possible explanations of the phrase, none with much historical value, but illuminating for the implications.[4] It is barely possible that the phrase was based on the belief that Herod's mother was not considered a true convert to Judaism, but the later view that Jewishness was reckoned through the mother should not be pressed back into this period. In this period it seems that a wife was considered Jewish if she married a Jew. It is also barely arguable that the phrase implied that Herod was a "Godfearer" (to use a term common in New Testament scholarship) but was not a full convert

---

1. Strabo, *Geog.* 16.2.46: *anêr epichôriois. . . hierosynê.*

2. Eusebius, *Church History,* 1.6; Julius Africanus was born in Jerusalem and lived about 160–240 CE. See also 1.7.24, "Herod . . . had no drop of Israelitish blood."

3. Justin, *Dialogue with Trypho* 52, claims Ashkelon is the birthplace of Antipater, Herod's father.

4. It can hardly have come from Nicolas; more likely is an origin in some other Jewish source available to Josephus in the first century.

to Judaism through baptism, circumcision, and sacrifice,[5] but Herod's Judaism had more to do with his grandfather than with him. The third possible explanation of the phrase "half-Jew" is that a sufficient number of generations (usually three)[6] had not passed since his forebear's conversion, so Herod was still religiously disabled. Even if such a requirement obtained there might have been debate whether the third generation was to be reckoned inclusively or exclusively, although, generally speaking, in numeric matters such as the calendar, years would have been reckoned inclusively.[7]

Given the limited evidence and the absence of vigorous controversy on the point, it appears that Herod would have been reckoned a full Jew. We should therefore discount views that post-date Herod's death by a good bit which allude to Herod's disability or to his pagan origin, just as we must discount the revealing story that comes from Herod's own lifetime (told disingenuously by Josephus):[8] "Nicolaus of Damascus . . . says that [Herod's] family belonged to the leading Jews from Babylon. But he says this in order to please Antipater's son Herod. . . ." This extract, however, reveals two important facts about Josephus's use of sources: first, he can be critical of them, and second, he may be more dependent upon Nicolas (as he himself implies) in *Antiquities* than in *War*. Though we will have to return to such questions from time to time, here we can trust his rejection of one of the sources on which he was heavily dependent.

What can be said about Herod's background and the broader canvas on which his picture is painted? Our sketch is built up in successive layers, beginning with his parents' roots in Idumaea and Nabatea, and then the other political, cultural, and religious influences that shaped him.

---

5. Since the publication of an inscription from Aphrodisias in Asia Minor, skepticism about the category of "Godfearers" has been laid to rest. See J. Reynolds and R. Tannenbaum, *Jews and Godfearers at Aphrodisias,* Cambridge Philological Society Supplements, vol. 12 (Cambridge: Cambridge Philological Society, 1987), pp. 43–67.

6. Philo, *De virtutibus* 108: "Gentiles must not be spurned with an unconditional refusal, but be so far favored that the third generation is invited to the congregation and made partakers in the divine revelations, to which also the native born, whose lineage is beyond reproach, are rightfully admitted." See also *Spec. leg.* 1.52–53. The Temple Scroll (11QT) refers to four generations.

7. In an inclusive reckoning, his father Antipater and his grandfather Antipas both faced limitations, but Herod—the third generation—was fully Jewish. In an exclusive reckoning, it would only be Herod's children who were fully Jewish. Some have considered that the debate on the question may have revolved around Herod, his children, and his grandchildren, especially Agrippa I. Though there is no direct evidence of this, Philo—from the same period roughly as Agrippa I—is suggestive; later evidence in *m.Sotah* 7.8 attaches the issue of legitimacy to Agrippa I, but not connected with this matter in particular. In Herod's day there probably were no fixed rules. See *Ant.* 19.332 on Agrippa I, and note (c) ad loc. concerning a textual variant and other evidence.

8. *Ant.* 14.9; *War* 1.123. The story is patently false, but it reveals the depth of Nicolas's apologetic for Herod.

IDUMAEANS

Herod was an Idumaean. But his family origins lay in the desert in the tribe of Edom, as it was known in earlier times. Conflict between Israel and Edom was endemic. A parenthetic explanation (Gen. 25:30) describes the enmity between Jacob, the eponymous progenitor of Israel, and Esau, the eponymous progenitor of Edom, and suggests that Esau was called Edom because he was famished. The legend of an early brotherly relationship, though mythological, contained an element of reality; both tribes' origins were somewhat similar. Both were nomadic peoples with connections with the Arabian plateau, both settled in areas adjacent to the Rift Valley sometime during the second millennium BCE, the Israelites mostly to the west of the Jordan and the Edomites mostly to the east of the Jordan and south of the Dead Sea (the border between Edom and Moab was usually considered the brook Zered; see map 1). Gradually the Edomites moved westward, occupying areas in the northern Negev and southern Judea.[9] This pattern of settlement, though accelerated by the Babylonian victory over Judah in 587 BCE, showed little evidence of force of arms. The depopulation of Judah during the sixth century occurred at just the same time the Idumaeans (as they were called in Greek) were pushing westward, so that by the second century BCE they were settled on the southern border of Israel, occupying the area from just south of Bethlehem to near Beersheba, and from the Dead Sea to the coastal plain, though not to the coast. The chief city was Marisa.[10]

At the same time as the Idumaeans migrated to better land, another tribe whose origins are less clear moved from the Arabian plateau into ancient Edom. The paucity of written sources does not allow us to say whether the Idumaeans were pushed by these Nabateans or moved peacefully.

When the Hasmonean dynasty pursued an aggressive policy in the wake of their startlingly successful revolt (165 BCE and following), relations with the Idumaeans on their southern border were relatively good. Common cause made good sense for a period, since both occupied an uncomfortable position between two major powers: Syria under the Seleucids to the north of Judea and Egypt under the Ptolemies to the south-west of the Idumaeans.[11] But John Hyrcanus (135–104 BCE) disturbed the balance, pushing east into the Transjordan and south into Idumaea (*Ant.* 13.257–58). Josephus speaks of his "conquering" the Idumaeans and forcing their conversion to Judaism. This uniformly

---

9. On Idumaeans, including a brief account of this gradual process and Jewish-Idumaean relations, see A. Kasher, *Jews, Idumaeans and Ancient Arabs* (Tübingen: J. C. B. Mohr, 1988).

10. A. Kloner, "Mareshah (Marisa)," *NEAEHL* 3.948–57. The claim is sometimes made that Marisa was the birthplace of Herod, and this is not implausible; see E. D. Oren and U. Rappaport, "The Necropolis of Mareshah-beth Guvrin," *IEJ* 34 (1984): 114–53.

11. On all these points see further below.

held view has been reassessed; Strabo, *Geog.* 16.2.34, provides strong support: "The Idumaeans are Nabataeans, but owing to a sedition they were banished from there, joined the Judaeans, and shared in the same customs with them." The reassessment of Idumaean conversions means that Herod's attachment to Judaism resulted from his grandfather's voluntary adherence and willing "full" conversion to the Temple cult in Jerusalem and not from a forced submission to a bare-bones form of Judaism.

The challenge has been mounted by Aryeh Kasher.[12] With the two exceptions of heavily hellenized cities that had ceased to practice the traditional circumcision, the conversion of Idumaea was peaceful and voluntary, he claims, not under duress. With the exception of Marisa and Adora, Idumaea was annexed, not conquered.[13] Following John Hyrcanus's annexation, the rite of circumcision, which the Idumaeans already practiced, was given Jewish content. Later evidence confirms this picture. (1) When Pompey imposed his settlement on Judea two generations later in 63 BCE he did not detach Eastern Idumaea from Judea because he considered it fully Jewish. (2) No Idumaean delegation begged Pompey for separate status and a revival of the Idumaean cult. (3) In Herod's day there were still unconverted Idumaeans practicing the cult of Cos (or Kos), as one would expect if conversion was not forced but voluntary. (4) When, a century later, Jospehus wrote about Pompey's decision he said that he confined the Jewish nation within its own borders—an impossible turn of phrase had Idumaea been contending for a national identity. (5) Josephus also reports that, at the time of the Great Revolt of 66–74 CE, Idumaeans were especially prominent on the side of revolutionaries. (6) There are accounts of Idumaean disciples in the House of Shammai who were learned in Torah and punctilious in their observance.[14]

For our purposes the most important argument in favor of peaceful conversion is that: (7) not much later Alexander Jannaeus (103–76 BCE) appointed Herod's grandfather Antipas *stratêgos* ("praetor") of all Idumaea—an unusual degree of trust had Antipas only recently accepted Judaism unwillingly (see *Ant.* 14.10).[15] Kasher also points to the tendency for Idumaean nobility in this period to be integrated with Jewish national leadership: Hyrcanus II, a Hasmonean, married an Idumaean, and Herod, an Idumaean, married a Hasmonean. Kasher

---

12. Kasher, *Jews, Idumaeans*, pp. 46–78, to which I am indebted in what follows.

13. Kasher argues on the basis of careful comparison of *Ant.* 13.257–58; 15.254; Strabo, *Geog.* 16.2.34, and Ptolemy (as cited in Stern, *CRINT*, vol. 1, #146). He emphasizes that Josephus in *War* 1.63 refers to the conquest only of Marisa and Adora; he feels it is significant that there is no reflection of the problem of forced conversion in the *Mishnah*.

14. *Sifre Zuttah;* for details of the other arguments see Kasher, *Jews, Idumaeans*, esp. pp. 62–63.

15. Some have argued, most recently Kochman in a dissertation in Hebrew, that Idumaeans were always Jews and did not need "conversion" at all, merely reform. This view, as Kasher points out, is too apologetically motivated.

observes that even though Antipater, Herod's father, was vigorously pro-Roman and strongly hellenized, two of his children bore Hebrew names (Joseph and Salome), as did Herod's cousin, Achiab.

Kasher supplies a social-historical reconstruction in support of these views. When Hyrcanus I threatened Idumaea there was a voluntary agreement between him and the Idumaeans' strongly patriarchal leadership, perhaps including Antipas, to accept inclusion in Judea. The decision naturally was accepted by the majority of the tribe. Not all, of course, would have agreed; such holdouts surfaced two generations later, still bearing names that reflected the ancient Idumaean cultic attachment to Cos, such as Herod's brother-in-law, Costobar. Because some resisted and others in the two hellenized cities who had not been circumcised were compelled to be, it came to be viewed generally as forced conversion with compulsory circumcision.[16] Even if Herod's family came from Marisa, the picture so far as Herod was concerned is not significantly altered. The rapid rise of Herod's grandfather Antipas to a position of influence evidenced that the conversion was more voluntary than forced, though he might have become prominent in any case, since Antipas was wealthy and influential. Some of Herod's wealth two generations later must have derived from Antipas's sources of income (land, trade, flocks, investments, tariff concessions perhaps). On the whole, Kasher's analysis is successful and profoundly alters the general approach one takes to Herod's antecedents.

Herod probably grew up—if indeed the conversion was "full" and voluntary—in a family without doubt about its Judaism. He was the third generation descended from a full and willing proselyte to Judaism, and was regarded as a Jew by his contemporaries (*Ant.* 20.173; *War* 2.266: Herod was from *to genos Ioudaiôn* in the dispute among Caesarea's inhabitants over the status and character of the city). Later hesitations concerning Herod's Judaism cannot be shown to apply widely—if at all—at the time of Herod; the likeliest reconstruction is that the question was *sub iudice* and a matter of debate between various schools of interpretation in the first century BCE.

The Idumaean area was relatively small (see map 2): on the east they occupied the middle half of the shore of the Dead Sea, roughly centered on the present site of Masada; on the south the occupation line ran roughly east and west through Beersheba; on the west the line paralleled the coast-line, between five and fifteen miles inland; on the north the area ran from east to west between Bethlehem and Hebron, with a bump to the north at the western corner. The area is mostly rolling hill country, rising from the coastal plain that the Idumeans generally did not occupy through the Shephelah up to the relatively barren areas beyond the height of land, where the land drops rapidly away

---

16. Voluntary conversion does not necessarily mean it is enthusiastic; it can be as minimal as forced conversion. Kasher tries to meet this difficulty with some of the evidence noted above.

through a very rugged and arid area to meet the Dead Sea at nearly 1,300′ below sea level. The southern edge is relatively flat; beyond this border lived the Nabateans.

All in all the land was productive in a variety of ways; there were good grain, olive and fruit-growing areas, useful grazing lands for flocks of goats and sheep and herds of camels (Strabo, *Geog.* 16.2.2: "partly farmers"). Within its borders was the ancient city of Hebron, known for pottery and glass-blowing. Marisa and Adora, on the other hand, were in close touch with cultural currents of the Hellenistic world; Marisa in particular was *à la mode,* laid out on a Hippodamian plan, with a grid-iron of two main north-south and one main east-west streets.

Despite their uncomfortable position on Egypt's north-eastern flank, the Idumaeans prospered. Some of the land encouraged settlement; in the eastern and southern portions semi-nomadic grazing was the rule; in the west grain-growing predominated; in the central and northern areas olives and settled pursuits predominated. Their location near two natural transportation corridors encouraged contact with neighbors and may also have prompted involvement in the lucrative trade routes running through these corridors: one through Nabatean and Idumaean territory between Petra and Ashkelon, part of an overland trade route from the Arabian plateau;[17] the other a coastal route from Egypt to the Fertile Crescent, the Via Maris.

The Idumaeans were a classic example of a semi-nomadic people in the process of moving to a settled existence. By a curious stroke of good timing, they occupied a suitable piece of land that was largely empty and not much contested. The variety of land-forms was appropriate for mixed occupation and a mixed economy, itself a kind of transitional region, where several population centers could be developed, some on traditional sites,[18] some on relatively undeveloped land. Marisa, though an old site, had fewer religious attachments and was, therefore, appropriate for a fresh experiment in city-building. Transportation routes were adequate, except for a lack of an outlet to the sea.

Idumaeans were in transition culturally. While there was a strong sense of cultural differentiation at the beginning of the second century BCE that continued, even if in a muted fashion, during the next two hundred years, the main cultural trend was toward a higher degree of integration—first under the Hasmoneans and then under the Herodians. Idumaean settlement in the area to the

---

17. Petra, once an Edomite city, was a crucial transfer point; from Petra the route crossed the Rift Valley and headed north-west, eventually arriving at Ashkelon or Gaza on the Mediterranean, where goods could be transshipped anywhere in the Greek or Roman world.

18. Josephus, *War* 4.530, says "Hebron is a town of greater antiquity not only than any other in the country, but even than Memphis in Egypt, being reckoned to be two thousand three hundred years old." He also refers to it as "a small town" (*War* 4.529). See A. Ofer, "Hebron," *NEAEHL* 2.606–9.

south of Judea—a process that had been going on for several hundred years—led directly to the complementary process of assimilation to and integration with Judea. This policy had different characteristics under the Hasmoneans, Herod and the procurators, but it was remarkably successful. As Kasher has pointed out, there is good evidence both of passive Idumaean participation in the political and religious life of Judea and of strong and active involvement as vigorous defenders of Jewish religious autonomy and political freedom in the revolt of 66–74 CE.[19] At its outbreak, for example, the generals delegated to lead the Idumaeans were prominent Jewish religious leaders.[20] At the climax of the revolt (the account of which begins at *War* 4.208) Idumaeans rushed to mobilize all their forces in order "to defend the freedom" of Jerusalem (4.234), a better indication of their character than Josephus's scurrilous editorial description: "they were a turbulent and disorderly people, ever on the alert for commotion and delighting in revolutionary changes, and only needed a little flattery from their suitors to seize their arms and rush into battle as to a feast" (4.231).

While waiting to be let into Jerusalem to aid in its defense, Simon of Cathla, one of the Idumaean leaders,[21] delivered an important speech in which he claimed that the city "belongs to us all" (*War* 4.272), it is "the mother city" (274), its gates have been closed against the defenders' "nearest kinsmen" (278), its worship constitutes "national sacred rites" (279)—indeed, the revolt is a defense of "our common country" from both inside and outside foes (281). Once inside the city the Idumaeans slaughtered great numbers, including the chief priests and the high priest Ananus (*War* 4.314–18; see. also 7.267).[22] But Josephus exaggerates, for the Idumaeans are also reported (perhaps following a different source) to have been full of remorse for the events that followed their liberation of Jerusalem, and in dejection they went back home after first releasing two thousand prisoners from jail (4.345–54). While Josephus is not always to be trusted, especially in the speeches he puts in his actors' mouths, his rhetoric emphasizes feelings of kinship between Idumaeans and Jews. There is no discernible political or editorial reason Josephus might have exaggerated commonality between Idumaeans and Jews; the claim to closeness must make sense historically.

Josephus reports another revealing incident that took place about a hundred years earlier, associated with the beginning of Herod's efforts to consolidate

---

19. Kasher, *Jews, Idumaeans,* passim; see his Epilogue, pp. 206–11, and Appendix, pp. 214–39.

20. Jeshua son of Sapphas a chief priest, and Eleazar son of the high priest Neus (*War* 2.566). Josephus provides no explanation of the decision.

21. Along with John, James, and Phinehas! The combination of names is striking: three are names of three of the Twelve, and the fourth is the quintessential "zealot" name going back to the key figure in Num. 25.

22. In both places we have Josephus's own verdict on the Idumaeans, a verdict that needs to be moderated by the indications regarding their attachment to Judaism and to freedom.

the kingship bestowed on him by the Roman Senate. After landing at Ptolemais (Acco) in early 39 BCE, the districts of Idumaea, Galilee, and Samaritis (*War* 1.302) came over to Herod voluntarily. Despite the fact that he was Idumaean, however, when later the same year he rescued his mother and other family members from Masada, he did not leave them in Idumaea but sent them for safety to Samaritis (*War* 1.303), while he occupied Idumaea "to prevent any insurrection in favour of Antigonous." In two generations, then, Idumaea had apparently become sufficiently integrated into Judea that a leading Idumaean could count on only partial Idumaean support as king of the united territories, and in family matters not at all. By contrast, Idumaean support for the Hasmoneans is found in *War* 1.326, which reports defections to Antigonus from among Herod's supporters in Idumaea.[23] One final indication: when Herod died and revolt was raised in Idumaea, among other places, two thousand of Herod's veterans who had been settled on allocations there (presumably to guard the Nabatean frontier) rose and fought the troops loyal to Archelaus; this Idumaean revolt was not an indigenous revolt in favor of an autonomous state, religion, or culture (see *War* 2.55),[24] unless the veterans were originally Idumaeans. But this is inherently unlikely.

In brief, when these additional bits of evidence are added to Kasher's reassessment of the relationship between Idumaeans and Judeans, there is substantial support for the view that from Herod to the end of the revolt, the Idumaeans' strongest loyalty was to Judea. While they are not pictured as strongly devoted to a religious set of goals, religion was certainly an important part of their attachment to Judea. Except for a relatively small group, they did not intend merely to seize political opportunity, for they harbored no special ambition for local self-government.

This cultural change began with the "conquest" under Hyrcanus I; its aftermath suggests that it was, as Kasher claims, voluntarily supported by a large number of Idumaeans. In 39 BCE when they might collectively have viewed Herod as a dream come true, a segment of the Idumaeans preferred to attach their fate to the one remaining Hasmonean star, Antigonus. They did not rise in general revolt in 4 BCE; they sprang vigorously to the standard in 66 CE; they sought to defend the city of Jerusalem with all their resources in 69 CE; and they withdrew from the city when it was clear that Judaism was in deep trouble a little later. Given these indications of steady and loyal devotion to Judaism,

---

23. In the same place (*War* 1.325–26) Josephus reports serious troubles for Herod in Galilee also, where groups of partisans of both Antigonus and Herod vie with each other. The Herodian group is referred to as "the men of rank who were in favour of Herod," probably the earliest reference to "the Herodians."

24. Just as Samaritis had been the safest place for Herod to send his family in 39 BCE, so in 4 BCE it was Samaritis that remained the most loyal to the dispositions Herod had made in his will. As a result it was remitted a quarter of its taxes for not rising in the disturbances of 4 BCE; *War* 2.96.

Judea and Jerusalem, Josephus's negative evaluation of the Idumaeans needs modification. The fact is that the Idumaeans were acculturated to Judea and closely identified with its fortunes from the late-second century BCE to the mid-first century CE. The strong hellenizing tendencies in the cities of Marisa and Adora especially (exemplified in the new city design of Marisa) were slowed or even reversed in this period.[25]

There is little evidence of continued strong devotion to Cos in the literature (other than the use of Cos in proper names) and the archaeological record has not provided much direct and datable evidence.[26] Two religious sites in the area bear directly on an understanding of Herod: Mamre (Ramet el-Khalil) and Hebron (el-Khalil), both associated with the patriarchs, especially Abraham. The archaeological evidence—though there is no supporting literary or epigraphic evidence—suggests that Herod enclosed the traditional site of Mamre, just north of Hebron, with a finely dressed temenos wall, enclosing an area of about 150' by 200,' with a huge oak recalled traditionally as one of the oaks of Mamre at Abraham's altar to the Lord (Gen. 13:18; 14:13; 18:1).[27] Josephus says the oak had been there ever since creation (War 4.533; Ant. 1.196), and he associates it with Abraham (Ant. 1.186), though he does not say that the site was connected with Herod. The style of the stonework and the date of building point clearly to Herod as the patron, perhaps at an early point in his building activity.[28] For us the importance lies in its location in Idumaean territory and its association with Abraham's altar to Yahweh.[29]

---

25. Marisa was destroyed by the Parthians in 40 BCE and not resettled; it was effectively replaced by Beth Guvrin (Eleutheropolis).

26. Marisa was the largest and most important city in Idumaea; during the third century BCE, for example, it was mentioned in the Zenon papyri as a center of the slave trade with Egypt. Excavations identified a temenos in the eastern quarter of the city; it was not clear whether the structure in its middle (a three-chambered building) was a temple, and if so, to whom it was dedicated (one of the deities of the city was Apollo, perhaps Cos). The city itself was a modest size (480 feet by 450 feet) with walls and towers protecting it. The most important archaeological finds were painted tombs of the second century BCE, showing a mixture of Idumaeans, Sidonians, and Greeks (NEAEHL 3.956); the excavations, now covered over, were published by F. J. Bliss and R. A. S. Macalister, details and bibliography in NEAEHL.

27. Several (W. F. Albright, F.-M. Abel and B. Mazar) dispute this identification; at the time of Herod, however, it was thought to be associated with Abraham, so that Herod built his structure around this sacred site.

28. The history is complex, including evidence of Hasmonean (second century BCE; possibly John Hyrcanus), Herodian (late first century BCE), Hadrianic (second century CE), and Byzantine occupations or structures. The north wall has a long section of Herodian wall, including ceremonial entrances here and in the west wall. The Herodian work is similar to that at Hebron, in the Temple in Jerusalem and the Phasael tower in Herod's Palace in Jerusalem. The temenos, as reconstructed by Herod, may not have been completed. In Hadrian's rebuilding the functions were maintained but the associations of the place were altered. See I. Magen, "Mamre," NEAEHL 3.939–42; A. E. Mader, Mambre. Die Ergebnissen der Aussgrabungen im heiligen Bezirk, Ramat el-Halil in Süd-Palästina (Freiburg in Breisgau, 1957); R. de Vaux, "Mambre," DBSupl 5 (1957): 753–58.

29. Mamre was destroyed in the Great Revolt. In 130 CE, when he visited the East, Hadrian

Closely linked with Mamre was Hebron, a few miles away, where Abraham bought the caves of Machpelah as a family burial site at the time of the death of Sarah (Gen. 23:1–20; Num. 13:22). As the patriarchal burial place (Sarah, Gen. 23:19; Abraham, 25:9; Isaac, Rebekah, and Leah, 49:31; and Jacob, 50:13), Hebron became important after its defeat by Joshua (Josh. 15:13; 10:16–27); David, for example, lived and ruled there for seven years (2 Sam. 2:1–4; 5:5). While Nehemiah implies that Hebron was one of the places in which returning exiles settled (Neh. 11:25–36), it seems to have been during this period or a little later that Idumaeans settled it; Judah the Hasmonean, early in the revolt, took over Hebron and destroyed its fortifications at the same time as he attacked Marisa and Azotus (1 Macc. 5:65–68; about 164 BCE).

Hebron was thus a key site in the area to the south of Judah, not only as an important sacred place but also as an ancient urban area. Herod built there a fine and immensely powerful structure—the only Herodian building surviving today virtually intact—over the caves of Machpelah.[30] Functionally it protected the caves and covered them with a beautiful pilastered wall enclosing what was likely an open space[31] used for religious observances in connection with Abraham and the patriarchs.[32] The wall treatment and overall design approach were prototypes of the Jerusalem Temple.[33]

Both Idumaeans and Jews held Abraham as a common progenitor,[34] so the building of these memorials to Abraham at Hebron and Mamre allowed Herod to emphasize the unity of Idumaeans and Jews; they were acts of piety to please both and offend neither. These structures—perhaps among Herod's earliest— indicated Herod's true colors in religion and piety, for he had little reason to

---

ordered it rebuilt as one of three great public markets (alongside Acco and Gaza); following the Bar Kokhbah revolt, it was used as a slave market for Jewish prisoners (Jerome, *Commentaria in Jeremiam* 31; *in Zechariam* 9:2).

30. See C. Conder, *PEQ* (1881): 266–71; L. H. Vincent, E. J. Mackay, and F.-M. Abel, *Hébron: Le Haram El-Khalîl* (Paris: Éditions Ernest Leroux, 1923); "Hebron," *EJ* 8:226–36; D. M. Jacobson, "The Plan of the Ancient Haram el-Khalil at Hebron," *PEQ* 113 (1981):73–80; N. Millar, "Patriarchal Burial Site," *BAR* 11/3 (1985): 26–43; Ofer, "Hebron," 606–9 (though not dealing with the Haram in detail).

31. The reconstructions of both Mamre and Hebron show an open paved courtyard structure, with memorials in the open area. The degree of similarity is very great between the two, especially in this feature, the wall treatment, and the style of masonry.

32. The door into the enclosure on the main level is later; some speculate that there was a door on the lower level behind a later wall, and that this would imply that visitors originally had access to the caves before moving up an internal stair to the main "courtyard" level. Certainty on the reconstruction of the building is impossible, despite its remarkably fine state of preservation.

33. The enclosed area is 103 by 203 feet, with walls rising 60 feet above the floor that covers the caves. The pilasters are identical to those in the Jerusalem Temple; the stones, while not quite as large as those in Jerusalem, are similar in scale and in surface treatment.

34. This is being written in the wake of the massacre of Palestinian Muslims worshipping in the Haram in February 1994 by an extreme right-wing Israeli settler. The presence of a synagogue and a mosque in Herod's building is a continuing reminder of a related aspect to the point I am making here.

give a false impression here. They suggest that Herod's own convictions were rooted in the origins of the religious experience of Jews and Idumaeans, with no fundamental opposition between his Idumaean race and his Jewish religion.[35]

From his father and grandfather Herod inherited a generous measure of interest in the Hellenistic world, a fondness for things Roman, an acute sense of political opportunity, and perhaps an autocratic style. He also inherited from them a sense of rootedness in Idumaea and a real but not overly sophisticated attachment to Judaism (see chap. 10).

NABATEANS

The Nabateans have captured more scholarly and public imagination than Idumaeans. Interest in the Nabateans has been spurred through a number of causes: the wonderfully romantic impression both of Petra and of its modern discoverer, Jakob Burckhardt; the discovery of other Nabatean sites with rich artistic traditions, especially in sculpture and low relief; the Nabateans closeness to their desert roots; and their appearance of living on the margin of the civilized world.[36]

Though the evidence is slender, Herod's mother Cypros was either a Nabatean or—less likely—from some unnamed Arab tribe contiguous to the Nabateans:

> Antipater had married a lady named Cypros, of an illustrious Arabian family,[37] by whom he had four sons—Phasael, Herod afterwards king, Joseph and Pheroras—and a daughter, Salome. He had, by kind offices and hospitality, attached to himself persons of influence in every quarter; above all, through this matrimonial alliance, he had won the friendship of the king of the Arabians, and it was to him that he entrusted his children when embarking on war with Aristobulus.[38]

---

35. It is curious that Josephus (perhaps following Nicolas of Damascus's silence) makes nothing of these two largely unparalleled buildings—religious precincts with memorials but no other important appurtenances. A remote parallel is the memorial described in 1 Macc. 13:25–30: a walled precinct with seven pyramids to the Hasmoneans and columns adorned with trophies and carved ships.

36. On Nabateans in the context of the Near East, see Millar, *Roman Near East,* chap. 11.

37. *Gynaika tôn episêmôn ex Arabias.* . . . Jospehus's use of "Arabia" and "Arab" is not consistent enough to be certain that he means Nabatea, but he usually does; Antipater's friendship with, and his sending of his children to, "the king," strongly implies the Nabatean king, since there is no record of another "king of the Arabians."

38. *Ant.* 14.121 is less clear, sounds garbled, and is textually uncertain. It confirms that Cypros was from a distinguished Arab family, but says that Antipater found her among the Idumaeans. This is not impossible, though it would distinguish her origins from other Idumaeans. In 14.122 again the account is less clear than in *War* when it refers to Antipater courting "other princes, especially . . . the king of the Arabs."

If "Arabians" and "Nabateans" are one and the same in *War* and *Antiquities,* Cypros must have been connected with the Nabatean royal family, since her children were sent for safekeeping to the king. Herod's family, during their formative years, were thus known to Nabateans through the patronage of King Aretas III (85–62 BCE) or Obodas II (62–57 BCE); the family may have spent a period of time in Petra under Malichus I (57–ca. 28 BCE) when Herod was about fifteen years old.[39]

The Nabateans occupied ancient Edom as the Idumaeans moved to the south of Judea. By the third or second century BCE, Nabateans occupied an area east of the Dead Sea and Rift Valley southward beyond the head of the Gulf of Aqaba, and also an area to the west of the Rift Valley between the Idumaeans to the north, the Sinai peninsula to the south and the Egyptians to the west (maps 1 and 2). Their northern border varied a good deal; occasionally it may have reached as far as Damascus[40] but for most of the Herodian period it ran through Auranitis, east of the Sea of Galilee, beyond the Decapolis cities.

The Nabateans lived partly as semi-nomads and partly in urban centers (Petra above all, but also Bostra, Canatha [Qanawat], Dionysias [Suweida], et-Tannur, Mampsis [Kurnub], Avdat [Obodas], Nissana and others). Much of the early information about Nabateans is drawn from Diodorus Siculus (a contemporary of Herod's, using earlier sources), who mentions a number of tribes in the area described above. This view is undoubtedly correct for the earlier period he describes and it may even be partly correct for the Herodian period, though it is unlikely that Diodorus's information is first hand. By mid-first century BCE the Nabateans had become more sedentary; they had already seen the advantages of cooperation among the tribes and actively promoted such unity, including the incorporation of non-Arab peoples in the area. They established a Hellenistic style of kingship with Nabateans occupying the key positions, and this adoption of Hellenistic customs extended in a remarkable way to their religion and architecture.

Some parts of the Nabatean territory were fertile, particularly in the North where Auranitis grows a good grade of wheat. Other parts, especially to the east and south, were relatively infertile, though capable of supporting flocks and herds and limited agriculture. In the areas to the west of the Rift Valley the land varies from slightly rolling lands in the Negev to more inhospitable areas in the Sinai peninsula proper.

One of the most remarkable aspects of Nabatean culture was the ability to mine arid areas for water, thus cultivating marginal lands. They developed

---

39. On Nabatean kings, see Schürer, Appendix II, 1.574–86 with bibliography; Sullivan, *Near Eastern Royalty,* p. 215, suggests Cypros was the daughter of Aretas III.

40. Millar argues that Nabateans may have controlled Damascus during the late 30s CE; *Roman Near East,* pp. 56–57.

technologies for building efficient plastered cisterns and for multiplying the amount of water available to a field for agricultural purposes by building parallel walls in a herringbone pattern to bring water from higher uncultivated lands. Like Idumaeans, Nabateans were developing from a nomadic life on the Arabian plateau to a settled and partially agricultural style of life.

The Nabatean economy, however, was founded less on agriculture than on international trade. Its origins went back to the Nabateans' nomadic origins as traders between East and West, especially in the flourishing spice trade, but also in incense, silks, and cottons. In their settled location they were still able to control the trade in these commodities that came up the Wadi Sirhan, that kept to the southern overland routes through the Hejaz, or that came by sea to the head of the Gulf of Aqaba. Much of this trade passed through or near Petra, and much of what missed Petra had to pass through Nabatean lands on its way to the coast at Gaza or Ashkelon.[41] Petra was a particularly important trade entrepôt due to its location at the intersection of two main routes—the Hejaz trade route paralleling the Red Sea and the King's Highway from Aqaba to Damascus and beyond.[42]

The Nabateans were merchants. In addition to eastern trade they took advantage of their proximity to Jericho to be involved in the balsam trade. They may also have developed the bitumen trade exploiting the deposits in the Dead Sea (*Lake Asphaltitis* to the Romans).[43] They were skilled potters with an advanced technology for glazing and firing fine pottery that was an international commodity.[44] Much of the individual wealth of Nabateans was founded on their roles as merchants, and the wealth of their cities—especially Petra—was bolstered by income from international trade. They were much ahead of their time in certain respects, supplying—as Hammond puts it—packaged end products.[45] Herod must have benefitted from some of these activities. Trade was facilitated by the Nabatean use of Aramaic, the *lingua franca* of the eastern trading bloc. With no written language of their own they adopted—perhaps in response to economic opportunities—Aramaic as both a written and spoken language, despite the fact that their racial origins were Arabic.[46]

---

41. Perhaps even including the trade keeping to the Wadi Sirhan farther north and heading straight for Damascus, though Millar seems unsure. Some maritime trade from the East went straight to Egypt, thence overland to the Nile and then up the river.

42. On Nabatean trade see G. van Beek, *BA* 23 (1960):70–95.

43. Diodorus Siculus, *Bibliotheca* 19.94.4–5.

44. K. Schmitt-Karte, in Manfred Lindner, ed., *Petra und das Königreich der Nabatäer* (Munich: Delp, 1970), pp. 174–203; K. Schmitt-Karte, *Die Nabatäer. Spuren einer arabischen Kultur der Antike* (Hanover: Veröffentlichen der Deutsch-Jordanischen Gesellschaft, 1976).

45. P. C. Hammond, *The Nabateans: Their History, Culture and Archeology*. Studies in Mediterranean Archeology 37 (Gotheburg: Paul Aströms Forlag, 1973), p.69.

46. This seems the most reasonable reading of the evidence; though some have argued for Aramaic as the language of commerce and the written language, with Arabic being the everyday language, this must be "hazardous" (so Millar, *Roman Near East*, p. 402; see pp. 392–408).

Nabateans worshipped a pantheon of gods, centered on Dusares (*Du* = "he of," *Shara* = a region, probably in Edom), identified during the Roman period with Zeus/Jupiter. Dusares dominates the sources of the first century BCE to the first century CE, but may have been preceded by the North Arabian god Illah (*el, elohim* in Hebrew). The major goddess in the pantheon was Allat, identified with Athena, Aphrodite and Venus, and also with Ishtar/Astarte and Attargatis. Male gods included al-Kutba, Shailaqaum; female gods included Manawatu and al-Uzza. It was a religion that assimilated other deities without strain. Thus Ba'al Shamim from Phoenicia and from Palmyra,[47] Cos from Idumaea, and Isis from Egypt could find homes in Nabatea.[48]

The most important cult centers known archaeologically—at Petra, Dhiban, Obodas (Avdat), et-Tannur, and Si'a—had important features in common: a high and severely rectangular temple with an altar in front for sacrifice, a *temenos* reminiscent of but alien to both Hellenistic and Roman practice,[49] as well as a strong cubical sense of space with sophisticated surface decoration. Nabatean architecture, like its religion and culture and agriculture, was a unique response to the geographical, climatic, and ethnological influences on it.[50]

There was, however, variety in Nabatean towns, religious complexes, and building types. While Petra, for obvious reasons, is the best known and the most remarkable, no other Nabatean city is like Petra with its extensive use of rock-cut buildings. The Qasr Bint and the so-called Temple of the Winged Lion (both of ashlar masonry), together with stunning rock-cut tombs (the Khasneh, the Tomb of the Roman Soldier, the Urn Tomb, and many others), show Petra at its most impressive. Alongside Petra should be put the very different complexes at Obodas (Avdat), the heavily residential complexes at Mampsis (Kurnub), and the more remote religious site of et-Tannur. No simple description will cover the variety in this remarkably vigorous culture at the height of its powers in the first century BCE to the first century CE.

One site is particularly important in a study of Herod. His name occurs on a statue base found immediately to the right of the main entrance in the Naba-

---

47. Note the wonderful precinct at Palmyra dedicated to Ba'al Shamim, a century or so later than the one at Si'a.

48. A. Negev, "Nabatean Religion," *ER,* vol. 10, pp. 287–90.

49. Two forms of temple buildings have been identified typologically by Negev and others: one is a three-part form (porch, holy place, holy of holies, itself often tripartite), the other a square building within a larger walled *temenos.* Negev, "Nabatean Religion," p. 288; A. Negev, *Nabatean Archaeology Today* (New York: New York University Press, 1986), chap. 2; A. Negev, in *ANRW* 2.8 (1978): 520–686.

50. Hammond, *The Nabateans,* pp. 60–74. Earlier, see M. de Vogüé, *Syria Centrale. Architecture civile et religieuse de I au VII siècle,* 2 vols. (Paris: J. Baudry, 1865–77); H. C. Butler, *Architecture, Southern Syria,* Division II A, Publications of the Princeton University Archaeological Expeditions to Syria, 1904–5 (Leiden: Brill, 1907).

tean Temple of Ba'al Shamim at Si'a.[51] It was built in 33 BCE and the years following, though the extent of his involvement is uncertain (see chap. 8, Appendix B).

> To King Herod, master,
> Obaisath, son of Saodos
> placed the statue at his own expense.

The base shows that Herod accepted representational statues of himself (the statue itself is missing, though a foot remained when the base was found) and was willing to locate them in association with foreign gods.[52] Apparently Herod was not averse to images of himself as long as they were away from his Jewish subjects. Does the statue-base suggest Herod's direct participation in the building of this Temple, whether as donor (or one of them—there were several other statues alongside his) or as builder? Not directly; the inscription was dedicated to Herod and stems from a Nabatean; it offers neither reason nor role for him. Yet its placement on the porch implies a connection between Herod and the building. The style of the building is different from Herod's buildings[53] and so is the detail. So while we cannot be certain of his primary participation, the inscriptional evidence and the presence of his statue on the entrance porch support patronage of the Temple, perhaps in the form of a financial contribution.[54]

Another inscription refers to the *theatron*,[55] indicating not a theatral type of seating area but rather a porticoed forecourt fronting on the temple proper, providing seating for cultic ceremonies and festive meals. There were ritual baths at the entrance, an office for the keeper of the site, and places of sacrifice. None of the reconstructions of this complex have done justice to its dramatic use of the natural site hovering steeply over a perpetual river, the juxtaposition of the cult centers in the one site, or the rich decorative elements.

The time when the temple was built was bad for Herod. The struggle between Antony and Octavian was coming to a head, with Herod preparing to join forces with Antony, and he was having difficulty with Cleopatra VII, the

---

51. Religion provides the raison d'être for Si'a; in a three-temple complex, the Temple to Ba'al Shamim predominates over the Temple of Dusares, which has been located to one side.

52. This evidence is supported by the finding of three statue bases in Athens; he obviously was associated with other gods than the God of Israel; see further chaps. 8, 10.

53. It is typically Nabatean. The siting on a low ridge and the arrangement of courtyards is not unlike the Temple in Jerusalem; I take this to be the result of Nabatean influence on Herod, not vice versa.

54. See Millar, *Roman Near East*, pp. 395–96. See below on Athens (chap. 8 and Appendix B).
55. Ibid., pp. 394–95.

famous Queen of Egypt and Antony's lover (*War* 1.364–65). His relations with Nabatea were strained at about this time;[56] in 32–31 BCE, prompted by the machinations of Cleopatra, he raided Nabatea, attacking first Diospolis (no doubt Josephus means Dion) and then Canatha (Qanawat) where, after initial success, he fell into a trap laid by one of Cleopatra's generals. The result was a stunning defeat for Herod (*War* 1.366–68), though he later gained such a crushing victory near Philadelphia (Amman) that, according to Josephus, he was named "Protector" (*prostatês*) of the Arab nation (*War* 1.380–85; *Ant.* 15.108–60, and chap. 7).[57]

These events, military and political on the one hand, religious and architectural on the other, fit well together. After his victory near Philadelphia Herod remained dominant in the northern portion of Nabatea for a time, perhaps until Auranitis was given to him formally by Augustus in 23 BCE.[58] His role in the completion of the Temple of Baʿal Shamim at Siʿa was probably prompted by a desire to celebrate his victory at the one place where he had suffered a demoralizing defeat—near Canatha.

Two conclusions follow. (1) Herod had few compunctions about supporting other deities outside the Jewish homeland. He happily built memorials to Abraham in Idumaea—indirectly to the God of Israel who revealed himself to Abraham—while he built a temple at Siʿa to a competing god.[59] His actions in Idumaea would have generated a favorable reaction in both Idumaea and Judea; the building at Siʿa, however, would have been looked upon favorably by the Nabateans but viewed suspiciously by Jews. (2) Herod seized an opportunity to assist in building in his mother's Nabatea just as he had in his father's Idumaea. These appear to be parallel and complementary acts of piety (*War* 1.400, 462—probably on Nicolas's authority).[60]

---

56. The problem arose from Herod's guarantee of the tribute both he and the king of Nabatea had to pay to Cleopatra. Malichus refused to pay his share so Herod was responsible for the whole amount.

57. It seems unlikely that Herod would be named *prostatês* of Nabatea by the Nabateans, and there is no confirmation. The word has a range of meanings: "front rank man, leader, chief (especially of a democracy), ruler, chief administrator, guardian, patron, at Athens one who took charge of the interests of the *metoikoi*" (LSJ). The notion of guardian or patron seems the likeliest meaning here; perhaps the term was used by Herod, not by the Nabateans.

58. In 10/9 BCE a similar problem arose, triggered by a similar default in payment, this time by Obodas III (30–9 BCE), but occasioned by a revolt in Trachonitis. After demolishing the fortress at Rhaëpta, Herod settled three thousand Idumaeans in Trachonitis to assist in keeping the peace (*Ant.* 16.285; see all of 271–99, and below, chap. 11).

59. Jews might barely understand Baʿal Shamim ("the Lord of the Heavens") as equivalent to Yahweh. For a period Israel had understood its God as God of the Heavens, and the one title might be assimilated to the other; perhaps only Herod himself made the adaptation.

60. P. Richardson, "Religion and Architecture. A Study in Herod's Piety, Power, Pomp and Pleasure," *Bulletin of the Canadian Society of Biblical Studies,* 45 (1985): 3–29, esp. 16–19.

ITURAEANS

Like Nabateans, Ituraeans were Arabs whose eponymous ancestor Jetur was connected in Jewish tradition with Ishmael (Gen. 25:12–15; 1 Chron. 1:28–31).[61] Like Idumaeans, Ituraeans were open to strong Hellenistic and Roman influences; more important still, they had come under the influence of Judaism, though to what extent they had been deeply integrated into Jewish religion and society by Herod's day is debated.[62]

Ituraea comprised a fluctuating area in southern Syria (see map 1), centered on the southern end of the Anti-Lebanon mountains. At its greatest limits it extended from the headwaters of the Jordan and the area around Lake Huleh northward to include Mount Hermon, parts of both Lebanon ranges, the Beka'a valley between them through which the Litani River runs,[63] and possibly eastward through parts of Gaulanitis (the Golan), Batanea, Trachonitis, and Auranitis.[64] The territory shrank or expanded according to political fortunes, but probably never included Damascus.[65] It offered a mainly mountainous region with mixed land forms and some very fertile areas; according to Strabo, Ituraeans preferred the mountains because they were "robbers." Some of the area was thickly forested with the famous cedars of Lebanon and full of wildlife; other parts offered well-watered land for farms, vineyards and orchards. It included the headwaters of two major rivers and several minor ones—the Jordan, fed to a large extent by melt water from Mount Hermon's snowcap, flowing south; and the Litani, rising near Heliopolis and flowing south before taking a sharp turn west to the Mediterranean at Tyre. Just north of Ituraea was the source of the Orontes, in the Beka'a valley near Heliopolis, flowing north through Emesa and Apamea (Qal'at al Madiq) before turning west through Antioch (Antakya) to the Mediterranean at Seleucia. Ituraea's main cities were Chalcis, Abila (= Suq) for some of the time, and Heliopolis (Baalbek).

The region had earlier been a political borderland between the Ptolemaic and Seleucid kingdoms in the period following the division of Alexander the Great's empire. In 200 BCE the Syrian Seleucids under Antiochus III defeated the Egyptians under Ptolemy IV at Panias (Banyas) in the southern portion of Ituraean territory. For the previous century or more, Judea and the Jews had been under Ptolemaic rule; with the Battle of Panias everything changed. Judea

---

61. Schürer, "History of Chalcis, Ituraea and Abilene," 1:561–73, with bibliography.

62. See I. Shahîd, *Rome and the Arabs. A Prolegomenon to the Study of Byzantium and the Arabs* (Washington, DC: Dumbarton Oaks, 1984), pp. 5, 13–14.

63. Strabo, *Geog.* 16.2.10, 18, 20, specifically alludes to both mountain ranges and to Trachonitis. D. Baly and A. D. Tushingham, *Atlas of the Biblical World* (New York: World, 1971), "Lebanon-Anti-Lebanon: The Key to the Levant," pp. 98–101.

64. Schürer 1:561, n.1, gives texts of two inscriptions found in Auranitis. Despite this, he argues vigorously but not decisively against an eastward extension; p. 563, n.17.

65. Sullivan, *Near Eastern Royalty,* p. 71, linking Ituraean expansion to Seleucid weakness.

was soon to face a more aggressive Hellenism from Antiochus IV Epiphanes, though initially Syrian rule was benign. The menace eventually triggered a revolution under the Hasmoneans;[66] as the revolt gained assurance and as Syria weakened, the forces of Hellenism were swept back on a number of fronts. Judean control over the Ituraeans came in the brief reign of Judah Aristobulus I (104–103 BCE), or perhaps a bit earlier.[67] According to Josephus, it was Aristobulus who converted the Ituraeans to Judaism, "for he made war on the Ituraeans and acquired a good part of their territory for Judea and compelled the inhabitants, if they wished to remain in their country, to be circumcised and to live in accordance with the laws of the Jews" (*Ant.* 13.318).[68] Josephus's account may well be colored by his view that the Hasmoneans extended Judaism by force of arms and thus imposed their beliefs on others;[69] in the case of Ituraean acceptance of Judaism (like Idumaean), there is room for doubt about Josephus's view, though with respect to Ituraeans confirming evidence is lacking. Strabo's comments help somewhat. We must be content to note the parallels between Idumaeans and Ituraeans, placing a question mark behind statements about forced conversion.[70]

Hasmonean incorporation of areas north and east of Galilee into the Judean kingdom was reversed under Pompey's settlement of 63 BCE. He handed Panias, Gaulanitis and Lake Huleh back to the Ituraeans—consistent with his limiting the area of Judea—thus hampering Judea's economic prospects and weakening its political will.

Who maintained jurisdiction over Ituraea during the Herodian period is anything but clear.[71] When Herod came into public view for the first time it was as ruler of Galilee, appointed in 47 BCE by his father Antipater (*War* 1.203),[72] whom Julius Caesar appointed procurator of Judea when he confirmed Hyrcanus II as ethnarch (*War* 1.199–200; *Ant.* 14.143). A year later

---

66. See later in this chapter and chap. 4.

67. There is doubt whether he could have made so extensive a military campaign in such a brief reign; perhaps he led the Galilean-Ituraean foray while Hyrcanus I was still alive.

68. Josephus quotes Strabo (relying on Timagenes), who makes the process much less forced than does Josephus himself: "he acquired additional territory for them, and brought over to them a portion of the Ituraean nation, whom he joined to them by the bond of circumcision" (*Ant.* 13.319). In *Geog.* 16.2.18, 20, Strabo focuses on Ituraeans being "robbers"; he does not comment on the point on which Josephus quotes him, so presumably it was in his lost *Historical Sketches*.

69. Kasher, *Jews, Idumaeans,* pp. 79–80.

70. There were occasional Jewish rulers in Chalcis, including one of Herod's grandsons, also known as Herod (41–48 CE), during a portion of which he was responsible for Temple affairs in Jerusalem. Agrippa II also ruled Chalcis. Chalcis was a petty kingdom in the southern part of the Beka'a valley, sometimes separate from and sometimes a part of Ituraea; for details, Millar, *Roman Near East,* p. 238.

71. Sullivan, *Near Eastern Royalty,* pp. 408–9; Schürer 1.561–73.

72. On his putting down the brigand Hezekiah and the subsequent trial in Jerusalem, see chap. 5.

Sextus Caesar (a relative of Julius Caesar and governor of Syria) appointed Herod governor of some portion of Syria (*War* 1.213),[73] but what portion it is impossible to say, perhaps the area between the two mountain ranges or areas in Gaulanitis, Trachonitis, Batanea, and Auranitis. Nor is it clear what the appointment meant, since these regions were outside the territory governed by Antipater and within the bounds of the governor of Syria. His appointment may have been over areas occupied by Ituraeans, though they are not mentioned in the narrative at this point. The appointment was enlarged, according to Josephus, in 42 BCE by Cassius who, following the assassination of Caesar, was dominant in the East (see chap. 5). Josephus's use of the phrase "the whole of Syria" in this account is unclear,[74] but the safest interpretation is that it specified the role Herod played as strong man over Ituraea from his base in Galilee.[75]

When Herod was named king of Judea by the Senate of Rome (40 BCE),[76] his territory included Judea, Galilee and Peraea, and Ituraea too, for in 37 BCE Antony forced Herod to cede Ituraea (and Samaritis and parts of Nabatea and the coast land) to Cleopatra to satisfy her ambitions. The cession of territory implies that Herod had retained jurisdiction over Ituraea. Thus, between 47 and 37 Herod was confirmed several times in an Ituraean role.

The vagueness of the historical records prohibits too much speculation, but one deduction is in order: Herod's responsibilities focused on keeping the peace in this troubled area in south Syria, as a subordinate to the Syrian governor, whose troops were for the most part stationed in north Syria, while he was

73. The texts say Coele-Syria; *War* 1.213; *Ant.* 14.180.

74. *War* 1.225. *Ant.* 14.280 has "governor of Coele Syria," a likelier appointment since the former would be almost unimaginable. The best way to make sense of Josephus's texts is to presume he means a portion of Syria. On Coele-Syria as a geographic designation, see Millar, *Roman Near East,* pp. 121–23, and n.42 with bibliography cited there, including E. Bickerman, "La Coelé-Syria: Notes de géographie historique," *RB* 54 (1947): 256. The term floated; it did not have the connotations in antiquity that it now has. Most helpful is Strabo, *Geog.* 16.2.16–22: in 16–20 he discusses Coele-Syria proper, the area between the Lebanon and Anti–Lebanon Mountains; then in 21 he says the whole area between Seleucia (i.e., Syria) and Egypt-Arabia is called Coele-Syria, pointing out that "the country marked off by the Libanus and the Antilibanus is called by that name in a special sense" (see also 22). He is not confused but reports differing contemporary usages.

75. Compare with this Herod's later designation as "governor of Syria" with a kind of veto power, according to Josephus's implications, over legislation—an inherently unlikely situation also. Throughout this period Herod had been given responsibility for subduing brigands in Trachonitis, part of the territory often occupied by the Ituraeans. All these roles may cohere in some fashion. A full-scale study of the Ituraean problem is needed.

76. Meshorer, *Ancient Jewish Coinage,* pp. 5–30, argues that the year 41 (or 42) was decisive for Herod. When he began to mint coins (after his appointment as king) he referred back to his appointment as tetrarch as if it were the beginning of the regnal period, so the year-three coins—the only date ever to appear on a Herodian coin—refer to the year 40 BCE. See further Appendix B, chap. 8.

centered in Antioch.[77] From his appointment in 47 until 37, when Ituraea was stripped from him, Herod was occupied with putting down brigandage (not altogether successfully, since he again had to turn to this task in 23 BCE; see chap. 9), a responsibility that was a key to Herod's rise to power. His influence over Ituraea and south Syrian affairs was more than nominal.

Brigandage was a continuing problem in the area. Like the Nabateans and the Idumaeans, the Ituraeans had been semi-nomadic inhabitants of the desert areas of Arabia who had taken up small and often impermanent settlements in the area of today's northern Galilee, Golan, southern Lebanon, and southern Syria.[78] In the time of Herod some still occupied caves in the region, the origin of many of the "brigands" Herod had to put down in order to keep peace in the area.[79]

Zenodorus, against whom Herod's later actions were aimed, was the hereditary tetrarch and high priest of Ituraea,[80] who controlled regions east of the Jordan as far as Auranitis and Trachonitis. He had leased the territory of Lysanias (*War* 1.398), presumably Abila up the Barada River from Damascus and perhaps also Chalcis in the Beka'a valley. The former area was the home of brigands and robbers, who preyed particularly on the commercial interests of Damascus from caves in the volcanic outflow north of the Jebel Druze. Zenodorus, whether in reality or in public perception we cannot be certain, encouraged the robber bands for his own profit; according to Josephus he actually instigated them.[81] When Damascus complained to the governor of Syria, sometime in 24/23 BCE, Varro asked advice of Augustus. On learning that he was to clear out the bandits, Varro deprived Zenodorus of Batanea, Trachonitis, and Auranitis. Augustus formally added these areas to Herod's territory (*War* 1.398) because they needed a firm hand to keep them pacified and to prevent the inhabitants from disturbing Syria. The account in *Antiquities* highlights more complexities (15.349–64). Zenodorus must have retained his position and power, for he charged Herod in Rome before Augustus, unsuccessfully as it turned out. He was also strong enough to instigate the Nabateans to revolt against Herod.

---

77. On the stationing of army units see B. Isaac, *The Limits of Empire: The Roman Army in the East* (Oxford: Clarendon, 1990), esp. pp. 60–67; Millar, *Roman Near East,* esp. chaps. 2, 7, 8.

78. Brigandage as an occupation of the Ituraeans was frequently exaggerated, as if all Ituraeans were always brigands (see. Strabo, *Geog.* 16.2.18: "Ituraeans and Arabians, all of whom are robbers" [*katourgoi*]). Some Ituraeans were farmers, so the most that should be claimed is that in some regions of Ituraea there were some brigands.

79. This problem concentrated on Hezekiah, apparently a Jewish bandit-chief operating in the border districts between Galilee and Syria (perhaps Ituraean territory). See further, chap. 5.

80. On numismatic and inscriptional evidence, Schürer 1.561–73; on Lysanias, Sullivan, *Near Eastern Royalty,* pp. 207–8.

81. *War* 1.398–400; *Ant.* 15.342–60; Strabo, *Geog.* 16.2.18–20. In *War* the military action is ascribed to Varro; *Antiquities* is ambiguous but seems to point to Herod as the one who cleared the area.

Josephus connects this account (through a short panegyric on the close relations between Augustus, Agrippa, and Herod; *War* 1.399–400; *Ant.* 15.354–61), with the account of Herod's building activity at Panias. For a long time there had been a cult center in Ituraea dedicated to Pan. Panias (Banyas) was located on an important head water of the Jordan River, on the lower slopes of Mount Hermon. An underground stream emerges adjacent to natural caves; the combination of spring and caves with their entrances to the underworld was a natural location for a cult devoted to Pan. Inscriptions attest to the vigor of the cult center. Herod selected Panias for special attention. Sometime in 20/19 BCE he constructed a Temple to Augustus and Roma adjacent to the Pan cult center;[82] he may also have constructed a palace. The location—within Zenodorus's territory and outside Jewish territory—is suggestive. The offensiveness of a center for the Imperial cult was reduced. Being inside the territory of the Ituraeans, it had the same effect as Herod's buildings at Hebron and at Si'a, indicating his valuing of their religious traditions and his inclusion of them within the larger religious framework of his reign.

In the next generation Herod Philip renamed Panias *Caesarea Philippi* (to distinguish it from the great port his father had built he added his own name).[83] Later still, Agrippa II again renamed it, this time *Neronias* after his patron Nero. After Nero's fall the name reverted back to *Caesarea*, or *Little Caesarea* as it is referred to in the Rabbinic literature (*Qisariyon; t.Sukkah* 1:9). None of this later renaming, however, obliterates either its original significance as a center for Pan's worship or its role in homage to the glories of Rome's power, as those were vested in the majesty of the Emperor himself.

Ituraeans were minor players in Herod's drama, occasionally influencing events significantly. Yet Ituraea was not named in the final settlement of Herod's will, though it emerges in the pages of the New Testament as part of the territory of Herod Philip, "Tetrarch of the region of Ituraea and Trachonitis" (Luke 3:1). According to Josephus, Philip had received Batanea, Trachonitis, Auranitis, and some parts of Zenodorus's domain around Panias (*War* 2.95; *Ant.* 17.319).[84] Both descriptions appear to refer to the same area; Luke's account is the garbled version of someone unfamiliar with the geography. Philip got some territory that had been Nabatean and some that had been Ituraean, but little that had not already been Judaized, though to what extent it is not possible to say.

---

82. The site began to be investigated scientifically in the summer of 1988. It will be unusually productive, and already the relation of the complex of cult caves to the rest of the site has begun to be clarified.

83. A high percentage of Philip's coins picture a temple, almost certainly this Temple of Roma and Augustus. See further Appendix B and chap. 12.

84. The text reads "Innano" but it has long been conjectured—probably correctly—that this is a mistake for "Panias."

HASMONEANS

It should be clear by now that the Hasmonean dynasty created the conditions with which those active in the last half of the first century BCE had to cope. The results of the successful expansionist policies of John Hyrcanus I and Alexander Jannaeus had been rolled back by Pompey. Herod probably viewed the Maccabean frontiers as borders that should be regained—they were both natural and ancient. Of all the Maccabean gains lost in Pompey's reorganization, however, the most crucial was an outlet to the sea.

The Maccabean revolt came at an important point in the changing balance between Seleucids, Ptolemies, the Hellenistic kingdoms, and Rome, and was a harbinger of the future. Under Antiochus III Syria had replaced the Egyptian Ptolemaic kingdom in the affairs of Judea (200 BCE); he also expanded into Asia Minor and extended Syria's traditional hegemony over eastern areas including Babylonia. Syria was overextended, however, and the defeat of Antiochus III at Magnesia in 190 BCE was devastating for Syria's future. Antiochus IV Epiphanes, Antiochus's son, pursued a program fundamentally different from his father's, attempting to draw together his diverse kingdom through religious unity focused on Olympian Zeus (the Temple to Zeus Olympios in Athens was begun by Antiochus IV). His attempt to subvert the practices of Judaism—fundamentally altering his father's tolerance—was one element in a grand design aimed at an eventual confrontation with Rome.

In order to survive, Judaism had to resist. Revolt was inevitable. Syria was too preoccupied to resist a revolt effectively and Egypt was too weak to take advantage of it. Before long the Hasmoneans secured a treaty with Rome, drawing the threat of her presence into the equation.[85] In a surprisingly short time (from 167 to 142 BCE) Judea achieved political and religious autonomy. Judea was still a small, almost landlocked, state in remote hill country.[86] The next two generations of Jewish leaders—John Hyrcanus I (135–104 BCE) and then his two sons, Judah Aristobulus I (104–103) and Alexander Jannaeus (103–76)—expanded the country's size dramatically and made it a substantial power in the East. Hyrcanus I first took Madaba and Esbus (Heshbon) across the Jordan (128 BCE), then overran Idumaea (125 BCE).[87] Hyrcanus I also took cities—at various times—on the coastal plain (Azotus, Jamnia, and Apollonia). Finally he went north through Samaritis, the Carmel range and Scythopolis (Bet Shean), and may have occupied some of lower Galilee, as Klausner argues.[88] With the

---

85. *Ant.* 12.414–19; 1 Macc. 8:1–32; see Schürer 1.171–73, esp. n.33.

86. Simon succeeded in taking Joppa, and providing Israel with an important outlet to the sea. On Joppa (Yafo), Schürer 2.110–14.

87. J. Klausner, in *The World History of the Jewish People*, vol. 6, *The Hellenistic Age: Political History of Jewish Palestine from 332 B.C.E.*, ed. A. Schalit (New Brunswick, NJ: Rutgers University Press, 1972), p. 217, says correctly that "the Idumeans who were attached to their homeland chose the former [embracing Judaism] and henceforth became Jews in every respect."

88. Ibid., p. 219.

way to Galilee open, Aristobulus I annexed it (103 BCE), tying Jews who lived there more closely to Judea and preventing the Ituraeans from moving farther south.

Alexander Jannaeus expanded to the Mediterranean coast to enhance the economy of Judea, taking Mount Carmel, Dor, Strato's Tower (Caesarea Maritima), Gaza, Raphia, and Anthedon (96 BCE?). Later he went east of the Rift Valley, taking Hippos (Susita), Gadara (Umm Qeis), Abila (Qailibah), Dium, Pella (Fahil), Ammathus (Tell 'Ammata), Gerasa (Jerash), and Gedor ('Ain Jedur). Only Philadelphia (Amman) remained independent. Jannaeus fought on three fronts externally (suffering a serious reverse at the hands of Obodas I) in addition to facing internal dissension in a prolonged civil war.

Hasmonean expansion brought the country almost to its old borders under David and Solomon. Its military successes did not bring internal political peace, however—quite the opposite; expansion exacerbated the latent internal tensions. Probably in the period under Hyrcanus I, Aristobulus I, and Jannaeus, the religious divisions of such interest to New Testament scholars took place. Sadducees, Pharisees, Essenes (and perhaps what later became the Zealots) all had their roots in the late-second and early-first centuries BCE. Each had a different vision of Judaism, a different program for Judea's future and little tolerance of rival views (see chap. 10). What prompted these competing views was Hasmonean military success and political power, coupled with modifications to Israel's religion and culture.

Two internal problems, at root religious, troubled the nation during the reigns of these three rulers: on the one hand, the conjunction of priestly and royal power in one person, and on the other, the competing views of Sadducees and Pharisees. Hyrcanus I held the high priesthood.[89] He shifted his religious ground as time went on so that it was said of him that "he became a Sadducee." But something in this shift caused him concern, so he left instructions that at his death his widow should assume the royal power and his oldest son Judah Aristobulus I should become high priest. According to Josephus (*Ant.* 13.301), Aristobulus starved his mother to death and then assumed the title of king as well.[90] If this information is correct, Aristobulus I was the first Hasmonean to join political and religious power. After Aristobulus I's brief reign, his brother

---

89. Did he also claim a political role as well? Schürer still argues that his coins carried the Hebrew legend "John the High Priest and the congregation (*hever*) of the Jews," this last phrase referring either to the whole Jewish community or to a council or "senate" (see Schürer 1.211). Meshorer, *Jewish Coins*, pp. 41–55, has the better of the argument, maintaining that Alexander Jannaeus was the first Maccabean to mint coins.

90. Meshorer, ibid., argues further that none of the "Judah" coins are to be assigned to Aristobulus I. According to Strabo, *Geog.* 16.2.40, writing on the authority of Timagenes, Jannaeus was the first king-high priest.

Alexander Jannaeus inherited both the titles of his brother, high priest and king, as well as his brother's widow. Jannaeus's coins demonstrate the extent to which Hellenistic ideas had entered Judean life: they are bilingual, refer explicitly to Jannaeus's kingship, and they use symbols such as the cornucopia and anchor. Like his brother and father, he was Sadducean in his outlook. He advanced the Sadducees' role and status in Judea and punished harshly the Pharisaic leader of the civil war that raged for six years. Klausner argues that Alexander Jannaeus made peace with the Pharisees late in his reign, though this is not certain.[91]

During the late second century and early first century BCE, the religious and political lines were increasingly sharply drawn. Descendants of earlier Hasmonean leaders who had reestablished both religious autonomy and political independence in Judea deliberately joined religion and politics together in a unique position of national leadership. Competing forms of leadership, whether political or religious, were subordinated; the party most agreeable to these developments—the Sadducees—became dominant; the Pharisees were weak and faced a religious predicament that was nearly intolerable. At the same time the Hasmoneans moved in a direction that made them very like the Hellenistic kingdoms of the east. Contact with Syria in particular led to an increase in Hellenistic ideas and aspirations, and encouraged in later Hasmoneans notions of autocracy and absolutism.[92] The problem was, of course, that Judea was not just another Hellenistic monarchy.

This uneasy situation broke apart during the civil war in Alexander Jannaeus's reign (War 1.88, 91–98; Ant. 13.372–83) and during the reign of his widow Alexandra Salome (76–67 BCE).[93] At her death civil war broke out between her two sons, John Hyrcanus II and Judah Aristobulus II. The troubles to come were announced already at her accession to power, Josephus implies (War 1.109), when Alexandra appointed her elder son Hyrcanus to the high priesthood while she kept her younger son Aristobulus out of public view, following her husband's death-bed advice.[94] Jannaeus told his wife to assume

---

91. World History, 6.234–435; he adduces the numismatic evidence of inscriptions referring to the hever ha-Yehudim. See Meshorer, Jewish Coins, pp. 56–59.

92. See World History, 6.280–97. Klausner emphasizes Hellenistic influence in matters of domestic policy such as levying of taxes, the bureaucracy for running the country, land distribution, royal prerogatives, a hierarchy of royal "friends," and the like.

93. Alexandra influenced matters in Judea during three reigns, as the wife of Judah Aristobulus I, wife of Alexander Jannaeus, and queen in her own right. She has not yet received her due as a key figure in Jewish history. A full study is needed.

94. In Ant. 13.407 a somewhat different impression is given: Hyrcanus II preferred a quiet life while Aristobulus II was a man of action; in War Hyrcanus was disinclined to be involved in public affairs but Aristobulus was a hot-head. The two accounts can be reconciled. In these same passages Josephus records something of Alexandra's motives—again with different emphases—in her dealings with the Pharisees. See further chaps. 5, 10.

the royal power herself and to resolve the long-standing dispute between the Sadducees and the Pharisees by handing power to the Pharisees; in this way she would settle Jannaeus's religious and political problems. She apparently altered the degree of influence somewhat, though it is not clear if this was because of Jannaeus's advice or because she herself shared the piety of the Pharisees. The glowing attitude of the rabbinic literature toward Alexandra's reign may be accounted for on the basis either of her actions or her attitude toward the Pharisees.[95] Though Pharisaic influence is almost certainly exaggerated, it was recalled in some circles as a golden period; Josephus's evidence, though slender, is less clear, especially on internal matters.

HYRCANUS II AND ARISTOBULUS II

When Alexandra fell ill toward the end of her reign, Aristobulus II seized the opportunity to improve his position at the expense of his older brother Hyrcanus II. He assumed control over some fortresses that may already have been in the hands of "friends" of his father's (War 1.117; Ant. 13.422). According to War he declared himself king; in Antiquities he attempted to seize power (compare Ant. 13.426). These actions were prompted by fear of the Pharisees taking complete control (Ant. 13.423), an eventuality which, when linked to his view that Hyrcanus was ineffectual, was not unjustified. In short, he took preemptive action in concert with Sadducean military persons and an army from Lebanon and Trachonitis (an Ituraean army, or, as War 1.117 says, "a mercenary army"; see Ant. 13.427), establishing an unshakeable position before his mother's death. This was necessary, he believed, because his mother was in league with the Pharisees and they would support his brother after her death (War 1.118–19; Ant. 13.423–29).[96]

The role of Alexandra is evaluated differently by Josephus in his two accounts, and it is difficult to reconcile them or even to decide which to prefer over the other. On the one hand Alexandra caused the problems, partly because a woman should not have ruled, he implies, and partly because she exercised absolute rule (according to Antiquities). On the other hand she was pious, had the peoples' respect, and was skilled administratively (according to War).[97]

---

95. See Lev.R. 35.10; b.Ta'anith 23a; Sifra 110b. Her piety is mentioned in War 1.108–11, but omitted in Ant.; her relation to the Pharisees is described in War 1.110–14; Ant. 13.408–15.

96. There are two suggestive differences between War and Antiquities: (1) War has Aristobulus II declare himself king, a claim which, at the most, could only be inferred from Josephus's account in Antiquities; (2) Antiquities has Alexandra more on Hyrcanus II's side than does War (but see Ant. 13.429, where she is uninterested).

97. Ant. 13.430–32: "none of the weakness of her sex . . . inordinately desirous of the power to rule . . . valued the present more than the future . . . everything else subordinate to absolute rule . . . no consideration for decency or justice . . . desire for things unbecoming to a woman . . . left the kingdom without anyone who had their interests at heart . . . even after her death she caused

Where does the truth lie? Two things are clear: Alexandra preferred the Pharisees and gave them some power; she did not, however, settle the succession unequivocally. Thus, at her death open civil war broke out—if it was not already raging[98]—pitting Aristobulus II, an aggressive and charismatic pretender, against Hyrcanus II, heir to royal power and ruling high priest. Hyrcanus had moral authority and the support of the Pharisees on his side, Aristobulus had the forces, fortresses, and support of the Sadducees on his.

Not surprisingly, Aristobulus won. Hyrcanus fled,[99] and the brothers came to a one-sided settlement, imposed by Aristobulus II on his brother, by which the latter abdicated and the former took control as king; they also exchanged residences (*War* 1.120). The inadequacy of our sources appears from the fact that the account in *Antiquities* hints at a revision of the usual dates for this period. In *Ant.* (14.4) a precise date is given for Hyrcanus's assumption of royal power corresponding to 70/69 BCE, that is, two or three years before Alexandra's death.[100] This date dovetails with two other features—her illness (accounting for the need for a regent) and Aristobulus's raising the standard of revolt at the same time.[101] A reconstruction of this crucial period would then be:

Royal Power	**High Priest**
Alexandra 76–67	Hyrcanus 76–66
Hyrcanus regent 69–67	
Hyrcanus 67–66	
Aristobulus 66–63	Aristobulus 66–63
[none]	Hyrcanus 63–40

If this reconstruction is correct, Hyrcanus held effective royal power for something less than three years—for about two years under his mother while being

---

the palace to be filled with misfortunes and disturbances . . . nevertheless she had kept the nation at peace." *War* 1.107–12: "utter lack of brutality . . . won the affections of the populace . . . firmly held the reigns of government, thanks to her reputation for piety . . . strictest observer of the national traditions . . . intensely religious . . . she listened to [the Pharisees] with too great deference . . . they took advantage of an ingenuous woman . . . a wonderful administrator in larger affairs . . . strengthened her own nation . . . But if she ruled the nation, the Pharisees ruled her."

98. This is an attractive conclusion from the fact that Hyrcanus had already been entrusted with the kingdom during the latter part of Alexandra's reign (*War* 1.120; *Ant.* 14.4, perhaps in 69 BCE) and that Aristobulus was trying to seize royal power, having already seized several major fortresses.

99. Josephus refers anachronistically to the Antonia fortress; he means the Baris, as he goes on to say (*War* 1.118), though his source here imagines that the Antonia is merely a renamed Baris.

100. See Schürer 1.200–1, esp. n.1, re chronology.

101. See Marcus's note (e), at *Ant.* 14.4; he is incorrect about 20.243, however, which states that Aristobulus reigned for two (not three) years and six months. See Feldman's note (d) at *Ant.* 20.244; see 14.97.

groomed during her illness for kingship, and for a short while after her death. After his defeat Aristobulus held power as king, and probably also as high priest (see *Ant.* 14.41, 97; 15.41; 20.243) from 66–63, a period of two-and-a-half years (*Ant.* 20.243–44).[102] Hyrcanus was reinstated as high priest from 63 onward.

Herod's story began during Alexandra Salome's reign. Antipater, Herod's father, appeared publicly on the scene during her reign; Herod himself was born about 73 BCE, just in the middle of her reign; and the struggles between Hyrcanus II and Aristobulus II, her two sons, signalled the end of Hasmonean rule and created the situation in which Antipater and his son Herod could occupy the vacuum.[103]

ANTIPATER

Josephus introduces Antipater neatly at just this point. When he appears the reports of him are quite differently conceived, though perhaps reconcilable. In *War* Antipater is an "old and bitterly hated foe of Aristobulus" (1.123), in *Antiquities* he is a "friend of Hyrcanus" (14.8) who believed that Aristobulus "wrongly held royal power," having usurped his brother's position.[104] From the two accounts some essential points about Antipater can be pieced together: (1) he was wealthy; (2) his influence rested in large part on being governor (*strategos*) of Idumaea;[105] (3) the roots of his power lay in his father's courting of Arabs, Gazans, and Ashkelonites; (4) he believed that Aristobulus should be removed; (5) he was influential in Hyrcanus's councils and encouraged him to feel wronged; (6) he persuaded Hyrcanus to flee to Petra, after securing Aretas's support by promising to return a dozen Nabatean cities to their control (*War* 1.123–26; *Ant.* 14.8–18). Josephus believed that Antipater's sole motivation was to take advantage of Hyrcanus's weakness and ineffectiveness for his own ends (according to *Antiquities; War* implies it was fear of Aristobulus). Both parts of this view may be partially correct: Hyrcanus, though not so indecisive and weak as *Antiquities* suggests, did not lust for power as Aristobulus did; and Antipater may have been concerned that he not lose his position—indeed he wanted

---

102. *Ant.* 14.97 and 20.244 disagree on the length of time; the latter is more likely correct. It also correctly says that Hyrcanus was forced to give up kingship in 63 BCE, though he continued to be political figurehead and high priest.

103. On Alexandra and Herod, Schalit, pp. 564–66.

104. Antipater was also "a man of action and a trouble-maker" (14.8; *drastêrios . . . kai stasiastês*). These accounts are not in fundamental conflict, but the different tone is hard to account for, since even if *Antiquities* gives us Nicolas's view, as Josephus suggests when he refers to Antipater's origins in 14.9, Josephus is critical and apparently independent.

105. The term is used in Ptolemaic and Roman Egypt of the "military and civil governor" of a nome (so LSJ), and that is the closest analogy here. According to *Ant.* 14.10 it was Alexander Jannaeus who appointed Antipater *stratêgos*.

to enhance it by having a national position of influence and power. In the conditions that followed the "conversion" of the Idumaeans to Judaism, Antipater had a considerable opportunity to play an important role and to influence events.

From their temporary base in Petra and with massive support from Aretas (fifty thousand men says Josephus in *War* 1.126; fifty thousand cavalry plus men as well in *Ant.* 14.19!) Antipater and Hyrcanus defeated Aristobulus and laid siege to Jerusalem early in 65 BCE, a siege that was lifted by the intervention of Scaurus, Pompey's general in Syria, who seized the opportunity for direct Roman influence.

In the midst of his account in *Antiquities,* Josephus inadvertently underscores the religious tensions troubling the nation. Despite the fact that Hyrcanus was the legitimate high priest,[106] most priests in Jerusalem remained loyal to Aristobulus. Onias, a righteous man with a reputation as a prophet, was asked to curse Aristobulus by Hyrcanus's supporters;[107] instead he prayed for retribution on Hyrcanus, as a result of which he was stoned to death. The most convincing explanation of a priestly preference for Aristobulus is that legitimacy was thought less important than religious affiliation, so that Aristobulus's Sadducaic connections and beliefs were preferable to Hyrcanus's Pharisaic support, despite the fact that Hyrcanus was the eldest son of the previous high priest. This abandoning of traditional notions of legitimacy was a precursor of later Herodian and Roman practises of sitting lightly to legitimacy.

Scaurus, Pompey's quaestor, settled the brothers' squabble while Pompey was still busy in Armenia. Both combatants approached Scaurus, offering roughly equal bribes, as he moved with his forces from Damascus to Jerusalem in the spring of 65. He filled his pockets with Aristobulus's offer[108] and ordered Hyrcanus and Aretas to withdraw while he returned to Damascus. A pitched battle near the Jordan went decisively in favor of Aristobulus, whose fortunes now seemed secure.

Aristobulus had gotten the superior Roman officer to side with him militarily while the priestly Judean party supported him religiously; though he was the younger brother, he had parlayed his advantages—mostly his more forceful personality—into a successful coup d'état. Antipater went with Hyrcanus into

---

106. That is to say, legitimate in the eyes of the leaders, though hardly in the eyes of conservative priests, some of whom must have hankered after someone from the line of the last legitimate high priest, Onias III, deposed by Antiochus IV Epiphanes a century earlier.

107. *Ant.* 14.22–24; perhaps the person referred to in rabbinic traditions as Honi the circle drawer. This Onias may have been a descendant of the deposed family, and the request to have him curse Aristobulus may have been based on that relationship. Nevertheless, his preference for Aristobulus is perplexing.

108. According to *War* 1.127–28 (contrast *Ant.* 14.31) Scaurus thought Hyrcanus's case was more just but less promising.

a kind of exile, probably lasting for over a year and probably spent in Aretas's capital city Petra. His family—including his young son Herod—was already in Petra awaiting the outcome of the struggle for the throne of Judea, on which their fortunes ultimately rested. Since Petra was the home of Antipater's wife, she and her children would have been at home while political events unfolded to the north and west. Those events, associated with Pompey's intervention, will be dealt with later (chap. 5). The Romans, when presented with a destructive and unsettling civil war on the edge of their sphere of influence, seized the opportunity. Hasmonean inability to solve their dynastic, civil and religious affairs led inevitably to the extension of Rome's power in the area. Though Rome was already on a path that would lead to this result at some point, the fratricidal strife speeded up and reshaped the process.[109]

---

109. Sullivan, *Near Eastern Royalty,* esp. pp. 78–79, 213–17 (re Judea).

CHAPTER 4

Late Hellenism in the Near East

SYRIA

Syria, says Strabo, "is bounded on the north by Cilicia and Mount Amanus, . . . on the east by the Euphrates; and on the south by Arabia Felix and Egypt; and on the west by the Egyptian and Syrian Seas as far as Issus."[1] He refers in passing to "the bridge at Commagene," implying its importance in the politics and power of the region, and goes on to list the regions of Syria: Commagene, Seleucis of Syria, Phoenicia, and Judea. He notes that others divide Syria into three regions: Syria, Coele-Syria, and Phoenicia, with four other tribes intermixed with them—Judeans, Idumaeans, Gazans, and Azotians (16.2.2). These divisions are sensible and natural; Millar uses a similar scheme in his study:[2] "Tetrapolis and northern Syria," "Phoenician coast and its hinterland," "Eastern Syria Phoenice," "From Judaea to Syria Palaestina" (see map 3).

The land-forms of Syria indicate that in antiquity, as today, the region functioned as a geopolitical unit—not that it was always under a single ruler any more than it is today, but that the geography of the region contributed to an intricate set of relationships where changes in one area prompted changes in other regions. In the period of empire there was a tendency for the whole of Syria to be under one kingdom's control, though obviously it was not always so.

The major geographical barriers were north-south, the dominant one being the great Rift Valley that cut in a straight line north to south from Commagene (southern Turkey, the Taurus mountains) through Syria, Palestine, the Gulf of Aqabah, and the Red Sea and thence inland to southern Africa. In places the Rift Valley acted as a border, as when it dropped to 1300 feet below sea

---

1. Strabo, *Geog.* 16.2.1.
2. Millar, *Roman Near East,* pp. 225–386.

level at the Dead Sea; in other places it was the center of lush valleys, as in the Beka'a and the Orontes. In what is today Lebanon, a pair of mountain ranges bounded the Rift Valley; in Samaritis and Judea the mountains were more gradual but the drop into the Rift was steeper. The farther north, the more rainfall there was and the farther the rainfall penetrated into the desert regions; the farther south and east, the drier it was.

The land forms allowed relatively unhindered north-south travel; routes could be found that permitted good transportation. In the south there were routes on the seacoast, through the Jordan Valley, to the east of the Jordan Valley, through the Beka'a Valley, behind the Anti-Lebanon mountains, along the Orontes Valley, all manageable in antiquity as they are now. Three transverse features distorted normal north-south communications: the Mount Carmel range, jutting into the sea between Dor and Ptolemais and dividing the coastal plain in the south from Lower Galilee; the hills of Upper Galilee that interrupted links between Lower Galilee and the Phoenician coast; and the ranges both south and north of Antioch that blocked the easiest route between Syria and Asia Minor. Travel, whether commercial or cultural or military, had to move in and out from the seacoast according to the local conditions.

Syria was large and varied but integrated. It all was "Syria," whether for geographic and intellectual reasons (to Strabo among others) or for conquest and defense. Borders between autonomous or semi-autonomous states, as in the first century BCE and most of the first century CE, were relatively fluid. The inability to define the changing fortunes of Ituraea, for example, was true of other states. This changeability or fluidity influenced Herod's story; he and others expanded their borders as opportunities arose or contracted them as politics in the region required. The tendency to empire ran through the whole period. The Seleucids tried to retain control of a vast empire centered on Syria and were unsuccessful; the Ptolemies tried to extend their control through the whole of Syria, but obtained only about half, up to the natural border through Mount Hermon.

The Romans saw Syria as an extension of their inexorable march from west to east, which culminated in the decisive intervention by Pompey (see chap. 5). From the east, Parthia viewed Syria as the logical next step in their drive westward, offering a vital opening to the Mediterranean that Parthia's landlocked position south of the Caspian Sea denied them. By the beginning of our period they had moved westward to the upper Tigris and Euphrates Rivers.

This complex situation, the waning of two old dynasties—Seleucids and Ptolemies—and the rise of two new rivals—Romans and Parthians—made the mid-first century in Syria a particularly difficult period. In the clash of the titans it was not clear whether Parthia and the East or Rome and the West would win out. Nor was it clear how other states should respond: Should they throw their lot in with Rome? Or with Parthia? Should they create coalitions against both? Or should they carve out a small territory and hope for the best? Or should they maintain a tenuous neutrality?[3] Each of these approaches was tried.

Syria had a long and distinguished history. Among its glories had been early steps toward urban cultures, balancing the nomadism of most of its peoples. It was not a backwater waiting to be occupied but one of the centers of civilization, predating the glories of Rome or Parthia and even those of Greece. In the early Imperial years Syria was again a center of civilization, this time not of an indigenous culture but of a mixed Greek, Roman, and indigenous culture. Some of the great cities of the east flowered in the conditions following the struggle for empire: Antioch (Antakya), Laodicea (Latakya), Berytus (Beirut), Tyre, Heliopolis (Baalbek), Damascus, Palmyra, Bostra. In this flowering, as in the struggles, Herod was a significant figure.

DEPENDENT KINGDOMS

The richest and most important of the northern states was Commagene, which controlled the crossings of the Euphrates at Zeugma and Samosata. Commagene occupied a fertile series of valleys, had access to large iron deposits, and was at a crucial corner where Hellenic, Semitic, and Iranian lands met.[4] "Of all the monarchs owning allegiance to Rome the King of Commagene enjoyed the highest prosperity" (*War* 5.461). Commagene's position and prosperity opened it to serious difficulties that it did not manage to escape, for its river crossings were crucial in the coming conflict between Rome and Parthia. Again Josephus puts it neatly: "Samosata . . . would afford the Parthians . . . a most easy passage and an assured reception" (*War* 7.224).

It is not certain when Rome and Commagene first came into contact, but Parthia and Commagene were combatants as early as the 90s BCE, and it was a struggle Commagene could not win. Commagene became a "reluctant subkingdom, one of the many that warranted assumption by Tigranes of the title King of Kings."[5] Rome soon saw that its interests in the east would be considerably strengthened if it controlled Commagene. As a result, Antiochus I of Commagene allied himself to Rome (calling himself *philoromaios*)[6] during the period when Pompey was active in the east.

Antiochus's greatest monument was the tumulus and *hierothesaion* at Nemrud Dagh, on the summit of a seven-thousand-foot mountain in the Ankar range, just above the Euphrates River. There are rock-cut terraces on the north,

---

3. See the compressed but helpful comments of Sullivan, *Near Eastern Royalty*, pp. 17–24.
4. Sullivan, *Near Eastern Royalty*, p. 59.
5. Ibid., p. 193.
6. Ibid., p. 194.

east, and south-west sides of the tumulus, and the eastern courtyard has an impressive ensemble of sculptural and architectural monuments: a pyramidal altar, colossal seated Hellenistic statues (25 to 30 feet high), and bas-reliefs on standing stones. The reliefs provide a genealogy, the colossal statues a syncretistic pantheon.[7]

The epithet *philhellênos* that Antiochus's son took matched his father's *philoromaios* and recognized the Hellenistic grandeur of his father's monuments at Nemrud Dagh. He himself built another memorial to his mother, his dead sister, and his niece, with an inscription to another sister who became Queen of Parthia.[8] These cultural and political connections tell the tale of Commagene; it managed remarkably well to carve out a quasi-independent existence until its incorporation as a Roman province in 72 CE.

Farther south, centered on the city of Emesa, another north Syrian territory managed to remain quasi-independent until about the same period.[9] Emesa (Homs) sat on the Orontes River at just the point where the easiest route between the Mediterranean coastline and the interior crossed the river after a relatively narrow pass (the pass that was guarded in the Crusader period by the Krak des Chevaliers). The kingdom was an Arab state, "founded not so much on agriculture as on the pastoral life the Arabs preferred,"[10] mediating between the settled coast and the desert of the *skênitai* ("tent-dwellers" or later "Saracens"), much of which Emesa controlled. The Romans neither occupied Emesa nor raised taxes there,[11] perhaps because Emesa came early and enthusiastically to the side of Rome. Its kings were active in the downfall of the last of the Seleucids, hoping to take advantage of Syria's disintegration. When Parthia invaded in the 40s BCE, following the civil war in Rome, Emesa faced serious problems because of its longstanding alliance with Rome.[12]

Emesa was, however, slightly non-typical. As an Arab territory in an agriculturally desirable region, it seems not to have developed to its full potential as a settled population. Few significant remains comparable to those in other areas attest to its culture.

East of Emesa lay Palmyra (Tadmor), centered on an oasis marking a major

7. Apollo-Mithra-Helios-Hermes; Tyche; Zeus-Ahuramazda; Antiochus; Herakles-Artagnes-Ares; with lion and eagle statues flanking both ends. A similar row was on the west terrace. For a brief archaeological description, E. Akurgal, *Ancient Civilisations and Ruins of Turkey* (Istanbul: Haset Kitabevi, 1985), pp. 346–52.

8. Sullivan, *Near Eastern Royalty*, p. 197.

9. Millar, *Roman Near East*, p. 84

10. Sullivan, *Near Eastern Royalty*, p. 62; for a later period, Millar, *Roman Near East*, pp. 300–309.

11. Millar, *Roman Near East*, p. 34.

12. Cicero, for example, in 51 BCE refers to Iamblichus I of Emesa as "well-intentioned and a friend to our republic," quoted in Sullivan, *Near Eastern Royalty*, p. 200, referring to Cicero, *Attici*, 15.1.3.

east-west caravan route. Palmyra originated in the Stone Age, but more recently it stemmed from the Hellenistic period; its inclusion in the Roman sphere of influence is attested epigraphically from the early years of the first century CE.[13] Inscriptions from below the Temple of Bel attest a cult site in the same location as early as 44 BCE which is likely to go back even earlier; some of the tower tombs are from the same period, and are built in polygonal sandstone blocks, unlike the later ashlar masonry.[14]

The arid steppe on which Palmyra sits is watered by infrequent springs and winter rains from the Mediterranean that pass through Emesa. The wadis store a good bit of the winter rain naturally, permitting cultivation of cotton and grains. At Palmyra itself a spring runs from Jebel Muntar, thus forming the oasis that made it such an important desert post. The claim that Solomon "strengthened Tadmor in the desert" (2 Chron. 8:4) probably confuses this with the parallel references to Tamar in the Judean wilderness (1 Kings 9:17–18), though for such a confusion to arise, Tadmor/Palmyra must have had a long history as a defensible, rich, and independent city that was on major trade routes.

Palmyra was active on the Seleucid side in the battle of Raphia (217 BCE), according to a hint supplied by Polybius. Appian says Mark Antony plundered Palmyra after entertaining Cleopatra at Tarsus in 41 BCE[15] and comments that "being surrounded on their borders by the Romans and the Parthians, they were dealing skillfully with both. Indeed, they were merchants who transported from the Persian Empire Indian and Arabian products to be sold in the Roman Empire."[16] Pliny the Elder stresses Palmyra's nobility, richness of soil, and its isolation and suggests that it acted as a middleman between "the two great Empires," Rome and Parthia.[17] An inscription from Dura Europus on the Euphrates (34/33 BCE) refers to two Palmyrenes dedicating a Temple of Bel and Yarhibol outside the city.[18] Palmyra was another quasi-autonomous kingdom in the first century BCE; Arab with a strong Hellenistic influence and later with an equally strong Roman influence.

So Palmyra is mostly a later creation from the first century CE and onward. Its earliest structures, the Temples of Bel and of Nabu, date from the first and the third quarters of the first century CE respectively, so they do not reflect the city a century earlier. Further, the Hippodamian plan is not likely to have predated these structures, since neither was oriented to the gridiron. Some of its art and sculpture—static, objective, frontal—predates the first century CE and is a strong and vivid witness to the merging of Greco-Roman and oriental tradi-

13. Millar, *Roman Near East,* pp. 34–35, cites a boundary marker from 11–17 CE.

14. K. Michalowski, *Palmyra* (New York: Praeger, 1968), p. 6.

15. Appian, *Civil Wars* 5.9.

16. See also A. Bounni and K. Al-As'ad, *Palmyra* (Damascus, 1988), p. 13.

17. Pliny, *NH* 5.88.

18. Millar, *Roman Near East,* p. 298.

tions of Syria, Mesopotamia, and Persia, thus testifying to the cultural vitality and independence of the city in its late Hellenistic and early Roman phase.

Seleucid control of Syria was severely eroded during the early years of the first century CE, partly because Armenia intruded into Seleucid areas east of the Euphrates and partly because Alexander Jannaeus and other small kingdoms picked away at Syria's soft spots. During the intra-family struggles of the late second and early first century BCE, Damascus became the capital of a small kingdom, first under Antiochus Cyzicenus (ca. 111–95 BCE) and later under Antiochus XII (d. 84 BCE),[19] though there seem to have been short periods of both Armenian and Nabatean rule. For example, when the Ituraeans were pressing from the west and south, Damascus asked the Nabateans for help; like camels in the tent, Nabateans ended up controlling Damascus under Aretas III. For some time it was a political football until Pompey seized the city as one of the crucial centers of Syria (*War* 1.127; *Ant.* 14.29). The Seleucid Empire came to an end when Rome, grasping the occasion in 65/64 BCE, moved into this agriculturally rich, cultured, and strategic area. Later, Antony gave Damascus and other valuable territories to Cleopatra, from whom Octavian regained them for Rome.

Damascus, which owed its location to a torrential mountain river, the Barada, flowing down the east flank of the Anti-Lebanon mountains, was a crucial link in Syria. Though cut off from the Mediterranean by two mountain ranges and the Rift Valley, Damascus was at the juncture of ancient transportation routes that ran north and south, south-east along the Wadi Sirhan, and northeast to Palmyra.[20] There was also a road from Damascus up the Barada past Abila and Chalcis, in the Beka'a Valley, and thence over the Lebanon range to Berytus on the Mediterranean. Some of these roads out of Damascus were troubled by brigands associated with the Ituraeans (see chaps. 3 and 5) and constituted a wonderful opportunity for Herod to show his mettle. The rewards Herod reaped from his actions must in some way have been connected with the region Damascus controlled.

Reputed to be the oldest continuously inhabited city in the world, there are few remains from the first century BCE that allow much evaluation of Damascus's appearance or influence. Even Strabo gives very little indication of its character, except to claim that it was "a noteworthy city, . . . I might almost say even the most famous of the cities in that part of the world in the time of the Persian empire. . . ."[21] The enormous Temple of Jupiter (first century CE), almost as large as Herod's *temenos* in Jerusalem, suggests that at least in this

---

19. Numismatic evidence is certain for the years 84–72 BCE; see Bowersock, *Roman Arabia*, pp. 25–30, for details.

20. Millar, *Roman Near East*, pp. 36–37, 310–19.

21. Strabo, *Geog.* 16.2.20.

period and very likely also earlier, the city was built on a strict Hippodamian plan. Incorporated into the city plan (and still visible in a curved street) was a theater built by Herod; there was also a major Seleucid palace and a large, relatively enclosed *agora*. At about the same time (late first century BCE) a precinct dedicated to Roma and Augustus may have been located in Damascus, but that is uncertain.

The character of the city is hinted at by Nicolas of Damascus's description of his father, Antipater (a skilled orator who filled all the offices of the city and represented it before other cities),[22] by Nicolas himself (a historian of considerable talent), and by Nicolas's brother (a financial expert of some ability). Herod imported the latter two to advise him after Cleopatra had hired Nicolas to tutor her children. All of this suggests that Damascus was a typical Greek *polis* with the customary institutions of such a city, and that it afforded sophisticated educational opportunities for talented youths, providing training that allowed them to move in the highest circles of the Roman east.

Part of what made Damascus special was its large Jewish population (see *War* 2.561; cf. Acts 9:2, re synagogues [plural])—which was probably a significant factor during the Herodian period—as might be expected in a major commercial and communications center so close to Israel. Little can be said about Damascus's religious life until the mid-first century CE, though the Damascus document of the Dead Sea Scrolls, while probably not having anything to do with the Damascus itself, indirectly attests to the presence of Jews in Damascus.[23] It was an extensively hellenized city on the northeast edge of Herod's kingdom, though its Jewish community distinguished it from most other Hellenistic cities.

These late Hellenistic kingdoms, some dependent kingdoms of Rome, were intermarried in complex and multiple ways, as Sullivan has demonstrated in his brilliant analysis. The web of royal linkages provided what stability the region had; they had to depend upon each other in a self-supporting network of related dynasties.[24] While these kingdoms were more or less autonomous and their interests differed, and while there was rivalry and mistrust, each shared a common link with Rome, reinforced by ties of marriage and by the kinship system that flowed from these links. These were major factors in the dynastic politics of the Near East from the first century BCE to the second century CE.

Herod participated enthusiastically in this scheme as one of its key players. He occupied a critical piece of the geography of the region, holding the only land route between Syria and Egypt; he was on the border between the Arabian

---

22. Millar, *Roman Near East*, p. 314, citing *FGrH* 90 F 131, 132.

23. The Dead Sea community would not likely refer to Damascus unless there were Jews there to make it plausible.

24. Details in Sullivan, *Near Eastern Royalty*, passim.

plateau and the settled littoral; he had strong familial ties with two of the Arab groups, the Idumaeans and the Nabateans; and he developed marital ties with a number of other kingdoms. Not surprisingly, he figured prominently in the politics and culture of the Near East in the late first century BCE.

THE DECAPOLIS

A loose association of Hellenistic cities known as the Decapolis (*dekapoleis,* "ten cities") occupied an uneasy buffer zone between Syria to the north, Ituraeans to the north-west, Nabateans to the south and east, and Jews to the west.[25] Only rarely were there ten; the number fluctuated as cities arose and as the political winds blew in different directions.[26] Two cities were included in Herod's jurisdiction for a period, but all constituted a challenge to Judea, not so much in military terms as in cultural and religious matters (see map 4).

All but one of the cities were east of the Sea of Galilee and the Jordan valley. Several occupied advantageous sites in desirable areas that ensured favorable economic prospects and a good standard of living. Gerasa (Jerash), Abila (Tell Abil and Tell umm el-Ammad), and Canatha (Qanawat) were set in good agricultural areas. Others such as Hippos (Susita), Amathus and Philadelphia (Amman) were strongholds, easily fortified and defended. Gadara (Umm Qeis) was an important center of learning and philosophy south-east of the Sea of Galilee. As the home of Philodemus, Meleager the poet, Menipppus the Cynic, and Theodorus[27] it had an influential Cynic school with links to much larger

---

25. A. H. M. Jones, *The Cities of the Eastern Roman Provinces* (Oxford: Clarendon, 1937); A. Kasher, *Jews and Hellenistic Cities in Eretz-Israel* (Tübingen: J. C. B. Mohr, 1990); A. Kasher, U. Rappaport, and G. Fuks, eds. *Greece and Rome in Eretz-Israel* (Jerusalem: Israel Exploration Society, 1990); Millar, *Roman Near East,* pp. 408–14; A. Spijkerman, *The Coins of the Decapolis and Provincia Arabia* (Jerusalem: Franciscan Printing Press, 1978); I. Browning, *Jerash and the Decapolis* (London: Chatto and Windus, 1982); Schürer 2.1–97, 130–60; articles on the various cities in *NEAEHL;* H. Bietenhard, "Die syrische Dekapolis von Pompeius bis Traian," *ANRW* 2.9 (1970): 220–61. It is disputed whether they formed a true league: see T. Parker, "The Decapolis Reviewed," *JBL* 94 (1975): 437–41. Two important inscriptions, however (*IGL* 2631 = *IGR* 1057; *IGR* I.824), the less noted and earlier being almost decisively in favor of some form of administrative association. See B. Isaac, "The Decapolis in Syria: A Neglected Inscription," *ZPE* 44 (1981): 67; cf. Millar, *Roman Near East,* p. 92, 423–24, taking the opposite view. I am indebted to Elaine Myers for assistance in understanding the complexities of the Decapolis.

26. The earliest references are in Mark 5:20; 7:31; cf. Matt. 4:25. See Pliny, *NH* 5.74, who lists Damascus, Philadelphia, Raphana, Scythopolis, Gadara, Hippos, Dium, Pella, Gelasa (= Gerasa), and Canatha, but notes that others provide different lists. Ptolemy (*Geography* 5.14.18), for example, adds Abila, Lysanias (cf. Luke 3:1), and Capitolias, but he omits Raphana. Josephus rarely mentions the Decapolis as such (*Life* 342; 410; cf. *War* 3.446); in *Life* 349 he mentions specifically Hippos, Gadara, and Scythopolis, and in *War* 3.46 refers to Pella, Philadelphia, and Gerasa. Much later Stephan of Byzantium lists fourteen. Not all of these, of course, were factors during the Herodian period: Bosra, for example, came to prominence only later.

27. Strabo, *Geog.* 16.2.29, who, curiously, does not mention the Decapolis by name.

centers in other parts of the Roman world.[28] Decapolis cities were important cultural communities and some were also important economic centers, but none had access to the coast and maritime trade. Scythopolis (Bet Shean), the one city west of the Jordan, stood at the end of a direct route between some of these cities and the Mediterranean, just at the point where a north-south road along the Jordan met a main east-west route through the Plain of Esdraelon and the Jezreel Valley from Ptolemais (Acco). Once across the Jordan it was a simple matter to connect with Pella, with Gadara, and with Hippos, and the areas beyond each of these nearby cities. At Bet Shean excavations reveal how significant a center Scythopolis was; excavations at Fahil have concluded that Pella was less important than had previously been thought.[29]

Most of the Decapolis cities, being founded on older sites, had earlier histories but were refounded following the death of Alexander the Great. Pella, for example, was named after Alexander's birthplace in Macedonia and was settled by retired veterans; Dium was named after another Macedonian city; Scythopolis was named after a troop of Scythians who settled the city. Their development fell in the Ptolemaic and the Seleucid periods and largely within those spheres of influence. The hostility between Jews and Seleucids, especially during the early second century BCE as Judea was subjected to religious humiliation and then fought for its autonomy (chap. 3), formed the immediate backdrop of the Herodian period.

Herod's relations with the Decapolis were affected by this critical period under the Hasmoneans and the intervening period marking the beginning of Roman rule. Under the expansionist policies of John Hyrcanus, Aristobulus I, and Alexander Jannaeus, most of the cities were captured. Apparently they were not faced with the same choice as Idumaeans and Ituraeans—live as Jews or get out. Still, a considerable number left, there were not many converts to Judaism, and resentment at their treatment was stronger than in the case of Idumaeans and Ituraeans. The cities' inhabitants were rooted in Macedonia or Greece or Asia Minor, with no ethnic or religious affinities with the Jews, and they were thoroughly hellenized. For a generation or two, seven of the cities fell under the sway of the Hasmoneans. The loss of their traditional independence was bitter.

When Pompey intervened and ended the infighting between Hyrcanus II and Aristobulus II, following the death of Queen Alexandra, he restored the independence of these Hellenistic cities. In 63 BCE he imposed a settlement

---

28. J. Corbett, "The Pharisaic Revolution and Jesus as Embodied Torah," *Studies in Religion/ Sciences Religieuses* 15/3 (1986): 375–91; some attitudes in early Christianity to such things as wealth may have come from Gadara.

29. R. H. Smith and L. P. Day, *Pella of the Decapolis 2: Final Report on the College of Wooster Excavations in Area IX, The Civic Complex, 1979–85* (Wooster: The College of Wooster, 1989).

upon Judea aimed at bringing peace, the most important goal of which was to reduce Judea's territory by placing the free cities under the loose authority of the governor of Syria. In practice the cities must have reacquired a large degree of autonomy, certainly over coinage and probably over finances, judicial, cultural, and religious matters. Years later—up into the third century CE—coins of some of the cities continued to bear Pompeian-era dates that counted from the year 63 BCE.

The Decapolis cities flourished. Those that have been excavated and even some that have had only superficial investigation give evidence of thriving centers with theaters (Gadara and Gerasa each have two), hippodromes (Gerasa, Gadara, Bostra), amphitheaters (Scythopolis), baths and nymphaea, substantial public buildings and civic spaces (few cities could boast anything comparable to the Oval Piazza at Gerasa). Greek and Roman cults flourished in the Decapolis; the awe-inspiring remains of Gerasa's Temple of Artemis (second century CE) testifies to the cities' religious vitality; the earlier Temple of Zeus (first century BCE) was an imaginative place of Decapolis piety. Though much of the building came after Herod, the liveliness of these centers of Greek culture is not in doubt. The recent excavations at Scythopolis (Bet Shean) suggest that it may have been the most important Decapolis city. All, however, improved the general prospects of the region through roads, aqueducts, small harbors (for Hippos and Gadara on the Sea of Galilee), and other infrastructure projects.

Damascus was a special case; for the Herodian period it was not a part of the Decapolis; it may have been a part of the association during part of the second century CE. Unlike Damascus, most of the others had relatively small Jewish communities,[30] though contemporary evidence is not abundant.[31]

Herod's friendship with Augustus interfered with the development of the Decapolis cities; Augustus gave Hippos and Gadara,[32] east and southeast of the Sea of Galilee, to Herod in 30 BCE. Why these two and not others which also impinged upon the integrity of Herod's territory is not made clear by the sources. No doubt part of the reason was that both cities bordered the Sea of Galilee, interrupting natural transportation routes around the lake. But Scythopolis and Pella, too, affected circulation within Herod's kingdom, forming a barrier to north-south traffic along the Jordan, and both would have been ripe plums to hand over to Herod.

At the time of Herod's troubles with Zenodorus (see chap. 9), Gadara petitioned Marcus Agrippa against Herod (22/21 BCE), and in 20 BCE petitioned

---

30. Synagogues have been excavated at Gerasa (a sixth-century Byzantine church was built on an earlier third- or fourth-century synagogue) and Scythopolis (a Byzantine synagogue; there was also a Samaritan synagogue in Scythopolis).

31. Early in the Great Revolt several Decapolis cities suffered from the revolutionaries; in Scythopolis Jews opposed the Revolt (*War* 2.466–76).

32. Hippos: *Ant.* 15.217; Gadara: *War* 1.396; *Ant.* 15.217.

Augustus directly, both times without success. When Herod died in 4 BCE unnamed cities petitioned Augustus again to have their freedom restored; Hippos, Gadara, and Gaza were successful and were put under the governor of Syria.[33] These repeated attempts to be free from Judea suggest an unhappy relationship and Hippos and Gadara were a part of that unhappiness. Both were vigorously attacked and destroyed by the revolutionaries in 66 CE (*War* 2.459; in *Life* 42, Josephus accuses his opponent Justus of Tiberias of setting fire to both cities); both retaliated against the Jews when the tide turned (*War* 2.478). In a curious incident, Vespasian gave Agrippa II a motley crowd of prisoners—including many from Trachonitis, Gaulanitis, Hippos, and Gadara—to do with as he wished. The long and troubled confrontations led to the conclusion that Hippos and Gadara (perhaps other unnamed Decapolis cities) played particularly irritating roles for each other, directly related to the way they were used as pawns during the Herodian period. What they wanted was political freedom.

THE COASTAL CITIES

Like the cities of the Decapolis, many of the free cities on the coast had been taken over by the Hasmoneans. Gaza, Raphia, Rhinocorura, Azotus (Ashdod), Anthedon (later Agrippias; now Khirbet Teda), Joppa (Yafo), Jamnia (later Yavneh), Strato's Tower (later Caesarea Maritima), Apollonia (Arsuf), and inland Marisa, Adora, and Samaria (later Sebaste), were all at one time or another Judean, won either by force of arms or negotiation. All were freed by Pompey in his settlement of 63 BCE and were put under the loose supervision of the governor of Syria. A few years later a number of them were rebuilt by Gabinius (as was true of several cities of the Decapolis) including Gaza, Azotus, and Anthedon; he intended no doubt to restore their fortunes and bolster their position. The loss of Joppa was a particularly acute blow to Judea's economy since it was Jews' main outlet to the sea and international trade contacts to the west.[34] Though it was reacquired by Judea in 44 BCE under the auspices of Julius Caesar[35]—one of his numerous favorable actions toward Jews—to reinforce Judea's economy, Antony later gave it to Cleopatra (36/35 BCE) along with other coastal cities, Ituraea and Jericho. Joppa was ceded to Herod by Augustus in 30 BCE, together with the important cities of Gaza, Anthedon, Jamnia, and

---

33. Nicolas of Damascus in his autobiography (*De Vita Sua* in Constantius Porphyrogenitus, *Excerpta de Vertutibus et Vitiis,* in Stern, *Greek and Latin Authors,* #96 [pp. 248–60]); cf. also *War* 2.97; *Jews* 17.320.

34. Many of Alexander Jannaeus's coins bear an anchor on the obverse, including some lead coins that are likely to be the earliest of all Hasmonean coins. The anchor probably alludes to the taking of maritime cities. Meshorer, *Jewish Coins,* pp. 56–59.

35. Schürer 1.273–75.

Strato's Tower (at the same time as Gadara, Hippos, and Samaria).[36] Augustus did not give Herod Ashkelon, to which he may have had a family attachment;[37] nor did he receive authority over Dor or cities farther north such as Ptolemais (Acco).

Taking these additional territories into Herod's kingdom posed peculiar problems. The roots of some of the cities were in Philistia, their more recent roots were Ptolemaic. Some of them had substantial Jewish communities as a result both of natural emigration and of Hasmonean settlement, probably larger than in the corresponding Decapolis cities. Because of their location on the main north-south route between Egypt and Syria, the coastal cities were in touch with the cultural and intellectual currents of the day sooner and more intensely than inland cities.[38] The Decapolis and coastal cities alike were restive under Herod's rule. They shared one essential feature: all had known and some still enjoyed independence and autonomy in a large range of matters. Despite their varying backgrounds and differing histories, they also shared a recent renewal of freedom under Pompey's settlement. The flip-flopping back to Jewish rule was hardly welcomed by the majority of the population. During most of the first and second centuries CE the Decapolis and the coastal cities (especially Gaza, Ashkelon, and Dor) occupied independent positions. Farther north on the coastline, a whole string of Greek cities (Ptolemais, Tyre, Sidon, Tripolis, Balanea, Laodicea) perpetuated a similar cultural inheritance, against a Phoenician background. Berytus was the only Imperial and Latin foundation.[39]

The coastal cities were centers of a stronger and more self-confident form of Hellenism than could be found in any of the major cities of Judea. It is true that Greek ideas and institutions, not to mention Greek language and literature, had long influenced the Jewish heartland; evidence of this is clear and widely acknowledged.[40] To be sure, there were attempts to reverse the drift toward Greek ways of thinking and acting and feeling; most forms of sectarian Judaism were in one way or another a result of this struggle (see chap. 10).[41] But as the history of the Hasmonean family itself showed, Hellenism was impossible to resist.

Hellenism for the sake of Hellenism appeared as an ideal in Judea or Galilee

---

36. Chap. 8, Appendix B, on Herod's coinage, on the significance of a sea outlet.

37. His failure to obtain Ashkelon marginally strengthens the case for Marisa as Herod's birthplace.

38. Synagogues of various periods have been found at Gaza (including a Samaritan synagogue), Ashkelon, Ashdod, Jaffa, and Caesarea Maritima.

39. Millar, *Roman Near East,* pp. 264–95.

40. See V. Tcherikover, *Hellenistic Civilization and the Jews* (Philadelphia: Jewish Publication Society, 1959 [rpt. New York: Atheneum, 1970]); M. Hengel, *Judaism and Hellenism: Studies in Their Encounter in Palestine during the Early Hellenistic Period* (Philadelphia: Fortress, 1974).

41. The violence directed at the cities of the Decapolis and the coast during the Revolt was one form of an attempt to reverse the tide (*War* 2.459).

only in rare circumstances, but contact with these cities brought Jews face to face with the institutions of late-Hellenism: religious ideals, cultural and philosophical pursuits, architectural and civic forms, athletic embodiments of the ideal life. This was different from anything found within Judea proper, where only cities such as Caesarea Maritima and Sebaste, in areas that had already been extensively influenced by Hellenism and were not considered a part of the original homeland, were hellenized to the same extent. Despite these contrasts (still observable in the differences between the excavation results in, say, Scythopolis and Sepphoris), there was a pervasive spreading of Hellenistic cultural influences and ideals, including the Greek language, within Judea, Galilee, Peraea, and the other regions.

Given the character of these hellenized cities, it is striking that the literary and archaeological records are silent on the question of gifts by Herod to the Decapolis.[42] If Herod had been as strong a hellenizer as most make him out to be, some of these cities, close to his own borders and (in two cases) a part of his kingdom for more than twenty-five years, might have received some substantial benefit from Herod's largess. Closer links between Judea and the cities could only have been to the advantage of both: Herod needed good relations for the integrity of his kingdom, the cities could benefit from Herod's closeness to Imperial power. An interest in benefactions from both sides would have been expected.

The case is somewhat different with the coastal cities. Herod transformed one of them, Strato's Tower, into a remarkable showcase of his benefactions; Caesarea Maritima, as it came to be called, was a splendid blending of Roman technology, Hellenistic spirit, and a megalomaniac need for a "world-class" port.[43] Herod also refounded Anthedon and renamed it Agrippias in honor of his good friend Marcus Agrippa. Others, however, did not get any benefit from Herod's largess. Yet outside his own territories Ashkelon appears to have benefitted substantially,[44] as did the more northerly Phoenician cities (Ptolemais, Tyre, Sidon, and so on).

Several explanations, none fully satisfactory, are plausible. From the Decapolis side (especially Hippos and Gadara), continued antagonism toward Judea rooted in the treatment of the cities under the Hasmoneans might have made

---

42. He built in Damascus, but it was not a part of the Decapolis in his day. With the one exception of Si'a, a part of Canatha, he made no gifts or special endowments to the Decapolis that we know of, though he did to the coastal cities. See chap. 8.

43. For a readable account, K. G. Holum et al., *King Herod's Dream: Caesarea by the Sea* (New York and London: Norton, 1988).

44. L. E. Stager has challenged the traditional view that one of the excavated buildings in Ashkelon was in fact Herod's gift, attributing it instead to the Severan period; "Eroticism and Infanticide at Ashkelon," *BAR* 17/4 (1991): 34–53. *War* 1.422 (baths, fountains, colonnades) and 2.98 (a palace, unattributed, but probably Herodian; *Ant.* 17.321), does not clarify matters much.

them unhappy about accepting substantial gifts. From Herod's side, unhappiness because these flourishing cities had been taken away by Pompey might have continued to affect his potential generosity. Or Herod may simply have been neither as much of a hellenizer as he is painted nor so anxious to appeal to these centers of Hellenistic life (though we might consider his enthusiastic rebuilding of Caesarea Maritima and Sebaste). Of the cities that attracted his attention some had substantial Jewish numbers (e.g., Damascus, Ashkelon, Caesarea Maritima), and this may well have been the determining factor; perhaps the most satisfactory explanation is that there were relatively few Jews in the rest of the cities and hence few incentives to throw them favors aimed at improving the lot of Jews. Such a hypothesis would be consistent with the view that benefactions in the Diaspora were prompted by the need to assist Jewish communities there in their relations with their fellow citizens (see chaps. 8 and 11).

CHAPTER 5

From Petra to Rome
(64–40 BCE)

POMPEY, GABINIUS, AND ANTIPATER'S RISE TO POWER

Gnaeus Pompeius (106–48 BCE), called Pompey the Great (since 81 BCE) as a result of his considerable military reputation, entered the story of the Near East with two major successes: in 67 he had dealt quickly with the menace of the Mediterranean pirates, mostly centered in Cilicia,[1] and in the following year after a struggle in the Senate he had received the responsibility for the Province of Asia and the command of the armies in the Mithradatic War. These campaigns were of decisive importance for Rome's expanding empire, Pompey's personal reputation, and the Kingdom of Judea and its neighbors.[2]

Mithradates VI of Pontus (120–63 BCE) and Tigranes I of Armenia (ca. 94–56 BCE) had resisted Rome's growing aspirations to control the east; Tigranes had taken over Syria for part of the period, Mithradates had been in direct conflict with Rome as early as 88 BCE. As Cicero put it, this was "their opportunity to seize the province of Asia."[3] Pompey was already in Cilicia resettling the defeated pirates, in some cases in new cities such as Pompeiopolis, when word came of his new command against Mithradates. After gathering the available troops and setting up a naval blockade around the whole coast of Asia

---

1. Cassius Dio, *History* 36.20–23; L. Annius Florus, *Epitome of Roman History* 3.6.7–14; Appian, *Mithridatic War* 92–97, who stresses the eastern connections and connects his title "the Great" with these actions, incorrectly; he likens him to a "king of kings," using the Parthian royal title.

2. See the readable study by J. Leach, *Pompey the Great* (London: Croom Helm, 1978); on the pirates, pp. 66–74; on the eastern campaigns, pp. 74–101. The main primary accounts are in Plutarch, Appian, and Cassius Dio.

3. Cicero, *Selected Political Speeches* (Harmondsworth: Penguin, 1973), p. 36; for Pompey himself, p. 48. See also the lengthy accounts in Appian, *Mithridatic War,* esp. from 10 onward.

Minor, Pompey set off after Mithradates after covering one flank of the operation with an alliance with Phraates III of Parthia (designed to keep Tigranes busy). After difficult maneuvers in Galatia, Cappadocia, Pontus and eastward into the Caucasus region, Mithradates was driven from his own kingdom and north along the Black Sea's eastern coast (see map 3).[4] Pompey then turned to Armenia, aided by the defection of Prince Tigranes who had joined Phraates (Pompey's Parthian ally), in an attack on the kingdom of King Tigranes, his father. The elder Tigranes submitted, and in a typically generous gesture Pompey allowed him to retain the kingship of Armenia, but stripped him of all territories acquired by conquest: parts of Syria, Cilicia, Phoenicia, Cappadocia, and Sophene. The latter kingdom was given to Prince Tigranes for his support in the war, together with a promise to inherit Armenia on his father's death, though Prince Tigranes's subsequent actions soon resulted in his deposition and execution.

Pompey did not attempt to push Rome's borders east of the Euphrates; her influence would be exercised through two powerful native kings, Tigranes and Phraates. The main purpose of the eastern campaign was concluded in 66, though two aspects of the campaign remained, to pacify the Caucasus and to settle affairs in Syria. He took on the Caucasus himself, while sending Gabinius to Syria in mid-65 BCE.

Syria was disintegrating, with rival claimants to the throne: Antiochus XIII, last of the Seleucids, and Philip II, the pretender who held power from 67–65. Pompey confirmed Antiochus in power in 65 while two of his legates took Damascus toward the end of 65,[5] and Marcus Aemilius Scaurus was deputized to sort out the dynastic problems in Judea late in 65 or early in 64. He did so by accepting Aristobulus's bribe and ordering Aretas and Hyrcanus to withdraw (see chap. 3, re Hasmoneans). This Roman intervention put the young Herod and his father Antipater in Petra.

Meanwhile Pompey was mopping-up Mithradates' kingdom and arranging for the governance of these new Roman areas.[6] His arrangements were to shape in an extraordinary fashion the future of the region. By late 64 he moved from the Black Sea through Cappadocia and Commagene down to Syria,[7] where he

---

4. *Ant.* 14.53 refers to Mithradates' death, probably spring of 63, while Pompey was engaged in hostilities against Aristobulus; see *War* 1.138.

5. Schürer 1.134–36.

6. Leach, *Pompey,* pp. 88–89, lists the issues facing Pompey: self-governance, tribute, loans, candidates for the thrones, boundaries, garrisons, local customs, the *lex provinciae,* and rewards. These same issues concerned him in Judea, since the conditions were parallel.

7. On the way, according to Cicero, he made an enormous personal loan of forty million sesterces to the king of Cappadocia, Ariobarzanes—an indication both of Pompey's vast wealth and of the importance of the network of clients who owed their patron a great deal personally and (often) financially. On his financial dealings, Cicero, *Letters to Atticus* (Harmondsworth: Penguin, 1978), letter 115 (= VI.1), from Laodicea in 50 BCE.

deposed Antiochus XIII, reversing his earlier decision, annexed Syria and created another new province, incorporating into it some of the land held by Arab princes (see chap. 4). On the way to Damascus he settled problems in Apamea and Tripolis, including the "fortress of Lysias, of which the Jew Silas was lord" (*Ant.* 14.40), apparently just north of Apamea.[8] He came down the Beka'a Valley, through Heliopolis (Baalbek) and Chalcis in the southern part of the valley, and thence over the Anti-Lebanon range to Damascus.[9]

Aretas III was a different matter; the Nabatean kingdom was rich, powerful, influential, and of some significance geopolitically,[10] so Pompey had to handle him carefully. Fortunately there was no immediately pressing issue. Pompey had to handle Judea even more carefully, for there was a pressing problem. Scaurus's support of Aristobulus had only avoided a decisive struggle in 65 while it filled his pockets. In 64 the same players still faced each other: Aristobulus with his Roman support against Hyrcanus, Aretas III, and Antipater.

The parties sent delegations to Pompey in Damascus; later they appeared in person.[11] Aristobulus made several fateful mistakes in the presentation of his case: he accused Gabinius and Scaurus of accepting bribes (they had, of course, but it was stupid to accuse them publicly); he had as supporters young blue bloods filled with too great a sense of their own importance; and he left Damascus in high dudgeon over some real or fancied slight.[12] His case rested on Hyrcanus's disadvantages and weaknesses—still a popular ploy. Hyrcanus's case rested on his own legitimacy. Both claimed the royal crown, both had Jewish supporters with them reinforcing their claims. But a third case was made at Damascus by an independent delegation, arguing for a return to a purer form of theocracy (a view that was expressed more than once in the years to come).[13] In its strong form the argument was, first, that the nation was supposed to obey the priests of God, second, that both Hyrcanus and Aristobulus were trying to change that theocratic state, and third, the result would be that the nation

---

8. Schürer 1.237, n.14. There are several other such minor figures; it is not clear who they were, what role they played or what independence they had. See Sullivan, *Near Eastern Royalty,* pp. 79–80.

9. On the textual difficulty in *Ant.* 14.40, see Schürer 1.237, n.15.

10. Sullivan, *Near Eastern Royalty,* pp.74–75. Aretas III styled himself "Philhellene." Coins attest his rule over Damascus from 84 to 72 BCE, prior to the arrival of Tigranes from 72–69 or so. See also Shatzman, *Armies,* pp. 129–32.

11. Josephus's two accounts differ: a reasonable solution would combine them in such a way that Antipater (on behalf of Hyrcanus) and Nicodemus (on behalf of Aristobulus) appeared in Damascus in the fall of 64; in the spring of 63 the principals went to Damascus themselves. Aristobulus then left Damascus for Dium and Judea shortly after arriving (*War* 1.131–33; *Ant.* 14.34–36).

12. Aristobulus had sent Pompey a very beautiful golden vine—perhaps a decoration from the Temple? (*Ant.* 14.34–36, quoting Strabo). Intended as a bribe, for which he had no need, Pompey deposited the "vine" in the Temple of Jupiter Capitolinus in Rome.

13. Schürer 1.237, argues that this was a delegation of "the Jewish people"; it was more likely from the priestly aristocracy.

would become slaves (*Ant.* 14.41).[14] In this form, of course, the argument was unconvincing and overlooked much of the previous nine hundred years of history from Saul and David down to the Maccabees, but it testified to a religious conservatism connected not to royal power or wealth but to the priestly aristocracy. The competing positions reflected deep social and religious divisions in the country.

Pompey decided not to decide (*Ant.* 14.46). He was faced with a potentially dangerous civil disturbance, created in part by Scaurus's preference for the younger and more vigorous brother who held power to the disadvantage of the rightful claimant, Hyrcanus, who had a strong allied force and a hold on Idumaea, the southern portion of the country.[15] According to Josephus, Pompey worried over Aristobulus's capacity to "incite the country to rebellion" and over Hyrcanus's Nabatean involvement.[16] He would wait, therefore, until his arrival in Judea to settle the dispute (*Ant.* 14.46). Despite his own position of strength in Jerusalem, when faced with Pompey's uncharacteristic indecision, Aristobulus left Damascus for Judea. This was a serious miscalculation; while Pompey had not yet confirmed Aristobulus's position, absenting himself from Pompey's circle without leave and at a delicate point in the negotiations was an offensively arrogant breach of etiquette and political wisdom.[17]

Pompey pursued Aristobulus past Pella, across the Jordan and beyond Scythopolis to Alexandreion.[18] The superior Roman forces made Aristobulus indecisive, first trying to curry Pompey's favor and then making a show of resistance. He retired to Jerusalem with Gabinius, Pompey's legate, in pursuit, where he faced the inevitable siege (*War* 1.138–54; *Ant.* 14.54–74). Pompey could not let Aristobulus get away with such defiance. Though the city was not unanimously behind Aristobulus, he may have had support of a majority; his partisans were determined to resist Roman intervention. Outside the walls, Hyrcanus assisted Pompey; his supporters opened the city's gates, as those intent on war gathered in the Temple precincts to continue their resistance. The siege lasted three months. Jerusalem fell in the autumn of 63 BCE (*War* 1.149; *Ant.*

---

14. Book 14 of *Antiquities* is noteworthy for its references to the use of sources: 14.9, Nicolas; 14.35, Strabo; 14.68, Strabo, Nicolas, and Titus Livius; 14.104, Nicolas and Strabo; 14.111, Strabo; 14.138, Strabo following Asinius Pollio; 14.145–55 and 188–264, various decrees.

15. This seems the most natural way to read *Ant.* 14.42.

16. In *Ant.* 14.48 Josephus alludes to a Roman army that was being prepared to march against the Nabateans. If this is correct, Pompey had already decided in favor of Aristobulus's claims, since an attack on Hyrcanus's ally would make his position impossible; it might also suggest a half-formed intention to draw Nabatea under Roman control.

17. Pompey's intention must have been to create a patron–client relationship with one or the other of the appellants; Aristobulus's precipitate action was out of line.

18. Alexandreion, Docus, Threx, Hyrcania, Masada, and Machaerus formed a line of Maccabean fortresses through the Jordan valley. Alexandreion was the most important strategically. See Shatzman, *Armies*, pp. 72–82.

14.66)[19] with a considerable slaughter of the defenders. Pompey entered the Temple's Holy of Holies (*War* 1.152–53; *Ant.* 14.72–73), but did not touch anything "because of his piety, and . . . virtuous character." The next day the Temple was ritually purified at Pompey's orders and sacrifices were offered again.

> Arrogantly the sinner broke down the strong walls
> with a battering ram and you did not interfere.
> Gentile foreigners went up to your place of sacrifice;
> they arrogantly trampled [it] with their sandals.
> Because the sons of Jerusalem defiled the sanctuary of the Lord,
> they were profaning the offerings of God with lawless acts.
> . . . .
> The beauty of his glory was despised before God;
> it was completely disgraced.
> The sons and daughters [were] in harsh captivity,
> their neck in a seal, a spectacle among the gentiles.
>
> (Psalms of Solomon. 2:1–6)

> I heard a sound in Jerusalem, the holy city.
> My stomach was crushed at what I heard;
> . . . .
> They stole from the sanctuary of God
> as if there were no redeeming heir.
> They walked on the place of sacrifice of the Lord,
> [coming] from all kinds of uncleanness;
> . . . .
> [God] brought someone from the end of the earth, one who attacks in
> strength;
> he declared war against Jerusalem, and her land.
> The leaders of the country met him with joy. They said to him,
> "May your way be blessed. Come, enter in peace."
> They guarded the rough roads before his coming;
> they opened the gates to Jerusalem, they crowned her city walls.
> He entered in peace as a father enters his son's house;
> he sets his feet securely.
> He captured the fortified towers and the wall of Jerusalem,
> for God led him in securely while they wavered.
>
> (Psalms of Solomon, 8:4–5; 11–12; 15–19)

---

19. Schürer 1.239–40, n.23.

Hyrcanus, one of the leaders who met Pompey with joy and helped him to enter securely as if into a son's house, was reinstated as high priest as a reward for his support and for keeping the rest of the country quiet; some leaders were executed; tribute was demanded of Judea.[20] Yet Hyrcanus did not receive the royal power that was at the root of the dispute.

As in the cases of Pontus, Armenia, and to a lesser extent Parthia, Pompey redistributed land and political relationships with two complementary goals: to weaken the more powerful states and cement the numerous client relationships. The former is quite clear in the case of Judea. Pompey liberated more than a dozen cities, mainly those in the interior whose origins went back to Alexander the Great's program, together with the coastal cities that had fallen into Judea's hands during the Maccabean conquests.[21] (The parallel with the treatment of Tigranes is almost exact.) These freed cities were to be administered through the new province of Syria. Other territories were stripped away; Josephus explicitly refers to cities of Coele-Syria and to a "Roman governor appointed for that purpose" (*War* 1.155; *Ant.* is not so clear or specific), though the truth is hard to come by. Probably regions north and east of Panias and Mount Hermon acquired by the Maccabees were returned to Syria proper.[22] Pompey "thus confined the nation within its own boundaries" and laid it under tribute (*War* 1.154–55), suggesting that some natural borders had been crossed by unwarranted Maccabean expansions.

Pompey thought to solve the dynastic problems by removing one of the remaining Hasmonean families from the scene, taking Aristobulus and his children to Rome. On the way, Alexander, the eldest son, escaped and made his way back to Judea where he raised a large force, took Jerusalem, and almost "deposed" Hyrcanus (*War* 1.160), who "was not able to hold out against Alexander" (*Ant.* 14.82). This implies that Alexander had a large measure of popular support, especially in Jerusalem, and that Hyrcanus and Antipater were relatively weak. Only when Gabinius and Mark Antony arrived could Hyrcanus and Antipater gain the ascendancy again; Josephus sneeringly refers to those on the Roman side as "submissive Jews" (*Ant.* 14.84). Even after Jerusalem had been taken from him, Alexander held out in Alexandreion, Hyrcania, and Machaerus.[23]

---

20. Appian, *Syrian Wars* 50

21. Gadara, Hippos, Scythopolis, Pella, Samaria, Jamnia, Marisa, Azotus, Arethusa, Gaza, Joppa, Dora, Strato's Tower, and Dium (the last according to *Antiquities* only); Schürer argues that more, especially east of the Jordan, were liberated, 1.240, n.25.

22. Schürer 1.236 and n.25, re Jannaeus's campaigns east of the Jordan, in which he took Pella, Dium, Gerasa, Gaulanitis, Seleucia, and Gamla, most of which are mentioned as cities returned. The general reference to the Golan gives the sense of the area in question. He distinguishes two classes of territory, even in the less specific *Ant.* 14.75. Aharoni and Avi-Yonah, *Atlas,* suggest that Gaulanitis went to the Ituraeans, but I can find no evidence for this suggestion.

23. These three fortresses—all constructed originally by the Maccabees and extended and reinforced by Herod—continued to be key fortifications in Judea and Samaritis to the late first century CE.

Pompey dawdled on the way to Rome, for he did not arrive for his triumph until the winter of 62/61 BCE. According to Appian (*Mithridatic War* 116–17) the magnificent procession included 324 satraps, sons and generals of the kings he had defeated, including Tigranes, five sons of Mithradates, and Aristobulus king of the Jews, among others. Not in the procession but listed in an accompanying record was Aretas the Nabatean.[24] At the conclusion, says Appian, Pompey "did not put any of the prisoners to death as had been the custom of other triumphs, but sent them all home at the public expense, except the kings. Of these Aristobulus alone was at once put to death and Tigranes somewhat later," though in this last detail Appian must be incorrect.[25]

Josephus's narrative then turns to the Nabatean problem. Pompey sent Scaurus, who reached a negotiated settlement, as Appian also implies in a passing allusion, in which Aretas pledged obedience.[26] The army prepared for use against him had already been used against Aristobulus, whose duplicity or pride—it is not clear which—put him in the same category as Tigranes, the young prince who came over to Pompey's side and then reneged on the deal. In the settlement with Aretas, Antipater emerged as the key figure in three respects. (1) He was sent by Hyrcanus to relieve Scaurus when the Roman army was faced with lack of food and provisions. (2) He was sent as a relative of Aretas to negotiate an end to the hostilities, which he brought off successfully, only because (3) he himself personally guaranteed payment by Aretas of the three-hundred-talent tribute (*Ant.* 14.80–81; *War* 1.159, lacking the third point).

A five-year-gap in Josephus's narrative must have been filled with important events, not the least of which was guerrilla warfare organized by Aristobulus's son Alexander. The action must have been successful enough that Alexander acquired control of Jerusalem, but not so threatening that it required intervention by the governor of Syria. When Gabinius, however, who was already familiar with the region and with the main players, returned as governor in 57 after being consul in Rome in 58, he moved against Alexander.[27] To counter, Alexander refortified Alexandreion, Hyrcania, and Machaerus. In the ensuing battles between Gabinius and Alexander, one near Jerusalem and two at Alexandreion, Mark Antony distinguished himself (*War* 1.162–67; *Ant.* 14.84–89).

---

24. The procession contained Mithradates' twelve-foot-high solid-gold statue, seventy-five million silver drachmas, images of those not present in the procession, and representations of battle scenes. A tablet in the procession referred to his founding twenty cities in Syria and Cilicia and only one in Palestine (Seleucis, perhaps Abila).

25. See also Pliny, *NH* 7.97–98, without the details. Appian must be confused in this reference to Aristobulus's immediate execution, for Josephus refers to subsequent actions, leading up to his death in a very different fashion (*War* 1.171–84; *Ant.* 14.92–97, 123–26).

26. An important coin from 58 BCE minted by Scaurus (*M. Scaur. Aed. cur. ex S.C. Rex Aretas*) referred to King Aretas and portrayed him kneeling suppliant beside a camel.

27. Schürer 1.245–46; Sullivan, *Near Eastern Royalty,* pp. 208–23.

As a conclusion to these events in the mid-50s, Hyrcanus got back custody of the Temple. (It seems as if he had been replaced by Alexander as high priest for a portion of the troubled period, with the support of the priests, though Josephus does not actually say this.) The civil administration was altered: "The Jews welcomed their release from the rule of an individual [i.e. from monarchic rule] and were from that time forward governed by an aristocracy" (*War* 1.170); Gabinius also divided the country into five districts (*synodoi*), each with its own council (*synedrion*).

This is a somewhat misleading summary, for no sooner was this settlement imposed on Judea than Aristobulus escaped from his detention in Rome and headed back to Judea. He raised a large force of supporters and admirers and rebuilt Alexandreion—the key to holding the center of the country. Gabinius sent an army, one of whose leaders was again Mark Antony. Aristobulus countered by retiring across the Jordan to Machaerus, near which his army was defeated and he, a short time later, was captured. He was returned to Rome in chains but his children, including both Alexander and Antigonus who figured prominently in what followed, were allowed to stay in Judea in accordance with an agreement made with their mother.

Antipater continued to make himself useful to Gabinius and the Romans, most notably in the campaign in Egypt (intended to restore Ptolemy Auletes to the throne)—a dangerous foray in which Gabinius interfered in another province mostly for his own enrichment. In this action the Jewish colony at Leontopolis—whose main role was as military border guards—at first tried to stop the combined forces of Gabinius and Antipater.[28] They were then persuaded to let the forces go by unopposed. During the same period Aristobulus had escaped from Rome, raised a revolt in Judea, been captured and returned to Rome again; Alexander had also revolted again;[29] and Gabinius re-organized the government again in Jerusalem in accord with Antipater's wishes (*War* 1.178; *Ant.* 14.103). What Antipater wished is unstated in Josephus's accounts, but it is not unreasonable to imagine that it involved a primary role for himself. The earlier reorganization would hardly have been to Antipater's liking, and the second

---

28. *Ant.* 14.99; a number of points in this story are similar to the incidents of 48/47 involving Julius Caesar (see below). On Leontoplis generally, see Richardson and Heuchan, "Leontopolis and the Therapeutae," with literature cited there.

29. Has Josephus garbled this account, perhaps separating into several escapes and revolts what may have been a single event? There is hardly time for everything to happen that is compressed into this period. He has Alexander come to power again (*Ant.* 14.100; differently in *War*), though it is doubtful that he exercised rule since the revolt was short-lived. Antipater, "a man of good sense," interceded with the rebels; (*Ant.* 14.101; how he could have acted as a mediator when he was so enthusiastically on one side of the dispute is difficult to see). Antipater's appointment as spokesman underlines his growing role during this fractious period; some rebels responded to his appeals and changed sides, but most did not and a pitched battle was fought against Alexander's forces near Mount Tabor in Lower Galilee (*Ant.* 14.102).

seems not to have altered the basic subdivision into five regions. But the mystery remains.[30] To conclude this chaotic sequence of events, Gabinius, according to Josephus, marched against the Nabateans and then returned to Rome.[31]

Four features of Josephus's account stand out. (1) A major part of the army was Antipater's, and for the first time Antipater stood in the place of Hyrcanus; in the previous five-year period Antipater had acquired more power and responsibility. (2) Gabinius, after putting down a series of revolts by Aristobulus and his sons, felt it necessary to rebuild a number of cities that had been ravaged.[32] (3) Hyrcanus retained his important role as high priest and his nominal role as de facto leader of Judea, providing continuity and a semblance of local autonomy. (4) Antipater dominated the political life of Judea through his skillful management of relations with Rome and his recognition that Rome had to be appeased. Gabinius's period as governor (57–55 BCE) was fateful.

CAESAR, CASSIUS, ANTIPATER, AND ROMAN TROUBLES

The die was cast. Hyrcanus occupied the leading position though he may have been overshadowed by Antipater and Antipater's close association with the Romans. Aristobulus was in decline; he and his children had attempted on several occasions to wrest power from Hyrcanus, each time without success. The Romans were now unsympathetic to the claims of the younger brother whose position was weakened by the fact that his allies were ineffective. The future lay with Antipater and his children, though that was not apparent in the 50s. What may have been apparent was that Antipater and his family could not act independently of Rome, so Judea's future depended as much on what happened in Rome as on the events in Judea. The most important questions were social and political—the machinations of rival claimants for power in the unrest that had gripped Rome for half a century. Who would win was not yet clear. For Judea and Antipater the question was personal: whom should one support in the dying stages of the Roman Republic?

In 54 BCE Marcus Licinius Crassus Dives, a member of the first triumvirate that was formed, with Caesar and Pompey, in 59 BCE, replaced Gabinius as

---

30. See Schürer 1.267, who speculates that Hyrcanus stood in some way "at the head of the government of the country, . . . subject only to the control of the Roman general" (citing Bammel and Kuhn).

31. Josephus's encomiastic summary of Gabinius ("having performed great and brilliant deeds," *Ant.* 14.104) was not echoed in Rome where he was tried for extortion (guilty) and *maiestas* (acquitted). Cicero acted on the losing side in both cases!

32. Destroyed in the earlier difficulties when Pompey was active; see *Ant.* 14.88, "long been desolate." A few, however, may have been more recently ravaged in the guerrilla actions. *War,* for example, includes Gamala (= Gamla) as needing rebuilding, but it was not mentioned earlier in Pompey's settlement. Marcus, note *ad loc.,* suggests this is a corruption of Gaza, but this has little to commend it.

governor of Syria.[33] To raise money for his expedition against the Parthians he stripped the Temple in Jerusalem of its gold, including two thousand talents left untouched by Pompey when he had entered the Temple nine years earlier. Crassus lost his life near Carrhae in the expedition the following year.[34] The Parthian menace was held back by Cassius—later to be one of Caesar's assassins—who had been with Crassus but escaped and was now back in Syria. After securing Syria, Cassius went through Tyre to Judea where he bound Alexander to keep the peace (*War* 1.182; absent from *Antiquities*). Cassius's action was prompted by a revolt of Jews supporting Aristobulus, which Cassius put down at Tarichea (Magdala) on the shore of the Sea of Galilee. A large number of captives were sold into slavery and Peitholaus, the leader of the revolt, was executed at Antipater's request (*War* 1.180; *Ant.* 14.120).

Antipater again came to the fore, as an influential force upon Cassius (*War* 1.181; *Ant.* 14.121). Josephus notes Antipater's influence: his marriage to the noble Cypros; his cultivation of important friends; and his confidence in the king of Arabia—perhaps connected by marriage—regarding his children's safety. It is at this point that Josephus introduces Herod, with the Parthian menace still hovering over Rome, Antipater and Cassius in a good relationship, and Cypros with Antipater's children ensconced in Petra.

Meanwhile, Roman politics had become increasingly dangerous. Pompey had immersed himself in political activity after his triumph, for much of the period 59–55 BCE as an ally of the fast-rising Julius Caesar. When Gabinius returned from his governorship of Syria in 54, only to be charged with treason, extortion, and bribery, Pompey was faced with a crisis. The charge of treason derived from Gabinius's expedition to Egypt (assisted by Antipater) to restore Ptolemy to the throne, but it was seen as an indirect attack on Pompey who had participated in the decision. Pompey needed Gabinius to be acquitted, and he was successful in this.[35] The informal coalition between Pompey and Caesar was breaking up, however, with increasing friction, and by 50 Caesar's star was ascendant as he threatened Rome from the north.[36]

Josephus laconically connects these circumstances of extreme danger to the

---

33. Appian, *Civil Wars* 2.18: Crassus chose "Syria and the adjacent country because he wanted a war with the Parthians, which he thought would be easy as well as profitable."

34. Appian, *Civil Wars* 2.18; *Syrian Wars* 51; Josephus, *War* 1.179. In *Ant.* 14.105 he elaborates (no parallel in *War*) the details of this theft. Apparently Josephus draws this information from one or both of Nicolas of Damascus and Strabo; see 14.104.

35. Cicero, *Letters to Atticus* 92 (= IV.18), pp. 183–86, scathingly attributes the result to the prosecutor's incompetence and a corrupt jury. In the same letter he refers to a "whiff of dictatorship in the air."

36. Octavian's coins later used the star as a symbol of Julius Caesar and his apotheosis. The *sides Iulium* is found numismatically on statues of Caesar and in the pediment of the Temple of Divus Iulius. See P. Zanker, *The Power of Images in the Age of Augustus* (Ann Arbor: University of Michigan Press, 1990), pp. 33–36.

Roman state with Judea: "when Pompey fled with the Senate across the Ionian Sea, Caesar, now master of Rome and the Empire, set Aristobulus at liberty," putting two legions at his disposal with instructions to undercut Pompey's strength in the east by bringing Syria and Judea over to Caesar's camp (*War* 1.183; *Ant.* 14.123; Cassius Dio 41.18.1). Caesar's principle was familiar: my enemy's enemy is my friend. Since Pompey decisively backed Hyrcanus, Caesar freed Hyrcanus's enemy as a simple way to trouble Pompey. Pompey effectively stymied Caesar's strategy by having the proconsul of Syria (Pompey's father-in-law) poison Aristobulus and behead Aristobulus's son Alexander, a popular and troublesome leader. The younger brother, Antigonus, and other members of the family were protected by King Ptolemy of Chalcis.

Over the next eighteen years, changes in the balance of power in Rome brought about convulsions in Judean politics, frequently requiring a fast about-turn in political allegiances.[37] With Pompey's defeat at Pharsalus and his death in Egypt (in August–September 48 BCE) the positions of Antipater and Hyrcanus were in jeopardy. Josephus's account poses two interlocking difficulties: (1) What was the role of Antipater? (2) What was the relationship between Antipater and Hyrcanus?[38]

What was the role of Antipater? Antipater had a strong basis of power in Idumaea among his own people; even if he was not unopposed there—and it does seem likely that there were competing political, social, and religious programs there—Idumaea was still his main base. But he also had strong links with Nabatea so that it too could be considered a region of influence and support.[39] In addition, Antipater made common cause with minor Syrian dynasts such as Iamblichus (*War* 1.188; *Ant.* 14.129).[40] According to Josephus this was only one facet of a larger policy to develop attachments among "influential persons" (according to *War; Antiquities* says "princes") who could buttress his growing influence. These widening connections presupposed the kind of relationships Antipater had seen so effectively at work among his Roman friends—a system of client relationships involving reciprocal responsibilities and benefits. These relationships would eventually result in a series of marital links involving his children, grandchildren, and great-grandchildren.

At the same time the Romans or, with their consent, Hyrcanus gave Antipater additional responsibilities, the specifics of which are difficult to pin down. Three terms are used, inconsistently:

---

37. "Antipater, on the death of Pompey, went over to his opponent and paid court to Caesar," *War* 1.187; *Ant.* 14.127 does not note the turn-around.

38. I dismiss a common view (e.g., Jones, pp. 16–34) that Antipater had a longstanding "plan" or "ambition" to use the weak Hyrcanus to his own ends and to seize power, a plan that went back to the early 60s BCE. Similarly, Perowne; more satisfactory is Grant, p. 41.

39. *War* 1.187; *Ant.* 14.121–22. Though the accounts differ both appear to imply a marital link with the Nabatean royal family.

40. Sullivan, *Near Eastern Royalty*, pp. 200–202.

stratêgos: "general, leader, commander"; in Asia Minor, "chief magistrate of cities"; in Ptolemaic and Roman Egypt, "military and civil governor of a nome"; in Jerusalem, "officer with custody of the Temple"; in Alexandria, "superintendent of police."[41]

epitropos: "one in charge, trustee, administrator"; "governor, viceroy, executor, guardian."[42]

epimeletês: "manager, curator"; as an official title, of sacred matters or financial matters (e.g. Athens), of the market, harbor, weights and measures, of a magistrate; in Egypt, financial officer; deputy of an Emperor holding honorary local office.[43]

Antipater's role was probably a combination of military and financial deputy to Hyrcanus, with a broad sphere of influence (the most efficient explanation of the varying terms). As we shall see, a similar vagueness attaches to the descriptions of Herod.

As for the second question concerning the relationship between Antipater and Hyrcanus, Josephus's view of the relationship is best shown by *War* 1.183–94 and *Ant.* 14.127–37. Antipater acted energetically on behalf of Caesar; he assisted a Pergamene force under Mithridates (different from Mithradates of Pontus discussed earlier in this chapter) to cross the border at Pelusium; got an Arabian (Nabatean) force to join them; persuaded the Jewish garrison at Leontopolis to let them past; and led the charges in various military engagements in Egypt. As a result, Antipater became a client of Caesar's, getting Roman citizenship and freedom from taxation into the bargain.[44] For his part, Hyrcanus was confirmed as high priest.

Josephus's method of dealing with these matters is transparent, and a brief discussion here will help to clarify this for subsequent similar instances. *War's* view that Hyrcanus was inactive and was confirmed as high priest only to please Antipater must be taken from a source Josephus uses, without doubt Nicolas of Damascus.[45] *Antiquities* repeats the same view, though less strongly. But in *Antiq-*

---

41. LSJ. It is used of Antipater at 14.10; of Herod at *Ant.* 14.180, 280; *War* 1.213, 225; of Phasael and Herod at *War* 1. 203; *Ant.* 14.158; of Gabinius at *Ant.* 14.103; of Murcus at *War* 1.224.

42. LSJ. Used of Antipater at *War* 1.199; *Ant.* 14.143; the verb form is used of Herod and Phasael at *War* 1.244; used of all three at *Ant.* 14.166.

43. LSJ. Used of Antipater at *Ant.* 14.127, quoting Strabo in 14.139, and in *FGrH.* 190 F; used of Herod at *War* 1.225; contra *Ant.* 14.280. See Schalit, pp. 40–41, esp. n.126.

44. R. D. Sullivan, "The Dynasty of Judaea in the First Century," in *ANRW* 2.8: 296–354, points out that "the entire dynasty of Herod I could properly bear the *nomen* Julius, in that Herod's father Antipater had obtained Roman citizenship from Julius Caesar" (p. 313).

45. Without doubt, because Hyrcanus's role depends on an exaggeration of Antipater's—and by reflection Herod's—role and status, and Nicolas has this as a primary goal. This approach contin-

uities Josephus has other sources available to him in addition to those used in *War*, and in this instance he cites three by name: Strabo, following Asinius Pollio, saying that "Hyrcanus, the high priest of the Jews, also invaded Egypt," and Strabo, following Hypsicrates, saying that "the high priest Hyrcanus also took part in the campaign" (*Ant.* 14.138–39). Later on in *Antiquities,* Josephus cites a long series of decrees and other documents that he knows, apparently, from Rome. For example, he cites a decree of Julius Caesar (*Ant.* 14.190–95) promulgated just at the moment when Caesar had finished his Egyptian campaign and was on his way back to Rome via Syria (47 BCE), to the effect that Hyrcanus showed loyalty and zeal (*pistin kai spoudên*) by coming to Caesar's side in Egypt with fifteen hundred soldiers.[46] Hyrcanus "surpassed in bravery all those in the ranks," so Hyrcanus and his children were confirmed as high priests and ethnarchs "in accordance with their national customs (*kata ta ethê*) and given jurisdiction over their "manner of life" (*peri tês Ioudaiôn agôgês*); they were also freed from the imposition of billeted troops.[47] Though we need not concern ourselves with the many specific provisions of these decrees, several of which are controversial, it is relevant to point out that in none of them is Antipater linked with Hyrcanus.[48] We have no independent evidence of the relationship between Caesar and Antipater, though a decree dated 44 BCE (*Ant.* 14.200–201) refers to "these persons" (*toutous*) who "receive and fortify the city of Jerusalem," apparently distinct from Hyrcanus and his roles in the second half of the same sentence.[49] Despite his quotations from both literary and epigraphic sources, Josephus has no place in his account of the Egyptian campaign for Hyrcanus; he even implies once that Hyrcanus is elsewhere, for Antipater shows a letter from Hyrcanus to the Jews at Leontopolis (*Ant.* 14.131)!

Though Hyrcanus must have been with Caesar's forces in Egypt or involved in a closely related action, the spotlight falls on Antipater because of his energy, determination, bravery, and leadership (*War* 1.193–94). Josephus im-

---

ues into the accounts of Herod with, if anything, even more animus against Hyrcanus. See D. R. Schwartz, "Josephus on Hyrcanus II," in F. Parente and J. Seivers, eds., *Josephus and the History of the Greco-Roman Period* (Leiden: Brill, 1994), pp. 210–32.

46. In 14.139 it is *Antipater* who came with three thousand soldiers to the aid of Mithridates. It seems unlikely that the two forces were independent and complementary, likelier that they were the same (in which case the more sober reckoning is probably correct) or overlapping (in which case, perhaps Hyrcanus went to Caesar with fifteen hundred men who then sent him on to Mithridates, while Antipater went to Mithridates with fifteen hundred men; see. also 14.211–12).

47. See also the following grants, for publication in Tyre, Sidon and Ashkelon (*Ant.* 14.196–98).

48. Not only was Hyrcanus ethnarch and head of state, he appears in several decrees to have taken the initiative by sending envoys to seek out or to have confirmed treaties with Rome: *Ant.* 14.185, 217, 222, 223 (on behalf of Asian Jews), 233 (?), 241 (possibly Hyrcanus I). See also Josephus's general summary at 265.

49. This is probably a veiled allusion to Antipater, since it is he, according to Josephus, who rebuilt the walls.

plies that Antipater held the real power; Hyrcanus was a figurehead. But this implication is grossly exaggerated. Hyrcanus was not only present but actively involved, well known to Caesar for his bravery, and was rewarded on his own, not on Antipater's, account.

These impressions are confirmed by the subsequent vignette. Faced with a new challenge from Antigonus, who had picked up the cudgels against Hyrcanus following his father's and his brother's deaths, Antipater took the lead in resisting his appeal to Caesar, as a result of which Hyrcanus was confirmed as high priest and Antipater was made *epitropos* (*War* 1.195–200; *Ant.* 14.140–43). Josephus immediately cites two decrees concerning Jews, probably both from an earlier period and referring to Hyrcanus I, as if they pertained to Hyrcanus II, and he concludes these with a statement about the honor paid to Hyrcanus (*Ant.* 14.144–55). Again Josephus provides evidence about the importance of Hyrcanus II that contradicts his own evaluation of his passive uninvolvement.

Both *War* and *Antiquities* make Antipater the rebuilder of the walls of Jerusalem, the strong man who put down local disturbances, the friend of Caesar who accompanied him on his journey back through Syria from Egypt, the heavyweight who cajoled and threatened, and the organizer of the reconstituted regime (*War* 1.201–203; *Ant.* 14.156–57). In Josephus's view (no doubt following Nicolas), Antipater played the leading role. Hyrcanus was "sluggish" and "without sinew."[50]

HEROD AND HIS TRIAL

At this precise point (in *Antiquities,* in the same sentence as his description of Hyrcanus's lassitude) Josephus brings Herod onto the stage as Phasael's junior partner. Both were given important roles as strong men under Antipater and Hyrcanus in this new Judean administration—Phasael as governor (*stratêgos*) of Jerusalem and environs[51] and Herod in Galilee.[52] Within a couple of sentences, however, Josephus reverses their relative importance; Phasael could only emulate his younger brother by currying favor with the population of Jerusalem, keeping the city quiet, and not abusing his authority.

---

50. The former word (*nôthê, War* 1.203; *Ant.* 14.158) is a Stoic term indicating lack of fiber. The latter (*atonôteron, War* only; *bradyn* in *Antiquities*) refers to sinews of animals, especially the skeins of gut used in torsion machines such as catapults; not to have *tonos* makes one inferior, without punch.

51. With no explanation why Phasael controlled Jerusalem when both Hyrcanus and Antipater were there.

52. Both *War* and *Antiquities* emphasize Herod's relative youth, specified in *Antiquities* as fifteen years of age. This must be corrected from *Ant.* 17.148 (Herod was about seventy when he died), giving an age of about twenty-five.

Herod, by contrast, showed his energy by catching Hezekiah,[53] a brigand-chief (*archilêstês; War* 1.204–206; *Ant.* 14. 159–60; see chap. 3) on the borders of Syria, and then executing him. The location of the capture cannot be determined and does not matter much, but what is important is the light this sheds on Herod's actions and the dénouement. Four consequences flowed from this event: (1) Herod made a reputation among Syrians for his decisive action (though there is no mention of Galilean reactions to it for the moment); (2) Herod came to the attention of Sextus Caesar, a relative of Julius Caesar's, who was governor of Syria; (3) Antipater was treated as if he were a king and ruler of the whole area (*basilikê kai . . . hôs despotêi tôn holôn; War* 1.207; *Ant.* 14.162); (4) Antipater's attachment to Hyrcanus did not waver at all, he remained fully loyal.[54]

The picture being gradually built up by Josephus becomes quite complex, and before offering an independent view we must understand his point: Hyrcanus was inactive and Antipater acted in his place, yet Antipater's reputation rested upon the actions of his two oldest sons whom he himself had put in prominent positions. Put the other way round, their effective administration increased Antipater's credibility, and Antipater made Hyrcanus credible. Yet among them—both between the two brothers and between Hyrcanus and Antipater—there was little jealousy or resentment.[55] Parts of this picture are inadequate or inaccurate. Since these events are so important to Josephus's picture of Herod we must investigate the description of his trial.

Malicious aristocrats (*hoi prôtoi tôn Ioudaiôn*, as *Ant.* 14.165 puts it) created trouble for Herod by subverting the relationship between Hyrcanus and Antipater.[56] Behind the complaints lay concern over Hyrcanus's inactivity, the pretensions of Antipater and his children (both in *War*), the growing wealth of Antipater, the family's popularity, their friendship with powerful Romans (all in *Antiquities*). This is not only plausible but virtually certain, given the class

---

53. The same Hezekiah who was the father of Judas, who led a revolt in 4 BCE, following Herod's death (*Ant.* 17.271).

54. Schalit, p. 52: "Denn wir haben gesehen . . . dass Antipatros niemals danach getrachtet hat für sich und seine Nachkommen ein Königtum zu errichten. Niemals hat der besonnene Idumäer seinen Platz in Volksganzen vergessen. Er hat verstanden, dass er immer nur die rechte Hand, der Eingeber, der Lenker und der Volkszieher im Namen des Hohenpriesters und legitimen Fürsten aus den Hasmonäerhause sein konnte."

55. Both *War* 1.208 and *Ant.* 14.165 (more implied than stated) refer to resentment over Herod, a resentment promoted in Hyrcanus by aristocrats at court, and more a matter of Hyrcanus's passivity (*hêsychê*) than of feelings of *lèse-majesté*.

56. Though the accounts in *War* 1.208–15 and *Ant.* 14.163–84 differ in several important respects, most of my reconstruction is based upon features common to both, unless noted. On Herod's trial, see J. S. McLaren, *Power and Politics in Palestine* (Sheffield: JSOT Press, 1991), pp. 67–79.

structure of society and the make-up of the not-quite-royal court.[57] The accusations reflected their aspirations and their concerns at being undercut by *nouveaux riches,* whose relations with Rome were significantly better than their own. In not much more than fifteen years (from 63 BCE or thereabouts to 47) Antipater and his family had leaped into prominence and formed an alternative elite, more powerful and closer to both Hyrcanus and Rome, on whom Hyrcanus's security rested. The threat to old privileges was real.

Josephus's picture so far has one oddity. The nobles raised no concerns over Antipater's origins; while spreading dissension they overlooked Antipater's vulnerability ethnically: he and his family were Idumaeans. The point is important because it suggests that Antipater's origins were not such an issue as they later seemed to be. The courtiers attacked where the opening lay: Herod's execution of Hezekiah and his men, in violation, so they said, of Torah. Herod, with no royal authority, behaved as if he were a king.[58] The attacks worked; Hyrcanus summoned Herod to stand trial (in *Antiquities* before the Sanhedrin).[59]

A revealing additional comment in *Antiquities* concerns the role of the murdered men's mothers, who begged "the king"[60] for judgment. The mothers of the "brigands" came to Jerusalem to the Temple precincts (*en tôi hierôi*) and daily asked for justice for their children. These were pious Jewish women, the account implies, whose claims for justice carried weight. They were not riff-raff, as Josephus's favorite word *lêstai* might suggest; probably they were families dispossessed by the dislocations that had taken place in Galilee over the previous two generations—the result of a growing upper class under the Hasmoneans, accommodation with Ituraeans, changes in land tenure following Hasmonean extensions into Galilee, civil disturbances between the death of Queen Alexandra and Hyrcanus's confirmation in power, the Roman settlement imposed by Gabinius, and restoration of the royal estates in Galilee.[61] How Hezekiah and

57. On the elite, see M. Goodman, *The Ruling Class of Judea. The Origins of the Jewish Revolt against Rome A.D.* 66–70 (Cambridge: Cambridge University Press, 1987), esp. chaps. 1–5, focusing on the period 6–66 CE; R. Fenn, *The Death of Herod: An Essay in the Sociology of Religion* (Cambridge: Cambridge University Press, 1992).

58. S. Zeitlin, *The Rise and Fall of the Judean State* (Philadelphia: Jewish Publication Society of America, 1962), pp. 372–73, claims that Herod could not have been convicted and executed because he had not killed them himself, he was only the instigator.

59. The need to appear before the Sanhedrin is a dominant theme of *Ant.* 14.167–80; the Sanhedrin was bent on executing Herod, and Herod's threat to Jerusalem (14.181) follows from the Sanhedrin's actions against him. The sense of *War* 1.210–11 is fundamentally different, for the Sanhedrin is not even mentioned. See Schalit, pp. 43–48.

60. *Antiquities* does not get Herod's title right until the citation of the decrees in 14.190–267, in several of which Hyrcanus is correctly referred to as ethnarch (e.g., 14.191, 194, 196, etc.).

61. On the latter, see the allusion in *Ant.* 14.209 in one of the decrees: "places, lands and farms, fruits of the kings of Syria and Phoenicia" reverted to Hyrcanus and the Jews. On the question in general, see Fiensy, *Social History,* and R. Horsley, *Sociology and the Jesus Movement* (New York: Crossroad, 1989), esp. part 2; S. Freyne, *Galilee, Jesus and the Gospels* (Dublin: Gill and Macmillan, 1988), esp. part 2.

his band fit into this set of disturbances is unclear; they were probably neither revolutionaries nor thugs, but brigands by necessity, operating on the margins of society in the interstices between Galilee and Syria. They had considerable support among Galileans (only Syrians welcomed their executions) and among Jerusalemites (only they argued with Hyrcanus for Herod's trial). Hezekiah himself was probably a village leader of local stature.

Characterizing the brigands in this way helps to account for the trial of Herod, though other elements still need explanation. *Antiquities's* claim that "the" (or even "a") Sanhedrin was involved is doubtful.[62] *Synedrion* is used here for the first time by Josephus,[63] and even overlooking the convoluted question of the dating of the origins of the Sanhedrin, it is obvious that there are serious discrepancies in the accounts. *War* has no council involved in the trial and it portrays Hyrcanus as the prime actor. Even though *War's* portrayal of Hyrcanus is not altogether believable (he was first jealous of Herod [1.208], then angry [1.210], then loving [1.211]), and even though the description of Herod is not altogether convincing (he appeared with a troop large enough to protect and threaten but small enough to avoid the appearance of a coup d'état [somewhat similar in *Ant.* 14.169–70]), it is hard to avoid the conclusion that *Antiquities's* insertion of the Sanhedrin into the account is just that—a retrospective insertion. *War's* emphasis on the role of Hyrcanus is more nearly correct.[64]

The actions of Sextus Caesar fit this reconstruction better. He was concerned, quite plausibly, with Herod's danger from powerful aristocratic enemies and an insecure Hyrcanus who was receiving advice behind the scenes. Sextus wanted a strong military presence in Galilee keeping his southern flank quiet. Herod provided this. Given that his family was known to Julius Caesar and possibly viewed as a client of his, the motive for Sextus to protect Herod was relatively strong.[65] When the ethnarch Hyrcanus was also dependent on Caesar, his course of action was obvious. Sextus ensured, through advice and threats, that Hyrcanus acquitted Herod. Personal ties of loyalty and natural obligation were crucial in the episode.

Antiquities inserts a narrative concerning the Sanhedrin hearing into this complex incident (one absent from *War*). To judge from this account Herod

---

62. See McLaren, *Power and Politics,* passim.

63. Schürer 2.204–5. He argues that the five *synodoi* with councils established by Gabinius lasted only ten years at the most and that, with the appointment of Hyrcanus II as ethnarch, the Jerusalem *synedrion's* authority was extended to Galilee.

64. See McLaren, *Power and Politics,* who emphasizes that Hyrcanus made all the decisions, that Herod was ultimately responsible to Hyrcanus and acted as if he were, that Hyrcanus had capital jurisdiction, and that whatever role the Sanhedrin had it was not a permanent body (pp. 76–79).

65. A. Gilboa, "The Intervention of Sextus Julius Caesar, Governor of Syria, in the Affair of Herod's Trial," *SCI* 5 (1979–80): 185–95, who argues cogently that he insisted Herod be released not from the charge but from trial altogether.

stood before the Sanhedrin with his troops and so intimidated them that none would accuse him until Samaias (Shemaiah? Shammai?)[66] berated Herod fearlessly for his actions, his dress (in purple!), his haircut and demeanor. Then, turning on Hyrcanus and the Sanhedrin, he predicted (in an aside) that Herod would subsequently punish them and "the king." In another aside Josephus tells us that this actually happened, but that Herod honored Samaias both for this speech and a later one when he urged the people of Jerusalem to admit Herod and his army in 37 BCE.

Is Josephus's later account in *Antiquities* more accurate than his earlier account? The marks of a retrospective insertion are too obvious, the strains between this incident and the main framing story too great,[67] the setting in the Sanhedrin too artificial to reach such a conclusion. While it is possible that the Samaias story was an independent traditional account known to Josephus, *Antiquities* is not based on better sources at this point, and the value of this narrative for a reconstruction of the trial is almost negligible.

The conflicts in Josephus's accounts continue. *War* has Herod acquitted (1.211) because Hyrcanus loved him; *Antiquities* has Hyrcanus advise Herod to flee (14.177). *War* has Herod uncertain whether Hyrcanus really wanted him acquitted (1.212), so he goes to Damascus to join Sextus, while *Antiquities* has Herod go to Damascus "as if fleeing from the king" (14.178). *War* has the nobility continue to inflame Hyrcanus because of Herod's greater strength, while *Antiquities* has the Sanhedrin trying to strengthen Hyrcanus, who cannot act out of cowardice. *War* has Herod appointed governor (*stratêgos*) of Coele-Syria and Samaritis (1.213), while *Antiquities* makes his appointment to Coele-Syria (only) dependant upon a bribe.[68] The more restrained though still muddled account of *War* is more believable than the snide insinuations of *Antiquities,* too many of which bear the marks of editorial insertions. I conclude that Herod was in danger, that he appeared before Hyrcanus, that Hyrcanus was double-minded, in part because of the advice of his courtiers (later confused with the Sanhedrin), and that Herod was released. Uncertain of his standing with Hyrcanus he went to Damascus where Sextus gave him a subordinate military command under his own jurisdiction.[69] From this base he appeared to threaten

---

66. In *Ant.* 15.370 he is a disciple of Pollio, a Pharisee. See further in chap. 10.

67. To mention just one, in 14.174 the Sanhedrin was accused by Samaias of wanting to let Herod go for Hyrcanus's sake. In 14.177, when the main narrative resumes, the Sanhedrin was bent on putting Herod to death.

68. The reference to Samaritis seems quite implausible.

69. Coele-Syria has a disconcerting way of moving around in the ancient world. See Millar, *Roman Near East,* pp. 6, 423–24. In this instance it must mean a part of the area contiguous to that which Herod had already cleared of *lêstai,* perhaps southern Lebanon/upper Galilee, the Panias region, or parts of Gaulanitis and Trachonitis. *Koîlos* means "hollow," and the clearest use of the epithet is for the Beka'a Valley (the "hollow" between the Lebanon and Anti-Lebanon ranges), but it could be used of other areas between ranges or in valleys.

Judea. His military strength, surely not very great, appeared more formidable and his jurisdiction both in Galilee and Syria enlarged his area of operations.[70]

The incident was still not over. Hyrcanus's anxiety matched Herod's anger (*War* 1.214; *Ant.* 14.180); Herod marched on Jerusalem with an army to depose Hyrcanus (the last phrase absent from *Antiquities,* replaced by a reference to an arraignment of Herod before the Sanhedrin). Antipater and Phasael cooled Herod down, saying that he should merely threaten Hyrcanus, because Hyrcanus had helped him achieve such high office. The whole complex story concludes with Herod being satisfied with his show of strength before the nation as a prelude to his future expectations![71] Even in *War,* Josephus leaves no doubt about the future.

The main lines of Josephus's two accounts are clear. The relationships between Antipater and Hyrcanus and between Phasael and Herod were not threatened, but there was a serious problem between Hyrcanus and the young Herod, which probably reflected rivalry between Hyrcanus's aristocratic friends and the ambitious young man.[72] Herod, with the rest of his family, appeared threatening partly because of their widespread power bases. From a base in Idumaea they had achieved major advances: Antipater had a nation-wide administrative role under Hyrcanus; Phasael was governor of Jerusalem and its environs; Herod was governor of Galilee, with some role nearby in Syria. Even if Josephus has made the threat to Hyrcanus seem greater than it was, the positions of Antipater and his two sons must have been distressing to supporters of the Hasmonean dynasty and to those who thought they ought to be near the source of power to influence both the ethnarch and the way future events would unfold. A weakened Hyrcanus and a rapidly rising Idumaean family threatened their positions, as the outcome of the trial—which had been instigated by them and then backfired—had now shown.[73]

CIVIL WAR

Pompey was assassinated in 48 BCE, but his partisans continued to influence events in the east. Caesar put down continuing problems in North Africa. In

---

70. *War* 1.213 suggests that Herod was popular "with the nation" (*kat' eunoian tēn ek tou ethnous*), that is, the Jewish people; earlier *War* portrayed him as popular only in Syria (1.205).

71. *War* 1.215; *Ant.* 14.184. In both cases preceded by the assertion that Hyrcanus was a beneficent friend, indeed a benefactor (*euergetēs*) who had been influenced by evil counselors (*ponēroi symbouloi*). In both, Herod was the one wronged.

72. McLaren, *Power and Politics,* overlooks this element.

73. McLaren, *Power and Politics,* p. 189: "Jews seeking prominence were content to stand under the official head of state, whether Jewish or Roman. The main preoccupation of these Jews was to obtain a position of privilege and public status. . . . [and] to participate actively in decisions regarding policy." He goes on to comment on the rivalry these efforts created.

Syria, where Q. Caecilius Bassus assassinated Sextus Caesar and took over the province, those loyal to Caesar (including Antipater and his sons) sent troops in 45 BCE to Apamea on the Orontes to confront Bassus (*War* 1.216–17; *Ant.* 14.268–70). On March 15, 44 BCE, Julius Caesar was assassinated.[74] The reverberations of this "tremendous upheaval" (*War* 1.218) were felt everywhere, not least in the east where Cassius, one of the chief conspirators, soon arrived to take over Syria (43 BCE).[75] The Judean/Syrian vantage point hints at the difficulties faced by anyone who wished to be involved in—and perhaps to profit from—the great political and military issues that were deciding the fate of the world.

The situation in Syria changed dramatically with the arrival of Cassius; Cassius diplomatically won over the rivals, Bassus and Murcus, with their armies.[76] He then sought to put the conspirators' fortunes on a sound footing by a heavy tax on the cities of Syria. Antipater had to decide immediately between his obligation to Caesar and the de facto power of Caesar's assassin. Just as he had earlier changed allegiance from Pompey to Caesar, so now he shifted alliance from Caesar to his murderers. A high price was attached to peace with Cassius—seven hundred talents: Cassius was "exacting sums which it was beyond their ability to pay" (*War* 1.219).[77] The raising of the sum implies that Antipater called the shots—there is no mention of Hyrcanus, though that may be a result of Josephus's dependence on Nicolas, who underemphasized Hyrcanus. Yet Antipater did not have to raise the money, as one might have expected if his primary function were financial.[78] He farmed out the responsibility to Phasael and Herod and some others, including a Jew named Malchus.[79] The sum apportioned to Herod (and presumably to Galilee) was one-seventh of the

---

74. As I write this, on March 15 (!), an "In memoriam" notice appears in the *Toronto Globe and Mail*: "Caesar, Gaius Julius—foully murdered this day, the Ides of March in 44 BCE, by men whose names are not fit to appear here."

75. Appian, *Civil Wars* 4.57–59, points out that Cassius had been named next year's governor of Syria. The Senate gave him Crete as a temporary measure. His move to Syria, like Brutus's to Macedonia, was illegal, of course.

76. Appian, *Civil Wars* 4.58: Cassius "anticipated Dolabella by entering Syria, when he raised the standards of a governor and won over twelve legions of soldiers."

77. Josephus adds (*Ant.* 14.272), "Worst of all was his treatment of Judea"; there is no way to know whether there was a differential treatment of Judea. For confirmation and another view of the sum, see Syncellus, 1.576.

78. Evidence from Hyrcanus's coins has been interpreted to support the claim that Antipater had financial oversight in general and minting authority in particular. A number of coins that now are thought to be from Hyrcanus II's reign have a monograph "*A*" or "*AP*" in several different forms, probably reflecting the name Antipater and therefore probably pointing to his financial role. See Meshorer, *Jewish Coins*, pp. 41–52, 121–23; plates III, IV.

79. Apparently a friend and supporter of Hyrcanus (so *Ant.* 14.277). I use this form of the name to distinguish him from the Nabatean king, Malichus.

total, indicating the relative economic importance of Galilee[80] and the relative responsibilities of Herod, his brother (whose portion is not specified), and the other deputies. Cassius's strategy was not entirely successful; Malchus was so slow to respond (as perhaps were others) that Cassius would have executed him but for Antipater's intervention. Cassius then reduced four cities to servitude and threatened others that were dilatory; all these were saved by a special gift of one hundred talents from Antipater, though the gift derived originally from Hyrcanus.[81] There is an awkward sense of tension between Antipater's overall responsibility and his immunity from retribution when the levy was not delivered speedily enough: it is hard to reconcile his primary role, his farming out of the financial obligation, others' failures to comply, and his effectiveness interceding for them when their failure became evident. The account in *Antiquities* (which is to be preferred) clears up one element in the puzzle: Hyrcanus stood behind Antipater and acted in the emergency.[82]

In *Antiquities*, Josephus wants to emphasize—presumably because Nicolas made the point—the opportunity this levy gave Herod. He "thought it prudent to court the Romans and secure their goodwill at the expense of others" (*Ant.* 14.274; not in *War*). He deliberately moved quickly and prudentially to collect his share so that he again came to the approving attention of Roman officials in the east—this time it was Cassius.

When Cassius withdrew in 43 BCE Malchus had an opportunity to undercut Antipater, hoping to make Hyrcanus more secure on the throne (according to *Ant.* 14.277, though not in *War*). Clearly conditions in Judea were complex; Antipater was forced to withdraw to Peraea, where he had to raise troops, an unexpected reversal for someone at the right hand of the ethnarch. The narrative implies that Judean troops were under the control of Malchus. Where was Hyrcanus in all this? The Judean troops should have been his, and if there were such a threat to Antipater that he had to flee, why is there no hint that he was estranged from Hyrcanus? Why could Herod and Phasael have stayed in Jerusalem when Antipater could not? Why were their forces and arms not at Antipater's disposal?[83] Was Malchus an official of Hyrcanus's or a local strong man

---

80. At the close of Herod's reign, Galilee and Peraea had an annual income of two hundred talents, Philip's territories one hundred talents and Archelaus's territory four hundred talents. Though these areas were not identical to the earlier areas, the proportion of the levy for Galilee in 43 BCE was less ($\frac{1}{7}$) than in 4 BCE (about $\frac{1}{5}$); put differently, the profitability of Galilee increased through Herod's reign. Cassius's levy of seven hundred talents was equal to the total annual royal income of the larger kingdom in 4 BCE, a substantial sum.

81. This may make up the eight hundred talents to which Syncellus refers.

82. See *Ant.* 14.275: "Hyrcanus through the agency of Antipater sent him a hundred talents of his own money and so stopped his [Cassius's] hostile move." The less nuanced account in *War* 1.222 makes the gift Antipater's own. *Antiquities* is not an anti-Herodian alteration (against Laqueur) but either pro-Hasmonean or a correction of detail.

83. Herod was custodian of the armory in Jerusalem, while Phasael controlled Jerusalem.

unwilling to cooperate with the Romans, but one who saw Hyrcanus as the best figurehead? We cannot know; but the incident challenges views that exaggerate Antipater's power and minimize Hyrcanus's.

The details get murkier. While this standoff continued between Antipater and Malchus, with a minor reconciliation effected by Herod and Phasael (*War* 1.224), Octavian and Mark Antony set out after Cassius and Brutus (according to *War*, though its chronology is not sure) forcing Cassius to raise a Syrian army. The details of Herod's role are unclear: *War* says that Cassius and Murcus appointed Herod *epimeletês* of all Syria (perhaps as a financial expert), putting a force of cavalry and foot soldiers at his disposal, and they promised to make him king of Judea when the war was over (*War* 1.225); *Antiquities* 14.280 says he was entrusted with command of the whole army and was made *stratêgos* ("commander") of Coele-Syria—a larger responsibility, smaller title, and a more limited area, probably in southern Syria—also giving him ships and promises that he would be king.[84] Herod's friendship with Cassius apparently led to a military role somewhere in Syria, probably in the south, with some sort of force, probably small, and some promise of future honors. In other words, it is prudent to avoid either a maximalist or minimalist reading. It seems likely that some role in the region of southern Lebanon, southern Syria, and northern Jordan (in today's terms) was envisaged.

These events caused Antipater's death. Malchus got the wind up, either because of Herod's future promise and present power (*War* 1.226) or because of Antipater (*Ant.* 14.281). At a dinner party in the royal palace where Antipater and Malchus were being entertained by Hyrcanus, Malchus had Hyrcanus's wine steward put poison in Antipater's wine. He died after leaving the banquet. Though there is no suggestion in Josephus's account that Hyrcanus was implicated, we should ask what relationship existed between Malchus and Hyrcanus that Malchus felt free to use Hyrcanus's palace and servant to carry out his assassination.

Josephus then summarizes one of his main characters. Since Antipater is of such importance in Herod's story, the summary is relevant to our study. The difference between *War* and *Antiquities* is not what one might have expected; Antipater is praised in both accounts, but *Antiquities* is more flowery in its praise. Antipater is remembered as "distinguished for piety, justice and devotion (*eusebeia, dikaiosynê, spoudê*) to his country" (14.283), while *War* emphasizes his role in recovering and preserving the kingdom for Hyrcanus (1.226).[85] For a quar-

---

84. On the sequence of events, see Appian, *Civil Wars* 4.58–63. When he says that Cassius "left his nephew in Syria with one legion" (*apelipe*), he need mean no more than that; there is no necessary contradiction with Herod's role.

85. No simple theory accounts for praising Antipater (*Antiquities*) and emphasizing Antipater's support for Hyrcanus (*War*).

ter-century (from ca. 69–43 BCE) Antipater played an important role on behalf of Hyrcanus and his ethnarchy. Antipater's motives were mixed, no doubt, his support was equivocal, and relations were strained—but he was reliable, astute, and powerful in defense of Hyrcanus. His promotion of his sons was not anti-Hasmonean, though it led indirectly to the deposition and death of Hyrcanus, an end that was at least equally the result of the sibling rivalry between Hyrcanus and his brother Aristobulus and Aristobulus's children. Imputing a scheme to Antipater to put one of his sons on the throne is not supported by the evidence. For his part, Hyrcanus was not putty in Antipater's hands, but actively partici-pated in decisions, in military engagements, and in dealing with the Romans. We are not in a good position to evaluate the relationship between Hyrcanus and Antipater.[86] Yet this relationship was the stage upon which Herod played out the early scenes of his rise to prominence and power.

Malchus, Phasael, and Herod all played parts; on more than one occasion Malchus pretended to regret Antipater's death, while Herod and Phasael re strained their anger and plotted revenge against Malchus. In this power struggle amongst members of the elite, all appeared scornful of Hyrcanus. The difference was that Herod and Phasael, even after the wily Antipater had been assassinated, retained the confidence of Cassius; Malchus had broader popular support and planned to parlay that into a national revolt, taking the throne himself (*War* 1.232, 227–35; *Ant.* 14.284–93, especially 290). With Cassius's help Herod arranged Malchus's assassination at Tyre.[87] Herod's strong commitment to Rome never wavered.

Perhaps Malchus intended to support Hyrcanus and strengthen his inde-pendence; perhaps Hyrcanus was closer to Malchus than to Herod and Phasael. Both *Antiquities* (14.292, where Hyrcanus was struck speechless at Malchus's assassination) and *War* (1.235, where Hyrcanus acquiesced in the assassination out of fear) point to another of the uncertainties that bedevil our account. But of Herod's deliberate act and of Rome's support there can be no doubt.

This period (late 43 to early 42 BCE) was full of confusion and trouble. Following Malchus's assassination, Helix (a friend of Malchus) and Malchus's brother, apparently with the support of Hyrcanus, formed a coalition against Phasael while Herod was in Damascus. Phasael and Herod got the upper hand (though Malchus's brother controlled several fortresses including Masada) and

---

86. Josephus relied on the main outlines of Nicolas's account, and Nicolas wanted to give special prominence to Antipater and his family, especially Herod. The gaps in Josephus's accounts are a problem, like his limited descriptions of the social, political, economic, and religious condi-tions of the 40s. Appian's full account of events from the Roman side has no place for Hyrcanus, Antipater, or Herod.

87. *Ant.* 14.291 has Herod acting in concert with "heavenly power" (*daimôn*). The incident as a whole, while not showing Herod in a favorable light, does portray him indirectly as supporting Hyrcanus on the throne and opposing Malchus, who acts lawlessly.

a truce was arranged (*War* 1.236–38; *Ant.* 14.294–96). Samaritis was "in a sorry condition" (*Ant.* 14.284)—even "seditious" (*War* 1.229)—and Herod went there to restore order. At about the same time, there were disturbances in the north. Marion of Tyre,[88] seeking the borderlands with Galilee, still Herod's main power base and sphere of activity, was expelled by Herod from Galilean territory; Herod tried to buy Tyrian favor with his lenient treatment of Marion's soldiers. But Marion (*War* 1.239), Ptolemy of Chalcis (*Ant.* 14.297; *War* 1.239),[89] and the governor of Syria, Fabius (who had been bribed to this end), conspired to bring back Antigonus[90] so he could claim the throne of Judea.

The impression is of a fissiparous, volatile, and unstable region. The civil disturbances troubling Rome and the east provided a golden opportunity for local strong men to carve out their own spheres of influence. Thus, Phasael and Malchus competed as warlords around Jerusalem, Herod was strong man in Galilee and possibly in Samaritis, Malchus's brother controlled a number of fortresses, Hyrcanus II hedged his bets, the Nabateans waited to the east, Marion had pushed from Tyre into Galilee, Ptolemy of Chalcis threatened in the Beka'a valley, Antigonus took up a position with Ptolemy on Galilee's northern flank, and the governor of Syria feathered his own nest.[91] This picture might seem exaggerated with too much going on in one brief period. But the unrest in Rome and the rest of the Roman world, as well as in the east, supports the general correctness of Josephus's sketch. A not dissimilar portrayal, though limited mostly to Roman actions, is given by Appian.

In Judea the elite, indebted to the Hasmoneans, were pulled in two or three directions—toward Antigonus, the aggressive remaining member of the family, toward Hyrcanus, the legitimate and de facto holder of power, and possibly even toward Herod, a recently acquired member of Hyrcanus's extended family through betrothal. Others such as Malchus, Helix, and Phasael (and Herod should also be included here) had tried to secure their positions. The

---

88. On the independence of Tyre, Millar, *Roman Near East,* pp. 285–95, esp. 287–88; Tyre acquired *autonomia* from the Seleucids in 126/125 BCE.

89. Ptolemy, king of Chalcis in the Beka'a valley from 85–40 BCE, was brother-in-law to Antigonus; for the complex and rather lurid series of events, see *War* 1.103, 185–86; *Ant.* 14.39, 126; 13.392, 418.

90. Antigonus was the younger son of Aristobulus II; with the death of his father Aristobulus II and his brother Alexander in 49 BCE he became the leading rival to the throne, vying with Hyrcanus, his uncle, for undisputed control.

91. Josephus (*War* 1.240; *Ant.* 14.299) says that Herod engaged in a preliminary battle with Antigonus on the border between Galilee and Chalcis, as a result of which Herod was accepted by everyone in Jerusalem. Josephus links this acceptance in the very next sentence with his engagement (not marriage, contra *War*) to Mariamme, Hyrcanus's granddaughter through his daughter Alexandra and Aristobulus II's granddaughter through Alexander. The two data fit uncomfortably together; it is hard to see why defeat of one Hasmonean and betrothal to another would result in an increase in Herod's popularity. It is much likelier that his engagement to Mariamme was seen as a good thing but that his defeat of Antigonus was seen as a bad thing.

crucial element in the equation was how far to accept and act upon the realities of Roman power.[92] Opinions varied substantially. One thing is clear: Herod and Phasael accepted those realities and threw their lot in with the Romans and whoever held power. Hyrcanus aside, it is likely that the others seeking power did not; Antigonus, in particular, threw in his lot with the growing military power in the region, Parthia.

PARTHIA

During the second century BCE Seleucid power had weakened and then, in the early first century, collapsed. This development was marked in Judea by the Hasmonean revolt's success; in Asia Minor by the rise of Pontus, Galatia, Cappadocia, Cilicia, Commagene, and other similar states; in Syria proper by the independence of Emesa, Chalcis, Palmyra, and the coastal cities.[93] To the east the collapse encouraged Parthia's successes under Mithradates I (171–138 BCE) and Armenia's possession of Syria under Tigranes (83–69 BCE). The enduring sign of Seleucid weakness in Syria was Rome's encroachment on Syria's former areas of hegemony,[94] until Rome finally created the Province of Syria (64 BCE) and confirmed Hyrcanus II as ethnarch of Judea (63 BCE). These actions under Pompey in his campaigns in the east (66–63 BCE) included making peace with Armenia under Tigranes, on condition that Tigranes keep the Parthians at arm's length. So Pompey confirmed an earlier provision (in 84 BCE under Sulla) that had made the Euphrates the frontier between Rome's and Parthia's interests.[95] This meant that Rome now collided directly with Parthia rather than, as before, through a vassal state,[96] even if that point of contact was over a relatively short line along the Euphrates River (see map 3).[97]

The establishment of the Parthian Empire under Mithradates I (171–138

---

92. A. Lintott, *Imperium Romanum. Politics and Administration* (London and New York: Routledge, 1993), pp. 16–21, comments on the fusing of the patronage system with dependent kingships: "The Romans well understood the operation of patronage and were happy to make use of existing vertical social links in order to control societies. . . ." More cautiously, pp. 32–36, he points out that dependent kings were clients of the Roman people. See also the essays by J. Rich and by D. Braund in A. Wallace-Hadrill, ed., *Patronage in Ancient Society* (London and New York: Routledge, 1989), chaps. 5 and 6.

93. Sullivan, *Near Eastern Royalty;* see also chap. 4, above.

94. Appian, *Syrian Wars* 2: "This was the beginning of an open disagreement with the Romans as well. . . ," referring to Antiochus III's push westward in 196 BCE. See also 15, 38, 48, 50.

95. Sullivan, *Near Eastern Royalty,* pp. 20–24, 112–20, 300–318.

96. *CAH* 9.574–613; 10.71–75, 254–59; N. C. Debevoise, *A Political History of Parthia* (Chicago: University of Chicago Press, 1938).

97. Parthia comprised roughly an area from the Euphrates eastward on a line across the bottom of the Caspian Sea to the Oxus River, and thence south to the Persian border. It was bounded on the west and north by Palmyra, the new province of Syria, Commagene, Sophene, Armenia, Adiabene, and Atropatene.

BCE) and its extension under Phraates II (138–128 BCE) and Mithradates II (123–87 BCE) was another instance (similar to, but more successful than, the Idumaeans and Nabateans) of an originally nomadic group successfully adapting to the politics and the realities of a settled existence. It occurred at almost exactly the same time Rome was extending its sphere of influence incrementally eastward through acquisitions of various sorts. Both Rome and Parthia had developed impressive military capabilities; it was inevitable that the two great powers of the first half of the first century BCE would soon come into conflict.[98]

They did. Crassus, proconsul of Syria in 54 (following his consulship with Pompey in 55 BCE),[99] invaded Parthia with an army based on Gabinius's troops (and with Cassius Longinus, later Caesar's assassin, as quaestor). He crossed the Euphrates near Zeugma;[100] his army was disastrously defeated and he was killed on June 9, 53, at Carrhae (Haran), losing their military standards to the Parthians under Orodes II (55–38 BCE). As a consequence, Parthian "friendship" with Rome ended and their de facto border shifted westward to the Euphrates River. A third more fateful consequence soon emerged: Parthia was bent on moving straight on into Syria.

A second conflict occurred in 51 BCE when Cassius, who had had to assume the command after his escape from Carrhae, defended Syria against a Parthian advance that reached Antioch-on-the-Orontes. His successor, Bibulus (51–50 BCE), also had to resist the Parthians, which he did by successfully promoting internal strife.[101] When Bassus seized control of Syria on behalf of Pompey, he won the support of the Parthians, who strengthened his defense of Apamea against Caesar (45–44 BCE). With Caesar's assassination, Cassius returned to Syria and secured the east and its resources for the tyrannicides (see above). This put him in conflict with Dolabella, who had been appointed proconsul by Mark Antony. Cassius, with Murcus and Bassus,[102] defeated Dolabella at Laodicea (May, 43 BCE). Dolabella committed suicide, as Cassius and Brutus were to do in turn following their defeat at Philippi little more than a year later (42 BCE).

Parthians played a part in this internecine Roman warfare, attempting to weaken Roman power on their borders. Cassius's attempt to forge an alliance

---

98. Their early relations, first under Sulla and later, for a period, under Pompey, had been cordial; Sullivan, *Near Eastern Royalty,* p. 118.

99. In 60 BCE Pompey, Caesar, and Crassus had formed the "first triumvirate," renewed in 56 BCE. The joint consulship of two of them was a part of the agreement, as was the allocation of Spain to Pompey and Syria to Crassus. B. A. Marshall, *Crassus. A Political Biography* (Amsterdam: Hakkert, 1976), has argued for a significant improvement in Crassus's reputation, making a case for the war being not his own decision but a Roman one.

100. On the importance of Zeugma, see Millar, *Roman Near East,* pp. 29, 66.

101. Schürer 1.246–47, gives an outline, with primary sources and secondary literature. Sullivan, *Near Eastern Royalty,* p. 310, is slightly skeptical of this "propaganda distortion of the truth."

102. See Cassius's letter to Cicero from Magdala (Tarichea) in 43 BCE saying that Bassus has come over to him; Stern, *Greek and Latin Authors,* vol. 1, #71.

with them against Antony and Octavian had ended by the latters' success at Philippi. This brought Antony to Syria. The Parthians moved west in 40 BCE (still under King Orodes II, but with his son Pacorus as joint king), this time with a Roman as co-commander of the army! Q. Labienus had headed Cassius's embassy to the Parthian court in 43/42, but had been marooned by the defeat and death of Cassius. He stayed on to persuade Orodes to attack the Romans in 40 BCE; Labienus and Pacorus invaded and conquered Syria, then split their forces, Pacorus moving south to win Phoenicia (except for Tyre) and Judea, Labienus moving west into Asia as far as the coast of Ionia.

An unexpected glimpse of the unpredictable twists and turns of the period comes from a denarius minted in 40 BCE with a portrait of Labienus on the obverse surrounded by the legend Q.LABIENUS.PARTHICUS.IMP., and on the reverse a Parthian horse with a quiver hanging from the saddle. The coin combined the legendary skills of the Parthian cavalry[103] with Labienus's self-proclaimed right to the status of "Imperator" and the title "Parthicus."[104] His treason, as viewed by Romans loyal to Antony and Octavian, was rewarded with execution at the hands of P. Ventidius Bassus (not to be confused with Q. Caecilius Bassus) after a defeat at the Cilician gates in the Taurus mountains in 39 BCE. Ventidius rolled the Parthians back and reoccupied Syria and Palestine. But this runs slightly ahead of the story of Herod.

HEROD AND ANTIGONUS

During the late 40s, probably in 42 BCE, Herod was betrothed to Mariamme, the granddaughter of both rivals, Aristobulus II and Hyrcanus II, through Alexander on the one side and Alexandra on the other. The betrothal—she was probably still below marriageable age—was not consummated until 37 BCE, perhaps the point at which she turned fifteen or sixteen.[105] Herod's infatuation with her will be discussed in detail later. The relevance of the betrothal is threefold. First, Herod put aside Doris (the mother of Antipater), a Jew of Jerusalem,[106] taking on a new set of allegiances that he anticipated would

---

103. A "Parthian shot" was a bow shot by a mounted archer, seeming to ride away in disarray, who turned around on his horse and shot back toward the enemy.

104. The first portraits of living Romans on coins were by Pompey and then Julius Caesar. Labienus followed a recent innovation.

105. She was born sometime between 54 and 51 BCE; her father, Alexander (son of Aristobulus II), who was beheaded at Pompey's order in Antioch by Scipio (Pompey's father-in-law) in 49 BCE, was probably born in the early 70s, her grandfather was born around 103 or a little later. Zeitlin, *Rise and Fall*, p. 383, suggests 15–16 without giving reasons.

106. Interpreting *War* 1.241 to mean a person of standing in Judea (*gynaika tôn epichôriôn ouk asêmon*), in conformity with 1.432 ("a native of Jerusalem") and reading *Ant.* 14.300 as "the nation" (*gynaika dêmotin. . . ek tou ethnous*), not Herod's nation (or Idumaea). The double negative in *War*, "not ignoble" (*ouk asêmon*) contrasts with *Antiquities*'s "commoner" (*dêmotin*), though the latter may only mean "from the city." The question of origin affects the interpretation both of Herod's marriage policy and of the position, later, of Antipater (see chap. 2).

be more favorable.[107] Second, he became a grandson-in-law (to coin an ugly phrase) to Hyrcanus II, thereby adding another factor to the rivalries for preeminence in the disturbances of 42–40 BCE.[108] Third, he also became related to Antigonus, Mariamme's uncle, who had emerged as Herod's rival. It is difficult to evaluate how close this betrothal brought Herod into the family of Hyrcanus and Antigonus (and beyond that of Ptolemy of Chalcis, to whom the family was also related by marriage). Recalling that betrothal was the key step in establishing bonds of obligation and reciprocal duties, it was likely viewed as a significant matter, perhaps as a way of consolidating Judea in the wake of Roman and Parthian rivalry. In the absence of her dead father, Mariamme's grandfather Hyrcanus must have contracted the marriage for her.[109]

The betrothal in 42 BCE was a deliberate decision to incorporate Herod into the Hasmonean family.[110] Herod's side of the contract—putting Doris away—was a deliberate decision on his part to sever other ties and to develop his position within the Hasmonean household. His recent actions in Samaritis and Judea were likely carried out at the request of Hyrcanus, since Herod seems to have had no jurisdiction over either; his control over the Jerusalem armory also must have had the authorization of Hyrcanus.[111] Hyrcanus thus attempted to forestall a threat from Antigonus, who had placed himself under the protection of Ptolemy of Chalcis (*War* 1.239; *Ant.* 14.297).[112]

This change in the atmosphere worried the elite (*hoi dynatoi*; *War* 1.242) in Jerusalem who were opposed to changes in the status quo. They sent an embassy to Mark Antony in Bithynia (probably at Nicaea or Nicomedia) in 41 BCE to undercut Herod's and Phasael's positions by arguing that Hyrcanus was just a titular head and that the two brothers held de facto power. This was a partial misrepresentation: by his recent betrothal Herod had become the more dominant of the two brothers; by his own actions Hyrcanus must have participated in the arrangements, probably on strategic grounds, without relinquishing his own power. Moreover, though political groups would send a delegation to

---

107. If Hanson (see chap. 2 above) is correct, Herod may have been married twice before Doris; Herod's marriages to his own cousin and niece may have been his earliest ones and are mentioned last only because they are of lower status. If so, Herod would have ended these marriages too.

108. This might help to account for the curious fact, noted above, that Antipater had to flee to Peraea while Herod was able to stay in Jerusalem.

109. Zeitlin, *Rise and Fall,* claims Alexandra planned the betrothal, but she would hardly have been competent to do so.

110. So also Grant, pp. 42–44.

111. Since Herod's first military skirmish with Antigonus comes at just this point in the narrative, Herod's betrothal to Mariamme was a part of a policy by Hyrcanus to protect himself against Antigonus's usurping the throne (*War* 1.240; *Ant.* 14.299). In both accounts Josephus underscores Judea's approval of his actions.

112. Also on Antigonus's side were Fabius, governor of Syria, and Marion, despot of Tyre.

establish relations with Antony as the new power in the east (*Ant.* 14.301–2; *War* 1.242),[113] for an interest group to send a separate delegation was unusual. So when Herod also appeared, he would have been seen as the official representative of Hyrcanus and Judea.[114] He alone won the opportunity to speak to Antony, as the representative of the ethnarch and as an acquaintance through Antony's friendship with his father, Antipater. A bribe might have smoothed the way to Antony's ear, as Josephus claims. Whatever the factors, Herod established friendly relations between Hyrcanus, Antony and himself, and prevented an audience between his adversaries and Antony. Hyrcanus and Herod successfully changed sides for the third time, this time from Caesar's assassins to his avengers, especially Mark Antony.

Hyrcanus acted swiftly with another delegation to Antony (who had moved on to Ephesus in Asia later that year),[115] which did not include Herod and which obtained return of some captive slaves and of Judean territory,[116] presumably the territory seized by Marion and, according to Jospehus, seized back by Herod's action. This contradiction indicates how Josephus's archival research in Rome offers a different reading of events than Nicolas's, his main source. Herod was not as effective as Nicolas portrayed him; Hyrcanus was more effective.

As Mark Antony aimed toward a campaign in the east against Parthia,[117] he paused at Tarsus to call Cleopatra to account for her support of Cassius. The famous seduction scene took place on a golden barge.[118] Everything changed. Parthia was forgotten. Antony moved to Antioch (actually its suburb Daphne),

---

113. Plutarch, *Antony* 24, says that "obsequious rulers would flock to his door, while their wives would vie with one another in offering gifts and exploiting their beauty, and would sacrifice their honour to his pleasure." He contrasts Antony's reaction to victory to Octavian's hard work.

114. Josephus makes it appear that Herod was merely defending himself against accusations. This seems impossible: (1) as ethnarch, Hyrcanus would be expected to send a delegation; (2) Herod was now a member of Hyrcanus's family; (3) the other delegation cannot have had Hyrcanus's blessing; so (4) there was a strong need to counter the effect of that delegation.

115. Plutarch, *Antony* 24, comments that Antony was hailed as Dionysus, in a procession with women dressed as Bacchantes, men and boys dressed as satyrs and Pans.

116. *Ant.* 14.304–23; these decrees dovetail with others cited in *Antiquities,* none of which is found in *War.* The Jewish slaves had been sold at auction by Cassius (313); the territory was that taken by Tyre (313; see above re Marion; see also the decrees to Tyre in 314–18 re territorial adjustments to the pre-Cassius days, and 319–22). The general sense is of close relations with Judea (to Hyrcanus: "goodwill, friendliest feelings, your interests as my own, the welfare both of you and your nation"; to Tyre, referring to Judea: "our allies [*symmachois*], undisturbed possession of whatever they formerly owned"; "friend of the Roman people, allies"). Josephus says (323) that Antony wrote in similar fashion to Sidon, Antioch, and Aradus.

117. Plutarch, *Antony* 28, implies that he was heading to Parthia explicitly to attack Labienus.

118. Plutarch, *Antony* 25–29, in having Cleopatra appear to answer charges of assisting Cassius, overlooks the fact that many, including Hyrcanus and Herod, had done the same. Antony's messenger, Dellius, falls under her spell and advises her to go "in all the splendour her art could command," citing the *Iliad* 16.162 where Hera seduces Zeus. Part of Cleopatra's charm was her skill in

where another delegation of Judean nobles accused Herod and Phasael of unspecified crimes. Hyrcanus was present this time, supporting the brothers because of the marital bond (though that bond was relevant earlier than Josephus says). Herod and Phasael were defended by M. Valerius Messalla Corvinus (ca. 64 BCE—8 CE), originally a supporter of Brutus and Cassius who had switched allegiance to Antony (and then later to Octavian), a distinguished soldier, orator and patron of the arts. Antony heard both sides this time, asked Hyrcanus who was best qualified to rule, and then made Herod and Phasael tetrarchs—the first time the word is used in Josephus—entrusting them with the governance of Judea (*War* 1.244; *Ant.* 14.326 is slightly ambiguous).[119] When a larger delegation met Antony in Tyre to complain of Herod, prompted by Antony's imprisonment of fifteen of the delegates to Antioch (according to *Ant.* 14.326 Herod saved them from death), it met with more severe treatment.[120]

Josephus awkwardly reintroduces the Parthians into the narrative, stating that two years later Pacorus occupied Syria (actually in 40 BCE, a matter of months later). Antony's failure to move on into Parthia because of his dalliance with Cleopatra and his decision to go to Alexandria with her are linked by Plutarch, no doubt correctly:[121]

> At any rate Cleopatra succeeded in captivating Antony so completely that, at the very moment when Fulvia his wife was carrying on war in Italy against Octavius Caesar in defence of her husband's interests, and a Parthian army under Labienus . . . was hovering threateningly on the frontier of Mesopotamia and about to invade Syria, he allowed the queen to carry him off to Alexandria. (*Antony* 28)
>
> In the midst of these follies and boyish extravagances Antony was surprised by two reports. The first was from Rome to the effect that his brother Lucius and Fulvia . . . had been defeated and forced

---

languages; she needed no interpreter with Ethiopians, Troglodytes, Hebrews, Arabians, Syrians, Medes, or Parthians (27).

119. We must question the accuracy of Josephus's accounts (*War* 1.243–45; *Ant.* 14.324–29): with Hyrcanus, the ethnarch, there the decision cannot have taken the form Josephus gives it, especially *War*'s use of *archein* ("to rule," 1.244: the use of *proïstantai* in *Ant.* 14.325 is subtler, and need mean no more than "have precedence"). Hyrcanus had responsibility for Judea and for Jews; the question probably was the brothers' suitability for subordinate positions under Hyrcanus. Josephus's conclusion may still be correct: as tetrarchs they had authority over specific regions within Hyrcanus's territory.

120. Zeitlin, *Rise and Fall*, 1:387–88, argues that Cleopatra instigated the various delegations to Antony. Messala recognized Herod's strength and usefulness to Rome and defended Herod, not for his sake but to block Cleopatra. The hypothesis is too clever and not rooted in the real dynamics.

121. Appian's impression is kinder to Antony, *Civil Wars* 5.11.

to flee from Italy. The second . . . announced that Labienus in command of a Parthian army was making himself master of Asia, from the Euphrates and Syria as far west as the provinces of Lydia and Ionia. Then at last . . . Antony took the field against the Parthians and advanced as far as Phoenicia. (*Antony* 30)

In Phoenicia he changed his plans because of a letter from Fulvia and sailed for Italy with two hundred ships to meet Octavian and patch up their relationship. He delegated the Parthian responsibility to Ventidius, as we have already seen.

Antigonus now had a heaven-sent opportunity. Unlike Herod, his position was built on opposition to Rome, which was being successfully opposed by the Parthians. Herod and Phasael had lost their protector, Cassius, who was now dead, and had transferred their support to Antony, who was unlikely to trust them very much, and in any case had left the east. Pacorus (with a Parthian satrap, Barzaphranes) filled the vacuum in Syria. At just this moment Ptolemy of Chalcis died, though his son Lysanias maintained his father's alliance with Antigonus. A wider alliance with Parthia was inviting and strategic; together Lysanias and Antigonus promised one thousand talents and five hundred women to depose Hyrcanus and give the throne to Antigonus.[122] The Parthians advanced on Judea, Pacorus along the coastal route and Barzaphranes through the interior.[123] Another Pacorus, a cup bearer to Pacorus the king's son, went ahead to reconnoiter and help Antigonus, to whom a number of Jews attached themselves. After indecisive engagements, a small joint Parthian and Jewish force reached Jerusalem and besieged those in the royal palace. A skirmish in the market place involving Hyrcanus and Phasael (*War* 1.251) was slightly more decisive; the latter bottled up the invaders in the Temple courtyard and guarded them from adjacent houses. But local Jews supporting Antigonus killed the guard by setting fire to the houses, bringing Herod onto the scene to wreak vengeance (*War* 1.251–52; *Ant.* 14.335–36). The following accounts (*War* 1.253; *Ant.* 14.337–39) suggest that Antigonus had the support of the country population who were coming to Jerusalem for the feast of Pentecost (mid-40 BCE). They and the invaders held the Temple and much of the city, while Herod held the palace and Phasael the walls. Antigonus proposed Pacorus (the cup bearer) as a mediator to resolve the stalemate. Herod was rightly suspicious—how could Antigonus's ally act as mediator?—but Phasael "suspected nothing" (*Ant.* 14.341) and was persuaded to go off with Hyrcanus to Barzaphranes.[124]

---

122. *War* 1.248; *Ant.* 14.331 adds, "and to destroy Herod and his people."

123. Tyre resisted the Parthians; Sidon and Ptolemais admitted them.

124. Though Herod is the center of Josephus's story, it was Hyrcanus and Phasael who went to negotiate with Pacorus, Barzaphranes, and Antigonus. Herod was not at this stage in control of affairs.

The scheme worked; while Pacorus allayed Herod's continuing suspicions, Hyrcanus and Phasael met with Barzaphranes in Galilee and were then taken to Ecdippa (Achzib; Tell Akhziv), north of Ptolemais. They learned that Antigonus had bought the kingship and that all of them—including Herod in Jerusalem—were in immediate danger. Phasael was urged to flee for his life but would not abandon Hyrcanus (*War* 1.259; *Ant.* 14.346); instead he offered Barzaphranes a larger sum than Antigonus had. He was unsuccessful, but he was able to get a message to Herod in Jerusalem before being confined, confirming Herod's suspicions, while Alexandra,[125] Mariamme's mother, also told Herod of her suspicions. Herod fled ignominiously taking Mariamme, Alexandra, Cypros his mother, Salome his sister, his youngest brother Pheroras, his servants and supporters and what soldiers he could. After engagements with both Parthians and Jews[126]—much dramatized by Josephus—he got away first to Masada and then to Orhesa.[127] He left the family at Masada protected by a guard, dispersed other followers throughout Idumaea,[128] and went to Petra, hoping for Nabatean assistance. The Parthians plundered Jerusalem (though they left Hyrcanus's treasure alone, presumably out of deference to Antigonus) and countered Herod by destroying Marisa, the chief Idumaean city.[129] The Parthians handed Hyrcanus and Phasael over to Antigonus, who cut off Hyrcanus's ears (*Ant.* 14.366; *War* 1.270 says he bit them off) so that he could no longer be high priest. Phasael committed suicide by beating his head against the wall of his prison (or he may have been poisoned—Josephus gives both versions: *War* 1.271–72; *Ant.* 14.367–69). Antigonus was crowned king by Parthia, where Hyrcanus was taken captive (only in *War* 1.273).

The parallels between Antigonus's and Herod's taking the throne are remarkable and not frequently noted: each had the support of one of the two main military powers; each fought his way up to Jerusalem; each was supported

---

125. As both Thackeray and Marcus point out, *War* 1.262 must be wrong when it says Mariamme (Mariamme can hardly have played a part, for she was still in her mid-teens). *Ant.* 14.351 is a believable correction. In acting on Herod's behalf Alexandra was also acting in her father's interests.

126. One of which, at the later site of Herodium, was of some importance to him and was memorialized in his brilliant fortified palace there.

127. The account has the character of a vivid oral tradition. Or perhaps Josephus had access to Herod's *Memoirs*.

128. Despite its absence from the narrative Idumaea may have been more of a factor in the previous events than Josephus allows. According to Josephus (*Ant.* 14.363–64; *War* 1.268) Herod had already sent his treasure to Idumaea for safekeeping.

129. Marisa was never rebuilt after this destruction, but was replaced by the adjacent Beth Guvrin. Avi-Yonah observes that "the original Hippodamic plan was distorted in the final phase of city. . . . the inhabitants were apparently no longer prepared to accept the urban plan imposed on them . . ." (*NEAEHL* 3.949); "with the Hasmonean conquest the city took on a typically oriental character" (p. 951).

by some parts of the population and rejected by other parts; each killed the supporters of the other; each took vengeance on areas that opposed him.

Herod quick-marched toward Petra, hoping to get a loan to cover the ransom for his brother Phasael, using Phasael's seven-year-old son as surety. Malichus I, the Nabatean king (ca. 56–28 BCE), refused permission to enter his territory for fear of Parthian reprisals.[130] Forestalled by Malichus, he turned 90 degrees and headed for Egypt; at the border (Rhinocoroura) he learned of Phasael's death. Though Malichus had had a change of heart and sent messengers to make amends, Herod moved too quickly for them to catch up; in any case he was unlikely to accept the offered hand since he had decided on a dramatic course of action. He pressed on to Alexandria, where he was given a magnificent reception by Cleopatra, who offered him a commission to head an expedition (*War* 1.279).[131] Herod turned down her offer; braving the early winter weather he set sail immediately for Rome via Pamphylia and Rhodes.[132] There he assisted the city's restoration after its destruction in the civil war by grants of money, and bought a trireme to take him to Brundisium.[133]

Once in Rome, Herod told Antony of the Parthian occupation of Syria-Palestine and of his family's misfortunes. While Antony would already have heard of the Parthian advances under Labienus in Asia Minor and under Pacorus and Barzaphranes in Syria and Palestine, few would have arrived in the dead of winter to give him a first-hand account of the most recent state. Yet Parthia occupies only a small place in Josephus's account (*War* 1.284; *Ant.* 14.379, 384), though it was the main factor in the Senate's decision.[134]

Several points in Herod's reception in Rome should be noted:[135] (1) An-

---

130. *War* 1.274–76; *Ant.* 14.370–73; both suggest that Herod hoped to reinforce the ties of friendship between his father and the Nabateans and to get access to moneys Antipater had deposited in Petra. He failed in all these.

131. The later tensions between Herod and Cleopatra cast doubt on this offer; at the time (40 BCE) both were equally obligated to Antony and anxious to cooperate with the rising star. The expedition was likely to be a project of her own, for at just this moment (perhaps October 40 BCE) Antony and Octavian met in Italy and patched up their quarrel, carving up Roman territory between Octavian (the West), Antony (the East), and Lepidus (Africa); so Plutarch, *Antony* 30.

132. The account is reminiscent of Paul's trip to Rome; they had to jettison cargo and only barely made it to Rhodes (*Ant.* 14.377; *War* 1.280).

133. Only *Ant.* 14.378 mentions his assistance in the restoration of the city. But in other accounts (see 16.147 and *War* 1.424) the restoration of the Temple of Pythian Apollo is specifically mentioned, along with support of the shipbuilding industry. In 40 he probably bought a trireme (he could not have waited while one was built to specification, as Josephus suggests), and borrowed or promised funds for the Temple of Apollo (he would not have had funds at hand); later he supported the shipyards by ordering his new navy from there. See further, chap. 8.

134. Josephus emphasizes Antony's compassion for Herod's reverses, respect for his heroism, dislike of Antigonus, Octavian's respect for family connections with Herod (*War* 1.282–83); *Ant.* 14.382–83 is similar, but adds a bribe and Octavian's wish to do Antony a favor.

135. With this compare the differently nuanced discussion of Schalit, pp. 81–88.

tony initiated the scheme to appoint Herod king[136] (*Ant.* 14.382; *War* 1.282) and pressed the idea upon Octavian,[137] based on his reading of Herod's character. (2) Octavian did not know Herod well, but he was obligated to Antipater's family under the patronage system his adoptive father had built up, motivated by a strong sense of loyalty. (3) So small was the Roman world that Herod was presented to the Senate by the same M. Valerius Messala Corvinus who had defended Herod just a year earlier before Antony at Daphne. (4) Unlike Antony and Octavian, the Senate saw Parthia as the main issue and Antigonus's acceptance of the crown from the Parthians as indicative of his enemy status (*Ant.* 14.385),[138] as a result of which the Senate determined to get rid of Antigonus. (5) Though it is absent from the accounts, some of the participants must have concluded that Hyrcanus should be abandoned, because Herod was now a better man for the job.

Antigonus's pact with the Parthians was as much responsible for Herod's elevation as were his own abilities. Antigonus had strong support from among his people, as almost the last Hasmonean, but he had bad political instincts and bad advice. While his brother's and his father's resistance to Rome had tainted him, he compounded his difficulties by conspiring with Parthia, Rome's greatest rival for empire, despite having earlier been at the side of Caesar and therefore, presumably, of Octavian. Had Antigonus avoided entanglements with Parthia and remained on the Caesarian side, Judean history might have been very different. In some respects, Herod's most brilliant decision was to oppose Parthia vigorously.[139]

---

136. The title "king" had been in abeyance since Pompey's actions in 63 BCE. With Parthian permission, Antigonus had usurped the title and was using it on his coins, several types of which had "Mattityah high priest and the *hever* of the Jews" (or similar) on the obverse and "Antigonus the King" (*BASILEôS ANTIGONOU*) on the reverse. His most remarkable coin, probably dated to 37 BCE, had a menorah on the obverse with the inscription "Antigonus the King," and the table of shewbread with a reference to his being high priest on the reverse. This latter motif is similar to one on Herod's coinage, where it is usually understood as a tripod, probably pagan! For legends and photos, see Meshorer, *Jewish Coins.*

137. Other accounts give the same impression; all emphasize Antony's primary role. Strabo, *Geog.* 16.2.46, says that "Herod was so superior to his predecessors, particularly in his intercourse with the Romans and in his administration of affairs of state, that he received the title of king, being given that authority first by Antony and later by Augustus Caesar" (presumably referring to 31 BCE). Tacitus, *Histories* 5.9, says: "During the civil war . . . the eastern provinces passed under the control of Mark Antony and Judaea was conquered by the Parthian king Pacorus. But the invader was killed by Publius Ventidius, and the Parthians driven back across the Euphrates. . . . Antony gave the kingdom to Herod, and it was enlarged by the now victorious Augustus." Appian, *Civil Wars* 5.75, says: Antony "set up kings here and there as he pleased, on condition of their paying a prescribed tribute. . . . in Idumaea and Samaria, Herod. . . ."

138. Plutarch, *Antony* 33–52, gives close attention to the Parthian dimensions, including these early stages in 33–35.

139. See Jones, p. 43: "the Parthian invasion was in reality a stroke of luck for Herod, for it

So Herod was appointed king; he had been tried in the fires of eastern politics and not been found wanting by his political masters.

KING OF JUDEA

Josephus's vivid picture of Herod strolling out of the Senate House with Octavian on one arm and Antony on the other, led by consuls and magistrates to the Capitol to offer sacrifice and to lay up the decree just made, is charming and may even be accurate. From there the group went to Antony's house for a banquet (*War* 1.285; *Ant.* 14.388–89).

In a generalizing summary (only in *Ant.* 14.386–87) Josephus adds three comments: (1) Herod had not come to Rome hoping to be named king, since he accepted the usual Roman custom of granting it only to members of the existing ruling family. (2) He intended to propose as king Mariamme's brother, Aristobulus III, who was fourteen or fifteen years of age. (3) Antony had rammed these decisions through in seven days, after which Herod had left Italy. What is the truth of these additional claims?

Regarding Josephus's first comment, it is probably correct that Herod did not expect the Senate to confer the crown on him. Josephus's earlier mention of Cassius's intention is not especially believable (*War* 1.225; *Ant.* 14.280), and even if correct, there is little reason to suppose that Herod thought Antony and the Senate would approve Cassius's notion and appoint him king—perhaps the opposite. The most he could have hoped for was an enhanced role in Judea, either similar to his father's position or as regent until Aristobulus III could govern on his own.

Regarding the second comment, Herod's betrothal to Mariamme may have included the expectation that Herod would support Aristobulus as ethnarch or king once Hyrcanus was gone. Hyrcanus, captive in Parthia and disfigured to boot, was unable to carry out either office and was as good as gone. Herod concluded that now was the time to get Aristobulus appointed king, for he would be—as he well realized—in an unassailable position. Who knew how the winds might blow to give him more power during the years he would be regent? Josephus, therefore, may be right that honor, which bound Herod to Mariamme and Aristobulus, the only remaining Hasmoneans, prevented Herod from usurping the kingship.

As for Josephus's third comment, one of Herod's goals was to rid Judea of Parthian control. His decision to leave his family with a small guard at Masada and to go to Rome suggests that he intended to seek immediate Roman aid against the

---

enabled him to pose . . . as a champion of Rome who had lost his all. . . ." Grant, surprisingly, undervalues the Parthian element (pp. 50–52).

Parthians and Antigonus.[140] Had the Senate named Aristobulus king, Herod might have dallied in Rome, but now that he himself was king, returning to Judea to see to the safety of his family and the establishing of his new position was essential. Herod showed speed, determination and decisiveness; he made the return trip in winter. Josephus may be correct about the seven-day stay in Rome.

Was Herod elated? Awe struck? Full of new resolve? Fearful? Self-congratulatory? Perhaps the latter more than anything. At thirty-three years of age he had seen Rome, appeared before the Senate, been appointed king of Judea, was betrothed to the last Hasmonean princess, had fathered at least one potential successor,[141] come to the attention of Rome's leading figures, made a military reputation of some substance, been appointed by Roman governors to assist in the affairs of the neighboring province, been noticed favorably by the Queen of Egypt, and fought off attempts by the elite of Jerusalem to remove him. He had prevailed. The future was full of promise.

There were clouds on the horizon, however. Someone else occupied his throne, Parthia was in control in Judea, Rome's eastern policy was in disarray, the leading citizens of Jerusalem opposed him, Malichus of Nabatea (his nearest neighbor and kinsman) was duplicitous, and Lysanias of Chalcis (his other near neighbor and relation by marriage) was allied with Antigonus. More difficult, his credibility with Hyrcanus, Aristobulus III, and Mariamme must have suffered when he returned as king. And his kingdom needed rebuilding since the Parthians had plundered it.[142]

The first day of Herod's reign began sometime late in 40 BCE under such conditions, dated by Josephus to the 184th Olympiad (not quite correctly, for the Olympiad ended in July 40 BCE),[143] when Gnaeus Domitius Calvinus and Gaius Asinius Pollio were consuls.[144]

---

140. Antigonus was besieging Masada, where Joseph, Herod's next younger brother, was in charge. At the same time, Ventidius's counter-offensive against the Parthians was so successful that he was able to lead a small force to Jerusalem. He must not yet have received orders about Antigonus, for he extorted money from Antigonus and did nothing to relieve the position of Herod's family in Masada (*War* 1.286–89; *Ant.* 14.390–93).

141. Doris, his first wife had born him a son, Antipater, in about 45 BCE.

142. Antigonus's bronze coins had a copper content of only 68 percent; earlier Hasmonean coins averaged 82 percent. Meshorer, *Jewish Coins*, p. 60.

143. It is debated whether Josephus adheres to his dating for the beginning of Herod's reign. Some believe that some of his dates count from 37 BCE when Herod took control of Jerusalem. Others have argued that Herod back dates some of his coins to 42 BCE when he was named tetrarch, a suggestion that seems impossible.

144. Pollio is the more interesting of the two. His dates (76 BCE—4 CE) are very similar to Herod's own dates. He was a supporter of Caesar and Antony, consul in 40 BCE, and a successful military figure who built the first library in Rome from his plunder. He retired and became a significant literary figure, writing an important history of the civil wars in seventeen books (unfortunately lost) that was utilized by Plutarch, Appian, Strabo, and possibly Josephus. Herod sent his sons to live with him while getting their education. Calvinus was a less interesting and attractive figure.

CHAPTER 6

The Kingdom

GALILEE

Herod's elevation to kingship in 40 BCE came with four pieces of territory: Judea, Galilee, Peraea, and Idumaea, though the latter seems not to have been differentiated.[1] In the following years Augustus added Samaritis, Hulitis, Gaulanitis, Batanea, Auranitis, and Trachonitis, some of which were reallocated from Ituraea, some from Nabatea, some from Syria.[2] The result was a kingdom that, at its greatest extent, rivalled the kingdoms of David and Solomon. Only for a brief period under Herod's grandson, Marcus Julius Agrippa I, was the territory reunited.

Galilee had reasonably clear boundaries. Its southern border was the Carmel range with its continuation along the north face of Mount Gilboa, a northwest to southeast line from modern Haifa to the Jordan River; south of this line lay Samaritis. The northern boundary fluctuated, but ran roughly from the "Ladder of Tyre" (north of Acco, where the mountains drop into the Mediterranean) eastward to Lake Huleh, to the north of which was independent Tyre. On the east, Galilee was contained by the Jordan River and the Sea of Galilee/Lake Gennesaret. Its western boundary, even after the conquests of Aristobulus I and Alexander Jannaeus, was the territory of Ptolemais (Acco), a narrow strip of land that hindered Galilean access to the Mediterranean.

Galilee was not a single region; sub-regions revolved around the Megiddo Plain, the Bet Netofa Valley, and the Jezreel Valley, the most fertile parts of the area, though they were separated from each other by a series of hills (rising to

---

1. Appian, *Civil Wars* 5.75, allocates Idumaea and Samaria to Herod, but not Judea, Galilee or Peraea; perhaps he simply assumes the others. In a garbled account, Strabo, *Geog.* 16.2.46, gives Herod Judea.

2. On Idumaea, Ituraea, Nabatea, see chap. 3 above; on Syria, see chap. 4.

about six hundred meters) dominated by Mount Tabor. All of this, together with the hills south of the Beth Kerem Valley, comprised Lower Galilee. More rugged hills (rising to about twelve hundred meters) to the north constituted Upper Galilee, with few major valleys and constrained north-south routes through it. Since most of the physical features of both Galilees run east to west, there was difficulty with north-south traffic; the best roads crossed diagonally to the northeast. Josephus catches the situation well:

> Galilee, with its two divisions known as Upper and Lower Galilee, is enveloped by Phoenicia and Syria. Its western frontiers are the outlying territories of Ptolemaïs and Carmel, a mountain once belonging to Galilee, and now to Tyre. . . . On the south the country is bounded by Samaria and the territory of Scythopolis up to the waters of Jordan; on the east by the territory of Hippos, Gadara, and Gaulanitis . . . ; on the north Tyre and its dependent district mark its limits. . . . With this limited area, and although surrounded by such powerful foreign nations, the two Galilees have always resisted hostile invasion. . . . [T]he land is everywhere so rich in soil and pasturage and produces such a variety of trees, that even the most indolent are tempted by these facilities to devote themselves to agriculture. In fact, every inch of the soil has been cultivated by the inhabitants; there is not a parcel of waste land.[3]

He exaggerates. Not all the land could be cultivated. Particularly important in his description, however, is the notion that Galilee was surrounded by "foreign nations": Tyre, Ptolemais, Samaria-Sebaste, Scythopolis (Bet Shean), Gadara, Hippos, and Gaulanitis, to which could be added Panias to the north and Philoteria-Beth Yerah to the east.[4] Though this situation changed, there was always a strong presence around the edges of Galilee of cities (poleis) whose origins lay in Hellenistic civilization, going back to the conquests of Alexander the Great. The cities usually had their own territorial integrity, so that there was no necessary conflict between them and Galilee, apart from the natural opposition between rival peoples with dramatically different traditions. Each city had a contiguous rural area; in some cases (Hippos, Gadara, Scythopolis) one area abutted the other.

---

3. *War* 3.35–42. On his geographical descriptions, see P. Bilde, "The Geographical Excursuses in Josephus," in F. Parente and J. Sievers, eds., *Josephus and the History of the Greco-Roman Period* (Leiden: Brill, 1994), pp. 247–62, which argues that these are Josephan descriptions, reflecting a deep interest in geography.

4. Though the Tell of the last is today west of the Jordan, just where it drains the Sea of Galilee, in antiquity the city was east of the Jordan. The original line of the Jordan can still be seen west of the Tell. I am indebted for this point to Mordechai Aviam, who also suggests that Philoteria was a Decapolis city, though I cannot find the evidence.

The rainfall in the Galilee derived from prevailing westerlies coming from the Mediterranean with moisture-laden clouds. The more gradual rise in land, as compared with Judea, allowed the rain to come farther inland and distributed the rain more evenly, so that Lower Galilee averaged about 600 mm. and Upper Galilee about 800 mm. of rainfall per year.[5] The rainfall combined with the good soil in the valleys meant healthy crops, especially olives, grapes, and grains.[6]

The roads followed natural features. One followed the coastline—despite its difficulties as the road worked its way over the Ladder of Tyre—from Acco through Tyre, Sidon and Beirut up to Antioch; a branch of the Via Maris passed through Arbela and around the north of the Sea of Galilee; another branch linked Tiberias to Panias (Banyas) by a route east of the Jordan River; another linked Sepphoris with Legio and, farther south, Sebaste-Samaria; an east-west road joined Acco and Tiberias; another connected Panias and Tyre. While the explicit evidence for paved Roman roads is first century CE or later,[7] most of these routes functioned much earlier, to judge from literary evidence of travelers or armies or trade. There were other local tracks or dirt roads, the most important being the natural east-west route along the Beth Kerem fault line (from Acco to Chorazin through modern Karmiel), for which there is no evidence of a paved road in antiquity.

In the Hellenistic period, Upper Galilee was a hinterland to Acco-Ptolemais and Tyre. It was a region of small villages (some ninety-three Hellenistic sites have been identified in Upper Galilee alone), with relatively few larger centers. A characteristic pottery style, Galilean Coarse Ware, was found in the Hellenistic period at a number of these sites. Judaism began to flourish in Galilee in the Hasmonean period, following the victories of Judah Aristobulus I and Alexander Jannaeus. Though some sites were abandoned, many became Jewish towns and villages (138 Roman period sites have been identified in the Upper Galilee).[8]

The main city of Galilee during the early Jewish phase was Sepphoris (Zippori), located on a small hill just south of the Bet Netofa Valley and about halfway between the Mediterranean and the Sea of Galilee;[9] Gabinius had made it the capital of Galilee, though few remains of that period have been found. Other important towns were Yodefat (Jotapata), whose current excavations

---

5. Z. Gal, "Galilee," *NEAEHL* 2.449.

6. M. Aviam, "Galilee," *NEAEHL* 2.453, points to Galilee, already at the end of the Hellenistic period, being the most important olive oil production area in Palestine.

7. Ibid., p. 455.

8. Ibid., pp. 453–54, reporting on a survey of Upper Galilee. He identifies as larger settlements Kedesh (an important cult site probably dedicated to Apollo), Philoteria, Beersheba in Galilee, Horvat Devora below Mount Tabor.

9. See Z. Weiss, "Sepphoris," *NEAEHL* 4.1324–28, and literature cited there.

promise to disclose first-century Galilean life,[10] Beersheba in Galilee and Meroth. Jewish settlement was clearly demarcated at a later period, and may also
have been at an earlier period. For example, the sanctuary of Apollo at Kedesh,
together with a temple to Apollo and Diana in modern Lebanon and a temple
at Jebel Balat—all originating in the Hellenistic period—may mark the northern
edge of Jewish settlement.

The Galilee was a mixed area immediately prior to Herod's reign—parts
heavily Jewish as a result of Hasmonean policies, parts with mixed populations,
dominated around the edges by late-Hellenistic cities and religious sanctuaries
(especially in the west and north). It was an attractively fertile area that improved the economic prospects of whomever controlled it. It was extensively
farmed by a peasant population on small farmsteads, some owning the land
outright, some renting it as tenant farmers, some working as day-laborers. There
is little evidence for villas of wealthy landowners such as are found in other
regions of the Empire.[11]

JUDEA

Judea proper, the area founded on the ancient territory of Judah, was small,
from just north of Jerusalem to Beersheba and from the western edge of the
Judean plateau to the Dead Sea.[12] The southern half of this area was Idumaea,
a separate geopolitical unit in the early part of our period. Judea was bordered
on the west by the Shephelah, a rough limestone region of foothills, covered
with woods and thickets, that was largely infertile—a kind of no-man's land,
except for occasional large towns such as Marisa. Further north was the Sharon,
an uninhabited area of marshes and forests. Along the coastline was, in an earlier
time, Philistia; in the late Hellenistic period it was occupied by independent
cities.

A distinct "rain line" north-south through Jerusalem makes a strip of Judea
along the Rift Valley uninhabitable. It is a steep and rugged wilderness or desert
which, in a series of steps dropped almost four thousand feet (about 1250 me-

---

10. Yodefat was a walled town, founded in the late Hellenistic period, with extensive areas of
housing in the early Roman period filling the whole area inside the walls. Most of the walls predate
the revolt of 66 CE. Evidence of a public building has been discovered. Some houses had *miqvaoth;*
like Gamla, some sections of housing were terraced so that the rear wall of one house acted as the
foundation for the front wall of the next house.

11. See Fiensy, *Social History,* pp. 55–60. The evidence is "incomplete," even slight; what there
is comes from the Herodian period or later. It is important to note that Fiensy, in his descriptions of
royal estates, pp. 24–55, lists none in either Upper or Lower Galilee. The usual comments by
scholars of the Gospels about large landowners and estates are not yet based on firm Galilean
evidence.

12. See Baly and Tushingham, *Atlas,* pp. 112–15, an area of about 80 km (50 miles) by 32 km
(20 miles).

ters) to the Dead Sea.[13] Within the Judean hills themselves the rainfall was adequate, and the arable soil, mostly in the valleys and hillsides, sustained olives, grapes, and, in small contained areas, grain. Judea was constrained by natural topography, except for the flexible northern and southern borders. Unlike Galilee, which formed a kind of bowl, Judea was a plateau region of high hills (up to thirty-four hundred feet or eleven hundred meters).[14]

A north-south road through Jerusalem and Hebron ran from Samaria-Sebaste in the north to Beersheba in the south, meandering along as the topography required. Another road connected Jerusalem and Jericho, parallel to the Wadi Qelt and making more than 1,000-meter drop in only 22 or 23 kilometers (about 13 miles). Jerusalem was joined by major roads to the northwest with Joppa-Jaffa, and to the southwest to Marisa-Beth Guvrin-Eleutheropolis, beyond which lay Ashkelon and Gaza, and then Egypt.

The key to Judea was Jerusalem, the administrative capital of the region and the cult center of all Jews everywhere. There was heavy traffic from pilgrims to Jerusalem at the major festivals, probably in increasing numbers through the first century BCE and CE as the *pax Romana* brought easier travel, more disposable income, and fewer border problems. This meant that Judeans had very large demands made upon them for good roads, lodgings, food, water, and sacrificial victims such as pigeons (doves), sheep, and cattle. Jerusalem was the royal capital of Judea and the other regions associated with it, the military center as the main "fortress" of Jews and its chief arsenal, as well as the economic center for taxation, trade, and international links. This made it the ceremonial center, too, the place where all important visitors came to see the sights. As archaeological excavations have made clear, Jerusalem had the greatest concentration of the wealthy and elite; they were attracted by all the advantages of nearness to the religious and political administration, the center of economic and international influence.[15]

The city had been, almost from the beginning, a significant stronghold and was regularly strengthened, destroyed, and rebuilt.[16] It was a naturally defensible site, centered on the eastern hill (the ancient City of David and Mount Moriah); by the Hasmonean period it had expanded to include the adjacent western hill

---

13. This rain line is created by the steep rise between the Shephelah and the hill country of Judea, which forces moisture-bearing clouds up, cooling them so that their moisture is precipitated very quickly.

14. A. Ofer, "Judea," *NEAEHL* 3.815–16, for a survey.

15. See B. Mazar, Y. Shiloh, H. Geva, and N. Avigad, "Jerusalem," *NEAEHL* 2.698–757, esp. 717–57, for archaeological data; W. Mare, *The Archaeology of the Jerusalem Area* (Grand Rapids: Baker, 1987); and somewhat older, J. Wilkinson, *Jerusalem as Jesus Knew It* (London: Thames and Hudson, 1978); J. Jeremias, *Jerusalem in the Time of Jesus* (London: SCM, 1969), among others.

16. Continuously inhabited from the Chalcolithic period, it was first named in historic records in the Egyptian Execration Texts of the twentieth and nineteenth centuries BCE.

(today's Mount Zion). The deep valleys, especially on the east, west, and south (the Kidron and Hinnom Valleys) provided natural protection for Jerusalem, though it was open to attack from the north and northwest. To the east it was overlooked by Mount Scopus and the Mount of Olives, which stood at the watershed and looked down the Wadi Qelt to Jericho; even to the north and west it was overlooked by higher ground. The Gihon spring provided a secure water supply that had been developed so that it was within the walls.

Jerusalem was resettled by returning exiles from Babylonia (ca. 538 and 521 BCE), who rebuilt the ruined walls and restored the sanctuary, though in much meaner form than the original. Even two hundred years later it was still a small and poverty-stricken city. Its physical condition improved with Alexander's conquest of Judea in 332 BCE which was followed by a period of stability under the Ptolemies. Following the battle of Panias (200 BCE), Jerusalem was identified by the Seleucids as a target for transformation into a Greek *polis* (see chap. 3). When the Hasmonean revolt succeeded against Antiochus IV Epiphanes, Jerusalem expanded—especially under John Hyrcanus I and Alexander Jannaeus—with new residential areas, a new royal palace, improved and expanded walls, and extension of the Temple precinct. The dynastic squabbles of the later Hasmoneans and the Roman intervention under Pompey (63 BCE) and Gabinius (55 BCE) slowed Jerusalem's growth; Roman damage to the city's fortifications was repaired by Antipater, Herod's father (48/47 BCE).

Jerusalem was not the only heavily fortified place in Judea. The Hasmoneans built several wilderness fortresses overlooking the Rift Valley: Masada to the south, Hyrcania near the Wadi Kidron, Docus and Threx overlooking Jericho, and Machaerus on the eastern side of the Dead Sea. This system (anchored in the north by Alexandreion) defended Judea and Samaria from Nabateans and the Decapolis cities.[17] Whether there were other Maccabean "fortlets" along the southern border is less certain.[18]

In general, "the Judean hills . . . were the least densely populated component of the country's Central Mountain Masif . . . [and] population fluctuations were quite extreme."[19] During the Persian period the numbers declined seriously in the southern sector, especially in and around Hebron and farther south, though population density was maintained from Beth Zur to Jerusalem. In the Hellenistic period, settlement intensified (with an increase from seventy to

---

17. E. Netzer, "Masada," *NEAEHL* 3.973–85; J. Patrich, "Hyrcania," 2:639–41; E. Netzer, "Cypros," *NEAEHL* 1.315–17; Y. Tsafrir and I. Magen, "Sartaba-Alexandrium," *NEAEHL* 4.1318–20, and the literature cited in the various articles. On Machaerus, see V. Corbo in *Liber Annuus* 28 (1978): 217–31; 29 (1979): 315–26; 30 (1980): 365–70; 31 (1981): 257–86.

18. For a detailed analysis, Shatzman, *Armies,* p. 55: "the evidence is remarkably scanty or negative"; his view opposes that of Kasher, who hypothesizes an integrated set of Herodian fortifications. The strategy for the major fortresses just named was Hasmonean, not Herodian.

19. Ofer, *NEAEHL* 3.815.

ninety-one settlements according to the survey; from 111 acres to 150 acres in total), though even during periods of more intense settlement the density was not high, despite the area's proximity to Jerusalem. There were two main reasons: the land could not sustain a high level of population, and the region symbiotically joined settlements and semi-nomadic uses—a feature still observable today though less obviously. The main settlements outside Jerusalem were Hebron, Ziph, and Adoraim.[20]

In his description of first-century Judea, Josephus exaggerates, as he did in his description of Galilee:

> [Samaritis and Judea] consist of hills and plains, yield a light and fertile soil for agriculture, are well wooded, and abound in fruits, both wild and cultivated; both owe their productiveness to the entire absence of dry deserts and to a rainfall for the most part abundant. All the running water has a singularly sweet taste; and owing to the abundance of excellent grass the cattle yield more milk than in other districts. But the surest test of the two countries is that both have a dense population.[21]

Josephus does not claim an extensive agricultural enterprise for Judea as he had for Galilee. There was cultivation of various kinds, but much of the pastoral activity was raising sheep and goats, as it is today. There were plots of intensely cultivated land, but not large farms in most of the Judean hills. There were also manufacturing activities: stoneware for ritually clean kitchens was exported to Galilee; Jericho produced fine date wines and perfumes; bitumen was taken from the Dead Sea.

The heartland of Judaism, centered on Jerusalem, was more thoroughly Jewish than other regions. While there were some Idumaeans not fully converted to Judaism in southern areas, Romans in western areas, and Samaritans in northern areas, to a first approximation, Judea was Jewish territory governed by the laws and customs of Judaism.

SAMARITIS

Between Galilee and Judea lay Samaritis. The Mount Carmel-Mount Gilboa line marked its northern border, the Jordan River its eastern border, a somewhat indefinite line a few miles north of Jerusalem its southern border,

---

20. On all this see Ofer, *NEAEHL* 3.816.

21. *War* 3.49–55. Josephus lists the toparchies: "Gophna . . . , Acrabeta, Thamna, Lydda, Emmaus, Pella, Idumaea, Engadi, Herodion, and Jericho. To these must be added Jamnia and Joppa . . . and . . . Gamala, Gaulanitis, Batanea and Trachonitis." Of these, only Emmaus, Idumaea, Engaddi, Herodion, and Jericho are in Judea.

and the drop between the hill country and the Sharon its western border. When Josephus lumps together Judea and Samaritis (as he does in the excerpt above), he is not altogether fair to Samaritis, for it was more fertile than Judea.

It comprised three sub-regions: northern, southern, and western Samaritis.[22] Northern Samaritis, focused on Mount Shechem and Mount Ebal (940 meters), had wide cultivable valleys, frequent water sources, and good soil. The number of sites peaked in the Persian period, perhaps to be explained on the basis that "some of the Babylonian returnees settled in Samaria (and not only in Judah) in the fifth and fourth centuries BCE,"[23] while the decline in the Hellenistic period has been attributed to Samaritan opposition to Alexander the Great. In the early Roman period there was an increase, especially in the northwestern part of the region. Southern Samaritis was harsher, especially topographically. In contrast to northern Samaritis, the number and size of the sites declined strongly in the Persian period (to 90), with renewed prosperity in the Hellenistic period (by the Roman period the number of sites had risen to 215). Western Samaritis, characterized by clusters of small settlements and by groups of farmhouses, was more densely populated than either of the others. By the early Roman period some of these settlements had grown to small or medium sized towns.[24] Field towers, especially common in western Samaritis, began to be built in the Hellenistic period and may have been associated with Hasmonean settlements. In the late Hellenistic and Roman periods (and up into the Byzantine period) the clusters of farmhouses began to be replaced by larger estates.[25]

Samaritis permitted extensive agricultural development, especially in the western areas where the rainfall was especially good (550 to 700 millimeters per year); rainfall declined substantially in eastern Samaritis, as it did in the wilderness of Judea and for the same reasons (200–400 millimeters per year). Crops included grapes, olives, fruits, grain and vegetables, and of course sheep. Many of the hills were terraced in antiquity, as they are today, to inhibit erosion and improve productivity.

There was a north-south road through the hills from Samaria and Shechem to Jerusalem in the one direction and to Ginae (Jenin) and the Jezreel Valley in

---

22. For the following see the relevant articles by A. Zertal, *NEAEHL* 4.1311–12; I. Finkelstein, 4.1313–14; S. Dar, 4.1314–16; and I. Magen on the Hellenistic and Roman-Byzantine periods, 4.1316–18. See also S. Dar, "Samaria," *ABD* 5.926–31.

23. Zertal, *NEAEHL* 4.1312. There were 247 Persian period sites, but only 140 Hellenistic and 146 early Roman sites (by the Byzantine period the number had climbed to 358).

24. Dar uses Umm Rihan, a town of nine to ten acres, as an example. It included one hundred well-built courtyard houses, a well-organized network of streets, water supply, defensive structures, public areas (including a bath, shops, mausolea, a public building, oil presses). Most of these developments were Persian and Hellenistic. See *NEAEHL* 4.1314–15.

25. On towers and estates, see Fiensy, *Social History,* maps 2 and 3; plan 1; discussion on pp. 31–43.

the other; there was a main road southwesterly from Shechem to Joppa, and another northwesterly to Strato's Tower (Caesarea Maritima), continuing in a southeasterly direction to the Jordan Valley, past Alexandreion. There was also a southeast-northwest route along the Wadi Far'ah past Mount Ebal and on to Ginae. At this intersection a route cut through the Carmel Range along the Dothan Valley, connecting the Jezreel Valley with the Coastal Plain (still visible today).

Curiously, there was no evidence of destruction of Persian period settlements to account for the reduced number of Hellenistic sites. The Hasmoneans encouraged increased cultivation as they attempted to "judaize" Samaritis. Since it is not possible to differentiate Jewish from Samaritan sites (even tombs cannot be identified one way or the other with any certainty), changes in religious-ethnic makeup of the various towns and villages can not be analyzed.[26]

The main settlements were Samaria and Shechem-Neapolis (Nablus), both under the shadows of Mount Ebal and Mount Gerizim, the latter the main cult center of Samaritan religion; a fortified city on Mount Gerizim covered about seventy-five acres. Other settlements were at Narbata-Arruboth (Khirbet al-Hammam), Umm Rihan, Qasr el-Lejah, Qasr el-Haramiyye, Khirbet el-Buraq, Qarawat Bani Hassan, but only Narbata has been identified. The Hasmonean fortress at Alexandreion (Sartaba), on a mountain dominating the Jordan Valley at a strategic point, played an important role in the history of the Hasmoneans and the Herods.

The largest percentage of the population was Samaritan, though it cannot have been exclusively so. Strabo claims that the populations of Judea, Galilee, Jericho, Philadelphia, and Samaria-Sebaste were all "mixed stocks of peoples of Aegyptian and Arabian and Phoenician tribes."[27] He is obviously wrong both in his general characterization and in his more specific claim that Judeans were Egyptians! But his view—in the late first century BCE—that the populations of all the contiguous regions were mixed is important, though what that mixture was and how it altered between the Hasmonean period, the Herodian period, and the period of the Procurators cannot be clarified until there are many more detailed excavation results available, with sufficient data to distinguish between Samaritans and Jews.

GAULANITIS, BATANEA, AURANITIS, AND TRACHONITIS

Adjacent to Galilee on the east was Gaulanitis, some of which was Ituraean (see chap. 3).[28] Ancient Gaulanitis roughly corresponds to the modern Golan,

---

26. Magen, *NEAEHL* 4.1317–18.

27. Strabo, *Geog.* 16.2.34.

28. See Z. Ma'oz, N. Goren-Inbar, and C. Epstein, "Golan," *NEAEHL* 2.525–46; there are no corresponding surveys of the areas to the east and north. Still useful is G. A. Smith, *The Historical*

east of the Jordan and the Sea of Galilee and north to the slopes of Mount Hermon, bounded on the south and east by the Yarmuk and its tributaries. Most of the area is a basalt plateau covered by arable soil, punctuated by volcanic cones. Rainfall varies from 350 millimeters to 1,200 millimeters per year. The southern portion of the area is the most fertile, known for its oil, wine, and grain.

The road system in Gaulanitis was adequate: a north-south road ran from Panias down the east bank of the Jordan, past Lake Huleh, along the east side of the Sea of Galilee and then around the lake, or up to Gadara, or down the valley; an east-west road went through Bethsaida and Chorazin; an east-west road ran from Panias to Tyre in one direction and northeast to Damascus in another, or southeasterly through Batanea to Auranitis.[29] The roads around the lake and up to Panias and Damascus formed one of the major transportation routes in antiquity. Farther east, the King's Highway came north from Philadelphia and Gerasa to Damascus. A third, more informal, route ran southeasterly along the fault-line that forms the Wadi Sirhan, into the center of the Arabian Plateau.

Much of the area was uninhabited in the Persian and early Hellenistic periods, but beginning with the Seleucid victory at Panias growth was substantial (from 78 sites in the second century BCE, 33 of them Ituraean, to 108 in the first century CE). After the Syrian victory, as Damascus developed as a political and religious center, Gaulanitis's role changed. Populating the Golan improved the economic base and provided a defensive buffer; both factors increased in importance with Hasmonean control. Under both regimes, Gaulanitis was a frontier with a frontier's advantages and disadvantages.

Major settlements were few: Bethsaida-Julias on the northeast corner of the Lake (now being excavated), Gamla a few miles farther east on an easily defensible spur in a deep valley, Panias at the head waters of the Jordan on the lower slopes of Mount Hermon, Seleucia (Qusbiyye), and Hippos (Susita), the latter a Seleucid fortress but by the first century BCE part of the so-called Decapolis. Farther east in Batanea were Naveh and Dium.

An important feature of Gaulanitis, only now coming to light, is Ituraean culture in the Golan. They settled the area in the second century BCE, controlling for various periods Trachonitis, Mount Hermon, the northern Golan, and the Beka'a Valley in Lebanon (see chap. 3). In the early Roman period, while

---

Geography of the Holy Land (London: Hodder and Stoughton, 1902), pp. 540–47, 611–38. See also Schürer 2.10–15, who emphasizes the judaization of the regions and its dominant Jewish population (he points out that the Mishnah legislates for these areas in the second century CE: *m.Sheb.* 9.2; *m.Bik.* 1.10; *m.Taan.* 3.6; *m.Ket.* 13.10; *m.B.B.* 3.2; *m.Edu.* 8.7; *m.Men.* 8.3). He also discusses the Jewish organization of the regions east of the Jordan, 2:184–98.

29. Ma'oz et al., *NEAEHL* 2.537, gives information on the milestones found; these date to the second century CE mostly, but represent earlier road systems.

the region was coming under Herod's direct control, Ituraeans increased the number of their settlements. Typically these sites were small unwalled clusters of farmsteads, suggesting that despite their bad press in Josephus and other sources they were basically sedentary agriculturalists.[30] The early Roman period is best represented by Gamla, the city destroyed by Roman siege in 67 BCE. Gamla provides excellent evidence of a pre-destruction Jewish Golani town. It was planned and walled, with a coherent street system, terraced houses, a water system, one (or perhaps two) synagogues,[31] miqvaoth, and oil presses.

Beyond Gaulanitis lay Batanea, also an elevated plateau; its ancient name, the Bashan, meant "smooth or stoneless plain; fertile, fruitful."[32] Its broad, flat plains were suitable for cattle, agriculture—especially wheat (it was one of the important granaries of the Empire)—and timber. These factors made it suitable for large estates or for settling military veterans.[33]

Southeast of Batanea was Auranitis (the Hauran, Jebel Druze), a massive volcanic eruption that rises from the surrounding plateau to a height of 1,800 meters (5,900'). Rainfall (500–750 millimeters per year) and reasonably fertile volcanic soil meant that the regions around Canatha (Qanawat), Dionysias (Suweida), Bostra (Busra), and Salecah (Salkhad) were useful for agriculture, though their fields were filled with small stones and boulders, unlike Batanea.

North of Batanea and Auranitis lay Trachonitis (al-Leja; trachôn = "rough, rocky"), another volcanic area, but here characterized by innumerable small volcanic cones. It was inhospitable, not suited to settlement, though in places erosion created topsoil that washed into small valleys and depressions.[34] At a much later date, Philip the Arab came as Emperor from one corner of Trachonitis (he named Philippopolis [Shahbah] in his own honor).

Strabo refers to "the Trachones," perhaps meaning the Jebel Druze, for he describes it a "hilly and fruitful."[35] He then describes the Bekaʿa Valley as home

---

30. See Maʿoz et al., NEAEHL 2.535–36. Sixty-seven sites have been identified with distinctive Ituraean Golan Ware, all at elevations of 700 m or more, of which 33 sites were Hellenistic and 38 early Roman. Maʿoz provides a brief account of two of the three sites to have been excavated even on a limited basis: Horvat Zemel (with Ituraean pithoi, some with Greek inscriptions, dating from the second half of the second century BCE) and Horvat Namra (Roman period). In all, 143 early Roman sites have been identified. For critical comments on Maʿoz, see D. Urman, "Public Structures and Jewish Communities in the Golan Heights," in D. Urman and P. V. M. Flesher, eds., Ancient Synagogues: Historical Analysis and Archaeological Discovery, vol. 2 (Leiden: Brill, 1995), pp. 373–617, now the fullest assessment of Judaism in the Golan.

31. A lintel from another public building was discovered in the southwestern part of town.

32. See J. C. Slayton, "Bashan," ABD 1.623–24.

33. Herod settled Babylonian immigrant veterans in Batanea late in his reign; see B. Isaac, The Limits of Empire: The Roman Army in the East (Oxford: Clarendon, 1990), pp. 329–31. In the second century CE Judah ha-Nasi had a large estate in Batanea.

34. Herod settled Idumaean veterans in Trachonitis, not a very attractive reward for some of his own people.

35. Strabo, Geog. 16.2.16; he could mean some part of the Anti-Lebanon.

of the Ituraeans ("robbers," in 16.2.18), before returning his attention to Damascus, and "two Trachones, as they are called. And then, toward the parts inhabited promiscuously by Arabians and Ituraeans, are mountains hard to pass, in which there are deep-mouthed caves . . . " (16.2.20). This description applies best to Trachonitis and perhaps to Auranitis. When Josephus describes the region—he gives it only brief attention—he refers to it as having in his day a "mixed population of Jews and Syrians" (*War* 3.57).

It was legitimate, from the vantage point of Palestine, to think of these regions as a unit (which they were not). Gaulanitis and Batanea were immediately adjacent agricultural areas, useful for crops, raising cattle, and for natural resources such as timber. They had been part of biblical Israel (Bashan, Geshur), pieces of the kingdom of David acquired by conquest. Auranitis and Trachonitis, by contrast, were less useful except as buffers for defense. By incorporating this whole area into the kingdom, whether that of David or of Herod, Jews acquired an economically beneficial farmland, improved borders and, not insignificantly, control of the upper end of the Wadi Sirhan—perhaps the reason for the military settlements.[36] Between Trachonitis and the Anti-Lebanon mountains, particularly Mount Hermon, was an important trade route with Damascus and beyond it the rest of Syria, the fertile crescent, and Asia Minor.

PERAEA

Stretching along the Jordan River, south of Gaulanitis and Batanea (south of the Yarmuk River and Gadara), was Peraea (*peraios,* "on the other side"). Josephus describes it as follows:

> Peraea, though far more extensive [than Galilee], is for the most part desert and rugged and too wild to bring tender fruits to maturity. However, there, too, there are tracts of finer soil which are productive of every species of crop; and the plains are covered with a variety of trees, olive, vine, and palm being those principally cultivated. The country is watered by torrents which never dry up. . . . The northern frontier is Pella, . . . the western frontier is the Jordan; on the south it is bounded by the land of Moab, on the east by Arabia, Heshbonitis, Philadelphia and Gerasa.[37]

Josephus fails to mention Gadara which, along with Pella, formed Peraea's northern boundary. Since both *poleis* had their own territory, and since they

---

36. Herod's settlements sat between the end of the Wadi Sirhan and the international trade routes of the Damascus road system. They also, of course, protected pilgrims from Babylon on their way to Jerusalem (as Josephus says) and protected against Arab incursions.

37. *War* 3.44–47.

abutted each other, they blocked easy communication between Peraea and Galilee or Gaulanitis and Batanea. Like Galilee, Peraea was surrounded by Hellenistic cities: Scythopolis, Pella, Gadara, Gerasa, Philadelphia, and Heshbon.

The roads in Peraea completed several of the routes that have already been noted. The main north-south route was on the east side of the Jordan, though it did not go right to the Dead Sea but turned up to Philadelphia. A second main north-south route, the King's Highway, came from the Gulf of Aqabah and Petra through Heshbon, Philadelphia, Gerasa (Jerash), Adraa-Edrei (Dera), and on to Damascus. Jews would have used the Jordan valley road for most purposes. East-west roads came up to Gadara from both the Sea of Galilee and Pella, and thence to Capitolias, Adraa, and Bostra. Another road joined Scythopolis (Bet Shean), Pella, and Gerasa; farther south a road connected Neapolis-Shechem with Philadelphia; still farther south, a road joined Jerusalem with Philadelphia, through Jericho and Betharamphtha-Livias.

What Josephus says of Peraea's wild and desert areas is partly true, especially in some of its deep wadis and in the southern areas around the great fortress of Machaerus. But other parts were well watered both by rainfall and natural rivers,[38] and readily supported the agriculture to which he refers. The palms he describes were probably at the southern end of the valley opposite Jericho, as Pliny suggests, around Betharamphtha. Insufficient work has been done to give a clear picture of settlement patterns in Peraea.[39]

Across from Jericho were three sites in close proximity to each other where the ascent to Philadelphia began. Betharamphtha (Tell er-Rama), where Herod later built a palace (renamed both Livias and Julias),[40] Bethnamaris (Tell Nimrin, five miles north, mostly a late-Roman and Byzantine site, though with evidence of earlier occupation), and Abila (Khirbet Kefrein), about halfway between. Farther south on the Dead Sea was Callirrhoe (Zara), one of the great hot springs of antiquity with thirty-eight thermal water sources, where structures have been found from the late Hellenistic and early Roman periods.[41] This little corner of Peraea, off the beaten track, must have been a Peraean equivalent to

---

38. The Jordan valley rainfall is relatively small, varying from 380 mm in the north to 100 mm near the Dead Sea. In the hill country there is a good bit more: from 700 mm in northern Peraea to about 300 mm in southern Peraea.

39. R. G. Khouri, *The Antiquities of the Jordan Rift Valley* (Amman: Al Kutba, 1980), provides a useful summary of excavations. South of Pella at Tell es-Sa'idiyeh was a large Persian palace with a later Hellenistic fortress, still unidentified. Tell Deir 'Alla, a major site, was abandoned from the Hellenistic period onward. Tullul edh-Dhahab, still unidentified, was occupied in the Hellenistic and early Roman periods, with a casemate wall 5 m wide with 9 m square towers, six terraces, retaining walls, peristyles, and colonnades with Doric capitals. Extensive indications of iron smelting, using ore found a little farther east, were also found. The occupation of the site ended in the late first century BCE, possibly as a result of the earthquake of 31 BCE. See pp. 40–45, 51–54, 55–57.

40. Schürer 2.176–78.

41. Khouri, *Antiquities*, pp. 75, 86, 87–88.

Jericho with its royal palaces, palms and estates. Machaerus, the most important Hasmonean fortress east of the Jordan, was above Callirrhoe; it marked the southern end of Peraea, defending the Nabatean border. In the hill country Gedora (es-Salt),[42] Amathus (Tell 'Ammata?), and Ragaba (Rajib) were the most significant settlements.[43]

In Israelite times this was Gilead, famous for its "balm" (a resin of a pine or fir tree, perhaps from the Ajlun area).[44] The area was inhabited by Jews, especially the tribes of Reuben and Gad; by the late Hellenistic period the area must have had a mixed population of Jews, Greeks, Nabateans and other Arabs, and descendants of the Ammonites (see map 1).

The most remarkable Jewish structure in the area is Araq al-Amir in the Wadi es-Sir (west of Amman), a Tobiad palace with surrounding pool, other support structures, and caves (one of which has an inscription reading "Tobiah").[45] Some of the Tobiads were opposed to Jerusalem authorities in the Second Temple period.[46] Their palace, decorated with massive lions at the corners of the eaves and others at ground level, shows a late-third century BCE Jewish palatial residence, influenced by Hellenistic canons of taste but still functioning within Judaism. It is the only such structure that survives. Some of the surrounding Jewish population in Peraea may have followed a similar accommodation with Hellenism, though this is uncertain.

Peraea was home to many Jews in the early Roman period; it was a natural part of Herod's original kingdom in 40 BCE, along with Galilee, Judea and Idumaea, the four most heavily Jewish areas of Palestine. When it was later paired with Galilee as Herod Antipas's tetrarchy, it combined two areas with similar backgrounds and makeups.

CONCLUSION

These areas, with some coastal and Decapolis cities, formed Herod's kingdom at its greatest extent. Each region had natural advantages and economic benefits; each was part of "greater" Israel, historically identified as Israel a millennium earlier. Perhaps the near coincidence of Herod's kingdom with David's was not an accident of unrelated decisions by Augustus but the result of deliber-

---

42. Schürer 2.134, n.250, distinguishes Gedora from Gadara, no doubt correctly.

43. *War* 1.86, 89, 170; *Ant.* 13.356, 374; 14.91, re Amathus, its takeover by Alexander Jannaeus, destruction, and status as capital of a district under Gabinius. See *Ant.* 13.398 re Ragaba.

44. R. N. Jones, "Balm," *ABD* 1.573–74.

45. The structure is often referred to as a Jewish temple; this is impossible and the conviction that it is a palace has won the day.

46. Tobiads appear in the Lachish Ostraca, in the Zenon Papyri, in Josephus (*Ant.* 11.4); they were connected with the Oniad high priests and supported the Ptolemies—clearly a family to be reckoned with.

ate lobbying by Herod to have the borders extended so as to embrace areas heavily Jewish—or at least thought to have been—with no area beyond the historic limits. The original gift to Herod of Judea, Idumaea, Galilee, and Peraea was a foundation for later grants predicated on Herod's continued loyalty to Augustus, his ability to govern Jews effectively, and his demonstrated commitment to Rome's policies.

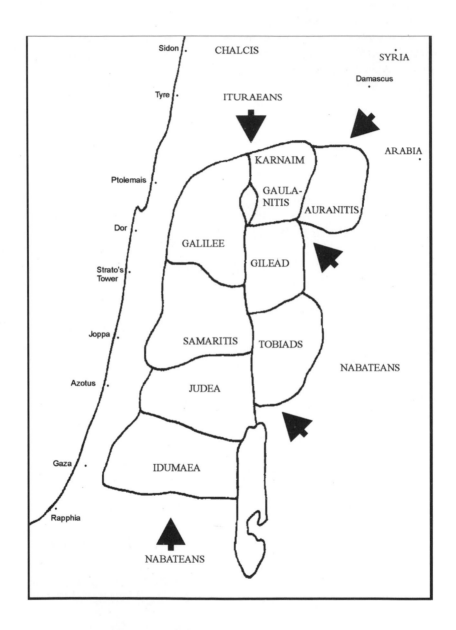

Map 1. Late Hellenistic and Pre-Hasmonean Palestine

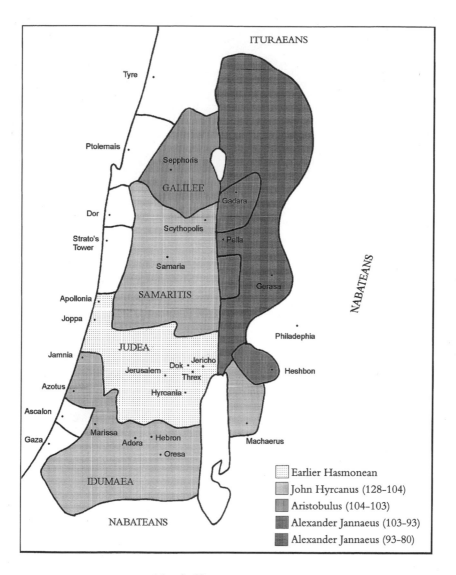

ITURAEANS

Tyre

Ptolemais

Sepphoris

GALILEE

Gadara

Dor

Scythopolis

Strato's
Tower

Pella

Samaria

SAMARITIS

Gerasa

Apollonia

Joppa

Philadephia

JUDEA

Jamnia

Dok · Jericho
Jerusalem · Threx

Heshbon

Azotus

Hyrcania

Ascalon

Gaza

Marissa

Adora · Hebron

Machaerus

· Oresa

NABATEANS

IDUMAEA

NABATEANS

	Earlier Hasmonean
	John Hyrcanus (128–104)
	Aristobulus (104–103)
	Alexander Jannaeus (103–93)
	Alexander Jannaeus (93–80)

Map 2. Hasmonean conquests

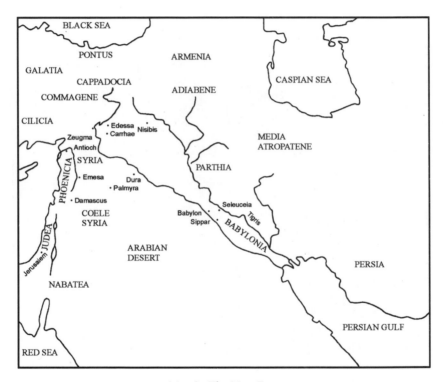

Map 3. The Near East

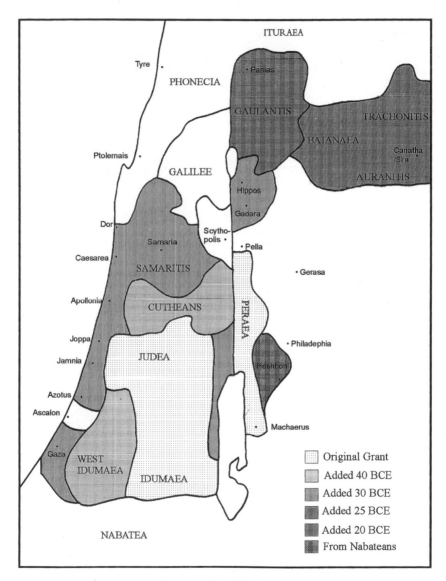

Map 4. Herod's kingdom

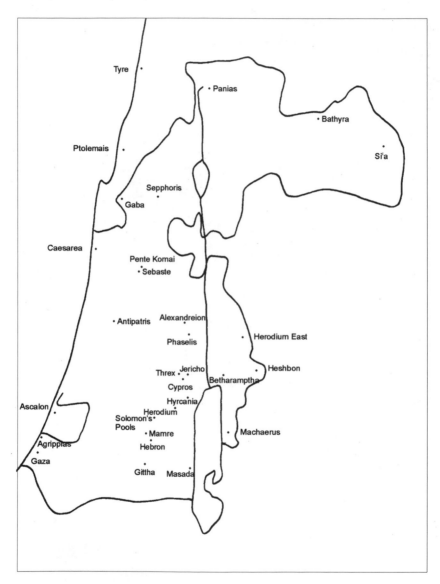

Map 5. Herod's building activity in his own regions

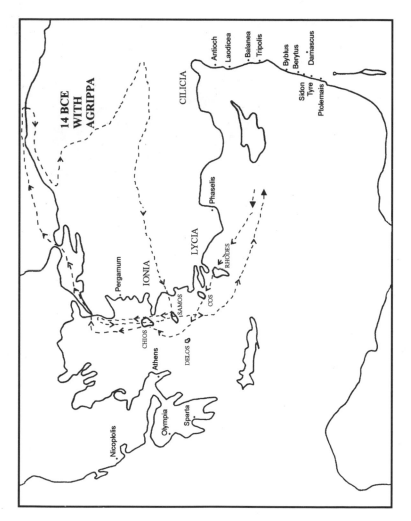

Map 6. Herod's building activity outside Judea, with the route of his expedition in 14 BCE with Marcus Agrippa

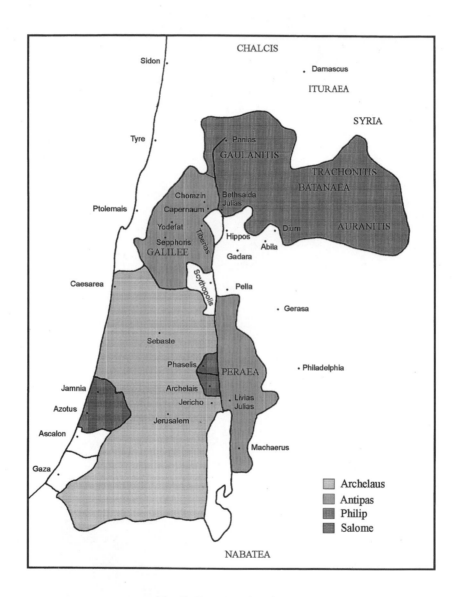

Map 7. Post-Herodian divisions

CHAPTER 7

From Rome to Rhodes
(40–30 BCE)

UP TO JERUSALEM: THE FIRST SEASON'S CAMPAIGN

Herod landed in Ptolemais in early 39 BCE, at about the same time that Ventidius was rolling back the Parthians. Antigonus's position as an ally of the Parthians was extremely tenuous, but the large degree of autonomy vested in Roman generals and their financial cupidity in looking after their own interests eroded Herod's efforts to fulfill the Senate's mandate. Herod was in a strong position with Antony waking from his military slumbers. The Parthians under Pacorus and Labienus (both would soon be dead) were in retreat, and Antigonus was on a limb that was about to be sawn off. Herod's first problem was the safety of his family members holding out in Masada.

Ptolemais (Acco), the only harbor with easy access to his territory, had never been a part of Israel (see chap. 6), but it was a customary entry point. From Ptolemais Galilee was open, and this was territory over which Herod had had control since 47 BCE. There he raised an army: some of his own men were loyal and available, others hitched themselves to Herod's rising fortunes, and numbers of non-Jews gathered to his standard. This army, "a not inconsiderable force of both foreigners and his countrymen,"[1] must have taken time to muster; in the meantime Antony, perhaps concerned about Ventidius and Silo's[2] non-cooperation, sent Dellius as his personal representative to assist Herod. Dellius was only partly successful, for when Ventidius and Silo later had an opportunity

---

1. *Xenôn te hama kai homophylôn: Ant.* 14.394; *War* 1.290.

2. Not further identified by Josephus, but referred to by Livy (*Periochae*) and Cassius Dio (48.41) as Peppedius or Poppaedius or Pompedius Silo. A Poppaedius Silo, Imperator of a northern group of rebels in the social war, defeated and killed Caepio in 90 BCE and Cato in 89, but was himself killed in 88. He could be grandfather to this Silo.

to rescue Herod's family (they had reached Jerusalem with a modest force) they failed to act, choosing instead to extort substantial sums from Antigonus (*War* 1.288–89; *Ant.* 14.392–93).[3]

In this first summer (39 BCE) Herod concentrated on Galilee, Ventidius put down local urban resistance (where is not specified), and Silo enjoyed Antigonus's hospitality in Jerusalem. Herod's Galilean campaign was successful; all but a few militants, says Josephus (too optimistically, as events unfolded), came to Herod's side. His base in his old territory was sufficiently solid that he turned to Masada and the relief of his family. Now a natural route from Galilee to Masada would have been down the Rift Valley—it was direct, straightforward, and had good roads most of the way—but it had been heavily fortified by the Hasmoneans, and all those fortresses (Agrippina[?], Alexandreion, Docus, Threx, Hyrcania, and Machaerus) were still occupied by soldiers loyal to Antigonus. Herod, therefore, had to take the Via Maris down the coast. The Via Maris had the advantage of a mostly neutral coastline, better roads, Idumaean reinforcements who might join him along the way, and Jerusalem would be in reach if that were feasible. Herod's main obstacle was Joppa (Yafo), the port left to Judea in the Pompeian and Gabinian settlements of 63 and 55 BCE (*War* 1.292; *Ant.* 14.396). As Herod approached Joppa, Silo left Jerusalem to join him, though Herod had to rescue Silo from a pursuing Jewish force; together they took Joppa.

With this success many more "country-folk" (*epichôrioi*) joined Herod (*War* 1.293; *Ant.* 14.398), enlarging his army considerably.[4] He moved south and east—bypassing Jerusalem and keeping as much as possible in Idumaea—and successfully relieved the siege of Masada, rescuing his family. On the way back he took Oresa (Khirbet Khoreisa, south of Hebron),[5] then marched up to Jerusalem where he was again joined by Silo. The show of force at Oresa attracted still more from Jerusalem to come over to his side (*War* 1.294; *Ant.* 14.399–400). Taking up a position on the west side of the city he proclaimed his good intentions and declared a general amnesty, even for his most vigorous enemies. Antigonus issued a counter-proclamation (*Ant.* 14.403–4; contrast *War* 1.296),

---

3. Josephus fails to integrate Ventidius and Silo adequately into his accounts. He has them in Jerusalem and extorting money from Antigonus before Herod lands, and then Dellius winning their cooperation. But in 39, at about this time, Ventidius was still dealing with Labienus; his march through Syria, and the opportunity to make a foray to Jerusalem, must have come only after Herod had landed. Thus even after Dellius was active on Herod's behalf at Antony's orders, Ventidius was still guilty of double-dealing. See also N. C. Debevoise, *A Political History of Parthia* (Chicago: University of Chicago Press, 1938), pp. 114–16; briefly in Schürer 1:282–83.

4. Some reinforcements were Idumaeans acting "out of friendship with his father," some joined "because of his reputation," some "for benefits received," but most "because of the hopes which they placed in him." These were additions to "all the Galilee" who joined Herod (*War* 1.292; *Ant.* 14.396).

5. See Abel, *Géographie* 2.350; Aharoni and Avi-Yonah, *Atlas,* p. 22.

arguing that even if he were deposed the kingship ought to have been given to someone of the royal family;[6] Herod, Antigonus said, was a commoner, an Idumaean, and a half-Jew (see chap. 2).

Winter was approaching (39/38 BCE), and Silo, showing his venality again, urged his troops to demand food, money, and winter quarters. Herod tried to prevent going to winter quarters, claiming the authority of Antony, Octavian, and the Senate. He foraged for food immediately and got supporters in Samaritis to bring supplies to Jericho.[7] But then, presumably because of Antigonus's successes, Herod changed his plans, dismissed the Romans to winter quarters in Idumaea, Galilee, and Samaritis, while his brother Joseph occupied other parts of Idumaea with the remaining forces.[8] Herod left his family in Samaria and went to Galilee to mop up, while Antigonus bribed Silo (*War* 1.302; *Ant.* 14.412) to quarter some troops in Lydda (Lod) in order to weaken Herod's position and show Antony how congenial he could be.

Failing to take Jerusalem must have been a cruel disappointment; both right and might had been on his side. Antigonus was vulnerable, though he still hoped, no doubt, that Parthia might reinforce him (*War* 1.289; *Ant.* 14.393). Without reinforcement, given Herod's Roman assistance, Antigonus's forces were strong enough only to sally from the walls but not enough to attack Herod directly. Breaking off the siege was a bitter decision, necessitated mainly by Silo's playing a double game with Antigonus. "And so the Romans put aside their arms and lived on the fat of the land" (*Ant.* 14.412).

It was a hard winter. Herod pushed on to Sepphoris in a heavy snowstorm, only to find that Antigonus's soldiers had abandoned it, though it was fully provisioned. So Herod proceeded against "brigands" occupying caves at Arbela (see chap. 10), though it is unclear whether these were all social brigands (as Josephus implies) or if they included soldiers from Sepphoris (since what Josephus describes sounds like a coherent military action; *War* 1.304–307; *Ant.* 14.413–17). Whatever the case, Herod was not entirely successful, for some "brigands" continued to hide in the caves.

Herod finally allowed his soldiers to take winter quarters after paying them

---

6. Josephus claims that Antigonus said there were many other suitable family candidates who "were priests." He must have had in mind Aristobulus III, his nephew, though at *Ant.* 14.489 Josephus refers to Herod's worry that Antigonus, if left alive after his defeat, might argue for his sons ruling in his place. If Josephus is correct, Antigonus staked his family's claim on their innovative linking of inherited priesthood and assumed kingship.

7. He was encamped on the west side of Jerusalem, so Jericho was not a natural place to camp. Antigonus may have controlled the roads between Samaria and Jerusalem; Herod intended to maintain the siege but to quarter most of his soldiers in Jericho over the winter. By this time Samaritis had been added to his territory; Appian, *Civil Wars* 5.75.

8. "To prevent any insurrection in favour of Antigonus," *War* 1.303. See chap. 3 for the significance and extent of Idumaean inclusion into Judea.

half a year's wages.[9] Silo fared less well; Antigonus cut off his supply of food and ordered the nearby inhabitants to move to the hills with all their supplies. To relieve the Romans' distress, Herod sent his youngest brother Pheroras to obtain supplies for Silo's troops.[10] Pheroras also used the winter to refortify Alexandreion, which had been abandoned and destroyed by Antigonus's soldiers.

Meanwhile Antony had roused himself.[11] Ventidius (late 39 BCE) triumphed over the Parthians and killed Labienus, the treasonous Roman.[12] As Ventidius reoccupied Syria he sent for Silo and Herod, anticipating a renewed Parthian campaign in the spring of 38 BCE, though first they were to complete the actions against Antigonus (War 1.309; Ant. 14.420). Herod seized the opportunity to be rid of Silo and sent him off. The Roman campaign was successful, though Herod missed it all; Pacorus was killed in the battle of Gindarus (9 June 38), northeast of Antioch-on-the-Orontes.[13]

Before joining Ventidius, Herod eliminated the remaining "brigands" in the Arbela caves (War 1.309–13; Ant. 14.421–30), a famous incident that can still be reconceived in the mind's eye today when standing above the cliffs. Herod combined ruthless efficiency and brilliant strategy, lowering soldiers in cages from above rather than attacking from below. Thinking the Galilean troubles over, Herod and his army hoped to face Antigonus in Samaritis for a decisive engagement. But the commander Herod left behind in Galilee was overwhelmed by an uncoordinated combination of brigands (who fled to the Huleh marshes) and tag-ends of Antigonus's soldiers (who fled to fortified places, probably Keren Naftali). So Herod again had to break off his main campaign against Antigonus to wipe out his opponents in Galilee; he fined the cities that had been sympathetic to their plight.[14]

UP TO JERUSALEM: THE SECOND SEASON'S CAMPAIGN

Following his victory over Pacorus (summer, 38 BCE), Ventidius sent Machaeras with two legions and a thousand cavalry to assist Herod (War 1.317;

---

9. Roughly one denarius a day; Herod paid them 150 denarii.

10. Ant. 14.418–19 is the more logical of Josephus's two accounts. The alternative (War 1.308) has Pheroras in charge of Herod's own commissariat. Both could be correct.

11. See Plutarch's account, Antony 33, of the tension between Antony and Octavian, Antony's reconciliation with his wife, the birth of a daughter, their wintering in Athens.

12. On Labienus, Schalit, Anh. VII, pp. 759–61.

13. War 1.317; Ant. 14.434; Plutarch, Antony 34; Cassius Dio says it was the same day fifteen years earlier that Crassus was killed. See Sullivan, Near Eastern Royalty, pp. 309–13.

14. The brigands in these actions fit well the notion of socially and economically disadvantaged Galileans who had lost lands and livelihood (see further chap. 10). The support of cities is one of the features that has led recent scholars to emphasize their social character (see War 1.314–16; Ant. 14.431–33).

Ant. 14.434). Herod should have been able to overcome Antigonus quickly, but Antigonus wrote Machaeras asking for his support, adding promises of a reward.[15] Machaeras rejected the bribe and went on his own to Jerusalem despite Herod's objections, was attacked by Antigonus and repulsed, forced to rejoin Herod at Emmaus (where Herod had moved, anticipating the coming campaign), and then angrily killed all Jews he met, including Herod's supporters.[16] Herod had been sold out once too often; enraged by Machaeras's betrayal he stormed off to see Antony, leaving his brother Joseph in charge. Though Machaeras pursued him and managed to calm him, Herod went to Samosata (Samsat) on the Upper Euphrates where Antony was fighting the Parthians. Herod probably saw Antony for more than one reason: to complain of Machaeras, to commit his support for Antony's campaign, and out of a desire to "display his courage" (*War* 1.321).[17] Though he exaggerates in praise of Herod, Josephus suggests that Herod contributed to Antony's war effort. Antony left Sossius in charge of Syria and left for Egypt;[18] Sossius, faithful to his instructions, sent two legions ahead with Herod into Judea and followed later himself.

The Parthian campaign occupied Herod's remaining summer campaign time. But disaster had struck in Judea. Joseph was inexperienced and exceeded Herod's orders; he took fresh but raw Roman soldiers and marched from Galilee to Jericho to gather grain. Antigonus ambushed these forces, cutting them to pieces, and decapitated Joseph. This left Galilee leaderless (Phasael was dead and Pheroras somewhere else), which triggered a peasant revolt against the nobility (*hoi dynatoi*),[19] in which Herod's supporters were drowned in the Sea of Galilee. Parts of Idumaea also revolted against Herod.[20]

Herod learned of these serious reverses as he paused in Daphne.[21] He marched south through Lebanon, where he was reinforced by a legion from Sossius and eight hundred "mountaineers" (probably Ituraeans),[22] and met the enemy near an unnamed fortress in Galilee, perhaps at Keren Naftali. After

---

15. According to *War* 1.317–18 Herod offered more money; *Ant.* 14.435 does not mention this. It is implausible that Herod should bribe Machaeras, who was there at Antony's explicit order and when Herod was king by the Senate's decision. See Schalit, pp. 93–94, and nn.136, 137.

16. *War* 1.319 refers to these as "Herodians" (*hoi Hêrôdeiôn*), reminiscent of the Herodians of the NT; see later (*War* 1.326; *Ant.* 14.450) "those of Herod" (*tous ta Hêrôdou*). The subsequent accounts differ in details; the main outline is clear.

17. *Ant.* 14.440–44 adds a highly encomiastic section, underscoring Herod's leadership and bravery, as a result of which he was greeted as "savior and protector" (*sôtêra kai prostatên*).

18. See Plutarch, *Antony* 34, re Sossius in Syria.

19. Another confirmation of the social reading of the brigands.

20. So *War* 1.326; *Ant.* 14.450 has Judea (probably the region between the two areas). The reference to Gittha in both texts may refer to a fortress in Idumaea.

21. According to *War* 1.328; *Ant.* 14.451, Herod had been informed of his brother's death in a dream.

22. There is no mention of Lysanias, Antigonus's ally, who held a substantial portion of the Beka'a Valley.

waiting out a heavy storm (early winter, 38–37 BCE), he was joined by Sossius's second legion. Antigonus's frightened forces evacuated the fortress without a fight (*War* 1.328–30; *Ant.* 14.451–53).[23] Herod hurried to Jericho where he intended to wreak vengeance. There he had a providential escape after a big dinner party when a roof collapsed and nearly killed him.[24] The following day he tried to engage the enemy in the fortresses guarding Jericho. When they withdrew Herod pursued them to Isana, putting himself between Jerusalem and a force under Pappus that had sallied into Samaritis to oppose Machaeras.[25] Herod laid several towns in the region to waste, prompting new recruits—many strongly opposed to Antigonus, some attracted by Herod's success, some merely wanting change (*War* 1.335). Herod would have marched straightaway on Jerusalem but for another severe storm. Josephus tells dramatically of another near-miraculous escape when Herod surprised some fully armed enemy soldiers (who had survived the battle) while almost alone at bath (*War* 1.340–41; *Ant.* 14.462–64).

A hard winter's campaign was almost over. Herod had fought his way a second time up to Jerusalem. By cutting the main road between Jerusalem and Samaria he had forced Pappus to engage him in a location of his own choosing or be stranded between his and Machaeras's forces in Samaritis. Antigonus blundered by making a feint into Samaritis; Herod had outwitted him, destroyed part of the enemy forces, and killed an experienced general.

Herod revenged his brother Joseph's death by sending the head of Pappus to Pheroras, to whom Pappus had sent Joseph's head. Having fought through most of the winter, Herod arrived at his capital in spring, 37 BCE.

THE BATTLE FOR JERUSALEM

Herod, like Pompey, approached the city from the north (*Ant.* 14.60; *War* 1.145). The Temple was protected on this side by a fosse cut into the bedrock, continuous with a small transverse valley that ran into the Kidron Valley to the east; above the fosse may have been the Baris—the Hasmonean fortress referred to often in the literature.[26] Only here was the ground outside the walls higher than the city within the walls, so it was a natural point of attack. In Roman fashion, Herod built earthen siege walls with towers at intervals and distributed his army around the whole city.

---

23. There are few Galilean fortresses, and no location is given. It may have been Agrippina (Jarmuth, site of Belvoir, the great Crusader fortress), or perhaps more plausibly the equally overlooked Hellenistic fortress of Keren Naftali, on the west side of the Huleh basin.

24. Josephus says this omen showed that Herod was a favorite of heaven (*War* 1.331; *Ant.* 14.455).

25. *War* 1.324 locates Herod's headquarters at Cana, but *Ant.* 14.450 is correct to say Isana, twenty miles north of Jerusalem. See Schalit, p. 96, n.141, and literature cited there.

26. See L. Ritmeyer, "Locating the Original Temple Mount," *BAR* 18 (1992): 24–45, 64–65.

In the midst of these preparations (probably in March) Herod went to Samaria to marry Mariamme, who was waiting there with other members of his family. Josephus's interpretation of this event, often accepted by critical scholars, is that Herod was contemptuous of his enemy (*War* 1.344), but it is not convincing. While Herod did expect to taste victory soon, the siege preparations were time-consuming and could be carried out by others more skilled than he at this aspect of warfare. An attack would not be ordered until all was prepared. A simpler and more convincing explanation of the Samaria trip is that Mariamme was now of marriageable age (see chap. 2). Herod had been divorced from Doris for almost five years.[27]

The promised reinforcements from Sossius appeared upon his return from his nuptials. The army now had two generals, eleven divisions of foot soldiers, six thousand cavalry, and an unspecified number of Syrian auxiliaries (*War* 1.345–46; *Ant.* 14.468–69). In an important aside Josephus adds (only in *Ant.* 14.469) that Antigonus had been declared an enemy of Rome, thus eliminating the possibility of Roman commanders self-interestedly dealing with Antigonus.

Though the details differ, *War* and *Antiquities* both convey vividly the atmosphere and the course of the attack: the zeal and bitterness of the defenders, the anxiety over the Temple, and prophetic expectations of deliverance. Herod pressed the siege, but the defenders countered by tunnelling under the siege works and harassing Herod's army (*War* 1.347–51; *Ant.* 14.470–75).[28] After six weeks, a specially picked group of soldiers scaled the walls and broke into the Temple precinct, at which time some of the stoas were burnt. Two weeks later they broke through the wall between the Temple and the Lower City (City of David). The last section of the city to be taken was the Upper City (Western Hill), though some priests were holed up in the Inner Court of the Temple maintaining daily sacrifice (*Ant.* 14.476–79; *War* 1.352).

Antigonus held out in the Baris.[29] When he emerged and threw himself at Sossius's feet (not Herod's!), Sossius made a bad pun and referred to him as

---

27. She was now between fifteen and seventeen years of age, a natural age of marriage in the Mediterranean world. The betrothal agreement would have set a date for marriage. Herod, anticipating a lengthy siege, seized a sensible opportunity. For confirmation of this calculation, see below for the age of Aristobulus. The claim in *War* 1.431–32 that he dismissed Doris and his son Antipater when he took the throne seems incorrect. Josephus also must be incorrect when he suggests that Mariamme brought trouble into his household before he came back from Rome, and that these troubles were exacerbated afterward. He ignores what he had argued more persuasively along the way, that the troubles began with Alexandra, Mariamme's mother.

28. In *Ant.* 14.475 Josephus refers to famine and a sabbatical year (see below for the date); it is probable that Josephus is correct when he says the sabbatical was the following year (37/36 BCE). His allusion reinforces the sense of difficulty under which the defenders worked.

29. A curious detail. Josephus implies and a reconstruction of the architectural history of the area suggests that the Baris was outside and north of the Temple precinct, near the main point of attack. If so, Antigonus was surrounded and cut off for some time.

Antigone,[30] though he treated Antigonus like an ordinary prisoner and put him in chains. The troops expected their usual booty after a siege, but Herod acted quickly to stop them. More importantly, according to Josephus, he stopped "his foreign allies" from seeing inside the sanctuary of the Temple (*War* 1. 354–55; *Ant.* 14.482–84). He paid the soldiers out of his own pocket, giving them their wages and something extra for the booty they failed to get. The siege ended in June of 37 BCE.[31] Sossius donated a golden crown to the Temple (*War* 1.357; *Ant.* 14.488), then took Antigonus to Antony at Antioch where he was executed.[32] Subsequently, Sossius was given the title Imperator and celebrated a triumph in Rome (3 September 34) for his Judean victory.[33]

---

30. Daughter of Oedipus and his wife—and mother—Jocasta; see Sophocles' *Antigone.*

31. On the date, see Schalit, Anh. IX, pp. 764–68 (August, 37 BCE); cf. Grant, p. 59 (August or September); Jones, p. 48 (July); Marcus, note (a) at *Ant.* 14.475 and note (d) at 14.480. The best solution is mid-37 BCE. Josephus refers at 14.475 to a famine and a sabbatical year (probably October 37—October 36 BCE; see *Ant.* 15.7), so Josephus is wrong in some of his calculations but right in his close association of the two events; he also dates the event twenty-seven years after Pompey's entry into Jerusalem (that is, 37 BCE, contra Marcus); at 14.487 Josephus gives the consuls (Marcus Agrippa and Cannius Gallus) in the 185th Olympiad (ended June 30, 37 BCE); he also suggests it was the fast day (*nêsteia,* the Day of Atonement) when the city fell, which fell on October 3 in 37 BCE; yet it was in the third month (implying the third month of the Olympiad, though that is manifestly impossible). As Schürer argues, 1.284–86 (n.11), it was probably the third month of the engagement and the fifth month of the siege. The two months or so difference would then be the period during which Herod celebrated his marriage in Samaria. The results: the army encircled the city in February, Herod was married in Samaria in March, he returned to Jerusalem in April, by which time Sossius was present, marching down from Syria at the beginning of the campaign season; the first wall was breached after forty days, sometime in late May, and the city was taken in June or July 37 BCE, after a siege of about five months.

Herod's coinage confirms the year 37 BCE for the conclusion of the siege. His "year three" coins were minted at the first opportunity after his victory. The third year from late 40/39 BCE is 37; the proposal that the third year should be reckoned from 42, when he was made tetrarch, is impossible, for that could hardly be celebrated as a royal appointment. His year three coins included some types similar to Antigonus's (tripod, palm branch), some were his own (helmets, shields, caduceus, pomegranate, aphlaston); all bore the legend in Greek "of Herod the king," similar to Antigonus's legend (also in Greek) "of Antigonus the king." All had a monogram, reminiscent of a Christian *chi-rho* symbol, that must have referred to the mint or mint-master. Sullivan, *Near Eastern Royalty,* p. 225, speculates that Herod "later abandoned this 'false' era and dated from his conquest of Antigonus, thus facilitating an amnesty and conciliating Jewish opinion." See further, Appendix B, chap. 8, below.

32. *Ant.* 14.489–90 claims that Herod still feared Antigonus, especially if he were given a hearing before the Senate and argued for his children taking precedence over Herod; so, says *Antiquities,* Herod bribed Antony to execute Antigonus. Cassius Dio claims (49.22) that he was crucified and had his throat slit; the earlier evidence says he was beheaded (Plutarch, *Antony* 36; Strabo, quoted in *Ant.* 15.9; *War* 1.357). The suggestion that this was unique in Roman history is not correct; what was unusual was carrying out the sentence without a decision of the Senate, though the Senate had already declared him an enemy of Rome.

33. See *PIR* 1 S 556; he minted a bronze coin at Zacynthus commemorating Judea's capture, see Grant, p. 59. Sossius was consul in 32 BCE; after verbally attacking Octavian in the Senate he

De facto power finally passed to Herod in mid-37; he had had the title "king" since late 40 BCE. (Josephus holds back from referring to Herod as king until 15.39 in *Antiquities* [though see 14.469], while in *War* he frequently refers to Herod as king or as *King Herod* since the incident in the bath at Isana [1.341]).[34] Kingship was now firmly Herod's; the Hasmoneans were effectively finished.[35] His first days in Jerusalem were spent in rewards and punishments. He destroyed Antigonus's supporters (only forty-five are mentioned) while he honored his own supporters, especially those who had espoused his cause while he was still a commoner (*War* 1.358; *Ant.* 15.1–7). He specially favored Pollion and Samaias the Pharisees,[36] one of whom had—as early as 47 BCE—predicted Herod's success and his eventual persecution of the elite (see chap. 3 and chap. 10).[37] Herod gave Antony money and valuables collected from among his dead and living opponents.

Any hope for continuing Hasmonean power lay in Hyrcanus II, Herod's old ally and patron (*Ant.* 15.11–17),[38] who had been held by the Parthians since his capture and disfigurement in 40 BCE. The new king of Parthia, Phraates IV (38–2 BCE), allowed Hyrcanus to live with the large Jewish community in Babylon where he received high honor because of his lineage and previous position as high priest and ethnarch.[39] Hyrcanus was anxious to return now that Herod was installed in Jerusalem; he anticipated repayment of favors he had done Herod. His Babylonian friends, however, urged him to stay, saying that his mutilation prevented his being high priest and that Herod was unlikely to be well-disposed.[40] But Herod wrote and promised a virtual share of the kingship;[41] his envoy Saramalla[42] took gifts to Phraates to get his cooperation. Josephus

---

fled to Antony with other senators. At Actium he commanded Antony's left wing, but following Antony's defeat he was pardoned.

34. Does this indicate a different source, perhaps even Herod's *Memoirs*? The story has a first-person ring to it; see also 1.349, 352, 354, 358.

35. *Ant.* 14.490–91, the concluding summary of book 14, underscores the accomplishments of the Hasmoneans as if Herod's story had been their story: it was a splendid house, occupied priestly offices, but it was marred by internal strife. Josephus is more interested in the Hasmoneans in *Antiquities*.

36. See Schalit, Anh. X, pp. 768–71.

37. If these were Shemaiah and Abtalion, as many think, it may be significant that both were proselytes.

38. *War* and *Antiquities* are relatively independent from here until *War* 1.387; *Ant.* 15.187. *Antiquities* has additional sources available, which Josephus has not integrated well, most of them having to do with Hasmoneans. On sources in *Ant.* 15–16, see S. J. D. Cohen, *Josephus in Galilee and Rome* (Leiden: Brill, 1979), pp. 53–57.

39. Sullivan, *Near Eastern Royalty*, pp. 314–18.

40. *War* 1.434 says, probably correctly, that Hyrcanus's countrymen had been instrumental in freeing him; it also reinforces the point made here, that they argued vigorously against his return.

41. *War* 1.434 suggests that Mariamme's marriage was also a factor.

42. Saramalla is described as the wealthiest man in all Syria. In 40 BCE, when he learned of the

adds that Herod invited Hyrcanus back only because he wanted Hyrcanus under his control (*Ant.* 15.18–20).

ALEXANDRA, CLEOPATRA, AND THE DEATH OF ARISTOBULUS III

Hyrcanus II left Parthia with Phraates' blessing and with financial help from the Jewish community; he returned to Jerusalem with full honors. The remaining Hasmoneans were reunited in Herod's household: Hyrcanus, his daughter Alexandra, his granddaughter Mariamme, his grandson Aristobulus III, and perhaps by now his first great-grandson by Herod and Mariamme. If Hyrcanus were unable to be high priest, because he was disfigured, then Aristobulus III— the nearest male relative of a previous high priest—should be, or so Alexandra argued, ignoring his age.[43] The minimum age for a high priest was not stipulated, but no contemporary evidence suggests the possibility of a priest, let alone a high priest, below the age of twenty.[44] Herod may have been justified in seeking another candidate. He selected Hananel, a member of a high priestly family from Babylon;[45] the simplest explanation is that Herod's choice derived from Hyrcanus's knowledge of the Babylonian community after his two-and-a-half-year stay there, and may have been on his advice (chap. 10). Herod could hardly have appointed someone without Hyrcanus's agreement.[46]

Alexandra took exaggerated offense at Herod's action; she asked Cleopatra to request the high priesthood for Aristobulus from Antony, a request he ignored (*Ant.* 15.23–24). Dellius, who had assisted Herod earlier, suggested that Alexandra have portraits of Mariamme and Aristobulus put before Antony as potential objects for sexual conquest to win Antony's support. What makes Josephus's account almost farcical is that Dellius was himself Antony's lover[47] and that Antony, despite his notorious sexual reputation, was too afraid of Cleopatra to act. Herod acted almost honorably: knowing fully his intentions, he told Antony that it was unwise to send Aristobulus, though Alexandra was

---

plans of Pacorus, Barzaphranes, and Antigonus to kill Hyrcanus and Phasael, he had advised them to flee.

43. Aristobulus was a younger brother of Mariamme's, who had recently become of marriageable age; Aristobulus was probably only fifteen or sixteen at this time. *Ant.* 15.29, 51, 56 refer to him as sixteen at this time, seventeen when appointed high priest, and not more than eighteen when he was drowned. These ages confirm the earlier calculation concerning Mariamme's age. Both were, as 15.25 puts it, "beautiful *children.*"

44. Schalit, pp. 101–102, esp. n.18; on priests in general, Schürer 2.243, nn.23–24; Sanders, *Judaism.*

45. *Ant.* 15.40; but in 15.21–23 he claims he was "a rather undistinguished priest from Babylon"; the former is likelier to be correct.

46. At *Ant.* 15.34 Herod claimed to have appointed Hananel only because of Aristobulus's youth.

47. Cassius Dio 49.39.

willing, because revolution might break out at his absence, since people hoped he would overturn Herod (*Ant.* 15.25–30)![48] All of this would play well on an operatic stage.

These early days revealed a pattern of family rivalry. (1) Herod accused Alexandra (and Cleopatra) of plotting against him; his consultations on the matter suggest a semblance of orderly government, though we have no indication of its form. (2) The honor and dishonor of family members were important, suggesting that family relationships were strained (see also *Ant.* 15.44). (3) Almost penitently, Alexandra backed down, satisfied with Herod's proposed course of action, and denied designs on royal power, of which no hint has yet been given.[49] (4) At the same time that Alexandra is portrayed as a culpable, scheming "royal," Herod is pictured more as sinned against than sinning; Josephus's unflattering portrait of Alexandra carries some conviction. (5) At the conclusion of the consultation all the players got something from the reconciliation: Aristobulus III got the high priesthood, though he was only seventeen,[50] Alexandra got increased honor from her son's new role, Mariamme got the satisfaction of her brother's appointment, and Herod got, as he thought, peace in the family (*Ant.* 15.31–41, cf. 42).

The reconciliation was superficial. Herod still feared Alexandra and so confined her to her palace where a watch was kept on her. She wrote again to Cleopatra, who urged her to come to Egypt with Aristobulus. Alexandra and Aristobulus left Jerusalem in coffins (anticipating ben Zakkai's escape from Jerusalem in 67 or 68 CE), intending to get to Alexandria.[51] Herod knew of the plot, let them proceed, then caught them red-handed. He took no immediate action, in part because, as Antony's paramour, Cleopatra was very powerful.[52]

Herod could no longer ignore the threat to his throne. He was prompted

---

48. The least believable part of this whole account is Herod's excuse to Antony, though behind Josephus's statement may lie Herod's concern that Aristobulus was a focus for others' aspirations to overturn him.

49. This is not as farfetched as it might seem (subsequent events reinforce the idea), for Alexandra's grandmother and namesake sat successfully on the throne for nine years and her friend Cleopatra currently occupied Egypt's throne successfully, so successfully that Herod feared their designs. Why should Alexandra not aspire to the throne as the daughter of Hyrcanus II and widow of Alexander (and thus daughter-in-law of Aristobulus II)?

50. Herod deposed Hananel, no doubt arguing publicly that his appointment had only been temporary, while he held it open for Aristobulus. The degree of offense in the deposition to which Josephus refers (he offers two previous examples, Onias III and Hyrcanus II himself) depended on the legitimacy of Hananel's appointment (Was he really from a high priestly family? Could he claim legitimacy equal to or better than the Hasmoneans?) and on the validity of Aristobulus's appointment (Was he of an appropriate age?). These questions admit no easy solutions.

51. Schalit, p. 110, n.47: "literarische Züge."

52. In passing Josephus offers Cleopatra's possible intervention on behalf of Alexandra as explanation, the first time that he suggests a serious breach in the relationship between Herod and Cleopatra; previously in 40 BCE she had asked him to become one of her military commanders.

to act by the evidence of Aristobulus's popularity at Tabernacles in 35 BCE. Once the festival was over the royal party left Jerusalem for the Hasmonean palace in Jericho, which Herod must have allowed Alexandra to retain.[53] As the young people frolicked in the huge swimming pool (observable today in the excavations), Aristobulus was drowned at Herod's orders (*Ant.* 15.50–56; *War* 1.437).[54] There was widespread mourning, but none matched Alexandra's grief; his death was a threat to her and meant that her grand design to replace Herod could not be carried out. She held her grief to herself and plotted revenge while Herod made a show of emotion and laid on a lavish funeral (*Ant.* 15.57–61).[55]

Once again Alexandra appealed to Cleopatra, at whose urging Antony[56] told Herod to answer charges of murder or conspiracy in Laodicea in Syria, a summons Herod could not refuse.[57] Leaving Joseph in charge,[58] with instructions to kill Mariamme if he should not survive his meeting with Antony, Herod went off.[59] As in a Shakespearian tragedy, Josephus's readers are permitted to see trouble brewing before it happens: Joseph revealed Herod's instructions to Mariamme; Herod's foes started a rumor that he had been tortured and executed; and Alexandra persuaded Joseph that they should flee to the Roman legion left guarding Jerusalem.[60] Her hopes for power were again dashed[61] when a letter from Herod arrived stating that, despite Cleopatra's arguments, Antony had cleared him and showered him with honor by inviting him to dine with him and to sit with him in judgment. Though Antony rebuffed Cleopatra and told her not to meddle in others' affairs, and though he refused to give her

---

53. *Ant.* 15.53, *tês Alexandras*.

54. The version in *War* is secondary. It does not mention the circumstantial details and claims (anachronistically) that Aristobulus was drowned by Gauls, though Herod had not yet inherited Cleopatra's Gaulish bodyguard.

55. In *War* 1.436–37 Herod's main antagonist is not Alexandra but her daughter Mariamme; Josephus presents there the standard picture of Herod consumed by his love for Mariamme, while she was consumed by her hatred of him—a hatred prompted both by his execution of her grandfather Hyrcanus and the drowning of her brother Aristobulus III.

56. Antony was now in Egypt (35–34 BCE) and on his way to invade Armenia and Parthia in 34 BCE. On the date, Schürer 1.288–89, n.5.

57. He rightly feared Cleopatra's malign influence on Antony: she "had never ceased doing her best to make Antony his enemy" (*Ant.* 15.65).

58. Not Herod's uncle but his brother-in-law, husband of Salome, as *Ant.* 15.81 has correctly; I take it that this is a duplicate, set later, of the same incident. Cf. also, correctly, *War* 1.441–42, where Josephus emphasizes Joseph's loyalty.

59. There is a strong parallelism between this account and a later one, with which there must be overlap and confusion (see below, chap. 9). The instructions about Mariamme do not fit as well here as later.

60. An important detail not noted elsewhere; three years after winning Jerusalem there was still a legion either helping Herod keep control or helping Antony keep Herod under the thumb.

61. "Through [Antony] they might recover the throne and so lack for nothing which it was proper for those of royal birth to have" (the plural links Mariamme and Alexandra together in the scheme, though the previous clause makes it clear that Alexandra was the initiator).

Judea, he did give her Coele-Syria,[62] the coastal plain, and Jericho (see *Ant.* 15.96).[63]

Herod's letter made Alexandra abandon her flight to the Romans. But another subplot emerged. Herod's sister Salome, who knew the details through her husband Joseph, who was in charge, along with Herod's mother Cypros, told Herod about Alexandra's plans. Salome accused her husband Joseph of adultery with Mariamme, which Mariamme vigorously denied.[64] Herod and Mariamme fought and made up, fell out again, and were reconciled again. Herod had Joseph executed and had Alexandra confined under guard (15.87).[65]

THE NABATEAN WAR

Having obtained substantial additional territories from Antony—who acted as a despot able to dispose of lands and peoples as he wished[66]—Cleopatra accompanied him on his campaign as far as the Euphrates, then returned via Apamea, Damascus and Judea.[67] Herod negotiated a lease-back (at the substantial

---

62. This term continues to confuse. To confuse matters further, it is not clear whether *Ant.* 15.79 and 92–95 are aspects of the same incident or not. In 79 she gets Coele-Syria, perhaps Chalcis in the Beka'a valley (so Marcus); in 92 she passed through Syria, accused Lysanias (of Chalcis) and had him killed. At the same time she asked for Arabia and Judea, but did not get all she wanted, only coastal cities south of the Eleutherus River (most of these were not in Herod's possession anyway; one or two may have been in Arabian territory). The likeliest reading is that there was one transfer of land, not two, that it comprised two separate but contiguous tracts: Chalcis, now that Lysanias was dead, and several coastal cities (probably Ptolemais, Dor, Strato's Tower, Joppa, Azotus, Ashkelon, and Gaza. Plutarch helps to clarify matters: "Phoenicia, Coele Syria and a large part of Cilicia . . . and the region which produces balsam and the coastal strip of Arabia Nabatea which stretches down to the Red Sea" (*Antony* 36). In 30 BCE Herod got many of these back from Augustus.

When Josephus says (*War* 1.440) that Cleopatra caused the deaths of both Lysanias and Malichus, king of Nabatea, he is not altogether accurate, for Malichus (56–28 BCE) seems to have survived Mariamme's death.

63. Jones, p. 49: the "first step in programme was to restore the empire of the Ptolemies to its ancient limits . . . "; similarly, Perowne, pp. 67–68.

64. *War* 1.438 puts matters differently. Herod "was paralyzed by his infatuation" with Mariamme, who was abusive to Salome and Cypros. They then charged Mariamme with three offenses: adultery, sending her portrait to Antony, and exposing herself to an unnamed person "powerful enough to resort to violence." All this happened prior to Herod's going to Laodicea.

65. See also *War* 1.441–44, with much the same story, though a different ending; *Ant.* 15.185–221, with Soemus, not Joseph, as the protagonist. Fuller discussion in chap. 9.

66. Plutarch, *Antony* 36: "The gift of these territories aroused deep resentment among the Romans. In the past Antony had bestowed tetrarchies and even the sovereignty of great peoples upon private individuals: he had deprived many rulers of their kingdoms, as for example Antigonus. . . . but nothing caused so much offence to his own countrymen as the shame of these honours conferred upon Cleopatra."

67. Antony's Parthian campaign was successful, especially its Armenian extension. Archelaus of Cappadocia received Lesser Armenia for his assistance.

sum of two hundred talents per year) of his own Jericho estates and (unspecified) parts of Arabia that were a part of Antony's gift to Cleopatra.[68] Jericho was
economically important to Herod because of trade in its balsam sap (used as a
headache and eyesight remedy)[69] and palm wine (which was exported as far as
Italy).[70] Such an arrangement was offensive to both Herod and Malichus and
helped to destabilize the region.

While Herod accompanied Cleopatra through Judea to her own border,
she tried to seduce him, according to Josephus (*Ant.* 15.97: "she was by nature
used to enjoying this kind of pleasure without disguise"). Josephus is unsure
whether her motive was passion or a complicated trap.[71] But Herod was not
interested, for his attitude toward her had changed; he was considering whether
to assassinate her—partly for revenge and partly to help Antony, even if Antony
did not know he needed this kind of help. Herod's friends advised him against
such dangerous plans, since Cleopatra was the most powerful woman of her
time and Antony was still in love with her (*Ant.* 15.101). So Herod simply
slipped away from her seduction and escorted her back to Pelusium, all the
while courting her with gifts (*War* 1.362–63; *Ant.* 15.103).

Following his Parthian-Armenian campaign Antony and Octavian's pact
began to fall apart,[72] with both sides preparing for war (33/32 BCE). We have
relatively poor information about the Middle East in this period, though there
were internal tensions in Judea and external problems with Nabatea.[73] To judge
from Josephus's accounts, Herod may have been guilty of some sharp dealing
in the leaseback arrangements (*War* 1.362; *Ant.* 15.96, 106–7). As the prime
lessee of the Jericho and Nabatean tracts of land, he paid Cleopatra two hundred
talents per year; he sublet the Nabatean territory back to Malichus and—if Josephus is accurate at this point—charged him two hundred talents per year. If so,
Herod got Jericho for nothing (15.107).[74] Malichus paid the requisite rent at

---

68. Herod then sublet the Arabian territory back to Malichus; *Ant.* 15.107.

69. Strabo, *Geog.* 16.763; Pliny, *NH* 12.111; cf. Schürer 1.298–300, n.36.

70. The two-hundred-talent rental (see also later) equalled half Herod's total income in 4 BCE
from all of Judea, Samaritis, and Idumaea, or the total income of Galilee and Peraea.

71. Josephus puts the uncertainty over motive in Herod's mind as well (*Ant.* 15.98).

72. Plutarch, *Antony* 37–52, has a vigorous account, including a good description of the hardships of winter campaigning (winter, 34/33 BCE); for the changing relationship between Antony
and Octavian, see *Antony* 53–60.

73. A small aside in *War* 1.364 hints at disturbances in Judea through the 30s. Josephus implies
that Herod did not capture the old Hasmonean fortress of Hyrcania until the outbreak of hostilities
between Antony and Octavian (it had been held by a sister of Antigonus's, about whom we otherwise know nothing). This suggests that Herod was not as successful as Josephus's sources claimed
and not as ruthless as his critics have argued. At about this time, according to later evidence, Herod
was faced with the defection of his brother-in-law, Costobar, who tried to go over to Cleopatra
and take Idumaea with him.

74. This interpretation, which seems plausible in view of the main accounts, may be called
into question later by *Ant.* 15.132, where Herod claims that each of he and Malichus had to pay

first, but then, as Antony and Cleopatra's position became less secure, he stopped. By 32/31 BCE relations were as strained between Malichus and Herod as they were between Antony and Octavian.

Herod intended to join Antony for the final showdown with Octavian (*Ant.* 15.109), but Antony told Herod to deal with Malichus first, about whom he had heard from both Herod and Cleopatra (*Ant.* 15.110). Cleopatra, however, was playing each side against the other, expecting to come out ahead whoever won the struggle (*War* 1. 365; *Ant.* 15.110). Cleopatra actually favored the Nabatean king, quite understandably, for if Malichus—and Antony—won she would get Judea, Samaritis, and Galilee, a preferable arrangement because her territory would then approximate the old Ptolemaic holdings, since she already controlled the coastal cities, Phoenicia, Chalcis (perhaps with other parts of Coele-Syria), and much of the Cilician coast lands, together with Cyprus. There may have been a grand design behind her strategy, though how much Herod discerned is uncertain.[75] He had to deal with one matter at a time, and his first priority, both in his own mind and in Antony's, was to deal with Malichus.

After several feints, Herod grappled with the Nabatean army at Dium.[76] His first international venture was successful, and he was well placed for a second victory as he moved across Batanea into Auranitis, where he met the Nabatean forces again, at Canatha (Qanawat). Herod was preparing a military encampment in good cautious Roman fashion when his soldiers—perhaps junior officers (*War* 1.369)—urged him to attack right away.[77] Herod was on the verge of success when Athenion, a general of Cleopatra's who had appeared neutral but actually favored the Nabateans,[78] intervened with Canathan soldiers (*War* 1.367; *Ant.* 15.116). The strengthened opposition turned Herod's victory into a slaughter;[79] Herod himself escaped to get reinforcements— reinforcements too few and too late. The most he was able to do was to conduct

---

two hundred talents; in years when Malichus defaulted Herod would, on this view, have had to pay four hundred talents. I think this unlikely: Josephus could have said it just that simply had he believed this. The amount is so large (the equal of the total income of Judea, Samaritis, and Idumaea) that Herod would quickly have gone broke. Jones, p. 50, assumes that the total was four hundred talents, but ignores the comparative data, as does Perowne, pp. 74–76.

75. In a speech, Herod claims (*Ant.* 15.131) that only his friendship with Antony protected the Nabateans from becoming slaves of Cleopatra. "Antony was careful not to take any measure that might seem suspect to us." He admits in the same place to having managed the leaseback arrangement.

76. Both *War* 1.366 and *Ant.* 15.111 say "Diospolis," but almost certainly it is Dium (Tell Ashari) that is meant, one of the less significant Decapolis cities in Gaulanitis. On Nabatean influence in the area, Millar, *Roman Near East*, pp. 391–400; 408–14.

77. In *War* 1.367 they implausibly took matters into their own hands and rushed the enemy.

78. He may have served in the forces of one or other Decapolis city in the region of Canatha. If so, Cleopatra would have been given some of the cities of the Decapolis in addition to Chalcis as a part of her gift of Coele-Syria.

79. Herod refers in a speech to Athenion's intervention as an "undeclared war" (*Ant.* 15.139).

guerrilla raids against Malichus (*War* 1.369; *Ant.* 15.120), and even that may be a bit of an exaggeration.[80]

Up to this point the portrait of Herod's military prowess has been very favorable; he was skilled, energetic, decisive, and a good commander.[81] He was near flawless in his actions against the brigands (*lêstai*), he assisted various Roman commanders including Antony effectively, he took over his kingdom slowly but in a workmanlike—and then magnanimous—way. Now he faltered. He won the first engagement at Dium, lost the second at Canatha, and had to fall back on trifling border raids. Herod suffered a substantial defeat at the hands of Malichus and Athenion, a defeat excused by Josephus (or his sources) on the basis that the fault was his soldiers' enthusiasm for battle.[82] Herod should have followed his own battle plan. Instead, he had to send envoys to sue for peace (*War* 1.371; *Ant.* 15.124).

The year 31 BCE was a low point for Herod.[83] He suffered the humiliation of Canatha, he was about to lose his patron Antony, and his kingdom was rocked by a major earthquake,[84] causing substantial loss of life, destruction of buildings, disruption, and loss of livestock.[85] This made the Nabateans bolder: they killed Herod's peace envoys "contrary to the universal law of mankind" (*War* 1.378; *Ant.* 15.136) and invaded Judea. Herod pulled all his forces back to Jerusalem and its environs.[86]

Having regrouped, mobilized fresh soldiers and offered sacrifices, Herod turned to the attack again (*War* 1.380; *Ant.* 15.147). He crossed the Jordan near Jericho and marched up toward Philadelphia (Amman), but stopped on the way to take a fortress. The Nabateans were aiming for the same fortress, though which fortress and whether either side was successful are not stated. It seems the Jewish army had the better of it, for they had water while the Nabateans

---

80. In *Ant.* 15.120 Josephus uses one of his favorite pejoratives, *lêsteia* ("brigandage"), of Herod!

81. The summary of Herod's character at *War* 1.429–30 (no parallel in *Antiquities*) argues that Herod was an "irresistible" fighter, a skilled bowman and javelin thrower, blessed with a strong body, a distinguished horseman, and an energetic huntsman.

82. *War* 1.429–30 reinforces this observation: "he rarely met with a reverse in war, and when he did, this was due not to his own fault, but either to treachery or to the recklessness of his troops."

83. *War* 1.370; *Ant.* 15.121; both refer to the seventh year of his reign, in both dating from 37 BCE, not 40.

84. The whole Rift Valley is an earthquake zone, where two plates butt against each other, one sliding along the other; every once in a while they let go with a great shudder.

85. The main showdown at Actium was later than his Nabatean struggle, for the earthquake of 31 BCE was in the spring and it *follows* the engagements at Dium and Canatha (*Ant.* 15.121), while Actium was 2 September 31 BCE.

86. He made a major speech, reported in two quite different versions (*War* 1.373–79; *Ant.* 15.127–46), in which Herod roused his troops for renewed battle; the differences are good examples of Josephus's different purposes and rhetorical flourishes.

did not; there were massive Nabatean army defections and the Jewish army gained victory.[87] Herod did not follow up this victory but withdrew again to Jerusalem. His revenge on the Nabateans for his crushing defeat earlier in the year must have been satisfying. As a result, says Josephus, Herod was called *prostatês,* "protector" or "patron" of Nabatea (*War* 1.385; *Ant.* 15.159).[88]

On 2 September 31 BCE, Antony was defeated at Actium. Though Herod might have wished to portray his victory over the Nabateans as parallel to Octavian's victory (Octavian had won over Antony and Cleopatra at Actium; Herod had won over Malichus and Cleopatra near Philadelphia), it could not be so presented. Such an interpretation would have been desperately self-serving, a playing with the facts that would not have impressed Octavian. That is to say, nothing in Octavian's victory reduced Herod's danger as a client of Antony's. Josephus emphasizes this sense of danger (*War* 1.386; *Ant.* 15.161–63) by claiming that Octavian could not think his victory complete as long as Herod was Antony's ally (so *War* 1.386). Herod's closeness to Antony, his strength in the past decade, was now a liability that put him in danger of Octavian's reprisals.

THE END OF HYRCANUS II

Herod had to clarify his position with Octavian immediately. First, however, he decided on a risky expedient. Hyrcanus II, by now just over seventy and no longer a threat,[89] was the only surviving male Hasmonean.[90] Herod determined to remove this one obstacle before he made a bold bid for Octavian's confirmation.[91] Herod's *Memoirs* claim that Alexandra, Hyrcanus's daughter and Mariamme's mother, caused Hyrcanus's death. She had pleaded with her father to write to Malichus asking for asylum. Hyrcanus reluctantly gave in and sent a letter to Malichus by Dositheus, a trusted friend, asking for an escort from Jerusalem to the Dead Sea. Dositheus took the letter to Herod,[92] who, after

---

87. Possibly it was the fortified palace of the Tobiads at Iraq al-Amir, with its perpetual river and fine water supply, or perhaps Gedor. The water problem suggests that it was late summer 31 BCE.

88. A standard term in a patronage context, though its implications here are not altogether clear. The term is used in Rom. 16:2 of Phoebe, who was Paul's *prostatis.*

89. Not 81, as *Ant.* 15.178 says explicitly, but probably about 71.

90. Schalit, pp. 131–41.

91. The details are not given in *War;* but *Antiquities* provides two lengthy accounts, 15.163–73 and 174–78, with a summary in 179–82. The first and longer account Josephus identifies as being from Herod's *Memoirs;* how much more of the preceding account might also be is not hinted at, but it is reasonable to suppose that some of the material only in *Antiquities* together with the improved sequence of events might derive from the same *Memoirs,* which seems to have been consulted in this work, but not in *War.*

92. Dositheus is described by Josephus (*Ant.* 15.160) as devoted to Hyrcanus and to Alexandra equally, and an enemy of Herod's because he was related to Joseph (Herod's brother-in-law whom he had had executed), and also related to some executed by Antony at Tyre. His action here seems odd.

reading it, instructed Dositheus to take it to Malichus. Malichus's reply granted Hyrcanus's requests;[93] Herod took the correspondence to his "council," which sentenced Hyrcanus to death.[94] Hyrcanus was executed (*Ant.* 15.163–73).

The second account (favorable to Hyrcanus) is an intentionally alternative explanation, for not only does it presuppose some of the same details (letters, horses) but it specifically undercuts charges of "revolution" and alleges that Hyrcanus's mild character was proof of his innocence (*Ant.* 15.174–78). From this view the correspondence was forged.[95] The details conflict: on the one hand, there is little suggestion in either account of Alexandra's actually coming under suspicion[96] and there is something implausible in an approach by Hyrcanus to Malichus just at the time Herod and he were engaged in war. On the other hand, earlier and later episodes involving Alexandra support the general picture given of her in the *Memoirs,* and a flight to Nabatea (only thirty-five miles or so away) was more feasible than flight to Egypt (at least seventy miles), where Alexandra might have expected a more enthusiastic, if less secure, welcome from Cleopatra.[97]

Hyrcanus had had a roller-coaster career (*Ant.* 15.179–82): he was high priest for nine years under his mother Queen Alexandra; he ruled for three months in 67 BCE; he was deposed by his brother Aristobulus II; he got his honors back for forty more years;[98] then Aristobulus's son deposed him, disfigured him, and sent him in chains to Parthia; then King Herod brought him back to the royal court under his aegis. Hyrcanus must have had a steel backbone to survive, but such a career may have unsettled him, and may help us to understand the rest of Josephus's epitaph: "he seems to have been mild and moderate in all things and to have ruled by leaving most things for his administrators to do, since he was not interested in general affairs nor clever enough to govern a kingdom. That Antipater and Herod advanced so far was due to [Hyrcanus's] mildness, and what he experienced at their hands in the end was neither just nor an act of piety" (*Ant.* 15.182).

---

93. Grant, pp. 90–92, leans toward this version.

94. For the second time Josephus reports Herod using a "council" for judicial reasons (the first was with Joseph); in matters affecting the throne and his own safety Herod did not act altogether alone.

95. Jones, p. 58, accepts this view.

96. As she should have done if the *Memoirs* were correct, though note *Ant.* 15.183, with its reference to continuing suspicions of Alexandra.

97. The distance of 300 stades is greater than the distance to the Dead Sea, contrary to what Josephus says. It would almost get them into Nabatean territory, which was what was needed in any case. Cleopatra's position was, of course, tenuous in the extreme following Actium.

98. Both parts are inaccurate; he did not get *all* honors back as he was called only ethnarch, not king; and it was only for twenty-three years. This is from a source favorable to Hyrcanus and the figure 40 is an indication of its view that Hyrcanus was the legitimate king from 67 BCE, almost forty years.

While most of this is confirmed by the evidence, Hyrcanus did occasionally take more of a hand in "general affairs" and he was probably clever enough to govern. He seems not to have desired power, and power was the name of the game; nor did he have sufficient suspicion to escape others' manipulation of him—by his brother Aristobulus, his nephew Antigonus, his viceroy Antipater, his daughter Alexandra, and Herod. But the one line of crucial importance in a study of the life of Herod is that "Antipater and Herod advanced so far [because of] his mildness" (*Ant.* 15.182). This is well put.

HEROD AND OCTAVIAN AT RHODES

In early 30 BCE Herod undertook another dangerous winter sea voyage, this time to Rhodes to play an extremely bold game: to confront Octavian's suspicions directly. Octavian knew well that Herod had been Antony's ally. Unlike other dependent kings, Herod had not abandoned Antony at the last moment.[99] From 40 BCE, when all three had walked arm in arm through the streets of Rome, Antony had been instrumental in Herod's position, and Herod had matched Antony's trust. Octavian had reason for thinking well of Herod: old ties derived from Julius Caesar's and Antipater's friendship that preceded Antony's link with Herod; Herod had limited Cleopatra's power in the region by defeating the Nabateans (who were also on Antony's side); he had supported Roman policy in the east effectively over the past decade. Given the difficulty of governing Judea, it was sensible to confirm Herod as king.

Herod, of course, did not know what Octavian was thinking. He had not been close to him personally and probably had no influential acquaintances in Octavian's entourage. He risked everything on a single throw, though he flirted with the possibility of defying Octavian and offering Antony his army and continued support.[100] But Antony's cause was hopeless. To retain power Herod had to go to Octavian and offer his support (*War* 1.387; *Ant.* 15.183). He appointed his younger brother Pheroras to manage affairs in his absence. Then he sent his children, Salome his sister, and Cypros his mother to Masada, and sent Mariamme and her mother Alexandra to Alexandreion, since relations with then were tense. The latter were in charge of Herod's steward, another Joseph, and

---

99. Plutarch, *Antony* 63, re Antigonus of Galatia and Lycaonia.

100. *War* 1.389–90 implies that Herod saw Antony or wrote to him in Egypt, advising Antony to kill Cleopatra and offering him support if he did so, an insinuation supported by *Ant.* 15.190–92. Plutarch, *Antony* 71, confirms that it was only in Egypt that Antony learned Herod had abandoned him; he sent Alexas to forestall Herod's changing sides (Plutarch, *Antony* 72). Nabateans actively campaigned against Antony and Cleopatra; when Cleopatra wanted to drag ships from the Mediterranean to the Red Sea to settle beyond the Egyptian border, Nabateans set fire to the ships.

Soemus, an Ituraean.[101] In the worst case scenario, Joseph and Soemus were to argue for kingship to pass to Herod's children and his brother Pheroras.

Herod, now forty-three years of age, came to Octavian, now thirty-three, in Rhodes, without his crown and other signs of his royal status.[102] He stressed his integrity and loyalty, saying he would be as loyal to Octavian as he had been to Antony. The transfer from one benefactor to another was duly concluded,[103] with Octavian expressing thanks that Antony had not taken Herod's advice. Had he done so, Herod could not have been pardoned but would have had to share Antony's defeat. Octavian accepted Herod more enthusiastically than Herod had any right to expect. He promised Herod he would reign "more securely than before" (*War* 1.391), confirmed him in this kingship, and bestowed additional honors on him (*War* 1.392–93; *Ant.* 15.195).[104] While in Rhodes, Herod interceded for Alexas of Laodicea, who had acted as go-between for Antony and Herod and may have been a special friend of Herod's (Plutarch, *Antony* 72; *War* 1.393), but Octavian executed him despite Herod's pleas.[105]

Octavian travelled triumphantly through Syria and Judea to Egypt in pursuit of Antony and Cleopatra (*War* 1.394; *Ant.* 15.199; Plutarch, *Antony* 74), confirming publicly that Herod's position had been enhanced by his shift to Octavian. Herod entertained him "with all the resources of his realm" at Ptolemais (*War* 1.394; *Ant.* 15.199–200) and accompanied him to the Egyptian border, where he provided water and wine and a gift of eight hundred talents that he could ill afford. Herod's generosity had a desired—though unexpected—result. Octavian returned the territories Cleopatra had held, as well as two cities

---

101. Their instructions, as in the previous threat to his own position in 34 when he went to Laodicea to meet Antony, were to kill both women if he did not survive (*Ant.* 15.184–86). The parallels between the incident here and that earlier in 15.65–87 are striking. It is unlikely that two such similar incidents occurred, especially when there is a coincidence of names. See below.

102. The accounts differ on several points: *War* 1.388–92 gives the conversation in direct speech, *Ant.* 15.188–94 in indirect speech.

103. Both here (*Ant.* 15.190, *euergetês*) and earlier, as when Julius Caesar and Antipater became friends, the language of clientism is used extensively. The accounts presuppose the patronage system, and can only be understood in the light of conditions of such a system, operating here at the highest levels of society. Though some features of this usage are now doubted (A. Lintott, *Imperium Romanum. Politics and Administration* [London and New York: Routledge, 1993], pp. 32–36, preferring "friends and allies" to "client kings"), Josephus presupposes the system of personal clientism. See A. Wallace-Hadrill, ed., *Patronage in Ancient Society* (London and New York: Routledge, 1989), esp. the essay by D. Braund, pp. 137–52.

104. During the preceding months a group of gladiators being trained for Antony in Cyzicus tried to join him in Egypt by travelling overland. Herod assisted the governor of Syria, Q. Didius, in preventing them reaching Antony, though why Herod's help should have been needed is not said (*War* 1.392; *Ant.* 15.195).

105. Plutarch hints that Octavian's hostility had to do with Alexas's support for Cleopatra and his encouragement to Antony to reject a marital reconciliation with Octavia, Octavian's sister.

of the Decapolis—Hippos and Gadara—and Samaria, the coastal cities of Strato's Tower (later Caesarea Maritima), Joppa (Yafo), Anthedon (later Agrippias) and Gaza, together with Cleopatra's bodyguard of four hundred Gauls (*War* 1.396–97; *Ant.* 15.217).

When Antony asked to retire to private life in Athens, Octavian rejected his appeal, but was willing to be lenient to Cleopatra if she would abandon Antony (Plutarch, *Antony* 72–73). Octavian had reached Alexandria; as Antony's troops gradually defected to Octavian, Antony tried to commit suicide, thinking Cleopatra dead, but he fumbled the attempt, and was carried to Cleopatra, in whose arms he died. She too tried unsuccessfully to commit suicide and lived on for some days, but was successful in a second attempt (Plutarch, *Antony* 73–87).

By the spring of 30 BCE, it was apparent to Herod's supporters and opponents alike that he had successfully finessed transfer of his loyalty to Octavian. With Cleopatra dead and Malichus weakened, Herod was preeminent in the east. He was without significant rivals externally; internally he had an increased kingdom with new outlets to the sea and no obvious claimants to his throne.[106] He was still married to Mariamme, who, now that Hyrcanus II was dead, added a degree of legitimacy to his reign in the eyes of traditionalists.[107]

---

106. In *War*, once this point is reached, Josephus (following his source) records additions to Herod's territory in 24/23 BCE, the addition of Zenodorus's territory, and Herod's appointment as procurator (*epitropos*) of all Syria (both in 20 BCE; *War* 1.398–400). He goes on to summarize his building activities (1.401–28), at which point (1.429–30) Josephus offers a summary that sounds as if his source were concluding its account. But then he picks up the story again, now focussing on Herod's tragic domestic problems, going right back to 40 BCE once again. This disrupted narrative flow shows Josephus's reliance on more than one source in *War,* and creates difficulties for historical reconstruction.

107. By now Herod had several potential heirs: Antipater, born to Doris about 45 BCE; Alexander, born about 36 to Mariamme; Aristobulus, also born to Mariamme about 35; two daughters, Salampsio and Cypros, born perhaps in 33 and 32, also to Mariamme. Another son (unnamed) survived infancy but died in Rome while being educated there (*War* 1.435). This crowded timetable of births is required by Jospehus's accounts.

CHAPTER 8

Herod's Buildings

INTRODUCTION

Several important studies of Herod have given due weight to his buildings. The reason is obvious: his buildings represent an enduring aspect to his career— observable today to even casual observers—and are the most easily appreciated aspect of his volatile and not always admired life. The buildings are stunning in their size, boldness, and complexity. In addition to non-technical appreciations of his work by scholars of Herod, an enormous amount of archaeological work has been done on his projects, usually because of their significance as examples of Second Temple Jewish structures. A few persons, most notably Ehud Netzer, have both an archaeological and architectural interest in his work, and this has resulted in some fine studies of individual projects.[1]

Herod's building activity can be approached from the point of view of geographic location, building type, chronological development, methods, materials, and strategy—all of which I will comment on before summarizing his work. Herod was not a megalomaniac advancing his own reputation—though this may be true in part—but he had clear and larger goals for advancement of Judaism in the Mediterranean world.

GEOGRAPHIC LOCATION

Following this chapter, Appendix A's list of Herod's projects is categorized primarily according to location; these projects covered most regions of the east-

---

1. Individual projects: see, for example, Netzer's editing of the field notes of Yigael Yadin in the official final publication of Masada. Studies of Herod: Schalit devotes about seventy-five pages to them, Grant covers the ground in parts of five chapters, Perowne gives over all of four chapters to his buildings. A recent introduction to New Testament archaeology by J. McRay has four full chapters surveying Herod's structures.

ern Roman Empire from Idumaea to Epirus (western Greece), including many intervening provinces and several islands of the Aegean. One obvious and one not so obvious feature emerge: first, a great deal of his building activity focused on his own region, especially Jerusalem and Judea; and second, there was no uniform pattern of distribution and there are some areas where there was no building at all (see maps 5 and 6).

To begin with the second issue first, contrary to expectations, Herod did not build farther west than the western coast of Greece. He was close to Augustus and dependent on Rome; he made several trips there; his male children were educated there; he had close friends there: these reciprocal contacts might have spawned an outburst of creative activity in the capital city. While one inscription might give evidence of a direct or indirect interest in a synagogue in Rome (see Appendix B), nothing dependable points to any Roman projects. He probably thought of Italy as Augustus and Marcus Agrippa's special field of action; certainly Italy was not an ideal place for Herod to parade his benefactions.

More surprisingly, Herod sponsored no projects in North Africa, including Egypt and Alexandria. After the deaths of Cleopatra and Antony there was little hindrance to such projects, unless Egypt's special relationship to the Emperor required care that one not appear to tamper in its affairs. Perhaps special factors in Herod's relationship with Egyptian Jews militated against benefactions, though there is no evidence of general strains or tensions.

Herod built in many other eastern provinces, though not in Macedonia, Galatia, Pontus and Bithynia, Cyprus, Crete, or Cappadocia (the latter still a dependent kingdom under his friend Archelaus), and relatively little in Asia (there is no recorded benefaction to Ephesus). Nor did Herod bestow his largess on any of the non-incorporated neighbors: Thracia, Commagene, Nabatea, Armenia, or Parthia. The literary evidence shows no buildings in the Decapolis cities, including Hippos and Gadara, that were under his control for a substantial part of his reign.

In his home territories, it is surprising that there are few benefactions in Galilee, Gaulanitis, and the adjacent regions, and relatively few in Peraea. (1) Herod's early career and his reputation were made in Galilee, and he might have recalled his glory days there through attention to noteworthy sites. He did not. Even Sepphoris benefitted little, according to both the literary and the archaeological record. (2) The common view that Galilee was a hotbed of dissent requiring control through force is contradicted by the fact that there is no record of any fortresses or fortified palaces having been built there. Herod's building activity indicates that Galilee must have been relatively quiet. (3) It would have been politic to locate public works projects in Galilee to strengthen its finances (as I shall argue is one of his motives); their absence suggests that such support was either unnecessary or undesirable. In Gaulanitis and the adjacent regions and in Peraea the issues are similar but less clear.

There was more building activity in Idumaea. The suggestion has been made that there was a large amount of building activity in Idumaea, in the shape of forts or "fortlets"; altogether about thirty or so sites have been proposed in various studies. Though this estimate is incorrect in my view, if even a small portion are to be attributed to Herod, were these fortlets for defense of Herod and his holdings, for intimidation of Idumaeans, for protection from Nabatea or Egypt? Until a more precise list of Herodian projects can be drawn up, and a pattern of fortlets seen, it is impossible to say.

In general, the majority of Herod's buildings were to be found in the heartland of his own territory, in Jerusalem and Judea and Samaria, including the coast lands. There was a surprising paucity of work in Galilee, Gaulanitis, and Peraea, with the evidence for Idumaea still uncertain. There was a wide distribution of work extending as far as Greece, but nothing in the western or southern portions of the empire.

The pattern fits three possible explanatory rationales. (1) These areas included the core of the late-Hellenistic world (excepting the absence of Macedonia) and may have been just the areas where a patron such as Herod would get special credit for his work. (2) They formed the eastern portion of the Empire in the early days of Augustus and represented a region of potential influence that would enhance Judea's stability. (3) It was here (excepting Alexandria and Rome, the two largest cities of the Empire) that the greatest concentrations of Diaspora Jews were found.

In the first rationale, this was where his buildings would be most appreciated, in the second where he could build most profitably and with least risk of treading on Augustus's toes, in the third where his involvement would be the most beneficial to world Judaism. The decision to stay away from areas not yet integrated into the Empire, such as Thrace and Commagene, may have been a political decision not to tamper with delicate political alliances.[2] Whether any of these explanations, or some combination of all of them, is on the mark cannot be known. That some explanation is needed, however, is hinted at by Josephus: "Often, however, [Herod's] noble generosity was thwarted by the fear of exciting either jealousy or the suspicion of entertaining some higher ambition, in conferring upon states greater benefit than they received from their own masters" (War 1.428). This comment of Josephus's helps provide an explanation of the absence of projects in a number of areas.

---

2. See the general comments in Sullivan, Near Eastern Royalty, pp. 9–24; Millar, Roman Near East, chaps. 1–2; A. Lintott, Imperium Romanum. Politics and Administration, (London and New York: Routledge, 1993), Part I.

MAJOR PROJECTS

Herod's benefactions cover a diverse range of projects. Some can be known in great detail from both literary and archaeological descriptions (Masada, Herodium, Caesarea Maritima); some from literary description but not from archaeological investigation (Antonia Fortress, Jerusalem Palace); some from archaeological excavations that are ignored in the literary remains (water works, Temple of Apollo in Rhodes). The farther away from Jerusalem the project is the less that is known, for Josephus and his sources are less interested in these and less knowledgeable. One class of benefactions—those to cities or regions in the Hellenistic world—is unknown in any detail.

Little can be said about these. All are outside Herod's territory and only one, Balanea in Syria, is at all near. Included are a few cities (Phaselis in Lycia, Pergamum, Athens, Nicopolis, Olympia) and several provinces, regions, or islands (Cilicia, Lycia, Ionia, Lacedaemon [Sparta], Rhodes, Chios, Samos). We have no detail at all about many. Athens is mentioned in passing (*War* 1.425), yet there are three inscriptions (see Appendix B) naming Herod—two from the Agora and one from the Acropolis—all three attesting a benefaction. Three cases are especially interesting. Josephus says that Herod built the majority of the public buildings at Nicopolis, which was founded by Augustus to celebrate his victory at Actium in 31 BCE over Antony and Cleopatra (*War* 1.425; *Ant.* 16.147). Silent as the excavations are on this point, Herod may have felt it appropriate to give dramatic force to his decision, late in the day, to support Octavian. According to Josephus (*War* 1.424), Herod made donations at Rhodes on several occasions for shipbuilding and on one occasion to the restoration of the recently-burnt Temple of Pythian Apollo. These contributions began in 40 BCE (*Ant.* 14.378) and continued well beyond 31 BCE, following his meeting with Octavian. At Olympia (*War* 1.426–27; *Ant.* 16.149) Herod endowed the games at a point when they had fallen on hard times, partly perhaps as a result of the earthquake of 36 BCE; he may have contributed to the restoration of the buildings, though the literature and inscriptions are silent.[3]

New cities were his most dramatic projects; all were in his own territory. The most remarkable were Caesarea Maritima—built on a Hellenistic site but so expanded as to make it unrecognizable—and Sebaste, built on the site of ancient Samaria, the capital city of the northern kingdom of Israel (see below).

Others were less grand but significant: his rebuilding of Agrippias (Anthedon), the new foundations of Antipatris (Aphek)[4] and of Phaselis (Fasayli). He established new military settlements, villages, or towns around which

---

3. See W. D. Dinsmoor, "An Archeological Earthquake at Olympia," *AJA*, series 2, 45 (1941): 399–427 ; M. Lämmer, "Eine Propaganda-Aktion des Königs Herodes in Olympia," in *Perspektiven der Sportwissenschaft* (Schorndorf: Hoffmann, 1973), pp. 160–73.

4. *NEAEHL* 1.67–72.

he settled demobilized veterans of his armies, presumably with civic structures though probably of a minor character. Those known are Gaba (Sha'ar ha-'Amaqim on the Plain of Esdraelon),[5] Pente Komai ("Five Villages," just north of Sebaste, where he probably settled six thousand colonists; *War* 1.405), Bathyra (in Batanea), and Heshbon (Hesban, in Peraea). There were military colonists in other areas (for example in Idumaea; see *War* 2.55), but no details survive. These colonies derived from a combination of need, availability of land, and strategic location.[6] Herod had large royal estates (Plain of Esdraelon, Western Samaria, Idumaea) or new land available to distribute (e.g., Batanea, Peraea),[7] which helped to shape their location.[8]

Some of the same general factors applied also to Antipatris, Agrippias, and Phaselis. The latter case is a good example.[9] Herod prized his huge royal estates in the Jericho area, from which he derived a substantial income.[10] A new city to the north of Jericho, extensively irrigated, would have stimulated new agricultural developments to complement Jericho's riches and encourage new trade. It was on an important north-south transportation route, easily accessible to Jerusalem.

Antipatris and Agrippias were also close to Herodian estates; Agrippias provided another (minor) outlet to the sea between Gaza and Ashkelon. Antipatris was a new town in the Sharon plain astride the main route between Jerusalem and Caesarea Maritima, with the added advantage that it was near the royal estates in Samaritis at Qiryat Bene Hassan.[11]

Caesarea Maritima and Sebaste were the most significant in complexity, size, and strategic importance. Caesarea Maritima was Herod's showpiece city; it was a major outlet to the Mediterranean, home for the Judean navy, the largest harbor in the Mediterranean. It rearranged trade patterns in the area. Produce, trade, and people flowed in both directions; it was a city where Hellenistic and Roman ideals jostled with Jewish convictions, where Roman, Greek, Jew, Nabatean, and Egyptian would rub shoulders daily. The city covered 164 acres and included a large number of state-sponsored or royal structures:[12] the

---

5. *NEAEHL* 4.139–40.

6. Note the social importance of land allocation in Italy by Marius, Sulla, Pompey, Julius Caesar.

7. Again note the similarity to the ways in which land was freed and distributed to demobbed veterans in Rome.

8. On royal estates, see Fiensy, *Social History*, chap. 2, pp. 24–48; S. Applebaum, "The Settlement Pattern of Western Samaria," in S. Dar, with a historical commentary by S. Applebaum, *Landscape and Pattern. An Archaeological Survey of Samaria, 800 B.C.E.–636 C.E.* (Oxford: BAR/IS, 1986).

9. Regrettably it has not been excavated, but a visit to the site immediately turns up evidence of the city.

10. Strabo, *Geog.* 16.2.41, emphasizes the wealth of the palms, fruits, and balsam products.

11. See Fiensy, *Social History*, pp. 38–42; *NEAEHL* 4.1316–18.

12. *NEAEHL* 1.270–91 and literature cited there.

harbor itself with its installations and warehouses; water and sewage facilities; walls; gates; streets; agora; hippodrome; theater; amphitheater; Promontory Palace; and the Temple of Roma and Augustus hovering over the whole at the focal point of the harbor.

Sebaste was different, symbolically valuable as the ancient capital of the Northern Kingdom of Israel. The Temple of Roma and Augustus in Sebaste was built directly over the old royal palaces of King Ahab, perhaps intended to make explicit the symbolic succession. Like Caesarea, Sebaste's new name and temple paid homage to Augustus; in both cities Herod could be less careful of local religious sensibilities. Sebaste was similar in size to Caesarea; though less complex, it covered 160 acres that included among state-financed projects walls, gates, streets, aqueducts, agora, hippodrome, theater, and the Temple of Roma and Augustus.[13]

FORTRESSES AND PALACES

The most dramatic of Herod's buildings, heavily overlaid with legend and well preserved in the archaeological record, Herod's fortresses were places of drama and excitement. Several variant types can be distinguished. (1) *Walls.* In a few cases Herod built or restored walls of cities: Caesarea Maritima, Sebaste, Jerusalem and—outside his territory—Byblos. He may also have built walls in a number of other places, not yet clearly established. (2) *Fortresses primarily.* The literary and archaeological records do not always allow certainty, but the following should be thought of mainly as fortresses: the Antonia in Jerusalem, Masada, Cypros, Docus, Alexandreion, Hyrcania, Machaerus, and perhaps also Herodium East (in Peraea). (3) *Fortresses with generous living quarters.* Several of Herod's forts seem oriented more to royal life than to protection: the towers Phaselis, Hippicus, and Mariamme incorporated into but hovering over the Royal Palace in Jerusalem and, of a quite different order, the Northern Palace at Masada and the Upper Palace at Herodium, near Bethlehem. (4) *Fortlets or unknown.* There may be a series of fortlets in Idumaea or Peraea.[14] A fortress call Agrippina probably occupied the site of the later Crusader fortress at Belvoir; and a fort still probably occupied the site of Keren Naftali, overlooking Lake Huleh. Esbus (Heshbon) may have functioned as a fortress for part of Herod's reign.

It is often claimed that these forts formed a system defending Herod's borders from external attack and providing internal security against the deep hatred of the people. One sequence of fortresses suggests a strong line of externally oriented strongholds, most of which would have been near enough to provide

---

13. *NEAEHL* 4.1300–1310.

14. See A. Kasher, *Jews, Idumaeans and Ancient Arabs* (Tübingen: J. C. B. Mohr, 1988), p. 155, which shows a security belt (also p. 154, n.64, and literature cited there).

internal security if needed: Masada, Machaerus, Hyrcania, Cypros-Docus, Alexandreion, and perhaps Agrippina. All were within signalling distance of each other, easily defended, and extremely strong. Three factors modify this view. (1) Without exception these forts went back to Maccabean foundations, when the need for this particular line of defense was pressing. Their genius, especially their brilliant locations, was Maccabean. The literary and historical evidence confirms that the Hasmoneans were more in need of defense and more anxious about security than Herod. Herod restored, refurbished, modernized, and improved them—especially the water systems and royal apartments—but these were his establishments in neither location nor purpose. (2) In Herod's day this line of defense made little sense. Though some of the forts played a strategic role in the first days of Herod's rule,[15] for the majority of his reign they were irrelevant as fortresses. The Jordan valley was not the natural border it had been in earlier days and there was no need for a major defensive line at that point, since he controlled almost the whole of the adjacent territory east of the Jordan (Peraea).[16] (3) In refurbishing them, the archaeology makes clear, attention was paid to the living amenities.[17] While they were fortified and in extremely strong positions (Hyrcania, Machaerus, and Masada, along with Herodium, were the last fortresses to fall in the Great Revolt), in Herod's day they were mainly wilderness retreats that could be used in an emergency as places of refuge, with basic royal amenities for an enjoyable visit if one needed solitude. Their remote locations also encouraged their use for executions.

At Jerusalem and Jericho there was a sequence of structures: in both cases the earliest Herodian palace was a reconstruction of a Hasmonean palace, superseded in both places by a purpose-built palace, in Jericho two later palaces. The Hasmonean palace at Jericho was the largest of the three, but the last of them, now known as the Winter Palace, is demonstrably the most interesting.[18] At Jerusalem the later Royal Palace was a vast affair with two large wings, raised on a podium to create a platform for the requisite structures, gardens, and pools, and overlooked by three great towers to the north.[19]

---

15. Alexandreion was rebuilt by Pheroras in 39/38 BCE.

16. Note that Herod's children, Antipas and Philip, were the ones to construct walls at several cities: Sepphoris, Bethsaida, Panias, Betharamphtha-Julias (*Ant.* 18.27–28).

17. There were strong points of similarity among these. They turned their backs to the exterior. There was an interior court around which living and service facilities were arranged. Much attention was paid to the collection of water and there was sometimes provision for a bath complex. There were a few imaginative elements in the design, with some gracious touches in the way the design was carried out—columns, capitals, paved courtyards, fresco work, stuccoed architectural decoration, and the like. But there is little evidence of intricate mosaics, elaborate fresco work, or spaces designed for pleasurable purposes, though some of that type of work is present, especially in Masada's Northern Palace.

18. See E. Netzer, *NEAEHL* 2.682–92.

19. Brief description by H. Geva, *NEAEHL* 2.736, with literature cited on pp. 756–57.

In Judea, in addition to the palaces at Jericho, was Herodium, one of Herod's most imaginative structures, a fortified palace with extensive related facilities clustered around the bottom of the hill, including at least two other palaces—the Intermediate Palace and the Lower Palace. Herodium was one of Herod's favorite places, a retreat near Jerusalem with facilities suitable for large-scale entertaining.

In Idumaea, Masada is known from both literature and archaeology. There were two main palaces, the earlier Western Palace and the Northern Palace, along with several minor residences for nobles. Both main palaces were significant, but the Northern Palace was far more interesting architecturally.[20] In Samaritis the only known palace, which was more of a fort, was at Alexandreion. On the coast land adjacent to Samaritis, the Promontory Palace at Caesarea Maritima has recently been re-excavated and provides excellent new evidence of a palace built purely for pleasure.

In Galilee there may have been a Herodian palace at Sepphoris (*Ant.* 17.271), of which no evidence has yet been found in the excavations there, though there is some evidence of Herodian-style masonry. It may be that the palace, like the theater, was built by Antipas. In Gaulanitis there may have been a palace at Panias. In Peraea Herod had a substantial but unfortified palace at Betharamphtha,[21] across the Jordan River from Jericho, still unexcavated; to judge from the extent of the tell it was of a considerable size (*War* 2.59, 168, 252; *Ant.* 18.27–28). The fortified palace at Machaerus, associated with the later beheading of John the Baptist, marked the border with Nabatea and was undoubtedly more fortress than palace. In Phoenicia Herod apparently had a palace at Ashkelon, though nothing is known of it.

Only four of these can be known in detail and are relevant: leaving aside the fortified palaces, the Winter Palace at Jericho, the Northern Palace at Masada, the Upper Palace at Herodium, and Promontory Palace at Caesarea Maritima. Coincidentally, these four palaces were much alike, all falling within the villa style that was such an interesting part of Roman architecture.[22] All had architectural flair, made dramatic visual impression, used circular elements, and showed up-to-date technology in a coherent solution. The four together make a good case for a single architectural genius behind Herod's buildings. All four used a site most patrons would have shied away from in horror and turned its disadvantages into an opportunity to show off, with flair, imagination, and drama.

---

20. E. Netzer, *Masada,* vol. 3 (Jerusalem: Israel Exploration Society, 1993).

21. Deduced from Josephus's comment that it was Antipas who threw up walls around Julias. This would confirm the earlier view that fortification was not a primary concern of Herod's.

22. See A. G. MacKay, *Houses, Villas and Palaces in the Roman World* (London: Thames and Hudson, 1975).

The Northern Palace at Masada is the most obvious example; it occupied a knife-edge with three platforms spread over a thirty-five meter (110 foot) vertical drop—the top platform being semi-circular, the middle circular, and the lowest rectangular.[23] It opened out on a view as spectacular as any villa anywhere in the Roman world, looking north up the Rift valley, east to the Dead Sea, and west to the wilderness. Less obviously dramatic, until one thinks about its main use in the winter months, was the Winter Palace at Jericho, set on both sides of the Wadi Qelt with the two sides mirroring each other and connected by a bridge over the wadi.[24] The flair lay in the rejection of the obvious solution—build near the oasis with its natural advantages of water, warm winter weather, abundant fruits and vegetables. Instead, like the Hasmoneans before him, Herod built away from the oasis, so that water had to be brought by aqueduct from up the wadi. The drama came from the opportunities inherent in having a torrent pass under the bridge whenever it rained in the hills east of Jerusalem. On the north side of the wadi was a fine villa, on the south side a magnificently executed garden, a huge pool, and an artificial mound with a splendid gazebo, perhaps with a small bath complex, the whole taking advantage of views of the oasis and the Dead Sea.

In the Upper Palace at Herodium the flair was in making a hill appear to be an artificial mound, constructing a circular palace to suit the conical top, with views of both wilderness and agricultural land just at the border line between "desert and sown," incorporating public and private spaces, together with a small bath.[25] The structure was designed for use as Herod's mausoleum after his death. The palace most recently excavated, the Promontory Palace at Caesarea Maritima, combined several features of the Northern Palace and the Winter Palace; it was focussed on a pool and was anchored to the shore by various service facilities around a large colonnaded courtyard; at the western (sea) end there were public or entertaining areas with a huge semi-circular vantage point to catch the sunset.[26]

These were the best—perhaps the only—true villas in Israel. Though large farmsteads have been discovered, there is little evidence that the elite in Jerusalem (quite wealthy, to judge from houses in Jerusalem) built country houses

---

23. The top level (the entrance) had living spaces, the middle level (still a controversial matter) probably was a whimsical circular gazebo, and the lowest level was the main retreat area, with a small three-room bath complex tucked out almost in mid-air underneath the floor level. See Netzer, *Masada* vol. 3, Part IV.

24. Netzer, "Jericho: Tulul Abu el-ʿAlayiq," *NEAEHL* 2.682–91.

25. The old view that the whole hill is artificial, often repeated in modern books, is simply false. The artificiality appears from the way, once the main structure's ring was built, fill was placed around it to smooth the transition from hill to building, thus seeming to finish off the natural hill in an obviously "artificial" manner, a perfect "breast" as Josephus says.

26. B. Burrell, K. Gleason, and E. Netzer, "Uncovering Herod's Seaside Palace," *BAR* 19/3 (1993): 50–52, 76.

for their pleasure and relaxation. Unlike the other end of the Empire—Gaul, Germany, Britain, and Spain, where the local elites delighted in villas—few existed in Judea, Samaria, and Galilee. More remarkable, however, is that some of the dramatic elements in these Herodian structures, notably the vertical drop at Masada's Northern Palace, pre-dated analogies in the Roman world.[27] The use of round elements was another distinctive element in Herod's palaces. Especially notable was Herodium's round structure to be used as a mausoleum, echoing the great Mausoleum of Augustus in Rome, whose date may well be later.

Herod's villas were technologically up-to-date (*opus reticulatum, opus quadratum, opus sectile*, with vaults both circular and barrel, full Roman baths, mosaics, plaster work, frescoes, painting in the latest style, and so on). They contained no decorative effects offending against the second commandment, though one might have expected him to suit himself in his private spaces. Apparently the lack of such art reflects his personal commitment to Judaism.[28]

Each of these palaces was a coherent solution to a deliberately chosen challenge. Each was primarily for private use, though all incorporated rooms that were intended for public or semi-public occasions. Each showed a delicate, refined hand at work, sensitively responding to the mixture of personal, public, site-related, and environmental challenges. Each focussed on the building's main purpose: view (Northern Palace), enjoyment of the sea (Promontory Palace), seclusion (Upper Palace), or dramatic natural climate (Winter Palace). The Royal Palace in Jerusalem may have had a distinctive feature, perhaps public entertainment and statecraft; regrettably little can be said about it.

RELIGIOUS BUILDINGS

The Upper Palace at Herodium was, in one sense, a religious building—it was a mausoleum. Consistent with this project, though different in the details, Herod built another circular structure as a family mausoleum in Jerusalem, just north of the Damascus Gate,[29] which has much in common with Augustus's mausoleum in Rome but pre-dates it. In the sequence of large, round, family tombs, the Herodian ones come early, perhaps at the beginning. Herod also built a memorial to David at the entrance to his tomb, which he plundered at a needy point in his career (*Ant.* 16.179–84).[30]

---

27. The nearest comparison to Masada is Tiberius's villa at Capri, built at the top and down the cliff face; it is forty or fifty years later.

28. It has been argued that in some of his baths the cold pool functioned as a *mikveh* (Masada and Cypros, to mention two). If correct, this adds to our understanding of Herod's practices.

29. E. Netzer, "Remains of an Opus Reticulatum Building in Jerusalem," *IEJ* 33 (1983): 163–75.

30. Enthusiastically but indecisively, H. Shanks, "Is This King David's Tomb?," *BAR* 21/1 (1995): 62–67.

In Hebron, Herod built a kind of maquette for the Temple in Jerusalem, a memorial for the Patriarchs and Matriarchs (Abraham and Sarah, Isaac and Rebecca, Jacob and Leah), the Haram al-Khalil. He built a similar memorial to Abraham just north of Hebron at Mamre, recalling the oaks that were located there according to the Bible. Located in Idumaea, both structures demonstrated an aspect of the early phases of Herod's religious program: he recalled common antecedents of both Idumaeans (Edomites) and Israelites.[31] In undertaking these projects he walked a fine line between those Idumaeans who, like his own family, had embraced Judaism and those who remained attracted to the old Edomite traditions.

He also participated in a Temple to Ba'al Shamim at Si'a, near Canatha (Qanawat, on the Jebel Druze). The evidence for this (see Appendix B) was found on a statue base with an inscription in the remains of the porch. He probably contributed financially to the project,[32] thus indicating an accommodation with Nabatean religious interests.

Herod's primary interest, with the exception of the Temple in Jerusalem, was the Imperial cult, for which he built three temples to Roma and Augustus:[33] one in Caesarea Maritima dominating the harbor and city center, one in Sebaste at the highest point of the city, and one in Panias alongside the grottoes dedicated to the god Pan.[34] From his confirmation as king in 31 BCE, Herod maintained a consistent loyalty to Augustus, to which he gave visible form with these three temples. He chose sites that were unlikely to offend: Strato's Tower, a long-time Hellenistic city, renamed Caesarea; Samaria, capital of the Northern Kingdom, renamed Sebaste; and Panias, long associated with the pagan god Pan. That there is no recollection of disputes over these temples indicates the success of his choices of sites.[35] All of these cities must have had a substantial number of Jews, who accommodated themselves, presumably, to this homage to the Emperor. Since the Jerusalem Temple offered prayers to God on behalf

---

31. The primary literature gives no indication of either as Herodian projects, though the construction evidence is unmistakable. These are good examples of the limited nature of the literary records.

32. The style and structure are typically Nabatean, unlike anything else that Herod was involved in or developed on his own.

33. Augustus insisted that temples for the cult be dedicated to Roma and him together. He prohibited Emperor worship in Rome itself, though he allowed it in other parts, especially in the East.

34. The first two have been identified in excavations; the last is currently being clarified in ongoing excavations. The excavator of the Pan caves believes that the Temple to Roma and Augustus is the largest of the small temples backed up against the cliff within which are caves and numerous inscriptions to Pan, though this seems unlikely to me.

35. *Ant.* 15.365 could allude to difficulties in 20 BCE when Herod remitted taxes to win back people's favor, lost by resentment at the dissolution of religion and the disappearance of customs; it is too general to be sure.

of the Emperor daily, it could be argued that the temples of Roma were merely an extension of that provision for homage to Augustus.

Outside his own territories Herod helped with other religious structures. Josephus tells us Herod built temples in Tyre and Berytus (Beirut), but he gives no details (*War* 1.422) and none have emerged archaeologically. Josephus also says that Herod restored the Temple of Pythian Apollo in Rhodes (*War* 1.424; *Ant.* 16.147) in addition to the gifts he gave for shipbuilding there. This temple has been extensively excavated and partly restored, though details of the construction history are lacking, so that we have no confirmation of Josephus's rather casual remark concerning Herod's involvement. The Temple to Pythian Apollo sits in a wonderfully articulated complex of civic buildings on the Acropolis in Rhodes, including a stadium, odeum, and terraces in the best Hellenistic manner.[36] Probably this temple also owes nothing to Herod apart from money. He may have helped to rebuild religious structures at Olympia that were shattered in a serious earthquake in 36 BCE. The statue base on the Acropolis in Athens may have celebrated a Herodian benefaction connected with the worship of Athena in the Parthenon, but there is no literary evidence of this.

Herod's enormous contribution to the rebuilding of the Second Temple—Josephus calls it a work of great piety (*War* 1.400–401)—needs a book in itself.[37] The rebuilding's organization and careful preparations, the quality and the enormous quantities of materials used, the vast scale and drama of the Temple, its innovations, its integration into the existing cityscape, the demand to continue regular worship—all are truly staggering. Determined to leave Judaism richer for his having been king, Herod undertook this project and persuaded the priestly hierarchy of its viability, even gaining their agreement to important innovations such as the courts of women and gentiles. Reactions were varied but generally positive: "He who has not seen the Temple has not seen a beautiful building" (*b.Baba Bathra* 4a). Some, though, must have been offended by the money lavished on it. Some, such as the folk responsible for the Dead Sea Scrolls, felt the new Temple was further evidence of the bankruptcy of the leaders of Judaism. Others, however, valued the employment the project provided; when the Temple was more or less finished in the early 60s, eighteen

---

36. Some of Herod's early coin types have a tripod like the tripods associated with the worship of Pythian Apollo. It is not clear whether this is intended as a deliberate reference to this renovation project or to the incense tripod in the Temple in Jerusalem. There is another shape of tripod altogether on several of Herod's coin types; the legs on this are more like the kind of tripod legs found in Israel. Since no representation of the tripod in the Temple is known, the question cannot be settled.

37. See P. Richardson, "The Social-Historical Significance for Gentiles and Women of Herod's Temple Architecture," in J. Halligan and Philip Davies, eds., *Second Temple Studies*, forthcoming.

thousand people were put out of work, a fact that helped to foment the great revolt, according to Josephus.

The Temple was to serve all Jews, though in fact it could serve only those who came to it. Synagogues provided for the rest. The records suggest that Herod built no synagogues, though nothing could have been more natural. There are two possible exceptions to this general picture. (1) There was a synagogue at Masada dating from the Sicarii occupation during the Great Revolt; an earlier stage may also have housed a synagogue, and if so, that earlier stage might have been associated with Herod's work at Masada.[38] (2) A fragmentary inscription, though its reading is uncertain, from the Jewish catacombs in Rome can be read to refer to a "Synagogue of the Herodians"; if that reading is correct, Herod was seen in some way as the synagogue's patron (Appendix B).[39]

Herod's buildings allow preliminary judgments on Herod's religious convictions. He was a Jew, committed to the Temple, accepting the commandments dealing with images and figurative representations. He was devoted to the Patriarchs and Matriarchs of Israel and to the dead members of his family. His commitment to Augustus was almost as strong as his commitment to Yahweh; he had no reservations about building temples to honor Augustus within his own kingdom. He also contributed to other cults, for example, to Ba'al Shamim, to Pythian Apollo, to temples in Tyre and Sidon, and perhaps to cults in Olympia and Athens (see chap. 10).

CULTURAL BUILDINGS

Theaters, hippodromes, stadia, amphitheaters, baths, and gymnasia were part of Hellenistic culture, though foreign to religious Jews. Part of the strangeness came from the activities held in such places (dramatic events, games, spectacles, nude athletic competitions, study of philosophy); part derived from the styles of the buildings, with their figurative decorations sometimes offensively portrayed; part related to the quasi-religious character of the events that took place there. That Herod built a number of such structures is important to his portrait.

Jerusalem was the most sensitive place in the Jewish world, yet it had had a gymnasium since before the Hasmonean revolt of 165 BCE (1 Macc. 1:14–15). Josephus says that Herod built a theater, a hippodrome, and an amphitheater. The theater was located on the north slope of Er-Ras (the south side of Wadi es-Shamm), a few hundred meters south of the Hinnom Valley, where it had a

---

38. Netzer, *Masada*, vol. 3, discusses the possibilities and concludes that its original Herodian structure was a stable, a view I find unconvincing.

39. P. Richardson, "Augustan-era Synagogues in Rome," in K. Donfried and P. Richardson, eds., *Judaism and Christianity in Rome in the First Century,* forthcoming.

view of the whole south wall of the city.[40] An amphitheater is once referred to by Josephus and a hippodrome twice (*Ant.* 15.268 for the former; *War* 2.44 and *Ant* 17.255 for the latter), though he may be sloppy in his terminology and may merely refer to the same structures.[41] The last two passages are incidental references to Pentecost pilgrims (4 BCE) being located south of the city. Josephus probably confuses hippodrome and amphitheater in these three passages; it seems likeliest that Herod built an amphitheater—possibly a hippodrome—on a flat site southwest of the city, not yet identified.[42]

In two of Herod's favorite places, Herodium and Jericho, he built similar facilities, in both cases developing unorthodox solutions. Just below the Intermediate Palace at Herodium he constructed a "course" of some kind, on axis with an important but mysterious "monumental building." No analogy exists for this combination of structures.[43] At Jericho he combined a hippodrome-like "course" with a theater-like building at one end, so that the viewing area was not along the sides, as in a hippodrome or stadium, but from the starting or finishing end.[44] These two unique solutions to spectacles were at his own private palaces, where the public would not attend. For public purposes more traditional structures were provided.

Examples of public arenas can be seen at Caesarea Maritima, where the Herodian hippodrome has been excavated parallel to the sea shore. It was damaged by wave action from the Mediterranean (it was built too close), and was later filled in and covered over. A new hippodrome was subsequently built on the east side of the city. Just south of the hippodrome Herod built a theater,[45] and in the northeast part of the city an amphitheater can be detected, though it

40. The shape of the cavea can still be seen. Test holes in the nineteenth century confirmed the identification, but no scientific excavation has been carried out. On theaters, see A. Segal, *Architecture and the Theatre in Eretz Israel during the Roman and Byzantine Periods* (Haifa: University of Haifa Press, 1991).

41. *Ant.* 15.268 distinguishes the "amphitheater" from and later than the "theater." He locates the former in the "plain," probably to be understood as the Rephaim Plain, southwest of the city proper.

42. *Ant.* 15. 268–91 incorrectly uses the word *theatron* for contests typically carried on in a hippodrome, stadium, amphitheater, or gymnasium, but not in a *theatron*. In the "trophies incident" the structure in question was for animal contests (15.274), suggesting strongly that the second building—where the trophies were hung—was an amphitheater.

43. There was no obvious provision for viewing areas for this course, though the Intermediate and Upper Palaces provided vantage points, suggesting a "private" purpose.

44. The theater-like structure at Jericho was, uncharacteristically, made of mud brick. The sides and rear face formed a rectangle, not a semi-circle as in other theaters built on a flat site, creating a space at the rear of the cavea. The site is almost on axis with the Winter Palace, though a good distance north of it.

45. The excavators concluded that the earliest phase of this much rebuilt theater was Herodian. The most recent excavations seem to imply that the hippodrome and palace, and possibly the theater, formed a carefully articulated trio of buildings.

is unexcavated. At Sebaste there was a Herodian phase of the still visible the-ater[46] and a stadium carved at one end into the hill on which the city sits.[47] Herod built a bath at Ashkelon, gymnasia in Ptolemais, Tripolis, and Damascus, and theaters in Sidon and Damascus (in Damascus the location of the theater can be determined from the semi-circular street pattern to the south of the Omayyed Mosque and on one side of "Straight Street").

Three statements summarize Herod's cultural building projects. (1) Herod built cultural facilities mostly in places where religious proclivities would not cause problems—hellenized cities in his own areas and Hellenistic cities else-where. (2) His attraction to these buildings prompted him to experiment with novel forms in places where only he and his guests used them. (3) The two such structures he built in the Holy City expressed his cultural convictions at the center of Judaism, but he located them outside the city and minimized their offense by using a limited decorative vocabulary.[48]

COMMERCIAL CONSTRUCTION AND INFRASTRUCTURE

Some large-scale constructions were intended to promote trade.[49] The most important was Caesarea Maritima with its enormous harbor installations, warehouse facilities, commercial space, and the like. Smaller but analogous facilities were provided in other new cities, especially Sebaste (at the center of a rich agricultural area), but also in Agrippias, Antipatris, Phaselis, and others. In Jerusalem, the Temple reconstruction provided for commercial activity along the streets adjacent to the Temple retaining walls.[50] Whether other parts of the city also had state-sponsored shopping or commercial facilities is not certain.

Two sites deserve special mention. (1) To the north of the Winter Palace at Jericho was a cluster of buildings whose purpose has not yet been fully clari-fied; likely they constituted a manufacturing or refining area, connected with the royal estates at Jericho. If confirmed, this fact would imply that Herod maintained a close watch on the products (perfumes, ointments, opobalsam, and date wine) he produced; if this could be generalized, it could have repercus-sions on the commercial and manufacturing activities near his other estates in

---

46. See J. W. Crowfoot, "Samaria Excavations: The Stadium," *PEFQS* (1934): 62–73, and plates I–VI.

47. At Sepphoris, the theater cut into the north slope of the city's hill shows no first-century BCE evidence, a conclusion that coheres with Josephus's silence.

48. The so-called trophies incident showed Herod's reserve with respect to decorative matters (*Ant.* 15.268–91).

49. On the economy in general, Z. Safrai, *The Economy of Roman Palestine* (London: Routledge, 1994).

50. Evidence for shops is quite certain along the south wall (below the terrace at the Huldah Gates), under the main pier supporting the outer end of the stair at "Robinson's arch," and along parts of the street beside the Western Wall.

western Samaria, the Plain of Esdraelon, Idumaea, and so on. (2) En Boqeq, at the southwest corner of the Dead Sea, had a small industrial installation producing pharmaceuticals and cosmetics;[51] nothing connects it directly with Herod himself, but it is possible—perhaps even probable—that he had a finger in that pie too. Under the procurators the area was an Imperial estate; perhaps it already was a royal prerogative under Herod.

Outside his own territories, Herod provided benefactions for commercial facilities at four locations, intended no doubt to impress upon citizens his interest in trade and commerce. At Tyre and Berytus he constructed "halls, porticoes . . . and markets" (*exedras de kai stoas . . . kai agoras, War* 1.422), referring in part to commercial activity.[52] At Antioch he repaved the main street and fitted it with colonnades—thus introducing the first covered shopping street. In Chios he rebuilt a *stoa* destroyed by Mithridates, possibly, but not certainly, a storehouse.

Herod's commercial and manufacturing interests show intriguingly in his dealings with the shipbuilding industry at Rhodes. Josephus's allusions to these dealings seem to indicate two related things:[53] benefactions in general to support the industry itself in whatever way was appropriate[54] and, following the construction of a trireme, giving his business to Rhodes when he needed large warships.

I use the modern term "infrastructure" to cover state projects: roads, sewers, reservoirs, and aqueducts are the most obvious needs. Herod was involved in far more of this type of work than the literary record tells us (since most ancient authors are not interested in such matters) or than we can infer from archaeology—the projects are not readily datable. There is no hint in the literature that Herod built roads, yet it is inconceivable that he was inactive on this front, given his new cities, relations with neighboring states, interest in trade and the economy. His extensive harbor facilities at Caesarea Maritima were undoubtedly state-funded; he probably provided minor harbor facilities elsewhere, as at Anthedon-Agrippias or Joppa.

Clearly visible in the archaeological record, and occasionally in the literary record, are provisions for water and sewage. The concern for waste removal at Caesarea Maritima is commented on by Josephus, who describes it as an engineering marvel.[55] There were sewers below the Temple court in Jerusalem,

---

51. M. Gichon, "'En Boqeq," *NEAEHL* 2.395–99.

52. The *stoa* originally was a long storehouse for grain and *agora* clearly meant market place.

53. At *War* 1.280 he commissions the building of a trireme to take him to Italy in 40 BCE. At *War* 1.424 he provides funds *eis nautikon* ("for shipbuilding"); at *Ant* 16.147 *pros naupēgian* ("for shipbuilding").

54. Shipbuilding sheds have been excavated alongside the harbor in Rhodes, though not from this period. A full report has never appeared.

55. The rise and fall of the Mediterranean flushed out the city sewer system, according to *Ant.* 15.340.

where the sacrificial cult created a very heavy load of blood and waste that needed to be carried away, and under the street west of the western wall.[56] Appropriate attention was given to similar projects in urban contexts such as Sebaste.

Water facilities are more obvious today.[57] In Jerusalem Herod built several major reservoirs, partly for citizens' needs and more particularly for the Temple's needs. This was presumably state work at Herod's direction. The following were in whole or part Herodian: the Pool of Israel (north of the Temple precinct), the Struthion Pool (at the Antonia Fortress), the Mamillah Pool (northwest of the Jaffa Gate), Hezekiah's Pool (northeast of the Jaffa Gate), the Sheep Pool (Pool of Bethesda at St. Anne's), possibly the Birkat Sitti Maryam (outside St. Stephen's Gate), and the Birkat es-Sultan (Serpent's Pool, southwest of the Jaffa Gate). Most were above the level of the Temple platform and could supply water for cultic purposes. Some were also intended for the city's general water supply.

Herod's most ambitious water project was Solomon's Pools, where water was collected within a bowl-shaped area south of Bethlehem and brought by aqueduct to the city—a distance of twenty-four kilometers as the aqueduct flows (another system in the Wadi Arub extended the length to sixty-one kilometers). The route followed the contours in some places, cut through the hills in another, and eventually approached Jerusalem along the Hinnom and Tyropoean valleys to enter the Temple across Wilson's arch at platform level. Of the three enormous reservoirs, one and maybe two were built by Herod; one was probably built by Pontius Pilate a generation later with money "borrowed" from the Temple resources. Herod revised installations at the Gihon Spring on the Ophel (City of David), at Warren's Shaft leading to Hezekiah's Tunnel, and at the Siloam and Hamra Pools at the junction of the Kidron and Hinnom valleys.

Herod's careful attention to water is confirmed by the evidence of other Herodian sites. All the fortresses had intricate water facilities—aqueducts, cisterns, collecting basins, and so on (traceable at Hyrcania, Herodium, Jericho, Docus, Cypros, Masada, Alexandreion, and Machaerus). Caesarea Maritima, Sebaste, Panias, and Phaselis all had extensive facilities. At Laodicea ad Marum in Syria Herod provided an aqueduct for the city.

In his own palaces he satisfied his needs with pools of different kinds: at Herodium, a large pool with a gazebo in the middle reached only by boat, the whole surrounded by stoas alongside a landscaped garden; at Jericho, a large pool with a more or less matching garden, overlooked by a central gazebo

---

56. It was carried away in sewers below the platform, one of which can still be seen in the south wall. From here the waste went—as the city waste does today—down Wadi Kidron past Mar Saba and to the Dead Sea.

57. On some of the following, *NEAEHL* 2.746–47.

crowning an artificial mound; at Caesarea Maritima, a pool in the interior of the palace with a statue in the middle; and at the royal palace in Jerusalem, "deep canals and ponds everywhere, studded with bronze figures, through which water was discharged, and around the streams were numerous cots for tame pigeons" (*War* 5.181–82). He built swimming pools at both Masada (south of the Western Palace) and at Machaerus, and perhaps elsewhere.

Water was the most crucial infrastructure need, for which Herod provided imaginatively. He tended to sewage facilities in his largest urban centers and provided significant commercial and industrial facilities. These kinds of facilities did not attract much attention from contemporary authors; the evidence is all the more impressive.

STRATEGY AND RATIONALE

The reasons for this largess—a program almost overpowering in its scope— were complex. It will not do to attribute such a program to megalomania or paranoia.[58] The reasons for it change as need and Herod's circumstances change, so ultimately the question requires reassessment of the social conditions of Herod's reign. In the following analysis I have conjectured the dating of many projects (see Appendix A), though most dates should be considered merely educated guesses.

When introducing a list of Herod's projects, Josephus says encomiastically: "Thenceforth he advanced to the utmost prosperity; his noble spirit rose to greater heights, and his lofty ambition was mainly directed to works of piety" (*War* 1.400; *kai to pleon tês magalonoias epeteinen eis eusebeian*). He then goes on to deal with Herod's piety toward Judaism and its cult center, piety toward his patrons Antony and Augustus and Agrippa, piety toward his family members, and then toward himself. Josephus's artificial approach integrates differentiated aspects of one quality: piety.[59] His unitary approach is attractive, but overlooks many factors.

---

58. P. Richardson, "Religion and Architecture. A Study in Herod's Piety, Power, Pomp and Pleasure," *Bulletin of the Canadian Society of Biblical Studies* 45 (1985): 3–29.

59. In *War* 1.400 Josephus attributes to Herod "utmost prosperity," "noble spirit" (or "moral stature"?), "superb generosity" (or "lofty ambition"?), and "works of piety." At the conclusion of the section (1.429–30) he summarizes his life: "Herod's genius was matched by his physical constitution. . . . He was blessed by good fortune. . . ." These contrast starkly with evaluations after his death: "the most cruel tyrant . . . , he crippled the towns in his own dominion, he embellished those of other nations, lavishing the life blood of Judea on foreign communities. . . . he had sunk the nation to poverty and the last degree of iniquity" (*War* 2.84–86, in the mouths of the Jewish delegation in Rome); "he was . . . cruel to all alike and one who easily gave in to anger and was contemptuous of justice. And yet he was as greatly favoured by fortune as any man . . ." (*Ant.* 17.191, in Josephus's own words).

A. GRATITUDE AND HONOR. Early in Herod's career, gratitude was a dominant motif—part of his "piety." Herod renamed the fortress in Jerusalem after his patron of the moment, Mark Antony. The same motive was evident in his gratitude to Rhodes for the help he received there on his way to Rome while fleeing from Antigonus in 40 BCE; though short of funds he assisted Rhodes to repair the damage caused by the war against Cassius (*Ant.* 14.377–78).[60] He was grateful to Rhodes a second time, when Octavian confirmed his kingship in 31 BCE. Gratitude was his earliest and his strongest motive as benefactor—exactly what one should expect in a society dominated by a patronage system with strong notions of honor. He accrued honor from large expenditures in memory of benefactors and communities that had helped him. What is startling is the extent of these projects.

B. SELF-PRESERVATION. The defensive line of fortresses along the Rift Valley were Maccabean foundations whose location and style were set. Their rebuilding was among Herod's first tasks. Parthia had just withdrawn, Nabatea continued to threaten, Antigonus was still active (until 37), and the population was not friendly. During the early and middle 30s, then, self-preservation and defense were considerations. As late as the 20s he fortified two major cities, Sebaste and Caesarea Maritima, as was customary at the time (see map 5).

It is easy to exaggerate, however. Two factors lessen defense as a motive. First, Herod did not continue to build fortified structures throughout his reign. As stability became a reality he built unprotected structures—the palaces at Jericho, Betharamphtha, and Caesarea, for example. Of the later projects, only Herodium was truly fortified, and its architectural character was strongly influenced by its eventual use as a mausoleum. Apart from the rebuilding of the Maccabean fortresses there is no evidence of a strong sense of self-preservation or of "paranoia" behind Herod's programs. A second factor that lessens defense as a motive is that there were *no* rebuilt fortresses in Galilee or Gaulanitis (there may have been a couple of existing ones), only a few in Peraea (Machaerus, and possibly Herodium East and Esbus), and one in Idumaea (Masada).[61] Peraea and Idumaea were the likeliest problem areas for Herod. The popular picture of Herod as an embattled monarch who kept his people in subjection by force of arms, with well-manned fortresses spread throughout his territory, does not persuade in an archaeological and architectural analysis. He may have kept people in some degree of subjection, but the motive of self-defense has been exaggerated.

---

60. Ironically, for Cassius had helped him in his career at a crucial moment.

61. On "fortlets" in Idumaea, see above. If accurate, danger from Nabateans was the likeliest reason, since Egypt had been incorporated into the Empire and Cleopatra was dead.

C. PERSONAL COMFORT. Herod liked creature comforts. Among early projects were renovations of Hasmonean palaces in Jerusalem (though no trace remains) and in Jericho (now extensively excavated). His delight in lavish surroundings never left him; he continued obsessively through the late 30s and 20s and into the 10s to build imaginative residences for himself, his family, and his guests. Enjoyment of his surroundings came out in smaller ways: gardens, pools, gazebos, small baths, vistas that overlooked the landscape or seascape, and attractive yet restrained decoration. We don't know if he ever relaxed to enjoy his buildings, but he created surroundings that would make life enjoyable.

D. PIETY. Another early rationale was "piety" (above, per Josephus), especially for family. Provision of suitable memorials was a concern of the upper classes, for which purpose Herod created a large circular family tomb in Jerusalem before the end of the 30s and Herodium as his own memorial in the 20s. He covered the caves at Hebron (associated with the Patriarchs and Matriarchs) with a memorial, in effect to distant ancestors,[62] as a focus for local piety (late 30s). In a project just north of Hebron at Mamre he memorialized Abraham alone.[63] In Jerusalem he tried to alter public opinion of his desecration of David's tomb by adding another grand memorial.

Herod's strategy in building memorials was closely related to religion; his interest in the Patriarchs and Matriarchs, for example, may have been intended to win approval among Idumaeans and Jews. His religious project at Siʿa at about the same time (32/31 BCE) was aimed to "normalize" relations with Nabateans following a period of conflict.[64] Early experiments with a strategy of "piety" were insignificant, however, compared to his interest in the Emperor cult and his relationship to Judaism (see below, and chap. 10).

E. ECONOMIC EXPANSION. Before Actium, none of Herod's projects had especially large or ambitious goals; all were specific reactions to particular needs. The projects were spread out, with not more than one or two going on at the same time as would be expected in a period of consolidation. After 30 BCE the pace and scale of his projects increased dramatically. Enormous projects were undertaken and several ran concurrently. At some point in the early 20s, accelerating in the late 20s and early 10s, Herod adopted a strategy of economic

---

62. It is remarkable that he gave equal weight to the Matriarchs.

63. The evidence for both these projects is archaeological; the early dates are conjectural.

64. Participation in a Temple of Baʿal Shamim could have angered Jews, though that danger was lessened by the possibility of seeing Baʿal Shamim as an alternative name for the God of Israel. In the Hebrew Bible God can be called *elohe hashamim*, an exilic title (Ezra 1:2; 2 Chron. 36:23; elsewhere in Ezra and Nehemiah 11 times; Jonah 1:9 "the Lord God of Heaven"; Dan. 2:18, 19, 28, 44; Gen. 24:7; Ps. 136:26). Israel could absorb the Canaanite title Baʿal into its understanding of God.

expansion. The building of Sebaste (27 BCE) signalled this phase, while he was still completing Masada, the theater and amphitheater in Jerusalem, and founding Pente Komai, Gaba, and perhaps Phaselis. In the late 20s his construction activities were staggering: Sebaste was still under construction (27–12), Caesarea (22–10), the Temple in Jerusalem (23–15 for the main parts), Herodium (23–15), Panias (ca. 20), Nicopolis (sometime after 27), and possibly the Northern Palace at Masada.

The projects during this period were broadly conceived (military settlements, new cities, trade facilities, religious buildings, personal comfort projects—several of which have already been noted), but the overall strategy seems to have been aimed to stimulate the economy of Judea, enhance its trade position, and secure full employment. "Public works" and "infrastructure" projects, most of which cannot be dated, were probably linked with these, and had the same general strategy.

F. CULTURAL INTEGRATION. The cultural buildings noted earlier, most constructed from the early 20s through the 10s, formed part of a strategy. Herod's motive was in part obtaining popular support, in part encouraging Roman culture. Many of the cultural buildings were built in three main cities inside his realm (Jerusalem, Sebaste, and Caesarea) and in several places outside his territory; they were built not when he was consolidating his position in the 30s, but later when he was seeking greater cultural integration.

In addition, features of other structures coincided with this thrust toward cultural integration; the Temple in Jerusalem included Roman features (the Royal Basilica, the stoas); many buildings incorporated Roman decorative elements (Corinthian and Doric columns, Pompeian interior decoration); and urban design elements reflected late Hellenistic civic patterns (Hippodamian plans, agoras). Herod minimized offensive elements, but he was a good Roman and a "Hellenist."

G. IMPERIAL PIETY. Following Octavian's acclamation as Augustus in 27 BCE, there was a growing development, especially in the east, of the Emperor cult, to honor him and the goddess Roma. Herod could probably have avoided participation; no one would have insisted that Judea—a monotheistic country—participate in building Sebasteia. But Herod embraced the Emperor cult, first at Sebaste (after 27), then Caesarea (sometime after 22), and Panias (sometime after 20), all sites where strong objections were not likely to arise. His rationale was simple: the Augustan age required "piety" toward Augustus, and Judea must participate to attain its proper place. The amount of popular support these shrines gained is uncertain.[65]

---

65. P. Richardson, "Religion, Architecture and Ethics: Some First Century Case Studies," *Horizons in Biblical Theology* 10/2 (1988): 19–49.

H. JEWISH PIETY. It will seem odd to those wishing consistency that just when Herod was engaged in building temples to Roma and Augustus he dealt with the priests in Jerusalem to rebuild the Second Temple. To take its place on the international scene Judea's cult center had to rank with the cult centers of others. Suspicion of Herod as patron of the Second Temple must have been intense; he was untrustworthy, perhaps even illegitimate. Precautions were taken, therefore, to ensure that God's worship continued uninterrupted and undefiled, that work would be speedily completed, and that the holy place would be built by priests.

This project alone (beginning in the late 20s and continuing to the end of his life and beyond) assured Herod a place in Jewish religious history. Perhaps Josephus's report is pointed in the right direction (*Ant.* 15.380–425, especially 382–87): Herod was motivated by prestige, by piety, and by the peace and wealth of Judea. It is almost impossible to imagine he wanted to undertake the work—or was able to get agreement from the priestly authorities—without a strong personal commitment to Judaism. Other aspects of his piety, and his innovation, show in the provision for women and Gentiles in the Temple.

I. INTERNATIONAL REPUTATION. As Herod moved onto the international stage in the 10s, especially with his expedition with Marcus Agrippa to the Black Sea and Pontus, his interest in international questions increased. Though active internationally as early as 40 BCE, by the 10s Herod was concerned for his own role and reputation. He was engaged in the Olympic Games, supported Diaspora Jewish communities in the Islands and in Asia Minor, invested in trade facilities elsewhere: all activities aimed to establish Judea as a premier province in the Empire. This objective came relatively late. It is ironic that it coincided with the disastrous deterioration in his personal life, the result of which was deterioration in his relations with Augustus and diminution of his reputation internationally (see map 6).

CONCLUDING COMMENTS

The evidence of Herod's benefactions, public works, and building activities might now be read differently from the usual way; it opens the way for a more integrated analysis of his reign and allows for a more generous evaluation of his role. A few additional comments are reuqired.

All of Herod's structures were up-to-date in both materials and methods of construction. Some of the design elements were ahead of their time; some of the innovations had no earlier Roman antecedents. His use of concrete that set underwater conformed to its contemporaneous mention by Vitruvius; the harbor at Caesarea was the largest experiment with this new technology at this period and was hugely successful. The organization needed to gather the materials, obtain the technical experts, and coordinate the work was prodigious. And early on Herod imported other innovations for wall, floor, and roof construction (the little vault at Herodium may be the earliest of its kind).

His designs were innovative also. The rebuilding of the Temple in Jerusalem best exemplifies this—not only its vast size, but such elements as the retaining walls, the brilliantly varied entrances and exits (including a bridge to the western hill, two pedestrian overpasses at the southern corners, a dramatic pair of tunnels and stairs to dramatize the holy place itself, and a bridge across to the Mount of Olives for the red heifer ceremony), a series of courtyards defining levels of holiness, and so on.

There remains an unanswerable question: Who was responsible for this remarkable body of work? We do not know if it was Herod or someone acting under him—and if the latter, was it one person or a whole stable of architects? Several factors point to Herod's important role: the combination of influences that reflected Herod's own background, the wide-ranging innovations, and the absence of references to architects when there must have been popular comment on the structures. At the least, Herod must have been a remarkable patron, perhaps even greater than either Augustus or Marcus Agrippa, the only two rivals he had in his period. At the most, he played an important architectural role himself.

Appendix A
LIST OF HEROD'S BUILDINGS

A. In Jerusalem

1. Antonia Fortress, with porticoes connecting it to Temple,
   apartments, cloisters, bath, four towers (site of al-Omariyya
   school)   [37–35 BCE]
   BJ 1.401; 5.238–46; AJ 15.292, 409, 424; 18.91–95; 20.30
2. Hasmonean Palace rebuilt   [mid-30s BCE]
   BJ 2.344; AJ 20.190
3. Royal Palace (Caesareum and Agrippeum—two
   buildings—with banqueting halls, one hundred guest rooms,
   cloisters, courtyards, and pools)   [23 BCE]
   BJ 1. 402; 5.156–83, 246; AJ 15.292, 318
4. Phasaelis, Mariamme, and Hippicus Towers   [mid–30s BCE]
   BJ 1.418; 2.46, 439; 5.144, 147, 161–75; 7.1–2; AJ 16.144;
   17.257   [possibly later]
5. Family Tomb (north of Damascus Gate)   [before 30 BCE]
   BJ 5.108, 507
6. Temple, Temenos, Courtyards   [23 BCE–64 CE]
      Sanctuary, BJ 1.401; AJ 15.380–425; 17.162; 20.219–22;
         cf. Pliny NH 5.70 (BJ 1.401 implies 23; AJ 15.380 implies
         20)   [23–22 BCE]
      Forecourts   [23–15 BCE]
      Temenos with retaining walls, various gates
      Royal Basilica, BJ 5.184–227
      Solomon's Porticoes (remodeling only?)
      Other Porticoes, AJ 17.259–63
      Exits and overpasses at south-west corner (Robinson's
         Arch) and south-east corner
      Bridge to upper city (Wilson's Arch)
      Streets and shops
      Plazas and Miqvehs outside Huldah Gates
      Water and sewage systems
      Gate, BJ 2.5
      Gate of Marcus Agrippa, BJ 1.416   [before 15 BCE]
      Golden Eagle, AJ 17.151   [before 15 BCE]
      Beautiful Gate
7. Memorial at entrance of David's Tomb (unknown)   [10 BCE]
   AJ 16.179–84; 7.392–94; 16.188
8. Theater (slope of south side of Wadi es-Shamm)   [before 28 BCE]
   AJ 15.268–91
9. Amphitheater (Rephaim Plain?)   [before 28 BCE]
   AJ 15.268
   Hippodrome (probably identical to previous)   [before 28 BCE]
   BJ 2.44; AJ 17.255

Aqueducts and Reservoirs

10. Solomon's Pools (south of Bethlehem, with aqueducts to
        Jerusalem and S. to 'Arrub)
11. Pool of Mamillah (Western Jerusalem)
12. Hezekiah's Pool (north of Petra Hotel)
13. Sheep Pool (St. Anne's), 5 porticoes (Herodian acc. to Jeremias)
14. Struthion Pool (Antonia Fortress)
15. Pool of Israel (at North wall of Temple Mount)
16. Birkat Sitti Maryam (at St. Stephen's Gate)
17. Gihon Spring; Hezekiah's Tunnel; Siloam and Hamra pools
18. Various aqueducts to serve the pools mentioned above and
        Temple needs

B. In His Own Territory

1. Alexandreion (Sartaba), fortified palace restored by Pheroras   [39/38 BCE]
    BJ 1.133–37, 161–72, 308, 334, 528–29, 551; AJ 13.417;
    14.48–52, 82–94, 394, 419; 15.84, 185; 16.13, 317; Strabo
    Geog. 16.2.40; m.Rosh Hash. 2.4
2. Hyrcania (Khirbet Mird), refortified palace with water system   [37 (32?) BCE]
    BJ 1.161, 167, 364, (664?) 684; AJ 13.417; 14.89; 15.366; 16.13;
    17.187; Strabo *Geog.* 16.2.40
3. Masada   [37–10 BCE]
    BJ 1.236–38, 264–67, 286–87; 2.408, 433–34,446–47, 653;
    4. 339, 516, 555; 7.252–407; AJ 14. 296, 361–63, 390–91,
    490; 15. 184; Strabo *Geog.* 16.2.44; Pliny NH 5.73
        Fortification: casemate wall around top
        Western Palace
        Other palaces
        Storehouses
        Administrative buildings
        Barracks
        Synagogue
        Baths
        Cisterns
        Northern Villa
        Pools and gardens
4. Machaerus (Makhwar), fortified palace with ramparts, towers,
    cisterns, adjacent town, aqueducts   [20s BCE]
    BJ 1.161, 164–77; 2.485–86; 4.555; 7.164–210; AJ 13.83,
    89–97, 417; 18.111; Strabo *Geog.* 16.2.40; m.Tamid 3.8;
    j.Shviit 9.2.38d
5. Cypros (Kipros) Fortified Palace above Jericho   [30s BCE]
    BJ 1.407, 417; 2.484; AJ 16.143

6. Docus (Jebel Qarantal) Fortress   [30s BCE]
   Strabo *Geog.* 16.2.40; 1 Macc 16:11–16; AJ 13.230–35; BJ
   1.54–56
7. Herodium West (= Har Hordos; Jebel el-Fureidis) Fortress   [23–15 BCE]
   BJ 1.265, 419–21, 673; 3.55; 4.55, 518–19;7.163; AJ 14.360;
       15.323–25; 16.13; 17.199 9.199? Pliny NH 5.70
           Upper palace with towers, apartments, cisterns
           Stadium or course
           Monumental building
           Pool with gazebo, gardens
           Large intermediate palace by course
           Other palaces, service buildings
           Aqueducts and cisterns
8. Herodium East (= Kh. es-Samra?) Arabian frontier   [after 30 BCE]
   BJ 1.41
9. Hebron, memorial to Patriarchs and Matriarchs over Cave of
       Macphelah   [30s BCE]
   BJ 4.530–33
10. Mamre (= Ramat et Khalil), memorial   [30s BCE]
    BJ 4.530-33
11. Si'a (near Canatha), temple of Ba'al Shamim   [32–31 BCE]
12. Jericho (= Tulul Abu el-Alaiq) BJ 1.407; Strabo *Geog.* 16.2.40
    Reconstruction of Hasmonean Palace   [37–35 BCE]
    Second Palace (now covered over)   [18–9 BCE]
    Winter Palace on Wadi Qelt
        Gardens and pools
        Strabo, *Geog.* 16.2.40
    Hippodrome *cum* theater, plus pavilion (= Tel es-Samrat)
        BJ 1.659, 666
    [Amphitheater ? probably part of above]; AJ 17.161, 175–78,
        194
    Adjacent town with manufacturing areas (perfume? wine?
        dates? balsam?)
    Aqueducts – Wadi Qelt
    Cemetery (= Nuseib el-Aweishireh)
13. Betharamphtha (= Tell Er Rama), palace; renamed Livias/
        Julias by Agrippa
    BJ 2.59, 168, 252; 4.438; AJ 17.277; 18.27; 20.159; Pliny NH
        13.44; Ptol. *Geog.* 5.15.6; Eus. Onom. 49.12; j. Shebit 9.2
14. Sepphoris (= Zippori), palace
    BJ 2.56, 574; AJ 18.27; 17.271
    Arsenal ?
15. Caesarea Maritima (Qesari)   [22–12 BCE]
        Harbor, mole, breakwater, towers, docks
        Warehouses and commercial buildings

Promenade
Temple to Roma and Augustus
Amphitheater
Theater
Hippodrome (all three for quinquennial games)
Promontory Palace (= Praetorium, Acts 23.35)
Walls and North gates
Aqueducts
BJ 1.156, 408–16; 2.266; AJ 14.76, 121; 15.293, 331–41;
16.136–41; 20.173

16. Sebaste (Shomeron)   [27–12 BCE]
Walls, gates, fortifications, AJ 15.292, 296–98
Colonnaded streets (probably later)
Temple to Roma and Augustus, AJ 15.298
Forum
Pre-Basilical building (later?)
Stadium (Pre-Herodian—Busink; Herodian—Netzer)
Theater (later?)
Aqueducts
BJ 1.64, 403, 415; AJ 13.275; 15.292–93, 296–98, 342;
16.136–41; Strabo Geog. 16.2.34

17. Panias (= Banyas), Temple to Roma and Augustus   [after 20 BCE]
Palace
Walls and fortifications?
BJ 1.404–406; AJ 15.363–64

18. Phasaelis (El Fasayili), new city   [after 30 BCE?]
BJ 1.418; 2.98,. 167; AJ 16.145; Pliny NH 13.4.44   [= 12–10?]

19. Ascalon (Tel Ashqelon), baths, fountains, colonnades, palace   [after 30 BCE]
BJ 1.422; 2.98; AJ 17.321

20. Antipatris (Afek), new city   [9 BCE]
BJ 1.417–18; AJ 16.142–43; 11.329; 13.390

21. Agrippias (Anthedon), port—refounded and rebuilt   [after 30 BCE]
BJ 1.87, 118, 416; AJ 13.357; 14.9

22. Pente Komai (= Fondaquma), village for soldiers, AJ 15.296   [27–20 BCE]

23. Gaba (Sha'ar ha-'Amaqim) military colony   [28–24 BCE ?]
Life 115–18; BJ 2.459; 3.36; AJ 15.294, 299; Pliny NH 5.19.75
(?)

24. Bathyra (Busr El-Hariri?), Babylonian military colony   [9–6 BCE]
Life 55–61; AJ 17.23-29 [=Samamim?]

25. Heshbon (Hisban near Amman), military colony refortified [28–24 BCE ?]

26. Esbus (fortress?), AJ 15.294, 299

27. Idumaean settlement in Trachonitis   [9/8 BCE]

Uncertain

1. Aroer, fortified town in Negev
2. En Boqeq, industrial installation near Dead Sea
3. Batanea, fortresses
4. Malatha, fortress (84x56 m.) settlement adjacent
5. Gittha, rebuilt by Machaeras for Herod, *War* 1.326
6. Agrippina (Jarmuth), at Belvoir
7. Oresa, BJ 1.266, 294; AJ 14.361, 400
8. Zif, fortress, 7 km south of Hebron
9. Adora (= Dura), fortress, BJ 1.2.6; AJ 13.9.1; 1 Macc 13:20
10. Tell Qasile (Joppa), Herodian public building in Stratum IV
11. Calirrhoe, hot springs
12. Gedor (east of es-Salt)
13. Keren Naftali (west of Lake Huleh)

C. In Phoenicia and Roman Province of Syria

1. Ptolemais (Akko), gymnasium, BJ 1.422
2. Damascus, BJ 1.422
      Gymnasium
      Theater
3. Tyre (= Sour) BJ 1.422
      Halls
      Porticoes
      Temples
      Market places
4. Sidon, theater (BJ 1.422)
5. Byblus, walls, BJ 1.422
6. Berytus (Beirut), BJ 1.422 [cf. AJ 19.335 re Agrippa I
      —amphitheater, baths, porticoes]
      Halls
      Porticoes
      Temples
      Market places
7. Tripolis (Trablus), gymnasium, BJ 1.422, 212
8. Laodicea-on-sea (Latakia), aqueduct, BJ 1.422   [36 BCE ?]
9. Balanea (near Latakia), lightened taxes, BJ 1.422
10. Antioch (Antakya), broad paved street, colonnade   [30 or 20? BCE]
      BJ 1.425; AJ 16.148, 427

D. In Asia Minor and Greece (mostly 14 BCE on occasion of visit with Marcus Agrippa)

BJ 1.400; AJ 15.12-15; 16.16ff (re Itinerary) 16.24 (re
   benefactions)
1. Unnamed towns in Cilicia, "tax relief," BJ 1.428

2. Lycia, "gifts," BJ 1.425
3. Phaselis in Lycia, "tax relief," BJ 1.428
4. Ionia, "liberality," BJ 1.425; AJ 12.125; 16.27
5. Pergamum, "Herod's offerings," BJ 1.425
6. Rhodes, restored city
   Rebuilt Pythian Temple   [40? BCE]
   Money for ship-building   [40, 30? BCE]
   BJ 1.280, 387, 424; AJ 15.183; 16.147; 14.378
7. Cos, revenue for gymnasiarch (endowment?), BJ 1.423
8. Chios, colonnades, money to repay loan from Augustus,
   AJ 16.18-19, 26
9. Samos, "gifts," BJ 1.425; AJ 16.23–24
10. Athens, "Herod's offerings," BJ 1.425
11. Elis, Olympic Games, endowed with funds   [12 (8?) BCE]
    restoration work? BJ 1. 426–27; AJ 16.149
12. Lacedaemon (Sparta) "Herod's offerings," BJ 1.425
13. Nicopolis, "the greater part of their public buildings" [after 29 BCE]
    BJ 1.425; AJ 16.147
15. Delos (?Syros) epigraphic reference
    possibly for gymnasium (*xystos*) at stadium

Appendix B

INSCRIPTIONS AND COINS

INSCRIPTIONS

Several important inscriptions mention Herod or other members of his family by name. They originate both from within his kingdom and from sites associated with Herod beyond his own borders (see maps 5 and 6).

1. Masada

> C. Sentius Saturninus, Consul
> Philonian wine from the estate of L. Laenius
> for King Herod the Jew

Thirteen Latin inscriptions, all in more or less the above form and on wine jugs' handles from a shipment of 19 BCE, were found at Masada.[66] The date supplied could refer to the vintage, but it probably refers to the date of shipment. The type of wine and the estate are not otherwise known, but it was probably from southern Italy. The handles were found in several locations: in storerooms (three), in building IX (one), in the northwest section of the wall near the synagogue (three), and in the floor of the Herodian-level of the synagogue (one). Different inscriptions are found on #817 (also referring to 19 BCE) and on #818 (to 14 BCE).

With varying degrees of completeness, the inscriptions refer to "King Herod the Jew," as the editor insists (*regi herodi iudaico*, not "Herod King of the Jews"). The attestation of a supplier of wine in Italy is good evidence for others' views of Herod as a Jew, and probably for his viewing himself in just this way.

In addition to these thirteen, six other jars were stamped with consuls' or others' names, one dated to 27 BCE (#795), "Year of Caesar's seventh and Agrippa's third consulate," and one (#796) to 26 BCE, possibly indicating Masada's well-advanced construction at that time. Evidence for products other than wine was clear: "honey" (#800), medicinal frankincense (#801), "honey wine" (#821), "apples from Cumae" (#822, perhaps also ##823–25), "fish sauce" (*garum;* #826, referring in lines 4–5 to the "king" and probably to "Herod the Jew" as in the previous cases; somewhat similarly up to #850). There were also Latin amphora stamps referring to Nepos and dates on the handles to 27–26 BCE (##946–47, see also ##948–50).

These jars provide evidence both of a wide range of imported products on

---

66. H. M. Cotton and J. Geiger, *Masada II: Latin and Greek Documents* (Jerusalem: Israel Exploration Society, 1989), pp. 133 and following with figures 795–950. The date is established from the consulship of Saturninus. These thirteen are numbers 804–16.

Masada at a relatively early period and of indisputable references to Herod the King as a Jew. The evidence is specially significant found in Judea and having come from Italy.

2.(a) IEJ 20 (1970):97–98 (Jerusalem)

Year 32 of King Herod, Benefactor, Friend of Caesar
Inspector of markets
Three minas

This Greek inscription on a limestone weight, with uncertain provenance, is in three lines, with the first running around the weight, and the other two lines within.[67] Year 32 corresponds to 9/8 BCE. The name Herod is signified by the first two letters of the name in a monogram. This is the only known Judean inscription referring to Herod as "Benefactor" (*Eu*[*ergetês*])and as "Friend of Caesar" (*philok*[*aisaros*]). (For Diaspora inscriptions to the same effect, see below.) The linking of Herod's kingship, benefactions, and relationship to Augustus in this Judean artifact is important, even if it is merely the weight of a Herodian official, the *agoranomos;* it stands as evidence that Herod had no compunctions about promoting his imperial connections.

2.(b) (Ashdod)[68]

In the time of King
Herod
pious
and friend
of Caesar

This is a new and persuasive reading of a lead weight from Ashdod that argues for a provenance under our King Herod, not Herod of Chalcis, the only other plausible suggestion. The argument can be strengthened by noting the anchor on the reverse, a symbol of Herod of Judea that was irrelevant to Herod of Chalcis (see plate X). The language is similar to 2(a) above, which might on the strength of 2(b) be read as "pious" (*eusebias*) rather than "benefactor" (*euergetou*). The two weights and their descriptions of Herod are coherent and important.

---

67. Y. Meshorer, "A Stone Weight from the Reign of Herod," *IEJ* 20 (1970): 97–98, plate 27, who believes that *euergetês* and *philokaisaros* do not otherwise appear in reference to Herod, but see below.

68. A. Kushnir-Stein, "An Inscribed Lead Weight from Ashdod: A Reconsideration," *Zeitschrift für Papyrologie und Epigraphik* 105 (1995): 81–84.

3. SEG 1277 (Jerusalem)

[In the reign of Herod the King]
in the 20th year, upon the high priest
[Simon, S]paris Akeonos
[a foreign resident] in Rhodes
[donated the] pavement
[at a cost of {?}] drachmas

A fragmentary Greek inscription found south of the Temple Mount by B. Mazar and his team in debris in a pool,[69] refers to a donor named Sparis or Paris, probably a Jew living in Rhodes.[70] The gift was some of the paving for the courtyard or, more likely given the location of the inscription, of the platform south of the Temple Mount. The inscription supports the earlier of the two possible datings for the start of construction on the Temple, ca. 23 BCE, since Herod's 20th year was 21/20 BCE (on the one reckoning; on the other it was 18/17 BCE). The form of the inscription conforms to many records of benefactions.

4. Delos (?Syros)

King Herod to the people of . . .

Three fragments of a very large Greek inscription were found in 1874 (sic), 1987, and 1988 on Syros.[71] The editor argues persuasively that the provenance of the inscription was Delos, not Syros, where no large buildings from antiquity have been discovered. The letters are 12 cm (4³/₄") high, on marble slabs that were part of the architrave of a large Doric building (*regulae* and *guttae* survive partially), probably from a portico or perhaps a porch. There was a Jewish community on Delos, but the grand building of which these fragments were a part could hardly have been a building for the community, as the reference to *dêmos* ("people") in the inscription makes perfectly clear. The editor argues for the *xystos* (a covered colonnade in a gymnasium attached to the stadium).

The inscription makes three important points: that Herod made benefactions to Greek communities where there were Jewish communities, but those

---

69. *SEG* 33 (1983): 1277, p. 184–85; B. Isaac, "A Donation for Herod's Temple in Jerusalem," *IEJ* 33 (1983): 86–92, plate 9B. The inscription was intended to be inserted in a wall. The reference to "year 20" must be a part of a regnal formula, linked with a reference to a high priest. The only king who ruled more than twenty years and who was not also high priest was Herod, hence the reconstruction; at the same time this allows identification of the high priest as Simon son of Boethos.

70. Isaac provides evidence, Ibid., pp. 90–91, for Jews in Rhodes.

71. E. Mantzoulinou-Richards, "From Syros: A Dedicatory Inscription of Herodes the Great from an Unknown Building," *Ancient World* 18/3–4 (1988): 87–99

donations were for the people (*dêmos*) at large; that he made very large benefactions sometimes, as this testifies; and that not all his gifts have survived in the literature (it was a plausible deduction that he might have given to Delos, but there was no evidence until the present detective work).

With this, Mantzoulinou-Richards links two other inscriptions, one of which (SEG 16.490) I have hesitantly included below. The other I hesitantly include here as an addendum.

> SEG 16.488 (Chios)
> [so and so was honored for such and such]
> which he repaired with his own money
> and for all the many and great things
> he donated to the city and for his perpetually
> providing anointment oil for the athletes
> for his virtuousness and his benevolence
> toward the city. The supervisor of the repairs
> was Apollonios, son of Apollonios the Philologist.

This dovetails with my number 10, below, in both titulature and name, Apollonios son of Apollonios. That dedication was made on Delos, before the Temple of Apollo; the honoree was not our Herod but his son Antipas, the tetrarch. This, on Chios, is arguably from the same period and directed to the same person, though nothing but plausibility links the inscription with any Herod. It does not seem correct to attribute it to our Herod.

5. OGIS # 415 (Siʿa)

> To King Herod, master,
> Obaisath, son of Saodos
> placed the statue at his own expense

The Greek inscription, now lost, was copied by W. H. Waddington from a statue base on the porch to the right of the entrance of the Temple of Baʿal Shamim at Siʿa. The Marquis de Vogüé found fragments of statues in the vicinity, some of less-than-life-size, including two heads that he took back to Paris. The statue of Herod was life-size, as determined from the foot still attached to the base. "Other fragments of this statue, and a badly mutilated torso, indicated to M. de Vogüé that Herod's effigy had been the special object of early Christian violence."[72]

The statue with its base was donated to the Temple of Baʿal Shamim by a

---

72. H. C. Butler, *Architecture, Southern Syria,* Division II A, Publications of the Princeton University Archaeological Expeditions to Syria, 1904–5 (Leiden: Brill, 1907), p. 379.

member of a family associated with Si'a (Obaisath and Saodos, Nabatean names, are known from other inscriptions at Si'a). The inscription referred to our Herod, the only member of the family known simply as "King Herod." It appears to recognize some involvement by Herod in the building of the Temple, the statue being a grateful recognition. Though the inscription is undated, the building's construction period was late 30s BCE, and the inscription may date from the same period.

Statues of Herod are unattested in Judea and Galilee; this is the nearest known statue to the Holy Land. That Herod appreciated recognition seems a reasonable deduction, though he accepted no such honors in Jewish territory where it would cause offense. His title was clearly "king," linked with a second term of honor, "master" or "lord," probably to be explained here as a term appropriate to the relationship between Obaisath and Herod, perhaps with Herod as patron. It is surprising that no inscriptions have been found in Herod's own territory that recognize his very extensive building activities, especially given the frequency of inscriptions recognizing the contributions of patrons in the Roman world. It is not clear whether this is accidental, or whether it was a deliberate policy on Herod's part to minimize his own role.

6. OGIS # 414; CIAtt 3. 550 (Athens, Acropolis)

> The people to King Herod
> friend of Romans
> because of his good works and good will toward the city.

Found behind the Parthenon on the Acropolis in Athens, the base, which must have carried a statue, was apparently the gift of the Athenian *dêmos* in gratitude to Herod. The inscription highlighted two aspects of Herod's relationship to the Athenians—his "good works" (*euergesia*) and his "good will" (*eunoia*). The impression Josephus gives in *War* 1.425 corresponds to this: Athens, among other cities, was "laden with Herod's offerings." Placing a statue on the Acropolis implied that a portion of his largess was devoted to improvements of some kind in that location; the most logical explanation would be contributions to some aspect of the cult of Athena, though other explanations are possible.

One of the descriptive phrases supplied in the inscription is part of the title of this book: King Herod was "friend of Romans" (*philoromaios*). The term is found in reference to others than Herod—it was the Greek equivalent of one part of the Latin phrase *rex socius et amicus populi Romani,* a designation given to client kings on occasion, and applied, for example, to Hyrcanus II as ethnarch.

7. OGIS 427; CIAtt 3. 551 (Athens, Acropolis)

> The people
> to Herod the pious King and friend of the Emperor
> because of his moral excellence and good works.

Dittenberger applies this to Agrippa I, also "King" (cf. Acts 12:1), but this is unlikely. The location in Athens, the usage "king," and the description of the person honored suggest Herod.

Found on the Acropolis in Athens, west of the Erechtheion, this must also have been connected with Herod's gifts to the city. This was more effusive, however, and struck two notes additional to those in 6, above. Herod was friend of the Emperor—a fact attested to in glowing terms by Josephus—as in 2(a) and 2(b), above. He was also not merely a person of "good works," but a person of "piety" (*eusebês*) and of "moral excellence" (*aretê*). Though discordant and overdone when compared to the usual evaluations of Herod's character, the terms used offer contemporary counter-evaluations of Herod. Josephus uses the term "piety" without blushing (see chap. 8), linked in part with Herod's relationship to Augustus. The inscription is thus consistent with literary sources.

8. *SEG 12 [1955] 150* [73] (Athens, agora)

The people
for Herod the pious King and friend of the Emperor
because of his moral excellence and good works

This inscription was found in the agora in Athens in damaged condition. It was restored in its initial publication so that it gave an identical reading to the previous one. Even the name is missing from this one, though, so it is not a certain testimony to Herod.

9. *OGIS 416 (Cos)*

Herod
—son of Herod the King—
Tetrarch
Philo Aglaos of the family of Nikon
his guest and friend.

The inscription was addressed to Herod's son, Herod Antipas, tetrarch of Galilee or possibly Philip, tetrarch of Gaulanitis, Auranitis, Batanea, and Trachonitis. Whomever, he was identified as "son of Herod the King" in an inscription from Cos, where the elder Herod had donated funds to sustain the office of a gymnasiarch. It confirms that "Herod the King" meant in antiquity our Herod, unless clarified specifically; it also demonstrates that other members of the family were known as Herod, both popularly and formally.

---

73. See also B. D. Merritt, "Greek Inscriptions," *Hesperia* 21 (1952): 340–80; see #14, p. 370.

10. OGIS 417 (Delos)

> The Athenian people and those
> living on the island,
> for Herod, son of Herod the King,
> Tetrarch
> on account of piety and good
> will shown to them
> when Apollonios, son of Apollonios of Phamnous was *epimelêtês*

Likewise dedicated to Herod Antipas (or Philip), specified as the "son of Herod the King," and using adjectives noted above, this inscription was found on Delos in front of the Temple of Apollo. Our Herod is not recorded as having given any benefaction to Delos, though as the discussion above (4) suggests, it is probable. The reference to Athens in the first line strengthens the possibility. Since Herod provided funds for rebuilding the Temple of Pythian Apollo at Rhodes, the Herodian association with Apollo is not far to seek.

11. CIJ 173 (Rome)

> . . . synagogue
> . . . of the Herodians
> . . . a blessing to all.

For this inscription, which may refer to a synagogue of the Herodians in Rome, see chapter 11, where I argue that the Jewish community in Rome, out of gratitude for Herod's constructive role with respect to Jewish privileges in the Diaspora at large, named a synagogue after him during his lifetime.[74] The Roman Jewish community also named synagogues after Augustus and Marcus Agrippa, and possibly after a governor of Syria, Volumnius, who was a friend of Herod's. The inscription, if reconstructed correctly, suggests that during his lifetime this particular Jewish community was more positive toward Herod than Josephus tells us they were at his death, when they joined the Judean delegation's vigorous criticism of him.

The next two generations of Herod's descendants were not generally identified in inscriptions by their relationship to Herod the King. Occasionally, despite Herod's own failure to use the adjective "great," Agrippa I and II have it used of them on inscriptions. Some of the terms applied to Herod recur in these inscriptions of the first century CE (the list is not complete). I translate only the portions immediately relevant to Herod's descendants.

---

74. Further, Richardson, "Augustan-era Synagogues in Rome."

12. (OGIS 418) "For the deliverance of the powerful King Agrippa . . ."
13. (OGIS 419) "Concerning great King Agrippa, friend of the Emperor, pious, and friend of the Romans . . ."
14. (OGIS 420) "Concerning great King Marcus Julius Agrippa, friend of the Emperor and friend of the Romans . . ."
15. (OGIS 421) "Concerning the great Marcus Julius Agrippa . . ."
16. (OGIS 422) ". . . for great King Agrippa . . ."
17. (OGIS 423) ". . . for King Agrippa the powerful."
18. (OGIS 424) "King Agrippa, friend of the Emperor [and friend of the Ro]mans . . ."
19. (OGIS 425) ". . . to the great powerful King Agrippa, his son Agrippa made it."
20. (OGIS 426) ". . . to the powerful King Agrippa."
21. (OGIS 428) ". . . daughter of King Julius Agrippa . . ."
22. (SEG 16.490) "The Great King . . . has sent another donation . . . a thousand denarii . . . [the courier] Philatas son of Philatas."

To summarize, the name Herod *simpliciter* was usually used of Herod of Judea; he was always referred to as "King" in these inscriptions (6–8, above, refer to King Herod). His son Antipas was sometimes called simply Herod, but he was tetrarch (not king) so there was no confusion. His grandson Agrippa I and great-grandson Agrippa II were usually called Agrippa, not Herod, or in the latter case sometimes with full name. The numismatic evidence is strong that Agrippa I referred to himself as "great" (*megas*). The inscriptions with this style then likely refer to Agrippa I also: 13, 14, 15, 16, 22, and 19, the last of which clearly indicates that the older Agrippa was referred to as "great" and the younger not. Number 21, above, must refer to Agrippa I, since it refers to his daughter, likely Berenice. Since both Agrippa I and II have the same full name it is not always possible to decide between them: thus, 21 seems uncertain, as are 17, 18, and 20.

King Herod was "friend of Romans" and "friend of the Emperor," and the other adjectives describing him are the sort of overblown descriptions expected in major benefactions: a person of "piety," "good works," "good will," "moral excellence." The distribution of inscriptions concerning Herod the King is revealing: Masada, Jerusalem, Ashdod, Si'a, Rome, Athens, Cos, and Delos. All were areas where Herod was active; in the cases of Athens, Cos, and Si'a there is confirming literary evidence of benefactions.

Since the language of inscriptions was so stereotyped, it is tenuous to identify the dedicatee by the language used. By comparison with the restraint in the inscriptional references to King Herod, those associated with his grandson and great-grandson were more exaggerated; for example the frequent use of *kyrios*, probably equivalent to "powerful," is noticeable. The designation "great" is absent from the epigraphic evidence for Herod, but is found in inscriptions of Agrippa I. This dovetails, as we shall see in a moment, with the absence of the adjective from his coins. When Josephus uses the term (in one very brief genealogical section in *Ant.* 18.130–36), he either takes a title known to be used of his own contemporary Agrippa II and applies it to his great-grandfather or, alternatively, he simply means the "elder" Herod.[75]

COINS

The epigraphic and numismatic evidence from Herod's reign agree both on the absence of the adjective "great" (*megas*) and on the presence of the title "king" (*basileus*). The two kinds of evidence are also generally consistent in the case of Herod Antipas (usually called "Tetrarch" on coins and inscriptions), in the case of Agrippa I (called "king and friend of the Emperor" on both, as well as "great"), and in the case of Agrippa II (who is the first to be called by his Roman names on both). The epigraphic and numismatic styles are remarkably similar.

Herod's coins were unilingually Greek, whereas the coins of Alexander Jannaeus were frequently bilingual and those of Mattathiah Antigonus (Herod's rival) sometimes bilingual. The coins of Hyrcanus II, with whom Herod's fortunes were so tightly bound in the years prior to 40 BCE, were always in Hebrew, though occasionally with Greek monograms (resembling those on Tyrian, Seleucid, and Ptolemaic coins) on the reverse that probably referred to Antipater, Herod's father and Hyrcanus's financial minister and head of the mint.[76] Many of Herod's earlier coins had similar disputed monograms; the interpretation of his monogram devices should follow the interpretation of the earlier ones.

The coins can be classified into two groups: dated and undated. All dated coins refer to "year three" and have a monogram; undated coins have no monogram. The device in all cases is very like a *chi-rho* or *tau-rho* symbol, frequently interpreted as an abbreviation for *tritos* (*TR*) or third. Since, however, the date is given in standard form on these and only these coins, this proposal

---

75. The first modern scholar to raise this question about *megas* was H. G. A. Ewald, *History of Israel* (London: Longmans, Green, 1874 [1843–55]), vol. 5, p. 473. Cf. J. M. Jost, *Geschichte des Judentums und seiner Secten* (Leipzig: Dorffling und Franke, 1857), p. 319, n.2; F. W. Madden, in W. L. Alexander, *Cyclopedia of Biblical Literature* (Edinburgh: Adam and Charles Black, 1864) 2: 286–92; F.W. Madden, *History of Jewish Coinage* (London: Bernard Quaritch, 1864), p. 83–84; E. M. Smallwood, *Jews*, p. 60, n.1.

76. Meshorer, *Jewish Coins*, p. 46, accepts Kanael's proposal in this regard; see B. Kanael, "The Greek Letters on the Coins of Yehohanan the High Priest," *BIES* 16 (1952): 52–55 (in Hebrew). The monograms include *alpha, alpha* contained within *pi, alpha* above *pi,* and either *alpha* (?) or *lambda* alone.

means that one group of coins had two ways of giving the date on the same face, while the other group had no date. Meyshan was the first to disagree with this theory, arguing that the monogram and date cannot say the same thing;[77] he claimed the monogram referred to the minting authority of Tyrus (Tyre). This suggestion is plausible, for Tyrian coinage was the accepted currency for payment of the Temple tax in Jerusalem.[78] Another interpretation of the dated coins is provided by Meshorer:[79] the monogram refers to "Tetrarch," that is, to Herod's appointment as tetrarch by Mark Antony in the year 42. Hence, Meshorer claims, year three counting from 42 is 40 BCE, the very year in which Herod was named king by the Senate in Rome. He suggests, in support of this, that "this self-confident monarch" would hardly wait for three years (i.e., until the taking of Jerusalem in 37 BCE) to mint his own coins, as the usual interpretation of year three supposes.

Attractive as Meshorer's argument seems, there are several contrary arguments. (1) The year of Herod's appointment as tetrarch may have been 41, not 42. (2) His appointment as tetrarch was jointly with his brother Phasael, of whom there is no mention; in any case he had been appointed "governor" by Cassius in 42, by Sextus Caesar in 46, and by his father, Antipater—acting for Julius Caesar—in 47, any of which dates would have done equally well. (3) It is almost inconceivable that he would offend the Senate that had appointed him with a claim to authority earlier. (4) The monogram can barely be interpreted as a convoluted way of saying *TETR* (see Meshorer, pp. 10–11), but the gymnastics smack more of modern contrivance than of ancient habits. (5) Herod arrived in his domain in early 39, not 40, and could only have begun minting coins then. (6) He was not half so "self-confident" in 39 when he was battling his way to power.

Meshorer claims that Herod minted these early year-three coins from 40 to 37, probably in Samaria, while he consolidated his hold; they were therefore competitive with Antigonus's coinage. The care with which these early coins were struck was part of the competition; later, when his hold was firm, his coinage was produced with noticeably less care (following Kanael). This argument, too, sounds forced.

I cannot offer a new interpretation of the data, but the following conclu-

---

77. J. Meyshan, "The Chronology of the Coins of the Herodian Dynasty," *Eretz Israel* (1950–51): 104–14 (in Hebrew), abbreviated in *PEQ* (1959).

78. Meshorer has argued that Herod may have minted later issues of Tyrian shekels himself, especially those with the monogram *kappa-rho* (= *kosmos romaion*? or, as Meshorer prefers = *kratos*—that is "power, authority"). See his later treatment, *Ancient Jewish Coinage,* esp. pp. 6–9. I have discussed aspects of Tyrian coinage in a paper to the SBL meetings, "Why Turn the Tables? Jesus' Protest in the Temple Precincts," *SBL Seminar Papers 1992* (Atlanta: Scholars Press, 1992).

79. Meshorer, *Ancient Jewish Coinage,* pp. 5–30; A. Strobel, *ANRW* 2.20.2: 988–1187, esp. 1063–83.

sions best agree with the evidence. (1) The dated and monogrammed coins were early and from a different mint than Herod's later mint in Jerusalem (the undated coins). (2) If the monogram referred to Herod's appointment as tetrarch, the earliest possible date for minting coins was 39 BCE. But it is likelier that the monogram referred neither to "year three" nor to "tetrarch" but to the minting authority, either Tyre or some person with the initials *TR*. (3) Herod may have minted Tyrian shekels in Jerusalem, with their approval of course, during a portion of his reign.

The undated coins can sometimes be interpreted on the basis of historical allusions, though different conclusions from Meshorer's are sometimes indicated. (1) The "anchor" coins probably referred to the construction of Caesarea Maritima, and were evidence of the importance Herod attributed to this new port in strengthening the economy, improving international contacts, and even allowing for the development of a navy.[80] (2) The unusual coin with an "anchor" and a "war galley" is more likely to refer to Herod's naval support for Marcus Agrippa's expedition against Pontus in 14 BCE, not to the founding of Caesarea Maritima. The expedition was important to Herod, built upon and cementing the close friendship between the two. It was the one time—so far as we know—that Herod's fledgling navy was used in a Roman action, and it provided an opportunity for Herod to visit many Diaspora Jewish communities. (3) The eagle design was associated, as Meshorer claims, with the construction of one portion of the Temple, perhaps the building of a gate over which the eagle was found. This was probably completed and so named when Marcus Agrippa visited the Temple in 15 BCE (contra Meshorer).[81] (4) The coin with the vine was later and rarer, also associated with the Temple project.

Every coin of Herod referred to his kingship, often in abbreviated form, consistent with epigraphic references to him; it was the one fixed datum in his view of himself.[82] Few of the symbols referred to Herod himself; most had to do with Jewish or Roman symbolism, not with his own rights or actions or honors.[83] This also is similar to the epigraphic evidence, especially the absence of inscriptions in the Holy Land. Meshorer notes that five of the seven symbols on the dated coins appear also on Roman republican coinage of the period 44 to 40 BCE (tripod, apex, palm branches, caduceus, and aphlaston). The two

---

80. The coins of Alexander Jannaeus and also of Agrippa I that use the anchor-type refer to a seaport for Judea, with the same motivations. See also the discussion of the Ashdod inscription, above.

81. Alternatively the eagle may be associated with Herod's assistance in the construction of the Temple of Ba'al Shamim at Si'a, where eagles of exactly this form decorated several of the gates. It should be dated to about 31 BCE.

82. All but a couple of coin inscriptions are in the genitive ("of King Herod"); the exceptions are in the nominative ("King Herod").

83. For the symbolism see Meshorer, *Ancient Jewish Coinage*, pp. 18–29.

additional symbols are the shield and fruit. The fruit Meshorer interprets as a poppy-head, not a pomegranate—associated with the worship of Demeter and Kore at Sebaste—wrongly claiming that Herod built the Temple of Kore, for which there is no evidence other than the proximity of that temple to his Temple of Roma and Augustus. Meshorer falls back lamely on the popularity of the cult to explain why Herod would mint a coin in the years 40–37, well before he had rebuilt Samaria and renamed it Sebaste in honor of Augustus. It is likelier the fruit is a pomegranate and is similar to Hasmonean use of this symbol.

In contrast, the symbols on the undated coins struck in Jerusalem reflect Jewish art, the Temple, or Jewish symbols, claims Meshorer: table = Temple furniture; diadem = symbol of royalty;[84] wreath = royalty;[85] palm branches = Temple ritual; vine = Temple; anchor = maritime cities and trade;[86] double cornucopia with caduceus = Moses' staff; single cornucopia = half of the value of the double; galley = Caesarea Maritima; eagle = divine power.[87]

The symbols on Herod's coins are often described as "ambiguous," capable of being interpreted by Jews in one way, by Hellenists in another. Meshorer's later work emphatically rejects this interpretation that he had earlier shared; he now suggests two stages, dated coins using Roman republican symbols and undated using Jewish symbols.[88] A theme of the dated coins was to win over the Samaritan population—he sees the poppy-head as decisive. The shield and helmet, which were not used in contemporary Roman coins, might be seen better not as representing Roman military support—so Meshorer—but as referring to the military struggle for Jerusalem. There were no blatantly military symbols in the undated coins except for the war galley, referring to a foreign, not an internal, military venture.

Noteworthy, however, is what was not found on Herod's coins. (1) There were no human representations; Herod conformed to Jewish sensibilities and his predecessors' usage.[89] (2) No coins followed Imperial or even Republican practice by noting Herod's military or political triumphs. The war galley hints

---

84. The diadem often has a *chi*-cross inside it. Meshorer argues that *chi* was a symbol of priesthood (citing *b. Kerithoth* 5.2) and that the combination symbolized the cooperation between the priesthood and the kingship.

85. Meshorer incorrectly states that one coin (#18) with a wreath reads "Herod the Great"; actually it reads Herod the King.

86. Alexander Jannaeus used the anchor and cornucopias also; Herod's issue may be intended to claim that he was successor to the Hasmoneans, after his marriage to Mariamme in 37 BCE.

87. Meshorer points to the important difference between a Roman eagle with wings outspread and the eagle on Herod's coins with wings folded in the Hellenistic manner. Eagles at Si'a and elsewhere in the Nabatean world also had folded wings.

88. Meyshan earlier had attempted to describe many of the dated-coin symbols as Jewish: e.g., the *thymiatêrion* was not a pagan symbol but a reference to a small altar in the Temple.

89. Tyrian shekels used to pay the Temple tax showed the god Melkart and an eagle.

at such an aim, but it was Marcus Agrippa's expedition, not Herod's. The coins merely identified Herod as king—no victories, no political ambitions, no honors. (3) The coins departed from Antigonus's types with menorah and table of shewbread (repeated on Titus's triumphal arch following the destruction of Jerusalem in 70 CE). A later *baraita* to *Avodah Zarah* 43a forbade such symbols: "A man may not make a house after the design of the Temple, . . . a table after the design of the table or a candelabrum after the design of a candelabrum. He may, however, make one with five, six or eight [branches], but with seven he may not make it even though it be of other metals." The status of the *halachah* at the time of Herod and Antigonus cannot be determined; while there is a Second-Temple grafitto with a seven-branched menorah and a shewbread table, first-century synagogues avoid symbols associated with the Temple prior to its destruction.[90] The attitudes that shaped the *baraita* may have been at work in Herod's time.[91] His avoidance of such symbols is as important as Antigonus's—the high priest's—use of them.

CONCLUSION

The inscriptions and coins can hardly be overemphasized in providing contemporary evidence of Herod's character. He maintained an unexpected reserve, followed convention, and was regarded effusively by others. The reserve—almost conservatism—was evident in the simple designation "King," recognition of him as a Jew, the absence of "great," avoidance both of human likenesses and of too-sacred symbolism. Herod followed convention in using Hasmonean symbolism (the double cornucopia and the pomegranate), possibly minting Tyrian coins locally used in paying the Temple tax, and using Roman republican symbols to tie himself to the Senate in Rome from which he derived his royal power. He was regarded externally as a important patron, a man of kindness, generosity, good will, and piety, a friend of Romans and of the Emperor. These features contrast with the usual picture; though none is inconsistent with Josephus's picture, the balance and composition are radically different.

---

90. P. Richardson, "Augustan-era Synagogues."

91. Later synagogues, third century CE onward, used "sacred" or even pagan symbols (zodiacs, Helios) in the decorative motifs, both in two- and three-dimensional applications.

CHAPTER 9

From Rhodes to Rome
(30–17 BCE)

THE DEATH OF MARIAMME

When Herod returned, reunited with Mariamme and satisfied with his successes, he found the family paralyzed with jealousies and tensions.[1] There is, however, great difficulty in sorting out what to make of the parallels, overlaps, and disagreements between *War* 1.441–43; *Ant.* 15.65–87; 15.185–87; 15.202–39 (see above, chap. 7, for one version; appended note, below). What follows seems a more plausible account; it seems likelier that the main episode involving Mariamme was part of a complex sequence falling at this juncture in the narrative.

The main outline appears to be the following. When Herod went to Rhodes he left his brother Pheroras in charge of matters (*Ant.* 15.185–87), with a steward named Joseph (confused in the tradition with Herod's brother-in-law Joseph, who was by now already dead) and an Ituraean named Soëmus in Alexandreion responsible for Mariamme and Alexandra. While there, Soëmus revealed that the two women were to be executed if Herod failed to return; perhaps he fell in love with Mariamme. When Herod returned with his good news he reinstalled all the women (including Salome and Cypros) in the palace in Jerusalem. He expected renewed sexual intimacies with his wife, but Mariamme refused his sexual advances (perhaps not unnaturally; she had had five children in seven years!). When he wanted to punish her, Salome and Cypros provoked Herod to greater hostility. Before he left Jerusalem to rejoin Octavian, Mariamme requested that Soëmus be given command of some part of Her-

---

1. On Mariamme, Schalit, pp. 566–70: Josephus attributes four characteristics to her: self-control (*enkrateia*), greatness of soul (*megalopsychia*), lack of fairness, contentiousness (*philoneikon*).

od's kingdom (*meridarch*), to which Herod agreed (*Ant.* 15.216); he then left to meet Octavian at Ptolemais, from which he accompanied him to the border with Egypt. After he returned from Egypt with promises of new powers and lands (*War* 1.396–97; *Ant.* 15.217), he left again to accompany Octavian back to Antioch (*Ant.* 15.218).

During these short visits in Jerusalem the relationship between Herod and Mariamme deteriorated, with passionate arguments and reconciliations, partly over sex, partly over her family, and partly over other men, perhaps including Soëmus (*Ant.* 15.218–22; see also 15.82–86; *War* 1.442). Salome, Herod's sister (or Salome and Cypros together), stirred the pot with stories of love potions and poison (*Ant.* 15.223–27; see also 15.80–81; *War* 1.443).[2] Herod learned from torturing a court eunuch that Soëmus had revealed his instructions to Mariamme (*Ant.* 15.229; see 15.87; *War* 1.441–42). This information convinced him that Soëmus was guilty of adultery with Mariamme, as a result of which Soëmus was executed and Mariamme was sent to trial. Altogether these unhappy events occupied more than a year.[3]

In this version of the story, Alexandra saved her own skin by abandoning her daughter Mariamme and confirming the truth of the accusations, especially of Mariamme's ingratitude to Herod (*Ant.* 15.232–36).[4] Mariamme went to her death silently and calmly (29 BCE).[5] Josephus writes her an epitaph: Mariamme was beautiful, dignified, and "unexcelled in continence," though she was quarrelsome and unreasonable and fond of speaking her mind; she let her feelings show before Salome and Cypros, whom she unwisely antagonized. Josephus's description suggests immaturity: she was less than 25 years old.

There is no more tragic episode in the story of Herod. Were Herod and Mariamme star-crossed lovers, mismatched spring and winter mates, spouses doomed by malicious women around them, or two persons caught in a web of national and international politics? Was Mariamme a passionate woman who attracted others without considering Herod's jealousy or a "royal" who abhorred the commoner in her husband? Was Herod a middle-aged tyrant who wanted to own his wife body and soul, or a vulgar man who could not win his wife's respect? Perhaps the truth lies in a complex combination of all of these.

Josephus provides his own analysis. Herod's remorse almost drove him out of his mind. He refused to believe she was dead and spoke to her as if she were still present (*War* 1.444). From the beginning his love for Mariamme had a divine madness to it, and in the end he suffered a sort of divine punishment

---

2. Schalit, pp. 571–73, refers to Salome as "the Satanic figure" (p. 571).

3. Some such complex and drawn out process seems required. Shorter versions appear only to tell a stripped down version of the story, sometimes in the service of other aims.

4. On Alexandra, Schalit, pp. 564–66; on Mariamme, pp. 566–73.

5. On her death, see also *b.BB* 3b; *b.Qid* 70b.

(*Ant.* 15.240–41). He tried distractions, lost interest in the kingdom, and went off to the wilderness; he became ill to the point that many thought he would die where he lay in Samaria (*Ant.* 15.242–46).[6] Herod's condition following Mariamme's execution was desperately serious. The kingdom was neglected; Herod was disabled and in danger of losing his grip due to his infatuation for this woman twenty years his junior. Through much of 28 BCE Judea was rudderless.

APPENDED NOTE

The background to Mariamme's execution is especially complex; several issues hang on the relationship of the accounts. The main problem is that there are two very similar incidents: in both, Herod left Jerusalem to face a test, once with Antony and once with Octavian; he entrusted Mariamme to someone else with instructions to kill her if he failed to return; the person in charge revealed this information to Mariamme; that person was accused of adultery and executed. *Prima facie* the accounts seem doublets, so it is important to decide what happened and when.[7]

First, the facts. *War* overlooks the earlier incident when Herod went to Antony in Laodicea in 35 BCE. But then we find: (1) that *War* 1.441–43 contains, within a somewhat garbled and unreliable section, an account of Herod's order to kill Mariamme in 30 BCE, an order that was explicitly addressed to Joseph, Salome's husband, and in the end both Joseph and Mariamme were executed.[8] (2) *Ant.* 15.65–87 parallels *War*'s account, but deals with the earlier incident before Antony at Laodicea; the person in charge of the realm and also guarding Mariamme was Joseph, Herod's uncle(!). The result was that while Herod was near to killing his wife he only executed Joseph, but his brother-in-law not his uncle. (3) In *Ant.* 15.185–239 there is a very long, somewhat interrupted account, which should probably be divided into two separate accounts. In the first, *Ant.* 15.185–87 and 202–208, Herod left Pheroras his brother in charge of matters while he went to Octavian at Rhodes, leaving Mariamme and her mother at Alexandreion in charge of Soëmus and Joseph, a steward (same name, although this account includes a flashback to the other Joseph and the earlier incident); Soëmus disclosed his instructions, which Mariamme deeply resented. When Herod returned from Egypt (not Rhodes!) he declared his love for her. (4) The remainder (*Ant.* 15.209–39) is a second, partly (though

---

6. During this period there was also, Josephus says, a serious plague; perhaps the plague accounts for some of Herod's symptoms.

7. Schalit, pp. 575–88; S. Sandmel, *Herod: Profile of a Tyrant* (Philadelphia and New York: Lippincott, 1967), pp. 164–65, makes a similar point.

8. This contains a "slip" at 1.441, which refers incorrectly back to Antony, who was already dead.

not entirely) independent account: it begins with a return from a sea voyage (from Rhodes, not from Egypt), drawing on materials found elsewhere (*War* 1.396–97 and 1.437), together with an altogether new incident involving a love potion and suspicions of poison. In the end Soëmus was executed and Mariamme was tried, while Alexandra rescued herself at Mariamme's expense.

The flashback (3 above) has secondary elements;[9] it is a formulaic attempt to overcome the obvious difficulty posed by the parallelism just noted and is worthless as evidence for the reliability of *Antiquities* at this point (contra Schürer, 1.302–303, n. 49). The similarities between (1), (2), and (3) (including the flashback), especially the references to Joseph the brother-in-law, Joseph an uncle (of whom we have no other evidence), and Joseph a steward, are perplexing. Were all different, all the same, or is there some confusion? The likeliest is that there is confusion. I conclude that Joseph, Herod's brother-in-law, was involved in an incident (probably not involving Mariamme) that led to his execution in 35 BCE, that the same name Joseph was attached to the later incident, as in (3), and prompted a story that Mariamme was involved in Joseph's death in 35. Number 2, above, is fabricated to explain Joseph's death on the occasion of Herod's return from his meeting with Antony. The resemblances between (1) and (2) thus are natural, because they ultimately refer to the same event, in 30 BCE, though (2) wrongly attributes it to 35 BCE and (1) wrongly imagines that it was in 30 that Joseph was executed. Each is partly right but mostly wrong. That leaves (3) and (4), which are presented as one discontinuous narrative. Both are set in 30 BCE, though some of the circumstantial details are garbled, because there are elements drawn from more than one tradition, as noted above. What is right about it is the following: Pheroras was left in charge; Joseph a steward and Soëmus were in charge of Mariamme; in the end more guilt attached to Soëmus and he was summarily executed; the sequence of events was long and complex and took about a year; Mariamme got a trial; Alexandra in the end abandoned her. But the comings and goings are mixed up, the reference to news of the deaths of Antony and Cleopatra is probably wrong; it may be wrong that Cypros and Salome were put in Masada for safety.

This analysis does not exhaust the problems or the possibilities, but it offers a fairly simple explanation of how matters might have stood. One way to summarize issues is to ask a series of questions:

—When did the incident happen? 35 BCE, 30/29 BCE, or both? In 30/29 BCE, with Mariamme's execution taking place in late-29 BCE.
—Which trip was it? To Laodicea, Rhodes, or Egypt? To Rhodes.

---

9. Schalit, pp. 131–41, points to the rhetorical character of *Antiquities*'s version, using literary *topoi* and an approach specially characteristic of the Peripatetic School, to which Nicolas of Damascus belonged.

—Who was in charge? Joseph the brother-in-law, Joseph an uncle, or Pheroras? Pheroras.

—Who guarded Mariamme? Joseph the brother-in-law, Joseph an uncle, or Joseph and Soëmus? Joseph and Soëmus, mostly the latter.

—Who made the charge of adultery? Herod, Salome, Salome, and Cypros or Alexandra? Uncertain, but probably Salome and Alexandra.

—Whose deaths resulted? Joseph and Mariamme, Joseph, or Soëmus and Mariamme? Soëmus and Mariamme.

The earlier incident in 35 BCE is incorrectly placed and told. Something happened in 35 BCE to cause Joseph's death but we cannot now get at the truth of it. In 30/29 BCE the more significant set of events occurred, and these are best reproduced, even if garbled, in the account in *Ant.* 15.185–239.

THE DEATHS OF ALEXANDRA AND COSTOBAR

Mariamme's death created a political vacuum, not because she was important in matters of policy but because of Herod's reaction. Vacuums are always filled. Few were ambitious and experienced enough to take control of events when Herod was almost totally *mentos non compos*. None of his children were old enough to insinuate themselves into a position of power. Antipater, the oldest, was about seventeen years of age in 28 BCE, but he shared his mother's fate of exclusion from the court. Herod's brother Pheroras had carried some responsibilities but usually kept a low profile. His sister Salome, though meddlesome, was loyal to her brother and would not usurp his position.

Only Alexandra, Mariamme's mother, had the will and cleverness to take over when Herod was ill in Samaria: she tried to occupy both the Antonia fortress (recently built by Herod)[10] and whatever fortifications existed on the site of the present citadel (possibly the three towers referred to as Phasael, Hippicus, and Mariamme).[11] Josephus exaggerates when he says that the person who controlled these fortifications controlled the whole nation, but their importance cannot be doubted. Alexandra appealed to their commanders to surrender to her and Herod's sons to forestall trouble if Herod died; she had in

10. More or less on the site of the earlier Baris, northwest of the Temple mount. Herod built the Antonia while Mark Antony was still alive; it overlooked the Temple, though the Temple precinct was not extended to the north until the late 20s. During this period there must have been a fosse between the fortress and the Temple perimeter. The Antonia was high enough to overlook the Temple—on a high rock outcrop—but it could not have been physically connected to the Temple.

11. The base of one still stands just inside the Jaffa Gate, left as a memorial to Roman might in smashing Jerusalem in the revolt of 66–74 CE. The masonry still standing was solid, though it had sumptuous apartments above.

mind Mariamme's children, all still young in 28 BCE (the oldest may have been eight).[12] Alexandra was proposing herself as regent of her grandchildren (*Ant.* 15.247–49).

The ploy, as bold as it was devious, failed. The commanders, including Achiab who continued to be close to Herod until his death in 4 BCE (*Ant.* 15.250–51),[13] were loyal. When a messenger brought word of Alexandra's attempt to Herod at Samaria he ordered her execution immediately without recourse to a "council." Alexandra's attempted *putsch* galvanized Herod into action. The two had long been at odds, and now that he had dealt with her he turned his attention to other dissidents. "He was in an ugly mood and . . . he found fault with everything" (*Ant.* 15.251); before long he had executed several old associates.

Costobar was the most notable of those executed: he was a close friend, married to Herod's sister Salome (after the execution of her first husband, Joseph), a noble Idumaean ("first in rank"; *Ant.* 15.253) whose family were priests of Cos; he remained loyal to the old ways (15.255). Herod had appointed Costobar governor of Idumaea when he married Salome in 34 BCE or thereabouts, but he resisted Herod's orders and refused to accept Judaism.[14] Worse still, Costobar approached Cleopatra (perhaps in 32/31 BCE, when Herod's hold was shaky and he was confronted by an aggressive Nabatean army) and offered his loyalty if she would ask Antony for control of Idumaea, hoping to achieve eventually a larger role for himself. Antony refused Cleopatra's request; he must have leaked the information to Herod, who was persuaded by his sister and his mother not to take any action against Costobar at the time (*Ant.* 15.256–58).

Salome soon divorced Costobar.[15] She charged that four associates of Herod (Costobar, Lysimachus, Antipater, and Dositheus) were planning revolt and that in 37 BCE—in the waning days of the siege of Jerusalem—Costobar had sheltered some Hasmoneans who had been effective in the defense against Herod. Instead of stopping deserters, those "who were in debt or followed a policy of opposition to the king" (*Ant.* 15.264), Costobar had hidden the sons of Baba on his own estate to curry their favor and for subsequent personal

---

12. Antipater must be excluded; though the oldest, he was brought back to the court only in 14 BCE when his mother returned to favor.

13. Achiab was a son of Phallion, Antipater's only known brother, who died in 40 BCE; he was probably about the same age as Herod. He had a sister (unnamed) and may also have had a brother, Antiochus, who was buried in Scythopolis. See S. Applebaum in *CRINT* 2.669.

14. Josephus does not actually say this; he only points to Costobar's priestly background and his belief that Idumaeans should not have to adopt Jewish customs. Costobar must have been circumcised according to Jewish custom and so a suitable partner for Salome, even if his beliefs were deficient, for Herod later refused Salome permission to marry Syllaeus unless Syllaeus was circumcised.

15. Above, chap. 2, re Hanson's study; several Herodian women divorced their mates. Though unusual, divorce by females fell within the realm of possible elite behavior.

benefit. A reward for their capture had elicited no response. When Salome told Herod all this some ten or eleven years later, he had them executed, eliminating the last male Hasmoneans (*Ant.* 15.259–66). Dositheus was likely the same person who brought about Hyrcanus II's death by divulging his letter to Malichus; Lysimachus is not otherwise known; the name Antipater sounds as though he may have been a relative of Herod's. To this list of elite persons executed can be added Soëmus and Joseph, Salome's husband (see above). Herod had lost support among the elite upon whom he counted.[16]

JUDEAN SOCIETY

We enter a period—roughly 28 to 23 BCE—when there are few chronological markers and a less coherent narrative, so that an account of Herod's career is difficult. Some of the general features of Judean society, however, can be reconstructed. The initial impression is of a troubled period, disturbed by natural disorders, religious difficulties, and a tendency in Herod to hold the population in subjection, though at a later stage (*Ant.* 15.326) all seemed to go well, both for Herod himself and for Judean society.

In 28/27 BCE there was a famine (*Ant.* 15.299–316). Though Josephus allows that the drought that helped to create the famine was a whim of nature, he explains theologically that God was angry. If the previous year (29/28 BCE) was a sabbatical year the situation was especially severe; the reduced diet for two years running weakened the population so that plague got a foothold (15.300–302).[17] The result was death and disease, with a severely restricted crop the following year (27/26 BCE).

"Necessity made them find new ways of sustaining themselves" (15.303). In truth it was Herod, not the people, who found these new ways. (1) He melted his gold and silver ornamentation and jewelry to a usable form for ex-

---

16. Note the summary, *Ant.* 15.266: "the kingdom was wholly in Herod's power, there being no one of high rank to stand in the way of his unlawful acts."

17. Two dates are possible: 28/27 (the likelier) and 25/24 BCE. In favor of the earlier date are the following. (1) *Ant.* 15.299 presupposes not 15.298 but 15.267, the death of Costobar. (2) The year was explicitly Herod's 13th: though some of Josephus's dates count from 37 (= 25/24), others count from 40 (= 28/27). (3) The "same year" refers to the building of Sebaste, which was begun in 27 BCE. (4) The year 29/28 was a sabbatical year when fields were left fallow; seed stored up during that year was used up sowing the fields in 28/27, when food supplies were stretched. If in *that* year there was a drought, the consequences would be exactly as Josephus describes, with no seed-grain and inadequate food. (5) *Ant.* 15.243 puts the plague in the period when Herod was disabled. In favor of 25/24 are: (1) the natural sequence at the end of this section of the text, so that the expedition to Arabia Felix in 25/24 follows directly from the natural disasters ("at this time" in 15.337); (2) The completion of Sebaste's reconstruction may be meant at 299. Both points strain the meaning of the text. See Schürer 1.290–91, n.9.

change.[18] (2) He sent this to his friend Petronius, governor of Egypt, who gave Judea's needs priority over others'.[19] (3) Herod doled out relief provisions sparingly, especially to those capable of producing food. (4) He arranged for the aged and infirm to get food from bread-kitchens. (5) He countered the loss of flocks of sheep, which provided wool and hides for winter clothing, in some unspecified way. (6) He allocated food supplies to neighboring Syrian cities.[20] (7) And if the above chronology is correct, his rebuilding of Sebaste was a famine-relief project. These remedial actions, unusual in their day, brought about a "reversal of attitude" inside Judea because of Herod's good will and protection (*eunoia kai prostasia, Ant.* 15.308, and 309–10),[21] an improvement in his relations with his neighbors in Syria (15.311–14), and an international reputation for generosity and innovation (15.315–16).[22]

It seems from Josephus that Herod's actions constituted a national relief program. There is even a sense that this was the beginning of a state economy along new lines, with a hint of economic weapons used positively in the international sphere; first in getting relief from Egypt where the drought was less severe (the annual flooding of the Nile lessened variations in food supply) and then in Herod's using his grain in dealings with others. But the most noteworthy aspect of the relief program was Herod's personal contribution to the efforts, both in establishing the programs and in stripping his own palaces of precious metals to provide the funds.[23]

During the mid-20s a second issue troubled Judea. Because Herod had the kingdom entirely in his control with no high-ranking rivals, he could depart "from the native customs and . . . [corrupt] the ancient way of life" (*Ant.* 15.260–67). Josephus provides a list. (1) Herod established quadrennial athletic contests in Jerusalem, with a theater and an amphitheater,[24] inviting contestants to vie for generous prizes (15.268–71) in athletic events, music, drama, and

---

18. Not to "coinage" as Josephus says, for Herod never minted gold and silver coins—probably gold and silver bullion for trade.

19. The prefecture of Egypt poses problems. Petronius became prefect in 25 BCE, not altogether too late for the above chronology but troublesome. The greatest need for famine relief would have been in 26, the second year of the drought. A second problem, see later, is that Aelius Gallus may have preceded Petronius as governor. If so Josephus has their responsibilities incorrectly, with consequences for the chronological scheme. It is arguable that the problems arise from Josephus's composite account and that the Gallus expedition should precede the famine account.

20. It is probably this to which Josephus alludes in *Ant.* 15.327, when he says Herod "treated the Gentile cities skilfully and humanely, and he cultivated the local rulers."

21. *Eunoia* appears in several of Herod's inscriptions. See Appendix B, chap. 8.

22. These accounts must derive from Nicolas in their enthusiasm for Herod. While exaggerated, there is truth to them.

23. In the famine of 46 CE Queen Helena of Adiabene likewise came to the aid of Jerusalem, buying grain in Cyprus and Egypt.

24. Or possibly a hippodrome, but probably not both; see chap. 8.

chariot races.[25] (2) One of Herod's buildings was decorated with offensive reminders of Rome's power,[26] some of which were thought to offend Israel's aniconic Torah.[27] Outrage focused on the "trophies," thought by critics to comprise images (*eikonas*) surrounded by weapons. Herod first attempted to reassure his critics and then, when this had no effect and the protesters continued to claim that he had contravened national customs,[28] he took representatives to see the trophies. He showed them there were no images at all, just bare wood covered with ornaments.[29] His embarrassed critics outwitted themselves; they thought the coverings attempted to reduce offense by concealing the images (admitting there was no visible offense). The unveiling left them doubly embarrassed.[30]

The perception that Herod opposed national customs continued even after this incident dissipated the vigor of the protests (*Ant.* 15. 280–81). How widespread this muted opposition was is not clear. Nevertheless, ten persons entered into an assassination conspiracy, not unlike the plot against Julius Caesar fifteen or twenty years earlier. Concealing daggers under their cloaks, the conspirators headed for the theater, where Herod had already gone. When he was warned of the conspiracy by an informer, he returned to the palace. The conspirators were rounded up, then proudly confessed and were executed. The informer was torn apart by a crowd, which led to reprisals against those participating in the lynching (15.282–90). According to Josephus, conflicts over the laws (*hyper tôn nomôn* = *toroth*) upset Herod so much that he reduced the freedom of his citizens to limit the possibility of rebellion (*apostasis*, 15.291).

---

25. This last allusion suggests a hippodrome.

26. Josephus says the theater, but he probably means the amphitheater, since the decorations do not fit a theater well.

27. The so-called trophies incident (*Ant.* 15.272–79) refers to inscriptions in honor of Octavian/Augustus, gold and silver trophies recalling previous wars, displays of garments and vessels, a supply of animals for gladiatorial combat. All were objectionable, though the degree of offense was a matter of dispute. Two factors may be noted. (1) The gymnasium Jews established in Jerusalem for educational and athletic purposes in the (pre-Maccabean) Seleucid era had been maintained into the Roman period. (2) Herod's structures were outside the city—the theater south of the West Hill, the amphitheater on the plain, probably meaning to the southwest beyond the modern railway station.

28. The phrase *en têi polei* seems wrong, given the likelihood that both theater and amphitheater were outside the city.

29. 1 Macc. 13:27–30 describes the Maccabean tombs at Modein in a way that suggests a similar "offense," though this display of trophies created no problems. "Over the tomb of his father and brothers Simon raised a lofty monument and faced back and front with polished stone. He erected seven pyramids, arranged in pairs, for his father and mother and four brothers. He contrived an elaborate setting for the pyramids: he surrounded them with tall columns [a stoa?] surmounted with trophies of armor as a perpetual memorial, and with carved ships alongside the trophies, plainly visible to those at sea."

30. This probably occurred shortly after 28 BCE, the year the first quadrennial games were held. The buildings were constructed between 31 (Actium) and 28 BCE.

Josephus provides evidence for Herod's wish for security: (1) a palace in Jerusalem;[31] (2) the Antonia fortress; (3) reconstruction of Samaria (renamed Sebaste);[32] (4) Caesarea Maritima, which Josephus understands as a fortress *for* the entire nation;[33] (5) a military settlement at Gaba, not far from Megiddo; (6) Heshbon in Peraea, also a military settlement; (7) other garrisons "throughout the entire nation" to restrain revolts; (8) reconstruction of Samaria (noted for the second time) as a walled city with a military settlement, Pente Komai, nearby (15.292–98).[34] This impressive list joins important and not so important projects, and puts a damaging "spin" on their collective role within Herod's public policy.[35]

The "spin" is just that; the list gathers disparate projects (note the sloppy double reference to Samaria/Sebaste, and the duplicate reference to Caesarea) from the mid-30s to the late-teens. It refers to military settlements whose intention may have been partly security, but more obviously were an obligation to retiring veterans. The centerpieces were huge urban projects, Sebaste and Ceasarea, whose purposes were neither military nor for security; given their location, character, and appurtenances, they were intended to stimulate the economy, to honor Augustus, and perhaps also, in the case of Sebaste, to express gratitude for nurturing Herod back to health.

The selection of material in *Antiquities* is not matched in *War;* descriptions that praise Herod for generous relief of the natural disasters Judea faced are juxtaposed with others that pillory him for religious problems and for general oppression of the population. While these descriptions stand in tension with each other, the inevitable tendency is to prefer one portrait to the other, typically the negative side. Josephus's own view (or that of his source) is that Herod used a carrot-and-stick approach: he kept his subjects fearful of speedy punishment but he was considerate when there was a crisis (15.326) and he was "well spoken of among foreign nations" (15.316).

Two things are certain. First, Josephus's attempt to portray the mid-20s as difficult and troublesome—though successful and partly correct—is partly artificial, for much of his evidence comes from earlier and later periods. Second,

---

31. The restoration of the Hasmonean palace took place in the mid to late 30s; the building of his new grander palace was later, perhaps 22 and following; Josephus may mean the three towers of Phasael, Hippicus, and Mariamme, the dating of which is uncertain—possibly late 30s or even as late as 12–10 BCE.

32. Probably 27 BCE and following; Josephus claims that this was a "rampart against the entire nation," that it was only a day's travel from Jerusalem, and that it could be used to control affairs in the city (Jerusalem) and the countryside. Its construction began just after Herod recovered from his illness there.

33. Built 22–10 BCE; though walled, it was hardly a fortress for the nation.

34. We should add (9) the building of Herodium (15.323–25) as a fortified palace with a "city" at its base (built 23–15 BCE).

35. See chap. 8 for an assessment of Herod's fortifications within his overall building policy.

the two internal events that fell most clearly in this period—the famine and the trophies incident—give a benign picture of Herod, on the one hand benevolent and on the other inoffensive. The assassination attempt with its consequences, certainly not benign, was the action of a small group. In sum, the only information we have is mixed; Josephus speaks with forked tongue, though his own estimate is mostly negative. Are the benign impressions more likely to give a correct picture?

HEROD AND AUGUSTUS

Octavian was proclaimed Imperator Caesar Augustus on 16 January 27 BCE; from then on he was to be known as Augustus. The Senate's Act of Settlement conferred new powers, the consequences of which were far-reaching. In Judea the effects were as much seen as felt. There was a spurt of new building activity (duplicated in other parts of the Empire but nowhere as quickly and as visibly) associated with the name of Caesar Augustus: Caesarea Maritima with its harbor separately named Sebastos—the Greek equivalent of Augustus (see *Ant.* 15.331–41); the renamed and rebuilt city of Sebaste, (15.342); the naming of one part of Herod's splendid Jerusalem palace Caesareum (15.318); the three Temples to Roma and Augustus, at Caesarea Maritima, Sebaste, and Panias (among the three earliest Sebasteia). It was all part of a trend.[36]

> Octavian's leadership was confirmed both by the Senate and by the people. Even so, he still wished to be regarded as the representative of the people, and hence while he undertook the whole care and supervision of public business on the ground that it demanded a special degree of attention, he announced that he would not personally govern all the provinces, and that those he did take on, he would not continue to govern permanently. In the event, he handed over the weaker provinces to the Senate, on the ground that they were at peace and free from war, but he kept the stronger under his authority, arguing that they were insecure and exposed to danger and either had enemies near their frontiers or were capable of starting a serious rebellion on their own initiative. The purpose of the decision, as he explained it, was that the Senate should enjoy without anxiety the fairest territories in the Empire, while he should confront the hardships and the dangers. But the real object of this arrangement was that the senators should be unarmed and

---

36. Josephus comments on this generally in *Ant.* 15.328–30: his ambition encouraged a "flattering attention . . . to Caesar and the most influential Romans," forcing him to depart from Jewish customs by the founding of cities, erecting of temples, honoring of statues, and so on.

unprepared for war, while he possessed arms and controlled the troops. . . . Octavian took charge of the rest of Iberia . . . , all the Gauls . . . , together with Coele Syria, Phoenicia, Cilicia, Cyprus and Egypt. . . . [O]thers . . . had either been left autonomous or entrusted to the rule of one kingdom or other. . . .[37]

(Cassius Dio 53.16)

Though this analysis was improved by hindsight (Dio was born around 163/164 CE), it is clear, brief, and largely correct. The division between senatorial and imperial provinces, with the east falling to Augustus, and the quasi-independent role of the "kingdoms" that enjoyed their own laws fits the period under discussion.[38]

When Octavian had finally put his plans into effect, the name Augustus was conferred on him by the Senate and the people. . . . Octavian had set his heart strongly on being named Romulus. But when he understood that this aroused suspicions that he desired the kingship, he abandoned his efforts to obtain it and adopted the title Augustus, as signifying that he was something more than human, since indeed all the most precious and sacred objects are referred to as *augusta*. For this reason, when he was addressed in Greek, he was named *Sebastos,* meaning an august individual.

(Cassius Dio 53.16)

Other writers commented on Augustus's role and powers; of special interest is Philo, a Jewish philosopher who was concerned about the status of Judaism within the Empire and knowledgeable of Torah but willing to accommodate the fashions of the Roman world. The context of these remarks is his description of the embassy to Gaius (Caligula), defending the loyalty of Alexandrian Jews in their dispute with the Greek community.

What about the Emperor whose every virtue outshone human nature. . . . [A]lmost the whole human race would have been destroyed in internecine conflict and disappeared completely, had it

---

37. This and the next translation are taken from the translation of I. Scott-Kilvert, *Cassius Dio, The Roman History: The Reign of Augustus* (Harmondsworth: Penguin, 1987).

38. Augustus's authority described here was not static. In 23 BCE he received an expanded degree of authority over all provinces, increased authority within Rome's bounds, and more responsibility over the Senate's agenda (Cassius Dio 53.22). At the same time he took charge, following famine and flood and civil disturbance, of the grain supply. When he returned from the east in 19 BCE he took on the role of commissioner of morals and other civic responsibilities "believing them to be necessary, but absolved them from the requirement of an oath" (Cassius Dio 54.10).

not been for one man, one *princeps,* Augustus, who deserves the title of "Averter of evil." This is the Caesar who lulled the storms which were crashing everywhere, who healed the sickness common to Greeks and barbarians alike. . . . This is he who not merely loosened but broke the fetters which had confined and oppressed the world. . . . This is he who set every city again at liberty, who reduced disorder to order, who civilized all the unfriendly, savage tribes and brought them into harmony with each other . . . and who hellenized the most important parts of the barbarian world.

(Philo, *Legatio,* 143–47)[39]

I quote these assessments of Augustus extensively because they convey best the attitude of educated independent-minded persons toward Augustus. That a contemporary Jew, living in Alexandria, could say such startling things about Augustus, even allowing for his rhetorical purpose, underscores Octavian's awesome role. It also shows how a dependent king such as Herod, recently confirmed in his position after having been opposed to Octavian, might think about Augustus and his responsibilities to him.

Augustus's policy on kingdoms is enunciated by Suetonius: "He nearly always restored the kingdoms which he conquered to their defeated dynasties, rarely combined them with others, and followed a policy of linking together his royal allies by mutual ties of friendship or intermarriage, which he was never slow to propose. . . . He also brought up many of their children with his own, and gave them the same education."[40] The description fits Augustus's dealings with Herod precisely. Though Augustus toyed with the idea of extending Herod's kingdom, in the end he did not, consistent with the policy described by Suetonius. Augustus approved, consistent with Suetonius, ties of intermarriage with other sovereigns and he brought up Herod's male children at court in Rome with his own children and grandchildren. Herod fit exactly Augustus's pattern for dealing with dependent kings.

Of particular importance was Augustus's attitude toward Jews and Judaism; regrettably there is no reference to Jews or Judea or Herod in the *Res gestae,* Augustus's own account of his accomplishments and his career written at the end of his life.[41] So we have no first-hand description, though there are several second-hand accounts, some of which will be dealt with in chapter 11. Philo, who followed events from Alexandria, provides some help. Just after the passage

---

39. The translation is E. M. Smallwood's (*Philonis Alexandrini Legatio ad Gaium* [Leiden: Brill, 1970]).

40. Suetonius, *Augustus* 47–48.

41. See P. A. Brunt and J. M. Monroe, *Res gestae divi Augusti: The Achievements of the Divine Augustus. Introduction and Commentary* (Oxford: Oxford University Press, 1967). The only full text was found in the Temple of Roma and Augustus at Ankara.

quoted above Philo points out that Alexandrian Jews ignored Augustus for forty-three years; there were no dedications in their synagogues (actually *proseuchai*, "houses of prayer"), while the city itself built a wonderful Sebasteion to Augustus that overlooked the harbor (*Legatio* 148–51). Philo turns this "neglect" on its ear, saying that Augustus maintained "firmly the native customs of each particular nation no less than of the Romans, and . . . he received his honours not for destroying the institutions of some nations in vain self-exaltation," with which he links Augustus's "approval of the Jews, who . . . regarded all such things with horror" (*Legatio* 153–54). Philo emphasizes that Augustus knew the Jewish community and their houses of prayer in Rome and he knew that they sent money to Jerusalem. He even claims that Augustus "adorned our temple . . . and ordered that for all time continuous sacrifices of whole burnt offerings should be carried out every day at his own expense" (*Legatio* 155–58). This maximal interpretation was not correct at every point, but that a Jew maintained these views shortly after Augustus's death—while the Temple still stood and in a less favorable political climate—is testimony to Augustus's tolerance.

Herod's relationship with Augustus took shape in this atmosphere. (1) He was dependent upon Rome and Augustus, with the degree of independence that other kings enjoyed. He could not pursue independent external initiatives, but he had considerable freedom domestically; he could practice and promote Judaism and he could tend to the well-being of his country's laws and customs. (2) With respect to Judaism, Rome's attitude was lenient. Philo comments on Augustus's own support of daily sacrifice in the Temple, on the duties of Jews everywhere to the Jerusalem Temple, on synagogue worship, and on conditions in Alexandria, Rome, and Jerusalem. Much of what we know of Augustus tends in the same direction, with tolerance almost approaching approval. (3) Octavian had, however, become *Augustus/Sebastos*, offered honors that pushed even that title to its limits, especially in the east, where religious precincts such as the one Philo describes at Alexandria were built to Roma and Augustus. Because of Jewish religious particularity, Herod might have sought exemption from these honors to Augustus, yet he was one of the first to recognize the Emperor cult. (4) The relationship between Augustus and his client kings was a delicate balancing act between local internal matters and Imperial policy. Other less obvious factors may also have played a part: the two personalities, the behavior of their children in Rome, the reception of each other on state visits and the like.

A warm friendship between Augustus and Herod survived intact for almost thirty years, though with ups and downs, particularly when both were having trouble with their respective successions. Herod did what he said at Rhodes he would do: he transferred loyalty to Octavian and served him faithfully.[42] Herod

---

42. Josephus's occasionally exaggerated claim about how close the friendship was, together with the negative evidence of the *Res gestae* and contemporary writers, suggests Herod rarely was a source of problems for the Emperor.

was a secure point in Rome's eastern policy, supplying troops when necessary, keeping his region quiet, showing the loyalty required of clients, and maintaining open trade routes.

Herod's first opportunity to show his worth in foreign ventures came in 25/24 BCE when Aelius Gallus (governor of Egypt) took an expedition of ten thousand Roman soldiers into Arabia Felix, accompanied by auxiliary forces of one thousand Nabateans (led by Syllaeus) and five hundred of Herod's soldiers (Strabo, *Geog.* 16.4.22–24; see *Ant.* 15.317), with several purposes: first, to reconnoiter the Arabian peninsula, which lay well beyond usual definitions of Roman interests; second, to establish Roman dominance among the Sabeans (modern Yemen),[43] thereby controlling the eastern trade routes; and third, perhaps to vault past the Nabateans with their dominance in the region.[44] These purposes suited Herod's interests, though the presence of Nabateans, especially Syllaeus, did not.

The campaign was a disaster. Soldiers suffered from serious illnesses—perhaps sunstroke and scurvy—and the majority died either from these or in battle with the Sabeans.[45] The bright face Augustus put on it (*Res gestae* 26), that the army "advanced . . . to the town of Meriba," may be technically accurate but conceals that there was neither long- nor short-term benefit.[46] The cause of the defeat, according to Strabo, was Syllaeus, the Nabatean "administrator" (*epitropos*) under King Obodas, who misled and misguided the expedition, particularly the marine part. If Strabo's account of Syllaeus's treachery is even partially correct, however, it was a miracle both that Syllaeus was not executed on the spot and that later (about 19 BCE) Herod considered him a candidate for his sister's hand. Strabo's invective against Syllaeus is suspect;[47] the disaster arose more from unforeseen conditions (the heat of the Yemen, the unknown waters of the Red Sea). From Strabo's neglect of Herod and from *Antiquities*'s very brief notice, it is probable that Herod stayed home. It was just

---

43. See Strabo, *Geog.* 16.4.21, re Sabeans, Syrians, and Nabateans. According to 2.5.12 Strabo joined his friend Aelius Gallus up the Nile as far as Syene.

44. Strabo, *Geog.* 16.4.22, says "to explore the tribes and the places, not only in Arabia but also in Aethiopia . . . [and to win] the Arabians over to himself or [to subjugate] them. Another consideration was the report. . . that they were very wealthy." Strabo emphasizes trade and exploration.

45. Cassius Dio 53.29; Strabo, *Geog.* 16.4.24, in a wonderful exaggeration, says only two persons died in one battle, only seven altogether from war, because the Sabeans were such terrible fighters; the rest died from "sickness and fatigue and hunger and bad roads."

46. Cassius Dio says they "advanced as far as the place called Athloula," on the Egyptian side of the Red Sea (53.29), making it more of a fiasco.

47. Aelius Gallus and Strabo were friends, so dropping all the blame onto Syllaeus protected Gallus's reputation: "if Syllaeus had not betrayed him, he would even have subdued the whole of Arabia Felix" (*Geog.* 17.1.53). The Syllaeus affair was concluded only in 6 BCE when he was executed in Rome, after overreaching himself in his dispute with Herod (see chap. 11).

as well he did not go, for the expedition lasted much longer than expected (perhaps parts of two years).

Herod developed his friendship with Augustus through his children's education. In 22 BCE Alexander and Aristobulus went to Rome "to present themselves to Caesar" (*Ant.* 15.342–43).[48] They stayed first with Pollio[49] and then with Augustus himself (see Suetonius's comment, above), who showed the greatest consideration. They would be about fourteen and thirteen, approximately the right age for education in grammar following primary instruction in rhetoric.

Questions about Antipater, Herod's eldest son, arise naturally. Nothing can be said, however, until he reappears in the narrative of *Antiquities* and *War* later (about 13 BCE), when his trip to Rome is presented as his first visit, designed to introduce himself to Augustus. Given the shame and disgrace he suffered when Doris was divorced and banished in 42 BCE (Antipater was about three years of age), he would not have been sent to Rome for schooling. The first contact between Augustus's family and Herod's was this occasion in 22 BCE when Alexander and Aristobulus, the last of the Hasmoneans, were educated under Augustus's watchful eye—when Augustus, in addition, gave Herod the right to name his own successor (*Ant.* 15.344).[50]

The brothers stayed for five years; in 17 BCE Herod went to Rome to bring them home (*Ant.* 16.90–130; *War* 1.445) because of their antagonism to him. Other children also went to Rome for their education. Another of Mariamme's children, who had gone at the same time as Alexander and Aristobulus probably, died there; we know nothing further of him, not even his name. At the appropriate ages Archelaus, Antipas, and Philip went to Rome and were treated generously by the Emperor, some of them being "brought up by a certain Jew"

48. Jospehus, as so often, says "at this juncture," with a reference to the conclusion of the rebuilding of Sebaste, which was completed before Caesarea Maritima was undertaken: Sebaste, ca. 27–22 BCE; Caesarea Maritima, ca. 22–10 BCE. According to Josephus the boys were proud of their Roman education (*War* 1.479; *Ant.* 16.203–204).

49. With which Pollio is an interesting but not hugely important question. There are two candidates, Asinius Pollio and Vedius Pollio (a more recent suggestion by R. Syme, "Who was Vedius Pollio?," *JRS* 5 (1961): 25–30, especially the brief addendum: "Perhaps Vedius Pollio"; see also G. W. Bowersock, *Augustus and the Greek World* (Oxford: Clarendon, 1965), p. 55, n.3. Feldman has argued that Asinius Pollio was interested in Judaism, was bookish and, after a public career (consul in 40 BCE when Herod was named king by the Senate), turned to a scholarly life, writing an important history of the period (on Vedius Pollio, see Cassius Dio 54.23; L. H. Feldman, "Asinius Pollio and Herod's Sons," *Classical Quarterly* 35 [1985]: 240–42; D. Braund, "Four Notes on the Herods," *Classical Quarterly* 33 [1983]: 239–42). Asinius seems more likely, based on both inclination and acquaintance with Herod. The recent preference for Vedius derives partly from the assumption that both Herod and Vedius were scoundrels; birds of a feather flocked together.

50. This is phrased, appropriately, in the singular. Augustus would not welcome splitting the kingdom. The concession had partly to do with his Augustus's confidence in Herod, partly with his experience of the Hasmonean brothers in Rome. See chap. 2.

(*Ant.* 17.20). We have no coherent information about any of the stays in Rome (length, nature of the education, contacts with Augustus's family, other friends),[51] but it is likely that Augustus knew Herod's sons, though he himself was absent from the city for a portion of their time in Rome, part of it spent visiting their father in Judea.

At about the same time (24/23 BCE) Augustus added Trachonitis, Auranitis, and Batanea to Herod's kingdom.[52] The central figure in the drama was Zenodorus, who had become "Tetrarch and High Priest," according to coins, of some unnamed portion of the region. Following the execution of Lysanias, he took over part of Chalcis and later held portions of the Huleh region (or perhaps leased them from Cleopatra; she had arranged for Lysanias to be executed by Antony because she wished title to the area). This whole area was part of the Ituraean hegemony (see chaps. 3 and 6), and Zenodorus was probably an Ituraean prince or noble[53] who controlled lands east and southeast of him. Josephus claims that Zenodorus encouraged Trachonites to harry and plunder the traders and inhabitants of Damascus who used a nearby route to the south (*War* 1.398–99; *Ant.* 15.343–48). It is not clear who got rid of the brigands: according to *War* it was M. Terrentius Varro, governor of Syria 24–23 BCE; according to *Antiquities* Varro asked Augustus's advice (who advised, "drive them out and give the area to Herod") and let Herod pacify the region and put a stop to the depredations after he had been granted the land,[54] after which Zenodorus travelled to Rome to complain of Herod's behavior (*Ant.* 15.349). The later account of *Antiquities* is the more plausible, though the action may have been joint. If Augustus intended to grant this troublesome area to Herod, he may have done so on condition that Herod pacify it.

Soon after, Marcus Vipsanius Agrippa was named Augustus's "deputy" for the east (23 BCE), a general responsibility that continued until 13 BCE, though he did not live in the east for the whole period.[55] At the time of his appointment he took up residence in Mitylene on Lesbos; Herod paid his respects there as soon as possible (23/22 BCE).

Agrippa was an extremely powerful figure, *praetor urbanus* in 40 BCE (when Herod was named king), governor of Gaul in 39–38, consul in 37, 28, and 27 BCE, a lifelong friend of Octavian/Augustus and a leading strategist in his victory

---

51. In the next generation, however, there are good sources for Agrippa I's inclusion in the top levels of society; he was a boyhood friend of Germanicus, Gaius, and Claudius, so well-connected with Senate and Imperial family that he acted as go-between when the Senate negotiated with Claudius over the throne. The same was true, to a lesser extent, of Agrippa II.

52. *War* 1.398 laconically refers it to "after the first Actiad," 23 BCE or shortly thereafter; *Ant.* 15.343 relates it to his children's stay in Rome.

53. Schürer 1.561–73, esp. 566. A full study of these problems and this area is required.

54. See Cassius Dio 54.9.

55. Cassius Dio, for example, says Augustus "once more dispatched Agrippa to Syria" (54.19).

at Actium. He was designated successor to Augustus (Cassius Dio 53–54) and then was commanded to divorce his second wife (Augustus's niece) in order to marry Augustus's daughter Julia (21 BCE). His importance was further enhanced when his new wife gave birth to successors for Augustus: Gaius, Lucius, and Agrippa Postumus. Agrippa was wealthy, successful, powerful, and influential;[56] he "was advanced by Augustus to the supreme position" (Cassius Dio 54).

Agrippa and Herod were close friends. In a startling exaggeration Josephus says (following *War*'s account of Zenodorus), "what Herod valued more than all these privileges was that in Caesar's affection he stood next after Agrippa, in Agrippa's next after Caesar" (*War* 1.400; *Ant.* 15.361).[57] The friendship was natural: both were rooted in the countryside, fabulously wealthy, ambitious patrons of public works, keen supporters of Augustus, and imaginative military commanders. They were thrown into a closer cooperation through Agrippa's *proconsulare imperium* over the east. Josephus's description of these mutual relationships must derive from Nicolas of Damascus, for in a fragment of his *Universal History* that survives, Nicolas describes how in 16 or 15 BCE Julia arrived unexpectedly in Ilios (Troy) and almost lost her life in a flash flood. Angrily, Agrippa fined them one hundred thousand silver drachmae; the citizens begged Nicolas to ask Herod to intervene on their behalf, which he did successfully.[58]

The friendship stood Herod in good stead, though it laid certain demands upon each. For example, the Gadarenes sent a delegation to Agrippa in Lesbos to complain about the city's position within Herod's kingdom, shortly after Herod had returned to Judea (22 BCE). Agrippa dismissed the complaint without hearing it and sent the delegation to Herod in chains, who let them off (*Ant.* 15.356).[59] The affair bubbled for a couple of years until Augustus made a state visit to Syria in 20 BCE (Cassius Dio 54; *Ant.* 15.354);[60] then, with the support of Zenodorus who posed as their protector (*Ant.* 15.355), Gadarenes denounced Herod's tyrannical rule. Their case rested on accusations of violence, pillage, and overthrowing temples (*Ant.* 15.357).[61] When some of the delegation committed suicide because Augustus's views became known, he dismissed the charges.[62] Augustus gave parts of Ituraea (Lake Huleh and Panias) to Herod after

---

56. See M. Reinhold, *Marcus Agrippa* (Geneva, NY, 1933).

57. See *Ant.* 15.350: "Herod . . . was one of his closest friends and companions."

58. *FGrH* 90 F 134; quoted in R. K. Sherk, *Rome and the Greek East to the Death of Augustus* (Cambridge: Cambridge University Press, 1984), 98C.

59. Note the evaluation: "he had . . . the reputation of being the most inexorable of all men toward those of his own people who sinned, but magnanimous in pardoning foreigners."

60. He had completed the seventeenth year of his reign, an instance of a date being reckoned from 37 BCE.

61. This last is particularly odd. Evidence of temples in Gadara is confined to literary, numismatic, and artifactual data, for no temples have yet been excavated. I am indebted to Elaine Myers for a study of this question.

62. Marcus suggests in the Yarmuk River below Gadara, but the case was probably being heard in Antioch.

Zenodorus's support for the Gadarenes evaporated. In a further mark of his esteem, Augustus gave Herod procuratorial responsibility in Syria, probably confined to border regions, though Josephus's description makes it sound more extensive and important (*Ant.* 15.360; *War* 1.399).

Herod obtained financial and political independence for his brother Pheroras by getting Augustus to carve off Peraea (*Ant.* 15.362; *War* 1.483). The incident offers important political insights: Herod could not make the disposition himself; he arranged it to secure Pheroras's position against his own sons, Alexander and Aristobulus, who at this very time were in Rome under the aegis of Augustus; Pheroras acquired a share of Herod's rule and was made financially secure with a grant of one hundred talents per year plus the income of Peraea; to enhance his position he was married to Herod's wife's sister (a sister of Mariamme I, daughter of Alexander and Alexandra; *War* 1.483).

Augustus visited Herod in his own territories (Cassius Dio and Josephus both say that he visited Syria; Cassius Dio 54; *Ant.* 15.354). Given Herod's decision to build a Temple to Roma and Augustus at Panias and its mention at this point in the narrative (15.363–64), it was probably at Panias that Herod entertained Augustus. From there a royal procession to Sebaste (named in Augustus's honor and recently completed) with its Temple to Roma and Augustus, then a visit to Caesarea Maritima (also named in his honor) with its remarkable harbor installations and its Temple to Roma and Augustus, now under construction, would be logical. Though the itinerary is conjecture, it allows Herod the advantage of displaying the sites honoring his patron.

The picture is grossly incomplete, and surprisingly so given Nicolas's knowledge of Augustus, Agrippa, and Herod. The description of the friendship of Agrippa and Herod with Augustus and with each other is certainly true of Agrippa and Augustus, probably true of Agrippa and Herod, but unproven of Herod and Augustus. Herod made few visits to Rome and Augustus made only the above mentioned visit to Judea. Nothing is known of how Augustus was entertained; apart from the conjectured building of the Temple of Roma and Augustus at Panias to celebrate a visit, no memorials of the princeps's trip to Herod's regions have survived. The infrequent contact is difficult to explain. Yet in the specific challenges Herod faced he had support from both Augustus and Agrippa, not least in the Zenodorus and Gadara affairs: he gained Trachonitis, Auranitis, Batanea, Huleh, and Panias as a result, and was confirmed as ruler of Gadara.

INTERNAL MATTERS

Other matters absorbed Herod's time and energy during this same period. He continued to be troubled by family concerns, primarily his own marital status in the mid 20s. Mariamme I was dead, executed in 29 BCE. He had divorced his first wife, Doris, and dismissed her and her son from the palace. Two of Herod's marriages, one to a cousin and one to a niece, are impossible to place on a timeline (see chap. 2), since Josephus's decision to list them last may not be chronological.[63] The following list of marriages is more likely to be correct: (1) Doris (47 BCE); (2) Mariamme I (37 BCE); (3) his niece (probably about 30/29 BCE); (4) his cousin (about 28 BCE); (5) Malthace (27 BCE); (6) Cleopatra of Jerusalem (25 BCE); (7) Mariamme II (24 BCE); (8) Pallas (say about 22 BCE); (9) Phaedra (20 BCE); (10) Elpis (about 18 BCE); (11?) Doris brought back to the royal court (about 14 BCE).[64] Herod contracted eight of his ten or eleven marriages in the brief period under consideration. Curiously, the marriages to his niece and his cousin were the least remembered; not even their names are recorded. They were probably of little account, quickly ended, and resulted in no issue—merely marriages of convenience to tide Herod over the period during and after Mariamme's execution.

His marriage to Malthace, a Samaritan, came in the year be began reconstruction of Sebaste and immediately after his life-threatening illness. The marriage did nothing for his political or religious reputation in Judea and he had no pressing reason to court Samaritans, who had been surprisingly supportive of Herod. A simple explanation is best: it was a marriage of love or at least attraction. Malthace must have been resilient; she survived in a position of influence longer than any other of his wives, from 27 to 4 BCE. She died during the hearings in Rome over the succession where she was active on her sons' behalf.[65] Herod married Cleopatra of Jerusalem (to distinguish her from Herod's nemesis, Cleopatra VII of Egypt), of whom nothing is known; she may have been a daughter of a Jerusalem noble. Since Malthace was not divorced, to judge from the position she occupied, from this period on Herod had multiple wives. He also married a second Mariamme whose father was a priest—Simon son of Boethos, from Alexandria (see also chap. 10). When Herod saw her beauty he wanted to marry her. Since her status was not high enough to be the wife of the king,[66] Herod took the simple expedient of deposing the current high priest, Jesus ben Phiabi, and elevating Simon in his place when he contracted marriage with Simon's daughter (see *Ant.* 15.320; 17.19; *War* 1.562).

These three marriages (Malthace, Cleopatra of Jerusalem, and Mariamme II) must have run concurrently, all contracted between 27 and 23 BCE or there-

---

63. Hanson makes them the first two, coming before his marriage to Doris.

64. This list differs in some details from Hanson's excellent work. See for additional detail, Appendix, chap. 2.

65. In two lists (*War* 1.562; *Ant.* 17.20) her children are listed in what is likely the wrong order; Archelaus was probably the older.

66. Others of his wives may have had the same problem, though no comments are made in these cases.

abouts.[67] About marriages with Pallas, Phaedra and Elpis nothing is known;[68] they probably occurred in the years 22 through 19. To complicate matters, in 14 BCE Herod brought Doris and her son Antipater out of disgrace (see chap. 11); they had married thirty-three years earlier and had been divorced for twenty-eight years. The tension, in a household with as many as seven wives living together over a long period of time with several children and their struggles for precedence, can hardly be imagined.

Financial problems struck again in 20 BCE or a little earlier (*Ant.* 15.365, referring back to 15.354 and Augustus's visit). Previously the combination of sabbatical year, drought, famine, and plague had required Herculean efforts and caused a large drain on Herod's finances. In this instance Josephus does not say that there was a famine, though this is often deduced: "Herod remitted to the people of his kingdom a third part of their taxes, under the pretext of letting them recover from a period of lack of crops. . . ." The occasion was almost certainly another sabbatical, in the year 23/22 (the previous one was 30/29),[69] so it should be dated to 22/21. Several factors stand out. (1) Herod was concerned to win "the good will of those who were disaffected"; there was disagreement but not famine. (2) "They resented his carrying out of such arrangements [remission of taxes?] as seemed to them to mean the dissolution of their religion and the disappearance of their customs"; this seems a reference to letting land lie fallow for the sabbatical year.[70] The sabbatical had deepened the problems seven years earlier; now Herod may have encouraged the people to make no more than minimal provision for the sabbatical. (3) He remitted one-third of the taxes to alleviate the hardships; Roman decrees, cited by Jospehus, recognized the hardship of sabbatical years and occasionally taxes were remitted on those occasions. Herod was following his masters' practice—not a popular course. (4) It seems likely that conservatives, perhaps landowners not affected in he same way as smallholders, objected to Herod's tampering with the divine order of things. (5) Herod "instruct[ed] them to apply themselves at all times to their work," perhaps a reference to idleness popularly associated with not working the fields during sabbatical years.[71]

---

67. The latter date derives from *Ant.* 15.323, which refers imprecisely to Herod's marriage with Mariamme II occurring at about the time he undertook the building of Herodium, possibly even as a wedding present for her.

68. Probably in this order since both *War* 1.562 and *Ant.* 17.19–21 agree on this despite other differences.

69. I calculate there were sabbatical years in 37/36 BCE, 30/29 (with a famine in 28/27), 23/22, 16/15, 9/8, 2/1, 6/7 CE, 13/14, 20/21, 27/28, 34/35, 41/42, 48/49, 55/56, 62/63, and 69/70, the final year of the siege of Jerusalem.

70. It is hard to see what other religious custom could have been dissolved by tax relief, unless Herod tampered with the Temple tax, which was unlikely.

71. Tacitus, *Histories* 5.4: "We are told that the seventh day was set aside for rest because this marked the end of their toils. In course of time the seduction of idleness made them denote every seventh year to indolence as well. Others say that this is a mark of respect to Saturn. . . ."

Remission of taxes was a different strategy from that adopted during the previous financial hardships, when he purchased grain in Egypt for general distribution. The problems and measures were different, but two factors were similar: an increased degree of state manipulation of the economy, and a substantial degree of benevolence and social welfare. Though Judea was hardly a welfare state, there was more economic interference and more religious accommodation such as the sabbatical year than conservatives wished to see.

Other actions of Herod went against or beyond Jewish law. He intended to remove injustices by acting harshly against malefactors, suggesting social dislocation and brigandage (although the word is not used here) both in the countryside and in Jerusalem (*Ant.* 16.1). Housebreakers were to be sold into slavery and deported, a more severe penalty than Torah's because release was not envisaged.[72] The new measure was thought tyrannous and led to more dislike (*Ant.* 16.1–5). Another internal problem characterized this period: state "supervision" of the population. Josephus notes prohibition of meetings and of normal association, secret police, strict punishment, both secret and open incarceration in Hyrcania (Herod's most dreaded fortress), and executions (*Ant.* 15.366). In a statement that sounds as if it were lifted from Suetonius's account of Nero, Herod was rumored to go out and about in disguise to learn peoples' attitudes to him (15.367).

Herod demanded an oath of loyalty to him and his rule (15.368), though Josephus says two groups were excused, Essenes and followers of Pollion and Samaias (15.369–70).[73] The exact nature of the oath is not given, but in the east oaths were not unknown, as the following makes clear:

> Of Imperator Caes[ar,] son of the god, Augustus the twelfth consulship, third year (of the province), on the day before the Nones of March in Gangra in [camp?,] the oath completed by the inhabitants of [Pa]phlagonia [and the] R[omans] who do business among them: I swear by Zeus, Earth, Sun, and all the gods [and] goddesses, and Augus[t]us himself that I will be favorably disposed toward [Cae]sar Augustus and his children and descendants all the time of my [life] in word and deed and thought, considering as friends those whom they may consider (friends) and holding as enemies those whom they may judge to be (enemies). . . . In the same words was this oath sworn by all the [inhabitants of the land] in the temples of

---

72. According to Josephus, thieves were subject to a fine of four times (Philo says twice; *Spec. leg.* 4.2) the amount stolen; if the fine could not be paid the thief was to be sold, but only to a fellow Israelite so that in a sabbatical year he would in the ordinary course of events be released. Note how this resonates with tax relief, above.

73. On the oath, Grant, p. 204; P. W. Barnett, "*Apographê* and *apographesthai* in Luke 2:1–5," *ExT* 85 (1974): 372–80; on Essenes, see *Ant.* 18.18–22; *War* 2.119–61.

Augustus throughout the districts (of the province) by the altars [of Augustus]. . . .[74]

The general intent was similar. Given the point at which this incident falls in Josephus's narrative, the oath was probably instituted when Augustus was in Judea;[75] it would have highlighted treaty relationships between Judea and Rome, given special prominence to Augustus and minor (possibly still explicit) reference to Herod. If the oath cited above is relevant, it may have been connected with the Temples of Roma and Augustus in Sebaste and at Caesarea Maritima, then under construction. Since an oath was a religious act, it fits well in this period when "religion" and "customs" were matters of controversy and exemptions from the oath were allowed to some who argued on special religious grounds.[76]

At exactly this time Herod began his most important building project, the complete reconstruction of the Temple in Jerusalem (see chap. 10). It is dated differently in our two sources: *Ant.* 15.380 says the eighteenth year of his reign (dating from 40 = 23/22; dating from 37 = 20/19); *War* 1.401 says the fifteenth year (dating from 40 = 26/25; dating from 37 = 23/22). The obvious, and overlooked, solution is that 23/22 was the year construction started.[77] Regardless, it was a massive undertaking, another of the religious issues of the late 20s and early teens. At this point we need only highlight several of Josephus's claims: (1) the money came from Herod's own pocket; (2) he was motivated by the popular acclaim that might accrue (*Ant.* 15.380 for both); (3) it was possible only because of Judea's prosperity;[78] (4) sustained peace and harmonious relations with Rome also were factors (*Ant.* 15.387); (5) the project outshone for its piety and beauty all his other projects at home and abroad (15.384); (6) careful preparations reduced objections and ensured speedy conclusion of the essential parts of the work (15.388–90), so that the *naos* (the Temple proper) was completed in one-and-one-half years.

Finally, an internal problem that would become a major external challenge stirred below the surface. Just before his death (20 BCE), Zenodorus had sold

---

74. 6 March 3 BCE: IGR III.137; OGIS 532; ILS 8781; cited in Sherk, *Rome and the Greek East* (Cambridge: Cambridge University Press, 1984), #105.

75. An oath to Herod without reference to Augustus is inherently unlikely.

76. Might this form part of the background to Jesus' prohibition of oaths?

77. That is, *Antiquities* reckons from 40, *War* from 37. Schürer 1.292, n.12, is overly positive about a connection between Augustus's visit and the beginning of construction; nothing in the narrative makes this connection explicit—no visit, no association of ideas.

78. This is found in Herod's speech (*Ant.* 15.382–87; see 383, 387); it is almost certain to be correct, however, given the immensity of the project; the notion of special prosperity is supported by the tax holiday referred to above. See E. Gabba, "The Finances of King Herod," in A. Kasher, U. Rappaport, and G. Fuks, eds., *Greece and Rome in Eretz-Israel* (Jerusalem: Israel Exploration Society, 1990), pp. 160–68.

Nabatea a portion of his territory known as Auranitis (Jebel Druze). Though Nabateans considered this region or some part of it theirs (Bosra, Qanawat, and Si'a all have early Nabatean remains), Augustus had included it as part of his gift to Herod in 23/22 (*Ant.* 15.351–52). Nabatea tried several stratagems to get it back, partly legal and partly military. For Herod the most unsettling aspect of this was that his soldiers stationed or settled there who did not share the general prosperity enjoyed by the country shifted their support to Nabatea. Mindful of his obligations as a dependent king to keep peace within his realm and avoid foreign entanglements not sanctioned by the emperor, he bided his time (*Ant.* 15.352–53).

TO ROME

While we may not know of all of Herod's visits to Rome, there seem remarkably few. One occurred in 17 BCE,[79] when he went to see Augustus and his sons, and to bring the boys home. Alexander and Aristobulus had been there five years and completed their schooling, so Augustus "permitted [Herod] to take them home" (*Ant.* 16.6). Possibly a third unnamed brother had recently died and Herod was taking the body home.

When they arrived in Judea, now mature young men of about nineteen and eighteen, there was great interest in them. They were rich, royals, Hasmoneans, intimates of the Imperial family, and educated in Rome (*Ant.* 16.7). But in Judea they upset the uneasy balance. Salome and her supporters feared they might come to power and make reprisals for accusations resulting in Mariamme I's death. The rumor mill turned; it was mooted that the boys were opposed to their father—not implausibly—for his part in their mother's death. Herod's affection, never great, began to lessen (see *War* 1.445–47).

For a time it was standoff. Herod arranged marriages (his trip to Rome may have included negotiating Augustus's permission) for Alexander[80] and Glaphyra, daughter of fellow dependent king, Archelaus of Cappadocia; and for Aristobulus with Berenice his cousin, daughter of Herod's sister Salome. This latter union must have been tense, for Aristobulus's new mother-in-law was his mother's main accuser. The other marriage had more chance of success, though Glaphyra would have known nothing of Judaism and her children's status might be in question.[81]

---

79. His first visit was in 40 BCE, his second in 17 BCE, a third in 13/12 BCE (see chap. 11); there was one other later one. His other contacts with Augustus were only slightly more numerous: in 31 BCE in Rhodes, in 20 in Syria and Judea.

80. The older of the two, contra Hanson.

81. Aristobulus and Berenice had five children: Herod of Chalcis (d. 48 CE), Marcus Julius Herod Agrippa I (d. 44 CE), Aristobulus, Herodias (first married to Philip, then to Antipas); and another Mariamme. Alexander and Glaphyra had two children, another Alexander and Tigranes IV.

CHAPTER 10

Herod and Religion

INTRODUCTION

In 40 BCE the Senate did not appreciate or care that the Hasmoneans, with whom they had lost patience, claimed the high priesthood of the Temple cult in addition to kingship. In 153/152 BCE Jonathan had become high priest, and since 104 BCE Hasmonean high priests had considered themselves kings (see *Ant.* 20.241: Aristobulus was "the first to hold both offices"). The linkage was a key to their position in the early first century, though not all were as bold as Alexander Jannaeus in using both titles on their coins.[1] Mixing political and religious authority may have been a latent weakness of the dynasty, but unquestionably it gave them great power and prestige. After the death of Alexander Jannaeus in 76 BCE, his widow Alexandra, who assumed royal power, appointed her oldest son, Hyrcanus II, as high priest.[2] This temporary expedient did not hold; before her death her two oldest sons' rivalry weakened the state and provided a pretext for Pompey's takeover in 63 BCE.

There is little to indicate popular concern over the linkage of high priest and king, an innovation not known in Israel before (though see *Ant.* 13.372–73). But deep antagonism arose within two circles: the authors of some of the Dead Sea Scrolls, following priestly ideals, believed it an offense and the Pharisees, according to Josephus, saw it as inappropriate (*Ant.* 13.288–92). One effect may be imagined; the ruling elite must have included more priestly figures and the countervailing power of a lay elite must have been diminished, which

---

1. Alexander Jannaeus first struck coins using his royal title ("Yehonatan the King" in Hebrew; or "King Alexander" in Greek); then he struck coins describing himself as "Yehonatan the High Priest and the *hever* of the Jews." Later, he overstruck "royal" coins with the "high priestly" legend.

2. Later series of his coins identify him as "Head of the *hever* of Jews." Some of his coins have a monogram, usually identified as a reference to Herod's father Antipater.

would explain the prevailing view in the first century CE that the priests were the ruling elite. When Herod took over as king he faced a substantial problem, for most of the upper class supported Antigonus, the son of Aristobulus II and the opponent of Hyrcanus II, Herod's ally.

HEROD AND THE TEMPLE

Greek has a variety of words connoting in one way or another "elite." *The Lexicon of Semantic Fields* lists fifty-seven words marking either status distinctions in general or high status.[3] A study of Josephus's use of these words has not, so far as I know, been done; in what follows I will deal with a small portion of the relevant evidence.

With respect to the priestly elite—and not all priests were elite—several factors need to be considered. (1) The high priests were a natural part of the religious elite—indeed at the center of it—by virtue of family associations, functions within the cult, and permanent residence in Jerusalem. During many periods, especially when Israel was not independent, the high priest, whom outsiders naturally approached as an authoritative spokesman, held effective power within Judaism. (2) Other priests living in Jerusalem tended to share this elite status, for they had regular contact with the high priest and other authorities. By contrast, priests who lived at a distance from Jerusalem were in the city only two weeks in the year, could not know what was happening, and could not influence decisions much. (3) For 120 years the Hasmonean family had been at the center of this religious elite. The honor ascribed to them made the family unique; even during Alexandra's rule, when high priesthood and kingship were separated, political and religious power resided in the one family. (4) While the ruling class in Judea was larger than one family or even one group such as wealthy priests, during the Hasmonean period there was a tendency for wealth, power, and status to flow toward the friends, supporters, and associates of the Hasmoneans, a good number of whom were priests.[4]

Herod's relations with the elite are not traced by Josephus specifically or in detail. He executed some, he took others' property, he undercut the previous power structures and obliterated the remaining vestiges of allegiance to the Hasmonean family. This much is reasonably clear, if not well documented.

---

3. Excluding those indicating low status. See Louw and Nida, 87.1–57. I have in mind such words as *dynatos* ("powerful"), *megalos* ("great"), *eugenês* ("well-born"), *topos* ("position"), *klêsis* ("station" or "calling"), *bathros* ("standing"); various words denoting "honor," such as *timê, kleos, dokimos, entrepomai,* and so on.

4. In the excavations of the Western Hill in Jerusalem some buildings have been identified as priests' houses; they are remarkably large and richly finished. While priests were not supposed to hold land, this regulation did not seem to apply in this period; some priests were also large landowners.

What is less clear is the extent to which he created his own ruling elite, though it seems likely—politically necessary—that he did so. Certainly members of his extended family took on that role; it appears that there were transfers in land ownership and social dislocations that were likely the result of shifts in wealth and power. Occasionally he held councils or courts, to which he turned for support, implying a social and religious elite. A limited few families held the high priesthood during Herod's and his children's years in power, so we can conclude that the religious elite was reshaped. In short, a transformation of the upper layers of society was underway.

The high priest and his associates were important during the Herodian era. For the Temple cult and Judaism to function, a valid high priest must be in office. The Hasmoneans had altered the traditions about the high priest, both with respect to heredity (though Aaronite, they were not from the family of Zadok) and to function (no one had previously dared to link king and high priest).[5] The recollection of a break with tradition in the matter of high priest was found most obviously at Leontopolis (in the Delta region in Egypt), where a rival temple continuing the sacrificial cult was founded either by Onias III or Onias IV, the former being the legitimate high priest in 174 BCE when Antiochus IV Epiphanes deposed him. The sense of a break was also felt among Essenes, who abandoned Jerusalem while they waited for a legitimate priesthood and temple to be re-established in the messianic age under their own leaders.[6]

Despite these complexities, Herod's first brief experiment following his victory over Antigonus was to appoint Hananel,[7] a Babylonian of "high priestly family" (*Ant.* 15.40–41) to the office (15.22),[8] whom he subsequently deposed. Josephus says the deposing was unlawful and had only happened twice before—first by Antiochus IV Epiphanes replacing Jason with Menelaus, and second by Aristobulus II removing his brother Hyrcanus II to appoint himself. Herod deposed Hananel to appoint Aristobulus as high priest,[9] partly to satisfy his wife

---

5. The issue of priesthood is very complex. For general introductions from different intellectual vantage points see the articles in *ABD* and *IDB,* along with Sanders, *Judaism.* For the Maccabean family pedigree, see 1 Macc. 2:1.

6. Some have argued that it can also be found in the Sadducees, who incorporate in their name the revered name of Zadok. This seems to me unlikely.

7. See J. Neusner, " The Jews East of the Euphrates and the Roman Empire I. 1st–3rd Centuries A.D.," *ANRW* 2.9.1 (1976): 46–69, esp. pp. 50–52.

8. In *Ant.* 15.22 Josephus refers to Hanael as from an undistinguished priestly family, an editorial attempt to poke fun at Herod's choice. The reference to his being of high priestly family is likelier to be correct. It is tempting to think that Hyrcanus II played some part in the appointment, since he was now disqualified as a result of his disfigurement and so could have no further priestly ambitions. Josephus refers to a friendship between Herod and Hananel prior to Hananel's appointment (15.40), so Hananel may have returned to Judea with Hyrcanus.

9. *Ant.* 15.31–41; 20:247–48. This is Aristobulus III, son of Alexander and Alexandra (both of

Mariamme and partly to confer a notion of legitimacy on his fledgling reign. The appointment was not a success, for Aristobulus was too successful in presenting himself as a focus of Hasmonean aspirations. According to Josephus (*Ant.* 15.50–56; 20.248), Herod had him drowned in a pool at Jericho in the Hasmonean palace.[10]

Josephus summarizes the traditional view of the high priest (*Ant.* 20.224–51) by emphasizing that he must be "of Aaron's blood and that no one of another lineage, even if he happened to be a king, should attain to the high priesthood" (*Ant.* 20.226).[11] He provides no list of the Herodian family's appointments after Aristobulus III, summarizing that Herod "abandoned the practice of appointing those of Asamonaean lineage as high priests . . ." (20.247); "After Aristobulus' death Herod ceased to entrust the high priesthood to the descendants of the sons of Asamonaios" (20.249). Note that Josephus refers to this merely as a practice, not a legal requirement;[12] so far as we know, there were no male descendants who could have followed in the Hasmonean line after the murder of Aristobulus III.

Elsewhere Josephus provides information about the mixed bag of Herodian high priests:

> Hananel (37–36/35 BCE) and Aristobulus III (35);
> Hananel again (35–30);[13]
> Jesus son of Phiabi (30–24);
> Boethos (24–5);
> Simon son of Boethos (5);[14]
> Matthias son of Theophilus (5–4);
> Joseph son of Ellemus (for one day in 4; not Herod's appointee);
> Joazar son of Boethos (4).

Four were deposed: Hananel (his first appointment), Jesus son of Phiabi, Boethos, and Matthias. Of Hananel's end we have no information; Joseph son of Ellemus was irrelevant because he was a one-day replacement necessitated

---

Hasmonean descent) and brother of Herod's wife, Mariamme I. He is not be confused with Aristobulus II, brother of Hyrcanus II, whose parents were Alexander Jannaeus and Queen Alexandra.

10. J. Gray, *A History of Jerusalem* (London: Hale, 1969), p. 155, speculates that Herod's motive had to do with Alexandra's political links with Cleopatra VII.

11. Does Josephus intend this as a hint of the illegitimacy of kings and high priests being one and the same person—and thus a slight on his own lineage as a Hasmonean (see *Life* 1–6)—or as a hint that Herod wished to hold both positions?

12. Is he here indirectly expressing his disapproval of all high priests outside the line of Onias III?

13. On this chronology the end of Hananel's second term coincides with the death of Hyrcanus II, whose friend and "client" he may have been.

14. It is possible that Boethos and Simon were the same person.

by Matthias's semen impurity. With respect to permanence of office, the picture is not pretty, though in a thirty-year period (35–5 BCE) there were only three high priests.

Personal considerations were a factor in several appointments: Aristobulus III was Herod's wife's brother; Boethos was Herod's future father-in-law; Joazar was Mariamme II's brother. These, like Archelaus's two appointments after Herod's death, were deliberate attempts to connect Herod's family with religious authority,[15] though it was not a vital consideration, for some were not so linked (Hananel and Jesus son of Phiabi), suggesting a political-religious issue at stake left unmentioned by Josephus.

Hananel may have been of high priestly descent.[16] Babylonians represented a large community of Jews, many of whom were priests, of whom some must have been from high priestly families. The coincidence of Hyrcanus II's return from Babylon and Hananel's appointment implies a deliberate attempt to draw the Babylonian Jewish community more closely to Judea. Given the conflict between Rome and Parthia, it may indicate an interest in staking out an eastern "sphere." Appointing a Babylonian priest as high priest must have seemed to some an unacceptable innovation, to others an enlightened opening to the Diaspora.[17]

Jesus son of Phiabi is mysterious. Apart from texts in Josephus, *Mishnah,* and *Tosephta,* the only place his name is attested is in the cemetery at Leontopolis (Tell el-Yehudiyeh) in the Delta region in Egypt.[18] It seems probable Herod's appointee was from Leontopolis. Why? First, just as Herod had attempted to draw in the Babylonian Diaspora more closely to Judea, he would have wanted to connect the large Egyptian community to Judea. (The fact that the next high priest, Boethos, was an Egyptian from Alexandria, supports this view, though in this case Herod's motives were connected with his forthcoming marriage.) Second, Leontopolis was the site of the temple built by Onias III or IV.

---

15. He followed the Hasmonean precedent, without being able to link king and high priest in the one person as they did.

16. If preference is given to *Ant.* 15.40–41 over 15.22; 20.247 implicitly supports the latter.

17. Sanders, *Judaism,* chap. 18 (on the Pharisees) claims that all high priests were brought up in Jerusalem and trained for the job (p. 396). If this were true it would provide a social-religious setting for the claim of Josephus that Pharisaic views were influential (cf. also pp. 397–98); but clearly some of Herod's appointees were not.

18. In a list of high priests who prepared the ashes of the Red Heifer (*m. Parah* 3.5) Hanamel (sic) is referred to as an Egyptian, followed immediately by "Ishmael son of Piabi." The Mishnaic tradition appears to have transposed the epithet "Egyptian" from Phiabi, where it belongs, to Hananel, where it does not. This Ishmael, a high priest appointed by Valerius Gratus (cf. *Ant.* 18.34), was likely son of our Phiabi. Another Ishmael b. Phiabi is referred to in *m. Sota* 9.15, "When R. Ishamael b. Phiabi died the splendour of the priesthood ceased," who was appointed high priest in 59 CE. The recollections of a son and grandson of Jesus b. Phiabi attest this family's status in proto-Rabbinic traditions.

It was modelled on the Temple in Jerusalem (*Ant.* 13.67) and had a tradition of high priests going back to the last of the Zadokite line to function in Jerusalem. Undoubtedly some viewed this as the legitimate line. No evidence links Phiabi with Onias III and the hypothesis that Herod was seeking a more "legitimate" high priest is speculative, yet the connection between Phiabi and Leontopolis is suggestive.[19]

Herod began the reconstruction of the Temple in 23 BCE.[20] Presuming a preliminary period for negotiations with the authorities, training the workers,[21] gathering the materials, and so on, the project was initiated while Jesus son of Phiabi was high priest (30–24 BCE) and construction began while Boethos was high priest. Is it coincidence that both were Egyptians, and that one may have been associated with the Temple at Leontopolis? I think not.[22] It is tempting to suppose that Jesus ben Phiabi was involved in the planning of the Temple project based on his experience at Leontopolis, and I offer one conjecture along this line.[23] In the Herodian reconstruction there is a sequence of courtyards of increasing degrees of holiness and purity: courts of Gentiles, of women, of Israel, of priests, and then the sanctuary and the holy of holies.[24] The Hasmonean Temple, like the Temple of Zerubabel and the first Temple, had some of these gradations (outer court, holy place, and holy of holies). However, there was neither a court of Gentiles nor a court of women;[25] both were innovations of the Herodian structure, yet they were accepted in the *Mishnah* with little suggestion of dispute.[26]

---

19. See A. Kasher, *Jews in Hellenistic and Roman Egypt* (Tübingen: J. C. B. Mohr, 1985), pp. 119–35, 346ff.; M. Stern, "Social and Political Realignments in Herodian Judaea," *Jerusalem Cathedra* 2 (1982): 40–62.

20. See chap. 9, above. The alternative is 20 BCE; both dates depend upon Josephus's evidence.

21. Only priests were used for the sanctuary in order not to incur ritual impurity (*m. Eduyoth* 8.6).

22. E. Bammel, "Sadduzäer und Sadokiden," *Ephemerides Theologicae Lovaniensis* 55 (1979): 107–115, links Boethos too with Leontopolis.

23. For details see P. Richardson, "The Social-Historical Significance for Gentiles and Women of Herod's Temple Architecture," in J. Halligan and P. Davies, eds., *Second Temple Studies,* forthcoming.

24. In *m. Kelim* 1.6 there are ten degrees of holiness: Israel, walled cities, Jerusalem, Temple Mount, Rampart, court of women, court of Israelites, court of priests, between the altar and the porch, sanctuary, and holy of holies.

25. In 1 Macc. 9:54–57 there is a curious aside concerning Alcimus, high priest and "leader" of the renegade and godless, who began to tear down the "wall (*teichos*) of the inner sanctuary." Schürer suggests (1.175, n.6) this implies that Alcimus intended to remove the barrier between Gentiles and the Holy Place; since Gentiles were not allowed into the outer court, this seems anachronistic and Schürer's suggestion impossible (though *m. Middoth* 2.3 says the destruction made 13 breaches in the Soreg). Perhaps Alcimus was redefining the courtyards; Jonathan rebuilt them as they had been (1 Macc. 10:10–11, 44–45; 14:15). On Alcimus, see U. Rappaport, *ABD* 1.145

26. Two mishnaic traditions are relevant to the question of a dispute. In *m. Sanhedrin* 1.5, where the general issue is which court was competent to try which kinds of cases, one instance is

The 19th-century excavators of Leontopolis discovered a slightly more formal series of spaces than existed in the Maccabean structure: a two-part sanctuary as at Jerusalem with two more sequential and architecturally independent
courtyards. There was no evidence to suggest how these courtyards were used,
but the number of spaces more or less coincided with the spaces in the Herodian
Temple. Other evidence of an extra court is found in 11QT in the Dead Sea
Scrolls.[27] We have this situation, then. The first Temple (and Ezekiel's vision)
had an inner court (the sanctuary and its adjacent areas) and an outer court. In
the late second century a tradition developed (11QT) of a more complex structure with three "courtyards," the outer of which was for women and proselytes.
During the same period a rival temple was built at Leontopolis, which expanded
the number of courtyards, though we do not know exactly how. Later, the
Mishnah recalls two unascribed traditions of debates about extension of the
courts, and the resolution of those debates in favor of an essential integrity
with the Temple proper. Further, both Josephus and the Mishnah describe the
Herodian Temple's courtyard arrangement.

All this suggests an alternative tradition, associated in part with a "sectarian" group, in part with Leontopolis, and in part with a mainstream Jewish

cited as follows: "they may not add to the City or the Courts of the Temple save by the decision
of the court of one and seventy"; and in m. Shebuoth 2.2: "It is all one whether a man enters into
the Temple Court or into any space that has been added to the Temple Court, since they may not
add to the [Holy] City or to the Courts of the Temple save by the decision of a king, a prophet,
Urim and Thummim and a Sanhedrin of one and twenty [judges]. . . ." Strictly speaking, both
traditions refer to additions to the space of the Temple courts, not to changes in the number of
courts. The texts, however, imply (see below) that there was debate about the alterations and the
enlargements of the courts and that Herod's alterations had approval of a legally constituted court
or combination of authorities (Shebuoth allows "a king, a prophet, Urim and Thummim" to be
involved in the decision, perhaps requiring that a combination must conspire to the same end).
The debate could apply to both Maccabean and Herodian additions, but in either case there would
have been a debate. On the sequence of stages in the development of the precinct, see K. Ritmeyer
and L. Ritmeyer, " Reconstructing Herod's Temple Mount in Jerusalem," BAR 15/6 (1989):
23–53.

27. 11QT describes the ideal temple of a reconstituted Jerusalem in the messianic period.
Though some details are uncertain, there are three courtyards, the outer one being an enormous
space of 1600 cubits (almost half a mile) square for "daughters" and "strangers" (i.e., women and
proselytes; see cols. 36–40, esp. 40). Around the Temple Mount is a narrow "rampart" with twelve
steps up to it, beyond which only "the children of Israel shall ascend to enter my sanctuary." These
arrangements are similar to the provision for a court of the Gentiles in the Herodian Temple, but
with a major difference: the separation between Israelite and non-Israelite is outside the Temple
precincts rather than inside. 11QT predates the Herodian period (perhaps the second half of the
second century) and may be connected with 4QMMT (see L. Schiffman, ABD 6.348–50). M.
Wise, A Critical Study of the Temple Scroll from Qumran Cave 11 (Chicago: Oriental Institute, 1990),
argues that the Temple Scroll is associated with New Jerusalem traditions, and that the huge size of
the court is consistent with the city plan of the New Jerusalem (p. 83); he argues for a Temple
Source lying behind 11QT that he dates around 190 BCE (p. 99).

view prior to and associated with the Herodian structure. An Egyptian influence—the high priest—was one element in these developments.[28]

JOSEPHUS'S ACCOUNT OF HEROD AND THE TEMPLE

Josephus is at his encomiastic best in his description of Herod's rebuilding of the Temple (*Ant.* 15.388–425; *War* 5.184–237).[29] There are few such circumstantial descriptions of buildings in antiquity;[30] rarer still is an account of motive (for Herod, see *Ant.* 15.380–87). While we cannot trust this report of Herod's speech any more than we can trust Josephus's reports of other speeches, some elements appear to be historical because they cohere with circumstances at this point during Herod's reign, correspond with the point of the undertaking, and, most important, run counter to Josephus's own evaluation of Herod.[31] Thus, I believe the finances for reconstruction of the Temple derived from funds under Herod's control, not Temple funds, a combination of personal and state money available to him because Judea was relatively prosperous and secure.[32] Herod's motives included having his name go down in history, improving the image of Judea internationally, and expressing his Jewish piety.

Herod was acting as a patron not of one region, interest group, association, or segment of society, but as benefactor of all Jews everywhere. The project was deeply symbolic, for it was nothing less than the re-imaging of the cult center of the main monotheistic religion of the period. The grandeur of the design, far from being incidental, was aimed at altering the image of Jews in the Roman world. The Temple's innovations, its size, and the speed at which the project was carried out—even its implied competition with other precincts—all

---

28. The more striking departure from the first Temple is the innovation of the women's court, which the *Mishnah* accepts without comment. When might the social conditions be ripe for such a development? Perhaps in the period of Queen Alexandra, when her oldest son (Hycanus II, whom she apppointed to the position) was compliant with her wishes. She was pious and might have welcomed a place in which to participate; on this showing, her commitment to the Pharisaic position ensured little dispute about these matters since she had their concurrence already. In the end I do not accept this attractive notion (suggested to me by John Sandys-Wunsch), because it requires an unlikely silence among all the sources.

29. Sanders, *Judaism,* pp. 59–60, prefers the account in *War,* correctly, though he is overly critical of the complementary account in *Antiquities* and skeptical of Josephus then having access to other sources.

30. Though we have a number in Pliny (*NH*), Philo (*De vita*), Pausanias and Vitruvius, *On Architecture.*

31. Josephus's own evaluation of Herod, especially in *Antiquities,* tends to be negative, though not unformly. It would be contrary to Josephus's purpose to present Herod in such glowingly favorable terms in a speech he composed, so Josephus is probably relying upon a source, likely Nicolas of Damascus, but possibly Herod's own *Memoirs.*

32. With so many diverse projects on the go at the same time Herod may have been overspending. See E. Gabba, "The Finances of King Herod" in A. Kasher, U. Rappaport, and G. Fuks, eds., *Greece and Rome in Eretz-Israel* (Jerusalem: Jerusalem Exploration Society, 1990), pp. 160–68.

suggested more than bringing up to date an old place of worship. Together with avoidance of offending Jews' sensibilities, of interrupting worship, and of ritual impurity during construction, the motives appeared even greater. The reconstruction enhanced Jews' self-image in Judea, the Diaspora, and in the rest of the Roman world. Herod, of course, improved his own reputation at the same time.

Was the reconstruction program successful? Absolutely. The only disputes were over the courtyard extensions, not the details.[33] Many of the references to Herod in rabbinic literature indicate a surprisingly favorable reaction to this project,[34] even though the traditions themselves are not altogether reliable:

> He who has not seen the Temple in its full construction has never seen a glorious building in his life. Which Temple?—Abaye, or it might be said, R. Hisda, replied, The reference is to the building of Herod. Of what did he build it?—Rabbah replied, Of yellow and white marble. . . . He intended at first to overlay it with gold, but the Rabbis told him, leave it alone for it is more beautiful as it is, since it has the appearance of the waves of the sea.
>
> (*Gemara, Sukkah* 51b; cf. also *b.Baba Bathra* 3b)

> Likewise we find [withholding rain] happened in the days of Herod when the people were occupied with the rebuilding of the Temple. [At that time] rain fell during the night but in the morning the wind blew and the clouds dispersed and the sun shone so that the people were able to go out to their work, and then they knew that they were engaged in a sacred work.
>
> (*b.Ta'anith* 23a; see *Ant.* 15.245)

> But how could Baba b. Buta have advised Herod to pull down the Temple . . . [with a lengthy derogatory discussion of Herod]. . . . Now tell me [scil. Herod] what amends can I make. [Baba b. Buta] replied: As you have extinguished the light of the world [the Rabbis] . . . go now and attend to the light of the world [the Temple, of which] it is written, *And all the nations have become enlightened by it.* . . . Herod replied, I am afraid of the government [of Rome]. He said: Send an envoy, and let him take a year on the way and

---

33. See above. I leave to one side the "eagle incident," discussed in detail in chap. 1, above.

34. If Herod and the Essenes got on reasonably well together, as many scholars think (I am not fully convinced), their attitude to his building is perplexing.

stay in Rome a year and take a year coming back, and in the meantime you can pull down the Temple and rebuild it. . . .

(b. Baba Bathra 3b)[35]

These approving comments on the Temple, despite highly critical comments
on Herod's life, illuminate two aspects of the reconstruction. First, it had the
approval of the authorities, including one named contemporary, Baba b. Buta.
Second, Rome was lukewarm, and it was only b. Buta's clever advice or, according to Josephus, Herod's close friendship with Rome (Ant. 15.387) that
made it possible. Both points are potentially important. The rebuilding of the
Temple required masterly negotiations, both inside and outside the country. It
could have created massive dissent in Judea if it were commonly perceived to
be against Torah or impious in any way; and it could have angered Rome,
either because Herod was too independent or because the Temple created a
focus for dissent among the Diaspora. The project avoided the Scylla of internal
unhappiness and the Charybdis of external opposition, despite the fact that it
was the greatest religious precinct in the Roman world and that Herod was
redefining the arrangements for Israel's temple worship.[36] This balancing act
was a major coup, a masterful piece of religious diplomacy.

HEROD AND GROUPS OR PARTIES

Herod's closest contacts were inevitably with the representatives of the cult
center in Jerusalem, as is shown in his attention to the rebuilding of its sanctuary
and direct involvement in the appointing—and deposing—of the high priest.
Josephus gives extensive evidence of both. At the same time, Herod may have
been interested in other religious groups; investigation of these matters is seriously limited by imbalances in the sources.[37] Party perceptions of Herod are

---

35. Several features of this passage require comment: (1) Josephus's report that the *naos* took
three years to build is reflected; (2) there was a process of discussion and debate, with the rabbis in
full agreeement; (3) Rome was not happy with a new Temple to the Judean God; (4) Herod's
earlier hostility to the Pharisees underlies the story, and his rebuilding of the Temple was seen as
recompense for his earlier actions; (5) the approval of the building did not alter later rabbinic views
of Herod himself.

36. It is surprising that Herod was able to get assent. His scheme derived some of its details
from neither Jerusalem Temple traditions nor proto-Rabbinic traditions but from an earlier and
independent—and possibly sectarian—seer and from a rival temple in Egypt. No small feat.

37. Jospehus is interested in and describes various groups, yet the Qumran library ignores
Herod while tradition fails to preserve early literature of Pharisees or their successors and obliterates
Sadducean evidence. Literature from other hypothesized groups (e.g., zealots, Herodians, baptists,
Sicarii) is absent and Christian literature is not contemporaneous.

largely non-existent, and those few we have are skewed. Nevertheless, we will examine the available evidence.

Herod and Brigands

In his primary account of "three schools" (*War* 2.119–66) Josephus includes descriptions of Pharisees, Sadducees, and Essenes. He sets this description just at the point when Archelaus was deposed by Augustus, Coponius appointed as procurator, and Judas the Galilean started a tax revolt, all in the year 6 CE (*War* 2.117–18). Judas was a "sophist" (or possibly "scribe") who "founded a sect of his own, having nothing in common with the others," a fourth group contrasted with the other three. Josephus's general motive in *War* is to blame everything on revolutionaries, so Judas's actions must not contaminate the three respectable groups in Judaism, hence the avoidance of language for the "fourth philosophy" implying group or party.

War's and *Antiquities*'s description of "brigands" (deliberately leaving out references in *Life* that help to understand Jospehus's own reactions) should not be thought to define a specific group. Josephus would not wish his readers to think of them as a formal group, and he may be correct that they are not. The tendencies, however, that led ultimately to a "fourth philosophy" coalescing into the "zealots" predated the Revolt and even 6 CE. Since the incidents are crucial to understanding Herod several points need to be made.[38] (1) Herod's actions against Hezekiah (a "brigand chief") and his group of "brigands" on the Syrian frontier brought peace to Galilee and Herod to the attention of Sextus Caesar; as a result, however, Herod was brought before a Jerusalem court (*War* 1.204–11; *Ant.* 15.158–67; see *War* 2.56). (2) Herod rid the caves of Arbela of bandits and their families (*War* 1.309–13; *Ant.* 14.420–30). (3) In a closely related action against promoters of disturbances who fled to marshes and fortresses around Lake Huleh,[39] Herod fined some towns that had supported nearby brigands (*War* 1.314–16; *Ant.* 14.431–33). (4) He dealt with a "revolt" of Galileans against nobles and "partisans of Herod" who were drowned in the Sea of Galilee (*War* 1.326; *Ant.* 14.450). (5) Herod had to quell (general) disturbances (*War* 1.364). (6) He brought peace and security to Trachonitis and Abila by taking action against Zenodorus who himself was not a brigand but used brigands to pillage Damascenes and increase his income (*War* 1.398–400;

---

38. On brigands in the Empire, see Cassius Dio, 5.28; 75.2; Pliny, *Letters,* 6.25; *CIL* 8.2495; 3.8242. On brigands in Palestine, Strabo, *Geog.* 16.2.18–20; 16.2.37. Literature includes E. J. Hobsbawm, *Bandits* (New York: Penguin, 1985); R. Horsley and J. Hanson, *Bandits, Prophets, and Messiahs* (Minneapolis: Winston, 1985); B. Isaac, "Bandits in Judaea and Arabia," *Harvard Studies in Classical Philology* 88 (1984): 171–203; J. D. Crossan, *The Historical Jesus* (New York: HarperCollins, 1991), chap. 9.

39. The most likely fortress was a Hellenistic structure on Keren Naftali on the west side of the Huleh basin.

Ant. 15.344–48; *War* 2.215).[40] (7) He settled Zamaris and five hundred Babylonian Jews in Batanea to bring security to Trachonitis, creating a (tax free) buffer zone (*Ant.* 17.23–29).[41]

From these accounts it is clear there is "social brigandage" at the beginning of Herod's reign, in the unsettled days of the 40s and 30s; in several cases the brigands had families, close connections with towns, and religious or upper-class support. The descriptions are not of incidental bands of true "brigands" but of uprooted peasants who maintain connections with their neighbors and even their social superiors, a picture of social dislocation spawned by economic change and consequent hardship. Dispossessed landholders, concerned for survival, preyed on those who had more (perhaps who had taken the little they had). Some—maybe many—chose brigandage.

Herod sided with Judean upper-class needs and Roman political aims. Rome had long had problems with social radicals—on land and sea, in the provinces and in Italy, in east and in west. Herod linked himself firmly with the effort to rid the Empire of pirates and brigands—a goal endorsed by Pompey, Mark Antony, and others of his mentors. In so doing, he came into conflict as a young man with Jewish authorities, though their motivation in trying him on a capital charge was not clear; it appears to be connected with Herod as a threat to the elite's control of the levers of power in Jerusalem.[42]

The locations of the brigands cohere with this interpretation: on the Syrian frontier, in the Huleh marshes, in Trachonitis and Abila. All were inaccessible areas in the northern part of Herod's kingdom where it was relatively easy to hide yet close to towns. The exceptions to this pattern were the caves of Arbela (in a good agricultural area, well settled, and overlooking a major north-south road); around the Sea of Galilee when Herod's people were drowned (also a settled area); and at Sepphoris (see *War* 2.56) when, just after Herod's death, Hezekiah's son Judas raided the royal arsenal. These three locations suggest collusion between townsfolk and brigands; but all support the claim of social content to the brigands' actions.[43]

Prior to the expansionism of the 20s and 10s, with its attendant prosperity,

---

40. Some independent confirmation of the problem is found in the *Treatise of Shem* 7:18ff ("earthquake in Galilee," "robbers in the Hauran and Damascus," "plague in Galilee") and 11:1 ("robbers from Palestine").

41. These prospective settlers had paused in Antioch-on-Orontes, though they had already been given, according to Josephus, a place to settle in Ulatha by the Roman governor Saturninus, despite the fact that this was Herod's territory. This is all quite confusing.

42. It could not have had much to do with execution of Jews if they were genuine revolutionaries. The court's action implied that Hezekiah had considerable respect in Jerusalem; only on such a basis does the action of the Jerusalem authorities make sense.

43. Zamaris's settlement in Batanea was intended to provide safety from brigands for Babylonian pilgrims travelling to Jerusalem for festivals, suggesting that those disturbances were not caused by Jewish brigands.

there was a social activism that turned Jews to revolution, "brigandage" as Josephus calls it. This soft underbelly of Herod's rule occurred especially (not exclusively) in Galilee. Sometimes those driven to such harassment of the upper classes and merchants did not lose the support of their neighbors. Herod tried to eliminate this social unrest but—despite Josephus's assurances to the contrary—he was not altogether successful (point 7, above, was late in his career). Many of these folk were the common people (the ʿamme ha-aretz) of the New Testament. While religion might have been a factor, it was not a dominant issue.

Herod and Sadducees

Sadducees, a group that must have existed during Herod's reign, were at the other end of the social ladder.[44] When Josephus describes the three or four "schools" at 6 CE (see above), he implies that they had been around for a long time. His accounts of Sadducees and Pharisees in that period assures that he is correct that Sadducees precede Herod; he moves his earliest reference back to the time of Jonathan Maccabeus (160–143 BCE; *Ant.* 13.171–72) when, according to him, a Sadducee named Jonathan inflamed the problems between Hyrcanus I and Pharisees (especially one Eleazar) and induced Hyrcanus to join the Sadducees and punish anyone observing Pharisaic regulations (*Ant.* 13.288–96). Sadducees accepted only written regulations (*nomima ta gegrammena*); those handed down by the "fathers" need not be observed (13.297). They had the confidence of the wealthy alone (*tous eutropous monon*), with no following among the populace (13.298). Josephus repeats these claims when he gives his main account (18.16–18): the Sadducees held to nothing but the laws, they were disputatious (*War* 2.166, "boorish"), yet they accomplished nothing when in office because they had to follow Pharisaic opinions (see *b. Yoma* 19b, *Niddah* 33b).[45]

Surprisingly, Josephus never refers directly to the Sadducees in either of his accounts of Herod's life; between the death of Hyrcanus I (104 BCE) and the deposing of Archelaus (6 CE) there are 110 years when Sadducees do not surface. Should we then say nothing about Herod and the Sadducees, or are they present in other ways? One line of argument has been to say that high priestly families are all Sadducean, especially the House of Boethos, because Boethusians =

---

44. See Sanders, *Judaism,* chap. 15.

45. See C. Wassén, "Sadducees and *Halakah,*" in Richardson et al., *Law in Religious Communities in the Roman Period: The Debate over Torah and Nomos in Post-Biblical Judaism and Early Christianity* (Waterloo, ON: Wilfrid Laurier University Press, 1991), chap. 8; J. LeMoyne, *Les Sadducées* (Paris: Gabalda, 1972); J. Z. Lauterbach, in *Rabbinical Essays* (Cincinnati: Hebrew Union College Press, 1951), pp. 23–48; A. J. Saldarini, *Pharisees, Scribes and Sadducees in Palestinian Society* (Wilmington, DL: Glazier, 1988).

Sadducees,[46] so, in considering Herod and the Sadducees all we need do is analyze Herod and the high priests. This, however, imports rabbinic views together with later social notions into the reading of Josephus. A more promising approach examines matters of class and status, as Josephus strongly hints with his emphasis on their standing and wealth. Goodman, for example, claims with good reason that

> Sadducaism was adopted by those who did not need [the comfort of belief in the bodily resurrection, angels and spirits]. Against the whole ethos of the Old Testament . . . the Sadducees maintained that God exercised no influence at all on human actions and that a man could choose for himself whether to do good or evil, being entirely responsible for his own fortune or misfortune. . . . Such ideas in other societies have seemed attractive to political rebels who, rejecting the notion that their poor social position was divinely ordained, used their own efforts to seek change; in Roman Palestine, by contrast, Sadducaism embodied a smug self-congratulation about the status quo that only the rich could accept.[47]

This points in the right direction. It is not that Sadducees were not religious[48] but that this was not the most distinctive feature in Herod's day;[49] rather than focus on some supposed association between Sadducees and high priests we should investigate social status and outlook.[50] A careful analysis of high status terms such as "wealthy, powerful, and high-born" used by Josephus is still needed.

Josephus is not entirely consistent in his use of the available terms, and conditions did not remain static. During Herod's reign the Sadducees as a *religious* entity faded out of focus—though not out of sight—and were replaced by a social elite, partly as a result of Herod's elimination of members of the ruling

---

46. See Stern, "Aspects of Jewish Society," *CRINT* 2.609–12; for an alternative view, G. Porton, "Sadducees," *ABD* 5.892–95 (see literature cited there).

47. M. Goodman, *The Ruling Class of Judea. The Origins of the Jewish Revolt against Rome AD 66–70* (Cambridge: Cambridge university Press, 1987), p. 79

48. Their name is usually taken to refer to Zadok, high priest at the time of David.

49. Sanders, *Judaism,* considers the question in his typically forthright way (pp. 317–40, esp. p. 318); his appproach would be sounder if he were to analyze each set of questions (Sadducees, aristocrats) independently. Though he says he will give a history of the aristocracy, he actually gives a history of high priests and chief priests. His treatment of "lay" aristocrats is under chief priests, at pp. 329–31.

50. The exaggeration of Sadducean religious views is prompted by the sources available: Josephus, the New Testament, and the rabbinic literature all have an interest in portraying them as religious rivals to the Pharisees, debating the same issues. Some of this must be true, but Judean society was not permanently engaged in halakhic discussions.

elite at the time he took power and partly due to a natural diminution of one set of factors in favor of a new set under Herod. Not all high priests or ordinary priests were Sadducees in affiliation or inclination. Herod's practice of bringing in high priests from elsewhere (Babylon, Leontopolis, Alexandria) contributed to the disaffiliation of priests from the party with which scholars have for so long imagined them to have been associated. Indeed the group itself faded out of sight during his reign. Why would a Babylonian or Alexandrian high priest associate himself with an outmoded group when he owed his appointment to Herod? It is likely that, as Josephus's silence suggests, Sadducees were not much of a factor during Herod's reign; an elite ruling group around Herod held the levers of power.[51]

Herod and Pharisees

The situation is both similar and different; on the one hand Josephus's first reference to Pharisees is in the Maccabean context just discussed (*Ant.* 13.171–72), and his main account in *War* comes in 6 CE (*War* 2.119, 162–64). Josephus also includes several circumstantial accounts of Pharisaic activity in the Maccabean period that fill out his picture at that early period. Unlike the Sadducean situation, however, Josephus directly connects Herod and the Pharisees.

Josephus's earliest account is historically situated in the same dispute mentioned above (*Ant.* 13.288–98) between Jonathan (a Sadducee) and Eleazar (a Pharisee), when Hyrcanus I deserted the Pharisees, abrogated the regulations (or oral Torah) and lost his popular support—for the Pharisees had the support of the masses.[52] A generation later, the pious Queen Alexandra, widow of Alexander Jannaeus, yielded power to the Pharisees at Jannaeus's suggestion (*War* 1.107–14; *Ant.* 13.401–29); her strict observance made her defer to similarly strict Pharisees, so that they assumed "royal authority" and executed Diogenes, a friend of Jannaeus's (*Ant.* 13.410).[53] Later, the powerful (*dynatoi*) came with Aristobulus to the palace in a barefaced attempt to help Aristobulus seize power because they feared Pharisees (13.423).[54] Incidentally, this brings to view one

---

51. Similarly Porton, "Sadducees," though he is more skeptical of their social status. He fails to note the absence of Herodian period evidence. See also J. N. Lightstone, "Sadducees versus Pharisees," in J. Neusner, ed., *Christianity, Judaism and Other Greco-Roman Cults*, 3:206–17, and LeMoyne, *Sadducées*.

52. Eleazar, who "liked dissension" (*Ant.* 13.288), argued an important matter of principle with Hyrcanus: whether the throne and the high priesthood should be combined. Sadducees were on Hyrcanus's side of the debate, which suggests an association at that stage between Sadducees and ruling power, with a less elite set of affinities for the Pharisees.

53. One of the few named Sadducees in our sources; the name is suggestive of hellenizing tendencies. Was he named after a Cynic (Diogenes of Sinope), a Stoic (Diogenes of Babylon), or an Epicurean (Diogenes of Tarsus)?

54. The provenance of the *Psalms of Solomon* is still not settled: they came from a pietist group, not unlike the Pharisees and probably from before the time of Herod. Their invective was directed

further factor in the decline of the Sadducaic party: if Aristobulus's powerful supporters—some of whom (like Diogenes) were Sadducaic—continued to support him after Herod's father, Antipater, took the side of Hyrcanus II, there would have been a strong antipathy between Antipater's family and Sadducees.

When Herod first came to prominence in 47 BCE as the Galilean administrator who cleared out Hezekiah's "brigands," he was brought before a court. Josephus says that Samaias (or more likely Pollion)[55] berated the court for its timidity; without attacking Herod directly Samaias predicted that Herod would punish them and the king (*Ant.* 14.172–74), implying that Herod would rule. The unexpected result was that Herod held Samaias in greatest honor (175–76). When Herod took Jerusalem he punished his opponents and honored his supporters, but especially Pollion, a Pharisee, and Samaias his disciple (*mathêtês*), because they had urged the city to admit Herod without further opposition.[56] Pollion and Samaias appear a third time in Josephus's accounts, when they and their disciples were excused from taking an oath of support of Herod (*Ant.* 15.368–70). In a duplicate account of the same event set much later (*Ant.* 17.41–45) the oath was to Augustus and Herod together; when six thousand Pharisees refused to take the oath Herod's brother's wife paid the fine.[57] Pharisees ruled the women of the court (*Ant.* 17.41), especially Pheroras's wife; after they predicted that Herod would fall and the throne would pass to Pheroras and his wife (*Ant.* 17.43), Herod executed those responsible for this prediction, a court eunuch and household members "who approved of what the Pharisee [singular] said."[58] In the "eagle affair" (*War* 1. 648), Judas and Matthias, two men learned (*sophistai*) in traditions of the fathers (*ta patria*) and probably Pharisees, were executed with some of their followers for tearing down a golden eagle from the Temple gate (see chap. 1).

This provides an odd assortment of data. (1) There were no shared values between Herod and the Pharisees; he made no special concessions to them as a group, nor did they to him.[59] (2) Herod had grudging respect for and conceded

---

against the Hasmoneans (e.g., 2:3–18; 8:14–17; 17:20) and Pompey (e.g., 2:1–2, 19–21, 25–29; 8:18–22).

55. On Samaias and Pollion, Schalit, Abh. X, pp. 768–71 (Hillel and Shammai).

56. This account shows that Josephus earlier made a mistake, that the previous incident involved Pollion—not Samaias—the likelier person since he is the older of the two; for our purposes it matters little which persons are involved or who exactly they are, for the main issue is their affiliation.

57. She was an (unnamed) Hasmonean; her father was Alexander, her sister Mariamme I, Herod's dead wife.

58. See the important remarks on this passage by A. I. Baumgarten, "Rivkin and Neusner on the Pharisees," in Richardson et al., *Law in Religious Communities,* chap. 7, esp. pp. 119–20, who stresses the source's hostility to Pharisees.

59. Sanders, *Judaism,* chap. 18, esp. p. 391, argues for the Pharisees being initially well-disposed to Herod: on the one side were Alexander Jannaeus, Aristobulus II, Antigonus, and the "eminent"; on the other Pharisees, Queen Alexandra, Hrycanus II, and Herod's family.

to Pollion and Samaias, as a result of which he made concessions to others. (3) Herod was contemptuous of Matthias and Judas, whom he executed along with their closest followers. (4) As a whole the Pharisees refused an oath of allegiance, but so did the Essenes. (5) Some Pharisees found supporters in the royal court, especially Pheroras's wife and other women, to whom they predicted the fall of Herod and his immediate family; these Pharisees were also executed. The last three incidents came late (6–4 BCE) and imply fresh fears of Pharisaic power as Herod aged and his control slipped.[60] At this point they seem willing to confront Herod and dabble in court affairs.[61] As Baumgarten has pointed out, the evidence argues strongly against Neusner's view that during the Herodian period the Pharisees changed from a political group to a table fellowship: "the Pharisees *as a group* must have been working against Herod."[62] There was hostility toward Herod, with mutual respect between himself and Pollion and Samaias. At some points, especially in the middle of his reign, direct confrontation was avoided.

Herod and Essenes

For reasons he never makes clear, the Essenes fascinate Josephus. In both long accounts of the "schools" (*War* 1.119–66 and *Ant.* 18.11–25) Josephus devotes more space to the Essenes than to any of the others—in *War*'s account forty-two of forty-eight paragraphs. Throughout the relevant accounts he names almost as many Essenes as Pharisees and Sadducees combined.[63] He is obviously well disposed to them; his tone is more approving than of either Sadducees or Pharisees, though his own views remain uncertain.[64] The Essenes had the greatest piety and sanctity; unlike Pharisees and Sadducees, Essenes were not hostile to other groups, though they still engaged in current affairs.

---

60. G. Alon, "The Attitude of the Pharisees to the Roman Government and the House of Herod," *Scripta Hierosolymita* 7 (1961): 53–78, gives six reasons for Pharisaic opposition: (1) he was unfit because not Jewish; (2) he suppressed the Sanhedrin; (3) he appointed and deposed high priests; (4) he introduced Greek civilization; (5) he evicted Jews, as at Caesarea, and replaced them with non-Jews; (6) he failed to be independent of Romans. None of these is as compelling as Alon thinks, but there are elements of truth to each.

61. Sanders, *Judaism*, p. 393: "Herod's true supporters distrusted the Pharisees and watched them carefully," alluding especially to Nicolas.

62. Baumgarten, in Richardson et al. *Law in Religious Communities*, p. 120, his italics; similarly, Sanders, *Judaism*, chap. 18.

63. Essenes: Judas (*War* 1.78), Simon (2.113), Manaemus (*Ant.* 15.373), later John (*War* 2.567); Pharisees: Eleazar (*Ant.* 13.288), Pollion and Samaias (15.1–4, cf. 14.172–76), and possibly Judas and Matthias (*War* 1.648); Sadducees: Jonathan (*Ant.* 13.171), possibly Diogenes (*War* 1.113).

64. I am persuaded by S. Mason, *Josephus on the Pharisees* (Leiden: Brill, 1991), that Josephus's personal views were more in conformity with Bannus's religious outlook; cf. also Mason's *Josephus and the New Testament* (Peabody, MA: Hendrickson, 1992); contra Sanders, *Judaism*, pp. 532–33, n. 9.

Following the death of Hyrcanus I (104 BCE), Aristobulus's assassination of his brother Antigonus was prophesied by Judas the Essene (*War* 1.78–80; *Ant.* 13.311–13) who was active in the Temple court (*to hieron*).[65] One description contains a suggestive sentence: "[The Essene] is made to swear tremendous oaths . . . that he will forever keep faith with all men, especially with the powers that be (*malista de tois kratousin*), since no ruler (*tini to archein*) attains his office save by the will of God" (*War* 2.139–40). Is this a reference to secular or religious authority? The language is ambiguous, but it seems likelier to refer to secular rulers.[66] It seems that the Essenes' community life, their non-involvement in official religious activities together with their notion of "divine right" of rulers allowed them relative quiet during the Herodian period.

The closest connection between Herod and the Essenes occurred about 20 BCE when Herod required an oath of loyalty (*Ant.* 15.368–70).[67] Herod excused not only Pollion and Samaias and their disciples, but also the Essenes; in the former case Josephus implies a limited number of Pharisees, in the latter all Essenes. Josephus highlights Herod's positive attitude toward the Essenes: "Herod [held] the Essenes in honour and [had] a higher opinion of them than was consistent with their merely human nature" (*Ant.* 15.372). Josephus intends this statement as an introduction to the virtuous prophet Manaemus (373–79). While Herod was a schoolboy, Josephus says, Manaemus addressed him as "king of the Jews" (*basilea Ioudaiôn*) and explained that he would rule happily "for you have been found worthy of this by God." He instructed Herod to love justice and piety but predicted that he would not, and so God's wrath would be shown at the end (376).[68] Later, in the middle of his reign, Herod called for Manaemus and asked about its length, receiving an evasive answer in the region of twenty or thirty years;[69] "and from this time on he continued to hold all Essenes in honor" (378). It is not certain whether Josephus thinks there was a connection between his account of Herod and Manaemus and the immediately

---

65. They had not yet been barred from it, as *Ant.* 18.19 claims (probably incorrectly). The lengthy account of *War* 2.120–61 claims they were spread throughout every city (124), despite its general sense that they lived a withdrawn—not an urban—communal life (see also Philo, *Quod Omnis* 76, who says they lived in villages and avoided cities). The presence of an Essene gate in Jerusalem on the southern slope of the Western hill hints at an Essene quarter in Jerusalem, surprisingly close to where priests, according to the archaeological evidence, lived.

66. The clause in 140 refers to "all people," whereas in 141 he refers explicitly to members of the sect. Though it is possible that Josephus intends a reference only to community rule, as the next clause suggests, he probably, like Paul in Romans 13, refers to the state.

67. In *Ant.* 17.42–43 an oath was also required; see above, on Pharisees.

68. *Epi tê katastrophê ta biou tês ant' autôn orgês epomnêmoneuomenês* (with an odd hint of 1 Thess. 2:16). This legendary prophecy about Herod must have come from Nicolas of Damascus, yet it is useful to underscore the essentially placid relationship between Herod and the Essenes.

69. If there is substance to this account, it must have occurred before 21 BCE (or 18?), the twentieth year of Herod's rule. The following account ("at this time") provides an explicit date, the eighteenth year of his reign (either 23 or 20).

following description of Herod's rebuilding of the Temple (15.380–425); the coincidence of timing and the fact that both accounts speak of Herod's piety may sufficiently account for the sequence.[70] Such generous assessments of the Essenes were not characteristic of Herod's behavior and were not paralleled by a similarly generous treatment of other groups.[71]

We get additional insight from the Dead Sea Scrolls,[72] about which I make a few obvious comments. (1) Despite their invective and the fact that a number of the DSS are dated to the late first century BCE or early first century CE, they have no unmistakable references to Herod; community antagonism did not focus on Herod or his children.[73] (2) That hostility focused on the later Hasmoneans who departed from the way they ought to have walked and were opposed to the community and its Teacher of Righteousness.[74] (3) In other works the invective shifts toward the Romans (*Kittim*), especially in the *War Scroll,* which anticipates a thirty-three-year war between the Sons of Light and the Sons of Darkness, attitudes that are analogous to, though not the same as, those in the Psalms of Solomon (see chap. 5).[75] (4) Though many of the scrolls presuppose that the cult center in Jerusalem was defiled, there is no particular antagonism toward the cultic buildings themselves.[76] If, as seems likely, 11QT was earlier

---

70. But see earlier in this chapter and chap. 8, concerning the foreshadowing of Herod's court-yard arrangements in 11QT, a document preserved only at Qumran. R. H. Eisenman's view that the laws of 11QT appear to presuppose some features of Herod's practices is attractive (see *James the Just in the Habakkuk Pesher* [Leiden: Brill, 1986], p. 89), and the connections between 11QT's description of the Temple and Herod's Temple are suggestive. On the whole, Wise and others have the better of the argument.

71. They can hardly be attributed to Josephus's putative sources such as Nicolas, or to a current attitude to Essenes at the time of writing, since they had been wiped out. Possibly they could be attributed to Josephus's own interest in the Essenes, but I think it likelier that there is some truth to his description of Herod's attitude.

72. I incline to the view that the majority of the DSS are from the community at Qumran or their affiliates, and that the group was connected to those described by Josephus as Essenes. These qualifications are necessary as a result of the intensive scholarly investigation of the documents in the last decade or so, particularly of 11QT, 4QMMT and other fragmentary materials.

73. Contrast *Testament of Moses* 6.1–9.

74. 4Q175, "A Messianic Anthology," is a good example: "Behold, an accursed man, a man of Satan, has risen to become a fowler's net to his people, and a cause of destruction to all his neighbours. And [his brother] arose [and ruled], both being instruments of violence. They have rebuilt [Jerusalem and have set up] a wall and towers to make of it a stronghold of ungodliness . . . in Israel, and a horror in Ephraim and in Judah. . . ."

75. For example, 1 QpHab, cols 4,6: "Interpreted [this concerns] the commanders of the Kittim who, on the counsel of [the] House of Guilt, pass one in front of the other; one after the other [their] commanders come to lay waste the earth." "And [the Kittim] shall gather in their riches, together with all their booty, *like the fish of the sea.* And as for that which He said, *Therefore they sacrifice to their net and burn incense to their seine:* Interpreted, this means that they sacrifice to their standards and worship their weapons of war."

76. Sanders, *Judaism,* pp. 362–63, 376–77, distinguishes helpfully between two views among Essenes, that at Qumran being the more sectarian and exclusivist (cf. 1QS 9.4–5; 1QSa 1.3).

(though not necessarily from progenitors of the community), it would have served the community's purposes to connect the Temple of the end-times in later documents with the impiety of Herod's rebuilding.[77] This connection does not occur, however. Even a description of New Jerusalem (5Q15) lacks a comment on the present Jerusalem.

No passage in the DSS alludes clearly to Herod. The community's interest in the Maccabean period was not matched by an interest in Herod and his period. The silence is striking.[78] This dearth of evidence confirms Josephus's positive reports on Herod's relationship with Essenes. There is another curious synchronism; the original excavators of Qumran held that the buildings were deserted from the earthquake of 31 BCE until the early first century CE.[79] Perhaps a reduced sense of antagonism led to reduced activity at Qumran. This can hardly be certain, but evidently there was no *increased* tendency to withdraw as a result of Herod.

Herod and Herodians

A few minor New Testament allusions to "Herodians" (Matt. 22:16; Mark 3:6; 12:13) have stimulated a concern that "Herodians" be put in their proper historical and literary context.[80] Historical analysis suggests three main possibilities: first, "Herodians" is a late term, imported into the New Testament texts because the group was relevant at the time of writing (the name then derived from Agrippa II); second, that "Herodians" was historically correct during the lifetime of Jesus, and reflected a setting in the life of Antipas (or in the early

---

77. 4Q174 has something of this force: a House will be built in the last days into which various classes of persons will not enter: "This is the House into which [the unclean shall] never [enter, nor the uncircumcised,] nor the Amonnite, nor the Moabite, nor the half-breed, nor the foreigner, nor the stranger, ever. . . . " It is participants, not structures, that matter. 4Q174 is in tension with 11QT, with its provision for women and proselytes.

78. In the following description of Philo's, by contrast, one or the other half refers to Herod (*Quod Omnis* 89–91): "Many are the potentates who at various occasions have raised themselves to power over the country. They differed both in nature and the line of conduct which they followed. Some carried their zest for outdoing wild beasts in ferocity to the point of savagery. They left no form of cruelty untried. They slaughtered their subjects wholesale, or like cooks carved them piecemeal and limb by limb whilst still alive . . . till justice who surveys human affairs visited them with the same calamities. Others transformed this wild frenzy into another kind of viciousness. Their conduct showed intense bitterness, but they talked with calmness. . . . They fawned like venomous hounds yet wrought evils irremdiable and left behind them in the cities the unforgettable sufferings of their victims as monuments of their impiety and inhumanity. Yet none of these . . . were able to lay a charge against this congregation of Essenes. . . ." Which part might refer to him, and which to Alexander Jannaeus or Aristobulus or Antigonus or Archelaus is not clear.

79. J. T. Milik, *Ten Years of Discovery* (London: SCM, 1959), pp. 52–54, 93–94; cf. Schürer 2.587.

80. W. Braun, "Were the New Testament Herodians Essenes? A Critique of an Hypothesis," *RB* 14 (1989):71–84; see literature cited there.

development of Jesus-traditions, associated with Agrippa I); or third, "Herodians" had a longer history, anchored originally in Herod's lifetime.

In favor of the latter view, toward which I lean, are three factors. (1) Several phrases in Josephus suggest a Herod-party; it is hardly to be doubted that Herod had his supporters, though it is not certain that a party coalesced around him.[81] (2) It is not easy—though not impossible—to understand why a Herodian party should be associated with Antipas (who only ruled Galilee), and only slightly easier to see why there might be one associated with Agrippa I, since he did acquire the whole realm for three years or so. One would have to suppose that early Christian tradition created references to the party, then failed to remove them when they became inappropriate three years later (44 CE), and that they then survived until they came to be written down. (3) It seems historically implausible to posit a group developing after 55 or 60 CE associated with Agrippa II, and then getting almost immediately into the Gospels.[82]

An active group coalescing around Herod and the Herodian family is more plausible. The group's convictions were straightforward: Judea needs a king; here is a family with power and prestige and the confidence of Rome; expectations of a new messianic king are pie in the sky; if Judea is to survive as a nation it must rally round Herod, for he offers stability and an appropriate accommodation with Rome. It was hoped that Augustus would give Herod more territory, improving national prospects and creating a greater kingdom than David's and Solomon's. In addition, Herod was owed gratitude for his building of the Temple and strengthening of Jerusalem. So it seems likely that the primary referent in *hêrôdeioi* and *hêrôdianoi* was to King Herod, with continuing support of later family members. Herodians owed their standing to Herod, and their continuing positions of influence to the close relationship he established with the Imperial family. Such views may not have been held by a large number, but some of the elite and powerful's interests coincided with Rome's and their positions depended on their links with the Herodian family.

CONCLUSION

The above analysis sheds light on contemporary attitudes to Herod and on his relationships with several competing groups. The group with which he had the most cordial relationship—after Herodians—was likely to have been Essenes. The situation was more complicated than we can now know given the

---

81. H. H. Rowley, "The Herodians in the Gospels," *JTS* 41 (1940): 14–27, correctly argues (following Bickerman) that Josephus's *hêrôdeioi* are equivalent to "Herodians," in good Greek form, whereas *hêrôdianoi* is a Latinization. It is also equivalent to *hoi ta hêrôdou phronountes* (see *Ant.* 14.450; *War* 1.326; 1.319; *Ant.* 14.436; *Ant.* 15.1; *War* 1.358).

82. After 66 CE and Agrippa II's forceful activity on the side of Rome there was not likely to be a "Herodian" party of much consequence.

available data; no group is recorded as holding explicit views of Herod, so the analysis has been inferential and provisional. One author, who might speak for a group, had an explicit view of Herod; in the name of Moses, he says:

> And a wanton king, who will not be of a priestly family, will follow them. He will be a man rash and perverse, and he will judge them as they deserve. He will shatter their leaders with the sword, and he will (exterminate them) in secret places so that no one will know where their bodies are. He will kill both old and young, showing mercy to none.
>
> Then fear of him will be heaped upon them in their land, and for thirty-four years he will impose judgments upon them as did the Egyptians, and he will punish them. And he will beget heirs who will reign after him for shorter periods of time. After his death there will come into their land a powerful king of the west who will subdue them, and he will take away captives and a part of their temple he will burn with fire. He will crucify some of them around their city.
>
> (*Testament of Moses* 6:2–9)

The technique and language are not unlike those of some of the DSS, and this may be from a related group, though to date no fragment of the *Testament of Moses* has been found in the scrolls. That the subject is Herod is certain: a non-priestly king who executed many leaders, who ruled for thirty-four years, who had heirs that followed him (only one of whom had a shorter reign).[83] That it is not a Christian document is implied by the absence of the standard Christian canard against Herod—his "slaughter of the innocents." The description is basically social and not religious; what is more, the author says that the people and the leaders deserved their punishment.[84] The "powerful king from the west" refers to Varus's suppression of the revolts at Herod's death, when some portions of the Temple were burnt (*War* 2.49), some people deported, and some crucified—a set of actions known in the Rabbinic literature as "Varus's War."

---

83. Sanders, *Judaism,* pp. 455–57, dates it from 4 BCE to 30 CE; more correctly, it must be from between 6 CE and 30 CE. After 30 CE two of his sons had reigned longer than he had.

84. See also the description in Philo's *Quod Omnis,* quoted at length, above.

CHAPTER 11

From Rome to Jericho
(17–4 BCE)

AUGUSTUS, MARCUS AGRIPPA, AND HEROD

In 17 BCE Augustus marked the tenth anniversary of the "restoration of the Republic," when he had been named princeps and had assumed the title Augustus.[1] In 16 BCE, the previous year, the office of princeps had been extended for another five years; "then [Augustus] conferred upon Agrippa a number of privileges which were almost equal to his own, in particular the tribunician power for the same period" (Cassius Dio 54.12). Like Herod, Augustus imagined plots against him and even wore a breast-plate beneath his tunic in the Senate—antiquity's bullet-proof vest; he eliminated a number of his opponents (Cassius Dio 54.15). Again like Herod, he had reformed the laws and begun a program to distribute grain (Cassius Dio 54.16; *War* 1.424).[2]

The most obvious similarity between Augustus and Herod concerned their respective successions. Augustus had no sons of his own, but he acquired stepsons—Tiberius and Drusus—when he married Livia.[3] When he instructed Marcus Agrippa to marry his daughter Julia, an important aim was that they should have children who might succeed him, with Agrippa regent if necessary.[4] Gaius Caesar was born to Agrippa and Julia in 20 BCE and Lucius in 17 BCE; Augustus

---

1. On Augustus and Herod, Schalit, pp. 554–62

2. See in general *CAH* 10.146–51. Herod copied Augustus in several of these activities.

3. Nero Claudius Drusus was born in 38 BCE to Tiberius Claudius Nero and Livia, at about the time of her marriage to Octavian. Tiberius Julius Caesar, the future Emperor Tiberius, was born in 42 BCE.

4. On M. Agrippa, J.-M. Roddaz, *Marcus Agrippa* (Rome: École Française de Rome, 1984); H. Signon, *Agrippa. Freund und Mitregent des Augustus* (Frankfurt: Societas Verlag, 1978); R. Meyer, *Marcus Agrippa. A Biography* (Rome: Bretschneider, 1965).

adopted both grandsons as heirs before the end of 17.[5] At just this time, Herod was in Rome concerned with his problems of succession. Both had children they could not or did not rely upon: Herod the children by Doris and Mariamme I, Augustus his stepchildren from Livia's previous marriage.

Augustus dispatched Agrippa to the east while he and Tiberius went to Gaul (Cassius Dio 54.19).[6] The princeps remained away from Rome for three years, Agrippa for almost five. On learning that Agrippa had come east again, Herod went to meet him at Lesbos in 16/15 BCE.[7] He invited Agrippa to visit Judea (*Ant.* 16.12), which he did in 15 BCE. Herod showed off his new cities, Caesarea Maritima and Sebaste, took him on a tour of his fortresses—especially Alexandreion, Herodium, and Hyrcania[8]—and entertained him royally. They visited Jerusalem, where a massive work force labored on the complete rebuilding of the Temple into one of the most dramatic religious precincts in the Roman world. Agrippa paid for a sacrifice in the Temple and offered a feast for the people. Herod named one of the gates of the Temple after Agrippa and renamed Anthedon, a rebuilt coastal town, Agrippias.[9]

This grand tour would have been remarkable. Agrippa would have been impressed by the number of recently completed building projects and the major ones still under construction, especially those dedicated to Augustus and the Imperial family, of which he was an integral part. As a past commissioner of Rome's water supply, he would have been particularly interested in Herod's extensive water projects;[10] while the technology was borrowed, the applications were specific to Herod's kingdom. Herod, for his part, gained honor from the visit of his patron and the evidence it provided of his closeness to Augustus. The people—at least those who did not resent having dealings with the Romans—must have been impressed by Herod's high stature in the Roman power structure, for Agrippa was Augustus's son-in-law, father of his adopted children, and putative regent. And as a military commander, Agrippa was a figure to be reckoned with in his own right. The two retinues would have created a splen-

---

5. Cassius Dio 54.18. To Augustus's great distress, Gaius, after being made heir apparent (*princeps iuventutis*) in 5 BCE, died in 4 CE in Lycia on his way back from Parthia; Lucius died at Marseilles on his way to Spain in 2 CE.

6. Augustus used Tiberius's military capacities, though he did not want him as heir.

7. It is either at this point, or more likely later during their expedition together, that the incident involving Julia's near death at Ilium / Troy and Herod's intercession with Agrippa on behalf of the people of Ilium took place (chap. 9). Josephus has it out of sequence.

8. Herodium, the only totally new building of the three, had just been completed. Sebaste and Caesarea were still under construction, but the majority of the work was completed.

9. Nicolas refers to this visit in his speech before M. Agrippa in Ionia (*Ant.* 16.55–57).

10. In Jerusalem, Caesarea, Sebaste, Herodium, Jericho, Phaselis, Sepphoris, Alexandreion, Hyrcania; Agrippa's itinerary seems deliberately planned to show off these particular features. Some were rather innovative and all showed clearly the exaggerated water problems in Herod's kingdom.

did show; likely they paused to enjoy spectacles at the various theaters, stadia, amphitheaters, and hippodromes that Herod had provided for such occasions.[11]

The visit was cut short as winter approached; Agrippa had to return before the sailing season closed. He must have learned of troubles in the Black Sea before leaving, for he dispatched Polemon, king of Pontus, to deal with Scribonius and his new wife Dynamis, daughter of a former king of Pontus.[12] Though Scribonius was executed, hostilities were not yet concluded (Cassius Dio 54.24); so Agrippa, while still in Judea, sought Herod's assistance for a campaign in the Crimea the next spring (14 BCE).[13]

Herod set off with his new navy once the sailing season reopened.[14] He hoped to catch Agrippa at Lesbos, but was delayed by contrary winds at Chios—time he used to win new friends and to make benefactions to repay a loan to Augustus and to restore a damaged stoa. He carried on to the Hellespont and Byzantium, and finally caught up to Agrippa at Sinope in Pontus (see map 6).

THE DIASPORA

The strain between Herod and various sectors of Judean society was not matched in Diaspora Judaism.[15] Jews outside Judea had no obvious reasons to be at odds with Herod and several reasons to be favorably disposed. Unlike Judean Jews, they did not need to deal daily with Herod's authoritarianism. The factors that led to often harsh policies at home—internal security, participation in Rome's foreign policy, liberal economic measures—in a reflex fashion impelled generous measures abroad. Jews at a distance from Judea benefitted from Herod's closeness to Rome; they too were engaged in the same balancing act. We have little direct evidence of Herod's policy in the Diaspora, however; most

---

11. Philo, *Legatio,* 294–98, has Agrippa I speak glowingly to Caligula of M. Agrippa's visit—the grandfather of the one to the grandfather of the other.

12. Polemon was a close parallel to Herod. He had been a supporter of Antony who had fought against the Parthians in 40–39 BCE, but his reward was that he had lost part of his territory in Cilicia because of Antony's generosity to Cleopatra. He fought on Antony's side at Actium, but Octavian generously confirmed him in his kingship in 31 BCE despite that allegiance.

13. There were Jewish communities in the region; see *CIJ* 683–89.

14. I conclude the navy was new for several reasons: (1) Judea historically did not have much if any navy; (2) until Caesarea Maritima's great harbor was finished there was nowhere to shelter it; (3) Herod is reported to have made a substantial benefaction to Rhodes, which explicitly alludes to commissioning ships for his navy (one aspect of the benefactions was a grant to shipyards; *Ant.* 16.147); (4) he minted a coin type that clearly portrayed a warship (#55 in Meshorer, *Jewish Coins,* undated). Herod's earlier and more numerous coins with anchors allude to the harbor at Caesarea, not to a navy; Alexander Jannaeus had earlier celebrated his acquisition of a harbor similarly.

15. See Perowne, pp. 95–102, 149–51; Schalit, emphasizing the Roman Imperial cult, pp. 424–50.

is inferential but points in one direction. Herod's reign as "king of the Jews" led to a time of security and prosperity for the Jews of the Diaspora because he was also "friend of the Romans." By the mid-first century BCE so many Jews had emigrated that Josephus could say that "there is not a people in the world which does not contain a portion of our race" (*War* 2.398).[16] Contemporary literary evidence of Jews outside of Judea (Philo, Strabo, Tacitus, and Luke, for example) is extended by inscriptional and archaeological evidence.[17] The reasons for this largely voluntary exodus and the communities' political status do not concern us.

Two Diaspora communities in Egypt had sacrificial cult centers modelled on the Temple in Jerusalem: the older—at Aswan on the island of Elephantine—had served as home to a Jewish military colony,[18] the other—at Leontopolis north of Cairo—offered a reconstituted temple cult following the deposition of Onias III by Antiochus IV Epiphanes in 174 BCE (it was razed in 73 or 74 CE during the mopping-up after the Great Revolt). These cases, leaving aside Samaria, were untypical; they highlight the important fact that Jews elsewhere did *not* ordinarily practice sacrifice outside Israel. Even in Egypt, the large Jewish community was served typically by synagogues (more properly, "houses of prayer") and claimed substantial privileges of self-government, avoiding any sense of being a cult different from that practiced at Jerusalem.[19] Jewish communities adapted to life in a foreign country linguistically; in Alexandria in particular they spoke Greek and it was there that Jewish scripture, with a number of extra books, was translated into Greek in the period just prior to Herod.

Herod showed no interest in or support for Jews in Egypt. His long-standing problems with Cleopatra, finally resolved only by her suicide in 30 BCE, caused him—we may suppose—to turn away from Egypt. Its special status under the Emperor would also have made him wary of dabbling in its internal affairs. There was no particular reason to show a special concern for the Jews of

---

16. On the Diaspora, see Smallwood, *Jews,* chap. 6.

17. Philo, for example, a generation after the death of Herod lists the following in *Legatio* 281–82: Egypt, Phoenicia, Syria, Pamphylia, Cilicia, Asia, Bithynia, Pontus, Thessaly, Boeotia, Macedonia, Aetolia, Attica, Argos, Corinth, the Peloponnese, Euboea, Cyprus, and Crete. A generation or two later Luke repeats some of the above and adds: Parthia, Media, Elam, Mesopotamia, Cappadocia, Phrygia, Cyrene, Rome, and Arabia. Inscriptional evidence supports most of the above and adds numerous other locations including, for example, Malta, Aquitania, Moesia, Lycia. Archaeological evidence for synagogues confirms Jewish communities at Sardis (a remarkably wealthy community), Cos, Delos, Aegina, Ostia, among others.

18. Aramaic papyri from the community have shed considerable light on life in this outpost. The community was founded sometime in the fifth century BCE; it may no longer have been active in the first century BCE.

19. On Alexandrian Judaism, see A. Kasher, *Jews in Hellenistic and Roman Egypt* (Tübingen: J. C. B. Mohr, 1985).

Egypt, since the later troubles under Caligula did not characterize Herod's period. Nor was he concerned for Jews in North Africa (Cyrenaica, Tripolitania, etc.) or in Spain. He had contacts with the Jewish community in Rome and was interested in Jews in Babylonia, but his closest attention was given only to Jews in the Greek Diaspora, especially Syria, Asia Minor, and the Greek islands, where there were significant Jewish communities facing problems in their relations with the communities in which they were set. Here the spirit of Hellenism had taken firm root, Hellenistic architectural masterpieces were to be found, Hellenistic kingdoms flourished, Hellenistic institutions were deployed—all of interest to Herod. So it was not accidental that Herod interested himself in these Jewish communities; their quality of life reflected upon his activities in Judea. If Judaism could not flourish in Hellenistic areas, how could Hellenism be adapted to Judea?

These Jewish communities, like those in Egypt, read the Bible in Greek and used Greek daily. They focused their social and religious communal life around the local synagogue and maintained an attachment to Judea through payment of the half-shekel Temple tax and occasional visits to Jerusalem. Jews walked a tight-rope: their material well-being was tied up with their fellow-citizens but their spiritual satisfaction was connected with sacrificial worship that could only be carried out in distant Judea.

There was more than one way to handle this tension. The powerful Jewish community in Alexandria, for example, created a sense of ambitious exclusiveness that helped lead to the riots of 37 CE. The equally powerful community in Sardis was almost totally integrated into the city without antagonism or resistance.[20] There were reasons for misunderstandings and hostility toward Jews: there was sometimes a sense of exclusiveness; they were reluctant to compromise over matters such as food regulations; their attachment to the Jerusalem Temple drained money from the local economy; and they had special privileges that stemmed from successive acts of Roman leaders, not least of which was exemption from military service. Sometimes these factors resulted in an offensive anti-Judaism—almost anti-Semitism.[21] The evidence has been collected carefully by Stern and commented on by Sevenster.[22]

A SYNAGOGUE IN ROME?

Herod was concerned with this state of affairs and acted to ameliorate the conditions in the Hellenistic Diaspora. Though there is no literary record of his

---

20. I am persuaded that the important building in Sardis was a synagogue, but there is some reason for doubt.

21. See P. Richardson, ed., *Anti-Judaism in Early Christianity,* vol. 1 (Waterloo, ON: Wilfrid Laurier University Press, 1986), esp. the essays by W. Klassen, E. P. Sanders, and P. Richardson.

22. Stern, *Greek and Latin Authors*; J. N. Sevenster, *The Roots of Pagan Anti-Semitism in the Ancient World* (Leiden: Brill, 1975); T. Reinach, *Textes d'auteurs grecs et romains relatifs au judaïsme* (Hildesheim: Olms, 1963 [1895]).

having built anything in Rome,[23] a tenuous piece of evidence comes from there:[24] a fragmentary inscription[25] may refer to a synagogue of the Herodians.[26] The problem is a difficult one; several other readings are possible and, even if one were to accept the reconstruction *SYNAGÔGÊ TÔN HÊRÔDIÔN,* it would not be clear whether this is a reference only to Herodians or to Herod himself.

There are references to twelve or thirteen synagogues in the inscriptions from Rome. Among them are three named after important persons: a synagogue of the Augustans (Augustesians), a synagogue of the Agrippans (Agrippesians), and a synagogue of the Volumnians.[27] These probably allude to the Emperor Augustus, M. Agrippa, and Volumnius (procurator of Syria from 9 to 7 BCE)[28] and are three of the earliest synagogues in Rome among those known through inscriptions,[29] dating from the late first century BCE or the early first

---

23. Smallwood, *Jews,* discusses the history of the Jewish community in Rome and notes especially the influence of Jewish prisoners in 62 BCE (Pompey) and in 37 BCE (Sossius) and possibly in 53 BCE. See also H. J. Leon, *The Jews of Ancient Rome* (Philadelphia: Jewish Publication Society, 1960); L. V. Rutgers, "Roman Policy Towards the Jews," *Classical World* 13/1 (1994): 56–74.

24. Herod made three or four trips to Rome: in 40 BCE when he was named king by the Senate, in 17 when he went to fetch his sons home, in 12 when he went to resolve family problems and the succession, and possibly in 8 BCE. No details are given of contacts with the Jewish community in Rome on any of these visits, though it is reasonable to suppose there were some. Josephus says that Jews in Rome supported the delegation from Judea during the hearings concerning the succession before Augustus in 4 BCE (see chap. 1).

25. *CIJ* 173: the remaining text reads as follows:
. . . .]X X X
. . . .]GÔGÊS
. . . .]RODIÔN
. . .]EULOGIAPASIN
Before the second line the vertical stroke of either an *H* or an *I* is visible. The reconstruction of the text is not simple and has been debated in the literature. None of the proposals are very persuasive, because none seem to answer all the problems, both epigraphic and textual. See P. Richardson, "Augustan-era Synagogues in Rome," in K. Donfried and P. Richardson, eds., *Judaism and Christianity in Rome in the First Century,* forthcoming.

26. See Leon, *Jews of Ancient Rome,* pp. 159–62.

27. Augustans (*CIJ* 284, 301, 338, 368, 416, 496); Agrippans (*CIJ* 365, 425, 503); Volumnians (*CIJ* 343, 402, 417, 523).

28. See Leon, *Jews of Ancient Rome,* pp. 135–66; he accepts the attribution to Augustus but is skeptical of Volumnius, pointing out, quite correctly, that we know little of this shadowy figure and that there are a number of persons by the same name. He also is uncertain of the correctness of the attribution to Marcus Agrippa, appearing to look just as favorably on the supposition that the synagogue is named after either Agrippa I or Agrippa II of Judea.

29. Leon argues correctly that the synagogue of the Hebrews is the earliest synagogue in Rome, since this is the most natural description for any synagogue in the Diaspora; cf. the "synagogue of the Hebrews" (*syna[GÔGÊHEB]raiôn*) in Corinth, known from a fragmentary but late inscription. Other synagogues in Rome are the synagogue of the Calcaresians, of the Campesians, of Elaea, of the Secenians, of the Siburesians, of the Tripolitans, of the Vernaclesians.

century CE. The least convoluted interpretation of the inscriptions is that they attest to the strong sense of obligation the Roman Jewish community felt toward powerful figures, perhaps including Volumnius.[30] The main argument against this view is the question of whether or not Jews would name synagogues after such dignitaries, though such an *a priori* argument does not carry much weight. Similarly, one effective argument against the fourth inscription referring to Herod is also *a priori* and carries little weight: a synagogue could not possibly name itself after Herod. Frey has argued most tellingly for reconstructing the text and parsing the result to refer to a synagogue of the Herodians.[31] A number of scholars oppose this interpretation, most notably Leon.[32]

If two or three of the earliest synagogues in Rome were named after three persons associated with each other and with Judaism in the eastern Mediterranean, naming another after Herod was unexceptional;[33] these four persons were seen by Jews in Rome as supportive of Jews.[34] The naming was not for monetary support for the synagogue, not even in the case of Herod (such actions are unattested elsewhere), but for communal thanks to the honoree. The Jewish community in Rome, where Herod's role was slight, thought of him as a beneficent figure who advanced the conditions of the Diaspora. This evidence,

---

30. Volumnius is a hazy figure even in Josephus. All the references cluster in a short section (*War* 1.535–42; *Ant.* 16.277–369), but his descriptions seem to imply that there are two different persons, one of whom is one of *two* governors of Syria, the other is a military tribune. In fact both must refer to the same person, a military tribune who acts in close association with the governor of Syria in certain military matters, especially in connection with Herod's punitive expedition against Nabatea to slap down Syllaeus and to make King Obodas repay his loan. When permission was given for Herod to act, Volumnius participated in that decision. He was friendly with Herod, later carrying a letter to Augustus from Herod concerning Herod's two sons. Subsequently Volumnius was present at their trial in Berytus and, according to Josephus, urged a "pitiless sentence." The aftermath of the Syllaeus episode led, on the one hand, to Augustus's withdrawal of his intention to give Herod control of Arabia and, on the other hand, to Herod's settling three thousand Idumaeans in Trachonitis to keep the peace. Scholarly opinion against the identification of this Volumnius as the person honored in the naming of the synagogue is often based on the impossibility of someone involved in the trial of Herod's sons being honored in this fashion. But it is possible that Volumnius was remembered by Jews in Rome because he supported Judea against Arabia and, as a friend of Herod's, pressed Herod's claims in Rome.

31. *CIJ* lxxii, 124–26; see also A. Momigliano, "I nomi della prime 'synagoghe' romane e la condizione giuridica delle communità in Roma sotto Augusto," *Rassegna Mensile di Israël* 6 (1931–32): 283–92; S. Kraus, *Synagogale Altertümer* (Berlin and Vienna, 1922), pp. 247–59; G. La Piana, "Foreign Groups in Rome during the First Centuries of the Empire," *HTR* 20 (1927): 183–403, esp. 341–71.

32. Leon, *Jews of Ancient Rome*, pp. 159–62; also in H. J. Leon, "The Synagogue of the Herodians," *JAOS* 49 (1929): 318–21; H. J. Leon, "New Material about the Jews of Ancient Rome," *JQR*, n.s. 20 (1929–30): 301–12.

33. Smallwood, *Jews*, pp. 137–38, inclines toward a reference to Herod, but away from a reference to Volumnius.

34. Compare Egypt, in an earlier period, when several synagogue inscriptions referred to Ptol-

then, hints at a Herodian policy—or perhaps better, impact—on the Diaspora; it converges with other evidence of Herod's constructive effect on the status of Jews in western Asia Minor and the Greek islands.

THE DECREES

Two further lines of evidence support this picture: Roman interventions to safeguard Jewish Diaspora conditions and Herod's interaction with the Diaspora. The decrees to which we refer were concentrated in the period before and during Herod's early influence and the communities involved were almost entirely in Asia Minor and the adjacent islands, the areas most significant to Herod. The decrees are described by Josephus in two extended collections: *Ant.* 14.190–264 and 16.160–73. The former passage includes a summary by Josephus:

> Now there are many other such decrees passed by the Senate and the Imperators of the Romans, relating to Hyrcanus and our nation, as well as resolutions of cities and rescripts of provincial governors in reply to letters on the subjects of our rights. . . . [W]e have furnished clear and visible proofs of our friendship with the Romans, indicating those decrees engraved on bronze pillars and tablets which remain to this day and will continue to remain in the Capitol. . . .
>
> (*Ant.* 14.265–66)[35]

Most of the decrees responded to initiatives of Hyrcanus II, ethnarch and high priest.[36] Through most of this turbulent period (63 to 40 BCE) Hyrcanus II was dominant in Judea,[37] with Antipater and/or Herod at his side, advising on or executing the regime's policies. Hyrcanus II's weakness has been exaggerated; he certainly does not appear weak in these decrees.[38] Either he or someone else had a clear sense of what was needed from Rome to guarantee the conditions of Diaspora Jews. In the first decree cited by Josephus (*Ant.* 14.190–95) Hyrcanus II is "high priest and ethnarch of the Jews," a brave, loyal, and zealous

---

emy and Cleopatra (*CIJ* 1441, 1442, 1443) or Ptolemy and Berenice (*CIJ* 1440) or Ptolemy alone (*CIJ* 1449).

35. With this, compare the introduction in *Ant.* 14.186–89, which says that Asia and Europe were the key areas.

36. Most but not all. The Pergamum decree directed against Antiochus is earlier, and several others that cannot be easily dated may also be outside the period of Hyrcanus II.

37. On the similar turbulence in Rome during the two Triumvirates and the Civil War, see chap. 5.

38. *Ant.* 14.200, for example, cites a decree of Julius Caesar from 44 BCE, confirming an earlier permission (47 BCE) to fortify Jerusalem, not the request of an ineffective person; the refortification may have been carried out by Herod's father, Antipater.

supporter of Caesar in the campaign against Mithridates; it guarantees him and his children the offices of high priest and ethnarch "for all time" and gives them the same title Herod later had, "friend and ally" (*amicus et socius*). Addressed to Sidon, it says that "if . . . any question shall arise concerning the Jews' manner of life, it is my pleasure that the decision shall rest with them" (Hyrcanus and his children).[39] Hyrcanus's regime (including Antipater and later Herod) protected Jewish minorities, perhaps even as a defender of expatriate Jews.

The decrees dealt with problems Jews faced in the Diaspora: (1) collection and transmission of the half-shekel Temple-tax (see 14.227 [Asia-Ephesus], 214 [Delos], 251 [Pergamum]); (2) gathering of produce for the tithe or first-fruits (see 14.203 [Sidon], 245 [Miletus], 250 [Pergamum]); (3) Jewish communal meals and sacred rites (see 14.213–14 [Parium], 242 [Laodicea]); (4) observance of the Sabbath (see 14.242 [Laodicea], 245 [Miletus], 258 [Halicarnassus], 263 [Ephesus]); (5) places of assembly (e.g., 14.258 [Halicarnassus], 260 [Sardis]) and even residential quarters (Sardis again); (6) exemption from military service (see 14.226 [Asia-Ephesus], 228 [Ephesus], 232 [Delos], 237 [decree of Lentulus]); (7) adjudication of civil suits (e.g. 14.260 [Sardis]); (8) observing laws and customs and rites generally. The list speaks for itself; in parts of the Diaspora rights already granted to Jews had to be safeguarded. This was done by decrees promulgated in towns and cities, with a copy in the capitol in Rome, and by instructions to city councils reminding them forcefully of the need for tolerance.[40] Much of this activity occurred under Julius Caesar and Augustus, the former associated with Hyrcanus II, the latter with M. Agrippa.

A shorter collection is found in *Ant.* 16.160–73, prefaced a few paragraphs earlier by Nicolas's speech before Agrippa. The picture is the same: the issues were civic status (160), the Temple tax (160–61), and private concerns (160); the communities were Asia, Cyrene, Ephesus, and Sardis; the main player was M. Agrippa. Specific matters dealt with in the decrees included the Jerusalem tax (163, 166, 167, 169, 171, 172), sabbath observance (163, 168), and violation of synagogues (164).

SUIT OF THE IONIAN JEWS

The appeal of Ionian Jews to M. Agrippa as described by Josephus is well known. The appeal asked for support of their laws, exemption from Sabbath

---

39. In his note (e) on this passage, Marcus says this probably refers to "internal jurisdiction in Judaea." Perhaps, but in the context and in the light of similar decrees it is likelier to refer to Jews of Sidon living according to their laws and customs. It appears to give Hyrcanus rights over this nearby Jewish community. A similar set of circumstances is envisaged in the next decree (*Ant.* 14.196–98) addressed to Sidon, Tyre, and Ashkelon, that Hyrcanus is "the protector of those Jews who are unjustly treated," presumably in those cities.

40. For similar decrees, see R. K. Sherk, *Rome and the Greek East to the Death of Augustus*

court appearances, security of transport of the Temple-tax, exemption from military service and from some civic duties (*Ant.* 16.27–60). Nicolas of Damascus, at Herod's direction, spoke on their behalf.[41] He reminded Agrippa that Jews used the seventh day to study their customs and laws, that money for the Jerusalem Temple was often stolen, that taxes had been imposed on them, that they had been taken to court on holy days, and that these kinds of difficulties had already been dealt with by decrees of the Senate recorded on tablets in the capitol. Agrippa's friendliness was obvious (16.55), and in his formal decision he granted all Jewish requests, confirmed their rights and customs, and told the defendants not to cause the Roman government trouble. This last statement revealed how important "peace" was as a motivation for Rome's unusual concessions to a subject peoples.

Herod also was interested in the Diaspora; in the Ionian hearing Nicolas connected Herod with their suit. According to Josephus, Nicolas referred to Herod as "our king," commended him for his support of Agrippa's house, and for his honor and foresight and good faith, emphasizing Herod's benefactions through the Diaspora. He referred to Herod's father's help for Caesar in earlier years (*Ant.* 16.52) and Antipater's Roman citizenship (16.50–57; 14.127–37). To stress Herod's importance in the decision, Josephus says Agrippa granted all that the Jews asked "because of Herod's good will and friendship" (16.60).

This picture of Herod's closeness to Agrippa, his benefactions, and his family's dependability, recalls Antipater's service to Hyrcanus II and dovetails with the evidence from the various decrees and letters. Antipater and Herod played constructive roles in the Diaspora in the eyes of Jews and Romans; the Diaspora's advantageous position derived partly from this family.

The episode with Agrippa, Nicolas, and Herod was a small episode in a major trip (*Ant.* 16.16). As Herod assisted M. Agrippa in the Black Sea in the spring of 14 BCE, he was both adviser and friend (16.22). After returning by land through Paphlagonia, Cappadocia, and Great Phrygia, to Ephesus,[42] they went to Samos and then Ilium, where Herod reconciled Agrippa to the Ilians (*Ant.* 16.26). When Herod arrived again at Chios (with its significant Jewish community), he paid off the Chian debt to Rome.[43] The Ionian suit before

---

(Cambridge: Cambridge University Press, 1984), ##95 (Kyme, 27 BCE), 97 (Mytilene, 25 BCE), 100 (Alexandria, 10–9 BCE), 101 (several Asian examples, 9 BCE and following), 102 (five edicts of Augustus, 7/6 and 4 BCE).

41. On M. Agrippa and the Diaspora, Grant, pp. 175–82.

42. While no details are given the route probably was as follows: Sinope, *Heraclea, Ancyra* (Ankara), Caesarea (Kayseri), Archelais, *Iconium* (Konya), Antiochia, *Apamea, Colosse,* Hierapolis (Pamukkale), *Laodicea, Tralles,* and Ephesus. (Jewish communities are known in the italicized cities.)

43. The whole account has a strong undertone of the patronal system at work: note esp. 16.22, "his deferential behaviour on pleasurable occasions," 16.24, he paid all the benefactions and entertainment costs out of his own pocket.

Agrippa occurred at this point, after which Agrippa went to Lesbos and Herod to Samos before going home to Jerusalem. When he arrived there (16.62) he convened an assembly to report on Jews in Asia and their future prospects; to show his beneficence he remitted a quarter of his own people's taxes.[44]

Herod bettered Diaspora Jews' conditions; sometimes he did this directly—as in the suit of Ionian Jews and his visits to communities with substantial numbers of Jews—but mostly he worked indirectly through benefactions (above, chap. 8). There was a close correlation between the places benefitted and the locations of concentrations of Jews, yet he never made contributions, so far as we know, to the Jewish communities themselves, only to the whole city or province. When he claimed that Jews in the Diaspora would be unmolested in the future he did not mean that the underlying problems had been resolved but that he had helped to change attitudes by his generosity. When he ended his speech in Jerusalem with the remission of taxes (16.62; cf. 15.365) he was trying to avoid exactly the charge that in the end was laid against him, that there was a financial drain out of the country. For Herod, benevolence in the Diaspora and remission of taxes in Judea were complementary acts of generosity.

BENEFACTIONS

There is no recorded instance of Herod's building a Diaspora synagogue nor of monetary gifts to a Diaspora community (even if the proposal above of a synagogue of Herodians in Rome is correct, it was an honoring of him, not a benefaction from him). He aimed to improve attitudes of Greeks and Romans toward the local Jewish minority, not to improve materially the Jewish lot (see chap. 8). This reading of the benefactions agrees with the decrees and letters, and with Herod's intervention before M. Agrippa. In all cases the issue was the relationship between Jews and their neighbors. Herod hoped to impress the various communities with the open-handed and broad-minded concern of the Jewish homeland and its king.

In Asia Minor and Greece Herod assisted cities financially (to repay a loan, to lighten taxes, or for unspecified purposes). He also made strategic gifts: support of shipbuilding in Rhodes, endowment of the Olympic games,[45] and of a gymnasiarch at Cos. He underwrote local public works in Rhodes (rebuilding the Pythian Temple of Apollo), Chios (completing a stoa left unfinished for lack of funds), Nicopolis (near the site of Octavian's victory over Antony—"the

---

44. Once again this action came shortly after a sabbatical year (see above).

45. As a result of his generosity to the games he was named President for life according to Josephus (*Ant.* 16.149; *War* 1.426–27). Part of the benefactions may have gone to repair the Temple of Zeus, which had been damaged in an earthquake twenty or so years earlier.

greater part of the public buildings"), and also Pergamum, Samos, Athens, and Sparta (chap. 8, Appendixes A and B).[46]

In Syria his pattern was similar, except that the gifts were almost all civic constructions. Herod built in Ptolemais (gymnasium), Tyre (halls, stoas, temples, and market places), Sidon (theater), Byblus (walls), Berytus (halls, stoas, temples, and market places), Tripolis (gymnasium), Damascus (gymnasium and theater), Antioch (broad paved street and colonnades), Laodicea-on-Sea (aqueduct), and in nearby Balanea he lightened taxes (see chap. 8 and map 6). Josephus implies that there were more gifts when he says that he lists only those "greatest and most celebrated" (*Ant.* 16.146–49; *War* 1.422–28).

Self-aggrandizement is not a sufficient explanation for Herod's beneficence; the gifts, endowments, and benefactions testified to Herod's political *savoir faire*. They worked in two complementary ways, shaping Judea's external relations with provinces and cities and influencing relations between Jews in the Diaspora and their neighbors. Works aimed only at local Jewish communities would have exacerbated local tensions. It is in this general context that Josephus claims that "Caesar himself and Agrippa often remarked that the extent of Herod's realm was not equal to his magnanimity, for he deserved to be King of all Syria and Egypt" (*Ant.* 16.141).

THE HOUSEHOLD

Herod's Black Sea trip was an interlude, included in a section of material in *Antiquities* that has little overlap with *War*. With attention once again on Herod's domestic problems the accounts come back into an uneasy parallelism, though *Antiquities*'s account is fuller.[47] Josephus's theme is clearly "dissension" (*stasis, Ant.* 16.66; *War* 1.445, *orgē*), involving Alexander and Aristobulus (Mariamme I's children) and Salome and Pheroras (Herod's sister and brother). The two brothers returned from Rome in 17 BCE, but for the following couple of years Herod was occupied in matters of state: the visit to M. Agrippa, the visit

---

46. See the important argument of E. Gabba, "The Finances of King Herod," in A. Kasher, U. Rappaport, and G. Fuks, eds., *Greece and Rome in Eretz-Israel* (Jerusalem: Israel Exploration Society, 1990), pp. 160–68. Gabba points out that Herod could only lighten taxes by having held the tax concession.

47. Chronological problems, to which there is no simple solution, are intense in the ten-year period from 17 to 7 BCE. In what follows I have been guided by two conclusions: (1) the datable events must act as a framework into which other incidents are inserted as logic and necessity dictate, not necessarily as Josephus has them; (2) Josephus complicates the household dissensions in both *War* and *Antiquities*, probably because he has several sources for some events and has kept apart what he should have pulled together. Still, problems remain that defy resolution, though it is clear that family troubles were intense and occupied significant portions of the ten-year period. At different stages the problems focussed on different players: (1) Pheroras and Salome; (2) Alexander and Aristobulus; (3) Glaphyra; (4) supporters of Alexander and Aristobulus.

by M. Agrippa, the Black Sea expedition, and visits to numerous cities in Asia Minor requiring representations and benefactions.

Household dissension was exacerbated during these various absences (*Ant.* 16.73). There are differences in Josephus, however: in *War* the problems focus on the two youths and their resentment of Herod (they "eyed him as an enemy," *War* 1.445); in *Antquities* Salome tries to repeat her earlier success in getting rid of their mother. The boys were not blameless (according to *Antiquities*), but the initiative rested with Salome and Pheroras,[48] who outwitted the brothers by manipulating them into an overt display of *lèse majesté* against their father (*Ant.* 16.68–72). It is not necessary to choose between these two alternate explanations; they fit well together.

Later accounts of the problems created by Pheroras and Salome are probably misplaced and should be included prior to Herod's Black Sea trip, where they are more plausible.[49] During this phase of family troubles Pheroras and Salome worked in concert. They broke, however, when Pheroras accused Salome of wanting to marry Syllaeus. This event must have taken place in 15 BCE when M. Agrippa visited Jerusalem and she was attracted—and continued to be drawn—to a Nabatean noble who was trying to erode Herod's position, while Pheroras had parallel responsibilities in neighboring Peraea (*Ant.* 18.130; 16.194; *War* 1.483). From 14 or so onward, Josephus's view that Pheroras and Salome were of one mind is probably wrong.

Pheroras's responsibilities had grown through marriage,[50] political power, and income. Yet for all his importance, he is a shadowy figure. In 31/30 BCE he had been accused of an attempt to poison Herod, but he weathered this crisis unscathed (*War* 1.485–86; *Ant.* 16.198, retrospectively). In 20 BCE he was made tetrarch of Peraea, at Herod's suggestion and with Augustus's permission (*War* 1.483; *Ant.* 15.362, retrospectively). Not long afterward his wife, Mariamme I's sister, died (*War* 1.483, retrospectively), perhaps in 18 or 17 BCE. At this point, I conjecture, Herod pledged his own daughter Salampsio to his brother (about 16 BCE). Pheroras offended Herod by rejecting this linking of the two branches of the family, and deepened the offense by rejecting a second arranged wedding with another of Herod's daughters, Cypros.[51] Pheroras's stupidity is

---

48. Pheroras has generally played only a modest role, now his actions are emphasized in *Antiquities*.

49. Some of the later episodes in *War* 1.483–85 and *Ant.* 16.194–228 contain explicitly retrospective material that fits with this present material.

50. He was married to Herod's wife's sister, another daughter of Alexander and Alexandra, a sister of Mariamme I. This further complicates the antagonisms within the palace, for Pheroras's actions against the two youths were thus actions against his wife's sister's children.

51. Salampsio would have been about fifteen to seventeen years of age (she was born about 33 BCE), an appropriate age for betrothal; Pheroras was in his 60s. With the betrothal came a huge dowry of three hundred talents. Herod must have been tolerant of, or bemused by, Pheroras's late-life crisis; he then married Salampsio to her cousin Phasael and offered Pheroras his younger daugh-

almost unbelievable. He was in love with a slave woman (*War* 1.483; *Ant.* 16.194, 196, again retrospectively) whom he seems to have married despite Herod's objections (*War* 1.572, 578).[52] When he later resolved to divorce the slave and accept Herod's offer, even taking an oath not to consort with her further, he could not keep his promise and fell back into the former relationship. The result was that Herod became suspicious of his own brother (*War* 1.483–84; *Ant.* 16.194–95), and this made Pheroras easy prey for anyone who wanted to redress old scores (only *Ant.* 16.196–99).

Herod could not ignore renewed accusations of Pheroras, especially that years earlier he and Costobar, Salome's husband, had planned to flee to Parthia.[53] Now Pheroras implicated his sister Salome in a plan to marry Syllaeus, the chief administrative officer of Nabatea under Obodas and guide of the ill-fated expedition by Aelius Gallus years earlier to Arabia Felix (*War* 1.486–87; *Ant.* 16.200–228).[54] The range of these suspicions is remarkable: Pheroras's base of power was in Peraea, Costobar's had been in Idumaea, Syllaeus's was in Nabatea, and over all hung the threat of Parthia.

Pheroras had for years been waging a campaign against Herod's son Alexander; now he told Alexander that Herod was secretly in love with his wife Glaphyra (*Ant.* 16.206). Improbable as this was, the dénouement was even more improbable. When Alexander confronted his father, Herod went to Pheroras, outraged, but instead of punishing him said he would give him greater benefits. All rumors were believed, everyone misunderstood, love and hate were rampant. The scene in Josephus's account is overdrawn, like bad opera—and yet there must be some truth to the accusations, counter-accusations, and tortuous defenses.

Next, Pheroras told Herod it was all Salome's idea; she was present and denied all charges, countering that everyone was jealous of her (*Ant.* 16.207–15). She and Pheroras were now opposed to each other and Herod was antagonistic toward both (*Ant.* 16.216–19).[55] This leads dramatically into the details of the relationship between Syllaeus and Salome. Syllaeus's relationship to Obodas was like Antipater's to Hyrcanus II much earlier: "Obodas was inactive and

---

ter, Cypros, now in her early 20s. In sum, Pheroras was married to Mariamme I's sister and betrothed in quick succession to Mariamme I's daughters. Herod was determined to establish Pheroras's children as acceptable to popular opinion. See further, chap. 2, above.

52. Josephus refers to Pheroras's wife. Since his first wife had already died, this wife must be the ex-slave. This gives added point to the description of her airs with others in the family, airs that were resented from a slave.

53. Though Josephus tells this as if it is at the present, it must be retrospective, as Costobar had been executed in 28 BCE.

54. On Syllaeus, Schalit, pp. 613–16.

55. *Antiquities* has a lacuna between 16.218 and 219. The reader expects some dramatic consequence, and instead is offered a summary of Salome's character, an indication of the composite nature of the accounts.

sluggish by nature," so Syllaeus took control (*Ant.* 16.220).[56] He came to Jerusalem on a matter of mutual interest to him and Herod, saw Salome and fell in love; since she reciprocated his feelings, he asked Herod for her hand.[57] A condition of the marriage was Syllaeus's circumcision.[58] Syllaeus's ambitions with respect to the Nabatean throne conflicted seriously with identification as a Jew, so he refused.[59] The rest of Syllaeus's story must wait a bit.

All these events that Josephus puts later must have come before Herod's return from the Black Sea expedition (late 14 BCE); he says that Pheroras and Salome—more likely Salome alone—insisted that Herod was in danger from his two sons bent on revenging their mother, and that Archelaus of Cappadocia, Alexander's father-in-law, would help the boys make their case before Augustus (*Ant.* 16.73–74; *War* 1.447).[60] Herod took an uncharacteristically ambiguous decision to recall his oldest son Antipater to the royal court in 14 BCE (*Ant.* 16.78; *War* 1.448). Antipater had been only two or three years old when Doris and he were expelled; during the interval they were *persona non grata*.[61] His ambivalence lay in restoring Antipater to honor while hesitating about Alexander and Aristobulus, wanting Antipater to "serve as a bulwark against his other sons" (*War* 1.448) and so to "curb the recklessness of Mariamme's sons and warn them more effectively" by showing them "that the succession to the throne was not solely and necessarily their rightful due." Antipater was merely a "standby" (*Ant.* 16.79–80).[62] In some circumstances the ploy might have worked, now it added fuel to the flames. Alexander and Aristobulus thought Herod had dealt unfairly with them, and Antipater could now further undercut

---

56. See above, chap. 9, on Syllaeus and Aelius Gallus's intervention in Arabia Felix, when he was already the financial controller of Nabatea. He was probably about the same age as Herod and Salome.

57. In the kinship/marriage system that obtained, even a woman of mature years had to get her brother's consent. Herod, Josephus explicitly says, asked Salome's own views (*Ant.* 16.220–25).

58. Hinted at but not explicitly said except in the Latin manuscript tradition (*circumcidi; Ant.* 16.225). The demand is impersonal, "otherwise it is not possible." We should take this an indication of Herod's views, though this is not said.

59. It is difficult to date this event in the sequence of troubles. The claim that Syllaeus was a young man and the retrospective glance back to a period when Costobar was still alive suggest that, as I have argued above, it is out of order and belongs earlier. I have not dated it as early as some: Grant puts it in the mid-20s (Grant, pp. 141–44), Perowne in 20/19 (Perowne, pp. 153–54). It must come after Herod's return from Rome in 17 BCE and before the Trachonite revolt with Nabatean support. Some occasion must explain Syllaeus's friendly visit to Herod in Jerusalem: the likeliest occasion is Marcus Agrippa's visit to Judea in 15—hence these events were in that year.

60. *Ant.* 16.75–77 describes Herod as being perplexed over these accusation, not altogether plausibly, though *War* 1.448 gives much the same sense (Herod was "drugged").

61. Only in 14 BCE was Antipater given a royal match with the daughter of Antigonus; such a marriage could not have been contracted during the years of disgrace.

62. Schalit, pp. 588–92, 600–606, on Alexander and Aristobulus; pp. 596–99, 628–32, on Antipater.

his half-brothers' position. Antipater showed "remarkable adroitness" (*War* 1.450) in not being seen to attack them while skillfully doing just that (*Ant.* 16.82–84).

As Alexander's and Aristobulus's positions disintegrated and support disappeared, Antipater's improved. "Eventually his influence was strong enough to bring back his mother to Mariamme's bed" (*War* 1.451; *Ant.* 16.85). For three decades Doris had suffered the shame of divorce and expulsion from the royal court. Nine other women had shared Herod's bed and exchanged vows with him; seven of them had borne him children. Herod's firstborn—Doris's child—had been ignored. When Herod brought Antipater and then, at his suggestion, Doris back to the palace, both saw it as an opportunity for revenge.

The change in positions was formalized in Herod's second will in 13 BCE (see chap. 2), in which Antipater was named heir and his two half-brothers were excluded. He was given the trappings of royal position (*War* 1.451; *Ant.* 16.86) and accompanied Herod to Ionia to say goodbye to Agrippa on the conclusion of his duties in the east.[63] To complete his rehabilitation, Antipater continued to Rome with Marcus Agrippa to present himself, with Herod's new will, to Augustus.[64] Antipater benefitted from Herod's friendship with Agrippa, making his first visit to Rome in the company of the Empire's second most powerful leader. He had gifts for Augustus, so he had every reason to expect that he too would become Augustus's friend.

In 13 BCE, then, at the advanced age of thirty-two or so, Antipater's star shone more brightly than he could ever have imagined. He had been recalled to court, out-manoeuvred his two main rivals (other sons were still too young to be factors), been sent to Rome in the company of Agrippa to see the princeps, and now occupied sole place in Herod's will. Alexander and Aristobulus "were completely excluded from power" (*Ant.* 16.86).[65]

While in Rome Antipater "advanced in honour and bettered his position of preeminence," for Herod had written friends in Rome on his son's behalf (16.87). The Roman period (13–12 BCE) was a turning point in Antipater's development (so *Antiquities;* different in *War*): he maliciously waged a letter campaign from Rome against Alexander and Aristobulus (16.88–89), with the desired effect on Herod's own "anger and resentment."

---

63. The date is not certain. See Cassius Dio 54.28, who refers to Agrippa's return from Syria, then to his military expedition to Pannonia, saying that the one event (or possibly both) fell in the consulship of Marcus Valerius [Messalla Barbatus Appianus] and Publius Sulpicius [Quirinius], which was in 12 BCE, the same Quirinius who figured in the famous census in Syria in 6 CE.

64. *War* 1.573 says Antipater should be sent off to Rome, as if for his first visit there, and with a will, as here. It is tempting to suppose that this is another dislocation resulting from the use of several sources, though note the circumstantial character of the surrounding material.

65. Herod even contemplated their execution (*War* 1.451), though this is doubtful at this stage.

TO ROME AGAIN

In 12 BCE Herod packed up both sons,[66] jumped on board ship and headed to Rome "in order not to make a mistake through carelessness or rashness." Augustus was in Aquileia (*Ant.* 16.91; in Rome, *War* 1.452), where Herod accused his sons of planning patricide and treason (seizing the throne; see *Ant.* 16.92; 15.343). Herod emphasized their unfilial behavior in wishing his death despite his own generosity and restraint (*Ant.* 16.993–97). In bringing them to appear before Augustus on an equal footing, he had renounced his own precedence.

Alexander (now about twenty-four) and Aristobulus (about twenty-three) knew they had serious problems in strategy and substance. They could not counter-accuse Herod before Augustus, for this would confirm Herod's accusations. Yet they had to mount a defense or they would be found guilty (*War* 1.452–54 succinctly; *Ant.* 16.100–120).[67] Augustus's sympathies swung to the brothers and reconciliation. He cleared them of the charges but instructed them to obey Herod, and urged him to abandon his suspicions (*War* 1.454; *Ant.* 16.121–26).

Though Antipater was present, he played no part;[68] all four left together on the same ship. The mind boggles at the pretense: Antipater seemed pleased, Alexander and Aristobulus seemed reconciled, Herod seemed to have forgotten the whole episode. But no one was content and Augustus's forced reconciliation made no essential difference in the spectacle of a father taking the children of his favored wife to Rome to accuse them of patricide.

Herod sent Augustus a gift of three hundred talents for spectacles and poor relief in Rome; in return he received the management of all and the revenue of half the copper mines in Cyprus. Augustus also confirmed Herod's right to name his own successor.[69] Josephus claims, unconvincingly and without detail, that Herod wished to slough off his responsibilities immediately, but that Augustus refused him permission "to give up control of either his kingdom or his

---

66. *War* 1.452 says only Alexander; *Ant.* 16.90–91 says both, though in the following narrative Alexander takes center stage. It seems certain both were there together.

67. There are important differences. *War* is in indirect speech, *Ant.* in direct speech. In *Ant.* Alexander is hesitant, in *War* he uses powerful oratory because he was "an extremely able speaker" (if he was it was due to his education in Rome a few years earlier). In *Ant.* there is not a word of Antipater, though he was behind some of the allegations; in *War* Alexander "bitterly complained of Antipater's villainy."

68. *Ant.* 16.273 confuses two separate but related aspects of his trip to Rome in 12 BCE. It rightly refers to his accusations against Alexander, but it incorrectly says he had gone to leave Antipater in the care of Augustus. Antipater had gone to Rome the previous year with Marcus Agrippa, but was still in Rome when Herod and Alexander arrived.

69. See *Ant.* 16.127–29; *War* 1.455–56; on the will, see also *Ant.* 16.92 and *War* 1.454. Previously he had the right to name *one* successor; perhaps he now received the right to split the kingdom if he chose. See above, chap. 2.

sons [!] during his lifetime" (*Ant.* 16.129). Their route home took them past Cilicia, where they paused to be entertained by Alexander's father-in-law, Archelaus of Cappadocia (*War* 1.456; *Ant.* 16.131).[70]

<h3 style="text-align:center">THE NABATEAN WAR (12–9 BCE)</h3>

Just as Josephus is confused about the details of Pheroras and Salome, he is also confused about Herod's difficulties with Nabatea and Syllaeus. The troubles came in two stages. Before returning from Rome in 12 BCE there were troubles in Trachonitis on Herod's northeastern flank (*Ant.* 16.130). This region east of Gaulanitis and north of Auranitis had been troubled by brigandage earlier under Zenodorus, when Augustus had ceded it to Herod after its pacification (24/23 BCE; see chaps. 9 and 10). The settlement worked as long as vigilant supervision was given to the region, but the land itself was not good arable land and in Herod's absence revolt flared up. Though his generals looked after the problems, some of the leaders of the revolt crossed the border into Nabatea, not surprisingly, since there was a strong Nabatean influence in Auranitis (*Ant.* 16.130, modified by 16.271). Syllaeus encouraged their resistance to Herod, giving them a fortified place to occupy called Rhaëpta,[71] from which raiding parties "pillaged Judea [and] also all of Coele-Syria."[72] Raids from Nabatea continued for years (perhaps 12–9 BCE), even while Herod took reprisals against their Trachonite relatives. The troubles were worse than Josephus admits, for he refers to Herod "surrounding" Trachonitis—a strange word to use when it was his own territory.

The second stage began when Saturninus and Volumnius took office in Syria in 9 BCE, the former as governor, the latter as military tribune; Herod properly informed them of the raids and demanded punishment of the offenders. The new Roman officials were not yet ready to back Herod in this cross-border venture, so Herod raised the stakes by demanding repayment of a loan to Obodas, who was now in the waning days of his reign. Since Syllaeus held effective control as chief administrator (while angling to succeed Obodas), he was able to deny that the Trachonites were in Nabatea and to delay repayment of the loan. A face-off before Saturninus and Volumnius led to an agreement

---

70. Josephus implies that Herod made a trip to Rome following the reconciliation Archelaus of Cappadocia effected in 9 BCE (*Ant.* 16.271), which may be correct, though if so it fell in 8 BCE, but this cannot be the trip he refers to at this point, since much of the trouble with the Nabateans had to precede that trip. This trip, and those mentioned at 16.273 and 16.130, must be the same trip, the one in 12 BCE.

71. Location not known. Josephus says (*Ant.* 16.275) that this occurred after Syllaeus's failure to marry Salome. See earlier.

72. Josephus means parts of Judea, with parts of Gaulanitis, Batanea, Auranitis, Trachonitis, and Peraea.

between Herod and Syllaeus that the loan would be repaid quickly and that each would return the other's nationals; though no Nabatean nationals were found in Herod's regions, Trachonites were found in Syllaeus's.

These incidents require two comments. (1) While the Trachonite experience should not be generalized, it shows that some subject peoples—and they were subject peoples—were restive under Herod. The region was not altogether typical, but it affords good insight into the type of unrest that arose and the need for strong control. (2) Herod could not act independently; as soon as Nabatea sheltered the leaders, Herod could act only with the permission of the Syrian governor or Augustus. In this instance Saturninus and Volumnius effected a compromise that showed up the Nabatean subterfuge.

Syllaeus's reaction was natural. He went to Rome to complain of Herod's actions and Saturninus's support (*Ant*. 16.282).[73] With Syllaeus in Rome Herod could not intervene in Nabatea directly, but he got permission from Saturninus and Volumnius to attack Rhaëpta.[74] When he was successful, he reported this to the Roman authorities. In Rome, Syllaeus went to Augustus and inflated the devastation and the numbers (from twenty-five killed to twenty-five hundred!). Augustus was interested in only one question: had Herod crossed the border with a military force? The answer: yes.[75] Augustus angrily wrote Herod that from now on he was not a friend but a subject (*Ant*. 16.286–90). Augustus refused to hear Herod's embassy (*Ant*. 16.293). By now Obodas was dead and his position had been taken, without Augustus's permission, by Aretas IV;[76] Syllaeus was quietly working in Rome to be given the throne of Nabatea. Aretas countered by accusing against Syllaeus of poisoning Obodas, exercising royal power, seducing others' wives,[77] and borrowing money to finance his attempt on the throne. Augustus did nothing.

In the meantime (11 or 10 BCE) Herod settled three thousand Idumaeans in Trachonitis—no doubt veterans who were owed land grants—to assist in

73. Syllaeus stopped at the great Temple of Apollo near Miletus on his way to Rome to leave a votive tablet to Jupiter Dusares "for the safety of King 'Aboud" (Obodas), making a reference to "Syllaeus, the brother of the King." See Perowne, p. 155.

74. According to Josephus, *War* 1.474, no other sovereign had been empowered to reclaim fugitive subjects from another state, apparently a reference to this incident.

75. Perowne, p. 155, points out that this was just as Augustus was dedicating the Ara Pacis, the "Altar of Peace." Herod was, in effect, undercutting Augustus's claims to an unrivalled period of peace and security. See also G. W. Bowersock, *Augustus and the Greek World* (Oxford: Clarendon, 1965), p. 56.

76. Why should Augustus feel Nabateans had to consult him on the succession, since he had not yet declared Nabatea within the Roman zone? Rome's tentacles were extending into Nabatea, and that may be reason enough. Syllaeus may have been in Rome mainly to win Augustus's ear and the throne.

77. Strabo claims that Nabateans shared wives, and that children had intercourse with their mothers; *Geog*. 16.4.25–26.

keeping the peace. Now the Trachonites rose against the recently-arrived Idumaeans, while the Nabateans continued to refuse to give over the remaining brigands and to repay the money owed Herod, and Syllaeus, in Rome, enjoyed outwitting Herod (*Ant.* 16.283, 291–92). A little later, Herod created the town of Bathyra on the border between Batanea and Trachonitis,[78] settling it with five hundred Babylonian Jewish cavalry together with another hundred kinsmen under the leadership of Zamaris.[79] Zamaris and his cavalry had found a temporary position in Antioch, but Herod attracted them to his new settlement with generous promises of land, freedom from taxation, exemption from tribute and no further obligations, hoping to create a defensive bulwark (*problêma*) against Trachonitis.[80] The community kept the Trachonite brigands at bay, protected the Babylonian pilgrims going to and from Jerusalem for the festivals, and attracted new settlers—people who were "devoted to the ancestral customs" (so *Ant.* 17.26)[81]—because of its freedom from taxation, though this lasted only as long as Herod lived.[82]

At about this juncture Herod sent Nicolas to Rome to act for him. It was a low point for Herod, when his problems with Nabatea and with Augustus coincided with heightened difficulties with his children.

IN JERUSALEM

The story of Syllaeus required running ahead of Herod's story. To pick up the other main thread, it is necessary to go back to the arrival of Herod and his three sons in Jerusalem late in 12 BCE. They put the best face they could on their strained relationship. Herod called a council of all the people in the Temple to explain what had happened in Rome and, after giving thanks, he admonished his children and his courtiers (*War* 1.457; *Ant.* 16.132–33).[83] He also declared publicly the content of his third will, which reflected the reconciliation: Herod named all three sons successors, with Antipater taking precedence by virtue of age and position in the family,[84] and he resumed the right to name their "advis-

---

78. Location uncertain.

79. It is not clear how many were Jewish. Zamaris was, and the other one hundred were *suggeneis* (in the context, Jews); the mounted archers may not have been.

80. One of the oddities in this is that this was his own territory, subdued years earlier.

81. See *War* 2.461–65; *Life* 55–61, for incidents during the Great Revolt, the implication of which is that this was a pure Babylonian community.

82. *Ant.* 17.27–28 suggests that Philip, Agrippa I, Agrippa II, and the Romans all taxed them, the latter three heavily. On the next couple of generations, see *Ant.* 17.29–31; *Life* 46–61, 177–80, 407–409; *War* 2.421. One of them, Philip, figures prominently as Agrippa II's lieutenant.

83. At crucial moments Herod sometimes called general public meetings, as now and in 7 BCE during the crisis with Alexander and Aristobulus; see *War* 1.550.

84. It seems likeliest that Antipater was designated successor, with Alexander and Aristobulus his successors in turn. It may have been, however, that all three inherited in some unequal fashion as his last will stipulated. See earlier, chap. 2, and *War* 1.458–65; *Ant.* 16.133.

ers and attendants" (*syngeneis kai philoi; War* 1.460). He warned people neither to discount him because of his age (about sixty-two) nor to fawn over his children.

In the same year (12 BCE) Herod celebrated the completion of the construction of Caesarea Maritima and its splendid harbor[85] with quadrennial games. Livia sent some of her best treasures from Rome; envoys came from cities Herod had endowed in one way or another; spectacles and feasts were laid on. The magnificence of the new city made Judea a major player in the Mediterranean rim of countries—a place it had not had before. From now on Judea would take its place among the nations of the world, especially in the new trade opportunities such a port opened up. It is doubtful that anyone then alive had seen such a massive new city built virtually from scratch in a decade, with the potential to influence the fortunes of the country.[86]

With the increased fractiousness of his household (*Ant.* 16.188), the resentment of Alexander and Aristobulus and the manipulations of Antipater continued.[87] Supposed friends of the two brothers ("traitors") reported their words to Antipater, and magnified reports then found their way to Herod. Antipater kept his own thoughts and actions sufficiently discreet that they could be described as a "mystery of iniquity" (*kakias mystêrion, War* 1.470). He gave the impression of defending his two younger brothers, while subtly confirming the whispered accounts of their words and thoughts, making himself blameless and the king more suspicious.[88] In a relatively short period Antipater had insinuated himself into the most powerful position in the family. The king's siblings, Salome and Pheroras, supported Antipater, as did Ptolemy, the king's chief financial officer

85. The dating is awkward: in *Ant.* 16.136 Josephus refers to the tenth year of work and he refers to the twenty-eighth year of Herod's reign (from 40 BCE = 13/12, from 37 = 10/9); he also refers to the 192nd Olympiad, which would have begun in 12 BCE. At 15.341 he says twelve years of work. The best solution is that the construction was begun in 22, took 9/10 years, and was finished in 12 BCE.

86. Hoping to replenish his coffers for yet more grandiloquent benefactions, Herod broke open the tombs of David and Solomon, having heard that Hyrcanus I, a century earlier, had taken three thousand talents of silver and had left even more behind. He was disappointed and was deterred from further exploration by divine punishment of two persons helping him. Out of fear he built a new marble memorial at the mouth of the tombs to honor his two famous predecessors (*Ant.* 16.179–83); no remains have yet been found. See H. Shanks, "The Tombs of Silwan," *BAR* 20/3 (1994), pp. 38–51, esp. 49–51.

87. The account in *Ant.* 16.188–205 parallels *War* 1.467–84. The preceding section in *Ant.* 16.127–87 is full of awkward transitions and jumps in the narrative flow. Comparison with fragmentary parallels in *War* and elsewhere in *Ant.* underscores what Josephus himself tells us in 185–89, that he is using diverse sources and deliberately balancing the impression given by those sources, especially Nicolas, with a reading more favorable to the Hasmoneans, with whom Josephus links himself. The whole section is a patchwork.

88. *War* 1.467–72; *Ant.* 16.188–90, referring to the dissension in the palace being "like a civil war": *stasis gar ên hôsper emphyliou polemou kata tên aulên.*

and trusted friend,[89] and of course Doris, now in residence, conspired against her stepsons. The result was an inexorable flow of support away from Alexander and Aristobulus.[90] Their position was worsened by Glaphyra, Alexander's wife, who disdained everyone else in Herod's family, commoners all, including Herod's other wives. She almost succeeded in uniting the opposition (*War* 1.473–77; *Ant.* 16.191–93).[91] The palace, though split more or less along two-party lines, had a number of sub-plots being played out.

Herod may have sailed once again to Rome; if so, it was a brief and unexceptional visit whose purpose is not recorded.[92] It would have fallen early in the year 8 BCE after Augustus had ended his absence from Rome due to grief over the death of Drusus; Augustus left Rome later in 8 BCE on a campaign with Tiberius against the Germans (Cassius Dio 55–56). The visit may have had to do with obsequies connected with Drusus's death or more likely with the fourth anniversary of Agrippa's funeral, commemorated by gladiatorial contests in which everyone present wore black.[93] As with his previous absence in Rome, Pheroras and Salome—who must have patched up their earlier quarrel—used the time to undercut Alexander and Aristobulus further (*War* 1.483).

---

89. It is not as clear to me as it seems to most that there are two Ptolemies, one the brother of Nicolas (*War* 2.21; *Ant.* 17.225) and one the chief financial person (e.g., *War* 2.14, 16, 24; *Ant.* 17.219, 221, 228). They may be the same person, Nicolas's brother. While they seem associated with a different claimant to the throne in 4 BCE, this is more likely the result of sloppy writing or editing.

90. This impression is later altered during Josephus's account of the aftermath of the execution of Alexander and Aristobulus, where Antipater is less popular than the two brothers. While this ebbing and flowing of support is not impossible, it is more likely that Josephus's reports come from different sources who reflect their own opinions, and that those sources reflect quite discrete pockets of opinion, with Alexander and Aristobulus having support from the old nobility and Hasmonean supporters while Antipater has the support of pro-Herodian and anti-Hasmonean—perhaps "new"—nobles.

91. According to *Ant.* 16.193, Glaphyra's actions flowed from love of her husband and were directed especially against Salome's daughter Berenice, who was married to her brother-in-law Aristobulus. Though these relationships are convoluted, it is still hard to see how Alexander and Aristobulus could be so closely associated together when their two wives were at war with each other, and how Salome could work so hard for the young men's downfall when her own daughter would be implicated in their loss of status. According to *War* 1.478–80 (see *Ant.* 16.203–204), the problem was Aristobulus, who reproached Berenice for being a commoner while Glaphyra was a princess. She promised her mother that Herod's other wives would become weavers and the royal children village clerks in the future. *Ant.* 16.201 adds the further twist that Salome persuaded Berenice to withhold sexual relations from Aristobulus.

92. It is not supported by other evidence. It is possible that he stopped, either going or coming, at the Olympic Games. He was made President either at the Games of 12 or 8 BCE, the date is not certain.

93. M. Agrippa died in 12 BCE and was buried in Augustus's own mausoleum (Cassius Dio 54.28). Cassius Dio dates the commemoration to the year that Tiberius and Piso were consuls, 7 BCE, though he is imprecise (Cassius Dio 55.8). A celebration in 8 BCE, i.e., in the fifth year after

ARCHELAUS, EURYCLES, AND EUNUCHS

As the household tragedy continued to unfold, Josephus refers more and more often to evidence—notoriously unreliable—obtained under torture. What follows is tainted both by Josephus's motives and by the purported base on which it rests. Three trusted eunuchs in Herod's entourage were accused of, and confessed to, sexual relations with Alexander. Under further torture ("to please Antipater") they added that Alexander said his father was an old man with only a short time left who even died his hair black to appear young! Alexander was determined to inherit and had already, the eunuchs said, got leading men on his side, including generals (*War* 1.488–91; *Ant.* 16.229–34).

Herod overreacted; he instituted a reign of terror in which charges and counter-charges crisscrossed. No one was immune. In his near-paranoia (*War* 1.492–94; *Ant.* 16.235–40) he withdrew, leaving him even more at the mercy of family members who had axes to grind. Chief of these was Antipater, who spread more rumors about Alexander. When Herod submitted Alexander's friends to torture, he took their denials to be confirmation of their loyalty to Alexander and thus of the truth of the charges (*War* 1.493–95; *Ant.* 16.241–46). Under torture, one friend described how Alexander deliberately pretended to be shorter and less skillful in hunting than his father, but he added—much more dangerously—that Alexander and Aristobulus were planning to assassinate Herod in a hunting "accident," then go to Rome to seek Augustus's confirmation (*War* 1.496; *Ant.* 16.247–49).[94] When the palace was searched for evidence, it only turned up a letter from Aristobulus to Alexander complaining about Antipater's responsibilities and income (16.250).

All this confirmed Herod's fears about Alexander. Herod had him arrested (*War* 1.496; *Ant.* 16.251); in his more rational moments he still thought his son was not guilty, but he continued to look for evidence and torture Alexander's confidantes to get at the truth. Another of those "confidantes" revealed a plan in which Alexander's Roman friends would get Augustus to call Alexander to Rome, where he would accuse Herod of secret dealings with Parthia; in another plan, Alexander had poison ready for use (*Ant.* 16.251–53). In a bizarre episode, Alexander wrote "four books" in which he admitted to a conspiracy,[95] implicating Pheroras and Salome too. He even accused Salome of forcing him

---

his death, seems just as likely, since there was no fixed interval for such a commemoration; one was held for Drusus, who died in 9 BCE, in 6 CE (Cassius Dio 55.27).

94. In *War* this is called a falsehood; in *Ant.* it is not, and the confession is not under direct torture.

95. If by "book" (*biblos*) Josephus means what he himself calls a book, four books was a large document. Josephus excuses Alexander's actions on flimsy grounds: "perverse pride," "to punish his father's rashness," "to shame Herod," "to injure the kingdom" (*Ant.* 16.255), "to confront the perils," to attack "his enemies" (*War* 1.498).

to have sex with her (*Ant.* 16.256). Faced with these revelations, Herod sank more deeply into his tormented imaginings (*Ant.* 16.257–60).

At this stage (about 10 BCE) a voice of sanity appeared in the person of Alexander's father-in-law, Archelaus of Cappadocia, pretending indignation by saying he intended to execute his daughter and his son-in-law if Herod had not already done so. He reproached Herod for being too lenient. He gradually shifted blame away from Alexander onto others, especially Pheroras, using "chapter after chapter" of Alexander's four books. His conclusion was that since Alexander enjoyed high honor and expected to succeed Herod it was clear that Alexander had no reason to act against Herod (*War* 1.499–503; *Ant.* 16.261–66). This left Pheroras high and dry for having manipulated—or having seemed to manipulate—Alexander into opposition to his father. Archelaus, still playing the reconciler, manoeuvred Pheroras into confessing *his* guilt and asking Herod's forgiveness, while Archelaus stood beside Herod reinforcing the need for healing and reconciliation (*War* 1.504–507; *Ant.* 16.267–69), though he so indignantly argued for Alexander's divorce from Glaphyra that Herod swung around and insisted on maintaining the marriage (*War* 1.508–509). Archelaus achieved his goals brilliantly by playing on Herod's changeable nature. He returned to Cappadocia with rich presents, some eunuchs, and a concubine, escorted as far as Antioch by Herod and his court (*Ant.* 16.511–12; *War* 1.269–70).[96] Archelaus of Cappadocia wrote a report to Augustus on the affair, and recommended that Herod (or possibly Alexander?) go to Rome.[97]

In a parallel but destructive scene, Archelaus's reconciliation was totally undone by Eurycles of Sparta, acting with opaque motives.[98] Eurycles became

---

96. The concubine's name was Pannychis, meaning "All night"! At Antioch, Herod reconciled Archelaus with the governor, Marcus Titius. His period of office is not certain, but it must fall between 13 and 9 BCE, thus giving a *terminus ante quem* for this phase of Herod's family troubles. The result, 12–10 BCE or so, is not far wrong.

97. *War* 1.510 for both points, though my interpretation differs from Thackeray's translation; in the context *auton* could refer to Herod but seems not to ("the latter" in Thackeray's translation); it would be more natural to refer to the object of the previous clause, Alexander. In *Ant.* 16.270 the wording is almost as ambiguous, but in different ways. It is probable, but not certain, that it was Herod who agreed to go to Rome, but an impersonal is used of the written communication with Augustus (3 p. sg. perf. pass.; "it had been written"). Josephus himself misunderstands the situation; he carelessly connects an explicit allusion to a trip to Rome in the next sentence (*Ant.* 16.271; see later) with the hint that Herod may have gone to Rome. This can only refer to his earlier trip in 12 (cf. *Ant.* 16.130). I conclude that Augustus was informed, and that it was not clear who went to Rome (if anyone did) as a result of this conversation.

98. Gaius Julius Eurycles fought alongside Octavian at Actium, as a result of which he became a Roman citizen and ruler of Sparta. Herod probably got to know him on his visit to Olympia in 12 or 8 BCE (Eurycles is best known for his baths in Corinth, noted in Pausanias, east of the Lechaion Road); Augustus banished him around 2 BCE. See G. W. Bowersock, "Eurycles in Sparta," *JRS* 51 (1961):112–18; Bowersock, "Augustus and the East: The Problem of the Succession," in F. Millar and E. Segal, eds., *Caesar Augustus. Seven Aspects* (Oxford: Clarendon, 1984), pp.

a friend of Antipater and a supposed friend of Alexander and Aristobulus, though he intended, according to Josephus, to bring about the latters' deaths. Eurycles worked on Herod's fears, presenting Alexander as a potential patricide and praising Antipater as a loyal son. At the same time, the two brothers were accused of suborning the military leaders.[99] Eurycles soon left, but he had done his damage. A few years later he was banished by Augustus.[100]

Herod put Alexander and Aristobulus under house arrest (*Ant.* 16.320–21), though this was swiftly changed to chains when Aristobulus threatened Salome about Syllaeus and she took preemptive action by telling Herod (16.322–24). Salome must still have been attracted to Syllaeus, even during an intense conflict with Nabatea, so that an accusation that she "betrayed to [Syllaeus] all the things that were happening here" had added point (*Ant.* 16.322). Glaphyra was implicated in a scheme to flee to Rome via Cappadocia and her powerful father (*Ant.* 16.325–34; *War* 1.534–35). Volumnius, the military legate of Syria, and Olympus, a friend of Herod's, went to Rome with an account of the latest steps in the saga (7 BCE), stopping in Cappadocia to inform Archelaus of the danger his daughter—and by implication he—faced. Volumnius's presence may suggest continuing problems between Herod and the Nabateans, to which he could speak directly as military tribune; Olympus apparently was carrying Herod's information and requests concerning his children (*War* 1.535–36; *Ant.* 16.332–34).

THE EXECUTION OF ALEXANDER AND ARISTOBULUS

In Rome the messengers learned that Nicolas had successfully reconciled Herod and Augustus, undermined Syllaeus by exploiting dissensions within the Nabatean delegation, and documented Syllaeus's treachery (*Ant.* 16.335–38). A hearing pitted Syllaeus, Nicolas, and representatives of Aretas against each other, with Nicolas accusing Syllaeus of causing the deaths of Obodas and his friends,

---

169–88; Schalit, pp. 616–20. A supposed relationship between Jews and Spartans might have accounted for the beginning of a friendship between the two rulers (*Ant.* 12.226; 1 Macc. 12:21); I am obliged to a lecture by Christopher Jones for this background. On the incident see *War* 1.513–30; *Ant.* 16.300–310.

99. There was a letter to the commander of Alexandreion, which, Josephus explains, Alexander said was Herod's secretary's work; Josephus also claims that the secretary was ultimately put to death for forgery and that under torture the commander of Alexandreion did not shed any light on matters. Josephus holds back from saying that Alexander was not guilty. The accusation involved Jucundus and Tyrannus (in *War* 1.527 commanders of the king's cavalry, in *Ant.* 16.314 bodyguards); the details in *Ant.* 16.315–16 seem a doublet of the earlier accusation of a feigned hunting accident.

100. At the same time Euarestus of Cos, another Greek visitor, was in Judea (*War* 1,532–33; *Ant.* 16.312, differently but defectively); he was a friend of Alexander and spoke very positively to Herod about him.

borrowing money for illegal uses, committing adultery with Nabatean and Roman women, and deceiving Augustus—much the most serious charge (16.339–40). When Augustus raised old matters, especially Herod's invasion of Nabatea, Nicolas had the opening he needed to defend Herod. He told of Herod's loan to Syllaeus, his unsuccessful attempts to recover the money peacefully with Volumnius's and Saturninus's help, and their approval of Herod's limited action against Nabatea when faced with the Trachonites' revolt (16.341–50). Syllaeus's defense crumbled, and Augustus condemned him to death but sent him back first to face his creditors. Augustus was then reconciled to Herod.[101]

Augustus's nose was still out of joint because Aretas IV had not consulted him before declaring himself king (9 BCE). Augustus intended, therefore, to cede Nabatea to Herod, but he changed his mind when Olympus and Volumnius gave him Herod's letters about his sons. These revealed clearly the extent of Herod's family difficulties and his inability to take on new responsibilities, especially ones that would be as controversial as Nabatean matters. In the end Augustus confirmed Aretas IV as ruler of Nabatea (*Ant.* 16.351–55).[102]

Augustus did not interfere in the decisions about Herod's children;[103] he advised that if the children had been planning to assassinate Herod he should punish them accordingly and if they had only been planning to flee, as they maintained, he should merely admonish them. He instructed Herod to convene a council to hear the case in Berytus,[104] including at least Saturninus, governor of Syria, and Archelaus, king of Cappadocia (16.356–60).[105] Saturninus presided (*War* 1.538; in *Ant.* 16.368 he is a participant);[106] Alexander and Aristobulus were not allowed to be present.

Herod himself led off for the prosecution, exaggerating the evidence from their letters (*Ant.* 16.362–66; *War* 1.540). Saturninus thought the young men guilty, but not of a capital offense; Volumnius argued for a harsh sentence, with others present following Volumnius's view (*War* 1.541–42; *Ant.* 16.369). Since

---

101. This brief summary may be garbled. Syllaeus was allowed to return to Nabatea, possibly under some restrictions; it is unlikely that he had been condemned to death, given his subsequent role in the story; see later. Strabo says he was beheaded and implies that this took place in Rome; *Geog.* 16.782.

102. Aretas had a long and brilliant reign; he was responsible for many of the most innovative structures at Petra and for securing the independence of Nabatea for another century. Had Nabatea been given to Herod, the history of the whole region would have been different.

103. On the ends of Alexander and Aristobulus, Schalit, pp. 620–28.

104. See Millar, *Roman Near East,* pp. 274–85, 527–28, on Berytus as the one Roman colony of the region and a center of Latin and Roman culture and law.

105. *War* 1.537 omits the reference to Archelaus; in *Ant.* 16.360 Herod chose deliberately not to invite Archelaus.

106. *War* lists some of the participants: Saturninus, Pedamius (his legate), Salome, Pheroras, the aristocracy of Syria, except for Archelaus, some of Herod's friends.

the council's decision was only advisory, Herod could be as severe or lenient as whim dictated. He went to Tyre, where he met Nicolas on his way back from Rome (*Ant.* 16.370–72; *War* 1.543), who reported that opinion in Rome was that he should merely imprison the brothers.

On reaching Caesarea Maritima, Herod's barber and an old soldier whose son knew Alexander and Aristobulus tried to intervene; they and others suspected of siding with the brothers were stoned to death.[107] Alexander and Aristobulus were taken to Sebaste and strangled, then buried at Alexandreion (*War* 1.551; *Ant.* 16.394).

So ended the protracted affair of Mariamme I's two sons, the last of the Hasmoneans. Their execution—no matter how guilty they were—went beyond Herod's immediate need for security. It was a cold-blooded decision that Herod had considered for years and only now felt appropriate, even against the advice of reasonable persons. The length of time Herod meditated upon it makes it today, as then, repulsive. Herod in fact had nothing to fear from his sons, for Augustus would never allow patricides to succeed to the throne, since it would be a threat to peace and stability. Herod's reign was secure as long as he lived, and his ability to name his successor allowed him to stymie undue ambition after his death. If they had fled, they might have sniped at Herod but could not have dislodged him.

The final scene in this awful tragedy occurred in 7 BCE, the same year that Jesus was born,[108] when Herod is held to have massacred the "innocents" in Bethlehem (Matt. 2.16–18, citing Jer. 31:15). It seems likely that Herod's killing of his own children prompted the report of his murder of a larger group of children (see chap. 12). It is for this New Testament account that Herod has been remembered in stained glass and sculpture, especially in the medieval period that so loved the drama of extreme actions. Of the execution of his own children, the more terrible act, there is hardly a trace.

ANTIPATER

The main beneficiary of the executions of Alexander and Aristobulus was Antipater, because he was now Herod's best possibility as successor; Salome and Pheroras also benefitted through weathering the suspicions against themselves. Antipater became virtual co-ruler with Herod, yet the military opposed him and the people—who seemed to know that the recent executions were largely his doing—hated him. Antipater's worry over other rivals prompted him to

---

107. Three hundred in number according to *Ant.* (*War* 1.544–50; *Ant.* 16.373–93).

108. This date is predicated on the association of the "star" of Bethlehem with a triple conjunction of planets in that year.

take several defensive actions (*War* 1.552; *Ant.* 17.1–4):[109] he tried to buy Pheroras's support, sent presents to friends in Rome, and showered gifts on Saturninus and his staff in Syria (*War* 1.553–55; *Ant.* 17.6).

Herod, now sixty-eight or sixty-nine, had a large, complex, and warring family. He had to put his house in order if it were to survive. He still had nine wives (Josephus says all nine were still alive and living in the palace), seven sons, and five daughters, most of whom still survived (*War* 1.562–63; *Ant.* 17.19–22).[110] The details are covered in the text and table in chapter 2. His actions show his marriage policy at work. (1) He sent Glaphyra with her dowry back to her father in Cappadocia. (2) At Antipater's suggestion, he married Berenice (Aristobulus's widow) to Theudion, Antipater's mother's brother. (3) He married Salome to Alexas over Salome's vigorous objections, but with the support of the Empress Livia. (4) He provided for the upbringing of the seven children of Alexander and Aristobulus. (5) He promised Pheroras's daughter to Tigranes. (6) He betrothed a younger Mariamme (daughter of Aristobulus) to a son of Antipater. (7) He betrothed Herodias (another daughter of Aristobulus) to his own son Herod. (8) He married one of Salome's daughters to Alexas's son. In short, he tried to secure family interdependence by a series of interlocking marriages, hoping to reduce further internecine strife. He also, of course, aimed to secure the succession of the family line (*War* 1.552–53, 556–58; *Ant.* 17.12–15). Antipater was unhappy with these arrangements; he worried over the position of Pheroras and the interference of Archelaus of Cappadocia. Still, he was powerful enough at this stage to arrange his own marriage to Mariamme, the daughter of Aristobulus (*Ant.* 17.16–18; *War* 1.559–62).

With Herod disintegrating and withdrawing from effective participation, an alliance was formed between Antipater and Pheroras (*War* 1.567; *Ant.* 17.32–33). Party to this were four women: Pheroras's wife, mother, sister, and Doris, Antipater's mother. This "gang of four" behaved arrogantly toward Herod's youngest daughters, now about ten years old. Through most of the household troubles Salome and Pheroras had been allies; now, in the face of Antipater's power, they took different sides (as they had done once before), Pheroras with Antipater and Salome against him (*War* 1.568–70; *Ant.* 17.34–40).

Pharisees played an unexpected role in these internal dissensions. Pheroras's

---

109. Josephus mentions that Alexander and Glaphyra had two sons, Tigranes and Alexander; Aristobulus and Berenice had three sons and two daughters: Herod, Agrippa, Aristobulus, Herodias, and Mariamme. It is curious that these should enter the account, for they all were less than ten years of age at the time of their fathers' executions, whereas Antipater's other half-brothers were coming into an age when they could be perceived as rivals; Archelaus, for example, was now about sixteen.

110. There is an error in the translation in the Loeb edition at *War* 1.562, which refers to Antipas, not Antipater as the text says.

wife and the other women, Josephus claims, were deeply influenced by Pharisees to oppose Herod (see also chap. 10). On a previous occasion Pheroras's wife—his first wife—had paid their fine, so it is odd that here too it was his wife—his second wife—who conspired with the Pharisees.[111] The story of ambition and dissension may require modification to allow for religious differences prompted by the Pharisees.[112] It is worth noting that Doris—a Samaritan—participated in the discussions, and Salome—who may still have wanted to marry a Nabatean—objected. Herod ordered Antipater to end all connection with this group (*War* 1.572) and may have executed some of the secondary figures who followed Pharisaic beliefs (*Ant.* 17.44–45). He dealt with Pheroras's wife in a council, urging Pheroras to divorce her and ordering that she and Doris not meet. Despite these actions, Pheroras and Antipater continued their plotting; there was even a rumor that Antipater and Pheroras's wife had had an affair (*Ant.* 17.41–51; *War* 1.571–72). Antipater's position was not secure, despite the fact that he was Herod's heir (with Herod, Mariamme II's son, designated as his successor).

Antipater arranged with friends in Rome to be invited there (6 BCE), arguing that he should see Augustus and participate in the action against Syllaeus currently taking place (*War* 1.573; *Ant.* 17.52–53).[113] Syllaeus faced accusations by Antipater on the same issues raised earlier by Nicolas, by Aretas IV (in Petra) on grounds of unlawful executions, by Herod (in Jerusalem) on charges of bad debts, and by Fabatus (also in Rome) regarding subversion of Herod's guard (*War* 1.575–77; *Ant.* 17.54–57).[114] It is impossible to give a coherent account of Syllaeus's end: Strabo, who knew of his career, says laconically, "But the man who was responsible for this failure [of Aelius Gallus], I mean Syllaeus, paid the penalty at Rome, since, although he proclaimed friendship, he was convicted, in addition to his rascality in this matter, of other offenses too, and was beheaded."[115] One of his other offenses may have been assistance in procuring poison with which to assassinate Pheroras (*War* 1.583; *Ant.* 17.63).

---

111. Josephus continues to be imprecise about Pheroras's wife, who must be, as I have argued above, not Alexander's daughter but the ex-slave. It strikes an odd note that she was in the vanguard in these events.

112. At *Ant.* 17.43 the Pharisees, who could foretell the future, predicted that the royal power would come to Pheroras and his wife and children. If I am right in the reconstruction that Pheroras's wife is an ex-slave, the marriage could hardly have been seen as promising by Pharisees.

113. Josephus says Syllaeus went to Rome again, after a period of freedom following the previous case against him led by Nicolas. It is not clear why Syllaeus would go back to Rome to carry on his action against Herod; nevertheless, it is unlikely that Augustus had already decided on Syllaeus's death (*War* 1.574; *Ant.* 17.54).

114. Perhaps the Nabatean issues loomed especially large at just this moment because of renewed threats from Armenia and Parthia in 6 BCE; see Cassius Dio 55.10.

115. Strabo, *Geog.* 16.782, an exact contemporary and perhaps even in Rome at this period. Josephus, who knows and uses Strabo, does not refer to Syllaeus's end, nor does his account refer

In the meantime, Herod banished both Pheroras and his wife, though strangely he did not reduce his brother's authority in Peraea, to which they went. When Herod believed he was dying, Pheroras refused to return to see him; yet when Pheroras himself lay dying a short while later, Herod visited and cared for him, giving rise to a (false) report that Herod had poisoned Pheroras. Herod had Pheroras's body brought to Jerusalem in state, declared national mourning, and gave him an impressive funeral (*War* 1.578–81; *Ant.* 17.58–60). Shortly after the funeral rites, two of Pheroras's freedmen claimed he had been poisoned, implicating his wife in the use of poison masquerading as an aphrodisiac that came from Nabatea, either from Syllaeus or Syllaeus's widow. Herod reverted to more torture, which resulted in more accusations against Doris, Pheroras, and Antipater (*War* 1.582–90; *Ant.* 17.61–67). Salome's long-standing opposition to Doris now bore fruit, as Doris was divorced a second time and stripped of Herod's gifts (*War* 1.590; *Ant.* 17.68).

Soon another plot emerged implicating Antipater and Pheroras's wife in a poison attempt on Herod, while Antipater was in Rome, safely away from all suspicion. Pheroras's wife confessed, but she threw herself from the palace roof in an unsuccessful suicide attempt (*War* 1.592–94; *Ant.* 17.69–71), after which she accused Mariamme II.[116] Yet another accusation was made against Antipater, claiming he had sent a vial of poison to Doris to be used against Herod. There was another scheme to undercut Archelaus and Philip (currently in Rome for their education) through forged letters suggesting they were constantly complaining of their father (*War* 1.601–603; *Ant.* 17.79–81).[117] Herod brought the two young men back to Jerusalem.

Although the stew had been bubbling in Jerusalem for seven months, Antipater had apparently not had a whiff of it in Rome, though this seems almost miraculous.[118] With no sense of his own danger he wrote Herod that he was returning to Judea; Herod replied with news of the death of Pheroras, and in a second friendly letter he told him not to delay, promising vaguely to drop his complaints against Doris (*War* 1.608–609; *Ant.* 17.83–85). By now Antipater was on his guard, worried about his mother and the implications of Herod's divorcing her. Friends argued that he should not go on to Judea with the situa-

---

to treasonable conduct in the Arabian expedition. Though it is difficult to fit together all the factors in the story of Syllaeus, especially his almost three years on the loose in Nabatea (i.e., from about 9 to 6 BCE) while Aretas IV was in power, the execution was probably in Rome and in 6/5 BCE. There is a need for a study of Syllaeus.

116. Herod divorced her, relieved her father, Simon son of Boethos, of his high-priestly duties, and struck her son Herod from his will (*War* 1.595–600; *Ant.* 17.72–78).

117. Archelaus was now about sixteen years of age, Philip about fourteen.

118. Josephus attributes this variously to hatred of Antipater (none of the visitors from Jerusalem told him), to the "spirits of his murdered brothers" sealing everyone's lips (*War* 1.606; *Ant.* 17.82), to Herod's care in guarding the roads, and to fear for people's own safety (*Ant.* 17.82).

tion unclear, but others thought that his presence and the force of his personality would dissipate all suspicion. He sailed for Caesarea Maritima in late summer, 5 BCE (*War* 1.609–12; *Ant.* 17.86–87).

When he landed he immediately realized he was in deep trouble. Everyone either avoided him or abused him (*Ant.* 17.88; *War* 1.614). He could not escape, yet he still did not know the charges he might have to face, so he put on a brave front and determined to try to brazen his way through (*War* 1.615–16). Antipater was now about forty years old, experienced, ruthless, a survivor; he had been back in the royal court for ten years or so, during which he had rehabilitated his mother, eliminated his rivals, established links with some other family members, had himself named heir, shared Herod's royal power, and become a friend to Augustus. Given such remarkable successes, how could vague suspicions promoted while he was absent in Rome undercut his established position and a vigorous assertion of innocence?

Anticipating Antipater's arrival, Herod had asked Publius Quintilius Varus, the new governor of Syria, to visit Jerusalem and advise him in the matter of his son,[119] whom Varus must have known, since he had been consul (with Tiberius) in 13 BCE when Antipater was first introduced to Roman society by Marcus Agrippa. When Antipater entered his father's presence alone—his friends had been stopped at the palace gates—he received a cold reception and was told to prepare for his defense the next day on charges of attempted patricide. Only when he met his mother and his wife did he learn the whole story (*War* 1.617–19; *Ant.* 17.89–92).

Herod convened a council; relatives and friends, including friends of Antipater, were allowed to attend. Varus presided (Herod and Varus together according to *War*), with Herod as chief prosecutor against his son and Nicolas as assistant, leading some of the evidence. Antipater responded effectively (*War* 1.620–35; *Ant.* 17.93–105), so that at this stage there was a good bit of sympathy for him, even by Varus.[120] In round two Nicolas was at the forefront with a stinging indictment of Antipater (reported in detail in *Antiquities*) and an ineffective defense by Antipater calling on God as his witness. At the close, Varus

---

119. Varus was governor of Syria 6–4 BCE, after having been proconsul of Africa 7–6 BCE; he was married to Augustus's grand-niece. Perhaps Augustus dispatched him to the East because he had had experience there and because he thought Herod was becoming senile, so Bowersock, *Augustus and the Greek World,* p.22 (he suggests the same thing about Quirinius, pp. 24–25, 29, 42). The troubles after the death of Herod are known collectively as "Varus's War" in the Talmud, because he played such an important part. He committed suicide after sustaining one of Rome's worst-ever defeats in the Teutoberg Forest at the hands of Arminius in 9 CE (see Cassius Dio 56.18–24).

120. Herod's reactions are unclear; in *War* 1.636 he is furious, "knowing that the evidence [of Antipater] was true"; in *Ant.* 17.106 he is "shaken in his purpose, although unwilling to let this be seen."

left for Antioch after interviewing Herod privately and sending a report to Augustus (so *War* 1.637–40; see *Ant.* 17.106–32).

Only a few of the details are important to this analysis. (1) The prosecution presented an intercepted letter from Doris to Antipater as an opening step; the letter urged him not to return because the game was up. There was no refutation of this damaging evidence. (2) The prosecution argued that Antipater was utterly ruthless, for he already shared Herod's power and authority. (3) The prosecution's main point was that Antipater had engineered the executions of Alexander and Aristobulus and had fomented the family dissensions. (4) It was also contended that Antipater had involved Pheroras in the plot against Herod, turning Pheroras into a potential fratricide. There was no formal finding of guilt or innocence and no sentence. Antipater was imprisoned, waiting for Augustus's advice following the report to him.[121] No news was released to the population at large (*Ant.* 17.133).

What of Antipater's guilt? Certainly he was guilty of sowing dissension and of scheming to establish his own precedence, but those are not capital crimes. He was probably guilty of the fundamental accusation of scheming directly against Herod. (1) He was ambitious and forceful, and anxious to have sole rule in his father's place. (2) He had positioned himself both in Rome and in Judea to take over smoothly after Herod's death. (3) The circumstantial details, to which he had little defense except the most general responses, do not seem plausibly to have been fabricated by Herod or Nicolas or others (the Acme affair is the least plausibly fabricated).[122] (4) Though family tensions did not begin with his arrival on the scene in 14 BCE, they increased all the time he was involved. There are factors that seem to exonerate him: Augustus's (implied) support and Herod's paranoia weaken the accusations against Antipater. But there are few positive actions by Antipater that demonstrate "filial piety": he was thoroughly roguish, and he was embittered by years of exile and by Herod's obvious preference for his children by Mariamme. Yet Antipater must have been able, decisive, and energetic—cunning and malicious though he may also have been.

Herod restrained his instinct to execute Antipater immediately; he made renewed charges of plotting against him and of abusing Augustus's kindnesses.[123]

---

121. In *War*, by Varus, in *Antiquities*, by Herod, supplemented by an oral report.

122. At the same time these observations tend toward the conclusion that Alexander and Aristobulus were not guilty. But in this matter as in everything else we are so much at Josephus's mercy in the way he presents the information; it is his view, of course, that the other two were not guilty and that Antipater was.

123. In a last twist, there were charges of a plot, involving Acme, a Jewish slave to Augustus's wife Julia, who forged letters in Rome carried to Jerusalem concealed in a slave's tunic, all prompted by Salome's wish to marry the Nabatean Syllaeus. The details are Byzantine and do not matter much, except that the existence of the forged letter, according to *War* 1.644, made Herod wonder if the earlier letters implicating Alexander and Aristobulus had also been forgeries.

When Antipater remained silent, Herod thought to send him to Augustus (*War* 1.641–44; *Ant.* 17.134–43); but fearing Antipater's charm and his contacts in Rome he changed his mind again, held him in detention, and sent envoys to Rome with the evidence and a report (*War* 1.644–45; *Ant.* 17.144–45). At this point, now early winter 5/4 BCE, Herod fell seriously ill. He made a new will (see chap. 2), passing over Archelaus and Philip, for unstated reasons, in favor of Antipas, who was now sixteen or seventeen years of age, making generous provisions for Augustus and Livia and Salome (*War* 1.646; *Ant.* 17.146–47). His illness worsened and his behavior became unpredictable.

The end of the story, with Antipater's execution, is found in chapter 1 and need not be repeated; it includes the eagle incident, Herod's removal to Jericho, his final illness, death, and burial, and the dithering in Rome among the various claimants. Though it is not pretty, it is dramatic.

CHAPTER 12

The Herods and Christianity

HEROD: THE BIRTH OF JESUS AND THE MASSACRE OF THE CHILDREN

This study has focused on Herod—his world, policies, relationships, and character. There has been little opportunity to draw connections between him and the beginnings of Christianity, yet the connections of Herod and of his descendants with the early church were important to the nascent movement.

Herod's piety, for which I have in a limited way argued, did not extend to matters of theology, Torah, the future, or God's role for Israel—let alone issues such as sin, redemption, and atonement. He was a practical person, uninterested in differences of opinion or sectarian withdrawal from society unless those things affected him or the stability of his reign. Herod was a Jew; but Herod's Judaism, no doubt like that of many others, was simple and uncluttered. More significant for him was the maintenance of the faith of Israel alongside support for the Imperial cult. He had little interest in the messianic speculations that occupied some groups—such as those behind the DSS or early Christianity—within the apocalyptic stream of Judaism.[1] He may have been radically opposed to them, but his relatively benign attitude toward Essenes cautions against an overly simple view that Herod aimed to stamp out all messianic ideas.

One of the problems in assessing the New Testament accounts of the birth of Jesus is that messianic convictions motivated the New Testament writers. Matthew and Luke were convinced that Jesus fulfilled expectations for a coming messiah—a kingly messiah, even if not a "king" in the traditional sense of the word. It is not surprising, therefore, that in their own ways they weave their accounts of Jesus' birth around the conviction that he was the coming one

---

1. A recently published fragment from Qumran, 4Q521, is strikingly like a messianic description from an early strand of Jesus traditions in Luke 7:18–23.

of intertestamental expectation. This necessarily required that Jesus as messiah and Herod as king conflict directly in the birth accounts.

Is it plausible that Herod knew of Jesus' birth? When was this birth? How much overlap was there between Herod and Jesus? Though neither the birth nor the death of Jesus can be securely dated, I conclude that he was born in 7 BCE and died in 33 CE. His birth must have occurred before the death of Herod (Matt. 2:1; Luke 1:5), still to be dated—despite recent challenges—to just before Passover 4 BCE.[2] How much before? The census in the tradition of Jesus' birth which brought Mary and Joseph to Bethlehem cannot be used as a datum (see further below); this leaves one possible clue, fragile at best: the "star of Bethlehem."[3] If the tradition of the Magi has any value at all, it leads to the conclusion that Jesus was born sometime in 7 BCE. The conjunction would be interpreted by Zoroastrian astrologers to mean that a world ruler of the last days was born in Judaism; the start of their visit would have been occasioned by the dramatic celestial events.[4] They travelled to Jerusalem, the obvious place to ask, and were directed from there to Bethlehem. Such speculation hangs on slender threads; but for this account of Herod it has one consequence, that Herod may have heard of an astrological prediction of a "successor," a ruler of the last days. Given Herod's long-standing concern for the succession (seven wills, intra-family troubles, sibling rivalries, attempts to undercut his hold on power), rumors of a non-Herodian "king of the Jews"[5] would have enraged him—at least that is the view of the sources behind Matthew's birth story.[6] He therefore deviously tried to get the Magi to return via Jerusalem after they had located the baby so as to learn the location himself.

Herod did not know the scriptural basis for Jesus' birth at Bethlehem so, according to Matthew, he consulted with "all the chief priests and scribes of the people." The account first supposes a close, historically improbable, relationship between Herod, the scholars and the Temple authorities, so that the Sanhedrin happily revealed the location of the Messiah because "all Jerusalem" was upset by the news (Matt. 2:3–4). Second, the account presupposes Matthew's po-

---

2. See especially T. D. Barnes, *JTS* 19 (1968): 204–8; he refutes the challenge of W. E. Filmer, *JTS* 17 (1966): 283–98. More recently, O. Edwards, "Herodian Chronology," *PEQ* 114 (1982): 29–42, has challenged Barnes.

3. See generally, R. E. Brown, *The Birth of the Messiah* (Garden City, NY: Doubleday, 1977), pp. 166–70; H. Hoehner, *Chronological Aspects of the Life of Christ* (Grand Rapids: Zondervan, 1977), chap. 1.

4. See E. Stauffer, *Jesus and His Story* (London: SCM, 1955), pp. 36–37, re the Star Almanac of Sippar; P. I. Schaumberger, "Textus cuneiformis de stella Magorum," *Biblica* 6 (1925): 446–47.

5. The title "king" (or "king of the Jews" as in *Ant.* 14.36) was first used by Alexander Jannaeus; his successors, including Herod, used the title regularly, almost unfailingly: see chap. 8, Appendix B, on coins and inscriptions.

6. Matt. 2:4 has Herod ask about the "Messiah," a tendentious shift in the tradition from the Magi's "King."

lemic against the chief priests, elders and scribes (see Matt. 27:4; Mark 15:31).[7] This consultation between Herod and the chief priests and scribes was the first instance of a hostility that would lead, according to Matthew, to the cross. The Magi saw through the opposition and returned home from Bethlehem by a different route after leaving their gifts with Mary.

The homage by Eastern visitors has an appropriate ring to it for that period. A significant instance of such homage was Tigranes the Younger of Armenia, who submitted himself and his nation to Rome in 66 BCE,[8] leaving his daughter as a hostage.[9] Queen Helena of Adiabene paid homage to Jerusalem upon her conversion, bringing substantial gifts intended to reduce the effects of the famine in the 40s CE.[10] Dignitaries came when Herod completed Caesarea Maritima; even the Empress Livia sent a generous gift (*Ant.* 16.136–41). In Jesus' case homage was momentary, for divine interventions removed both the Magi and Joseph's family (in both cases by way of dreams that gave travel instructions). Herod's intention to kill Jesus had an important place in Joseph's dream, so he and the family stayed in Egypt until Herod's death.

According to Matthew, Herod angrily killed the boys under the age of two in Bethlehem and in the area around it, a scene that has shaped both artistic and popular views of Herod,[11] yet there is little in the story that carries historical conviction. The differences between Matthew's and Luke's birth accounts,[12] together with the incident's absence from Josephus's account of the excesses of Herod's final years, work against the account's accuracy. Brown speaks of the verisimilitude of these accounts, but correctly distinguishes between that and historicity; plausibility does not guarantee accuracy. Brown's argument for a strong theological element (particularly motifs drawn from Old Testament accounts), especially in Matthew's narrative, is convincing.[13] Luke does not know the tradition of the "massacre" and merely connects Herod with John the Baptist's birth—not Jesus' (Luke 1:5)—just as he connects John the Baptist's ministry—not Jesus'—with chronological data in 3:1–2.

---

7. See B. Przybylski, "The Setting of Matthean Anti-Judaism," and E. Buck, "Anti-Judaic Sentiments in the Passion Narrative according to Matthew," in P. Richardson, ed., *Anti-Judaism in Early Christianity* (Waterloo, ON: Wilfrid Laurier University Press, 1986), pp. 181–200 and 165–80. Much of Matthew's polemic is taken over from Mark.

8. Sullivan, *Near Eastern Royalty,* pp. 284–85.

9. Cassius Dio 63.1–7; Suetonius, *Nero* 13; the incident is alluded to in *War* 2.379.

10. *Ant.* 20.17–96; *War* 2.520; 4.567; 5.55, 119, 147, 252; 6.355–56; her importance is indirectly attested in *War* 2.388, in Agrippa II's speech on the eve of the Revolt in 66.

11. As much in modern films and videos as in medieval stone or on canvas or vellum; in operas, novels, and plays.

12. Note the differences in general and the particular differences in Matthew's explanation of how Joseph and Mary got to Nazareth compared to Luke's explanation of how they got to Bethlehem.

13. Brown, *Birth of the Messiah,* pp. 165–230, esp. 188–90, 225–28.

In brief, these accounts suggest the following:[14] (1) both John the Baptist (Luke 1:5) and Jesus (Matt. 2:1) were born late in Herod's reign; (2) the birth of Jesus may have been in 7 BCE, two-and-a-half years before Herod's death; (3) the tradition of the "massacre of the innocents" reflected Herod's succession problems and the execution of three of his own children;[15] (4) the flight to Egypt derived from scriptural allusions that were plausible because of the difficult conditions in Judea at the end of Herod's reign.

Herod's abominable behavior is described accurately in the *Testament of Moses* 6:2–6: "An insolent king will succeed them. . . . He will slay the old and the young, and he will not spare. And he will execute judgments on them, just as the Egyptians did."[16] This does not prove the historical accuracy of the Christian tradition of the incident, since it makes only a very general comment on Herod, but it shows how Christians shaped their history to conform to prevailing assessments of Herod. His connection with Christian origins is limited to this brief overlap between Jesus' birth and his death. Christian writers established a connection to show how Herod's anxiety over a successor was relevant to the birth of the Messiah. In making this point, they claimed that Jesus was the true "king" of Israel, replacing the wicked Herod.

ARCHELAUS OF JUDEA, THE THRONE CLAIMANT, AND QUIRINIUS'S CENSUS

Archelaus was born to Herod and Malthace in about 23 BCE;[17] he married first another Mariamme, then Glaphyra, daughter of Antiochus of Cappadocia.[18] This latter union was contrary to a strict construction of Torah for two reasons: Glaphyra already had children, so the provision for Levirate marriage did not apply, and her second husband was still alive.

The intra-family antagonisms following Herod's death have already been described (chap. 1); everyone had a view, but no solution suited all. The position as Herod's primary successor was Archelaus's to lose. He managed to do just that by his brutal slaying of pilgrims at the Passover following his father's death in 4 BCE. Whether this incident created his reputation or added to an already unsatisfactory opinion is unsure, but subsequent difficulties suggest that

---

14. See Brown's reconstruction of pre-Matthean tradition; pp. 104–119, Table 7.

15. Augustus's reported remark, "I would rather be Herod's pig than his son" (Macrobius, *Saturnalia* 2.4.1), emphasizes revulsion at Herod's treatment of his children.

16. On the date, see J. Priest, in Charlesworth, *Pseudepigrapha,* 1:920–21 and literature cited there, especially G. W. E. Nicklesburg; chaps. 6 and 7 belong to the early Christian period.

17. Biographical information in *War* 2.111–17; *Ant.* 17.339–55; 18.1–108; Philo, *Legatio;* Cassius Dio 55.27; Strabo, *Geog.* 16.2.46; as well as coins and inscriptions. See above, chaps. 2, 8 (Appendix B).

18. Glaphyra was his own sister-in-law (widow of his half-brother Alexander, whom Herod had executed) and the divorced wife of King Juba of Mauretania. An important inscription in Athens refers to Glaphyra and Juba.

Archelaus was the least suited to reign of the three main heirs. For many Jews the best solution was to turn political responsibility over to the Syrian governor, with local religious autonomy in Jerusalem. Despite its attractions, Augustus rejected that solution and implemented Herod's final will (with a few alterations); Archelaus received the central, largest, wealthiest, and most difficult portions of Judea, Samaritis, and Idumaea (see map 7).

His unsuitability is indirectly reflected in the New Testament in the parable of "the entrusted money" (Luke 19:11–27; Matt. 25:14–30). The Lukan form of the parable is substantially different from Matthew's, with a different story-line.[19] A narrative has been merged, because of the common journey motif,[20] with the Q parable to create the present Lukan form.[21] When the parts are disentangled, the non-Q narrative emerges as self-contained:

> (11) As they heard these things he proceeded to tell a parable, because he was near to Jerusalem, and because they supposed that the reign of God was to appear immediately. (12) He said therefore, "A nobleman went into a far country to receive a kingdom and then to return. [. . .]" (14) But his citizens hated him and sent an embassy after him saying, "We do not want this man to reign over us." (15a) When he returned, having received the kingdom, [. . .] (24a) he said to those who stood by, [. . .] (27) "But as for these enemies of mine, who did not want me to reign over them, bring them here and slay them before me."[22]

While the original story of "the claimant to the throne" may have been fuller, even in this arbitrarily reconstructed form it is coherent; what is more, its removal improves the Q parable.

The elements of the story that bear on Archelaus are not found in the superscription (where a different applicational motif connects it with a near-expectation of the end) but in the story itself.[23] The nobleman goes to a far

---

19. J. Kloppenborg aptly remarks that this creates "serious source critical disputes"; *Q Parallels* (Sonoma, CA: Polebridge, 1988), p. 200.

20. Though there are cases where parables have been spliced together (e.g. Matt. 22:1–10, 11–14), there are no obvious cases of an editor uniting a parable and a story.

21. See J. Jeremias, *The Parables of Jesus* (London: SCM, 1963), pp. 58–63 (another parable of Jesus, joined at a pre-Lukan stage); B. B. Scott, *Hear then the Parable* (Minneapolis: Fortress, 1989), pp. 217–35; F. D. Weinart, "The Parable of the Throne Claimant," *CBQ* 39 (1972): 505–14.

22. Kloppenborg, *Q Parallels,* p. 201. For reconstructions of the Q traditions, see J. Kloppenborg et al., *Q Thomas Reader* (Sonoma, CA: Polebridge, 1990), pp. 72–73; I. Havener, with A. Polag, *Q: The Sayings of Jesus* (Wilmington, DL: Glazier, 1987), p. 146.

23. The origin and purpose of the introduction is not clear. The story does not require v. 11 as its introduction, some elements of which sit uneasily with the story itself. The strongly eschatological conclusion suggests that the story and the introduction were added to the parable at the same

country to seek a kingdom, followed by an embassy of embittered citizens rejecting his reign. When he returns after receiving the kingdom, his enemies are slain. If the subject was Archelaus the details are close, though not correct in two respects: Archelaus did not receive the "kingdom" (he was made ethnarch) though he did make such a claim (the inaccuracy is required by the story line), and he killed many *before* he left, though others were killed by Varus when putting down the revolts triggered by Herod's death.[24]

The parable of "the entrusted money" that frames this story did not include these elements; why should Luke, or earlier Christian tradition, incorporate historicizing details that referred to a long-deposed ruler? (1) Luke displays an interest in the Herodian family, so this insertion is consistent with his general editorial stance. (2) Luke or his source saw an opportunity to make an additional theological point, that those who did not serve Jesus adequately would be punished; in making Archelaus a prototype of Jesus' retribution we find an unexpected association between the Herods and the Messiah. (3) The revised Lukan parable (unlike Matthew's) is set in a deeply eschatological context more appropriate to the Archelaus story than the Q parable, indicating a willingness to read Herodian history as preparatory to the eschatological climax of history. (4) Luke's setting of the story is Jericho (Luke 18:35), a redactional setting he borrowed from Mark[25]; the story of Herod's succession was also centered in Jericho where his last will was written, his son Antipater executed, his own death occurred, and—according to Josephus—a great crowd of nobles threatened with death.

Archelaus continued badly after his return from Rome, so that in 6 CE delegations went from Judea and Samaria to Rome to plead for his removal.[26] As a result of the delegations, Archelaus was banished to Vienne in Gaul; his wife Glaphyra chose to share his exile. Rome decided to govern Judea, Samari-

---

stage, and possibly that there was some connection between the introduction and the story. The introduction can be read as evidence for "the throne claimant" being originally a parable of Jesus, but this is not certain.

24. The dependent status of Judea required such trips and several claimants fit. Antipas could be the subject of the story, since he later travelled to gain a kingship (see below); the brutality of the story's actions and his immediate exile without returning home speak against this identification. Philip also went to Rome to get a kingdom, again without brutality. Herod, of course, went to Rome in 40 BCE, though his objective was not to get a kingdom.

25. In Luke 18:35 Jesus approaches Jericho, taken over from Mark 10:46. Matthew, who also follows Mark, has Jesus depart from Jericho. Luke 19:1 (no parallels) sits uneasily with Luke 18:35 but maintains the Jericho setting. Matthew's setting for the parable of the entrusted money is Jerusalem. Archelaus's main building projects were located in the same region (rebuilding the Winter Palace in Jericho and the new city of Archelais, named after himself, a few miles north.

26. *Ant.* 17.342–44; in 345–48 Josephus recounts Archelaus's dream before going to Rome, interpreted by Simon the Essene as a prediction of the impending end of his rule. His wife Glaphyra also had a predictive dream (349–53) anticipating her own death, the result, according to Josephus, of her non-Torah marriages to Alexander, King Juba, and Alexander's half-brother Archelaus.

tis, and Idumaea directly in order to—as Josephus puts it—liquidate Archelaus's estate (*Ant.* 18.26). A census was held while Quirinius was governor of Syria and Cumanus procurator of Judea, noted in Luke 2:1–4 (cf. Acts 5:37). There have been various attempts to fit the census of 6 CE into the circumstances before Herod's death, but all have foundered.[27] The insuperable difficulty is that during Herod's reign "Roman taxes could not possibly have been levied in Palestine";[28] a census was only possible in the altered circumstances after Archelaus's exile.[29] Luke backdated the census of Quirinius and then used it as the reason for Joseph and Mary's trip to Bethlehem.

Luke knew, perhaps from someone in his circle, an account of the census at the end of Archelaus's rule and a story about a throne claimant at the beginning. Their inclusion was due not to deep theological concern but more likely to familiarity; in the case of the census Luke made an incorrect deduction.[30] Though Archelaus lived on in Vienne for another decade (he died around 16 CE), his influence was felt only tangentially by Christians. Yet the road that led to revolt in 66 CE may well have begun in the unsettled conditions that became so clear during Archelaus's reign.[31]

PHILIP OF BATANEA, AURANITIS, GAULANITIS, TRACHONITIS, AND ITUREA

When Archelaus left Philip in charge during the power-struggle in Rome following Herod's death, Varus, the governor of Syria, encouraged him to take ship for Rome to claim a share of the power. Varus's role requires explanation, the best being the most obvious—he recognized Philip's ability, as Philip's long and quiet rule over the areas Augustus had allocated him bore out. Philip was cooperative, reasonable, and just.[32] He stayed in his own regions, refusing to meddle in others' affairs, and died still in possession of his tetrarchy, but childless, in 33/34 CE.[33]

Philip's territories were contiguous but diverse; the majority of the popula-

---

27. Schürer 1.399–427; generally on the procurators, 1:357–98.

28. Schürer 1.420.

29. *Ant.* 18.26 correctly dates Quirinius's census to the thirty-seventh year after Actium (6 CE).

30. A possible source may be Manaean of Antioch (Acts 13:1).

31. See M. Goodman, *The Ruling Class of Judea. The Origins of the Jewish Revolt against Rome AD 66–70* (Cambridge: Cambridge University Press, 1987), and R. Fenn, *The Death of Herod. An Essay in the Sociology of Religion* (Cambridge: Cambridge University Press, 1992).

32. Biographical details of Philip: *War* 2.1–117, 167–68, 181; *Ant.* 17.23–30; 18.27–28, 106–108, 189, 237, 319; Luke 3:1; Mark 8:27 pars.; Pliny *NH* 16.74; Ptolemy 5.15.26; Philo, *Legatio* 326; Cassius Dio 59.12; Tacitus, *Annals* 12.23. The coins are especially important for aspects of Philip's program. Secondary sources: Schürer 1.336–40; Jones, *The Herods of Judea;* A. Reville, "Les Hérodes et le rêve hérodien," *Revue de l'histoire des religions* (1893): 283–301; (1894): 1–24.

33. Philip's death is put by Josephus in the twentieth year of Tiberius and the thirty-seventh year of his rule (*Ant.* 18.106), allowing cross-referencing with the date of his accession.

tion was non-Jewish (see chap. 6 and map 7). In areas of Gaulanitis close to the Sea of Galilee, as at Gamla, there was a high percentage of Jews; there had been settlements of Babylonian and Idumaean Jews in Philip's father's days in other areas. These settlers—somewhat analogous to the modern Jewish settlements on the West Bank—would be loyal to the Herods. But in most other parts of Gaulanitis the majority was non-Jewish, in some cases, as with Ituraeans, converted to Judaism. Philip managed to keep his tetrarchy quiet, despite its religious and racial mix, while he went further than other Herods in displaying Roman conventions and symbolism on his coins. To manage this balancing act with no hint of revolt or instability took considerable skill.

Born about 20 BCE to Herod and Cleopatra of Jerusalem, Philip was brought up in Rome—like his brothers—at the Imperial court and was only sixteen when catapulted into power. He had a mild case of his father's building craze; during his reign he embellished Panias, where Herod had built a Temple to Roma and Augustus, and had the city renamed Caesarea Philippi, partly in his own honor and partly in the Emperor's. He linked his name with the Emperor's (both Augustus and Tiberius) on his coins, too, which had two dominant motifs: a portrait of the Emperor and a representation of the facade of the Temple to Roma and Augustus. In one instance (possibly a mistake) his own name surrounds Augustus's portrait; in a second instance Augustus's portrait is linked with Livia's. The latter type may be associated with Philip's renaming of Bethsaida after Livia/Julia[34] and his rebuilding of the city.[35] In *War* 2.168 both projects come after the death of Augustus, while in *Ant.* 18.26–28 they come during Augustus's reign—the more likely conclusion.[36] Given the wealth of Philip's region and his father's example, it is surprising he did not build more. Canatha and Bosra, for example, were developing cities; while there is some doubt about their constitutional status (Bosra may have been part of Nabatea and Canatha part of the Decapolis) there is no record of Philip making benefac-

---

34. Livia was Augustus's wife's usual name; when she was adopted into the *gens Iulii* under Augustus's will she was renamed Julia Augusta (14 CE). She should not be confused with Augustus's daughter Julia, who was born 39 BCE of Augustus and Scribonia, betrothed to Mark Antony, and married to M. Marcellus, then to M. Agrippa and then to Tiberius. Augustus banished her in 2 BCE to Pandateria; she died of malnutrition in 14 CE.

35. A claimant to the site's location is now being excavated, but it has turned up remarkably little evidence of first-century building activity. It has been reported that a small figurine of Augustus's wife has been found at Bethsaida, confirming the view that the city was named after her.

36. Josephus says that Bethsaida was renamed after Augustus's daughter (*Ant.* 18.28), but this is virtually impossible; Philip acquired power in 4 BCE, Julia was banished in 2 BCE. In the previous sentence Josephus says that Herod (i.e., Antipas) renamed Betharamphtha after the Emperor's wife Julia; this could only have occurred after 14 CE. Josephus seems confused in this paragraph, both chronologically and in detail. It is likely that both Antipas and Philip named cities after Julia, the late Emperor's wife, after 14 CE, as Josephus says in *War* 2.168. Why he should say later in *Ant.* that Bethsaida was named after Augustus's daughter is a mystery. Either city may for a short while have been called Livias; see Hoehner, *Herod Antipas*, pp. 87–91.

tions to them, and this despite the fact that Herod had been involved in the important precinct at Si'a, just outside Canatha.[37]

Little attention has been given to the claim of one tradition that several of the Twelve in the Christian movement came from Philip's territory: in John 1:43–44, Andrew, Peter, and Philip are all from Bethsaida.[38] There is a subtle rivalry in Nathanael's sarcastic comment about Jesus being from Antipas's Galilean territory (John 1:46), together with an indication of a relationship with Gentiles ("Greeks" in John 12:20–22) on the part of Philip and Andrew. The impression that Jesus had a foothold in Gaulanitis emerges also from the synoptic accounts, in three different ways: (1) his withdrawal to "the other side," Philip's side; (2) the disciples' confession at Caesarea Philippi; and (3) Jesus' "woes" on Capernaum and Chorazin, both in Galilee.

First of all, on several occasions (Mark 4:35; 5:1 [probably = Gergesa]; 6:45, and 8:22) Jesus went to "the other side" where he variously withdrew (6:46; 4:35), healed (8:22–26), and exorcised (5:2–20).[39] Mark's tradition implies, though Mark does not develop the idea, that once at least this action was connected with Antipas's concerns about Jesus' identity and his relation with John the Baptist (Mark 6:14–16; see 6:17–29, on John the Baptist's death, and 1:14).[40] Admittedly not explicit, his withdrawals and even the awkward itinerary of Mark 7:24–9:50 seem to have had a political motivation.[41] When Jesus wanted to be away from Antipas, Philip's territory was the preferred place. Even the call of the disciples, which tradition locates at Capernaum, is thought of as a withdrawal, either from the capital region at Sepphoris or from Peraea.

Second, Luke's story line handles Mark's itinerary differently. In Luke 9:10 Jesus' withdrawal (explicitly to Bethsaida, contrast Mark 6:30–32) follows immediately the "sending out of the twelve," since Luke has put his account of

---

37. Schürer 2.140–42 on Canatha, who claims the city may have belonged to Herod and certainly belonged to Agrippa II. It is not clear what Schürer thinks of its position during Philip's reign.

38. Brown, *John* 1:82, suggests that John thinks of Bethsaida as in Galilee (John 12:21; cf. Ptolemy, *Geog.* 5.16.4). Possibly, but this would not affect the question of their home city. The synoptic tradition puts the call scene in Galilee, near Capernaum; it does not suggest where the disciples were from, except by inference.

39. J. A. T. Robinson, *The Priority of John* (London: SCM, 1985), pp. 197–211.

40. By contrast, in Mark 1:14; Luke 4:14, Jesus "came into" or "returns to" Galilee, presumably from Peraea. At the same point Matthew (4:12) explicitly has Jesus "withdraw" from Nazareth to Capernaum, presumably because it is farther from Sepphoris, the capital.

41. The itinerary in Mark 7:24–9:50 uses the following markers of place: "he arose and went away to the region of Tyre and Sidon" (7:24); "he returned from the region of Tyre and went through Sidon to the sea of Galilee, through the region of the Decapolis" (7:31); "and they came to Bethsaida" (8:22); "and Jesus went . . . to the villages of Caesarea Philippi" (8:27); "and [he] led them up a high mountain" (9:2); "they went on from there and passed through Galilee. And he would not have anyone know it" (9:30); "and they came to Capernaum" (9:33). This connectedness is unusual in Mark. I am indebted for this point to Linda Wheatley-Irving.

John the Baptist much earlier (3:19–20), with the result that the feeding of the five thousand is in Gaulanitis. When Luke departs from Mark's order and records Peter's confession, he fails to locate the incident, meaning that he places it in Philip's region near Bethsaida. Mark and Matthew both emphasize the location in Caesarea Philippi, also in Philip's territory but farther north at Panias. Despite these differences all three Gospels agree in locating the confession in Philip's territory.

Third, Jesus' "woes" on Chorazin and Bethsaida (Matt. 11:21; Luke 10:13) and Capernaum (Luke 10:15; Matt. 11.23) are relevant. All three towns had observed Jesus' mighty works—a sufficient opportunity to turn the citizens to repentance and to the conviction that the Kingdom of God had arrived (Luke 10:8–12). By linking Bethsaida with Chorazin (in Galilee), Luke underscores the similarity of Jesus' ministry in Philip's and Antipas's territories, for without a ministry around Bethsaida the woe would fall flat. Luke's setting in the context of the seventy suggests heavy redactional interests, but the saying itself is likely authentic even if the setting is secondary. The setting in Matthew is substantially different and at the redactional level (Matt. 11:20) shows that it is Jesus' mighty works, not those of the seventy or the twelve, that are at issue. The woe, therefore, is evidence of Jesus' close association with the region ruled over by Philip the tetrarch.[42]

These tantalizing hints suggest that for some part of his "Galilean" activity Jesus spent time in Philip's territory or farther afield. All the Gospels see this as withdrawal—not a natural extension from a Galilean ministry but a hiatus. Whether the hiatus was motivated by political necessity and personal safety is less clear, though such a conclusion would be reasonable. One of the most significant acts for Jesus' self-understanding—Peter's confession that Jesus was Messiah—took place during the withdrawal, and near a pagan cult-center dedicated to Pan, where an important Imperial cult center was located.[43]

Another clue comes from John 6:15. A crowd's wish to make Jesus king (in Philip's region, John 6:1) hints at the rivalry among Herod's children with respect to kingship. While Philip was content to remain tetrarch, a few years later Antipas went to Rome seeking a crown for himself, just as Archelaus had sought the crown many years earlier. Like Archelaus, though for different reasons, Antipas was deposed for his troubles. The report of Jesus being proclaimed

---

42. When Mark refers to "the region of the Decapolis" (7:31; contrast Matt. 15.29, which implies "upper Galilee") he means either Philip's territory (which connects with several Decapolis cities—Hippos, Dium, Abila, Canatha, Capitolias, Gadara) or those cities themselves. When Mark has Jesus surreptitiously re-enter Galilee (Mark 9:30) he hints that Jesus' time in these regions was to avoid notice. The phrasing of 7:31 suggests that he took a road from Sidon to Caesarea Philippi, and thence to the Sea of Galilee, avoiding Galilee.

43. See P. Richardson, "Religion, Architecture and Ethics: Some First Century Case Studies," *Horizons in Biblical Theology* 10/2 (1988): 19–49.

king across the lake from Antipas has a poignant ring. The incident—if it is historical[44]—was unlikely to have taken place in Galilee; it fits better in Gaulanitis where Philip was more easy-going. The allusions to Jesus' withdrawals and the biographical indications of Philip's character cohere; the other side was a safe haven where Jesus could withdraw in safety, a place where he spent time preaching and must have had a following.

ANTIPAS: THE DEATHS OF JOHN AND JESUS

Antipas, son of Malthace and full brother of Archelaus, was born about 21 BCE[45] and was educated in Rome. In Herod's final will Antipas was named tetrarch of Galilee and Peraea, a proposal Augustus confirmed. His being named sole heir in the previous will gave him a strong position in the arguments before Augustus in Rome in 4 BCE and accounted for some of his family support. Antipas first married the daughter of Aretas IV of Nabatea, his neighbor to the east and south; when he divorced her to marry his own niece, Herodias, he incurred Aretas's hostility, which later played a part in his downfall.

Antipas's links with Rome were strong. He may have mediated in the power struggle between Rome and Parthia in 36 CE, offering a banquet in honor of Artabanus and Vitellius (Emperor briefly in 69 CE) in a pavilion on a bridge across the Euphrates River.[46] His rush to communicate the news of the successful mediation to Tiberius was consistent with that role (see *Ant.* 18.101–

---

44. C. H. Dodd, *Historical Tradition in the Fourth Gospel* (Cambridge: Cambridge University Press, 1963), pp. 212–17; Robinson, *Priority*, pp. 199–212.

45. Biographical details of Antipas: *War* 2.167–68, 181–83; *Ant.* 18.27–28, 36–38, 101–105, 109–29, 240–56; Mark 6:14–29 pars; Luke 3:19–20; 13:31–33; 23:6–16. Main secondary sources: H. Hoehner, *Herod Antipas: A Contemporary of Jesus Christ* (Cambridge: Cambridge University Press, 1972); V. E. Harlow, *The Destroyer of Jesus: The Story of Herod Antipas* (Oklahoma City: Modern Publishers, 1954); Jones, pp.176–83; Schürer 1.340–53; H. Hoehner, "Why Did Pilate Hand Jesus over to Antipas?," in E. Bammel, ed., *The Trial of Jesus: Cambridge Studies in Honour of C. F. D. Moule* (London: SCM, 1970), pp. 84–90; F. F. Bruce, "Herod Antipas, Tetrarch of Galilee and Peraea," *Annual of the Leeds Oriental Society* 5 (1963–65): 6–23; J. D. M. Derrett, "Herod's Oath and the Baptist's Head," *BibZeit* 9 (1965): 49–59; 233–46; C. Saulnier, "Hérode Antipas et Jean le Baptiste: Quelques remarques sur les confusions chronologiques de Flavius Josèphe," *RB* 91 (1984): 362–76; M. L. Soards, "Tradition, Composition and Theology in Luke's Account of Jesus before Herod Antipas," *Biblica* 66 (1985): 344–64; J. E. Via, "According to Luke, Who Put Jesus to Death?," in R. Cassidy, ed., *Political Issues in Luke-Acts* (Maryknoll, NY: Orbis, 1983), pp. 122–45.

46. Josephus does not explicitly say that Antipas was the broker between the representatives of the two great powers; indeed there are problems with his account. Suetonius and Cassius Dio (by implication Tacitus) place the event not under Tiberius but under Gaius; see Schürer 1.351 for discussion. On Parthians, see N. C. Debevoise, *A Political History of Parthia* (Chicago: University of Chicago Press, 1938); M. A. R. Colledge, *The Parthians* (London: Thames and Hudson, 1967); on the meeting on the Euphrates, K. H. Ziegler, *Die Beziehungen zwischen Rom und dem Partherreich* (Wiesbaden: F. Steiner, 1964).

105), and it is hard otherwise to account for his presence at such an important and potentially explosive meeting.[47] Whatever his role, he occupied a "high place" in the circle of Tiberius's friends (*Ant.* 18.36) and founded Tiberias on the west shore of the Sea of Galilee in the Emperor's honor,[48] modeled in plan on Hellenistic lines. With a council (like a *polis*) and a magistrate (*archôn*), both experiments in hellenization,[49] Tiberias was the first Hellenistic city in the region designed for Jews.[50] At about the same time, Antipas renamed the town of Betharamphtha in Peraea after Tiberius's mother (Augustus's wife), Julia. Earlier he had undertaken to restore Sepphoris and to make it "the ornament of all Galilee" (*Ant.* 18.27); it, too, may have been modelled on a Hellenistic city.[51]

Antipas's territory fell into two parts: Galilee and Peraea (see chap. 6 and map 7), separated by a few miles of the Decapolis but almost contiguous. Peraea—the rougher area—was associated with John the Baptist while Galilee—the richer area—was associated with Jesus. Not surprisingly, Antipas figures more prominently in the Gospels than other Herodian princes. He appears first in Luke 3:1 ("Herod being the Tetrarch of Galilee")[52] at the beginning of John the Baptist's ministry "in the wilderness"; which wilderness is not specified but Peraea is likeliest. In Luke's account, Herod shuts John up in prison because John reproved him "for Herodias, his brother's wife" (Luke 3:19–20).[53] Josephus also mentions this incident at some length (*Ant.* 18.109–19), interpreting John's execution as the cause of Antipas's defeat at the hands of Aretas IV.

Josephus and the Gospels are concerned with John's death, but they weight

---

47. Vitellius's anger at Antipas's action is hard to square with a generous view of the role of Antipas. Josephus accepts at face value that there was an "offense," which might suggest Antipas was merely a bystander. Suetonius ignores Antipas in the meeting (*Vitellius* 2): Vitellius used "masterly diplomacy."

48. Tiberias reveals substantial remains of an impressive late-Hellenistic city; see *NEAEHL*. Josephus's description of its founding is muddied by a curious insistence that the city was built on top of existing graves, that Antipas knew it was contrary to Torah to build there (*paranomon*) and that he had to settle the city forcibly with unwilling Galileans and others, for whom he built houses and to whom he allocated land on condition that they not leave the city (*Ant.* 18.37–38). These were unlikely arrangements for a city founded to honor the Emperor; its later history as an important city of Rabbinic learning undercuts Jospehus's account; Josephus alludes to a large "house of prayer" in 66 CE (*Life* 277). See Hoehner, *Herod Antipas,* pp. 91–100.

49. Smallwood, *Jews,* p. 183; see *War* 2.641; *Life* 64, 169, 284, 300, 313, 381, re the council (*boulê*).

50. M. Avi-Yonah, "The Foundation of Tiberias," *IEJ* (1951–52): 160–69.

51. S. Freyne, *Galilee, Jesus and the Gospels* (Philadelphia: Fortress, 1988), p. 137; Schürer 2.174; Z. Weiss, "Sepphoris," *NEAEHL* 4.1324–28; E. Netzer and Z. Weiss, *Zippori* (Jerusalem: Israel Exploration Society, 1994).

52. Antipas is typically referred to both in the New Testament and in Jospehus as "Herod the Tetrarch."

53. Luke gets John out of the way before Jesus' baptism by relocating the description of John's arrest from its place at Mark 6:17–18; he retains the placing of the previous pericope at Luke 9:7–9//Mark 6:14–16.

the issues differently. Antipas had married the daughter of Aretas IV, the Nabatean king whose reign was so important in the cultural development of the
region. The two may have been distantly related, since Antipas's grandmother
was a Nabatean princess, perhaps of the royal family. His marriage to Aretas's
daughter must have had political motivations (see chap. 2), for Nabatea shared
a lengthy border with Peraea.[54] After a long marriage Antipas fell in love with
Herodias, the wife of one half-brother (*Ant.* 18.109) and the daughter of another,[55] and promised to marry her, ousting Aretas's daughter. She learned of
the pact, however, and without telling Antipas fled to Machaerus, the fortress
on the border between Peraea and Nabatea, from which she slipped quietly
over the border to Petra. Deeply offended, Aretas defeated Antipas resound-
ingly (36 CE).[56] Hostilities between dependent kings were anathema to Rome;
when Antipas informed Tiberius, the Emperor instructed Vitellius, governor of
Syria, to bring Aretas or his head to Rome.

Josephus mentions John the Baptist in his description of the destruction of
Antipas's army, explaining that "some of the Jews" thought it was divine vengeance for Antipas's execution of John.[57] According to Josephus, Antipas worried over the size of John's crowds; he feared a revolt and decided to strike first,
taking John to Machaerus where he was put to death.

This account in Josephus both supports and contradicts the New Testament
version of John's death. Mark states that John was imprisoned for his criticism
of Antipas's marriage to Herodias because the marriage contravened Torah.
Antipas was afraid to kill John, and was tricked into it by Herodias—who had
a grudge against John—using her daughter as the bait.[58] In both accounts, the
arrest and execution of John followed Antipas's marital difficulties: in the New
Testament this provides the full explanation of John's death; in *Ant.* the reason
is social and political, fear of a popular uprising triggered by the eloquence (and
possibly the social and religious content) of John's preaching. The identity of
Herodias's first husband is unclear. In Mark and some manuscripts of Matthew
her first husband was "Philip" (not in Luke and some manuscripts of Matthew);
in Josephus her first husband was "Herod," Antipas's half-brother.[59] At this

---

54. Schürer 1.342 speculates that Augustus may have encouraged the match; see Suetonius,
Augustus 48: he "followed a policy of linking together his royal allies by mutual ties of friendship
or intermarriage, which he was never slow to propose."

55. See below on the identity of Herodias's first husband. She was the daughter of Aristobulus.

56. *Ant.* 18.109–114; Jospehus hints at a quisling role for "refugees" from Philip's tetrarchy.

57. In a famous passage (*Ant.* 18.116–19) Josephus describes John as "the Baptist," "a good
man," exhorting Jews to "lead righteous lives, to practice piety, and to join in baptism."

58. Mark 6:17–29//Matt. 14:3–12. On the whole episode see Hoehner, *Herod Antipas,* chap.
7 (pp. 110–71). Matthew waffles over whether Antipas wanted to kill John, while Mark (with
Matthew, illogically, following him) suggests regret on his part over John's death.

59. Hoehner discusses the problems and various solutions; see *Herod Antipas,* pp. 131–36. It
seems near certain that Herodias was not married previously to Philip the Tetrarch, but to another

point in the late 20s Herod's family was closely bound up with Christian origins, for John's ministry was the essential introduction to the story of Jesus and John's death was the precondition for focusing solely on Jesus. Antipas thus shapes the connection between John and Jesus in the Gospels.

Josephus does not connect John, Jesus, and Antipas.[60] The New Testament does, so I turn to its description of Antipas's connections with Jesus. The pericope that precedes the account of John's death (Mark 6:14–16//Luke 9:7–9// Matt. 14:1–2) begins with Jesus' public notoriety and the extension of his role through the "sending out of the Twelve." Antipas either heard of the events (according to Mark and Luke) or of Jesus (according to Matthew) and either he (Matthew and the end of Mark's pericope) or others (Mark and Luke) claim that the explanation was to be found in a resurrected John the baptizer.[61] According to Luke—and Luke alone—Antipas wanted to meet Jesus.[62] The next major section in all three Gospels involves Jesus' withdrawal from Galilee, moving for a period to Gaulanitis, Ituraea, the region of the Decapolis and Phoenicia (Mark 6:30–9:30; see above). Is the sequence historically correct? Should we deduce that Jesus withdrew from Galilee because Antipas had noticed him? Mark seems to take the sequence seriously, for when Jesus finally returned to Galilee (Mark 9:30) and Capernaum (9:33) the opposition had increased and remained intense until the end. In his view the period in Philip's territory and the adjacent areas was a hiatus, a period of calm before the coming hostilities. Mark's locating of the withdrawal is deliberate, but not necessarily incorrect; he implies that there is a connection between the death of John in Peraea, Antipas's awareness of Jesus in Galilee, and Jesus' withdrawal elsewhere.

This view is strengthened by an analysis of Luke, who follows Mark in this section with substantial omissions. He includes, however, two other brief notices of Antipas. At 8:1–3 he describes a tour by Jesus and the Twelve with a number of women—including Joanna the wife of Antipas's steward Chuza[63]—

---

half-brother known to Josephus only as "Herod." Hoehner argues that his name was Herod Philip, but this is required only by the desire to preserve the New Testament's reliability.

60. The still-debated passage in Josephus concerning Jesus (*Ant.* 18.63–64) comes not much before his account of John (18.116–19). In the Jesus passage there is mention neither of John nor of Antipas; the account is set firmly and appropriately in the context of the narrative about Pilate (18.55–62).

61. Why does Mark introduce Antipas into the narrative at all? He does not give him a place later in the trial, as Luke does, and has no special interest in him; perhaps to provide a transition to John's execution?

62. The pericope is heavily redacted. Mark's incorrect attribution of "kingship" to Herod is removed by Luke and Matthew. Matthew collapses the two discrete statements about John—by some and by Herod—into one statement, by Herod. Luke makes Herod uncertain who Jesus is, and has him express the wish to see him, and then omits the following pericope so that the focus stays entirely on Jesus.

63. On Chuza's origin, see Hoehner, *Herod Antipas*, pp. 303–306. The name Chuza appears in

who supported them financially. In Luke 13:31–33 some Pharisees warn Jesus that Antipas wanted to kill him. These may well be remnants of an independent tradition about Jesus.[64] The several hints of connections between Jesus and Antipas here and in the trial suggest links—both positive and negative—with Antipas's household.

The Gospels thus provide two independent traditions about Antipas and Jesus: those behind Mark and those behind Luke. In Mark, Antipas was troubled by reports of Jesus' works and their relation to John the Baptist's. Antipas concluded from these reports that the one he beheaded had been raised to life to continue his work; so Jesus withdrew to regions outside Galilee. In Luke, a more benign explanation of Antipas's knowledge of Jesus is implied—Antipas learned of him through Joanna—but a more deliberate intention is given; Antipas wanted to kill Jesus. Luke's tradition suggests that this decision came relatively late. His final version retains both views in an unresolved juxtaposition, further muddied by Luke's revision of Mark's tradition (6:16) that Antipas was anxious to "see" Jesus (Luke 9:9).

A possible historical sequence was "judicial notice" by Antipas, Jesus' withdrawal and return, and a decision to take action. This coheres with Mark's view that during Jesus' time in Jerusalem "Herodians" attempted to get him to declare himself on taxes payable to Rome (Mark 12:13–17//Matt. 22:15–22//Luke 20:20–26),[65] a matter of no small interest to the Herods. The setting of the incident was, however, Jerusalem; the main actor was not Antipas himself but a small group of persons politically committed to the fortunes of the family of Herod, probably deriving from the days of Herod the Great.

"Herodians" appear again in the Gospels at Mark 3:6 (absent in the parallels) and at Mark 8:15 (where "Herodians" is a textual variant).[66] The latter is too allusive to be useful. The former is, however, important as evidence of Mark's conviction (though not Luke's or Matthew's) that the Herodian party

two Nabatean inscriptions, leading Hoehner to speculate that he may have been a Nabatean chief steward of Herod's estates. Perhaps his main role was in Peraea.

64. I here presuppose Proto-Luke, a first edition of Luke before Mark was incorporated into it. At this point in the narrative, Proto-Luke includes the account of John's question to Jesus and his response (Luke 7:18–35), the remainder of that chapter, Jesus' travels with Joanna, Mary, and Susanna and the Twelve (8:1–3). It then jumps to 9:51, Jesus' decision to go to Jerusalem, the appointment of the seventy, and eventually, as he draws near to Jerusalem, the warning about Antipas. For more consideration of the theory, see P. Richardson, "Gospel Traditions in the Church in Corinth (with apologies to B. H. Streeter)," in G. F. Hawthorne and O. Betz, eds., *Tradition and Interpretation in the New Testament* (Grand Rapids: Eerdmans, 1987), pp. 301–318, and literature cited there.

65. Luke does not mention "Herodians" (in both Mark and Matthew they are linked with the Pharisees); Luke attributes the incident to the scribes and chief priests (Luke 20:19).

66. The variant at 8:15 is strongly attested and is not so obviously secondary as most suggest; contra, B. Metzger, *A Textual Commentary on the Greek New Testament* (London and New York: United Bible Societies, 1971).

was committed early on to Jesus' destruction. This notice is either wrong or anachronistic, since such a conclusion so early in the ministry is hardly conceivable.[67] The correction of Luke is more plausible: "they . . . discussed with one another what they might do. . . ."

A summary to this point might be helpful. (1) Both John the Baptist in Peraea and Jesus in Galilee were in Antipas's territory. (2) John's death can confidently be attributed to Antipas, when Antipas had political difficulties with Nabatea over his divorce from Aretas's daughter; his fear of John derived from John's popularity. (3) As a result of John's death Jesus withdrew from Galilee. (4) When Jesus headed toward Jerusalem Antipas concluded that Jesus was dangerous. (5) A Herodian party supported this view.

One of the distinctive elements in Luke's trial narrative is its inclusion of an appearance before Antipas and a second appearance before Pilate.[68] When Pilate realized that Jesus was Galilean and Antipas was in Jerusalem (Luke 23:6–16), he sent Jesus to the tetrarch. Antipas was "very glad" to see Jesus and wanted to see some "sign" (*sēmeion*) by him;[69] when his questions met with silence, he contemptuously sent Jesus back to Pilate.[70] Pilate again tried to release Jesus because neither he nor Antipas had discovered guilt worthy of death (Luke 23:14–15).[71] From this, Luke concludes that Pilate and Antipas became friends. If Luke is independent at these points, should it be preferred over Mark,[72] and did Luke get the Antipas incident right?

A major difficulty in Luke's narrative is that it makes more complex a set of events that is already complex enough,[73] so it is hard to know what credence

---

67. If the implications of Mark 3:6 are taken seriously, the Pharisees reached their view about the need for Jesus' death on the basis of his sabbath healing; the Herodians were already committed to his destruction. E. P. Sanders catches the essence of the difficulty (*Jewish Law*, pp. 96): "An author's hand is responsible for the sequence of disputes in Mark 2:1–3:6, and though they contain authentic bits little more can be said. Historical reconstruction cannot rest on their details."

68. While the weight of opinion holds that Luke's trial account is dependent on Mark's, I hold the view that it is a parallel but independent account.

69. When Pilate was in Jerusalem he resided in Herod's palace on the site of today's Citadel, and Antipas up the street in the old Hasmonean palace.

70. Luke omits Mark 15:16–20 (the soldiers mocked Jesus and put a purple robe on him), but similar events followed the Antipas-incident. He also omits the release of a prisoner at Passover (Mark 15:6–10).

71. On the incident: Hoehner, *Herod Antipas,* pp. 224–50, especially 233–39, largely repeated in his "Why Did Pilate Hand Jesus over to Antipas?"; J. B. Tyson, "Jesus and Herod Antipas," *JBL* 79 (1960): 239–46; M. L. Soards, "Tradition, Composition and Theology in Luke's Account of Jesus before Herod Antipas"; J. Blinzler, *Herodes Antipas und Jesus Christus* (Stuttgart, 1947); J. Blinzler, *Der Prozess Jesu,* 4th edition (Regensburg, 1963).

72. See D. Catchpole, *The Trial of Jesus* (Leiden: Brill, 1971).

73. In the earlier stages of the trial Luke has the simpler version, with only one hearing before the council; Mark presupposes both a night meeting and a daylight meeting. But then, according to Luke, Jesus was taken to Pilate, to Antipas, back to Pilate, then to crucifixion.

to give this episode. Several historical factors bear on the evaluation. (1) Was Antipas legally competent to deal with Jesus in Jerusalem? (2) Were Antipas and Pilate at odds, and if so, did that relationship change? (3) How did Antipas's views in the trial square with indications of his (and a Herodian party's) wish to be rid of Jesus?

First, was Antipas legally competent to deal with Jesus in Jerusalem? The issue of competence turns on Roman law: where was a trial conducted, where the crime was committed or in the criminal's place of residence, and was it conducted by magistrates of the one location or the other? This last question is simply answered; magistrates rarely handed over jurisdiction to a visiting magistrate. Given that a trial should be conducted by the "home magistrate," it would be understandable if he were to hand him over for a preliminary hearing or the like. Pilate might, for the reasons hinted at in the narrative, plausibly have asked Antipas to have a look at Jesus, but he was not obliged to hand Jesus over.[74] Would Antipas have been competent? Trial in the place of ordinary domicile only came in later,[75] so Pilate could not have evaded jurisdiction even if he wished to do so, though he could still have sent Jesus before Antipas.

Second, regarding the relationship between Antipas and Pilate, we have no direct evidence—and only slender threads of indirect evidence—that the two were at odds. Since Antipas was the logical person to inherit Judea, Samaritis, and Idumaea when Archelaus was deposed in 6 CE (in one earlier will he was the sole heir), he would have been unhappy being subordinate to a succession of Roman prefects of Judea. He had specific reasons to be unhappy with Pilate's actions and maybe with Pilate's attitude in general. (a) The "standards incident," when embossed images of Caesar were set up in Jerusalem, was deeply resented by Jews (*War* 2.169–74; *Ant.* 18.55–59); though Antipas was not an important actor in this issue, Philo suggests he shared the revulsion and helped persuade Tiberius to force Pilate to remove the offending images (*Legatio ad Gaium* 299–305). (b) In the "aqueduct incident" Pilate sequestered Temple funds[76] to build an aqueduct; the accounts suggest a mainly Jerusalem resistance, though it could still have been known to Antipas.[77] (c) The "Samaritan incident" was not likely to disturb Antipas or the Jewish people in general (*Ant.* 18.85–89), and in any case occurred toward the end of Pilate's time in Judea.

---

74. So Hoehner, *Herod Antipas*, pp. 224–50.

75. A. N. Sherwin-White, *Roman Society and Roman Law in the New Testament* (Oxford: Clarendon, 1963), pp. 28–31.

76. The *Corban*, according to Josephus in *War* 2.175–77; the word is missing in *Ant.* 18.60–62.

77. In *Antiquities* these incidents are followed immediately by the description of Jesus (18.63–64), which includes a reference to Pilate's role in his death. In *War* the incidents are followed by the account of Agrippa I's unsuccessful accusation of Antipas before Tiberius. When Agrippa indiscreetly let it out that he hoped that Gaius (Caligula) would become Emperor, Tiberius threw him in prison (*War* 2.178–80).

(d) The "Galilean incident" (Luke 13:1) refers to Galilean pilgrims in Jerusalem for a festival who felt the severity of Pilate's police action. None of this material allows us to gauge the depth of animosity between Pilate and Antipas, if any, nor is there any evidence of later friendship. The conclusion: any animosity between them is not improbable but has by no means been proven.[78]

Third, what of Antipas's finding of no guilt in the informal hearing and the indications that he sought to kill him? The evidence for a decision to kill Jesus is slanted, probably exaggerated, and perhaps a result of a "Herodian" party's views. But it is not altogether implausible, given Antipas's execution of John; since Jesus did not personally attack Antipas, he probably felt Jesus was not as guilty as John was.[79]

Did Antipas hear Jesus before Pilate's sentencing? If Luke's narrative is independent of Mark's, the plausibility of an Antipas-hearing is increased, and some of Luke's and Mark's differences would have to be resolved in favor of Luke.[80] Yet if Antipas had a role in the trial, four episodes would need to be squeezed into a very busy morning: a hearing before the Sanhedrin, a trial before Pilate, an interview with Antipas, and a second Pilate episode.[81] Perhaps not an impossible schedule, but an extremely tight one.

Pilate's patron in Rome was Sejanus, Tiberius's chief lieutenant, who was opposed to Jews. When Sejanus was executed in 31 CE on a charge of treason, the career of protégés such as Pilate would have altered. In Jesus' trial, according to John 19:12, Pilate was accused of being no friend of Caesar's if he let Jesus go.[82] Pilate's position, following the fall of Sejanus, as a member of Tiberius's inner circle was threatened by doubts of his allegiance; to take a pretender to kingship lightly might have made Pilate, like Sejanus, guilty in Tiberius's eyes, adding a contextual dimension that the trial of Jesus otherwise lacks.[83]

---

78. An important feature of *Antiquities*'s view of Pilate is that his long term of ten years was a result of Tiberius's appointments policy (*Ant.* 18.176–77): he kept in check the rapaciousness of governors attempting to recoup their finances during short terms.

79. Antipas's finding is implied in Pilate's words in Luke 23:15 (see Acts 4:27): the latter supports the claim of a role for Antipas in the trial, though unlike Luke 23:15 it emphasizes Antipas's guilt.

80. Mark's two hearings before the council, the mocking of Jesus by the council, the finding of blasphemy, and so on, would be Markan redaction.

81. Mark's order has a similar problem: hearings before the Sanhedrin both at night and during the day, and before Pilate. The sparest account is Luke's without the Antipas hearing: hearings before the Sanhedrin and Pilate, but I am inclined to follow Luke's full account, and to consider the possibility of the trial incidents taking more than one day.

82. See especially E. Bammel, "Philos tou kaisaros," *Theologische Literaturzeitung* 77 (1952): 205–10; for a convenient survey, Brown, *John* 2:879–80, 893–96. Note especially Tacitus, *Annals* 6.6.8, quoting Marcus Terrentius: "the closer a man's intimacy with Sejanus, the stronger his claim to the emperor's friendship." See E. M. Smallwood, "Some Notes on the Jews under Tiberius," *Latomus* 15 (1956): 327, who holds there is a connection between the incidents described above and Sejanus's anti-Jewish policies, citing Philo, *In Flacc.* 1; *Legatio* 159–61.

83. B. Levick, *Tiberius the Politician* (London: Croom Helm, 1976), p. 136, doubts the plausibility of the connection as an explanation of Pilate's activity; she suggests "stupid offensiveness."

Antipas's character was passive, indecisive, and weak; he was perplexed and hesitant about John the Baptist; he was opposed to Jesus yet wanted to see him, and then he found him not guilty. He fell from power pursuing the title "king," which he did not specially want, prodded by his wife's ambition, but Antipas failed to reckon with Agrippa's closer relations with Gaius and Aggripa's hostility toward him. A half-hearted appeal to Gaius to be recognized as a king, after forty-one years as tetrarch, was not likely to persuade a new Emperor enjoying his power and wishing to reward loyal friendships. A different side to Antipas is hinted at in Agrippa's claim that he conspired with Sejanus against Tiberius[84] and was in league with Artabanus of Parthia against Gaius, stockpiling weapons for seventy thousand soldiers, a charge that was likely groundless, but Antipas was ineffective in refuting it.[85] So Antipas and Herodias fell: they were exiled to the city of Lugdunum in Gaul.[86]

THE HERODIAN FAMILY

The descendants of Herod continued in the next generations to be on the fringes of early Christian developments. Agrippa I and Agrippa II, especially, touched the lives of Christians directly, but throughout the first century the primary effect of the family of Herod continued to be on Judaism. Herod's grandson, Agrippa I, succeeded Philip and then Antipas and then for a brief period (41–44 CE) was king of most of the former regions of Herod. On his way to Gaulanitis he passed through Alexandria and was the occasion of a major riot, which left a very important mark in the historical literature, especially in Philo's *Legatio ad Gaium* and *In Flaccum,* thus providing invaluable descriptions of Alexandrian Judaism. Aggripa I was involved in Caligula's attempt to put a statue of himself in the Temple in Jerusalem and was a player in the succession game on the death of Caligula when Claudius was named Emperor. His unexpectedly early death is reported in Acts in terms not unlike those in Josephus's description. Surprisingly, Agrippa I is remembered in glowing terms in the Jewish literature, despite his delusions of grandeur: he named himself in coins and inscriptions "the great king" (see chap. 8, Appendix B). It is an irony of history that Herod came to be called "Herod the Great," when neither he nor his contemporaries used this adjective, while Agrippa, who self-consciously adopted this nomenclature, has been refused "the Great" in subsequent tradition.

Agrippa II, Herod's great-grandson, never acquired the position his father had. He was close to power—especially to Vespasian, Titus, and Domitian—but

---

84. In the light of the trial of Jesus, the Sejanus accusation is intriguing but probably groundless.

85. Josephus, however, says that Antipas confirmed he had such weapons, *Ant.* 18.240–56.

86. There is confusion over which Lugdunum. The more likely possibility is modern Lyon on the Rhone, a thriving center of Roman culture in the first century, though another Lugdunum, near the border with Spain, might have been meant.

he acquired neither the full title nor full lands that he wished. In the revolt of 66–74 CE he was firmly on the Roman side against his own people, trying to persuade them to abandon hope of independence in a world dominated by Roman power.

The Herodian family served Rome faithfully for almost two hundred years, from Antipater's helping Julius Caesar through to the bit players of the early second century CE. As a family, they were truly remarkable—the best known family of antiquity for the longest period of time—full of challenges for the ancient historian who wishes to understand the relationships between Rome and a minor state such as Judea during the most formative period in Western civilization. The family showed the complexity of the relationships, the over-lapping and competing interests, the tensions between independent national goals and inclusion in the larger world of Rome, as well as the social and reli-gious forces acting on them.

Individually, each member of the Herodian family had obvious warts, none more easily seen than Herod's. In the end, one's view of the whole family and of Herod himself depends on one's view of Rome: should the Herodian rulers have joined it or fought it? If indeed Judea was better off joined with Rome, then the Herodian family, especially Herod himself, did about as good a job as could be done. Like his great-grandson Agrippa II, Herod faced movements of resistance and revolution. Both could have supported movements of withdrawal from Rome; neither did. Herod, in fact, ruthlessly put down any resistance movement, creating a repressed but flourishing society, while tarnishing his own reputation, not the least in Christian history.

Herod was not a monster; he had the good of his people at heart, just as he had the best interests of Rome in view. He was "King of Jews"; he wished no other position and had no intention of reshaping Judaism into a new muta-tion. He also was "Friend of Romans"; he had no wish to withdraw from the opportunities and benefits that this bestowed. It is in the tension between these two that he and his family lived their lives and made their reputations.

CHAPTER 13

"The Achievements of King Herod" (4 BCE)

A copy is here set out of the achievements of King Herod and of his expenditures in restoring Judean pride and self-confidence. The original is engraved on bronze tablets at Caesarea Maritima, with copies in Jerusalem, Sebaste, and Panias.

1. At the age of twenty-five years I was appointed governor of Galilee; I raised an army at my own expense to suppress brigandage in the region and put down Hezekiah, who was oppressing the Galileans.

2. Three times I was appointed *epitropos* [procurator] of Syria, first by Sextus Caesar, then by Cassius Longinus, and finally by Caesar Augustus. I brought peace to southern Syria and assisted in its financial management.

3. I served Hyrcanus, the last of the Hasmonean kings, faithfully with forces that I raised and paid for myself, and I fought vigorously against his brother Antigonus, who tried to usurp his throne. When Antigonus allied himself with Parthia, Rome's enemy, I fought their forces though my army was badly outnumbered. I also fought the armies of Chalcis, Ituraea, and Nabatea in various campaigns, inflicting severe defeats on them.

4. During the Roman civil wars I ensured Judea's security through well-chosen alliances. After the great Caesar was assassinated and his murderers were brought to heaven's retribution, I was appointed tetrarch of Galilee and later king of Judea by the Senate in Rome.

5. I accompanied my troops in support of Sextus Caesar at Apamea, Mark Antony at Samosata, and Caesar Augustus at Alexandria. My troops supported

---

This chapter is modelled on Augustus's *Res gestae*; see P. A. Brunt and J. M. Monroe, *Res gestae divi Augusti: The Achievements of the Divine Augustus. Introduction and Commentary* (Oxford: Oxford University Press, 1967). *Res gestae* refers to "things achieved"; though what follows is wholly imaginary, it approximates how Herod might have wished to be remembered.

Aelius Gallus in Rome's campaign against the Sabaeans in Arabia Felix. I built and equipped the first Judean navy at my own expense, and with it I accompanied Marcus Agrippa on his campaign against Pontus in the Black Sea and Sinope. I ensured peace in the East by keeping peace in Judea.

6. When I was elevated to the kingship, Judea was a small landlocked state. To the original territory of Judea, Galilee, and Peraea were added Samaritis and Western Idumaea. I successfully persuaded Augustus to return territory unlawfully given Cleopatra. Augustus added to my kingdom the coastal cities of Gaza, Azotus, Joppa, Strato's Tower, and Anthedon, together with Gadara and Hippos. Later, I was granted rule over Batanea, Trachonitis, and Auranitis to mark my pacification of the regions from brigands. Augustus added Hulitis and Panias to my territory, formerly comprising Ituraea. By these extensions the kingdom of Israel was increased during my reign to match that of the blessed King David and King Solomon, restoring our country to its former greatness.

7. I secured for the Jews in the Diaspora the freedom to worship the God of Israel, to live where they wished, to follow the dietary laws, to send the Temple-tax to Jerusalem, not to serve in the army, and not to profane Sabbaths. Because of my friendship with Augustus and Marcus Agrippa decrees were passed in numerous cities guaranteeing these rights and privileges. In gratitude, the Jewish community in Rome named synagogues after Augustus, Agrippa, and me.

8. With the agreement of the Lord's high priests and as a mark of my piety I rebuilt the Temple of the Lord of the Universe, blessed be he, in Jerusalem. I trained priests to do the work, gathered materials from the four corners of the world, and prepared stones and timbers ahead of time. Not a day of sacrifice was left unmarked, nor did a day of rain slow the workers on the divine project. The structure was paid for at my own expense.

9. Judea's economy was strengthened during my reign through friendlier contacts with other peoples, improved trade routes, and enlarged harbors; by massive public works projects, increased population, and new cities.

10. When earthquakes, famines, or plagues shook the nation, I provided supplies of grain, tax relief, and support for the elderly and the infirm.

11. I increased exports of dates, opobalsam, wine, olive oil, and asphalt, and encouraged the pottery, perfume, and glass industries.

12. In recognition of my assistance, Augustus granted me control over and half the revenues of the copper mines in Cyprus.

13. I improved social justice with new laws while encouraging support of Torah. I suppressed dissension among the people and even in my own family, and I put an end to revolutionaries who tyrannized the common people.

14. I was on the friendliest of terms with all true worshipers of the Lord, including members of our nation in the Diaspora. I did not encourage sectarianism, but worshipped the God of Israel in his Temple.

15. I shared my rule with others, first with Hyrcanus, then with my brothers Phasael, Joseph, and Pheroras, and with my brother-in-law Costobar. I married my children to others of equal status within and outside Judea. My sons were educated in Rome to equip them better to rule in Judea.

16. In Jerusalem, in addition to the Temple, I rebuilt walls and defensive towers for the security of the people, constructed palaces, public buildings, shops, theater, amphitheater, aqueducts, and cisterns.

17. Samaritis was reincorporated into Judea; I rebuilt Samaria, renaming it Sebaste to mark my friendship with Augustus, and provided it with walls, towers, stoas, agora, temples, aqueducts, a theater, and a stadium.

18. Likewise I built Caesarea Maritima, making its harbor the largest on the Inland Sea and using all the latest technology. It, too, has walls, towers, stoas, aqueducts, religious buildings, a palace, a theater, a stadium, and an amphitheater, all built by me in honor of my patron Augustus.

19. New cities were built on my instructions at Phasaelis, Antipatris, Agrippias, Pente Komai, Gaba, Bathyra, and Heshbon. I settled veterans on allotments of land which I paid for from my own resources.

20. In addition to the Temple in Jerusalem, may the Lord be praised, I showed my piety in a memorial to the Patriarchs and Matriarchs in Hebron, another to Abraham at Mamreh, one to King David in Jerusalem, and in tombs for my own family. I built temples to Roma and Augustus in Caesarea, Sebaste, and Panias, reconstructed a temple in Rhodes, and helped complete a temple in Si'a.

21. I was made President of the Olympic Games for life to reward my contributions there. For the people of Damascus, Ptolemais, Sidon, Berytus, Tripolis, and Delos, I built facilities for games and festivals. I instituted games in Jerusalem, Caesarea, and Sebaste, where the competitors honored me with their prowess. Inscriptions and monuments honor my assistance in Athens, Chios, Cos, Samos, Pergamum, Phaselis, Cilicia, and Lycia.

22. I improved public facilities in Tyre, Byblus, Laodicea-on-sea, Balanea, Antioch, and Sparta. At Nicopolis, near where Augustus Caesar triumphed over Rome's enemies, I constructed most of the public buildings.

23. I secured the borders of Judea, built fortresses and walls where necessary, and established friendly relations with Judea's neighbors.

24. In recognition of my role I was appointed "protector" of Nabateans.

25. At my own expense I stimulated the economy, engaged in public works, offered tax and famine relief, and built religious and cultural buildings.

26. In Jerusalem, Caesarea, Sebaste, Herodium, Phaselis, Jericho, Sepphoris, and other cities I improved the water supply with aqueducts bringing purest spring water great distances, all at my own cost.

27. The blessed Augustus, long may he rule, and the late lamented Marcus Agrippa honored me with their friendship and trust. As "friend and ally," I was

as vigilant for the interests of Rome as for my own peoples' interests. Other cities sought my help in achieving justice in their dealings with Rome.

28. At the time of writing I am in the seventieth year of my age and will soon be gathered to my fathers. My body is to be laid in Herodium, my mausoleum and favorite retreat. May Judea long be blessed under Rome's beneficent oversight and the rule of my children and children's children. Dated at Jericho in January, in the consulship of C. Calvisius Sabenus and L. Pasienus Rufus, year one of the 193rd Olympiad and year 37 of my reign.

SELECT BIBLIOGRAPHY

PRIMARY SOURCES

Jewish Literature

Josephus. *Josephus,* ed. and trans. H. S. Thackeray, R. Marcus, and L. H. Feldman. Cambridge, MA: Harvard University Press, Loeb Classical Library, 1926–81.

Philo. *Complete Works,* ed. and trans. F. H. Colson and G. H. Whitaker. Cambridge, MA: Harvard University Press, Loeb Classical Library, 1929–62.

The Dead Sea Scrolls

García Martínez, F. *The Dead Sea Scrolls Translated: The Qumran Texts in English.* Leiden: Brill, 1994.

Vermes, G. *The Dead Sea Scrolls in English.* 4th ed. London: Penguin, 1995.

Yadin, Y., ed. *The Temple Scroll.* English ed. Jerusalem: Israel Exploration Society, 1983.

Apocrypha and Pseudepigrapha

Charlesworth, J., ed. *The Old Testament Pseudepigrapha.* Garden City, NY: Doubleday, 1983.

Rabbinic Literature

Danby, H., trans. *The Mishnah.* London: Oxford University Press, 1933.

Epstein, I., gen. ed. *The Babylonian Talmud.* London: Soncino, 1935–52. Reprint, 1961.

Hammer, R. *Sifre: A Tannaitic Commentary on the Book of Deuteronomy.* English trans. New Haven and New York: Yale University Press, 1986.

Neusner, J., et al., trans. *The Tosefta.* New York, 1977–86.

Greek and Latin Authors

Appian.

Appian's Roman History, trans. H. White. Cambridge, MA: Harvard University Press, Loeb Classical Library, 1912–13—includes *Civil Wars, Mithridatic War,* and *Syrian Wars.*

Cicero.
  Selected Letters, trans. D. R. S. Baily. Harmondsworth: Penguin, 1978.
  Selected Political Speeches, trans. M. Grant. Harmondsworth: Penguin, 1973.
Cassius Dio.
  Roman History, ed. and trans. E. Cary. Cambridge, MA: Harvard University Press, Loeb Classical Library, 1914–27.
  The Roman History: The Reign of Augustus, trans. I. Scott-Kilvert. Harmondsworth: Penguin, 1987.
Diodorus Siculus.
  Bibliotheca, ed. and trans. C. H. Oldfather, C. L. Sherman, C. B. Welles, R. M. Greer, and F. Walton. Cambridge, MA: Harvard University Press, Loeb Classical Library, 1933–67.
Eusebius. *Church History.*
  Ecclesiastical History, ed. and trans. K. Lake and J. E. L. Oulton. Cambridge, MA: Harvard University Press, Loeb Classical Library, 1926–32.
  The History of the Church. Rev. ed. Harmondsworth: Penguin, 1989.
Lucius Annius Florus. *Epitome of Roman History,* trans. E. Seymour. Cambridge, MA: Harvard University Press, Loeb Classical Library, 1929.
Nicolas of Damascus. *Fragmenta historicorum graecorum,* ed. C. Müller, T. Müller, et al. Paris: Didot, 1873–70.
Pausanius.
  Description of Greece, ed. and trans. W. H. S. Jones. Cambridge, MA: Harvard University Press, Loeb Classical Library, 1918–35.
  Description of Greece, trans. P. Levi. Harmondsworth: Penguin, 1979.
Pliny the Elder.
  Natural History, ed. and trans. H. Rackham, W. H. S. Jones, and D. E. Eichholz. Cambridge, MA: Harvard University Press, Loeb Classical Library, 1938–63.
Plutarch.
  Makers of Rome: Mark Antony, trans. I. Scott-Kilvert. Harmondsworth: Penguin, 1965.
Strabo.
  Geography, trans. H. L. Jones. Cambridge, MA: Harvard University Press, Loeb Classical Library, 1917–32.
Suetonius.
  Lives of the Caesars, ed. and trans. J. C. Rolfe. Cambridge, MA: Harvard University Press, Loeb Classical Library, 1914, 1951.
  Twelve Caesars, ed. M. Grant. Harmondsworth: Penguin, 1979.
Tacitus.
  The Annals of Imperial Rome, trans. M. Grant. Harmondsworth: Penguin, 1977.
  The Histories, trans. K. Wellesley. Harmondsworth: Penguin, 1986.
  Histories and Annals, trans. C. H. Moore and J. Jackson. Cambridge, MA: Harvard University Press, Loeb Classical Library, 1925–37.
Vitruvius.
  De architectura, trans. F. Granger. Cambridge, MA: Harvard University Press, Loeb Classical Library, 1931–34.

NUMISMATIC SOURCES

Kanael, B. "The Greek Letters on the Coins of Yehohanan the High Priest." *BIES* 16 (1952): 52–55 (in Hebrew).

Klimowsky, E. W. "Agrippa I as BASILEUS MEGAS." In *Recent Studies and Discoveries on Ancient Jewish and Syrian Coins*. Vol. 1. Jerusalem: Israel Numismatic Society, 1954.

Madden, F. W. *History of Jewish Coinage*. London: Bernard Quaritch, 1864.

Meshorer, Y. *Ancient Jewish Coinage: Herod the Great through Bar Cochba*. Vol. 2. New York: Amphora, 1982.

———. *Jewish Coins of the Second Temple Period*. Tel Aviv: Am Hassefer, 1967.

———. "A Stone Weight from the Reign of Herod." *IEJ* 20 (1970): 97–98.

Meyshan, J. "The Chronology of the Coins of the Herodian Dynasty." *Eretz Israel* (1950–51): 104–14 (in Hebrew); abbreviated in *PEQ* (1959).

Spijkerman, A. *The Coins of the Decapolis and Provincia Arabia*. Jerusalem: Franciscan Printing Press, 1978.

EPIGRAPHIC AND DOCUMENTARY SOURCES

Brunt, P. A., and J. M. Monroe. *Res gestae divi Augusti: The Achievements of the Divine Augustus. Introduction and Commentary*. Oxford: Oxford University Press, 1967.

Cagnat, R., ed. *Inscriptiones Graecae ad Res Romanas Pertinentes*. Rome: Loerma, 1964 [1811].

Cotton, H. M., and J. Geiger. *Masada II: Latin and Greek Documents*. Jerusalem: Israel Exploration Society, 1989.

Dessau, H. *Inscriptiones Latinae Selectae*. Dublin: Apud Weidmannos, 1974 [1892].

Dittenberger, W. *Orientis Graeci Inscriptiones Selectae*. Leipzig: Hirzel, 1903–5.

Frey, J. B. *Corpus Inscriptionum Iudaicarum*. 1936– .

Isaac, B. "A Donation for Herod's Temple in Jerusalem." *IEJ* 33 (1983): 86–92.

Jacoby, F. *Die Fragmente der Griechischen Historiker*. Leiden: Brill, 1954 [1876].

Kushnir-Stein, A. "An Inscribed Lead Weight from Ashdod: A Reconsideration." *Zeitschrift für Papyrologie und Epigraphik* 105 (1995): 81–84.

Mantzoulinou-Richards, E. "From Syros: A Dedicatory Inscription of Herodes the Great from an Unknown Building." *Ancient World* 18/3–4 (1988): 87–99.

Reinach, T. *Textes d'auteurs grecs et romains relatifs au judaïsme*. Hildesheim: Olms, 1963 [1895].

Reynolds, J., and R. Tannenbaum. *Jews and Godfearers at Aphrodisias*. Cambridge: Cambridge Philological Society, 1987.

Stern, M. *Greek and Latin Authors on Jews and Judaism*. Jerusalem: Israel Academy of Sciences and Humanities, 1974–84.

REFERENCE WORKS

Aharoni, Y., M. Avi-Yonah, et al. *The Macmillan Bible Atlas*. 3rd ed. New York: Macmillan/Jerusalem: Carta, 1993.

Baly, D., and A. D. Tushingham. *Atlas of the Biblical World*. New York: World, 1971.

Bury, J. B., S. A. Cook, and F. E. Adcock, eds. *The Cambridge Ancient History.* 1st and 2nd eds. Cambridge: Cambridge University Press.

Buttrick, G. A., ed. *Interpreter's Dictionary of the Bible.* New York: Abingdon, 1962.

Eliade, M., ed. *Encyclopedia of Religion.* New York: Macmillan, 1986.

Freedman, D. N., gen. ed. *The Anchor Bible Dictionary.* New York: Doubleday, 1992.

Liddel, H. G., R. Scott, and H. S. Jones. *A Greek-English Lexicon: A New Edition.* Oxford: Clarendon, 1940.

Louw, J. P., and E. A. Nida. *Greek-English Lexicon on the New Testament Based on Semantic Domains.* 2d ed. New York: United Bible Societies, 1989.

Picot, L., ed. *Dictionnaire de la Bible Supplément.* Paris: Letouzey, 1928.

Roth, C., ed. in chief. *Encyclopedia Judaica.* Jerusalem: Keter, 1972.

Stern, E., ed. *New Encyclopedia of Archaeological Excavations of the Holy Land.* Jerusalem: Israel Exploration Society, 1993.

Temporini, H., et al., eds. *Aufstieg und Niedergang der römischen Welt.* Berlin: de Gruyter, 1972– .

THE LIFE OF HEROD AND THE HERODIAN DYNASTY

Braund, D. "Four Notes on the Herods." *Classical Quarterly* 33 (1983): 239–42.

Bruce, F. F. "Herod Antipas, Tetrach of Galilee and Peraea." *Annual of the Leeds Oriental Society* 5 (1963–65): 6–23. Edwards, O. "Herodian Chronology." *PEQ* 114 (1982): 29–42.

Fenn, R. *The Death of Herod: An Essay in the Sociology of Religion.* Cambridge: Cambridge University Press, 1992.

Gabba, E. "The Finances of King Herod." In *Greece and Rome in Eretz-Israel,* ed. A. Kasher, U. Rappaport, and G. Fuks. Jerusalem: Jerusalem Exploration Society, 1990.

Grant, M. *Herod the Great.* New York: American Heritage, 1971.

Hanson, K. C. "The Herodians and Mediterranean Kinship." Parts 1–3. *Biblical Theology Bulletin.* "Part 1: Geneaology and Descent," 19 (1989): 75–84; "Part II: Marriage and Divorce," 19 (1989): 142–51; "Part III: Economics," 20 (1990): 10–21.

Jones, A. H. M. *The Herods of Judea.* Oxford: Clarendon Press, 1967 [1938].

Otto, W. *Herodes: Beiträge zur Geschichte des letzten jüdischen Königshauses.* Stuttgart, 1913.

Perowne, S. G. *The Life and Times of Herod the Great.* London: Hodder and Stoughton, 1956.

Reville, A. "Les Hérodes et le rêve hérodien." *Revue de l'histoire des religions* (1893): 283–301; (1894): 1–24.

Sandmel, S. *Herod: Profile of a Tyrant.* Philadelphia and New York: Lippincott, 1967.

Schalit, A. *König Herodes. Der Mann und sein Werk.* Berlin: de Gruyter, 1969.

Stern, M. "Social and Political Realignments in Herodian Judea." *Jerusalem Cathedra* 2 (1982): 40–62.

THE HERODS AND CHRISTIANITY

Bammel, E., ed. *The Trial of Jesus: Cambridge Studies in Honour of C. F. D. Moule.* London: SCM, 1970.

Blinzler, J. *Herodes Antipas und Jesus Christus*. Stuttgart, 1947.

———. *Der Prozess Jesu*. 4th ed. Regensburg, 1963.

Braun, W. "Were the New Testament Herodians Essenes? A Critique of an Hypothesis." *RB* 14 (1989): 71–84.

Brown, R. E. *The Birth of the Messiah*. Garden City, NY: Doubleday, 1977.

———. *The Gospel According to John*. Garden City, NY: Doubleday, 1978 [1966].

Catchpole, D. *The Trial of Jesus*. Leiden: Brill, 1971.

Corbett, J. "The Pharisaic Revolution and Jesus as Embodied Torah." *Studies in Religion / Sciences Religieuses* 15/3 (1986): 375–91.

Crossan, J. D. *The Historical Jesus*. New York: HarperCollins, 1991.

Derrett, J. D. M. "Herod's Oath and the Baptist's Head." *BibZeit* 9 (1965): 49–59.

Dodd, C. H. *Historical Tradition in the Fourth Gospel*. Cambridge: Cambridge University Press, 1963.

Freyne, S. *Galilee, Jesus and the Gospels*. Philadelphia: Fortress, 1988.

Harlow, V. E. *The Destroyer of Jesus: The Story of Herod Antipas*. Oklahoma City: Modern Publishers, 1954.

Havener, I., and A. Polag. *Q: The Sayings of Jesus*. Wilmington, DL: Glazier, 1987.

Hawthorne, G. F., and O. Betz, eds. *Tradition and Interpretation in the New Testament*. Grand Rapids: Eerdmans, 1987.

Hoehner, H. *Chronological Aspects of the Life of Christ*. Grand Rapids: Zondervan, 1977.

———. *Herod Antipas: A Contemporary of Jesus Christ*. Cambridge: Cambridge University Press, 1972. Reprint, Grand Rapids: Zondervan, 1980.

———. "Why Did Pilate Hand Jesus over to Antipas?" In *The Trial of Jesus: Cambridge Studies in Honour of C. F. D. Moule*, ed. E. Bammel, 84–90. London: SCM, 1970.

Horsley, R. *Jesus and the Spiral of Violence*. San Francisco: Harper and Row, 1987.

———. *Sociology and the Jesus Movement*. New York: Crossroad, 1989.

——— and J. Hanson. *Bandits, Prophets, and Messiahs*. Minneapolis: Winston, 1985.

Jeremias, J. *Jerusalem in the Time of Jesus*. London: SCM, 1969.

———. *The Parables of Jesus*. London: SCM, 1963.

Kloppenborg, J. *Q Parallels*. Sonoma, CA: Polebridge, 1988.

——— et al. *Q Thomas Reader*. Sonoma, CA: Polebridge, 1990.

Malina, B. J. *The New Testament World: Insights from Cultural Anthropology*. Louisville: John Knox, 1981.

Przybylski, B. "The Setting of Matthean Anti-Judaism." In *Anti-Judaism in Early Christianity*, ed. P. Richardson. Waterloo, ON: Wilfrid Laurier University Press, 1986.

Richardson, P. "Gospel Traditions in the Church in Corinth (with apologies to B. H. Streeter." In *Tradition and Interpretation in the New Testament*, ed. G. F. Hawthorne and O. Betz. Grand Rapids: Eerdmans, 1987.

———. "Why Turn the Tables? Jesus' Protest in the Temple Precincts." *SBL Seminar Papers 1992*. Atlanta: Scholars Press, 1992.

Robinson, J. A. T. *The Priority of John*. London: SCM, 1985.

Rowley, H. H. "The Herodians in the Gospels." *JTS* 41 (1940): 14–27.

Saulnier, C. "Hérode Antipas et Jean le Baptiste: Quelques remarques sur les confusions chronologiques de Flavius Josèphe." *RB* 91 (1984): 362–76.

Scott, B. B. *Hear then the Parable*. Minneapolis: Fortress, 1989.

Soards, M. L. "Tradition, Composition and Theology in Luke's Account of Jesus before Herod Antipas." *Biblica* 66 (1985): 344–64.

Stauffer, E. *Jesus and His Story*. London: SCM, 1955.

Tyson, J. B. "Jesus and Herod Antipas." *JBL* 79 (1960): 239–46.

Via, J. E. "According to Luke, Who Put Jesus to Death?" In *Political Issues in Luke-Acts*, ed. R. Cassidy. Maryknoll, NY: Orbis, 1983.

Weinhart, F. D. "The Parable of the Throne Claimant." *CBQ* 39 (1972): 505–14.

Wilkinson, J. *Jerusalem as Jesus Knew It*. London: Thames and Hudson, 1978.

ARCHAEOLOGY, ICONOGRAPHY, AND ARCHITECTURE OF THE NEAR EAST

Avigad, N. *Discovering Jerusalem*. Jerusalem: Shikmona, 1980.

Ben-Dov, M. "Herod's Mighty Temple Mount." *BAR* 12 (1986): 40–49.

———. *In the Shadow of the Temple*. Jerusalem: Keter, 1982.

Burrell, B., K. Gleason, and E. Netzer. "Uncovering Herod's Seaside Palace." *BAR* 19/3 (1993): 50–52, 76.

Bounni, A., and Al-As'ad. *Palmyra*. Damascus, 1988.

Browning, I. *Jerash and the Decapolis*. London: Chatto and Windus, 1982.

Busink, T. A. *Der Tempel von Jerusalem*. Leiden: Brill, 1970, 1980.

Butler, H. C. *Architecture, Southern Syria*. Division II A, Publications of the Princeton University Archaeological Expeditions to Syria, 1904–5. Leiden: Brill, 1907.

Corbo, V. "La fortezza di Macheronte." *Liber Annus* 28 (1978): 217–31; 29 (1979): 315–26; 30 (1980): 365–70; 31 (1981): 257–86.

de Vaux, R. "Mambre." *DBSupl* 5 (1957): 753–58.

Dinsmoor, W. D. "An Archeological Earthquake at Olympia." *AJA* 2d ser. 45 (1941): 399–427.

Holum, K. G., et al. *King Herod's Dream: Caesarea by the Sea*. New York and London: Norton, 1988.

Jacobson, D. M. "The Plan of the Ancient Haram el-Khalil at Hebron." *PEQ* 113 (1981): 73–80.

Khouri, R. G. *The Antiquities of the Jordan Rift Valley*. Amman: Al Kutba, 1980.

Kloner, A. "Mareshah (Marisa)." *NEAEHL*, ed. M. Stern. Jerusalem: Israel Exploration Society, 1994, 3.948–57.

Kraus, S. *Synagogale Altertümer*. Berlin and Vienna, 1922.

Levine, L. I., ed. *The Jerusalem Cathedra: Studies in the History, Archaeology, Geography and Ethnography of the Land of Israel II*. Jerusalem and Detroit, 1982.

MacKay, A. G. *Houses, Villas and Palaces in the Roman World*. London: Thames and Hudson, 1975.

Mader, A. E. *Mambre. Die Ergebnissen der Aussgrabungen im heiligen Bezirk, Ramat el-Halil in Süd-Palästina*. Freiburg in Breisgau, 1957.

Magen, I. "Mamre." *NEAEHL*, ed. M. Stern. Jerusalem: Israel Exploration Society, 1994, 3.939–42.

Mare, W. *The Archaeology of the Jerusalem Area*. Grand Rapids: Baker, 1987.

Mazar, B. *The Mountain of the Lord*. New York: Doubleday, 1975.

———, Y. Shiloh, H. Geva, and N. Avigad. "Jerusalem." *NEAEHL*, ed. M. Stern. Jerusalem: Israel Exploration Society, 1994, 2.698–757.

Michalowski, K. *Palmyra*. New York: Praeger, 1968.

Milik, J. T. *Ten Years of Discovery in the Wilderness of Judea*. London: SCM, 1959.

Millar, N. "Patriarchal Burial Cite." *BAR* 11/3 (1985): 26–43.

Momigliano, A. "I nomi della prime 'synagoghe' romane e la condizione giuridica delle communità in Roma sotto Augusto." *Rassegna Mensile di Israel* 6 (1931–32): 283–92.

Netzer, E. "Cypros." *NEAEHL,* ed. M. Stern. Jerusalem: Israel Exploration Society, 1994, 1.315–17.

———. "Jericho: Tulul Abu el-ʿAlayiq." *NEAEHL,* ed. M. Stern. Jerusalem: Israel Exploration Society, 1994, 2.682–91.

———. *Masada*. Jerusalem: Israel Exploration Society, 1993.

———. "Masada." *NEAEHL,* ed. M. Stern. Jerusalem: Israel Exploration Society, 1994, 3.973–85.

———. "Remains of an Opus Reticulatum Building in Jerusalem." *IEJ* 33 (1983): 163–75.

Ofer, A. "Hebron." *NEAEHL,* ed. M. Stern. Jerusalem: Israel Exploration Society, 1994, 2.606–9.

Oren, E. D., and U. Rappaport. "The Necropolis of Mareshah-beth Guvrin." *IEJ* 34 (1984): 114–53.

Patrich, J. "Hyrcania." *NEAEHL,* ed. M. Stern. Jerusalem: Israel Exploration Society, 1994, 2.639–41.

Richardson, P. "Augustan-era Synagogues in Rome." In *Judaism and Christianity in Rome in the First Century,* ed. K. Donfried and P. Richardson. Forthcoming.

———. "Early Synagogues as Collegia in the Diaspora and Palestine." In *Voluntary Associations in the Ancient World,* ed. J. S. Kloppenborg and S. G. Wilson. London: Routledge, 1996.

———. "Religion and Architecture. A Study in Herod's Piety, Power, Pomp and Pleasure." *Bulletin of the Canadian Society of Biblical Studies* 45 (1985): 3–29.

———. "Religion, Architecture and Ethics: Some First Century Case Studies." *Horizons in Biblical Theology* 10/2 (1988): 19–49.

Ritmeyer, K., and L. Ritmeyer. "Reconstructing Herod's Temple Mount in Jerusalem." *BAR* 15/6 (1989), 23–53.

Ritmeyer, L. "Locating the Original Temple Mount." *BAR* 18 (1992): 24–45, 64–65.

Segal, A. *Architecture and the Theatre in Eretz Israel during the Roman and Byzantine Periods*. Haifa: University of Haifa Press, 1991.

Smith, R. H., and L. P. Day. *Pella of the Decapolis 2: Final Report on the College of Wooster Excavations in Area IX, The Civic Complex, 1979–85*. Wooster: The College of Wooster, 1989.

Tsafrir, Y., and I. Magen. "Sartaba-Alexandrium." *NEAEHL,* ed. M. Stern. Jerusalem: Israel Exploration Society, 1994, 4.1318–20.

Urman, D., and P. V. M. Flesher, eds. *Ancient Synagogues: Historical Analysis and Archaeological Discovery*. Leiden: Brill, 1995.

Vincent, L. H., E. J. H. Mackay, and F.-M. Abel. *Hébron: Le Haram El-Khalîl*. Paris: Éditions Ernest Leroux, 1923.

Vogüé, M. de. *Syria Centrale. Architecture civile et religieuse de I au VII siècle*. Paris: J. Baudry, 1865–67.

Weiss, Z. "Sepphoris." *NEAEHL,* ed. M. Stern. Jerusalem: Israel Exploration Society, 1994, 4.1324–28.

Yadin, Y. *Masada: Herod's Fortress and the Zealot's Last Stand.* New York, 1966.

Zanker, P. *The Power of Images in the Age of Augustus.* Ann Arbor: University of Michigan Press, 1990.

GEOGRAPHY AND ETHNOLOGY OF THE NEAR EAST

Abel, F.-M. *Géographie de Palestine.* Paris: Lecoffre, 1967 [1933].

Akurgal, E. *Ancient Civilisations and Ruins of Turkey.* Istanbul: Haset Kitabevi, 1985.

Applebaum, S. "The Settlement Pattern of Western Samaria." In *Landscape and Pattern: An Archaeological Survey of Samaria, 800 B.C.E.–636 C.E.,* ed. S. Dar. Oxford: BAR/IS, 1986.

Aviam, M. "Galilee." *NEAEHL,* ed. M. Stern. Jerusalem: Israel Exploration Society, 1994, 2:453.

Bickerman, E. "La Coelé-Syria: Notes de géographie historique." *RB* 54 (1947): 256.

Bietenhard, H. "Die syrische Dekapolis von Pompeius bis Traian." *ANRW* 2.9 (1970): 220–61.

Bilde, P. "The Geographical Excursuses in Josephus." In *Josephus and the History of the Greco-Roman Period,* ed. F. Parente and J. Sievers. Leiden: Brill, 1994.

Bowersock, G. W. *Roman Arabia.* Cambridge, MA: Harvard University Press, 1983.

Colledge, M. A. R. *The Parthians.* London: Thames and Hudson, 1967.

Dar, S. "Samaria." *ABD,* gen. ed. D. N. Freedman. New York: Doubleday, 1992, 5.926–31.

Debevoise, N. C. *A Political History of Parthia.* Chicago: University of Chicago Press, 1938.

Hammond, P. C. *The Nabateans: Their History, Culture and Archeology.* Studies in Mediterranean Archeology 37. Gotheburg: Paul Aströms Forlag, 1973.

Isaac, B. "The Decapolis in Syria: A Neglected Inscription." *ZPE* 44 (1981): 67.

Kasher, A. *Jews, Idumaeans and Ancient Arabs.* Tübingen: J. C. B. Mohr, 1988.

Lindner, M., ed. *Petra und das Königreich der Nabatäer.* Munich: Delp, 1970.

Maʿoz, Z., N. Goren-Inbar, and C. Epstein. "Golan." *NEAEHL,* ed. M. Stern. Jerusalem: Israel Exploration Society, 1994, 2:525–46.

Millar, F. *The Roman Near East, 31 BC–AD 337.* Cambridge, MA: Harvard University Press, 1994.

Negev, A. *Nabatean Archaeology Today.* New York: New York University Press, 1986.

———. "Nabatean Religion." *ER,* ed. M. Eliade. New York: Macmillan, 1986.

Parker, T. "The Decapolis Reviewed." *JBL* 94 (1975): 437–41.

Schmitt-Karte, K. *Die Nabatäer. Spuren einer arabischen Kultur der Antike.* Hanover: Veröffentlichen der Deutsch-Jordanischen Gesellschaft, 1976.

Slayton, J. C. "Bashan." *ABD,* gen. ed. D. N. Freedman. New York: Doubleday, 1992, 1.623—24.

Smith, G. A. *The Historical Geography of the Holy Land.* London: Hodder and Stoughton, 1902.

Sullivan, R. D. *Near Eastern Royalty: 100–30 BC.* Toronto: University of Toronto Press, 1990.

Ziegler, K. H. *Die Beziehungen zwischen Rom und dem Partherreich*. Wiesbaden: F. Steiner, 1964.

JUDEAN SOCIETY

Alon, G. "The Attitude of the Pharisees to the Roman Government and the House of Herod." *Scripta Hierosolymita* 7 (1961): 53–78.

Bamberger, B. J. *Proselytism in the Talmudic Period*. New York: KTAV, 1939.

Bammel, E. "Sadduzäer und Sadokiden." *Ephemerides Theologicae Lovaniensis* 55 (1979): 107–15.

Baumgarten, A. I. "Rivkin and Neusner on the Pharisees." P. Richardson et al., *Law in Religious Communities in the Roman Period: The Debate over Torah and Nomos in Post-Biblical Judaism and Early Christianity*, chap. 7. Waterloo, ON: Wilfrid Laurier University Press, 1991.

Finkelstein, L. *The Pharisees: The Sociological Background of Their Faith*. 3rd ed. Philadelphia: Jewish Publication Society of America, 1962.

Gilboa, A. "The Intervention of Sextus Julius Caesar, Governor of Syria, in the Affair of Herod's Trial." *SCI* 5 (1979–80): 185–95.

Goodman, M. *The Ruling Class of Judea. The Origins of the Jewish Revolt against Rome A.D. 66–70*. Cambridge: Cambridge University Press, 1987.

Hengel, M. *The Zealots*. Edinburgh: T. & T. Clark, 1989.

Hobsbawm, E. J. *Bandits*. New York: Penguin, 1985.

Isaac, B. "Bandits in Judaea and Arabia." *Harvard Studies in Classical Philology* 88 (1984): 171–203.

Jost, J. M. *Geschichte des Judentums und seiner Secten*. Leipzig: Dorffling und Franke, 1857.

LeMoyne, J. *Les Sadducées*. Paris: Gabalda, 1972.

Lightstone, J. N. "Sadducees versus Pharisees." In *Christianity, Judaism and Other Greco-Roman Cults*, ed. J. Neusner. Leiden: Brill, 1975.

Mason, S. *Josephus on the Pharisees*. Leiden: Brill, 1991.

Neusner, J. *From Politics to Piety: The Emergence of Pharisaic Judaism*. Englewood Cliffs, NJ: Prentice-Hall, 1973.

―――. *The Rabbinic Traditions about the Pharisees before 70*. Leiden: Brill, 1971.

Richardson, P., et al. *Law in Religious Communities in the Roman Period: The Debate over Torah and Nomos in Post-Biblical Judaism and Early Christianity*. Waterloo, ON: Wilfrid Laurier University Press, 1991.

Saldarini, A. J. *Pharisees, Scribes and Sadducees in Palestinian Society*. Wilmington, DL: Glazier, 1988.

Smith, M. "Palestinian Judaism in the First Century." In *Essays in Greco-Roman and Related Talmudic Literature*, ed. H. A. Fischel. 183–97. New York, 1977.

Wassén, C. "Sadducees and *Halakah*." P. Richardson et al., *Law in Religious Communities in the Roman Period: The Debate over Torah and Nomos in Post-Biblical Judaism and Early Christianity*, chap. 8. Waterloo, ON: Wilfrid Laurier University Press, 1991.

Wise, M. *A Critical Study of the Temple Scroll from Qumran Cave 11*. Chicago: Oriental Institute, 1990.

SOCIAL, POLITICAL, AND CULTURAL HISTORY OF THE JEWS

Brooke, G. J., ed. *Temple Scroll Studies*. Sheffield: JSOT Press 1989.

Cohen, S. J. D. *From the Maccabees to the Mishnah*. Philadelphia: Westminster, 1987.

———. *Josephus in Galilee and Rome*. Leiden: Brill, 1979.

Davies, P. R., and R. T. White, eds. *A Tribute to Geza Vermes: Essays on Jewish and Christian Literature and History*. Sheffield: JSOT Press, 1990.

Ewald, H. G. A. *History of Israel*. London: Longmans, Green, 1874 [1843–55].

Falk, Z. W. "Jewish Private Law." *CRINT*, ed. S. Safrai and M. Stern, 1.504–34.

Farmer, W. *Maccabees, Zealots and Josephus*. New York: Columbia University Press, 1957.

Feldman, L. H. "Josephus." *ABD*, gen. ed. D. N. Freedman. New York: Doubleday, 1992.

Fiensy, D. A. *The Social History of Palestine in the Herodian Period*. Lewiston, NY: Mellen, 1991.

Freyne, S. *Galilee from Alexander the Great to Hadrian, 323 B.C.E to 135 C.E: A Study of Second Temple Judaism*. Wilmington, DL: Glazier, 1980.

Goodman, M. *State and Society in Roman Galilee: AD 132–212*. Totowa, NJ: Rowman and Allanheld, 1983.

Gray, J. *A History of Jerusalem*. London: Hale, 1969.

Hengel, M. *Judaism and Hellenism: Studies in Their Encounter in Palestine during the Early Hellenistic Period*. Philadelphia: Fortress, 1974.

Kasher, A. *Jews and Hellenistic Cities in Eretz-Israel*. Tübingen: J. C. B. Mohr, 1990.

———. *Jews in Hellenistic and Roman Egypt*. Tübingen: J. C. B. Mohr, 1985.

———, U. Rappaport, and G. Fuks, eds. *Greece and Rome in Eretz-Israel*. Jerusalem: Israel Exploration Society, 1990.

Lämmer, M. "Eine Propaganda-Aktion des Königs Herodes in Olympia." In *Perspektiven der Sportwissenschaft*. Schorndorf: Hoffmann, 1973.

Leaney, A. R. C. *The Jewish and Christian World 200 BC to AD 200*. Cambridge: Cambridge University Press, 1984.

Leon, H. J. *The Jews of Ancient Rome*. Philadelphia: Jewish Publication Society, 1960.

Mason, S. *Josephus and the New Testament*. Peabody, MA: Hendrickson, 1992.

———. "Priesthood in Josephus and the Pharisaic Revolution." *JBL* 107 (1988): 657–61.

McLaren, J. S. *Power and Politics in Palestine*. Sheffield: JSOT Press, 1991.

Neusner, J. *Judaism in the Beginning of Christianity*. Philadelphia: Fortress, 1984.

Parente, F., and J. Sievers, eds. *Josephus and the History of the Greco-Roman Period*. Leiden: Brill, 1994.

Rajak, T. *Josephus: The Historian and his Society*. Philadelphia: Fortress, 1983.

Rhoads, D. M. *Israel in Revolution, 6–74 C.E.: A Political History Based on the Writings of Josephus*. Philadelphia: Fortress, 1976.

Richardson, P., ed. *Anti-Judaism in Early Christianity*, vol. 1. Waterloo, ON: Wilfrid Laurier University Press, 1986.

Russell, D. S. *The Jews from Alexander to Herod*. London: Oxford University Press, 1967.

Rutgers, L. V. "Roman Policy towards the Jews." *Classical World* 13/1 (1994): 56–74.

Safrai, S., and M. Stern, eds. *Compendia Rerum Iudaicarum ad Novum Testamentum (CRINT)*. Assen: van Gorcum/Philadeplphia: Fortress, 1974– .

Safrai, Z. *The Economy of Roman Palestine*. London: Routledge, 1994.

Sanders, E. P. *Jewish Law from Jesus to the Mishna*. London: SCM, 1990.

———. *Judaism: Practice and Belief, 63 BCE–66 CE*. London: SCM, 1992.

Schalit, A., ed. *World History of the Jewish People*, 1st ser. *The Hellenistic Age: Political History of Jewish Palestine from 332 B.C.E to 67 B.C.E.* New Brunswick, NJ: Rutgers University Press, 1972.

Schürer, E. *The History of the Jewish People in the Age of Jesus Christ*. New English edition. Vols. 1–3. Rev. and ed. G. Vermes and F. Millar. Edinburgh: T. and T. Clark, 1973–87.

Schwartz, D. R. "Josephus and Nicolaus on the Pharisees." *JSJ* 14 (1983): 151–71.

———. "Josephus on Hyrcanus II." In *Josephus and the History of the Greco-Roman Period*, ed. F. Parente and J. Seivers. Leiden: Brill, 1994.

Sevenster, J. N. *The Roots of Pagan Anti-Semitism in the Ancient World*. Leiden: Brill, 1975.

Shatzman, I. *The Armies of the Hasmoneans and Herod*. Tübingen: J. C. B. Mohr, 1991.

Smallwood, E. M. *The Jews under Roman Rule*. Leiden: Brill, 1976.

———, trans. *Philonis Alexandrini Legatio ad Gaium*. Leiden: Brill, 1970.

Stern, M. "Social and Political Realignments in Herodian Judaea." *Jerusalem Cathedra* 2 (1982): 40–62.

Sullivan, R. D. "The Dynasty of Judaea in the First Century." *ANRW* 2. 8: 296–354.

Tcherikover, V. *Hellenistic Civilization and the Jews*. New York: Atheneum, 1970 [1959].

Zeitlin, S. *The Rise and Fall of the Judean State*. Philadelphia: Jewish Publication Society of America, 1962.

ROMAN HISTORY

Bowersock, G. W. "Augustus and the East: The Problem of the Succession." In *Caesar Augustus. Seven Aspects*, ed. F. Millar and E. Segal. Oxford: Clarendon, 1984.

———. *Augustus and the Greek World*. Oxford: Clarendon, 1965.

———. "Eurycles in Sparta." *JRS* 51 (1961): 112–18.

Feldman, L. H. "Asinus Pollio and Herod's Sons." *Classical Quarterly* 35 (1985): 240–42.

Isaac, B. *The Limits of Empire: The Roman Army in the East*. Oxford: Clarendon, 1990.

Jones, A. H. M. *The Cities of the Eastern Roman Provinces*. Oxford: Clarendon, 1937.

Jones, H. M. S. "The Princeps," vol. 10 *CAH*, ed. J. B. Bury, S. A. Cook, F. E. Adcock. Cambridge: Cambridge University Press.

La Piana, G. "Foreign Groups in Rome during the First Centuries of the Empire." *HTR* 20 (1927): 183–403.

Leach, J. *Pompey the Great*. London: Croom Helm, 1978.

Levick, B. *Tiberius the Politician*. London: Croom Helm, 1976.

Lintott, A. *Imperium Romanum. Politics and Administration*. London and New York: Routledge, 1993.

Marshall, B. A. *Crassus. A Political Biography*. Amsterdam: Hakkert, 1976.

Millar, F., and E. Segal, eds. *Caesar Augustus. Seven Aspects*. Oxford: Clarendon Press, 1984.

Meyer, R. *Marcus Agrippa. A Biography*. Rome: Bretschneider, 1965.

Reinhold, M. *Marcus Agrippa*. Geneva, NY, 1933.

Roddaz, J.-M. *Marcus Agrippa*. Rome: École Française de Rome, 1984.

Shahîd, I. *Rome and the Arabs. A Prolegomenon to the Study of Byzantium and the Arabs*. Washington, DC: Dumbarton Oaks, 1984.

Sherk, R. K. *Rome and the Greek East to the Death of Augustus*. Cambridge: Cambridge University Press, 1984.

Sherwin-White, A. N. *Roman Society and Roman Law in the New Testament*. Oxford: Clarendon, 1963.

Signon, H. *Agrippa. Freund und Mitregent des Augustus*. Frankfurt: Societas Verlag, 1978.

Syme, R. "Who was Vedius Pollio?" *JRS* 5 (1961): 25–30.

Wallace-Hadrill, A., ed. *Patronage in Ancient Society:* London and New York: Routledge, 1989.

INDEX OF REFERENCES TO ANCIENT TEXTS

Hebrew Bible

Genesis
13:8	60
14:13	60
18:1	60
23:1–20	61
24:7	193n.64
25:9	61
25:12–15	68
25:30	54
49:31	61

Numbers
13:22	61
25	58n.21

Joshua
10:16	27, 61
15:13	61

2 Samuel
2:1–4	61
5:5	61

1 Kings
6:23–29	18
9:17–18	85

1 Chronicles
1:28–31	68

2 Chronicles
8:4	85
36:23	19n.64

Ezra
1;2	193n.64
2	193n.64

Nehemiah
11:25–36	61

Psalms
136:26	193n.64

Jeremiah
31:15	288

Daniel
2:18	193n.64
2:19	193n.64
2:28	193n.64
2:44	193n.4

Jonah
1:9	193n.64

New Testament

Matthew
2:1	296
2:3–4	296
2:4	296n.6
2:11	298
2:16–18	288
4:12	303n.40
11:20–21	304
11:23	304

New Testament (*continued*)

Matthew (*continued*)

14:1–2	308
14:3–12	307n.58
15:29	304n.42
22:1–10	299n.20
22:11–14	299n.20
22:15–22	309
22:16	259
25:14–30	31n.42, 299

Mark

1:14	303n.40
2:1–3	310n.67
3:6	259, 310n.67
4:35	303
5:1	303
5:2–20	303
6:14–29	305n.45
6:14–16	303, 308
6:17–29	303, 307n.58
6:17–18	306n.53
6:30–39	308
6:30–32	303
6:45–46	303
7:24–9:50	303
7:31	304n.42
8:15	309
8:22–26	303
8:27	301
9:30	304n.42
9:33	308
10:46	300
12:13–17	309
12:13	259
15:6–10	310n.70
15:16–20	310n.70
15:31	297

Luke

1:5	296, 297, 298
2:1–4	301
3:1	72, 88n.26, 297, 301, 306
3:19–20	304n.45, 306
4:14	303
7:18–35	309n.65
7:18–23	295n.1
9:7–9	306n.53, 308
9:9	309
9:10	303
10:8–12	304
10:13	304
10:15	304
13:1	312
13:31–33	304n.45, 309
18:35	300, 300n.25
19:11–27	31n.42, 299
20:19	309n.65
20:20–26	309
23:6–16	304n.45, 310
23:15	312n.79

John

1:43–44	303
1:46	303
6:1	304
6:15	304
12:20–22	303
12:21	303n.38
19:12	312

Acts

4:27	312
5:37	27, 37, 301
9:2	87
13:1	301n.30

Romans

13	257n.66
16:2	169n.88

Apocrypha and Pseudepigrapha

1 Maccabees

1:14–15	186
2:1	242n.5
5:65–68	61
8:1–32	73n.85
9:54–57	244n.25
10:10–11	244n.25

10:44–45	244n.25
13:25–30	62n.35
13:27–30	224n.29

Psalms of Solomon

2:1–6	99
2:1–2	255n.54
2:3–18	255n.54
2:19–21	255n.54
2:25–29	255n.54
8:4–5	99
8:11–12	99
8:14–17	255n.54
8:15–19	99
8:17–20	255n.54
8:18–22	255n.54

Testament of Moses

6:1–9	258n.73
6:2–9	261
6:2–6	298

Treatise of Shem

7:18	251n.40
11:1	251n.40

Josephus

Antiquities

1.186	60
1.196	60
1.326	260n.81
1.358	260n.81
8.74	18
8.81–83	18
12.414–19	73
13.67	245
13.171–72	252, 254
13.171	256n.63
13.257–58	54, 55n.13
13.288–98	252
13.288–92	240
13.288	254n.52, 256n.63
13.301	74
13.311–13	257
13.318	69
13.319	69n.68
13.356	144n.43
13.372–83	75
13.372–73	240
13.374	144n.43
13.392	118n.89
13.401–29	254
13.407	75
13.408–15	76n.95
13.410	254
13.418	118n.89
13.422	76
13.423–29	76
13.423	254
13.429	79n.96
13.430–32	76n.97
14.4	77, 77n.98, 77n.101
14.8–18	78, 79n.104
14.9	53n.8, 98n.14
14.10	55, 78
14.19	79
14.22–24	79n.107
14.29	86
14.31	79n.108
14.34–36	97, 97n.9
14.34	97n.11
14.35	98n.14
14.39	118n.89
14.41	98
14.46	98
14.48	98n.16
14.53	96n.4
14.54–74	98
14.66	99
14.68	98n.14
14.72–73	99
14.75	100n.22
14.80–81	101
14.82	100
14.84–89	101
14.84	100
14.88	103n.31
14.91	144n.43
14.93–97	101n.25
14.99	102n.28

Josephus (continued)

Antiquities (continued)

14.100	102n.29
14.103	102, 106n.42
14.104	98n.14, 103n.31, 104n.34
14.105	104n.34
14.111	98n.14
14.120	104
14.121–22	105n.39
14.121	62n.38, 104
14.123	105
14.126	118n.89
14.127–37	106, 271
14.127	105n.37
14.129	105
14.131	107
14.138	98n.14
14.139	106n.43, 107, 107n.46
14.140–43	108
14.143	69, 106n.42
14.144–45	108
14.145–55	98n.14
14.156–57	108
14.158	106n.41, 108n.50
14.159–60	109
14.162	109
14.163–84	109n.56
14.165	109, 109n.55
14.167–80	111n.59
14.169–70	111
14.172–76	256n.63
14n.174	112n.67
14.177	112, 112n.67
14.178	112
14.180	70n.73, 106n.41, 113
14.181	111n.59
14.184	113n.71
14.185	107n.48
14.186–89	269, 269n.35
14.190–267	110n.60
14.190–264	269
	4.190–95
	107
14.196–98	107n.47, 270n.39
14.200–201	107

14.200	269n.38
14.211–12	107n.46
14.217	107n.48
14.222	107n.48
14.223	107n.48
14.265	107n.48
14.268–70	114
14.272	114n.77
14.274	115
14.275	115n.82
14.277	115
14.280	70nn.73–73, 116, 129
14.281	116
14.283	116
14.284–93	117
14.284	118
14.291	117n.87
14.292	117
14.294–96	118
14.297	118, 122
14.299	118n.91, 122n.111
14.300	121n.106
14.301–2	123
14.304–23	123n.116
14.324–29	124n.119
14.325	124n.119
14.326	124
14.331	125
14.335–36	125
14.337–39	125
14.341	125
14.346	126
14.351	126n.125
14.363–64	126n.128
14.366	126
14.367–69	126
14.370–73	127n.130
14.377	127n.132
14.378	127n.133
14.379	127
14.382–3	127n.134, 128
14.384	127
14.386–87	129
14.390–93	130n.140
14.392–93	154

14.394	153n.1	15.40–41	242, 244n.16
14.396	154, 154n.4	15.40	162n.45
14.398	154	15.44	163
14.399	154	15.50–56	164, 243
14.403–4	52, 154	15.51	162
14.412	155	15.53	164n.53
14.413–17	155	15.56	162n.43
14.418–19	156n.10	15.57–61	164
14.420–33	250	15.65–87	218
14.420	156	15.65	164n.57
14.421–30	156	15.79	165n,62
14.431–33	156n.14	15.81	164n.58
14.434	156n.13, 157	15.92–95	165n.62
14.435	157n.15	15.96	166
14.436	260n.81	15.97	166
14.440–44	157n.17	15.98	166n.71
14.450	157n.20, 158n.25, 250,	15.101	166
	260n.81	15.103	166
14.451–53	158	15.106–7	166, 166n.68
14.451	157n.21	15.110	167
14.455	158n.24	15.111	167n.76
14.462–64	158	15.116	167
14.468–69	159	15.120	168, 168n.80
14.470–75	159	15.121	168n.83, 168n.85
14.475	159n.28	15.124	168
14.476–79	158	15.127–46	168n.68
14.482–84	160	15.131	167n.75
14.487	160n.31	15.132	166n.74
14.488	160	15.136	168
14.489–90	160n.32	15.147	168
14.489	155n.6	15.159	169
14.490–91	161n.35	15.160	169n.92
15.1–7	161	15.161–63	169
15.1–4	256n.63	15.163–73	169n.91, 170
15.7	160n.31	15.174–78	169n.91170
15.9	160n.32	15.178	169n.89
15.11–17	161	15.179–82	169n.91, 170
15.18–20	162	15.182	170, 171
15.21–23	162	15.183	170n.96, 171
15.22	242, 242n.8, 244n.16	15.184–86	172n.101
15.23–24	162	15.185–239	218, 220
15.25–30	163	15.185–221	165n.65
15.29	152n.43	15.185–87	215
15.31–41	163, 242n.9	15.187	161n.38
15.34	162n.46	15.188–94	172n.102

Josephus (continued)

Antiquities (continued)

15.190   172n.104
15.195   172, 172n.104
15.199–200   171
15.202–39   216
15.202–8   218
15.209–39   218
15.216   217
15.217   173, 217
15.218–22   217
15.218   217
15.223–27   217
15.228–30   226
15.229   217
15.232–36   217
15.242–46   218
15.243   222n.17
15.247–49   221
15.250–51   221
15.253   221
15.255   221
15.256–58   221
15.259–66   221
15.264   221
15.266   222n.16
15.267   222n.17
15.268–91   187n.42, 188n.48
15.268–71   223
15.272–79   224n.27
15.280–81   224
15.292–98   225
15.298   222n.17
15.299–316   222, 222n.17
15.300–302   222
15.303   222
15.308–16   223
15.316   225
15.317   230
15.318   226
15.320   235
15.323–25   225n.34
15.323   236n.67
15.326   222, 225
15.331–42   226

15.340   189n.55
15.342–44   231
15.243–49   232
15.344–48   251
15.350   233n.57
15.351–53   239
15.354–55   233, 234
15.357   233
15.360   234
15.361   233
15.362–64   234
15.362   274
15.365   184n.35, 236
15.366–70   235
15.368–70   255, 257
15.372–79   257
15.373   256n.63
15.380–425   195, 247, 258
15.380   238
15.382–87   238n.78
15.387–90   238
15.387   249
16.1–5   237
16.6   239
16.16   271
16.22   271
16.24   271n.43
16.26   271
16.27–60   271
16.55–57   263n.9
16.62   272
16.68–72   274
16.73–74   276
16.73   274
16.75–77   276n.60
16.78–80   276
16.85–89   277
16.90–130   231
16.91   278, 278n.66
16.100–126   278
16.127–29   278n.69, 279
16.130–31   279
16.130   279n.70, 285n.97
16.132–33   281, 281n.84
16.136   282n.85

16.146–49   273
16.147   177, 185, 189, 264n.14
16.149   177, 272
16.160–73   269, 270
16.179–84   183, 282n.86
16.188–205   282nn.87–88
16.188   282
16.191–93   283
16.193   283n.91
16.194–228   274n.49, 275
16.194   274
16.198   274
16.200–228   275
16.201   283n.91
16.203–4   231n.48, 283n.91
16.220–25   276n.57
16.220   276
16.229–53   284
16.255   284n.95
16.256–69   285
16.265–66   269
16.270–71   285n.97
16.271   279, 279n.70
16.273   278n.68, 279n.70
16.277–369   268n.30
16.282   280
16.283   281
16.286–90   280
16.291–92   281
16.293   280
16.300   286n.98
16.312   286n.100
16.315–16   286n.99
16.320–38   286
16.339–69   287
16.360   287n.105
16.370–72   288
16.373–93   288n.107
16.394   288
16.395–404   29n.36
16.511–12   285
17.1–4   289
17.6   289
17.12–22   289
17.19   235, 236n.68

17.20   232, 235n.65
17.23–30   301n.32
17.23–29   251
17.27–31   281n.82
17.32–40   289
17.41–57   290
17.41–45   255
17.42–43   257n.67
17.43   290n.112
17.54   290n.113
17.58–71   291
17.63   290
17.72–78   291n.116
17.79–81   291
17.83–85   291
17.86–105   292
17.106   133, 292n.120, 293
17.134–47   294
17.149–67   15
17.160   15
17.191   191n.59
17.219   283n.89
17.221   283n.89
17.228   283n.89
17.259   17
17.271   181
17.300   25n.25
17.303   21n.19
17.339–55   298n.17
17.342–48   300n.26
18.1–108   298n.17
18.11–25   256
18.16–18   252
18.18–22   237n.73
18.19   257n.65
18.26–28   302, 302n.36
18.26   301
18.27–28   180, 181, 301n.32, 305n.45, 306
18.36–38   305n.45, 306
18.55–62   308n.60, 311
18.60–62   311n.76
18.63–64   308n.60, 311n.77
18.85–89   311
18.101–5   305

Josephus (*continued*)

Antiquities (*continued*)

18.106–8	301nn.32–33
18.109–29	305n.45
18.109–14	307n.56
18.109	307
18.130	274
18.176–77	312n.78
18.189	301n.32
18.237	301n.32
18.240–56	305n.45
18.319	301n.32
19.329	31n.41
19.332	53n.7
19.335	31n.41
20.17–96	297n.10
20.173	56
20.224–51	243
20.241	240
20.243–44	78, 78n.102
20.243	77n.101
20.244	77n.101
20.247–48	242n.9, 243, 244n.16

Life

42	91
46–61	281n.82
55–56	281n.81
64	306n.49
169	306n.49
177–80	281n.82
277	306n.48
284	306n.49
300	306n.49
313	306n.49
342	88n.26
349	88n.26

War

1.63	55n.13
1.78	256n.63, 257
1.86	144n.43
1.88	75
1.89	144n.43
1.91–98	75
1.103	118n.89

1.107–14	254
1.107–12	76n.97
1.108–11	76n.95
1.109	75
1.113	256n.63
1.117	76
1.118	77n.99
1.120	77, 77n.98
1.123–26	78, 79
1.123	53n.8
1.127–28	79n.108, 86
1.131–33	97n.11
1.138–54	98
1.138	96n.4
1.149	98
1.152–53	99
1.154–55	100
1.155	100
1.159	101
1.160	100
1.162–67	101
1.170	102, 144n.43
1.171–84	101n.25
1.178	102
1.179	104n.34
1.180	104
1.181	104
1.182	104
1.183–94	106
1.183	105
1.185–86	118n.89
1.187	105n.37
1.188	105
1.193–94	107
1.195–200	108
1.199–200	69
1.199	106n.42
1.201–3	108, 108n.50
1.203	69
1.204–11	250
1.204–6	109
1.207	109
1.208–15	109n.56
1.208	109, 111
1.210–11	110n.59, 111, 112

1.212	112
1.213	70, 70n.73, 106n.41, 112, 113n.70
1.214	113
1.215	113n.71
1.216–17	114
1.218	114
1.219	114
1.224	106n.41, 116
1.225	70n.74, 106n.41, 116, 129
1.226	116
1.227–35	117
1.229	118
1.232	117
1.236–38	118
1.239	118, 122
1.240	118n.91, 122n.111
1.241	121n.106
1.242	122, 123
1.243–45	124
1.244	106n.42, 124, 124m.119
1.248	125n.122
1.251	125
1.253	125
1.259	126
1.262	126n.125
1.268	126n.128
1.269–70	285
1.270	126
1.271–72	126
1.273	126
1.274–76	127n.130
1.279	127
1.280	127n.32, 189n.53
1.282–83	127n.134, 128
1.284	127
1.285	129
1.286–89	130n.140
1.288–89	154
1.290	153n.1
1:292	154, 154n.4
1.293	154
1.294	154
1.296	154
1.302–3	59
1.302	155
1.303	155n.8
1.304–7	155
1.308	156n.10
1.309–16	250
1.309–13	156
1.314–16	156n.14
1.317	156, 156n.13, 157n.15
1.319	157n.16
1.321	157
1.324	158n.25
1.326	59, 59n.23, 157n.20, 250
1.328–30	158
1.328	157n.21
1.335	158
1.340–41	158
1.341	161
1.344	159
1.345–46	159
1.347–51	159
1.352	159
1.354–55	160
1.357	160, 160n.32
1.358	161
1.362–63	166
1.364–55	67
1.364	166n.73
1.365	167
1.366–68	67
1.366	167n.76
1.367	167, 167n.77
1.369	167, 168
1.370	168n.83
1.371	168
1.373–79	168n.86
1.378	168
1.380–85	67
1.380	168
1.385	169
1.386	169
1.387	161n.38, 171
1.388–92	172n.102
1.389–90	171n.100
1.391	172
1.392–93	172, 172n.104

Josephus (continued)

War (continued)

1.393	172
1.394	172
1.396–97	173, 217, 219
1.396	90n.32
1.398–400	173n.106
1.398–99	232 232n.52, 234
1.398	71, 71n.81
1.399–400	72, 251
1.400–401	185
1.400	67, 191n.59, 191, 233
1.401	238
1.405	178
1.416	16
1.422–28	273
1.422	185, 189
1.424	177, 185
1.425	177
1.426–27	177, 272n.45
1.428	176
1.429–30	168nn.81–82, 173n.107, 191n.59
1.432	121n.106
1.434	161nn.40–41
1.435	173n.107
1.436–7	164n.55
1.437	164, 219
1.438	165n.64
1.440	165n.62
1.441–44	165n.65
1.441–43	216, 218
1.441–42	164n.58
1.442	217
1.444	217
1.445–47	239
1.445	231, 273, 274
1.447–48	276
1.451	277, 277n.65
1.452–54	278, 278n.66, 278n.69
1.455–56	278n.69, 279
1.458–65	281
1.460	282
1.467–84	282nn.87
1.470	282
1.473–77	283
1.474	280n.74
1.478–80	283n.91
1.479	231n.48
1.483	234, 274, 274n.49, 275, 283
1.485–86	274
1.486–87	275
1.488–96	284
1.498	284n.98
1.499–509	285
1.510	285n.97
1.513	286n.98
1.527	286n.99
1.532–33	286n.100
1.534–36	286
1.535–42	268n.30
1.537	287n.105
1.538	287
1.540–42	287
1.543	288
1.544–50	288n.107
1.550	281
1.551	288
1.552–62	289
1.562	235, 235n.65, 236, 289n.110
1.567–70	289
1.571–73	280
1.572	275
1.573	277n.64
1.574	290n.113
1.575–57	290
1.578–90	291
1.583	290
1.592–94	291
1.595–600	291n.116
1.601–3	291
1.608–9	291
1.609–12	292
1.614–35	292
1.636	292n.120
1.637–40	293
1.641–46	296n.10
1.644	293n.123
1.648–55	15

1.648	255, 256n.63
1.656–73	18
2.1–117	301n.32
2.1–100	18n.11
2.14	283n.89
2.16	283n.89
2.20–22	22
2.21	283n.89
2.24	283n.89
2.44	187
2.48	17
2.49	261
2.55	59, 178
2.56	27, 250, 251
2.59	181
2.80	25nn.25–26
2.82–83	21n.19
2.84–86	191n.59
2.95	72
2.96	59n.24
	2,97
	91n.33
2.111–17	298n.17
2.113	256n.63
2.119–66	250, 256
2.119–61	237n.73
2.119	254
2.120–61	257n.65
2.139–40	257
2.162–64	254
2.166	252
2.167–68	301n.32
2.168	181, 302, 303n.36
2.169–74	311
2.175–77	311n.76
2.178–80	311n.77
2.212	251
2.252	181
2.388	297n.10
2.398	265
2.421	281
2.459	91, 92n.41
2.461–65	281
2.466–76	90n.31
2.478	91

2.520	297n.10
2.561	87
2.566	58n.20
2.567	256n.63
2.641	306.49
3.35–42	132n3
3.44–47	142n.37
3.46	88n.26
3.49–55	157n.21
3.57	142
3.446	88n.26
4.208	58
4.231	58
4.234	58
4.272	58
4.278–79	58
4.281	58
4.314–18	58
4.335–54	58
4.529	57n.18
4.530	57n.18
4.533	60
4.567	297n.10
5.55	297n.10
5.119	297n.10
5.181–82	191
5.184–237	247
5.252	297n.10
5.461	83
6.355–56	297n.10
7.224	83
7.267	58

Philo

De virtutibus

108	53n.6

In Flaccum

1	312

Legatio ad Gaium

143–47	228
148–51	229
153–54	229
159–61	312

Philo (*continued*)
Legatio ad Gaium (*continued*)
281–82   265n.17
294–98   264
299–305   311
326   301n.32

Quod omnis probus liber sit
76   257n.65
89   259n.78

De specialibus legibus
1.52–53   53n.6
4.2   237n.72

Dead Sea Scrolls

Community Rule (1QS)
9.4–5   258n.76

Messianic Rule (1QSa)
1.3   258n.76

Commentary on Habakkuk (1QpHab)
4   258n.75
6   258n.76

Temple Scroll (11QT), 246, 246n.27, 258, 258n.70

Acts of Torah (4QMMT), 246n.27

Rabbinic Literature

MISHNA
Baba Batra
3.2   139–40n.28
Bikkurim
1.10   139–40n.28
Eduyyot
8.7   139–40n.28
Kelim
1.6   245n.24
Ketubot
13.10   139–40n.28

Menachot
8.3   139–40n.28
Middot
23   245n.25
Parah
3.5   244n.18
Sotah
7.8   53n.7
9.15   244n.18
Ta'anit
3.6   139–40n.28

TOSEFTA
Sukkah
1.9   72

MIDRASH
Leviticus Rabbah
35.10   76

Other Ancient Literature

APPIAN
Civil Wars
2.18   104nn.33–34
4.58–63   116
4.58   114n.76
5.9   85
5.11   124n.121
5.75   128n.137, 131n.1
Mithridatic War
10   95n.3
92–97   95n.1
116–17   101
Syrian Wars
2   119n.94
50   100n.20
51   104n.34

AUGUSTUS
Res gestae
26   230

CICERO
Attici
15.1.3   84n.12

CASSIUS DIO
History of Rome
36.20.3   95n.1
41.18.1   105
49.22   160n.32
49.39   162n.47
53.16   227
53.22   227n.38
53.29   230nn.45–46
54.9   232n.54
54.10   227n.38
54.12   262
54.15–16   262
54.19   232n.55
54.28   227, 283n.93
55–56   283
55.8   283n.93
55.10   290n.114
55.27   284n.93, 298n.17
56.18–24   292n.119
59.12   301n.32

Corpus Inscriptionum Iudaicarum (CIJ)
173   267n.25
284   267n.27
301   267n.27
338   267n.27
343   267n.27
365   267n.27
368   267n.27
402   267n.27
416   267n.27
417   267n.27
425   267n.27
496   267n.27
503   267n.27
523   267n.27

DIODORUS SICULUS
Bibliotheca
19.94.4–5   64n.43

EUSEBIUS
Church History
1.6   52
1.7.24   52

Die Fragmente der griechschen Historiker (FGrH)
190F   106n.44

HOMER
Iliad
16.162   123n.118

JEROME
Commentaria in Jeremiam
31   60n.29
In Zechariam
9:2   60n.29

JUSTIN
Dialogue with Trypho
52   52

L. ANNIUS FLORUS
Epitome of Roman History
3.6.7–14   95n.1

NICOLAS OF DAMASCUS (STERN, M., *Greek and Latin Authors*)
#96   91n.33

PLINY
Natural History
5.74   88n.26
5.88   85
7.97–98   101n.25
12.111   166n.69
16.74   301n.32

PLUTARCH
Antony
24   123n.113
25–29   123n.118
28   123n.117
30   124–25
33–52   128n.138
33   156n.11
34   157n.18
36   160n.32, 165n.62
71   171n.100
72–73   173
72   171n.100, 172
73–87   173
74   172

PTOLEMY
Geography
5.14.18   88n.26
5.15.26   301n.32
5.16.4   303n.38

STRABO
Geography
2.5.12   230n.43
16.2.1   81
16.2.2   57, 81
16.2.10   68
16.2.16–22   70n.74
16.2.16   141n.35
16.2.18   68, 69n.68, 71, 71n.81, 142, 250
16.2.20   68, 69n.68, 86, 142, 250
16.2.29   88n.27
16.2.34   55, 55n.13, 139n.27
16.2.37   250n.38
16.2.40   74

16.2.41   178n.10
16.2.46   52n.1, 13, 131, 298n.17
16.4.21   230n.43
16.4.25–26   280n.77
17.1.53   230n.47

SUETONIUS
Augustus
47–48   228n.40
Nero
13   297n.9

SYNCELLUS
1.576   114n.77

TACITUS
Annals
12.23   201n.32
16.22   1n.1
Histories
5.4   232n.71
5.9   128n.137

INDEX OF MODERN AUTHORS

Abel, F.-M., 60n.27, 61n.30, 154n.5
Aharoni, Y., 100n.22, 154n.5
Akurgal, E., 84n.7
Al-As'ad, K., 85n.16
Albright, W. F., 60n.27
Alexander, W. L., 211n.75
Alon, G., 256n.60
Applebaum, S., 178n.8, 221n.13
Aviam, M., 132n.4, 133nn.6–8
Avigad, N., 135n.15
Avi-Yonah, M., 100n.22, 126n.129, 154n.5, 306n.50

Baly, D., 68n.63, 134n.12
Bamberger, B. J., 42n.32
Bammel, E., 103n.30, 245n.22, 305n.45, 312n.82
Barnes, T. D., 296n.2
Barnett, P. W., 237n.73
Baumgarten, A. I., 255n.58, 256, 256n.62
Belloc, H., 12n.3
Betz, O., 309n.64
Bickerman, E., 70n.74
Bietenhard, H., 88n.25
Bilde, P., 132n.3
Blinzler, J., 310n.71
Bliss, F. J., 60n.26
Bounni, A., 85n.16
Bowersock, G. W., 27n.29, 86n.19, 231n.49, 280n.75, 285n.98, 292n.119
Braun, W., 259n.80
Braund, D., 199n.92, 172n.103, 231n.49

Brown, R. E., 296n.3, 297, 297n.13, 298n.14, 303n.38, 312n.82
Browning, I., 88n.25
Bruce, F. F., 305n.45
Brunt, P. A., 13n.7, 228n.41, 315
Buck, E., 297n.7
Burckhardt, J., 62
Burrell, B., 182n.26
Butler, H. C., 17n.7, 65n.50, 206n.72

Cassidy, R., 305n.45
Catchpole, D., 310n.72
Charlesworth, J., 298n.16
Cohen, S. J. D., 42n.32, 161n.38
Colledge, M. A. R., 305n.45
Conder, C., 61n.30
Corbett, J., 89n.28
Cotton, H. M., 203n.66
Crossan, J. D., 250n.38
Crowfoot, J. W., 188n.46

Dar, S., 138n.22, 138n.24, 178n.8
Davies, P., 185n.37, 245n.23
Day, L. P., 89n.29
Debevoise, N. C., 119n.96, 154n.3, 305n.46
Derrett, J. D. M., 305n.45
de Vaux, R., 60n.28
Dinsmoor, W. D., 177n.3
Dittenberger, W., 208
Dodd, C. H., 305n.44
Donfried, K., 186n.39, 267n.25

Edwards, O., 296n.2
Eisenman, R. H., 258n.70
Epstein, C., 139n.28
Ewald, H. G. A., 211n.75

Falk, Z. W., 37n.14
Farmer, W., 27n.30
Feldman, L. H., 11n.2, 77n.101, 231n.49
Fenn, R., 20n.16, 27n.30, 29n.34,
    110n.57, 301n.31
Fiensy, D. A., 110n.61, 134n.11, 138n.25,
    178n.8, 178n.11
Finkelstein, I., 138n.22
Flesher, P. V. M., 141n.30
Frey, J. B., 268
Freyne, S., 110n.61, 306n.51
Fuks, G., 88n.25, 238n.78, 273n.46

Gabba, E., 238n.78, 247n.32, 273n.46
Gal, Z., 133n.5
Geiger, J., 203n.66
Geva, H., 135n.15, 180n.19
Gichon, M., 189n.51
Gilboa, A., 111n.65
Gleason, K., 182n.26
Goodman, M. D., 20n.16, 22n.22,
    27n.30, 29n.34, 110n.57, 253, 253n.47,
    301n.31
Goren-Inbar, N., 139n.28
Grant, M., 16n.3, 105n.38, 122n.110,
    128n.139, 160n.33, 170n.93, 174n.1,
    237n.73, 271n.41, 276n.59
Gray, J., 243n.10

Halligan, J., 185n.37, 245n.23
Hammond, P. C., 64, 64n.45, 65n.50
Hanson, J., 27n.30, 38, 38n.18, 39,
    39nn.20–23, 40nn.24–26, 41,
    41nn.27–31, 42nn.33–34, 43nn.35–38,
    44nn.40–42, 45, 45nn.43–44, 46,
    122n.107, 221n.15, 235nn.63–4,
    250n.38
Harland, P., 28n.32
Harlow, V. E., 305n.45
Havener, I., 299n.22
Hawthorne, G. F., 309n.64

Hengel, M., 27n.30, 92n.40
Heuchan, V., 102n.28
Hobsbawm, E. J., 250n.38
Hoehner, H., 33n.4, 34nn.5–7, 35,
    35nn.8–9, 36nn.10–12, 296n.3,
    302n.36, 305n.45, 306n.48, 307nn.58–
    59, 308n.63, 310n.71, 311n.74
Holum, K. G., 93n.43
Horsley, R., 27n.30, 110n.61, 250n.38

Isaac, B., 71n.77, 88n.25, 141n.33,
    205n.70, 250n.38

Jacobson, D. M., 61n.30
Jeremias, J., 135, 299n.21
Jones, A. H. M., 88n.25, 105n.38,
    128n.139, 160n.31, 165n.63, 166n.74,
    170n.95, 301n.32, 304n.45
Jones, C., 285n.98
Jones, H. S., 33n.2
Jones, R. N., 144n.44
Jost, J. M., 211n.75

Kanael, B., 211n.76, 212
Kasher, A., 54n.9, 55, 55nn.12–15, 56,
    56n.16, 58, 58n.19, 59, 69n.69, 88n.25,
    136n.18, 179n.14, 238n.78, 245n.19,
    265n.19, 273n.46
Khouri, R. G., 143n.39, 143n.41
Klassen, W., 266n.21
Klausner, J., 73, 73nn.87–88, 75, 75n.91
Klimowsky, E. N., 12n.4
Kloner, A., 54n.9
Kloppenborg, J., 299n.19, 299n.22
Kraus, S., 268n.31
Kuhn, E., 103n.30
Kushnir-Stein, A., 204n.68

Lämmer, M., 177n.3
La Piana, G., 268n.31
Lauterbach, J. Z., 252n.45
Leach, J., 12n.5, 95n.2, 96n.6
LeMoyne, J., 252n.45
Leon, H. J., 267n.23, 267nn.28–29, 268,
    268n.32
Levick, B., 312n.83

Lightstone, J. N., 254n.51
Lindner, M., 64n.44
Lintott, A., 119n.92, 172n.103, 176n.2

Macalister, R. A. S., 60n.26
MacKay, A. G., 181n.22
Mackay, E. J. H., 61n.30
Madden, F. W., 211n.75
Mader, A. E., 60n.28
Magen, I., 60n.28, 136n.17, 139n.26
Malina, B. J., 38n.19
Mantzoulinou-Richards, E., 205n.71, 206
Ma'oz, Z., 139n.28, 140n.29, 141n.30
Marcus, R., 77n.101, 126n.125, 160n.31,
    165n.62
Mare, W., 135n.15
Marshall, B. A., 120n.99
Mason, S., 256n.64
Mazar, B., 60n.27, 135n.15, 205
McLaren, J. S., 109n.56, 111n.62,
    111n.64, 113nn.72–73
McRay, J., 174n.1
Merritt, B. D., 208n.73
Meshorer, Y., 70n.76, 74nn.89–90,
    91n.34, 114n.78, 128n.136, 130n.142,
    204n.67, 211n.76, 212, 212nn.78–79,
    213, 213n.83, 214, 214nn.84–85,
    214n.87, 264n.14
Metzger, B., 309n.66
Meyer, R., 262n.4
Meyshan, J., 212, 212n.77, 214n.88
Michalowski, K., 85n.14
Milik, J. T., 259n.79
Millar, F., 20n.17, 62n.36, 63n.40,
    64n.46, 66nn.54–55, 69n.70, 70n.74,
    71n.77, 81, 81n.2, 84nn.9–11, 85n.13,
    85n.18, 86n.20, 87n.22, 88n.25,
    92n.39, 112n.69, 118n.88, 120n.100,
    167n.76, 176n.2, 285n.98, 287n.104
Millar, N., 61n.30
Momigliano, A., 268n.31
Monroe, J. M., 13n.7, 228n.41, 315
Murray, T. J., 18n.10
Myers, E., 88n.25, 233n.61

Negev, A., 65nn.48–49
Netzer, E., 20n.15, 136n.17, 174, 174n.1,

180n.18, 181n.20, 182nn.23–24,
    182n.26, 184n.29, 186n.38, 306n.51
Neusner, J., 242n.7, 254n.51, 256
Nicklesburg, G. W. E., 298n.16

Ofer, A., 57n.18, 61n.30, 135n.14,
    136n.19, 137n.20
Oren, E. D., 54n.10

Parente, F., 106n.45, 132n.3
Parker, T., 88n.25
Patrich, J., 136n.17
Perowne, S. G., 174n.1, 264n.15,
    276n.59, 280n.73, 280n.75
Polag, A., 299n.22
Porton, G., 253n.46, 254n.51
Priest, J., 298n.16
Przybylski, B., 297n.7

Rappaport, U., 54n.10, 88n.25, 238n.78,
    245n.25, 273n.46
Reinach, T., 266n.22
Reinhold, M., 233n.56
Reville, A., 301n.32
Reynolds, J., 53n.5
Rich, J., 119n.92
Richardson, P., 17n.6, 28n.33, 67n.60,
    102n.28, 185n.37, 186n.39, 191n.58,
    194n.65, 209n.74, 215n.90, 245n.23,
    252n.45, 255n.58, 256n.62, 266n.21,
    267n.25, 297n.7, 304n.43, 309n.64
Ritmeyer, K., 245n.26
Ritmeyer, L., 158n.26, 245n.26
Robinson, J. A. T., 303n.39, 304n.44
Roddaz, J.-M., 262n.4
Rowley, H. H., 260n.81
Rutgers, L. V., 267n.23

Safrai, Z., 188n.49
Saldarini, A. J., 252n.45
Sanders, E. P., 28n.31, 162n.44, 242n.5,
    244n.17, 247n.29, 252n.44, 253n.49,
    255n.59, 256nn.61–62, 256n.64,
    258n.76, 261n.83, 266n.21, 310n.67
Sandmel, S., 218n.7
Sandys-Wunsch, J., 247n.28

Saulnier, C., 305n.45
Schalit, A., 13, 13n.8, 16n.3, 75n.92,
    78n.103, 106n.43, 109n.54, 110n.59,
    127n.135, 156n.12, 157n.15, 158n.25,
    160n.31, 161n.31, 161n.36, 162n.44,
    163n.51, 169n.90, 174n.1, 216n.1,
    217n.2, 217n.4, 218n.7, 219n.9,
    255n.55, 262n.1, 264n.15, 275n.54,
    276n.62, 285n.98, 287n.103
Schaumberger, P. I., 296n.4
Schiffman, L. 246n.27
Schmitt-Karte, K., 64n.44
Schürer, E., 13n.6, 16n.1, 63n.39, 68n.61,
    68n.64, 71n.80, 74n.89, 77n.100,
    88n.25, 91n.35, 96n.5, 97nn.8–9,
    97n.13, 99n.19, 100nn.21–22, 101n.27,
    103n.30, 111n.63, 120n.101, 139n.28,
    143n.40, 144n.42, 154n.3, 160n.31,
    162n.44, 164n.56, 166n.69, 222n.17,
    232n.53, 238n.77, 245n.25, 301nn.27–
    28, 301n.32, 303n.37, 305nn.45–46,
    306n.51, 307n.54
Schwartz, D. R., 106n.45
Scott-Kilvert, I., 227n.37
Segal, A., 187n.40
Segal, E., 285n.98
Seivers, J., 106n.45, 132n.3
Sevenster, J. N., 266, 266n.22
Shanks, H., 183n.30, 282n.86
Shahîd, I., 68n.62
Shatzman, I., 97n.10, 98n.18, 136n.18
Sherk, R. K., 233n.58, 238n.74, 270n.40
Sherwin-White, A. N., 311n.75
Shiloh, Y., 135n.15
Signon, H., 262n.4
Slayton, J. C., 141n.32
Smallwood, E. M., 40, 211n.75, 228n.39,
    265n.16, 267n.23, 268n.33, 306n.49,
    312n.82
Smith, G. A., 139n.28
Smith, R. H., 89n.29
Soards, M. L., 305n.45, 310n.71
Spijkerman, A., 88n.25
Stauffer, E., 296n.4

Stager, L. E., 93n.44
Stern, M., 55n.13, 91n.33, 120n.102,
    245n.19, 253n.46, 266, 266n.22
Streeter, B. H., 309n.64
Sullivan, R., 33n.1, 63n.39, 68n.65,
    69n.71, 71n.80, 80n.109, 83nn.3–6,
    84n.8, 84n.10, 84n.12, 87, 87n.24,
    97n.8, 97n.10, 101n.27, 105n.40,
    106n.44, 119n.93, 119n.95, 120n.98,
    120n.101, 156n.13, 160n.31, 161n.39,
    176n.2, 297n.8
Syme, R., 231n.49

Tannenbaum, R., 53n.5
Tcherikover, V., 92n.40
Thackeray, H. S., 126n.125, 285n.97
Todd, E., 41n.27
Tsafrir, Y., 136n.17
Tushingham, A. D., 68n.63, 134n.12
Tyson, J. B., 310n.71

Urman, D., 141n.30

van Beek, G., 64n.42
Via, J. E., 305n.45
Vincent, L. H., 61n.30
Vogüé, M. de, 65n.50, 206

Waddington, W. H., 206
Wallace-Hadrill, A., 119n.92, 172n.103
Wassén, C., 252n.45
Weinhart, F. D., 299n.21
Weiss, Z., 133n.9, 306n.51
Wheatly-Irving, L., 303n.41
Wilkinson, J., 16, 16n.5, 135n.15
Wise, M., 246n.27

Yadin, Y., 174n.1

Zanker, P., 104n.36
Zeitlin, S., 110n.58, 121n.105, 122n.109,
    124n.120
Zertal, A., 138nn.22–23
Ziegler, K. H., 305n.46

INDEX OF PLACES

Abila, 68, 71, 74, 86, 88, 88n.26, 101n.24, 143, 250, 251
Acco. *See* Ptolemais
Achzib. *See* Ecdippa
Actium, 3, 169, 170n.97, 177, 193, 264n.12, 285n.98
Adiabene, 199n.97
Adora, 55, 55n.13, 57, 60, 91
Adoraim, 137
Africa, 13n.7
Agrippias. *See* Anthedon
'Ain Jedur. *See* Gedor
Alexandreion, 98, 98n.18, 100, 101, 102, 139, 154, 179, 180, 181, 190, 216, 263, 263n.10
Alexandria, 106, 124, 127, 163, 173, 175, 228, 229, 244, 254, 265
Amman. *See* Philadelphia
Ammathus, 74, 88, 144
Antakya. *See* Antioch-on-the-Orontes
Anthedon, 74, 91, 173, 177, 178, 188, 189, 263, 316, 317
Anti-Lebanon mountains, 86, 97, 142
Antioch-on-the-Orontes, 3, 5, 6, 11, 23, 71, 82, 83, 120, 121, 123, 124, 133, 156, 160, 189, 217, 251n.41, 273, 281, 317
Antipatris, 177, 178, 188, 317
Apamea, 68, 97, 114, 120, 165, 315
Aphek. *See* Antipatris
Aphrodisias, 53n.5
Apollonia, 73, 91
Arabia, 71, 166, 268n.30

Arabia Felix, 13n.7, 81, 230, 275, 316
Arbela, 133, 155, 250
Arethusa, 100n.21
Armenia, 86, 95, 96, 100, 119, 119n.97, 175
Ashkelon, 4, 40, 52, 52n.3, 57, 57n.17, 64, 92, 92n.37, 93, 94, 135, 178, 181, 188
Asia Minor, 53n.5, 73, 82, 89, 95, 106, 119, 127, 142, 195, 266, 269, 272
Arsuf. *See* Apollonia
Arus, 23
Aswan, 265
Athens, 3, 5, 8, 66, 67n.57, 73, 173, 177, 186, 207, 208, 210, 273, 317
Atropatene, 119n.97
Auranitis, 4, 8, 24, 26, 63, 67, 68, 68n.64, 70–72, 131, 140–42, 167, 232, 234, 239
Avdat, 63, 65, 275
Azotus, 24, 40, 61, 73, 91, 92n.38, 100, 204, 210, 316

Baalbek. *See* Heliopolis
Babylon, 9, 53, 73, 136, 161, 162, 244, 254, 266
Balanea, 92, 177, 273, 317
Banyas. *See* Panias
Bashan. *See* Batanea
Batanea, 4, 8, 9, 24, 68, 70–72, 131, 137n.21, 140, 141, 141n.33, 142, 167, 232, 234, 251, 251n.43, 281, 316
Bathyra, 178, 281, 317

Beersheba, 54, 56, 133n.8, 134, 135
Beirut. *See* Berytus
Beka'a Valley, 68, 69, 69n.70, 71, 81, 86, 97, 112n.69, 118, 140, 141
Berytus, 5, 31, 83, 86, 93, 133, 185, 189, 268n.30, 273, 287, 318
Betharamphtha, 23, 143, 180, 192, 302,n.36, 306
Beth Guvrin. *See* Marisa
Beth Kerem, 133
Bethlehem, 52, 54, 56, 288, 288n.108, 296, 301
Bethsaida, 140, 180, 302, 302n.36, 303, 304
Beth Shean. *See* Scythopolis
Bithynia, 175
Black Sea, 3, 96, 195, 264, 271, 276, 316
Bostra, 63, 83, 90, 141
Britain, 183
Brundisium, 127
Busra. *See* Bostra
Byblos, 179, 273, 317

Caesarea Maritima, 2, 4, 24, 56, 92n.38, 93, 94, 177, 178, 179, 181, 182, 184, 187–92, 194, 213, 214, 225, 226, 231n.48, 234, 238, 263, 263n.10, 264n.14, 271n.42, 282, 288, 292, 297, 315, 317
Caesarea Philippi. *See* Panias
Calirrhoe, 4, 6, 18, 143, 144
Cana, 158n.25
Canatha, 63, 67, 88, 88n.26, 93n.42, 167, 167n.78, 168, 168n.85, 184, 302
Capernaum, 303, 303n.38, 308
Capitolias, 88n.26
Cappadocia, 13n.7, 35n.8, 39, 42, 96, 96n.7, 119, 175, 271, 276, 279, 285, 286, 289
Capri, 183n.27
Chalcis, 68, 69n.70, 71, 86, 97, 105, 118, 118n.89, 165n.63, 167, 167n.78, 232, 315
Chios, 3, 189, 206, 264, 271, 272, 317
Chorazin, 133, 140, 303, 304

Cilicia, 81, 95, 96, 101n.24, 119, 264n.12, 279, 317
Coele-Syria, 2, 5, 7, 70nn.73–74, 81, 100, 112 112n.69, 116, 165, 165n.62, 167, 167n.78, 279
Commagene, 81, 83, 84, 96, 119, 175, 176
Cos, 3, 55, 56, 60, 65, 208, 210, 221, 317
Crete, 175
Cypros, 179, 180, 190
Cyprus, 167, 175, 223n.23, 278, 316
Cyrene, 13n.7

Dacia, 13n.7
Dalmatia, 13n.7
Damascus, 4, 5, 12, 63, 64, 64n.41, 68, 71, 83, 86, 87, 88n.26, 90, 93n.42, 94, 96, 97, 98, 112, 117, 140, 142, 143, 165, 188, 232, 273, 318
Daphne, 128
Dead Sea, 56, 57, 63, 64, 82, 134–37, 143, 169, 170, 182, 190n.57
Delos, 205, 206, 209, 270, 318
Dhiban, 65
Dionysias, 63, 141
Diospolis, 67
Dium, 74, 88n.26, 89, 100nn.21–22, 140, 167, 167n.76, 168, 168n.85
Docus, 98n.18, 136, 154, 179, 180, 190
Dor, 74, 82, 92, 100n.21
Dura Europus, 85

Ecdippa, 126
Edom, 60, 65
Egypt, 5, 13n.7, 54, 57, 57n.18, 60n.26, 64n.41, 73, 81, 91, 102, 105–8, 127, 135, 157, 163, 170, 172, 173, 217–19, 223, 223n.19, 223n.23, 237, 265, 266, 268n.34, 297
Eingedi, 137n.31
Elephantine, 265
Eleutheropolis. *See* Marisa
Emesa, 68, 84, 85, 119
Emmaus, 23, 137n.21, 157
En Boqeq, 189
Ephesus, 9, 123, 175, 270, 271

Epirus, 175
Er-Ras, 186
Esbus, 73, 143, 179, 225
es-Salt. *See* Gedora
Ethiopia, 13n.7
et-Tannur, 63, 65
Euphrates River, 81, 82, 83, 85, 86, 96,
    119, 119n.97, 120, 157, 165, 305

Fahil. *See* Pella
Fasayli. *See* Phaselis

Gaba, 178, 194, 225, 317
Gadara, 24, 74, 88, 88n.26, 89, 90, 91, 93,
    100n.21, 132, 140, 142, 143, 173, 175,
    233n.61, 234, 316
Galatia, 13n.7, 26n.27, 96, 119, 175
Galilee, 2, 4, 7, 9, 11, 19, 23, 24, 26, 59,
    69–71, 71n.79, 73–74, 82, 93, 108,
    110–11, 113, 115, 115n.80, 118,
    118n.91, 126, 131–33, 133n.6, 134,
    135, 137, 139, 143–45, 153–57,
    166n.70, 167, 175, 183, 192, 207, 252,
    303, 305, 306, 308–10, 315–16
Gamla, 100n.22, 103, 134n.10, 137n.21,
    141, 302
Gaul, 13n.7, 183, 313
Gaulanitis, 8, 24, 26, 68–71, 91, 100n.22,
    112n.69, 131, 132, 137n.21, 139, 141–
    43, 175, 176, 181, 192, 279, 302, 304,
    305, 308, 313
Gaza, 24, 57n.17, 64, 74, 91, 92, 92n.38,
    100n.21, 103, 135, 173, 178, 316
Gedor, 74, 169n.87
Gedora, 144
Gennesaret. *See* Sea of Galilee
Gerasa, 74, 88, 88n.26, 90, 90n.30,
    100n.22, 140, 143
Gilead, 144
Ginae, 138
Golan. *See* Gaulanitis
Greece, 83, 89, 272
Gulf of Aquaba, 63, 64, 81, 143
Gush Halav, 10

Hebron, 4, 56, 57n.18, 60, 61, 61n.30,
    135, 137, 184, 193

Heliopolis, 68, 83, 97
Herodium, 3, 6, 8, 20, 20n.15, 126n.126,
    137n.21, 179, 181–83, 187, 190, 193,
    225n.34, 263, 263n.10, 317
Heshbon. *See* Esbus
Hinnom Valley, 190
Hippos, 24, 74, 88, 88n.26, 89, 90,
    90n.32, 91, 93, 100n.21, 132, 140, 173,
    316
Homs. *See* Emesa
Horvat Devora, 133n.8
Hulata, 8, 131
Hyrcania, 6, 98n.18, 100, 101, 136, 154,
    190, 237, 263, 263n.10
Hycanium, 19

Idumaea, 4, 7, 11, 23, 23, 42, 53–56, 59,
    60n.26, 62, 65, 67, 71, 73, 78, 105,
    113, 121, 126, 126n.128, 131, 134,
    137n.21, 144, 145, 154, 155, 157,
    157n.20, 166n.70, 175, 176, 179, 181,
    184, 192, 192n.61, 221, 299, 311, 315
Ilios, 233
Illyrica, 13n.7
India, 13n.7
Israel, 15, 87, 153
Ituraea, 24, 68, 68n.61, 69, 69n.70, 71,
    72, 82, 91, 131, 233, 308, 315

Jamnia. *See* Yavneh
Jebel Muntar, 85
Jenin. *See* Ginae
Jerash. *See* Gerasa
Jericho, 1, 4, 6, 15, 18, 19, 21–23, 91,
    135–37, 137n.21, 139, 143, 144, 155,
    155n.7, 157, 158, 166, 168, 178, 180–
    82, 187, 187n.44, 188, 190, 193,
    263n.10, 243, 294, 300, 300n.25, 317,
    318
Jerusalem, 2, 4, 6–10, 12, 17n.9, 18, 23,
    29, 32, 35, 43, 52n.2, 55, 58, 59, 60,
    64, 69, 69n.70, 79, 86, 98, 100, 101,
    106, 108, 108n.51, 112, 113, 115,
    115n.83, 118, 118n.91, 121, 122,
    122n.108, 125, 126, 130, 130n.140,
    130n.143, 134, 135, 136, 137, 144,

Jerusalem (*continued*)
154, 154n.3, 155, 155n.7, 157, 158,
160n.31, 161, 164, 168, 169, 175, 176,
177, 179, 180, 182, 183, 185–86, 190,
191, 190–94, 196, 204, 210, 212, 214,
216, 217, 218, 221, 223n.23, 224n.27,
225, 226, 228, 236n.69, 238, 241, 242,
249, 251, 255, 260, 263, 265, 266, 281,
291, 296, 310, 311, 312, 313, 315, 317
Jezreel Valley, 89, 131, 138, 139
Joppa, 73n.86, 91, 92n.38, 100n.21, 136,
137n.21, 139, 154, 173, 189, 316
Jordan, 54, 116
Jordan River, 23, 68, 73, 89, 90, 98,
100nn.21–22, 102, 131, 133, 140, 142,
144, 180, 181
Jordan Valley, 82, 88, 98n.18, 139,
143n.38, 180
Jotapata. *See* Yodefat
Judah, 54
Judea, 1–11, 13, 13n.7, 19, 20, 22–26,
26n.27, 28, 30–32, 37, 54, 55, 56, 58,
59, 60, 63, 67–70, 73–75, 81, 82, 88–
93, 95, 96, 96n.6, 97, 98, 100, 100n.22,
102, 103, 105, 114n.77, 115, 118, 119,
121, 121n.106, 122, 122n.111, 123–25,
129–31, 133–35, 137–39, 144, 154,
157, 165, 165n.62, 166, 166n.70, 167,
168, 171, 172, 175, 176, 181, 183, 194,
195, 204, 207, 218, 222, 225, 228, 234,
237, 238, 239, 241, 244, 247, 248, 260,
263–66, 268n.30, 269, 272, 279n.72,
279, 282, 291, 293, 299, 300, 300n.24,
301, 311, 315–18

Kedesh, 133n.8, 134
Keren Naphtali, 156, 157, 158n.23, 179,
250n.39
Kidron Valley, 158, 190
Khirbet el-Buraq, 139
Khirbet Kefrein. *See* Abila
Khirbet Khoreisa. *See* Oresa
Kos. *See* Cos
Kurnub. *See* Mampsis

Laodicea, 5, 83, 92, 96n.7, 120, 164,
165n.64, 172, 190, 218, 270

Latakya. *See* Laodicea
Lebanon, 68, 70n.74, 71, 76, 82, 112n.69,
116, 140, 157
Legio, 133
Leontopolis, 102, 102n.28, 106, 106, 242,
244, 245, 246, 254, 265
Lesbos, 3, 232, 233, 263, 264
Litani River, 68
Livia. *See* Bethsaida
Lod. *See* Lydda
Lydda, 155

Macedonia, 89, 114n.75, 175
Machaerus, 4, 98n.18, 100, 101, 102, 136,
143, 154, 179, 180, 181, 190, 191, 307
Madaba, 73
Magdala, 10, 120
Magnesia, 73
Mampsis, 63, 65
Mamre, 60, 60nn.28–29, 61, 61n.31, 184,
193
Marisa, 54, 54n.10, 55, 55n.13, 56, 57, 60,
60nn.25–26, 61, 91, 92n.37, 100n.21,
126n.129, 134, 135
Masada, 56, 59, 98n.18, 117, 126, 129,
130n.140, 153, 154, 174n.1, 179, 180–
83, 183n.27, 186, 190, 191, 203, 210,
219
Memphis, 57n.18
Meroth, 134
Mesopotamia, 86
Modein, 224n.29
Mount Carmel, 73, 74, 82, 131, 137, 139
Mount Ebal, 139
Mount Gerizim, 139
Mount Hermon, 68, 72, 82, 140, 142
Mount of Olives, 17, 17n.9, 136, 196
Mount Scopus, 136
Mount Tabor, 102n.29, 132

Nabatea, 4, 42, 53, 62n.37, 67, 67n.56,
70, 105, 131, 166, 169, 170, 175, 181,
239, 275n.56, 279, 280, 280n.76, 287,
287nn.101–2, 291, 305, 307, 315
Nablus. *See* Shechem
Narbata-Arruboth, 139

Naveh, 140
Neapolis. *See* Shechem
Negev, 54, 63
Nemrud Dagh, 83, 84
Neronias. *See* Panias
Nicaea, 122
Nicopolis, 177, 194, 272
Nissana, 63
North Africa, 113, 175, 266

Obodas. *See* Avdat
Oresa, 154
Olympia, 185, 186
Orontes, 68, 82, 84

Palestine, 81, 101n.24, 121, 127, 142, 144
Palmyra, 5, 65, 65n.47, 83–86, 119
Pamphylia, 127
Panias, 2, 8, 24, 68, 72, 72n.84, 112n.69,
    132, 133, 136, 140, 180, 181, 184, 190,
    194, 226, 234, 302, 303, 304, 315–17
Pannonia, 13n.7
Paphlagonia, 26n.27
Parthia, 13n.7, 82, 83, 96, 100, 119, 120,
    123, 125–29, 155, 161, 170, 192, 244,
    263n.5, 275, 305, 313, 315
Pella, 74, 88n.26, 89, 90, 100nn.21–22,
    137n.21, 142, 143
Pelusium, 106, 166
Pente Komai, 178, 194, 225, 317
Peraea, 4, 6, 7, 11, 23, 24, 26, 70, 93, 115,
    115n.80, 131, 142, 143, 143n.38, 144,
    145, 166n.70, 175, 176, 179, 181, 192,
    234, 291, 305–8, 309n.63, 310, 316
Pergamum, 270, 273, 317
Persia, 86
Petra, 4, 12, 57, 57n.17, 62–65, 78–80,
    96, 126, 127n.130, 307
Pharsalus, 105
Phasaelis, 24, 40, 177, 178, 188, 190, 194,
    263n.10, 317
Philadelphia, 67, 74, 88, 88n.26, 139, 140,
    143, 168
Philippi, 3, 120
Philoteria, 132, 132n.4, 133n.8

Phoenicia, 65, 81, 96, 121, 125, 167, 181,
    308
Plain of Esdraelon, 89
Pompeiopolis, 95
Pontus, 95, 100, 106, 119, 175, 195, 264,
    316
Ptolemais, 59, 82, 89, 92, 93, 125n.123,
    131, 132, 133, 153, 172, 188, 217, 273,
    317

Qailibah. *See* Abila
Qal'at al Madiq. *See* Apamea
Qanawat. *See* Canatha
Qiryat Bene Hassan, 178
Qasr el-Haramiyye, 139
Qasr el-Lejah, 139
Qumran, 259
Qusbiyye. *See* Seleucia

Ragaba, 144
Rajib. *See* Ragaba
Raphana, 88n.26
Raphia, 74, 85, 91
Red Sea, 64, 81
Rhinocorura, 91
Rhodes, 3, 127, 172, 177, 185, 189, 192,
    205, 216, 218, 219, 264n.12, 272, 317
Rift Valley, 54, 57n.17, 63, 81, 82, 86,
    134, 154, 168n.84, 182, 192
Rome, 1, 1n.1, 2, 3, 6, 8, 12, 18, 19, 21,
    21n.19, 23, 26, 30, 31, 32, 34, 71–73,
    80, 83, 84, 85, 86, 95, 96, 100–103,
    105, 107, 110, 118–20, 123, 125, 127–
    30, 159, 175, 184, 209, 210, 212, 228,
    229, 231, 232, 234, 238, 239, 244, 249,
    251, 260, 263, 267, 269, 270, 272, 273,
    277, 278, 280, 281, 282, 283, 285,
    285n.97, 288–94, 300, 305, 307, 309,
    312, 314, 317, 318

Salecah, 141
Salkhad. *See* Salecah
Samaria. *See* Sebaste
Samaritis, 4, 7, 11, 24, 59, 59n.24, 70, 72,
    82, 100n.22, 112, 112n.58, 118, 131,

Samaritis (*continued*)
  137–39, 155, 156, 158, 166n.70, 167,
  181, 299, 311, 316
Samos, 271, 272, 273
Samosata, 83, 315
Sappho, 23
Sardinia, 13n.7
Sardis, 266, 266n.20, 270
Scythopolis, 73, 88n.26, 89, 90, 90n.30,
  93, 98, 100n.21, 132, 143, 221n.12
Sea of Galilee, 24, 63, 88, 90, 131, 132n.4,
  140, 250, 251, 302, 206
Sebaste, 2, 23, 24, 91, 93, 94, 100n.21,
  132, 133, 135, 139, 159, 160n.31, 177,
  178, 179, 184, 188, 190, 192, 194, 214,
  220, 221, 222n.17, 225, 226, 231n.48,
  234, 238, 263n.10, 288, 315, 317
Seleucia, 100n.22, 140
Sepphoris, 9, 11, 23, 93, 133, 155, 175,
  180, 181, 188n.47, 251, 263n.10, 303,
  306, 317
Shechem, 138, 139
Shephelah, 56, 134, 135n.13
Siʿa, 4, 17n.7, 65, 65n.47, 66, 66n.51, 67,
  72, 93n.42, 184, 193, 206, 207, 210,
  214n.87, 239
Sicily, 13n.7
Sidon, 5, 93, 125n.123, 133, 186, 188,
  270n.39, 273, 317
Sophene, 96, 119n.97
Spain, 13n.7, 183
Suq. *See* Abila
Susita. *See* Hippos
Suweida. *See* Dionysias
Syria, 2, 5, 7, 8, 13n.7, 21, 23–28, 30, 54,
  68–70, 70n.74, 71, 71n.79, 73, 74, 81–
  84, 86, 87, 90–92, 95–97, 100, 101,
  101n.24, 105, 107–9, 111, 113,
  113n.70, 114, 114n.75, 116, 118, 119,
  119n.97, 120, 121, 124, 125, 127, 131,
  142, 154n.3, 156, 157, 160n.31, 164,
  172, 190, 223, 134, 166, 289

Tadmor. *See* Palmyra
Tarichea. *See* Magdala
Tarsus, 85, 121, 123
Tell Abil. *See* Abila
Tell ʿAmmata. *See* Ammathus
Tell er-Rama. *See* Betharamphtha
Tetrapolis, 81
Thracia, 175, 176
Threx, 136, 154
Tiber River, 3
Tiberias, 133, 306
Tigris River, 82
Trachonitis, 4, 8, 19, 24, 26, 67n.58, 68,
  68n.63, 70, 70n.75, 71, 72, 76, 91,
  112n.69, 131, 137n.21, 140, 141,
  141n.34, 142, 232, 250, 251, 279, 280,
  281, 316
Transjordan, 54
Tripolis, 92, 97, 188
Troy. *See* Ilios
Tyropean Valley, 190
Tyre, 2, 5, 68, 83, 92, 93, 117, 118,
  118n.88, 121, 124, 125n.123, 131, 132,
  133, 169n.92, 185, 186, 189, 213,
  270n.39, 273, 317

Umm Qeis. *See* Gadara
Umm Rihan, 139

Via Maris, 57, 133, 154

Wadi es-Sir, 144, Wadi Qelt, 135, 136,
  182
Wadi Sirhan, 64, 86, 140, 142, 142n.36

Yafo. *See* Joppa
Yavneh, 24, 40, 73, 91, 100n.21, 137n.21
Yodefat, 10, 12, 133, 134n.10

Zara. *See* Calirrhoe
Zeugma, 83, 120
Ziph, 137

INDEX OF SUBJECTS

Abraham, 60–62, 67

Achiab (Herod's cousin), 221

Acta Diurna, 1n.1

Aelius Gallus (governor of Egypt), 230–31, 290

Agrippa, Marcus (Augustus's son-in-law): death of, 283; in the East, 232–34; gate of, 16–18; and Herod, 93, 262–64, 274, 277; and Jews, 269–72; as patron, 175, 196, 233; petitions to, 90

Agrippa I, Marcus Julius (Herod's grandson), 12, 31n.41, 53n.7, 131, 209–11, 260, 313

Agrippa II, Marcus Julius (Herod's great-grandson), 72, 91, 209–11, 259, 313

Alexander and Aristobulus (Herod's sons), 29, 33–38, 41, 44, 231, 239, 273–79, 281–88

Alexander (son of Aristobulus II), 100–105

Alexander Jannaeus (king), 73–76, 86, 211, 240

Alexandra (mother of Mariamme I), 126, 162–65, 169, 171, 216–21

Alexandra Salome (queen), 74–78, 110, 240, 241, 254

Antigonus Mattathias (son of Aristobulus II), 102 105, 108, 118–119, 122–28, 153–60, 211, 241

Antiochus I of Commagene, 83–84

Antiochus IV Epiphanes, 69, 73, 242, 265

Antipas (Herod's grandfather), 52, 55

Antipas (Herod's son), 19–26, 36–38, 40, 208–209, 211, 231, 259, 294, 303, 305–313

Antipater (Herod's father), 53, 62, 69, 78–80, 95–117, 136, 211, 255, 271

Antipater (Herod's son), 19, 34–38, 41, 121, 220, 231, 276–79, 281–94, 300

Archelaus (Herod's son), 19–26, 36–38, 40, 44, 231, 250, 291, 294, 298–301, 304

Archelaus of Cappadocia, 276, 279, 285–87, 289

Aretas III of Nabatea, 97, 101

Aretas IV of Nabatea, 280, 286–87, 305, 307

Aristobulus I, Judah (king), 69, 73–74, 240

Aristobulus II, 75–78, 96–98, 100, 102, 105, 170, 242, 254–55

Aristobulus III (brother of Mariamme I), 129–30, 162–65, 242–44

Aristobulus (Herod's son). *See* Alexander and Aristobulus

Augustus (Octavian): and Antony, 121, 125, 128–30, 166–69; and dependent kings, 228–29; as emperor, 194, 226–29; gifts to Herod, 90–92, 131, 144–45, 172–73, 232–34, 239; and Herod, 171–73, 216–19, 226–34, 262–64; and Jews, 228–29, 267–72; and

Augustus (Octavian) (*continued*)
  Marcus Agrippa, 233; mausoleum,
    183; oath of loyalty, 237–38; as pa-
    tron, 175, 196; petitions to,
    90–91; pursuit of Antony and
    Cleopatra, 172–73; ratification of
    Herod's will, 20–29, 33, 37,
    39–40; *Res gestae,* 13
Auranitis. *See* Gaulanitis, Batanea, Auran-
    tis, Trachonitis; Nabateans

Baba, sons of, 221–22
Barzaphranes (satrap of Parthia), 125–26
Bassus, Q. Caecilius, 114, 120
Batanea. *See* Gaulanitis, Batanea, Aurantis,
    Trachonitis
Berenice (Herod's niece), 239, 289
Boethos (high priest), 243, 252
brigands, 71–72, 86, 109–113, 141–42,
    155–57, 232, 250–52, 255
buildings, 174–215. *See also* individual
    types of buildings: memorials, pal-
    aces, temples, and so forth
Brutus, 120

Caesar, Julius, 69, 91, 103–108, 111, 113–
    14, 171, 270
Caesar, Sextus (governor of Syria), 70,
    109, 111, 114, 212
Calvinus, Gnaeus Domitius (consul), 130
Cassius Longinus (assassin of Julius Cae-
    sar), 70, 114–17, 120, 125, 129
civil war, 75–78
Cleopatra VII of Egypt, 66–67, 70, 86,
    91, 123–24, 127, 162–69, 172–3,
    219, 221, 232, 265
Cleopatra of Jerusalem (Herod's wife), 40,
    43, 235, 302
coins, 211–15
Corvinus, M. Valerius Messalla, 124, 128
Costobar (husband of Salome), 44, 56,
    221, 275
Crassus, Marcus Licinius (member of first
    triumvirate), 103, 120
Cypros (Herod's mother), 62–63, 80, 126,
    171, 216–20
Cypros (Herod's daughter), 43, 274

Dead Sea Scrolls, 185, 240, 246, 258–59,
    261
Decapolis, 88–91, 304
Dellius, 153, 162
Diaspora, 175–76, 205–6, 244, 264–73
Dolabella, 120
Doris (Herod's wife), 34, 39, 41, 44, 121–
    22, 130n.141, 231, 234, 263, 272,
    283, 289–91
Dositheus, 169–70, 221–22
dowry, 38–39
dynastic networks, 87

economic development, 193–94, 213,
    223, 236–37, 264
Egypt, 57, 107, 217, 223, 242, 244–47,
    265–66
elites, 109–13, 130, 135, 157, 183, 222,
    240–42, 251, 253
Elpis (Herod's wife), 40, 43, 235
embassy: of Decapolis to Rome, 24, 30;
    of Gadara to Agrippa, 233; of Jews
    to Antony, 123–24; of Jews to
    Rome, 23, 25, 30
Essenes, 237, 256–59, 260
Eurycles of Sparta, 285–86

famine and drought, 222, 236
fortresses, 101, 136, 154, 159, 179–83,
    192, 225, 263

Gabinius, 91, 95–104, 133, 136
Gaius Caligula (emperor), 227, 266, 313
Galileans, 131–34, 175–76, 304, 306
Gaulanitis, Batanea, Auranitis, Trachoni-
    tis, 139–42, 250–51, 279–81,
    301–2, 308. *See also* Ituraeans
Glaphyra (Herod's daughter-in-law), 39,
    44, 239, 275, 283, 285–86, 289,
    300
godfearers, 52–53
gymnasia, 186–88, 273

Hananel (high priest), 162, 242–43
Hasmoneans: conquests, 54–56, 69, 73–
    76, 89, 91, 131; end of, 161, 169–

70, 221–22, 241, 288; rivalry among, 76–80. *See also* under individual names

Hellenism: in coastal cities, 91–94; in Decapolis, 88–91; in dependent kingdoms, 83–88; in Diaspora, 266; in Galilee, 132; in Judea, 92–93, 188; in Syria, 81–83

Herod
  achievements, 315–18
  appointments
    in Galilee, 180–115, 118
    in Judea, 70, 124–26, 127–30, 161, 171–73, 203–15
    in Syria, 116, 234
  as architect, 196
  and Augustus, 226–34, 278–79
  benefactions, 93–94, 127, 174–77, 272–73
  birth, 76
  buildings, 174–215
  children's education, 231, 239
  death, 18–20
  deterioration, 284–94
  evaluations of, 30–32
  extent of kingdom, 141–45
  family finances, 38–40
  flight from Jerusalem, 126
  genealogy, 40–51, 155
  the "Great," 12, 209–11, 215
  as hellenizer, 18, 93
  as Idumaean, 54–62, 155
  illness, 15–16, 19, 294
  images of, 66, 206–209
  and Ituraeans, 68–72
  as Jew, 42–43, 52–53, 55, 195, 203–204
  and Marcus Agrippa, 232–34, 262–64
  marriages, 41–45, 87–88, 121–22, 129, 216–20, 234–36, 289
  "massacre of the innocents," 288, 296–97
  military actions, 67, 86, 153–62, 167–68, 214–15, 230–31, 264, 271–72
  as Nabatean, 62–68

oath of loyalty, 237–38, 255–56
as patron, 181, 192, 196, 204–215, 233–34
piety, 193–95, 207–9, 247
and priests, 162
siege of Jerusalem, 158–60
and Syria, 70
trial of, 108–13

Herodians, 157, 250, 259–60, 309–10
Herodias (Herod's grandaughter), 305, 307
Hezekiah (brigand-chief), 71n.79, 109–12, 250
hippodromes, 90, 186–88
Hyrcanus I (king), 56, 59, 73, 108, 254
Hyrcanus II (king/ethnarch), 55, 69, 75–78, 96–100, 103–13, 114–17, 119, 122, 126, 161–62, 169–71, 222, 242, 269–70

Idumaea, 54–62, 78–79, 105, 110, 126, 154, 176, 221 280–81
imperial cult. *See* temples: Roma and Augustus
infrastructure, 90, 188–91
Ituraeans, 68–72, 86, 139–42, 232–34. *See also* Gaulanitis, Batanea, Aurantis, Trachonitis

Jerusalem: administrative and religious capital, 135; during the Great Revolt, 58; siege by Herod, 158–60; siege by Parthians, 125; siege by Pompey, 98
Jesus, 31n.42, 296–313
Joazar, son of Boethos (high priest), 243
John the Baptist, 297–98, 304, 306–308
Joseph (Herod's brother), 155, 157, 158
Joseph (Herod's brother-in-law), 164–65, 216, 218, 222
Joseph (Herod's steward), 171, 216, 218–20
Joseph, son of Ellenus (high priest), 243
Josephus: as author, 11–12, 76–77, 102n.29, 116–17, 218–20,

Josephus (continued)
    225–26; and Nicolas, 31n.40,
    106–108, 114, 233
Judas (son of Sepphoraeus), 15, 21, 255
Judaism: in coastal cities, 92–94; in Da-
    mascus, 87; in Decapolis, 90–91;
    decrees in favor of, 107–8; in
    Roman Empire, 227–28, 264–66,
    269; in Rome, 266–69. See also
    society
Judas the Galilean, 250–51
Judea, 134–37; connection with the sea,
    91; reduction of by Pompey, 100;
    as Roman province, 25–29
Julia (Augustus's daughter), 233, 262

kinship, 40–45

Labienus, Quintus, 121, 124, 153
Livia (Augustus's wife), 36, 39
Lysanias of Abila, 71
Lysanias of Chalcis, 125, 130, 232
Lysimachus, 221–22

Machaeras (Roman commander), 156–58
Malchus (friend of Hyrcanus II), 114–17
Malichus I (king of Nabatea), 127, 130,
    166–70, 173
Malthace (Herod's wife), 35, 40, 43, 235
Manaemus (Essene), 257
Marcus Agrippa. See Agrippa, Marcus
Mariamme I (Herod's wife), 34, 41–43,
    121, 129, 159, 162–63, 171, 216–
    20, 234, 244, 263
Mariamme II (Herod's wife), 35, 235,
    244, 291
Marion of Tyre, 118
Mark Antony, 66, 70, 91, 100, 102, 121–
    30, 156–57, 160, 162–69, 171–73,
    219, 257, 273
Matthias, son of Margalus, 15, 21, 255
Matthias, son of Theophilus (high priest),
    243
memorials, 60–62, 83–84, 183–84,
    224n.29
messiah, 295–96, 300, 304

Mithradates of Parthia, 119–20
Mithradates VI of Pontus, 95–96, 101
Murcus, 114, 120

Nabateans, 62–68, 78, 86, 101–03, 105,
    126, 166–69, 230, 238–39,
    279–81
Nicolas of Damascus: as author, 13, 53, 87;
    as Josephus's source, 106; as prose-
    cutor, 292–93; in Rome, 21–22,
    281, 286–88
nymphaea, 90

Obodas (king of Nabatea), 230, 275–76,
    280
Octavian. See Augustus
Olympic games, 185–86, 195, 272
Onias (high priest), 242, 265
Onias (prophet), 79

Pacorus (cupbearer), 121, 125
Pacorus (son of Orodes II of Parthia), 121,
    124–26, 153
palaces, 72, 126n.126, 136, 144, 179–83
Pallas (Herod's wife), 40, 43, 238
Pappus, 158
Parthians, 82, 104, 119–28, 153–56, 305
patronage, 45, 106, 192, 263
Peraeans, 142, 234, 274
Petronius (governor of Egypt), 223
Phaedra (Herod's wife), 40, 43, 235
Pharisees, 75–76, 240, 252, 254–56, 290,
    309
Phasael (Herod's brother), 108, 113, 114,
    117, 124–27, 157, 212
Pheroras (Herod's brother), 39, 43, 126,
    157, 171, 216, 218, 220, 234, 255,
    274–75, 282, 285, 288–91
Phiabi, Jesus ben (high priest), 235, 243,
    245
philhellênos, 84
philokaisaros, 204, 207–8, 210, 312n.82
Philip (Herod's son), 19–26, 35–38, 40,
    72, 208–09, 231, 291, 294, 301–5
philoromaios, 84, 207, 210
Pollio, Gaius Asinius (consul), 130, 231

Pollion (Pharisee), 161, 237, 255–56
Pompey, 12n.5, 55, 73, 79, 89, 91, 95–
    105, 113, 119, 120, 136, 240, 251
Pontius Pilate, 190, 310–12
priests: high priests, 74, 102, 108, 126,
    129, 162, 170, 235, 240–47, 253;
    legitimacy of, 79; power of, 74,
    241
proselytes, 56
Ptolemaic dynasty, 68–69, 73, 82, 136
Ptolemy (brother of Nicolas of Damascus),
    19, 22
Ptolemy of Chalcis, 118, 122, 125

Quirinius, 301

revolts: Great Revolt, 58, 265; Hasmo-
    nean, 73, 119; at Herod's death,
    23, 27, 59; of 6 CE, 250
Rome: end of the Republic, 103–21,
    167–69; expansion to east, 82–87,
    96–103, 119–21, 130; and Jews,
    229, 269–72
Roxana (Herod's daughter), 39
royal estates, 110, 134n.11, 166, 178

sabbatical year, 222, 236
Sabinus (procurator of Syria), 21, 23, 26
Sadducees, 74–76, 252–54
Salampsio (Herod's daughter), 39, 43, 274
Salome (Herod's sister), 19–24, 36–38,
    40, 44, 126, 171, 239, 273–76,
    282, 284–86, 289, 291
Salome (Herod's daughter), 39
Samaios (Pharisee), 112, 161, 237, 255–56
Samaritans, 118, 137–39, 235
Sanhedrin, 110–13, 312
Saturninus, 279, 287, 289
Scaurus, 79, 96, 101
Sejanus, 312–13
Seleucid dynasty, 68–69, 73, 82, 86, 96–
    97, 119, 136
Silo, 153–156
Simon, son of Boethos (high priest), 235,
    243
society: Babylonian, 161–62, 244; Gali-

lean, 110–11, 118, 133–34; Go-
    lani, 140–42; Judean, 31–32,
    73–76, 109, 118, 136–37, 222–26;
    Peraean, 142–44; Samaritan,
    137–39
Soemus (Ituraean), 172, 216, 218–20, 222
Sossius (Roman commander), 157–60
stadia. See hippodromes
Strabo, 13
Syllaeus, 44, 221n.14, 230–31, 274–76,
    279–81, 286–87, 290
synagogues, 186, 209, 229, 265–69, 272

taxation, 28, 114–15, 215, 236–38, 272,
    273n.46
Temple of Jerusalem: Agrippa's gate, 16–
    18, 213; and Augustus, 229; and
    M. Agrippa, 263; "eagle affair,"
    15–18, 255; extension of, 136;
    Pompey's entry, 99–100; rebuild-
    ing of, 185–86, 196, 205, 238,
    245–49; size and setting of, 86,
    158
temples: Apollo, 134, 185, 209, 272; Ar-
    temis, 90; Athena, 185; Ba'al
    Shamim (Si'a), 17n.7, 65–67, 184,
    206–07; Bel, 85; Diana, 134; Ele-
    phantine, 265; Jupiter, 86; Leonto-
    polis, 244–47, 265; Nabatean,
    65–67; Nabu, 85; Pan, 72; Roma
    and Augustus, 72, 87, 184–85,
    234, 302; in Tyre and Berytus,
    185; Zeus, 90. See also Temple of
    Jerusalem
theaters and amphitheaters, 90, 186–88,
    223–24
Tiberius (emperor), 262, 283, 302, 305,
    311–13
Tigranes I of Armenia, 95–96, 101, 119
Torah (law), 28, 31–32, 224, 252, 254,
    295, 298
Trachonitis. See Gaulanitis, Batanea,
    Aurantis, Trachonitis; Ituraeans
trade and commerce: Idumaean, 57;
    Judea, 135, 137, 178, 188–91; Na-
    batean, 64; Palmyra, 85; Syria, 82
Tyrians, 188, 212

Varro (governor of Syria), 71, 232
Varus (governor of Syria), 23, 26, 261, 292, 300, 301
Ventidius Bassus, 121, 125, 130n.140, 153–56
veterans, 59, 177–78, 239
villas, 182–83
Vitellius (governor of Syria), 305, 307
Vitruvius (architect), 2, 195

Volumnius (procurator of Syria), 267–68, 279, 286–88

water and aqueducts, 63–64, 90, 189–91, 263, 311

Zamaris, 251, 281
zealots, 29
Zenodorus, 71–72, 232, 233, 238–39, 250